STUDIES IN CULTURAL HISTORY

When Time Shall Be No More

When the trumpet of the Lord shall sound,
And time shall be no more,
And the morning breaks eternal bright and fair,
When the saved of earth shall gather,
Over on the other shore,
And the roll is called up yonder, I'll be there.

—"When the Roll is Called up Yonder"
   by James H. Black, 1921;
   in *Spiritual Songs and Hymns*
   (Nappanee, Indiana,
   E. V. Publishing House, 1935)

When Time Shall Be No More

Prophecy Belief in Modern American Culture

P A U L   B O Y E R

The Belknap Press of
H A R V A R D   U N I V E R S I T Y   P R E S S
Cambridge, Massachusetts
London, England

Library of Congress Cataloging-in-Publication Data

Boyer, Paul S.
   When time shall be no more : prophecy belief in modern American
culture / Paul Boyer.
      p.   cm.—(Studies in cultural history)
   Includes bibliographical references and index.
   ISBN 0-674-95128-X (alk. paper) (cloth)
   ISBN 0-674-95129-8 (pbk.)
   1. United States—Religion—1945–   2. Millennialism—United
States.   3. United States—Religious life and customs.   4. Bible
—Prophecies.   5. Twentieth century—Forecasts.   6. Prophecy
(Christianity)   I. Title.   II. Series.
BR526.B58   1992
231.7′45′0973–dc20   91-45302
                        CIP

For my brothers
WILLIAM E. BOYER and ERNEST L. BOYER
with love and admiration

CONTENTS

Illustrations follow pages 144 and 280

Preface

Shortly after the publication in 1841 of my work "On the Second Coming of Our Lord before the Millennium," a brother in the ministry met me in the street. "I hear, Brother R.," said he, "that you have published a book on the premillennial coming of our Lord." I replied that I had, and that if he would call on me I would give him a copy of the work. He thanked me for my offer, but never came for the book. Just as we were about to separate he laid his hand on my shoulder, and in a very persuasive tone said, "My dear brother, do let me advise you to stop your studies of the prophecies. I never knew a man who began to study them and to write on them who did not ultimately go crazy."

—William Ramsey, D.D., 1857

While still of comparatively sound mind, I should say a few words about this book and how it evolved.

When Time Shall Be No More explores a strand of American popular thought that has received little scholarly attention: the conviction that the course of history, and the sequence of events that will herald the end of the world, are foretold in the Bible. I advance two related arguments: first, that prophecy belief is far more central in American thought than intellectual and cultural historians have recognized, and second, that in the years since World War II the popularizers of a specific belief system—dispensational premillennialism—have played an important role in shaping public attitudes on a wide range of topics from the Soviet Union, the Common Market, and the Mideast to the computer and the environmental crisis.

Most Christians throughout history have believed in God's providential oversight of history and in a final eschatological consummation. Most still do today, to judge by the formal credal statements of all major Christian groups. The writers who are my subject represent a subset of that vast host of believers. These are individuals who are *deeply preoccupied* with eschatology, who place it at the *center* of their theological speculations, and who teach that God at the beginning of time determined a *specific, detailed* plan for history's last days—a plan revealed in the Bible with minute particularity, though in symbolic language and veiled images. They are committed (sometimes obsessively so) to elucidating these prophetic mysteries and using them to illuminate and explain the course of contemporary history.

To some, this belief system may seem too bizarre or atavistic to merit the time and attention I have expended on it. Is one really justified in devoting four or five years of one's scholarly life to a topic whose evidence includes Rapture wrist watches ("One Hour Nearer the Lord's Return"); dashboard signs that say "If you hear a trumpet, grab the wheel"; and earnest discussions of the meaning of the Beast's horns or the statue's toes in the Book of Daniel?

Further, the sheer abundance and ephemerality of sources at this level of popular belief can be daunting. Where does one begin? When does one stop? How does one determine the relative influence of specific books? What does it actually mean to say that a book has sold two hundred thousand copies, a million copies, or twenty million copies? Would a research strategy involving statistical quantification or in-depth interviews with a scientifically selected sampling of prophecy believers have been more valuable than the text-based approach I have adopted?

All these concerns and potential caveats are well founded, and I have wrestled with them myself. Yet the pervasiveness of prophecy belief in contemporary American thought, obvious in even the most cursory study of public-opinion data and surging to the fore at moments of crisis such as the 1991 Persian Gulf War; the ubiquity of prophecy popularization in contemporary mass culture; and the neglect of the topic by historians all persuaded me to pursue the topic despite the difficulties it poses.

To be sure, there have been second thoughts. At times in my research, as I shook my head over some particularly bizarre interpretative flight, I doubted whether this material merited all the attention I was giving it. Certainly prophecy belief is pervasive, but is that justification enough? Was my study akin to devoting years of research and hundreds of pages of scholarly prose to the supermarket tabloids whose headlines endlessly scream of UFOs, Elvis sightings, two-headed babies, and the latest escapades of Liz or Teddy?

On balance, I still believe the topic merits the protracted attention I have given it. In contrast to other mass-culture material, prophecy writing, even at its most outlandish, is linked to a *religious belief system.*

As prophecy writers address contemporary concerns and seek the largest possible audience, they must also ground their work, however tenuously, in a text that most Americans (and certainly most of their readers) revere as divinely inspired. Anyone interested in the history of ideas must surely find fascinating, as I do, the way these divergent pressures—the impulse toward contemporaneity and the constraints of scriptural integrity and long-standing interpretive conventions—shape the prophecy books that endlessly pour from the presses. Among other goals, I have tried to offer a case study in the persistence and adaptability of a belief system whose roots stretch back to the beginnings of recorded history, but whose latest formulations are as up-to-the-minute as today's *New York Times* headlines.

The genre of prophecy interpretation is an example of a collective discourse conducted at the mass level. Individually, most of the authors lack stylistic or intellectual distinction. The writing is generally pedestrian and formulaic, the ideas for the most part banal and derivative. Yet viewed more broadly, and from a perspective of decades and even centuries, the genre is an engrossing one. In the first place, it evolves in complex, intriguing ways. Outmoded themes are quietly abandoned and new themes introduced, elaborated, modified, and subtly altered within a subculture in which the premium is on continuity and regard for "biblical inerrancy," not innovation and creativity. From a Darwinian perspective, the adaptive mechanisms by which prophecy belief survives and flourishes, given the constraints imposed upon its expositors, are fascinating indeed.

This belief system is also noteworthy because of the psychological and even ontological function it performs for those who embrace it. Prophecy belief is a way of ordering experience. It gives a grand, overarching shape to history, and thus ultimate meaning to the lives of individuals caught up in history's stream. Here, I believe, is a key to its enduring appeal.

But if prophecy belief plays its private role for individuals, it has social ramifications as well. For it influences the worldview of those who embrace it. Of course, this "influence" is neither absolute nor easily separable from the multiplicity of factors that shape popular views on public issues. Belief in prophecy obviously coexists with and interacts with other agendas, purposes, and motivations.

For evidence of the contingent and partial role of prophecy belief in molding its adherents' worldview, we need look no farther than former President Ronald Reagan. His belief in Russia's demonic end-time destiny was deep-seated and well documented. Yet Reagan eagerly accepted glasnost and at the end of his term strolled in Red Square with the ruler of the empire foreordained (so his prophecy mentors insisted) to attack Israel in the last days and be destroyed in consequence. Most Americans of lesser visibility are similarly subject to a variety of ideological cross-currents, of which prophecy belief is only one.

Yet simply because prophecy belief does not *absolutely* determine most people's worldview, we cannot safely dismiss it altogether. If nothing else, I hope this study will establish that one cannot fully understand the American public's response to a wide range of international and domestic issues without bearing in mind that millions of men and women view world events and trends, at least in part, through the refracting lens of prophetic belief.

As to my research approach, I can offer only the feeble justification that, as an intellectual historian, reading texts—rather than marshaling statistics or interviewing subjects—is what I know best. But I do not dismiss the value of aggregate or interview-based studies, and it is my hope that other researchers will undertake such projects. Indeed, Robert Jay Lifton and Charles B. Strozier of the Center on Violence and Human Survival at the John Jay College of Criminal Justice, City University of New York, are conducting an interview-based study of apocalyptic belief, and I look forward to the results of their work.

This volume grew out of my 1985 study, *By the Bomb's Early Light: American Thought and Culture at the Dawn of the Atomic Age*. In researching that work, I discovered that many religious writers of the early postwar years found the atomic bomb foretold in Bible prophecies of Earth's fiery destruction. The article I originally planned to write surveying this theme has now become a chapter of the present book. But as I explored the subject, I realized that its far-reaching ramifications could not be encompassed within the confines of a single essay, and *When Time Shall Be No More* began to take shape.

I started systematic research in 1987–88, during a year as visiting professor at the University of California at Los Angeles. There I especially benefited from the proximity of Fuller Theological Seminary in Pasadena, with its extensive holdings of prophecy books, including the personal library of Wilbur M. Smith, an important mid-twentieth-century prophecy writer. In 1988–89, as Henry R. Luce Visiting Professor of American Culture at Northwestern University, I enjoyed easy access to Chicago's Moody Bible Institute, another major repository of prophecy works. In all these venues, as well as here now in Madison, I also frequented evangelical Christian bookstores, with their array of current paperbacks in the prophecy field.

Beginning in the summer of 1989 I pursued my research and writing at the Institute for Research in the Humanities at the University of Wisconsin, where a half-time research appointment provided incomparable scholarly opportunities. My colleagues in the Old Observatory, the institute's home, have endured numerous interim reports on my work, in formal seminar settings and in countless lunchtime discussions, and despite their bemusement at the offbeat nature of the topic, they have offered helpful critical responses. If this book falls short, I certainly cannot blame the three universities that offered such generous opportunities to pursue the project under optimal conditions.

Over the past four years I have read some one hundred pre-1945 prophecy books and over two hundred published since 1945. I have also read the published papers of eight prophecy conferences between the 1870s and the 1970s, held in America or, in one case, in Israel, and I have perused about twenty-five prophecy newsletters and religious periodicals devoted to the subject. Thus when I speak generically of what "prophecy writers" say on a given topic, the generalization grows out of this immersion in the sources. In most cases the three or four sources I cite for a specific interpretation could be duplicated many times over.

A word about citation form. Works are cited in the notes in the order that they are quoted or mentioned in the text. Of course, all omissions from within quoted passages are indicated by ellipses. Prophecy popularizations sometimes defy accurate dating; like textbooks, they are often reprinted again and again over a span of many years, with material added, deleted, and revised in successive editions. A book first published in the 1930s, for example, might have been reissued in the 1960s with allusions to the nuclear threat or the founding of the state of Israel. Where possible, I have cited the publication date relevant to the specific material I am quoting or discussing. Any errors in citation reflect these difficulties and are not deliberate.

Five writers on Bible prophecy, including John F. Walvoord, a master of the genre whose books have sold several million copies, graciously granted me interviews. In addition to Fuller Seminary and Moody Bible Institute, I did research at Dallas Theological Seminary in Texas and Gordon Conwell Seminary in Massachusetts. To experience at first hand the social context of prophecy belief, I attended services held by touring prophecy expositors at Shalom Christian Center and Madison Gospel Tabernacle in Madison, and a prophecy seminar sponsored by the Seventh-day Adventist Church.

The decision to cease doing research and turn to writing is always somewhat arbitrary. As Hans Schwarz wrote in 1972, "Most books are never really finished but gradually abandoned." I made the decision to conclude the research phase of this project when I discovered that I had read and taken extensive notes on the same prophecy book *twice*, and when the Bible I was using began to drop open of its own accord to Ezekiel 38, even as the pages of the Book of Revelation fell out entirely!

Finally, to balance the rather alarming quote with which I began, let me close this preface with a more reassuring one, from Cotton Mather in 1691: "I confess *Apocalyptical Studies* are fittest for those Raised Souls, whose *Heart Strings* are made of a Little *Finer* Clay, than other men's." If this book does push me over the edge—the fate William Ramsey's friend predicted for him in 1841—at least I will be interesting company.

When Time Shall Be No More

The Hidden World of Prophecy Belief

Surely the Lord God will do nothing, but he
revealeth his secret unto his servants the prophets.

—Amos 3:7

New Year's Day 1988 found me seated in a lounge at Los
Angeles International Airport, waiting for an incoming
passenger. Academic that I am, I had brought along some
research to pass the time: a paperback entitled *How to Recognize the
Antichrist*. At the bar a middle-aged man and woman laughed and
talked, seemingly oblivious to my presence. But as the man left, he
stopped at my table and demanded, "Well, do you think you'll recognize him?" Caught off guard, I mumbled that I wasn't sure, since I
hadn't yet finished the book. "I think he exists now," said the man
earnestly. "Actually, I'm kind of pleased, because the sooner the
better."

This is a book about what may seem, to some, a strange and alien
byway of American thought. It is about a world where the number
"666" and terms such as "Gog," "Magog," "Antichrist," "Mark of the
Beast," and "Armageddon" are as familiar as "Form 1040," "Saddam
Hussein," "VCR," "MasterCard," and "Hiroshima" are to the population as a whole. Those who inhabit this world take very seriously
the Bible's apocalyptic sections and derive from them a detailed
agenda of coming events. Adopting the eclectic approach advised by
the prophet Isaiah—"For precept must be upon precept, precept upon
precept; line upon line, line upon line; here a little, and there a
little"[1]—prophecy interpreters, like hobbyists assembling a picture
puzzle or artisans crafting a mosaic, painstakingly build from hundreds of Bible verses a picture of the final days of human history—a
picture strikingly similar to the world of today.

How widespread are these beliefs? The question is crucial, for it
would be folly to devote several years of research to a belief system
embraced by a handful of cranks. Much evidence (some direct, some

inferential) suggests that, despite gradual erosion in the twentieth century, prophetic belief remains deeply rooted in the United States as
the century ends. According to a 1983 Gallup poll, 62 percent of
Americans had "no doubts" that Jesus will come to earth again. A
1980 poll by the same organization found that 40 percent of Americans regarded the Bible as "the actual Word of God, . . . to be taken
literally word for word," while another 45 percent viewed the Bible as
divinely inspired, if not literally inerrant. (In a 1988 poll offering a
slightly different set of options, 31 percent of the respondents
supported the "actual-Word-of-God, to-be-taken-literally-word-for-
word" formula, while 25 percent endorsed the following language:
"The Bible is the inspired word of God. It contains no errors, but
some verses are to be taken symbolically rather than literally.") Such
beliefs have direct relevance, of course, for how one interprets the
Bible's prophetic and apocalyptic passages. In the 1988 poll, 80 percent of the respondents expressed the conviction that they will appear
before God on Judgment Day.[2]

Of course, such findings must be used with caution. Simply because an individual avows such beliefs when asked by a polltaker does
not mean that they necessarily impinge vitally on his or her daily life.
I have found it helpful to visualize the world of prophecy belief as a
series of concentric circles, at the center of which is a core group of
devotees who spend much time thinking about the Bible's apocalyptic
passages and trying to organize them into a coherent scenario. These
are the men and women who attend prophecy conferences; raise the
topic in Sunday school classes and Bible study groups; and avidly de-
vour the prophecy paperbacks, cassette tapes, and study aids that annually pour into the market. The historian Dwight Wilson, in a valuable 1977 study of U.S. prophecy belief, conservatively estimated the
number of firmly committed *premillennialists* at 8 million.[3] (Premillennialists, whose ideas we shall explore in some detail, believe in Jesus
Christ's bodily return *before* His thousand-year earthly reign, com-
monly called the Millennium.)

Next in this concentric series one finds those believers who may
be hazy about the details of biblical eschatology, but who nevertheless
believe that the Bible provides clues to future events. These are the
citizens of whom George Gallup, Jr., and Jim Castelli wrote: "Americans revere the Bible but by and large they don't read it. And because
they don't read it, they have become a nation of biblical illiterates."

(Six of ten adult Americans, Gallup and Castelli reported, have no idea who delivered the Sermon on the Mount; fewer than half can name the New Testament's first four books.)[4] This group, comprising many millions of Americans, is susceptible to popularizers who confidently weave Bible passages into highly imaginative end-time scenarios, or who promulgate particular schemes of prophetic interpretation.

In the outer circle are those superficially secular individuals who exhibit little overt prophecy interest, but whose worldview is nevertheless shaped to some degree by residual or latent concepts of eschatology, the theology of last things. One may hypothesize that in times of crisis, or when confronted by particularly troubling world trends, members of this group may listen with more than passing attentiveness to those who offer the Bible as a guide to events, or be particularly receptive to ostensibly secular works that are nevertheless apocalyptic in structure and rhetoric.

Among U.S. Protestants, prophecy belief usually comes embedded within a larger religious matrix that goes by the label "evangelicalism" or (to use a somewhat more specialized and restrictive term) "fundamentalism." This sector of American Protestantism grew significantly and gained dramatically in public visibility in the two decades after 1970—years when the more liberal, so-called mainstream denominations lost ground. A 1978–79 study by the Princeton Religious Research Center concluded that 22 percent of Americans could be classified as evangelical. In a 1986 Gallup poll, 32 percent of the respondents described themselves as "born-again" or "evangelical" Christians. Although this figure represented perhaps a 10 percent decline since 1900, it still encompassed a formidable number of citizens. (Meanwhile, from 1973 to 1983, membership in the United Methodist Church and the Presbyterian Church U.S.A.—two quintessentially mainstream denominations—fell by 8 percent and 15 percent respectively.) The authors of a 1980 study of U.S. religion found "a strong tide" running in favor of evangelicalism; another in 1984 pronounced evangelicalism "the dominant religious force" in America.[5]

The vitality of U.S. religious life in the 1970s and 1980s, spearheaded by a resurgent evangelicalism, stood out with particular vividness when contrasted with the situation in Western Europe. In the mid-1970s, when 56 percent of Americans told pollsters they considered religion "very important" to them, only 27 percent of western Europeans so described their feelings. In 1989, when Gallup and Cas-

telli gave the United States a rating of sixty-seven on their Religion
Index (based on various indicators), West Germany, Norway, the
Netherlands, Great Britain, and France all had scores in the thirties,
with Denmark bringing up the rear with twenty-one![6]

Several evangelical denominations, notably the nearly 15-
million-strong Southern Baptist Convention, represented bastions of
premillennial belief in the seventies and eighties. While the Southern
Baptists, America's largest Protestant denomination, historically
stressed congregational autonomy and avoided official credal statements, fundamentalists gained control of the denomination in 1979
and insisted on biblical inerrancy as a test of orthodoxy. Other strong-
holds of prophecy teaching were the nation's fast-growing pentecostal
and charismatic denominations, with some 8 million members by the
end of the 1980s, including the 2.1-million-member Assemblies of
God Church, which grew by 95 percent between 1973 and 1988; the
Church of the Nazarene (562,000 members by 1988); and thousands
of independent "Bible churches," "Gospel tabernacles," and "Christian fellowships" scattered over the land. The belief system of these
groups, which were characterized by a strict morality, fundamentalist
theology, and "spirit-filled" worship services (often including speaking in tongues and prayers for divine healing), had a strong eschatological component.[7]

The Jehovah's Witnesses, Seventh-day Adventists, Church of Jesus Christ of Latter-Day Saints (Mormons), and Herbert W. Armstrong's Worldwide Church of God, which total millions of members,
promulgated particular versions of end-time belief through their
churches, door-to-door visitation, and ubiquitous magazines such as
the Witnesses' *Watchtower* and the Worldwide Church of God's *Plain
Truth,* distributed free in airports and elsewhere. Even within mainstream denominations that did not emphasize prophecy, many evan-
gelically inclined members took prophetic claims seriously.[8]

Belief in Bible prophecy also pervaded parts of Africa and Latin
America proselytized by evangelical and pentecostal missionaries.
Prophecy belief was widespread, for example, among evangelical
sects in Nigeria that had several million members. Prophecy popularizations were routinely translated into Spanish for circulation in Central and South America (as well as among Hispanic Catholic converts
to evangelicalism and pentecostalism in U.S. cities). Prophetic modes
of thinking even survived in Europe. Followers of the Northern Ire-

land firebrand Ian Paisley remained convinced that the Pope is the Antichrist, the demonic figure expected to rule the world briefly just before Jesus Christ's Second Coming. Many Greeks, a 1989 visitor reported, viewed the European Common Market as a forerunner of the Antichrist—a favorite theme of U.S. prophecy expositors.[9]

With a revitalized evangelicalism creating a receptive cultural climate, prophetic belief was disseminated in these years by America's omnipresent religious broadcasters, including luminaries such as Jerry Falwell of Virginia, Michigan's Jack Van Impe, Oral Roberts of Tulsa, and shoals of Southern California electronic preachers. Charles Taylor's "Today in Bible Prophecy," based in Huntington Beach, California, aired on more than twenty stations nationwide and globally via the Spacenet, SATCOM, and Galaxy communications satellites. Pat Robertson's Christian Broadcasting Network (CBN), which in the 1980s served more than three thousand cable systems, and the Trinity Broadcasting Network (TBN) brought prophecy-oriented shows to homes across the nation and, by satellite, around the world. Radio disseminated prophetic teachings as well, through such widely broadcast programs as the Michigan-based "Back to the Bible Hour" and David Webber's "Southwest Radio Church" of Oklahoma City (heard five days a week over 130 stations) and hundreds of preachers who regularly held forth on local stations from coast to coast. In the early 1980s, National Religious Broadcasters, an evangelical trade association, included 922 radio stations, 65 television stations, 535 radio producers, and 280 TV and film producers.[10]

Hundreds of prophecy paperbacks fed an apparently insatiable market. *The* nonfiction bestseller of the 1970s, with 9 million copies in print by 1978 and 28 million by 1990, was a popularization of premillennialism, Hal Lindsey's *Late Great Planet Earth* (1970). A 1977 movie version narrated by Orson Welles appeared in theaters nationwide. Lindsey followed up with a stream of prophecy books such as *There's a New World Coming* (1973) and *The 1980s: Countdown to Armageddon* (1980). The latter, with its stark opening pronouncement, "*The decade of the 1980s could very well be the last decade of history as we know it,*" enjoyed over twenty weeks on the *New York Times* bestseller list.[11]

Boasts of "over 100,000 sold" or "250,000 in print" adorned many prophecy paperbacks. Salem Kirban's 1968 prophecy work, *Guide to Survival,* went through sixteen editions by 1988, selling half a million copies. The publisher of Paul Billheimer's 1975 prophecy popularization, *Destined for the Throne,* reported sales of over 650,000 by 1988, including 160,000 distributed as premiums by TBN. John F. Walvoord's timely 1974 paperback, *Armageddon, Oil, and the Middle East Crisis,* sold 750,000 copies. Capitalizing on the surge in prophecy interest triggered by the Persian Gulf crisis, *The Late Great Planet Earth* and *Armageddon, Oil, and the Middle East Crisis* appeared in revised editions in 1990–91, and David Wilkerson's *Set the Trumpet to Thy Mouth* (1985) found more than a million buyers.[12] Comparable statistics recurred over and over in the world of prophecy publishing.

Prophecy books published before World War II, and even in the nineteenth century, regularly appeared in updated versions in the late twentieth century, frustrating the historian trying to pinpoint particular passages but further testifying to the exuberant vitality of the genre. A 1918 prophecy book reappeared in fresh guise in 1964 with the notation, "173rd thousand." An 1896 prophecy work was reissued half a century later with updated references to radio and the movies. Julianne Booth's *Book of the New Testament for Children* (1981) offered juvenile readers an introduction to eschatology:

> Last of all is the Book of Revelation.
> It's full of mysterious information
> Given us by divine inspiration,
> Visions that tell of the end of days,
> And urge us now to seek God's ways.[13]

The awesome sales figures of prophecy books tended to be overlooked, since for the most part these works were not issued by the big New York houses, but by publishers located in Grand Rapids, Waco, Tulsa, or Eugene. (Hal Lindsey, who broke through to megabestsellerdom, proved the exception. His *Late Great Planet Earth,* first published by the Zondervan Corporation of Grand Rapids, was acquired for mass-market distribution by Bantam Books, which subsequently issued *The 1980s: Countdown to Armageddon.*) A 1978 *New York Times Book Review* feature on the surging sales of prophecy books urged those interested to "take a look at the catalogues of the more than 80 houses prospering west of the Hudson," but few heeded the advice. (The media giants, however, soon realized that prophecy could mean big money: in 1977, ABC acquired Word Books, a Waco evangelical house with a thriving prophecy list; in 1988, Harper and

Row paid some $57 million for Zondervan, a major prophecy publisher.)[14]

The marketing of prophecy books, too, diverged from the beaten track. While most general bookstores, airport bookshops, and outlets such as B. Dalton and Waldenbooks contained a "Prophecy, New Age, and Occult" section (or some variant thereof), the genre's natural habitat was the nation's six thousand Christian bookstores, where they were thick on the shelves.[15] In 1987 Logos Books, a Los Angeles Christian bookstore near the UCLA campus, stocked no fewer than eighty-one separate prophecy titles.

Magazines such as *Moody Monthly, Eternity, Christianity Today,* and Falwell's *Fundamentalist Journal* also, with varying degrees of circumspection, spread the prophetic word. Evangelical seminaries and Bible schools—Dallas Theological Seminary and Chicago's Moody Bible Institute, for example—functioned as centers of prophetic teaching, with faculty and graduates who figured prominently among the authors of prophecy popularizations. (Hal Lindsey is a product of Dallas Theological Seminary, and John F. Walvoord is a former chancellor.) Prophecy aficionados could also choose from dozens of fugitive publications such as James McKeever's *End-Times News Digest;* Charles Taylor's *Bible Prophecy News;* Peter Lalonde's *Omega Letter;* and Salem Kirban's *Rapture Alert Newsletter,* which in 1988 featured Mrs. Kirban's chicken-soup recipe along with predictions of the end. In Houston prophecy writer Hilton Sutton operated a twenty-four-hour prophecy hotline. Itinerant prophecy expositors held forth in charismatic and independent Bible churches across the land. Participants in the Bible Prophecy Seminars led by Seventh-day Adventist pastors as proselytizing devices received free mints, colorful worksheets illustrating the prophecies, and an impressive Certificate of Achievement at the conclusion.[16]

Evangelical churches and youth groups screened prophecy films with titles such as *Thief in the Night* and *The Road to Armageddon.* Tracts and Christian comic books disseminated the end-time message as well. The Rapture, the future moment when, according to many prophecy believers, all true Christians will rise to meet Jesus Christ in the air, was a favorite theme with the marketers of end-time kitsch. Salem Kirban and Leon Bates of the Texas-based Bible Believers' Evangelistic Association offered Rapture wrist watches with the words "ONE HOUR NEARER THE LORD'S RETURN" inscribed around the face; bumper stickers proclaiming "Beam Me Up, Lord," or "Warning: If the Rapture Occurs, This Car Will Be Driverless"; and full-color Rapture paintings, complete with crashing cars and planes, available in postcard format, as framed prints, and as laminated placemats. Prophecy belief, in short, loomed large on the landscape of U.S. evangelicalism in the twentieth century's waning decades.[17] (While the Second Coming is part of the Roman Catholic creed, Catholics do not as a rule, for reasons we shall explore, expend much energy on prophecy speculation.)

Prophecy belief filtered into secular mass culture as well, through novels such as *The Omen* (1976) by David Seltzer and, indirectly, through the genre some labeled "secular apocalyptic." Although the latter lies outside the purview of this study, its prevalence further testified to the upsurge of apocalypticism in these years. In *Terminal Visions* (1982), an illuminating study of "the literature of last things," the historian W. Warren Wagar explores the massive outpouring of apocalyptic fiction in the same years that popularizations of biblical prophecy enjoyed such a vogue. Wagar's list of more than three hundred novels, plays, poems, and science-fiction stories dealing with the end of the world, most published since World War II, includes highly varied titles such as Philip Dick and Roger Zelazny, *Deus Irae* (1976); Robert Merle, *Malevil* (1972); Michael Moorcock, *Dancers at the End of Time* (2 vols., 1972, 1974); Larry Niven and Jerry Pournelle, *Lucifer's Hammer* (1977); Douglas Orgill and John Gribben, *The Sixth Winter* (1979); Doris Piserchia, *A Billion Days of Earth* (1976); and James White, *The Dream Millennium* (1974)—and this enumeration, Wagar warns, "is far from a complete list."[18]

The movie versions of Seltzer's *Omen* (1976) and its sequels *Damien–Omen II* (1978) and *The Final Conflict* (1981) feature the birth, childhood, and career of Antichrist, the end-time ruler whose reign will come, according to prophecy believers, during a seven-year period known as the Tribulation that will follow the Rapture. *The Seventh Sign* (1988) was built around the seven end-time plagues prophesied in the Book of Revelation. In the 1984 hit *Ghostbusters,* a taxi driver quoted apocalyptic scriptures while Dan Ackroyd and his crew battled sinister supernatural forces. *The Rapture* (1991) featured Mimi Rogers as a sexually promiscuous telephone operator who is converted to fundamentalist Christianity just in time to experience the end of the world.[19]

Apocalypticism, sometimes explicitly biblical, cropped up in rock and pop music with surprising frequency, as in Barry Maguire's 1965 hit "The Eve of Destruction"; David Bowie's "[We've Got] Five More Years" (1972); the Sex Pistols' "Anarchy in the U.K." (1976) with its riveting first line, "I Am Antichrist"; Jean Siberry's 1984 "Mimi on the Beach" ("The great leveller is coming, and he's going to take those mountains and shove them in the valleys"); and Nick Cave's "City of Refuge" (1988), with its fire and brimstone imagery. Elvis Costello worked this vein in several songs, including "Waiting for the End of the World" (1977) and "Hurry Down, Doomsday (The Bugs Are Taking Over)" (1991).

"Apocalypse, in 9/8," part of the 1972 Genesis album *Foxtrot,* offered lyrics familiar to anyone even casually acquainted with the Book of Revelation:

> With the guards of Magog, swarming around
> The Pied Piper takes his children underground.
> The dragon's coming out of the sea,
> and the shimmering head of wisdom looking at me.
> . . . . .
> 666 is no longer alone,
> He's getting out the marrow in your backbone,
> And the seven trumpets blowing sweet rock and roll,
> Gonna blow right down inside your soul.

Another 1972 album, *666* (Antichrist's number, as recorded in Rev. 13:18), by a group called Aphrodite's Child, featured "The Seventh Seal," "The Four Horsemen," "The Beast," and other songs drawn from the Book of Revelation.[20]

Predictably, end-time motifs figured prominently in the lyrics of Christian rock groups such as DeGarmo and Key, whose video "Six, Six, Six" ran afoul of television guidelines in the mid-1980s for its graphic scenes of flames consuming a dapper-looking Satan in modish suit and dark glasses.[21]

The folk and gospel music genres also offered a rich harvest of apocalypticism. In 1973 the folk-music magazine *Sing Out* published "When Sorrows Encompass Me 'Round," a song about the Rapture. The Reverend Calvin Bridges' popular gospel song "Save Me Lord" included the following lines:

> Don't you see the signs?
> Wars and famine.
> It's all coming true
> Just like Jesus said.

You better believe my friend
One day this will all end.

Will you be welcome at the Kingdom's gate?
Just as sure as there's a heaven
He's coming back again
Just like he said.

At a 1990 Arkansas folk festival, a group electrified the audience with a haunting rendition of "Set Your Fields on Fire," a song about the Day of Judgment.[22]

The cultural preoccupation with the end penetrated even the worlds of Madison Avenue and mass marketing. A jingle in a 1990 Pizza Hut commercial contained these lines: "Beware of 666. It's the Anti-Pizza." A Los Angeles rug dealer advertised his going-out-of-business sale with the resonant headline, "THE END IS NEAR." The supermarket tabloids routinely offered "Amazing All-New Bible Prophecies" and "New Bible Cures and Predictions."[23]

At a different cultural level, Carl Orff's 1973 choral work, *De temporum fine comoedia* (Play about the end of time), based on the prophetic writings of the patristic theologian Origen, perhaps deliberately echoed—though with darker shading—Olivier Messiaen's *Quartet for the End of Time* (1940). In the visual arts, Richard Misrach's *Desert Cantos* (1987) presented a series of photographs of desert conflagrations eerily evocative of biblical images of Earth's fiery demise. In Robert Longo's sculpture "Seven Seals for Missouri Break," sinister jockeys emerge from a steel slab, recalling the death-dealing four horsemen of the Book of Revelation. And "New Visions of the Apocalypse," a 1988–89 exhibit at the museum of the Rhode Island School of Design, offered works by contemporary artists who drew on biblical images of the end even as they evoked an apocalypse that will be man-made rather than supernatural. The show's curator, Daniel Rosenfeld, explicitly linked the painters and sculptors affected by contemporary apocalypticism to earlier artists, including Albrecht Dürer and Michelangelo, influenced by biblical eschatology.[24]

The surge in prophecy interest epitomized by the success of *The Late Great Planet Earth* had deep roots. The story of Euro-American prophecy belief, as we shall see, begins with the Puritans (if not with Christopher Columbus). In the early post–World War II years, popular interest in Bible prophecy burgeoned under the impetus of the atomic bomb, the founding of Israel in 1948, and other factors. As early as 1953, prophecy writer Wilbur Smith observed, "Books on prophetic subjects are pouring from the presses . . . more frequently than ever before." In 1960, a professor at an evangelical seminary in Indiana spoke of the "amazing interest in predictive prophecy . . . within recent years."[25]

But popular attention to biblical prophecy, already at a high level, unquestionably intensified after 1970. Timothy Weber in 1978 described "the resurgence of . . . interest in prophetic themes" as "one of the most significant developments in American religion since the Second World War." Prophecy writers of the seventies often marveled at what one in 1975 called "the mushrooming interest" in the topic. One enterprising editor, candidly acknowledging that "Armageddon has become a growth industry," in 1979 put together an anthology of prophetic writings that he titled *Endtime: The Doomsday Catalog.* The *Atlantic Monthly* in 1982 featured as its cover story an overview of the prophecy phenomenon by a Rice University sociologist.[26]

Some evangelical leaders and established prophecy expositors lamented this wave of what *Christianity Today* in 1978 called "doomsday chic." "Prophecy is easily the hottest item in evangelical circles," observed the same magazine dryly in 1981. As early as 1975, *Eternity,* an old-line prophecy magazine, had surveyed the torrent of prophecy paperbacks and films and commented: "The whole field . . . has become the plaything of a lot of rampant imaginations . . . They have hopelessly complicated an otherwise beautiful and simple truth." But whether they approved or deplored the prophecy surge, none denied its reality. As Michael Barkun observed in 1983, "Far from suffering terminal exhaustion, apocalyptic literature is more popular in America now than at any time since the early nineteenth century."[27]

A wealth of anecdotal evidence underscores the ubiquity of prophecy belief in contemporary America. My Los Angeles airport experience proved only the first of many similar encounters. On a 1990 flight to the West Coast my seatmate, a Free Methodist minister in Washington State, told of a congregant immersed in the prophecies who expounds them at length to the pastor and fellow churchmembers.[28] My return–flight seatmate, a premillennialist missionary in Kenya, learning of my research, expressed her conviction that the world is growing worse as the end approaches. A pentecostalist in the row ahead joined in, adding his testimony to the truth of prophetic scripture.

A Wisconsin history colleague recalls that his grandmother, an otherwise benevolent soul, firmly believed that God will destroy the Soviet Union in the end times. A graduate student tells of teaching in a private school near Nashville; the seventh graders, terrified by reports that the Rapture would occur in September 1988, sat at their desks in nervous anticipation at noon on the appointed day. This same young woman describes a sister who, from being a partying undergraduate at Vanderbilt University, became a committed prophecy believer who now at family gatherings urges her father and siblings to prepare for the end. A professor at a college in Pennsylvania writes of students convinced that the 1990 Persian Gulf crisis heralded Armageddon. After the October 1989 San Francisco earthquake, a caller to Larry King's "Open-Phone America" TV show noted the (to him) portentous fact that a commentator had described the quake's "biblical proportions." He further claimed (incorrectly, as it turned out) that only government buildings had been demolished. King seemed mystified, but anyone attuned to the prophecy subculture could immediately understand: the Book of Revelation foretells earthquakes, and the destruction of the world's rulers, in the last days.[29]

Much anecdotal evidence relates to apprehension surrounding the mysterious number 666. A Madison retailer tells of customers who will not accept change of $6.66. A professor at Macalester College in St. Paul recalls the year her auto license plate included the fateful digits, and service-station attendants would ask nervously, "Is that the devil's car?" When the police chief of Horicon, Wisconsin, received an official license plate numbered 666 for 1989, he returned it after repeated comments by worried citizens. A historian friend recalls an early 1980s camping trip with his wife in a remote part of Michigan's Upper Peninsula. When the bill at a back-country store totaled $6.66, he writes, the shopkeeper "leaned forward, scrutinized me under rising brows, and informed me, with a mixture of what seemed like excitement and dread: 'That's the Devil's number.' As Mark Twain might have put it, we went away from there."[30]

Added to other forms of evidence, such stories help convey a sense of the pervasiveness of these doctrines. As the historian Leonard Sweet observed in 1979, only partly in jest, "Watching, waiting, and working for the millennium . . . has become, even more than baseball, America's favorite pastime."[31] This hidden world is not so hidden after all, if one knows where to look.

Nor can we dismiss prophecy belief as confined to some mythic southern Bible Belt, or as simply another export from southern California, where people spend too much time in the sun. Such stereotypes do, of course, have a grain of truth. For reasons rooted in history and demography, prophecy beliefs *are* probably more widely held in the South than in other regions, and they *do* proliferate in southern California with a special lushness. Certain cities of the Southwest and Far West—Dallas, Los Angeles, Oklahoma City—appear to have extra-heavy concentrations of prophecy devotees. Not only does the South have a much higher proportion of Protestants than any other region—74 percent as compared to 61 percent in the Midwest, 47 percent in the West, and 40 percent in the Northeast—but these include a high concentration of evangelicals and fundamentalists, among whom prophecy belief flourishes. In 1986, 48 percent of southerners described themselves as "born-again Christians," as compared to 31 percent of midwesterners, 28 percent of westerners, and 19 percent in the Northeast. About 10 percent more southerners, according to the polls, believe in the Bible's literal, word-for-word inerrancy than do respondents in other regions.[32]

While prophecy belief may be somewhat more pervasive in the South, in the post–World War II years (and certainly since 1970) it was clearly a *national,* not a strictly regional, phenomenon. With the spread of cable TV and communications satellites, prophecy-oriented evangelists reached a national and even global audience, and Christian bookstores that sold prophecy books by the millions dotted the nation. In Madison, Wisconsin, far from the Mason-Dixon line, seven evangelical bookstores and over fifty charismatic or evangelical "Bible-believing" churches disseminated the prophetic word as the 1990s began. "Prophecy conferences" in 1988–89 at two of Madison's larger charismatic churches—the Shalom Christian Center and the Madison Gospel Tabernacle—attracted hundreds of believers who followed the sermons in well-thumbed Bibles, took notes as the ministers expounded their interpretive schemes, applauded and chuckled appreciatively at ingenious applications of the prophecies to current events, and perused the paperbacks and cassettes offered for sale after the service. All America, not one region, is a "Bible Belt."

Furthermore, one should not too quickly stereotype prophecy belief as unique to the poor, ignorant, or unusually credulous. No doubt in late-twentieth-century America these beliefs are statistically more pervasive among the lower-income groups and those with less formal schooling. In the abovementioned 1986 poll, the proportion of Americans describing themselves as "born again" correlated inversely with education, falling from 38 percent among those lacking a high-school degree to 17 percent of college graduates. In a 1983 poll, 70 percent of adults without a high-school diploma said Jesus will come again, compared to 63 percent of high-school graduates and 50 percent of college graduates.[33]

But the correlation is far from absolute. Prophecy belief pervades all educational and income levels, including Ph.D.'s in computer science and multimillionaire Texas oilmen. A mid-1980s study of a "not particularly conservative" community college in Oregon found that one-third of the students believed in the Rapture.[34] One need only attend a service at the 26-thousand-member First Baptist Church of Dallas (the world's largest Southern Baptist congregation); Chuck Smith's Calvary Chapel in Orange, California; or any of hundreds of large evangelical congregations across America to realize that these beliefs are not solely a refuge of the desperate, the unlettered, or the disinherited. The Shalom Christian Center and the Madison Gospel Tabernacle are large, well-appointed edifices; on the evenings I attended, the parking lots were full of cars of considerably more recent vintage than my own. The upper-white-collar ranks of academics and professionals were probably underrepresented in the audiences, but the meetings were not by any means confined to the poor or ill educated.

The sociologist James Davison Hunter, analyzing data on evangelicals collected in 1978–79 by the Princeton Religious Research Center, found a similarly nuanced picture: evangelicals are *somewhat* lower in overall educational and income levels than their liberal Protestant counterparts, or than the national averages, but not dramatically enough to justify sweeping generalizations. Of the evangelicals in the sample, 38 percent were high-school graduates, 15 percent had done some college work, and 9 percent held college degrees. As for income, they were slightly overrepresented in the lower income quartile and underrepresented in the upper quartile, but most fell in the middle income levels. In a follow-up study in 1987, Hunter reiterated that evangelicals, while concentrated in the middle and lower social ranks, could be found at all points on the spectrum. Another sociologist, David Moberg, writing in 1975, agreed: "Some evidence may substantiate the generally lower than average social class position of evangelicals and especially of fundamentalists, but diversities are so great that stereotyped images of evangelicals as low-middle-class people are unwarranted."[35]

All of these social data offer suggestive clues to the characteristics of the "typical" prophecy believer, as do studies that find evangelicalism and biblical literalism more pervasive among women, blacks, and older Americans.[36] But in noting regional, educational, and other patterns, one ought not lose sight of the larger picture: the beliefs explored in this book *pervaded* U.S. thought and culture as the twentieth century drew to a close. Many millions of Americans of all races, regions, and socioeconomic levels embraced them. In noting the inverse relationship of education and belief in the Second Coming, for example, one ought not overlook that *50 percent* of U.S. *college graduates* await Jesus Christ's return. As Gallup and Castelli observed in 1989, the United States is nearly unique in the Western world with its "unmatched combination of high levels of education and high levels of religious belief and activity."[37]

Despite a vague awareness that prophecy belief is rampant "out there"—in the dark beyond the campfire, so to speak—academics have given these beliefs little systematic attention. Even scholars who have aided our understanding of popular eschatology in earlier eras reinforce the view that the subject is now of historical interest only. Marjorie Reeves, author of a valuable study of Joachim of Fiore, the twelfth-century monk whose prophetic interpretations contributed to a rich flowering of prophecy interest in the late Middle Ages, insisted in 1969 that "prophecy has now ceased to be of importance, except on the fringes of modern civilization." Christopher Hill, concluding his study of prophecy writings in Puritan England, claimed that such beliefs eventually "disappeared . . . into the world of cranks."[38] Yet in late-twentieth-century America, the "fringes" were very broad indeed, and the "cranks" numbered in the millions!

Even intellectual and cultural historians have paid surprisingly little notice to modern prophecy belief (or, indeed, to evangelicalism in general). The movies, advertising, and TV "sitcoms" receive well-deserved attention, but the cultural role of evangelical Protestantism goes largely unremarked. Popular-culture specialists who can learnedly discuss L. Frank Baum, Walt Disney, Bob Dylan, or Martin

Scorsese stare blankly if the names of major prophecy writers are mentioned. To resort to the anecdotal a final time, in the later 1980s academic friends and colleagues greeted my descriptions of my current research with bemused puzzlement. The name "Hal Lindsey" became for me a kind of litmus test; it rarely elicited a flicker of recognition.

Even historians of American religion have slighted the world of modern evangelicalism and charismatic Protestantism (although a growing company of scholars beginning with Timothy Smith, George Marsden, and Ernest Sandeen, and including Robert Mapes Anderson, Timothy Weber, Nathan Hatch, Joel Carpenter, Mark Noll, R. Laurence Moore, and William Trollinger, are gradually rectifying this omission).[39] Interestingly, it is not a historian but a political scientist, Michael Barkun, who has produced the most thoughtful and intellectually sophisticated work on prophetic belief in our own day.[40] We have a continuing stream of scholarly work on New England Puritanism, the Great Awakening, antebellum revivalism, the theological ramifications of Darwinism, the pre-1920 Social Gospel, and the intellectual impact of Reinhold Niebuhr, but then the flow slows to a trickle. As Nathan Hatch and others have noted, historians of U.S. Protestantism have focused more on liberal and ecumenical trends in the mainstream denominations than on evangelical belief and practice.

A Whiggish belief in progress still seems to inform the historiography of American religion: Protestant evangelicalism, important in its day, collapsed under the assault of modernism, secularism, and scientific naturalism. Certainly all these developments had their impact, yet history is not a zero-sum game: *pace* the undergraduate-bluebook version of history, one can recognize the force of new trends while at the same time understanding that deeply engrained belief systems do not vanish overnight. Whatever else it accomplished, the conservative resurgence of the 1970s and 1980s revealed the continued vitality of evangelicalism and fundamentalism.

Nor have the media given prophecy belief more than cursory attention. Magazines such as *Harper's* poke fun at it—printing an extract from a paperback arguing that Mikhail Gorbachev is Antichrist for its comic value, for example—but make little effort to understand it. The newsmagazines briefly noted what *Newsweek* labeled "The Boom in Doom" during Hal Lindsey's heyday, but otherwise displayed little interest. President Ronald Reagan's well-documented interest in prophecy briefly drew attention during the 1984 campaign, but media pundits confined themselves largely to inconclusive speculation about whether Reagan's beliefs might increase the likelihood that he would launch a nuclear war—admittedly not a trivial question—rather than an exploration of the theological sources or cultural meaning of these beliefs.[41]

A few writers outside academia have contributed to our knowledge of the cultural and political implications of contemporary prophecy belief. A. G. Mojtabai's *Blessed Assurance* (1986) noted the ubiquity of end-time belief in Amarillo, home of a hydrogen-bomb assembly plant, and offered illuminating reflections on its psychological function. In *Prophecy and Politics* (1986), the journalist Grace Halsell documented how particular readings of the prophecies led U.S. fundamentalist leaders to align themselves with the most expansionist, hard-line political groups in Israel.[42] But such studies are rare.

This book, then, is a foray into what, for many, will be intellectual terra incognita. My claim on the reader's attention, and my justification for devoting so many pages to a belief system seemingly so marginal and fantastic, is, first, that these beliefs are in fact far more pervasive than many realize and, second, that if one examines them attentively, themes emerge that tell us much about the larger worldview of those who embrace and promulgate them. What Christopher Hill wrote at the end of his study of Antichrist theories in seventeenth-century England applies equally well to prophecy belief in modern America: "In one sense we have been exploring a trivial blind alley in human thought: but at all points it trembles on the brink of major intellectual issues."[43]

Since the belief system to which we now turn is unfamiliar to many, I have tried to lay the groundwork carefully. This book therefore takes what may seem an excessively long time getting to its putative subject: prophecy belief in post–World War II America. I begin with the apocalyptic scriptures that underlie this belief system; briefly trace the history of Christian eschatological thought; and look with some care at the origins and development to 1945 of the most popular interpretive system, the so-called premillennial-dispensational system. At last, in Chapter 4, I turn to the central themes of popular prophecy belief since World War II, explore the ways these doctrines shaped the worldview of those who embraced them, speculate on their remarkable tenacity, and offer some concluding reflections on the future of prophetic belief in America. (Readers familiar with the biblical and historical background, or who simply wish to move quickly to the contemporary period, are of course free to begin with Chapter 4.) My aim throughout is not to ridicule or trivialize beliefs espoused by millions of Americans, but to understand them and to reflect on their meaning and implications.

With this introductory overview, let us turn now to a historical era more than two millennia in the past, when the apocalyptic texts still combed by contemporary prophecy expositors first came into being.

I

The Genre and Its Early Interpreters

1 *Origins of the Apocalyptic*

The prophetic beliefs that influenced the worldview of millions of Americans in the late twentieth century were grounded in the sacred texts of a far-distant era. In an age of computers, space travel, and genetic engineering, a genre of visionary writing that flowered from the middle of the second century B.C. to the end of the first century A.D., and whose roots go back much further, shaped countless believers' views of what lay ahead for humankind.

This genre, the apocalyptic, has complex sources. Historians of the ancient world find mythic outlines of history, conflict between cosmic forces of good and evil (or order and chaos), and eschatological visions in many ancient literatures, including Ugaritic, Akkadian, Babylonian, Egyptian, Canaanite, Greek, Hellenistic, and Roman. Early Persian mysticism had strong apocalyptic elements as well, although the problems of dating Persian texts make it difficult to discuss their influence with any confidence.[1]

Hesiod, a Greek poet thought to have lived in the eighth century B.C., believed that man's only hope lay in absolute submission to the gods. He envisioned history as a divinely ordered succession of worsening stages, descending from a golden age to a silver and on through bronze and iron—metallic symbolism that would reemerge in the Jewish Book of Daniel. In Hesiod's bleak view, the final stage, before Zeus destroyed humankind for its wickedness, would be marked by warfare and social discord: "Bitter sorrows will be left for mortal men, and there will be no help against evil."[2] Vergil's *Aeneid,* by contrast, foretold a "golden age" for Rome, with the Emperor Augustus as the promised deliverer.

In fragmentary Akkadian texts, the apocalyptic vision is of a tyrant whose rule will produce both human and natural disasters:

> A dreadful [man], son of a nobody, whose name is not mentioned, will arise.
> As king he will seize the throne, he will destroy his lords with weapons.

> Half the troops of Akkad will fall, in the gorges of Tupliash
> They will fill plain and hills.
> The people of the land will experience great scarcity.
> · · · · ·
> A prince will arise, three years will he exercise sovereignty.
> [The canals] and the rivers will fill up with sand.
> · · · · ·
> The rest of mankind [will descend] into the earth.
> Cities will decay, houses [will be desolate].
> Revolution, destruction will occur . . . [etc.]³

But if the apocalyptic had multiple sources, it reached its apogee among the Jews. Scholars have identified at least sixteen Judaic works in this genre. One Jewish source from circa 100 A.D. mentions the existence of *seventy* apocalypses. While many early peoples viewed history apocalyptically, as a reflection of the gods' titanic struggles, Judaism proved particularly congenial to this worldview. As Ruth Bloch has observed, the Jews' belief in a God "known primarily through his people's experiences on earth [produced] a particularly keen sense of the sacred significance of secular history." In addition, Judaism's linear conception of time, in which history has a distinct beginning and follows a clearly defined forward trajectory, further encouraged an eschatological vision of history culminating in a series of cosmic end-time events. As a deeply religious and comparatively weak people surrounded by powerful, warring neighbors, the Jews were further drawn to a cosmology involving supernatural conflict and the ultimate triumph of righteousness.⁴

The Jewish apocalyptic genre emerged from the earlier prophetic tradition, but is distinct from it. The Jewish prophets of the eighth to the sixth centuries B.C.—Amos, Joel, Isaiah, Jeremiah, Ezekiel, and the others—functioned primarily as preachers, focusing on the people's transgressions and foretelling the Lord's renewed favor if they repented and further woes if they did not. The prophets were present minded and specific as they addressed a people beset by enemies and continually straying from the path of righteousness.

The Jewish apocalypticists, by contrast, were learned stylists consciously creating a literary genre that relied heavily on symbol and allegory to reveal the divine plan underlying the surface flow of events. Taking the entire sweep of history as their subject, they portrayed in metaphorical language the future of the Jews, the fate of Israel's enemies, and the ultimate destiny of humanity and the universe itself. The prophets viewed the struggle between good and evil as an individual and corporate matter; the apocalypticists saw it in cosmic terms.[5]

Nevertheless, the two genres are closely related. Apocalyptic and eschatological passages appear in the works of the prophets, with their references to the end times and an approaching "Day of the Lord." Indeed, an apocalyptic passage much cited by contemporary popularizers for its alleged foretelling of a Soviet invasion of Israel (see Chapter 5) is embedded within the Book of Ezekiel. One scholar has seen in these early prophetic books "the dawn of apocalyptic."[6]

What, then, is an apocalypse? The word itself is Greek, meaning an unveiling of that which is hidden. The biblical scholar John Collins offers a useful definition: "A genre of revelatory literature with a narrative framework, in which a revelation is mediated by an otherworldly being to a human recipient, disclosing a transcendent reality which is both temporal, insofar as it envisages eschatological salvation, and spatial insofar as it involves another, supernatural world." Collins further distinguishes two major types of apocalypse: the *historical,* alluding to actual events, past or future, and the *otherworldly journey,* set entirely in a supernatural, extraterrestrial realm.[7] Another salient characteristic of the Jewish apocalypses is their pseudepigraphic character. The works are almost invariably attributed to some revered sage or semimythic leader of the past: Ezra, Enoch, Baruch, Abraham, Daniel, and the like. By this means the actual authors gave their texts added credibility and linked them to Jewish history and religious tradition.

What of the social context of the Jewish apocalypses? As Collins emphasizes, to speak of a single "apocalyptic movement" is misleading: although all apocalypses share certain common characteristics, the immediate events and circumstances, as well as literary convention, determined each one's specific shape and content. Since this mode of apprehending human destiny has historically appealed especially to those who see their era as a time of crisis, it is not surprising that the apocalypses that made their way into the canon and exerted the greatest continuing influence were those that emerged from periods of upheaval and danger, when the groups to whom they were addressed faced exile, persecution, or death. "Apocalyptic was born of crisis," writes David Noel Freedman; "it was underground literature, the consolation of the persecuted." While not all apocalypses fall into the "literature-of-the-oppressed" or "literature-of-crisis" category, as Bernard McGinn has reminded us, these are the ones that survive as living texts.[8] Of the three apocalypses most widely influential in late-twentieth-century America, the first two, from the Old Testament books of Ezekiel and Daniel, date from eras when the Jews faced extinction as a nation. The third, the Revelation of John, emerged at a time when the Christians of Asia Minor faced persecution and martyrdom at the hands of Roman authorities.

Since these three works loom so large in modern-day apocalyptic scenarios, an overview of their origins, content, and themes—as well as those of another key text, the "Little Apocalypse" of Mark 13—may be helpful. (All quotations are from the King James Bible, the translation preferred by most contemporary popularizers.) As we immerse ourselves briefly in apocalyptic texts that seem on first encounter forbidding if not utterly inaccessible, we can more fully appreciate the ingenuity with which later interpreters have teased from them complex patterns of meaning, detailed allusions to current events, and ominous future portents.

The Book of Ezekiel

The brief apocalypse incorporated in the Book of Ezekiel dates from the time of crisis in Jewish history precipitated by the depredations of the Babylonian king Nebuchadnezzar in the early sixth century B.C. In 597, engaged in a protracted power struggle with the Egyptians, Nebuchadnezzar captured Jerusalem and carried back to Babylon King Jehoiachin and his court, together with several thousand Jewish soldiers, priests, and artisans, beginning what would become a sixty-year exile. These first exiles viewed their captivity as temporary, but as war between Babylon and Egypt dragged on, Judea remained a battleground. In 586, after a year-long siege, Nebuchadnezzar sacked Jerusalem, destroyed the temple, and wrought a terrible vengeance on Zedekiah, who had acted as king in Jehoiachin's absence. Zedekiah's children were killed before his eyes, and he himself was blinded and carried a prisoner to Babylon.[9]

These horrifying events shattered the optimistic mood of the initial phase of the Babylonian exile and gave rise to the Book of Ezekiel, which foretells the Jews' restoration to their land and the destruction of future invaders.[10] As the work begins, Ezekiel identifies himself as a priest carried to Babylon with Jehoiachin, and places his initial vision in "the fifth year of king Jehoiachin's captivity," in other words, 592 B.C. The apocalyptic section of the work, however, found in chapters 37–39, is usually dated from a period after Nebuchadnezzar's destruction of the temple in 586.[11]

In chapter 37 Ezekiel is "carried . . . out in the spirit of the Lord" and set down in a valley full of dry bones, which by God's command come together and take on sinews and flesh. As the breath of life returns, they stand on their feet, "an exceeding great army." Explaining that the bones represent "the whole house of Israel," the Lord unfolds the vision's meaning and gives Ezekiel his prophetic mandate:

> Therefore prophesy and say unto them, Thus saith the Lord God, Behold O my people, I will open your graves, and cause you to come up out of your graves, and bring you into the land of Israel . . .
> And they shall dwell in the land that I have given unto Jacob my servant, wherein your fathers have dwelt; and they shall dwell therein, even they, and their children, and their children's children forever: and my servant David shall be their prince forever.

Ezekiel next reveals the fate awaiting the heathen "in the latter days"—not only Israel's neighbors, but more distant enemies as well. "Son of man," God declares as chapter 38 opens, "set thy face against Gog, the land of Magog, the chief prince of Meshech and Tubal, and prophesy against him." Gog, the Lord continues, together with "Persia, Ethiopia, and Libya . . . , Gomer, and all his bands; the house of Togarmah of the north quarters, and all his bands; and many people with thee," will invade an unsuspecting Israel seeking "to take a spoil and to take a prey." Undeterred by a challenge from "Sheba, and Dedan, and the merchants of Tarshish, with all the young lions thereof," the invaders advance on horseback in full battle array, coming "against my people of Israel, as a cloud to cover the land." But this invasion arouses God's fury, with terrible consequences:

> For in my jealousy and in the fire of my wrath have I spoken, Surely in that day there shall be a great shaking in the land of Israel;
> So that the fishes of the sea, and the fowls of the heaven, and the beasts of the field, and all creeping things that creep upon the earth, and all the men that are upon the face of the earth, shall shake at my presence, and the mountains shall be thrown down,

and the steep places shall fall, and every wall shall fall to the ground.

Afflicted "with pestilence and with blood, . . . overflowing rain, and great hailstones, fire, and brimstone," the terrified invaders turn on one another, and "every man's sword shall be against his brother." So great is the destruction that only a sixth of the attacking army survives. Meanwhile, fire falls on the land of Magog itself, "and among them that dwell carelessly in the isles: . . . and the heathen shall know that I am the Lord, the Holy One in Israel." With the invading armies destroyed by God himself, the Israelites burn their enemies' shields, spears, and bows and arrows in a conflagration that lasts for seven years. The stench of the dead is awful, and the burial of the bodies and cleansing of the land takes seven months. The Lord summons "ravenous birds of every sort, and . . . the beasts of the field" to gorge themselves on the remains:

> And ye shall eat fat till ye be full, and drink blood till ye be drunken, of my sacrifice which I have sacrificed for you.
> Thus ye shall be filled at my table with horses and chariots, with mighty men, and with all men of war, saith the Lord God.

The terrible vision closes with the Lord's reminder to Ezekiel that the Jews "went into captivity for their iniquity: because they trespassed against me, therefore hid I my face from them, and gave them into the hand of their enemies: so fell they all by the sword." But this divinely ordained suffering will end: when the Lord brings the Jews once more into Judea, they will worship him as before. Chapter 39 ends on a note of promise: "Neither will I hide my face any more from them: for I have poured out my spirit upon the house of Israel, saith the Lord God."

The Book of Daniel

This best-known of the Jewish apocalypses, which launched the genre as a distinct literary form, is dated by most scholars to the second century B.C., when Judea was once again under attack. Now the threat came from Antiochus IV of Syria, also known as Antiochus Epiphanes ("Illustrious"), who reigned from 175 to 164 B.C. A ruler of the Seleucid dynasty established in the late fourth century by Seleucus, a general of Alexander the Great, Antiochus from his capital in

Damascus sought to solidify and extend his realm by spreading Hellenistic culture and religion.

In pursuit of this goal (and to finance a campaign against Ptolemaic Egypt), he plundered the temple treasure in Jerusalem. Next, supported by a small cadre of hellenized Jews, Antiochus appointed his own high priests—first Jason and then Menelaus, renamed Jerusalem Antiochia, and established a gymnasium in the city as a center of Hellenistic cultic practices. Moving openly to destroy Judaism in 167, he forbade circumcision and Sabbath worship under penalty of death, forced Jews to take part in pagan rituals and to eat pork, and desecrated the Temple by erecting a statue of Zeus (called "the abomination of desolation" by Jewish writers) in place of the holy altar. These outrages gave rise to a resistance movement led by the Hasmonean family under Mattathias and his son Judah, nicknamed Maccabee. In 164, following Antiochus' death, the Maccabean rebels recaptured Jerusalem, purified the Temple, and rededicated it to God—a triumph commemorated in the Jewish festival of Hanukkah.[12]

The Book of Daniel dates from the period immediately following Antiochus' Temple desecration, and before the Maccabean restoration. The unknown author ascribed the work to a heroic figure, Daniel (linked by some scholars to a Ugaritic mythic figure of the same name),[13] and set it four hundred years earlier, in the time of the Babylonian captivity. Interwoven with the apocalyptic visions are the stories (beloved by generations of Sunday school teachers) of King Belshazzar's feast; Daniel in the lions' den; and Shadrach, Meshach, and Abednego in the fiery furnace.

In the first apocalyptic section, found in chapter 2, Daniel is called before King Nebuchadnezzar to interpret a dream the king's wise men have failed to decipher. The dream (distantly echoing the earlier imagery of Hesiod) is of a great statue with a head of gold, breast and arms of silver, belly and thighs of brass, legs of iron, and feet of mixed iron and clay. The statue's feet shatter when a huge stone "cut out without hands" falls upon them. As the statue crumbles, the stone grows into a mountain that fills the entire earth.

The statue, Daniel tells Nebuchadnezzar, represents four kingdoms of diminishing merit and glory. Nebuchadnezzar's own kingdom, Babylon, exemplified by the golden head, will be followed by three others. The last of these, though "strong as iron," will be divided, as symbolized by the ten toes, and become progressively weaker, as suggested by the incongruous juxtaposition of iron and clay. And what of the stone that destroys the statue? Here the eschatological theme emerges:

> And in the days of these kings shall the God of heaven set up a kingdom, which shall never be destroyed: and the kingdom shall . . . break in pieces and consume all these kingdoms and it shall stand forever.

Remarkably unperturbed by the prophesied demise of his kingdom, Nebuchadnezzar showers Daniel with honors for his prophetic gifts.

A second apocalyptic section beginning in chapter 7 recapitulates and embellishes the earlier imagery. Daniel himself now becomes the dreamer and various heavenly figures, including the angel Gabriel, become the interpreters. Four beasts arise from the sea: one like a lion with eagle's wings, human feet, and a human heart; another "like to a bear" with three ribs in its mouth; a third like a leopard with four wings and four heads; the fourth a "dreadful and terrible" monster with devouring iron teeth. This fourth beast has ten horns among which sprouts a "little horn" with human eyes and "a mouth speaking great things." This little horn destroys three of the other ten and makes war against "the saints." But the fourth beast is itself destroyed by "the Ancient of Days," a mysterious figure of awesome power. A fragmentary vision follows of a battle between a two-horned ram and a goat with "a notable horn" between its eyes that changes into four horns, among which the "little horn" again makes an appearance.

Gabriel partially interprets these visions, but the explanations themselves are cryptic. The beasts from the sea and the horned ram and goat, he says, represent successive kingdoms, this time explicitly identified as the Medes, the Persians, and the Greeks—the last destined to fragment into ten smaller kingdoms. The "little horn," Gabriel further reveals, represents a "king of fierce countenance" who will "destroy the mighty and holy people." "By him," the prophecy continues, "the daily sacrifice was taken away, and the place of his [the Lord's] sanctuary was cast down." This desecration will go on for 2,300 days, "and then shall the sanctuary be cleansed." The angelic interpreter also foretells the ultimate rule of righteousness. After the Ancient of Days destroys the little horn, "kingdom and dominion . . . shall be given to the people of the saints of the most High, whose kingdom is an everlasting kingdom, and all dominions shall serve and obey him."

After a prayer of confession for Israel's sins, Gabriel in chapter 9 reveals to Daniel that it will take *seventy weeks* for his "holy city to finish the transgression . . . and to bring in everlasting righteousness, and to seal up the vision and prophecy, and to anoint the most Holy." The first sixty-nine weeks will extend "from the going forth of the commandment to restore and to build Jerusalem unto the Messiah the Prince." After this, "the prince that shall come" will "confirm the covenant with many for one week" but "in the midst of the week he shall cause the sacrifice and the oblation to cease, and for the overspreading of abominations he shall make it desolate." Adding further complexity, a passage in the Book of Jeremiah is recalled (Dan. 9:2) in which "seventy days" actually meant seventy years, by which calculation "seventy weeks" (490 days) would, in fact, equal 490 *years*. As we shall see, few passages in all the apocalyptic scriptures have spawned such a vast body of interpretive speculation as Daniel's prophecy of the seventy weeks.

Following an interlude in which a mysterious robed figure with eyes like "lamps of fire" assures Daniel that the prophecies he is recording are true, chapter 11 offers a lengthy and complex prophecy of a ruler whose kingdom is "divided toward the four winds of heaven; and not to his posterity, nor according to his dominion which he ruled." The chapter foretells wars and dynastic alliances between "the king of the south" and "the king of the north"—actually three successive kings, the last of whom is "a vile person" whose "heart shall be against the holy covenant." In fighting the king of the south, the prophecy goes on, this ruler and his minions "shall pollute the sanctuary of strength, and shall take away the daily sacrifice, and they shall place the abomination that maketh desolate." This evil tyrant is notably arrogant and impious:

> And the king shall do according to his will; and he shall exalt himself, and magnify himself above every god, and shall speak marvelous things against the God of gods, and shall prosper till the indignation be accomplished; for that that is determined shall be done.
> Neither shall he regard the God of his fathers, nor the desire of women, nor regard any god: for he shall magnify himself above all.

But his doom is sealed. The Book of Daniel foretells a cataclysmic battle "at the time of the end" when the king of the north goes forth "with great fury to destroy, and utterly to make away many." But at the moment of his mightiest power "he shall come to his end, and none shall help him." In those days, the prophecy continues in chapter 12, now in a fully eschatological mode,

> There shall be a time of trouble, such as never was since there was a nation even to that same time: and at that time thy people shall be delivered, every one that shall be found written in the book.
> And many of them that sleep in the dust of the earth shall awake, some to everlasting life, and some to shame and everlasting contempt.

Daniel is now commanded to "seal the book, even to the time of the end." As two robed figures materialize by a river, Daniel asks, "How long shall it be to the end of these wonders?" The figure answers, "It shall be for a time, times, and a half; and when he shall have accomplished to scatter the power of the holy people, all these things shall be finished." When Daniel confesses, "I heard, but I understood not," he is given two seemingly contradictory clues to "the time of the end":

> And from the time that the daily sacrifice shall be taken away, and the abomination that maketh desolate set up, there shall be a thousand two hundred and ninety days.
> Blessed is he that waiteth, and cometh to the thousand three hundred and five and thirty days.

With a final instruction to Daniel to take a well-earned rest, the angelic interpreters fall silent and the book draws to a close.

The visions and revelations that crowd the Book of Daniel with dense imagery, cryptic allusions, and complex chronologies have for over two millennia challenged the ingenuity of prophecy interpreters. To modern-day popularizers elaborating a very old Christian interpretive tradition, the work foretells with amazing specificity not only Jesus' first coming, but also a sequence of events that still lies in the future, when (to suggest only the broadest contours) a ten-nation confederation (symbolized by the statue's ten toes) will be ruled by a satanic figure known as Antichrist (the "little horn"), who in history's final moments will be destroyed by Jesus Christ—the rock not made with hands—as he returns to earth in power and majesty.

Biblical scholars not committed to this futurist hermeneutic see the Book of Daniel as primarily historical in nature. A broad scholarly consensus views the book as mainly a reworking of the political and military history of the ancient Near East to the early second century B.C., with special attention to the wars, negotiations, and alliances between the Seleucid dynasty of Syria ("the king of the north") and the Ptolemaic rulers in Egypt ("the king of the south"). By this reading the statue's legs and feet in chapter 2, and the ten-horned beast of chapter 7, represent Alexander the Great and the kingdoms established in the wake of his conquests.[14]

A similarly strong scholarly consensus holds that the "little horn," the "vile person," the "king of fierce countenance," and "the prince that shall come" all refer to Antiochus Epiphanes, whose campaign to stamp out Judaism was at its peak when the work was composed. The allusions to the wicked ruler who will take away "the daily sacrifice," "pollute the sanctuary," and set up "the abomination that maketh desolate" clearly point to Antiochus' proscriptions against Jewish ritual and his desecration of the Temple.[15]

The weight of scholarly opinion views the Book of Daniel as a pseudepigraphic apocalypse written around 167 B.C. and predated to enhance its credibility. By presenting the manuscript as a newly discovered four-hundred-year-old text, the author could treat well-known historical events—Alexander's conquests, the wars of the Seleucids and the Ptolemies, Antiochus' persecutions—as *prophecies,* thereby increasing the authority of those passages that do, in fact, foretell future events. But, as John Collins has observed, the "real" history in the Book of Daniel is not chronicled simply for its own sake; it is transformed into an eschatological drama.[16] As with the apocalypse of Ezekiel 37–39, the work sought to assure faithful Jews reeling under assaults from external enemies that all these events were part of a divine plan that would culminate in the destruction of Israel's foes and the establishment of a righteous and everlasting kingdom.

While a work of learning and literary aspiration, the Book of Daniel is thus also a polemic, carefully crafted to persuade and convince. On the one hand, it implicitly rejects the Hasmodean family's open military resistance, arguing that the invaders will meet their doom by divine intervention, not human action.[17] On the other hand, it passionately urges faithfulness amid persecution and boldly condemns those

Jews seduced by Antiochus' hellenizing program. In describing the "vile" king of the north, the author emphasizes his flattery and his insinuating efforts to curry favor "with them that forsake the holy covenant." Not only Israel's external enemies, but Jews who collaborate with them, face a terrible fate. Given the political and military realities of the day, the promulgation of this work took considerable courage. As the author notes,

> And they that understand among the people shall instruct many: yet they shall fall by the sword, and by flame, by captivity, and by spoil, many days.[18]

Along with its historical content, all interpreters agree, the work also incorporates a transhistorical, apocalyptic element. Through most of the book, evil seems irresistible and ever increasing. Yet at key intervals, and again at the close, the author summons up an eschatological vision of the destruction of the wicked, the resurrection of the dead, and the triumph of righteousness. The power of this vision, penned at a moment when Judaism's survival hung in the balance, underlies the book's continuing appeal.

Jewish apocalyptic writing continued for the next 250 years or more, while Rome replaced Damascus as the threat on the horizon. In 63 B.C. the Romans captured Jerusalem and made Judea an outpost of empire. A revolt broke out in 66 A.D., and four years later a Roman army under Titus sacked Jerusalem, destroying and burning the temple. From this period of renewed crisis date several apocalyptic works, including those scholars have designated II Enoch, IV Ezra (the best, and best known), II Baruch, III Baruch, and others.[19]

The most recently discovered works bearing on the evolution of Jewish apocalyptic thought are the so-called Dead Sea scrolls that came to light in the 1940s and subsequently have been slowly translated and made available to the scholarly world. These scrolls preserve some of the writings of the Essenes, an ascetic sect that arose in Israel in the second century B.C. and lived a celibate, communal life at a Dead Sea site now called Qumran, from which they harshly criticized the priesthood in Jerusalem for laxness in religious observances.[20]

The Qumran scrolls contain copies of some early apocalypses, as well as much apocalyptic eschatology. One of the scrolls is an allegorical reworking of prophecies against Babylon in the Book of Habbakuk to make them apply to the Romans. The "hidden interpretation" of Habbakuk, the Essene writer declares, "refers to the Kittim [Romans], the fear and terror of whom are on all nations, . . . [and] who trample the land with their horses." As the Babylonians did earlier, he prophesies, the Romans will destroy the priesthood in Jerusalem for its wrongdoing. Another Qumran scroll, the Manual of Discipline, is explicitly eschatological, describing a battle between the Sons of Light and the Sons of Darkness "at the end of days."

The Essenes were among the last of the Jewish apocalypticists. With the failure of the Jewish revolt of 66–70 A.D. and a final one in 132–135 A.D., the rabbinate condemned this genre as futile and dangerous, and apocalypticism largely faded from Jewish thought.[21]

The "Little Apocalypse" of Mark 13

Meanwhile, the apocalyptic vision had been absorbed into early Christianity, where it would prove remarkably durable. Eschatology's precise role in the beginnings of Christianity has stirred much debate. Nineteenth-century liberalizing theologians, stressing Jesus' ethical teachings, downplayed the apocalyptic strand. With the appearance, however, of Johannes Weiss's *Die Predigt Jesu vom Reiche Gottes* (The sermon of Jesus on the Kingdom of God) in 1892, and of Albert Schweitzer's *Vom Reimarus zu Wrede* (1906), published in English in 1910 as *The Quest of the Historical Jesus,* theologians rediscovered the importance of end-time expectations in the early church. In an influential work of 1899, R. H. Charles explored the process by which the apocalyptic genre, with its roots in Jewish history and national hopes, metamorphosed into a Christian scenario of a worldwide end-time kingdom under the resurrected Christ.[22]

Awareness of early Christian apocalypticism again faded as liberal theologians emphasized the social-reform implications of the Gospel, but it reemerged strongly in the 1970s, thanks in part to two more German theologians: Klaus Koch, whose *Ratlos vor der Apokalyptik* (1970) appeared in English two years later as *The Rediscovery of Apocalyptic,* and Ernst Käsemann, who declared in an influential 1969 article that "apocalyptic was the mother of all Christian theology." Although McGinn and others have qualified Käsemann's flat assertion, emphasizing the interweaving of many different themes in early Christian thought, all scholars concede the centrality of eschatology.[23]

In addition to several noncanonical Christian apocalypses such as the *Apocalypse of Peter,* an early second-century work, apocalypticism pervades the earliest canonical Christian texts, notably the letters of Paul designated as I and II Thessalonians (the earliest known Christian writings, dating from about 50 A.D.) and I Corinthians. The epistle known as II Peter, thought to date from around 90 A.D., memorably describes the earth's destruction by fire—a passage much quoted after the atomic bombing of Hiroshima and Nagasaki.[24] The two short epistles called I and II John (whose precise dates remain in dispute) include several apocalyptic allusions as well as the only explicit references to Antichrist, usually identified with the Beast of Daniel and Revelation. This passage, for example, illustrates the early Christians' end-time preoccupations:

> Little children, it is the last time: and as ye have heard that antichrist shall come, even now are there many antichrists; whereby we know that it is the last time.[25]

Apocalyptic prophecies also appear in the Gospels, most memorably in Jesus' eschatological discourse to his disciples, the so-called Little Apocalypse, recorded in the thirteenth chapter of Mark (the oldest of the Gospels) and repeated, in slightly variant forms, in Matthew 24–25 and Luke 21. (These texts, based on collections of Jesus' sayings that circulated among the early Christians, began to be attributed to Matthew, Mark, and Luke early in the second century.)[26] In this final message to his disciples two days before his death, Jesus reveals the events of the last days. In the Matthew version, he foretells the destruction of the Temple ("there shall not be left here one stone upon another") and, answering his disciples' request for "the sign of thy coming, and of the end of the world," describes a sequence of events that will massively disrupt both the social and natural worlds: conflict among nations ("wars and rumors of wars"), famines, plagues, earthquakes, sinfulness, the persecution of believers. At last, when the "gospel of the kingdom" has been "preached in all the world for a witness unto all nations," Jesus goes on, "then shall the end come."

As the end draws still nearer, the sermon continues, a time of "great tribulation" will break out when "the abomination of desolation, spoken of by Daniel the prophet, [shall] stand in the holy place." Were this period not cut short, Jesus says, no life on earth would survive. Further, "false Christs, and false prophets" will deceive many with "great signs and wonders." But the Tribulation will end with dramatic suddenness: "As the lightning cometh out of the east, and shineth even unto the west; so shall also the coming of the Son of man be." This eschatological climax disrupts even "the powers of the heavens": the sun and moon darken, the stars fall. At this moment, "all the tribes of the earth . . . shall see the Son of man coming in the clouds of heaven with power and great glory."

Further responding to the disciples' request for the signs of the end, Jesus goes on:

> Now learn a parable of the fig tree; When his branch is yet tender, and putteth forth leaves, ye know that summer is nigh:
> So likewise ye, when ye shall see all these things, know that it is near, even at the doors.
> Verily I say unto you, This generation shall not pass, till all these things be fulfilled.

Together with Daniel's prophecy of the seventy weeks, the fig-tree parable has tempted generations of interpreters to seek clues to the precise time of the end. However, at just this point in the sermon, Jesus sternly cautions against date setting: "But of that day and hour knoweth no man, no, not the angels of heaven, but my Father only."

Nevertheless, he continues to provide more signs. As in the days of Noah (a time of universal wickedness), Jesus goes on, "so shall also the coming of the Son of man be." But despite all the warnings, the end will catch many unawares:

> Then shall two be in the field; the one shall be taken, and the other left.
> Two women shall be grinding at the mill; the one shall be taken, and the other left.
> Watch therefore; for ye know not what hour your Lord doth come.

After illustrating the importance of readiness with the parable of the wise and foolish virgins awaiting the bridegroom, Jesus concludes with a somber description of the final act of this end-time drama, the Last Judgment:

> When the Son of man shall come in his glory, and all the holy angels with him, then shall he sit upon the throne of his glory:
> And before him shall be gathered all nations: and he shall separate

them one from another, as a shepherd divideth his sheep from the
goats.
And he shall set the sheep on his right hand, but the goats on the left.
Then shall the King say unto them on his right hand, Come, ye
blessed of my Father, inherit the kingdom prepared for you from
the foundation of the world . . .
Then shall he say also unto them on the left hand, Depart from me,
ye cursed, into everlasting fire, prepared for the devil and his angels.

The Revelation of John

By far the best-known Christian apocalypse, and one that has im-
measurably influenced Western thought and culture, is the Revelation
of John, the final book of the Bible. In contrast to the Book of Daniel,
both fundamentalists and the scholarly community generally agree on
the dating of Revelation: the later years of the Emperor Domitian's
reign (81–96 A.D.), a time of persecution as Rome promulgated the
cult of emperor worship in the eastern empire as a way of solidifying
its power. To reject this cult, as many Christians did, was thus an act
of treason punishable by death.[27]

The work is addressed to the scattered Christians of Asia Minor
in their hour of affliction. Breaking with the tradition of pseudepigra-
phy, the author identifies himself as "John," a servant of Christ; a
"companion in affliction" to those he is addressing; and a prisoner on
Patmos, a small Aegean island forty miles off the coast of Asia Minor.
The work opens with seven letters to the churches of Asia Minor in
the form of angelic messages from Christ praising some and con-
demning others.

The apocalypse proper begins with chapter 4, as a door opens in
heaven and a voice "as it were of a trumpet" says to John: "Come up
hither, and I will show thee things which must be hereafter."[28] The
eighteen short chapters that follow record a series of cyclical, partially
overlapping, and densely symbolic visions.

First, John is shown a rainbow-enshrouded heavenly throne surrounded by twenty-four white-robed elders, seven lamps of fire, and
four winged beasts with eyes in front and back. At the right hand of
the figure on the throne is a book with seven seals that are successively
broken by Christ, represented as a slain lamb. The breaking of each

seal signals a further vision. These include four mounted figures ("the four horsemen of the Apocalypse") representing evils such as warfare, famine, and death. The opening of the fifth seal unfolds a glimpse of martyrs slain for their faith. The breaking of the sixth unleashes an earthquake and other upheavals in the natural order: the sun grows black, the moon turns to blood, stars fall to earth. People of all conditions, including "the kings of the earth, and the great men, and the rich men," vainly seek safety by hiding among rocks and in the mountains.

The breaking of the seventh seal offers a glimmer of hope, as 144,000 of the faithful, 12,000 from each of Israel's twelve tribes, together with "a great multitude, which no man could number, of all nations, and kindreds, and people, and tongues" who "came out of the great tribulation" and who "have washed their robes, and made them white in the blood of the Lamb," appear before the throne of God, who promises them eternal blessedness.

Chapter 8 opens with a half-hour of silence in heaven, after which seven angels blow trumpets, each signaling more bad news for humankind: hail, fire, and blood rain upon the earth; a third of all the trees and grass are consumed; a third part of the sea turns to blood; a falling star called Wormwood poisons the waters of the earth; again the sun, moon, and stars darken; and from "the bottomless pit" creep giant locusts with human faces, equine bodies, and stinging tails like scorpions to torment all who do not have "the seal of God in their foreheads."

> And I beheld, and heard an angel flying through the midst of heaven, saying with a loud voice, Woe, woe, woe, to the inhabiters of the earth. . .
> And in those days shall men seek death, and shall not find it; and shall desire to die, and death shall flee from them.

The sixth trumpet heralds the release of "the four angels which are bound in the great river Euphrates" who marshal an army of "two hundred thousand thousand" warriors riding horses breathing "fire and smoke and brimstone." This supernatural cavalry destroys one-third of mankind. As horrors mount, the chronicle becomes almost impossible to follow. Before the seventh angel sounds his trumpet comes an interlude in which an angel bearing a little book commands John to eat it: "And I took the little book out of the angel's hand, and ate it up; and it was in my mouth sweet as honey: and as soon as I had eaten it, my belly was bitter."

The long ensuing segment introduces specific temporal prophecies: Gentiles will occupy the Temple for forty-two months—an echo of the three and a half years of Daniel's prophecy. Two "witnesses" appear who cause worldwide drought, turn water to blood, and "smite the earth with all plagues, as often as they will." After 1,260 days a Beast arises from "the bottomless pit" and kills the witnesses who, after lying unburied on the streets of Jerusalem for three and a half days, are resurrected and lifted up to heaven. Another earthquake rocks Jerusalem. At last the trumpet sounds, proclaiming Christ's coming victory over the kingdoms of the world, the opening of a holy temple in heaven, and further catastrophes on earth: "lightnings, and voices, and thunderings, and an earthquake, and great hail."

Next, a mysterious woman in heaven "clothed with the sun, and the moon under her feet, and upon her head a crown of twelve stars," goes through the agonies of labor. A seven-headed, ten-horned red dragon appears, determined to eat the infant as soon as it is born. The woman delivers a male child, destined "to rule all nations with a rod of iron," who is caught up to God beyond the dragon's reach. War now breaks out in heaven itself, as the dragon, now identified as Satan, and his angels are defeated and driven to earth by the angel Michael and his hosts.

In chapter 13, the midway point in the apocalypse, a Beast, again described as having seven heads and ten horns, rises from the sea. Clearly drawing on the Book of Daniel, John describes it as having characteristics of a lion, a bear, and a leopard. One of its heads bears a mortal wound that has healed. Assisted by a second beast that also emerges from the sea (later called the false prophet), and granted "great authority" by Satan, the Beast for forty-two months rules "all kindreds and tongues and nations" and wars on the saints. By "speaking great things and blasphemies" and performing "great wonders" such as summoning fire from heaven and erecting a statue of himself capable of speech, the Beast wins many followers.

Terrible persecution follows. Those who refuse to worship the Beast's image are put to death. The Beast requires everyone, "both small and great, rich and poor, free and bond, to receive a mark in their right hand, or in their foreheads" in order to buy or sell. This mark apparently consists of either the Beast's name or its numerical equivalent:

> Here is wisdom. Let him that hath understanding count the number of the beast: for it is the number of a man; and his number is Six hundred threescore and six.

The vision now reverts to the Lamb, who appears on Mount Zion with the twenty-four elders, the four guardian beasts, harpists and singers, and the 144,000 redeemed saints "not defiled with women." Angels bring word of the fall of Babylon, describe the punishment awaiting those who accept the Mark of the Beast, and bless those who die in the Lord. Next appear two figures, one "like unto the Son of man" and the other an angel, swinging sharp sickles, "for the harvest of the earth is ripe."

> And the angel thrust in his sickle into the earth, and gathered the vine of the earth, and cast it into the great winepress of the wrath of God.
>
> And the winepress was trodden without the city, and blood came out of the winepress, even unto the horse bridles, by the space of a thousand and six hundred furlongs.

More plagues ensue, this time poured from "seven golden vials full of the wrath of God." "Noisome and grievous sore[s]" afflict the Beast's followers, the sea becomes "as the blood of a dead man," and the sun "scorch[es] men with fire." As darkness grips the Beast's kingdom, his worshippers "[gnaw] their tongues for pain." Huge hailstones fall; islands and mountains vanish; the world's cities collapse in an earthquake "such as was not seen since men were upon the earth"; and "unclean spirits like frogs" emerge from the mouths of the dragon, the Beast, and the false prophet. The sixth angel's vial dries up the Euphrates River, "that the way of the kings of the east might be prepared." This angel also sets the stage for the final conflict, "the battle of that great day of God Almighty," by gathering "the kings of the earth and of the whole world . . . into a place called in the Hebrew tongue Armageddon."

Next appears a "great whore . . . with whom the kings of the earth have committed fornication." Riding on "a scarlet colored beast" of the familiar seven-headed, ten-horned variety; bedecked with gold and precious stones; carrying a golden cup "full of abominations and filthiness of her fornications"; and bearing on her forehead the inscription "MYSTERY BABYLON THE GREAT, THE MOTHER OF HARLOTS AND ABOMINATIONS OF THE EARTH," the whore drinks the blood of saints and martyrs.

At this point the symbolism is partially interpreted. The Beast, an angel tells John, "was, and is not, and yet is." Now in perdition, the Beast will return to earth. His seven heads, the angel adds, represent "seven mountains, on which the woman sitteth." But the seven heads and ten horns also represent kingdoms past and yet to come:

> And there are seven kings: five are fallen, and one is, and the other is not yet come; and when he cometh, he must continue a short space.
> And the beast that was, and is not, even he is the eighth, and is of the seven and goeth into perdition.
> And the ten horns which thou sawest are ten kings, which have received no kingdom as yet; but receive power as kings one hour with the beast.

These ten kings make war with the Lamb, "Lord of lords, and King of kings," but they are crushed. In their fury, says the angel, "they shall hate the whore . . . , and shall eat her flesh, and burn her with fire."

Chapter 18 recounts the fall of Babylon and of the merchants who had "waxed rich through the abundance of her delicacies." Opulent and self-satisfied, Babylon is "utterly burned with fire." The memorable account of this event illustrates the descriptive power that assured John's apocalypse a permanent place in the world's literature:

> And the kings of the earth, who have committed fornication and lived deliciously with [Babylon], shall bewail her, and lament for her, when they shall see the smoke of her burning,
> Standing afar off for the fear of her torment, saying, Alas, alas, that great city Babylon, that mighty city! for in one hour is thy judgment come.
> And the merchants of the earth shall weep and mourn over her; for no man buyeth their merchandise any more:
> The merchandise of gold, and silver, and precious stones, and of pearls, and fine linen, and purple, and silk, and scarlet, and all thyine wood, and all manner vessels of ivory, and all manner vessels of most precious wood, and of brass, and iron, and marble,
> And cinnamon, and odors, and ointments, and frankincense, and

> wine, and oil, and fine flour, and wheat, and beasts, and sheep, and horses, and chariots, and slaves, and souls of men.
>
> And the fruits that thy soul lusted after are departed from thee, and all things which were dainty and goodly are departed from thee, and thou shalt find them no more at all.
>
> The merchants of these things, which were made rich by her, shall stand afar off for the fear of her torment, weeping and wailing,
>
> And saying, Alas, alas, that great city that was clothed in fine linen, and purple, and scarlet, and decked with gold, and precious stones, and pearls!
>
> For in one hour so great riches is come to nought. And every shipmaster, and all the company in ships, and sailors, and as many as trade by sea, stood afar off,
>
> And cried when they saw the smoke of her burning, saying, What city is like unto this great city!

Babylon falls silent and desolate: no more musicians or trumpeters; "no craftsman, of whatsoever craft he be"; no more voices of bridegrooms and brides—"for thy merchants were the great men of the earth; for by thy sorceries were all nations deceived."

After hymns of praise for Babylon's destruction, the apocalypse moves to its denouement: the ultimate struggle between the forces of good and evil. In a chapter of great solemnity, Jesus Christ emerges from heaven in full battle array, mounted on a white steed. His eyes are as flaming fire; he wears a blood-stained vestment; and his heavenly soldiers follow him, also riding white horses. This is the warrior-king, far removed from the lowly Jesus of Nazareth, avenging the world's accumulated injustices:

> And out of his mouth goeth a sharp sword, that with it he should smite the nations: and he shall rule them with a rod of iron: and he treadeth the winepress of the fierceness and wrath of Almighty God.
>
> And he hath on his vesture and on his thigh a name written, King of Kings, and Lord of Lords.

The battle is joined: "And I saw the beast, and the kings of the earth, and their armies, gathered together to make war against him that sat on the horse, and against his army." The actual combat, if any, remains offstage, but the outcome is clear: the Beast and the false prophet are defeated and "cast alive into a lake of fire burning with brimstone." The Beast's worshippers are put to the sword and—the imagery of Ezekiel comes to mind—scavenging birds gorge on their flesh.

His earthly followers defeated, Satan is sealed in the bottomless pit for a thousand years—hence, the *Millennium*—during which time Christ reigns on earth with those martyred by the Beast. Satan is released for a final battle, but again he is defeated, this time forever. At a solemn Last Judgment, all human beings who have ever lived are consigned to heavenly bliss or to torment in the lake of fire. With these events, recorded in chapter 21, history gives way to eternity—the endless reign of righteousness and justice described by John in one of the loveliest passages of all biblical literature:

> And I saw a new heaven and a new earth: for the first heaven and the first earth were passed away; and there was no more sea.
> And I John saw the holy city, new Jerusalem, coming down from God out of heaven, prepared as a bride adorned for her husband.
> And I heard a great voice out of heaven saying, Behold, the tabernacle of God is with men, and he will dwell with them, and they shall be his people, and God himself shall be with them, and be their God.
> And God shall wipe away all tears from their eyes; and there shall be no more death, neither sorrow, nor crying, neither shall there be any more pain: for the former things are passed away.

With further descriptions of the new Jerusalem, a warning against tampering with the prophecies that have just been unfolded, and a prayer for Christ's quick return, the Book of Revelation and the Bible itself draw to a close.

For centuries Revelation has challenged believers and unbelievers alike. Saint Jerome concluded that it contains "as many mysteries as it does words"; George Bernard Shaw flippantly dismissed it as the product of a drug addict's fevered brain.[29] The identity of the Beast and the whore; the composition of the armies that gather at Armageddon; the significance of Babylon, 666, the seven heads, and the ten horns—all these puzzles have stimulated a vast body of interpretive work both scholarly and popular. Revelation is like a glassy pool in which expositors find mirrored their own interpretive preconceptions. As Bernard McGinn has observed:

> It sometimes appears that Revelation is a book whose literary interest has been transferred from the text to the readers. In itself arcane and full of secret allegories at whose original refer-

ence we can only guess, it has offered all the more opportunity to researchers who can with impunity discover in its pages the message they themselves put there out of a sense that so menacing a document, full of hitherto misunderstood detail, can have application only to the unprecedented world-historical crisis of their own moment in time. Consequently the meaning of the book is, almost uniquely, identical with its various applications. We learn most about it from later interpretations which may be manifestly unacceptable to us.[30]

Still, as with the apocalypses of Ezekiel and Daniel, Bible scholars seek to root the work in the historical situation of its author and his immediate audience—a late-first-century Christian believer writing some sixty years after Jesus' death, and a scattered handful of fearful Christian communities. According to this so-called *preterist* (or presentist) interpretation, John was commenting on the dark events of his time, alluding in veiled language to the Roman emperors, including the current one, Domitian, and offering hope for the future.[31] By this interpretation, the "great whore" represents the cult of emperor worship and "Babylon" stands symbolically for Rome, the city of seven hills that was not only the seat of empire and commerce but also, for Christians, the vile metropolis from which emanated pagan wickedness and blasphemy. "The Beast" seems to symbolize both the Roman imperial system and a particularly demonic representative of that system. Many scholars believe that this individual is the Emperor Nero, who, Tacitus tells us, persecuted the Christians of Rome, blaming them for the fire that destroyed the city in 64 A.D. Nero committed suicide in 68 A.D., well before Revelation was written; but a myth that originated in Parthia and spread through the eastern empire held that he would return to life, assemble a vast army, and again seize power.[32] Among Christians this belief surely evoked nightmares of worse persecution ahead.

A number of passages in Revelation fit the *Nero Redivivus* myth, including the Beast's head wound that has healed; the cryptic reference to the Beast as one "who was, and is not, and yet is"; and the allusions to a seventh and eighth king—the Beast—to follow the present one. If one includes the short and turbulent reigns of Galba, Otho, and Vitellius, Domitian was the sixth emperor following Nero.[33] The Beast's number, 666, many scholars argue, also points to Nero. In Greek and Hebrew, each letter of the alphabet represented a number as well as a sound, inviting efforts to find the numerical value of names. The most prevalent system of *gematria* numbered the alphabet's first nine letters 1 to 9, the next nine 10 to 90, and the succeeding ones 100, 200, 300, and so on. By this system, "Neron Caesar" (a common early usage) totals 666 in Hebrew. "Nero Caesar" totals 616—the number that appears in some early manuscripts of Revelation.[34]

Somewhat in contrast to this emphasis on the work's historical specificity, other scholars view it as part of a vast body of ancient mythic material in which supernatural beings embodying good and evil wage war on a cosmic scale. "Every major culture of the ancient eastern Mediterranean world," writes Adela Yarbro Collins, "had at least one native version of such a combat myth." John drew not only on the Jewish apocalyptic tradition, Collins contends, but also on this large reservoir of mythic material. From this perspective, she maintains, the successive visions of Revelation are best read as "poetic expressions of human experiences and hopes."[35]

This reminder of the paradigmatic nature of Revelation's structure and motifs, and of the author's eclectic literary borrowings, while useful, ought not obscure the work's immediate historical context. Although "a creative literary artist expressing himself with material from a wide variety of sources" (as John Court has written),[36] John was also a Christian exile addressing an embattled and perhaps even terrified flock. Revelation offers not only a spiritualized version of current and future events reworked for literary effect, or a generalized mythic representation of the perennial clash of good and evil, but also a specific message both of warning and of hope to readers whom the author knows personally, concluding with an eschatological vision of Christ's imminent return, an end to suffering, and the inauguration of a heavenly kingdom of peace and justice. From this perspective, the work reveals with particular clarity the eschatological expectations that gripped the embattled early church.

Like the author of the Book of Daniel (and in contrast to the accommodationist message often found in the Gospels and the Pauline letters), John is radically hostile to the secular power of the state. But also like the author of the Book of Daniel, he does not urge violent resistance; Christ himself will punish the wicked rulers who are persecuting the faithful.[37] For men and women literally facing death at the hands of Roman soldiers, the message must have seemed both rigorously demanding and incredibly exciting.

These, then, are the apocalyptic texts that have comforted the faithful, intrigued the curious, and amused the skeptics for two thousand years. However one views their status as sacred texts, their imaginative power and poetic richness is undeniable, and it is hardly surprising that they became part of the living fabric of Western culture, influencing not only religious leaders and biblical interpreters, but also artists, composers, sculptors, and poets. The apocalyptic worldview, with its underlying assumption that human experience is moving toward a transcendent goal, profoundly shaped the Western view of history. Indeed, some have argued that Karl Marx's *Das Kapital,* with its vision of a classless utopia emerging from successive cycles of social upheaval and revolutionary violence, is the last great apocalypse of the Western intellectual tradition.[38]

Down to the Enlightenment, biblical apocalyptic was read with seriousness throughout Christendom, at all social and educational levels, for the clues it offered to God's divine plan. But as skepticism and rationalism gained ground in the eighteenth century, the academic and popular views of these texts gradually diverged. With the rise of historical-critical biblical study in early-nineteenth-century Germany, Friedrich Lücke and other scholars subjected them to close scrutiny, revising traditional attributions and datings, tracing parallel themes in the mythic traditions of other ancient civilizations, and exploring the historical context of specific apocalypses.[39]

At the popular level, particularly in America, the apocalyptic texts remained what they had always been: a vital source of doctrine, reassurance, and foreknowledge. Ordinary believers continued to pore over their pages and to look expectantly for the events they found predicted there. Even at this level, however, interest in prophetic interpretation fluctuated, waning in tranquil times and intensifying during periods of uncertainty, upheaval, and danger—most recently (or so I shall argue) in the post-1945 decades of nuclear menace, Cold War alarms, and unsettling technological developments. The next two chapters explore the earlier stages of this cyclical process, during which successive generations of believers sought to decipher the meaning of the Bible's apocalyptic texts, even as the specific historical situations that had spawned those texts receded farther into the past.

2   Rhythms of Prophecy Belief

From the dawn of Christianity, biblical apocalyptic has shaped Western thought. Even when downplayed by church doctrine, eschatological belief remained vigorously alive, influencing events in complex and unexpected ways. This chapter examines the shifting currents of prophecy belief before about 1800. We begin in the Near East within a century of Jesus' death and end in America at the time of the Revolution. As we traverse these vast reaches of time and geography, our focus will be on the changing dynamic of prophetic belief, and on those times and places when apocalypticism particularly influenced intellectual and social history. The aim is not merely antiquarian, but to establish more fully the historical rootedness of this belief system, and to suggest how this background can enhance our understanding of prophecy belief in present-day America.

Early Christianity and Medieval Europe

The eschatological hopes that sustained the first Christians remained alive in the years that followed, especially in the Eastern church. About 172 A.D. or earlier, a Phrygian prophet named Montanus proclaimed himself the Holy Spirit incarnate, said the Last Judgment was at hand, and asserted that John's prophesied New Jerusalem would soon descend in Phrygia. Meanwhile, he taught, Christians should practice asceticism and separation from the world. Montanist belief quickly spread through Asia Minor, North Africa, and parts of Europe.[1]

The patristic writer Irenaeus (ca. 130–ca. 200) knew Montanism well. A native of Asia Minor who became Bishop of Lyon, Irenaeus traveled to Rome in about 177 to discuss the movement with Bishop Eleutherius there. Irenaeus' most important treatise, *Against Heresies,* concluded with a survey of the biblical apocalypses. In Irenaeus' own prophetic timetable, patterned on the six days of creation and the day of rest, history extends for six thousand years, ending with Christ's return and the millennium, "the hallowed seventh day," which he described in lush, physically sensuous terms. The prolific Christian polemicist Tertullian of Carthage (ca. 160–ca. 220) looked favorably on the Montanists, though perhaps more for their rigorous ethics than for their apocalypticism. Montanism faded as an organized movement after condemnation by synods in Asia Minor and by Pope Zephyrinus in the early third century, but the millennialist impulse survived. Victorinus, the late-third-century Bishop of Pettau (in present-day Austria) and author of the earliest surviving commentary on the Book of Revelation, was a confirmed millennialist. Lactantius, a theologian much admired by the Emperor Constantine, introduced a strong apocalyptic strain into his *Divine Institutes,* written early in the fourth century.[2]

But millennialism met opposition as well, especially among the adherents of Gnosticism, a Hellenistic version of Christianity that arose in Alexandria and strongly influenced second-century Christian thought. Contemptuous of the imperfect material world in contrast to the spiritual realm of divine knowledge, or *gnosis,* Gnostics rejected notions of an earthly Kingdom of God. Origen (ca. 185–ca. 254), who headed theological schools at Alexandria and Caesarea, while not a Gnostic, was a Neoplatonist who sought to synthesize Christian belief and Greek philosophy. From this perspective Origen attacked Montanism as heresy and interpreted the prophecies allegorically: Antichrist symbolized evil; the thousand-year reign of righteousness described a spiritual reality achieved in the souls of individual believers, and so on.[3]

Anticipating charges leveled against modern-day fundamentalists, Origen attacked millennialists for misreading apocalyptic texts whose meaning "they do not perceive is to be taken figuratively . . . They think they are to be kings and princes, like those earthly monarchs who now exist." By such forced readings, he gibed, literalists were "refusing the labor of thinking." (Origen's rejection of apocalyptic literalism may have had a personal as well as a philosophical source: as a young man, following a practice viewed as praiseworthy in some Christian as well as pagan circles, he had castrated himself in a literal application of Jesus' words in Matt. 19:12: "For there are some eunuchs, which were so born from their mother's womb: and there are some eunuchs, which were made eunuchs of men; and there be eunuchs, which have made themselves eunuchs for the kingdom of heaven's sake. He that is able to receive it, let him receive it.")[4]

As Christianity triumphed, its millennialist strand faded. Once an embattled faith sustained by apocalyptic hope, Christianity by the third century enjoyed an increasingly secure position in the Roman world, a shift formalized by Constantine, who after coming to power in 312 not only tolerated but favored the new faith. He made Sunday a public holiday; granted privileges to the Christian clergy; and endowed various church institutions, including the Jerusalem holy places. He also arbitrated theological disputes and in 325 presided at the Council of Nicaea that codified the Church's fundamental creed.[5]

Increasingly linked to imperial power, the post-Constantinian Church downplayed its apocalyptic legacy. The Nicene Creed affirmed the eschatological hope ("shall come again with glory to judge both the quick and the dead"), but contained no reference to the millennium. Even the fall of a now-Christianized Roman Empire in the fifth century—Alaric sacked Rome in 410 and the Goths deposed the last Roman emperor in 476—did not, as in earlier crises, produce a wave of apocalypticism.

That it did not is in part attributable to Saint Augustine (354–430), the preeminent theologian—and literary stylist—of the early Church. Influenced by Tyconius, a North African Christian writer of the late fourth century, Augustine rejected the millennialism of his day for its coarse sensuality. In numerous polemical works, and above all in his masterpiece, *The City of God,* written between 413 and 426, he offered a subtle interpretation of history shaped by biblical eschatology but free of end-time speculation or predictions of a literal, earthly Kingdom of God. Rather, Augustine elaborated the metaphor of history as a struggle between two cities representing, in Peter Brown's nice phrases, "two fields of force" or "two great pyramids of loyalty" and symbolized typologically by Babylon and Jerusalem. Like Origen, he read biblical apocalyptic allegorically. The Beast of Daniel and Revelation, for example, pointed not to a specific person, but (as Shirley Jackson Case has put it) to "the community of unbelievers set in opposition to the faithful people of the city of God."[6] In such imagery, Augustine conveyed his sense of individuals, and all humanity, torn between the earthly and the divine. The combat so memorably depicted in John's Apocalypse did not await eschatological fulfillment; it was unfolding in the here and now:

Now let us hear, brothers, let us hear and sing; let us pine for the City where we are citizens . . . By pining, we are already there; we have already cast our hope, like an anchor, on that coast. I sing of somewhere else, not of here: for I sing with my heart, not my flesh. The citizens of Babylon hear the sound of the flesh, the Founder of Jerusalem hears the tune of our hearts.[7]

Augustine foresaw a Last Judgment at which the citizens of the two cities would be finally and forever separated, but otherwise his system was not strongly futuristic. Rather, with the coming of Christ, all history took on prophetic meaning:

God is the unchanging conductor as well as the unchanged Creator of all things that change . . . He is ordering all events according to His providence, until the beauty of the completed course of time, whose parts are the dispensations suitable to each different period, shall have played itself out, like the great melody of some ineffable composer.[8]

The recurrent musical imagery is noteworthy. Twentieth-century prophecy popularizers often portray God as a cosmic playwright stage-managing a vast melodrama, shifting about a huge cast of puzzled and unwitting actors. Augustine offered a different metaphor: God as composer and conductor, history as an indescribably lovely musical work, unfolding for the sheer pleasure of its human listeners.

Augustine's vision of the interpenetration of sacred and secular history profoundly influenced all future Christian eschatology, both Catholic and Protestant. He made the apocalyptic part of the everyday fabric of Christian life and belief, and to that extent reinforced eschatological awareness by embedding it in liturgy and preaching. But his approach also distanced Catholic thought from all literalist readings of prophecy, and especially from notions of an earthly millennium. With the condemnation of millennialism by the Council of Ephesus in 431, Augustine's views became orthodoxy. Indeed, church authorities went so far as to expurgate the works of Irenaeus and Victorinus, to eradicate all millennial taint. Bible translators from Jerome to Erasmus expressed doubt that Revelation should even be retained in the canon.[9]

While Catholic doctrine increasingly moved away from end-time speculation, apocalyptic thinking survived. In his 1970 work, *The Pursuit of the Millennium: Revolutionary Millenarians and Mystical Anar-*

chists of the Middle Ages, Norman Cohn focused on the proliferation of millennialism in "the obscure underworld of popular religion" among "the underprivileged, the oppressed, the disoriented, and the unbalanced." Cohn's medieval Europe, far removed from the society Henry Adams imagined as united in veneration of the Virgin in vast cathedrals such as Chartres, is a veritable cauldron of hermit messiahs, wandering visionaries, self-taught prophecy interpreters, and doomed social revolutionaries inflamed by apocalyptic expectations. For Cohn, the fearful speculation aroused by the approach of the year 1000 was only one incident in a succession of turbulent mass movements that germinated in a rich loam of popular millennialism.[10]

In reality, as Bernard McGinn and other scholars have made clear in recent years, apocalyptic speculation flourished at all levels of medieval society. Eschatological hope formed part of the ground of Christian belief, and thus of the medieval mentality. Monastic scholars and the most erudite theologians contributed to, and often cited, the vast body of verse prophecies known collectively as the Sibylline oracles. Modeled on Greek, Roman, and Hellenistic Jewish writings, these literary works wove images from Daniel and Revelation into imaginative narratives that were revised periodically as historical circumstances changed. In the later Middle Ages, guilds supported by the urban elites produced open-air dramas or miracle plays (the Oberammergau Passion Play is a surviving example) in which the Last Judgment and other end-time events figured prominently.[11]

Hildegard of Bingen, a brilliant twelfth-century German abbess, religious writer, and composer, recorded her visions of Antichrist and end-time events in works that enjoyed a wide influence. Issues of prophetic interpretation sparked intense debate at Oxford and the University of Paris in the late thirteenth century. As Marjorie Reeves observes in her study of prophecy in the later Middle Ages, not only society's marginal members but "sober historians and politicians" took very seriously speculation about the last days rooted in biblical apocalyptic.[12]

Medieval art underscores the ubiquity of end-time belief. Hildegard illuminated her apocalyptic visions with striking illustrations. Many medieval manuscript illuminations of the Book of Revelation survive. In a 1991 exhibit, "The Apocalypse and Other Visions in Medieval Illuminated Manuscripts," the J. Paul Getty Museum displayed holdings in this genre, including a superb mid-thirteenth-century example from the Abbey of Saint Albans in England. Medieval maps sometimes portrayed Gog and Magog as demons imprisoned behind a wall in northeastern Europe. Vast fourteenth-century tapestries at the cathedral museum in Angers, France, portray scenes from the Apocalypse. In 1498, on the eve of the Reformation, Albrecht Dürer issued a series of large woodcuts of the Last Judgment and other scenes from Revelation.[13]

Apocalyptic belief fueled support for the Crusades, launched between 1097 and 1270 to retake the Holy Land from its Islamic conquerers. Fired by visions of recapturing Jerusalem and thereby preparing the way for the New Jerusalem of John's Apocalypse, Europeans of all social levels—from the nobility to the peasantry and the urban poor—joined in the cause. Richard Coeur de Lion, setting out in 1190 on the Third Crusade, undertaken to drive Saladin from Jerusalem, stopped off in Messina to confer with the most famed prophecy scholar of the day, Joachim of Fiore. (According to a contemporary, Joachim told Richard that Saladin was Antichrist and that Richard would defeat him—a prophecy that failed.) Further acting on their end-time beliefs, the lower ranks of the Crusaders before embarking for Palestine sometimes conducted murderous campaigns against European Jewry. In the folk eschatology of the period (reinforced by some prophecy writers), Jews and Muslims alike were demonic agents of Antichrist. Indeed, it was widely believed that Antichrist himself would be a Jew—a conviction occasionally still found among post-1945 prophecy writers.[14]

Hildegard of Bingen was not alone in her Antichrist interest. Despite the allegorizing of Origen and Augustine, the terrifying figure of Antichrist—an amalgam of images from Daniel, Revelation, and extrabiblical sources—exerted a powerful grip on the medieval mind. The *Play of Antichrist,* a German religious drama dating from around 1160, enjoyed great popularity, as did a fourteenth-century English drama on the same subject. In Cohn's view, Antichrist functioned in this period (as he still does for millions) as "a gigantic embodiment of anarchic, destructive power." Yet in the texts, paintings, and dramas dealing with Antichrist, order and righteousness eventually triumph. Here is a key to the vitality of the Antichrist motif: in the Middle Ages, as in more recent times, the drama of Antichrist and his ultimate defeat expressed both the reality of evil and disorder and the sustaining vision of a very different social order rooted in justice, peace, and harmony.[15]

The most influential medieval apocalypticist was the man sought out by Richard Coeur de Lion, the Calabrian monk Joachim of Fiore (ca. 1135–1202). On Easter Sunday in 1183 or 1184, after a night of meditating on Revelation (and after years of intense biblical study), Joachim writes, "[I] suddenly perceived in my mind's eye something of the fulness [*plenitudo*] of this book and of the entire harmony of the Old and New Testaments." The result was his massive *Exposition on Revelation* and other writings. Toward the end of his life he summed up his understanding of the prophecies in intricate illustrations collected by his followers in the *Book of Figures*. Joachim's interpretation involved three overlapping ages, each identified with a figure of the Trinity: the Age of Law, presided over by God the Father; the Age of Grace, inaugurated by Jesus' birth; and a future Age of the Spirit, in which, after Antichrist's defeat, righteousness will prevail and mankind will devote itself to spiritual contemplation.[16] Joachim thus vigorously reintroduced millennarianism, rejected by Origen and Augustine. His tripartite scheme of history anticipates in rudimentary form the dispensationalism popularized by British and American prophecy writers in the nineteenth and early twentieth centuries, which similarly segments history into a series of divinely ordained stages, or "dispensations."

Although three successive popes encouraged Joachim, the troubling implications of his thought soon became evident. His eschatology diverged radically from Augustine's, which rejected a future millennium. The Fourth Lateran Council in 1215 condemned Joachim's view of the Trinity. Further, he held that in the Age of the Spirit the Holy Spirit would impart divine knowledge directly to individuals; the Church, if it survived at all, would be radically reformed along monastic lines.[17]

The Franciscan order, founded by Saint Francis of Assisi in 1209–1210, found highly congenial Joachim's prophecy of a new monastic order that would usher in the Age of the Spirit. Indeed, one branch of the order, the so-called Spiritual Franciscans, produced a rash of pseudo-Joachian prophecies criticizing the papacy's worldliness, commenting on current European politics, and explicitly portraying their order as the model of Joachim's Age of the Spirit. Following hints provided by Joachim, some of these writers went much further than he in offering a specific prophetic timetable. Noting that the Gospel of Matthew records forty-two generations from Abraham to Jesus (the Age of Law), they concluded that the Age of Grace (or Gospel Age), too, would last for forty-two generations. Assuming a generation to be thirty years, they foresaw the arrival of the Age of the Spirit in 1260. (This calculation gained further weight from the reference in Rev. 13:5 and elsewhere to "forty and two months"—1,260 years, if one figures a month at thirty days, as in the Hebrew calendar, and makes the usual day/year transposition.)[18]

Joachim of Fiore had an enormous impact on late medieval thought, reinforcing an already strong eschatological bent. Joachian manuscripts both authentic and spurious, complete with illustrations and elaborate charts (a staple of later prophecy writers as well), circulated through Europe and England stimulating apocalyptic speculation. Further, as Marjorie Reeves and Heiko Oberman argue, the pseudo-Joachian material, linking the Jews explicitly to Antichrist, helped to fuel an upsurge of anti-Semitism in late-medieval Europe—a theme explored more fully in Chapter 6.[19]

This resurgent interest in eschatology served many complex social functions; among them, it provided a vocabulary for writings and movements directed against the papacy, the corrupt clergy, and the ostentatious rich. As early as 1209, Parisian authorities burned at the stake a wandering preacher who had identified the Pope as Antichrist. In late-thirteenth-century Italy, a group called the Apostolic Brethren repudiated papal authority and proclaimed itself the new spiritual order foretold by Joachim. The movement's "low-born and illiterate" founder (Reeves's words) went to the stake in 1300.[20]

In thirteenth-century Germany, apocalypticism and social unrest combined with the political and territorial struggles between the papacy and successive German rulers to produce a widely believed myth that Frederick II, who ruled from 1220 to 1250, was the "Emperor of the Last Days" who would usher in the Millennium. The myth gained force when Frederick seized Jerusalem in 1229 and proclaimed himself its ruler. The pseudo-Joachian texts focusing on the year 1260 strengthened the end-time speculation surrounding Frederick. With his death in 1250, the legend took a new form: the departed ruler would *return* at the end of time to reform the government and establish righteousness. This belief spread across Germany in the fourteenth century and beyond. A hermit posing as the resurrected Frederick was burned at the stake by Frederick's successor, Rudolph. A second pseudo-Frederick met the same fate. (In some pseudo-Joachian manuscripts in Italy hostile to Frederick, the myth took a different form: the German emperor would return as Antichrist.)[21]

The "Frederick redivivus" myth played a complex role in late-medieval European society and politics, but clearly it functioned in part as a vehicle for venting hostility against corrupt priests and greedy rich men. A series of prophetic manifestos from the fourteenth to the early sixteenth centuries predicted that the resurrected emperor would lead a crusade against wrongdoers both civil and ecclesiastical. Writing in 1348, a conservative German monk, John of Winterthur, noted with horror the popular beliefs circulating about Frederick's return:

> As soon as he has risen from the dead and stands once more at the height of his power, he will marry poor women and maidens to rich men, and *vice versa* . . . . He will see to it that everything that has been stolen from minors and orphans and widows is returned to them, and that full justice is done to everyone . . . He will persecute the clergy so fiercely that if they have no other means of hiding their tonsures they will cover them with cow-dung.[22]

In the *Book of a Hundred Chapters,* a particularly bloodthirsty prevision of Frederick's return dating from early-sixteenth-century Alsace, an army of the poor attacks "the great men, both in the Church and amongst the laity." "Go on hitting them," Frederick exhorts his followers, "from the Pope right down to the little students! Kill every one of them!" All these millennial and apocalyptic pronouncements drew heavily on biblical prophecy. In the *Book of a Hundred Chapters,* for example, Frederick reappears on a white horse and establishes a thousand-year reign—details clearly drawn from Revelation.[23] Eschatology was a central concern of intellectuals in the Middle Ages; it also lay at the heart of popular religion and folk belief.

The fueling of radical social movements by apocalypticism emerges starkly in the Taborite uprising that convulsed early-fifteenth-century Bohemia. A radical sect that arose in the aftermath of Jan Hus's execution as a heretic in 1415, the Taborites took their name from a mountain south of Prague that they renamed Mount Tabor, traditional site of Jesus' Sermon on the Mount. At first protected by the Bohemian monarch, King Wenceslas, the Taborites became vulnerable after Wenceslas' death in 1419 as their social views turned more radical, their tactics more violent, and their millennialism more urgent.[24]

The movement's ideology reflected both its intellectual roots in biblical apocalyptic and the pseudo-Joachian literature and its social origins among the Bohemian peasantry and the poor of Prague. Once their persecutors were eliminated, the leaders preached, Christ would rule the world from their own Mount Tabor—establishing a kingdom free of suffering, war, and social distinctions. No clergy, church, or even books would be needed; everyone would receive divine knowledge by direct revelation. In the meantime Satan and his minions remained powerful. As one Taborite song implored, "Liberate us from the evil Antichrist and his cunning army."[25]

Convinced of their end-time role, the Taborites organized cooperative communities modeled on those of the early Christians. As Taborite preachers proclaimed Jesus' imminent return, many Bohemians sold their possessions and flocked to Taborite towns that they believed would be spared. Some tried to hasten the end by armed attacks on their opponents. Declared a Taborite tract: "Accursed be the man who withholds his sword from shedding the blood of the enemies of Christ. Every believer must wash his hands in that blood." For a time the Taborites held off an army of German and Magyar Catholics, but after a crushing defeat in 1434, their apocalyptic ardor dimmed and they soon vanished as an organized movement.[26]

Remote as it may seem from this book's subject, early Christian and medieval apocalypticism forms part of our story's historical context. Modern prophecy scenarios are in fact updated versions of very ancient ones. In some cases highly specific beliefs have been transmitted intact over 1,500 years or more. Irenaeus, for example, taught that Antichrist will reign on earth "for three years and six months"—precisely the time period mentioned by Hal Lindsey and other modern-day popularizers.

Further, the way these beliefs intermingled with other intellectual and social currents makes clear that apocalypticism has historically served many different and complex cultural functions. The same apocalyptic texts offered the disinherited a means of systematizing their grievances, the powerful an avenue of advancing their goals, and believers far from the public arena a language for expressing their deepest spiritual longings. For the Taborites, apocalyptic belief energized their fierce assault on the power elite of their day; for the Spiritual Franciscans (who despite their name could be highly political), Joachian teachings proved most helpful in furthering the interests of their order; for various German rulers, popular prophecy belief provided a useful weapon in buttressing their resistance to papal claims; and for people of the Middle Ages such as Hildegard of Bingen, the unknown illuminator of the Saint Albans Apocalypse, or the weavers of the Angers tapestries, apocalyptic belief could call forth creative energies that still speak to us across the centuries.

European intellectuals of the mid-fourteenth century, confronting the horrors of the Black Death, avidly drew on the common body of prophecy belief about Antichrist and the end times to place this terrifying plague in a meaningful context. A century and a half later, Christopher Columbus called on the apocalyptic scriptures and Joachian sources to give meaning to his career, eventually becoming convinced, as Pauline Moffitt Watts has shown, that "he was predestined to fulfill a number of prophecies in preparation for the coming of the Antichrist and the end of the world." Ancient and premodern apocalypticism, in short, underscores the protean nature of this belief system and its chameleon-like adaptability to many ends. As Bernard McGinn has written:

> Apocalypticism . . . could be used for a variety of purposes, not only in criticism of the powers of this world, but also in their behalf. The message of the apocalypticists was one of consolation and promise of reward, but there were other dimensions that we must not forget, such as those of historical illumination and martial exhortation. To neglect the full range of uses is to misunderstand the meaning of apocalyptic spirituality.[27]

The point is worth keeping in mind when we confront contemporary prophetic belief in all its diversity. The complex role of apocalypticism in earlier eras reminds us not to reduce it too quickly to a single explanatory mode, but to remain open to its multiple uses and functions.

The Reformation and Beyond

Prophetic belief played an important and complex role in the Protestant Reformation and its aftermath, particularly the upheavals in sixteenth- and seventeenth-century England that decisively shaped apocalyptic thought in colonial and revolutionary America.

In 1517, convinced of the doctrine of salvation by God's grace, faith, and the Bible alone (*sola gratia, sola fide, sola scriptura*), Martin Luther affixed his ninety-five theses to the door of Wittenberg's castle church. Three years later, rejecting a papal demand that he retract three pamphlets summing up his quarrel with Rome, Luther was excommunicated. Lutheranism, codified in the Augsburg Confession (1530) and supported by various princes, quickly spread across Germany. Through his hymns, catechisms, polemical tracts, and a vernacular translation of the Bible, Luther dominated the movement until the time of his death in 1546.[28]

Zurich's Ulrich Zwingli inaugurated Protestantism in Switzerland through a 1519 series of lectures on the New Testament. In tracts, sermons, public disputations, and theological works, Zwingli too shaped the evolving movement, stressing particularly the reformation of Roman liturgical practices. The Reformation's third great leader, the French-born John Calvin (Luther's junior by twenty-six years), studied theology, philosophy, and law in the 1520s; broke with Rome by 1533; and from 1536 on, except for a brief interval, led the movement in Geneva, where he and other Protestant elders organized as the Company of Pastors exercised both ecclesiastical and civil power, imposing orthodoxy, suppressing dissent, and enforcing a moral code based on Old Testament law. Calvin's *Institutes of the Christian Religion,* published in 1536 and much revised thereafter, emphasized both God's mercy and absolute power and man's helplessness. This work powerfully shaped the theology not only of Protestantism's Calvinist or Reformed branch, but of the movement as a whole.[29]

In England, meanwhile, the break with Rome occurred in a series of not-always-edifying stages. In 1533, having failed to secure a papal annulment of his marriage to Catherine of Aragon, Henry VIII defiantly married his mistress, the pregnant Anne Boleyn, an act that led to his excommunication. Over the next few years, Parliament and the English Catholic hierarchy rejected Rome's ecclesiastical rule and made Henry head of the Church of England. Henry remained loyal to Catholic doctrine despite his rejection of papal authority, but the movement toward full-fledged Protestantism, continuing under his son Edward VI, was largely accomplished during Elizabeth I's long reign.[30] By 1600 England, Scotland, Scandinavia, and much of Germany and Switzerland had embraced Protestantism, while strong Protestant minorities thrived in France and eastern Europe.

How did this transformation shape apocalyptic belief? To answer, we must look not only at the Protestants' struggle with Rome, but also at the larger social context of the day. For a time in the 1520s and 1530s, a volatile blend of apocalypticism and social unrest seemed about to explode into revolution. In 1524, as Luther's reform pushed forward, German peasants, miners, and urban artisans in some localities rose in an outbreak of violence. For months the so-called Peasants' War raged as the rebels, totaling perhaps three hundred thousand in all, issued demands and pillaged castles and monasteries. From its origins near the Swiss border, the uprising eventually engulfed much of southern and western Germany. The rebels' grievances, summed up in the Twelve Articles of 1525, reflected their discontent as Europe painfully moved to a postfeudal social order. They demanded the abolition of serfdom, an end to various feudal fees, the restoration of enclosed common lands and traditional hunting and fishing rights, and the right to choose their own pastors.[31]

A major figure in these events was Thomas Müntzer, a radical Thuringian Protestant pastor, theologian, and charismatic leader. Little interested in the rebels' economic grievances, the well-educated and widely read Müntzer was absorbed in apocalyptic speculation, which by the early 1520s had become an obsession with the end times and an imminent war of extermination against the godless. Initially of Luther's party, he had quickly turned against Luther. Though not the instigator of the Peasants' War, Müntzer became its principal theological defender and goaded the rebels of his region to new heights of violence. In an incendiary pronouncement of early 1525, issued as a coalition of German princes mobilized against the rebels, Müntzer invoked the language of biblical apocalypse to justify the peasants' cause. As the decisive battle took shape near Frankenhausen, he roused the ill-equipped rebels with a speech full of eschatological allusions. With God's help, he allegedly assured them, he himself would catch the cannonballs in his shirtsleeves. As the peasants sang hymns and looked for Christ's return to support their cause, the attack began. An estimated five thousand rebels died in the resulting slaughter; Müntzer himself was beheaded on May 15, 1525. By 1526 the uprising had been crushed. Estimates of rebels killed range as high as one hundred thousand.[32]

These years also saw the rise of the Anabaptists—religious radicals who rejected Luther's alliance with princely power in Germany and Calvin's theocracy in Geneva. Stressing the rebaptism of adult believers (hence *ana*baptists), personal piety, nonresistance, and separation from the world, the Anabaptists won support, especially among the poor, from Switzerland to the Netherlands. Eschatological hope burned brightly among the early Anabaptists. As Walter Klassen has written, "All Anabaptists were united in their conviction that the return of Christ was near" and that "Christ and Antichrist were locked in the final struggle." One leader, Melchior Hoffmann, especially dwelt on the approaching end in his preaching. Influenced by followers in Strasbourg, he came to believe that the New Jerusalem would arise in that city. Even though Hoffmann was imprisoned from 1533 until his death ten years later, "Melchiorism" remained an influential strand of early Anabaptism.[33]

The effort of men like Müntzer and Hoffmann to translate their apocalyptic beliefs into a radical overhauling of the established order convinced many that Anabaptism posed a dire threat. Such fears intensified early in 1534 when followers of a charismatic Dutch Melchiorite, Jan Matthys, on the invitation of the local Reformation leader, Bernhard Rothmann, gained power in the Westphalian city of Münster and proclaimed it (rather than Hoffmann's Strasbourg) the New Jerusalem.[34] The new order initially won broad support, including some of the town's elite. Residents who challenged Matthys' rule, among them many of the city's well-to-do, were driven out and their property confiscated. Transforming his apocalyptic vision into public policy, Matthys proclaimed that henceforth all property would be held in common. The Münster Anabaptists interpreted their rout of an army raised by the local Catholic bishop on February 9–11, 1534, as a sign of divine favor.

On the following April 5, Easter Sunday, having prophesied that the end of the world would occur on that day, Matthys led a small company of supporters against a besieging force; all were killed. He was succeeded by his convert Jan Bockelson (John of Leyden), a twenty-five-year-old tailor under whom the situation in Münster rapidly deteriorated. Citing divine instructions received in a trance, Bockelson imposed his absolute authority over an increasingly terrorized populace. Introducing polygamy (again at God's command), he took several teenaged wives in addition to Matthys' widow. Women who resisted were executed, together with scores of dissident males.

In September, when a wandering prophet hailed Bockelson as Messiah, he accepted the title. "Now I am given power over all nations of the earth," he proclaimed, "and the right to use the sword to the confusion of the wicked and in defense of the righteous." A cadre of Dutch supporters enforced Bockelson's rule; newly minted coins bore apocalyptic inscriptions such as "One king of righteousness over all"; Bockelson issued manifestos proclaiming Christ's imminent return and portraying Münster as a forerunner of the millennial kingdom.[35]

For Münster the end was indeed at hand. Early in 1535 an army representing the local bishop and several German states blockaded the city. As Bockelson and his inner circle lived opulently and commandeered what little food remained in the city, the starved populace ate rats, grass, shoes, and even corpses. In June the besiegers captured the helpless city, massacring Anabaptists who trustingly accepted offers of safe-conduct. As for Bockelson, Norman Cohn describes his end:

> At the Bishop's command he was for some time led about on a chain and exhibited like a performing bear. In January 1536 he was brought to Münster; and there he [and two close allies] were publicly tortured to death with red-hot irons. Throughout their agony the ex-king uttered no sound and made no movement. After the execution the three bodies were suspended from a church-tower in the middle of the town, in cages which are still to be seen there today.[36]

With the collapse of Münster's New Jerusalem, most Anabaptists gave up the effort to achieve an apocalyptic new order in the present age and turned to more peaceful and moderate leaders such as the Dutch Anabaptist Menno Simons. Nevertheless, Reformation leaders reacted with horror to the Peasants' War, the rise of Anabaptism, and the bizarre events in Strasbourg and Münster. Luther in vicious language urged the German princes to exterminate the rebellious peasants. Calvin in the *Institutes* denounced the "frenzied" Anabaptist "devils." Zwingli fiercely repressed Anabaptism in his part of Switzerland and acquiesced when Zurich's civil authorities executed an Anabaptist leader by drowning.[37]

The reformers' reaction to the Anabaptists' radical millennialism decisively shaped their eschatological thinking. In 1522, appalled by the radicals' use of apocalyptic rhetoric, Luther dismissed John's

Apocalypse as "neither apostolic nor prophetic" and relegated it to an appendix in his German New Testament. Luther eventually found greater value in Revelation, but his repudiation of all who sought in the work a clear key to current and future events profoundly influenced Lutheran theology. The Augsburg Confession denounced the Anabaptists' millennialism as "Jewish doctrine." Calvin, while accepting the Book of Revelation as canonical, granted it less authority than the Gospels and did not include it in his Bible commentaries. In his 1561 commentary on the Book of Daniel, Calvin offered a preterist interpretation in which the Beast stands for successive Roman emperors. Zwingli flatly dismissed Revelation as "not a book of the Bible."[38] Both the Lutheran and the Reformed theological traditions, then, began with a strong amillennial bias and suspicion of end-time speculation that they retain to this day.

Yet Luther remained profoundly eschatological throughout his career. He rejected not the Anabaptists' eschatology per se, but their effort to achieve the millennial kingdom by direct action and military force. At the same time, and somewhat contradictorily, Luther readily invoked the biblical apocalypses in attacking Rome. Drawing on centuries of popular belief, Luther in *Adversus exsecrabilem Antichristi bullam* (1520) insisted that Pope Leo X's bull denouncing Luther's published views could have come only from Antichrist. In the 1530 edition of his German Bible, and repeatedly thereafter, Luther identified the Pope as Antichrist in even more explicit and vehement terms. Other reformers followed Luther's lead. John Calvin, in several passages of the definitive 1559 edition of his *Institutes of the Christian Religion,* made the Pope/Antichrist connection. The 1560 Geneva Bible, prepared for English Protestant exiles in Calvin's Geneva, drew the same link. Protestant artists produced woodcuts of the Pope as a loathsome beast. "To prove the Pope Antichrist" would be superfluous, wrote an English pamphleteer in 1581, "considering how it is a beaten argument in every book."[39] Sinking deep into the Protestant consciousness, the Pope/Antichrist nexus shaped prophetic interpretation for centuries. One still finds hints of it in some post-1945 American popularizations.

The Reformation coincided with the expansion of the Ottoman Turks into eastern Europe and the Middle East, and this theme, too, affected the early Protestant leaders' eschatology. Luther, fearful of an Ottoman invasion, in his 1530 German Bible described the Turks as the Gog of Ezekiel 38. Catholic exegetes, too, saw the Ottoman threat in eschatological terms. A vast body of prophecy writing from the early sixteenth century on echoed this reading.[40]

The Reformation influenced Catholic interpretation of prophecy as well. While some Catholic polemicists simply turned the tables and identified *Luther* as Antichrist, most favored a different strategy. Since Augustine's day, as we have seen, Catholic theology had favored an allegorical or historicist reading of biblical apocalyptic. Confronted by Protestant vilification of the Pope as Antichrist, however, some Catholic theologians revived an older interpretive tradition looking to a future eschatological fulfillment, beyond history. In *Commentarius in sacram beati Joannis Apocalypsim* (1591), for example, the Spanish Jesuit Franciscus Ribeira offered such an interpretation of John's Apocalypse. Rooted in Reformation-era polemics, this so-called Futurist position, removing prophetic fulfillment from the present age altogether, supplemented the allegorical approach in coloring subsequent Catholic interpretation of the prophecies.[41]

In England, meanwhile, a rich literature of prophetic exegesis emerged from the religious ferment of the sixteenth and seventeenth centuries—a literature that profoundly molded early American thought. English polemicists avidly adopted the Continental reformers' labeling of the Pope as Antichrist. Luther's 1520 attack on the Pope as Antichrist, published in English in 1529, stimulated a wave of English imitators. The word *animal*, Christopher Hill speculates, may have replaced *beast* in everyday usage in these years because the latter became so completely identified with the Pope. Ingenious writers devised systems by which the pontiff's name totaled 666, the Beast's number according to Revelation 13:18.[42]

Writers at all social and intellectual levels interpreted the English Reformation in apocalyptic terms. In 1588, the year Protestant England defeated the Catholic Spanish armada, the future King James I issued a work proving, yet again, the Pope/Antichrist connection. (The dedication of the Authorized Version of the Bible published in 1611—the so-called King James Version—thanked James for this youthful effort to identify "the Man of Sin.") John Napier, the inventor of logarithms, in 1594 published *A Pleine Discoverie of the Whole Revelation of St. John*. Applying his mathematical genius to the books of Daniel and Revelation, Napier predicted that the current age would end in 1688. His work went through twenty-three editions in the seventeenth century. In Edmund Spenser's allegorical masterpiece *The Faerie Queene* (1596), Duessa, who represents the Catholic Church, is described as riding "a dreadful Beast with sevenfold head"—an instantly recognizable allusion. By this time, the theme had become a cliché. As one pamphleteer observed sardonically, "He who can swear that the Pope is Antichrist and that flesh is good on Fridays is a protestant." In Shakespeare's *King Henry V* (1599) Mistress Quickly, affectionately recalling the recently deceased Falstaff, mentions his frequent talk of "the whore of Babylon."[43] The double entendre must have amused earthy Elizabethan audiences familiar with both the eschatological and the ordinary meaning of the term.

England's preoccupation with prophecy intensified in the seventeenth century. In part, this trend reflected events in Europe. During the Thirty Years' War (1618–1648) English pamphleteers proclaimed their nation's duty to help preserve Protestantism against the assaults of Antichrist, embodied in the papacy. They also echoed Continental writers in finding continued prophetic significance in the rise of Ottoman power and of Islam in general. Soon, wrote one pamphleteer in 1615, "the Antichrist of Rome *and the Turk* shall be utterly destroyed." Christopher Angelos of Oxford University, a strongly anti-Turkish Greek, in 1624 identified Mohammed as Antichrist. Finally, a resurgence of millennialism in Continental Protestant thought during the Thirty Years' War, as represented in the work of the German theologian Johann Alsted, for example, stimulated millennial interest in England.[44]

But England's own political and religious upheavals supplied more than enough grist to keep the prophecy mills grinding. Through pamphlets, sermons, ballads, and woodcuts, Katharine Firth observes, "almost everyone could learn something about the applications of the prophecies to the national crisis." Prophecy also served new and more radical polemical ends in these years, as millennialism (again in Firth's phrase) became "a weapon for social revolution and civil war." In the early stages of the English Reformation, as Christopher Hill has shown, the authorities encouraged the Pope/Antichrist formula. Once unleashed, such speculation could not be controlled, and by the early seventeenth century it had turned against figures closer to home.

During the reigns of the first two Stuarts, Puritan pamphleteers identified Antichrist with Church of England bishops. The Tudor monarchs had cut off the Beast's head, they argued, but left his tail intact. One Puritan pamphleteer, in the earthy language of the day, called Anglican clerics "the excrement of Antichrist." Others identified Charles himself or the hated Archbishop of Canterbury, William Laud, as Antichrist.[45] In the margins of an anonymous 1640 pamphlet, Christopher Hill found handwritten calculations in which "WILL LAUD" totals 666, and the following verse, no doubt part of the oral culture of the time:

> I am the Beast. Count it who can
> This is the number. I am the man.[46]

Commenting on the versatility of the Antichrist image—the Pope, the Turk, Mohammed, Charles I, Bishop Laud (and soon Oliver Cromwell)—Hill perceptively observes, "One advantage of the symbolism . . . was its vagueness: it could conceal attacks on more than one target" and enable people to express their "confusion and shifting opinions" in uncertain times. Or, as a skeptic put it in 1663, people "set up a Jack-o-[lantern] of their fancy's framing, and then hoot at it for Antichrist."[47] The insight applies as well to late-twentieth-century U.S. prophecy popularizers.

Recognizing the subversive power of prophecy belief, the Stuarts tried to discredit it. Ben Jonson, a court favorite during the reign of James I, ridiculed Puritan apocalypticism in *Bartholomew Fair* (1614), in which Zeal-of-the-Land-Busy finds eschatological significance in a weird musical instrument he spies at the fair: the drum, he says, is "the broken belly of Antichrist, and thy bellows there are his lungs, and these pipes are his throat, those feathers are his tail, and thy rattles the gnashing of his teeth."[48]

From 1642 to 1660, as England experienced civil war, regicide, a commonwealth, and military dictatorship, end-time anticipation ran rife. John Milton, the poet of Puritanism, was but one of many who invested these events with high eschatological significance, viewing them as the prelude to the moment when "the Eternall and shortly-expected King shall open the Clouds to judge the severall Kingdomes of the World." The urgent apocalypticism of these years can scarcely be overstated. One William Sedgwick, drunk on the Millennium, predicted the end in two weeks, a rash venture in date setting that earned him the lifelong nickname "Doomsday Sedgwick." The coming "day of doom," reported an observer in 1647, was "the common talk about London." [49]

The career of Milton's teacher Joseph Mede (1586–1638), a prophecy scholar and fellow of Christ College, Cambridge, illustrates the ubiquity of prophetic interest in these years. While he sometimes indulged in the prevailing tendency to interpret current events apocalyptically, Mede's larger objective was to integrate the Bible's various prophetic and apocalyptic sections into a single, synchronous end-time narrative. So impressive did English Puritans find his 1627 work, *Clavis Apocalyptica* (Key to the Revelation), that the House of Commons ordered it translated and reprinted posthumously in 1643. This and Mede's other prophecy writings, collected in *Works of the Pious and Profoundly Learned Joseph Mede* (1672), circulated widely in England and America. Influenced by Alsted's eschatology, Mede embedded a future Millennium firmly in his prophetic scheme, stimulating a revival of this doctrine in the English-speaking world. [50]

With the defeat of Charles I in 1646 and his beheading in 1649, apocalyptic speculation surged among English radicals, largely drawn from society's lower ranks, who saw an egalitarian new order on the horizon. Like the Taborites and early Anabaptists, they invoked Bible prophecy to validate their expectations. In the millennial age, wrote Mary Cary in *A Word in Season* (1647), "not only men but women shall prophesy; . . . not only superiors but inferiors; not only those that have university learning but those that have it not, even servants and handmaids." For some visionaries, Oliver Cromwell himself became the Man of Sin impeding the New Jerusalem. One pamphleteer found that the title REX OLIVER LORD PROTECTOR could be made to total 666—provided one omitted the "L" from "LORD." Members of an anti-Cromwellian faction in the army called themselves "Fifth Monarchy" men, an allusion to Nebuchadnezzar's dream in which a divine kingdom of righteousness succeeds the four earthly kingdoms of the ancient world. In *A Brief Description of the Fifth Monarchy* (1653), William Aspinwall pictured the coming new order. [51]

The accession of Charles II in 1660 cooled this orgy of apocalypticism. Nevertheless, the portentous year 1666 brought widespread uneasiness, worsened by the great London fire of that year. Indeed, wrote the Quaker leader George Fox, every thunderstorm in 1666 produced expectations of the end. And it was in the late seventeenth and early eighteenth centuries that Isaac Newton pursued the exhaustive prophetic studies that ultimately supplanted his work on mathematics and optics. (Remarked Voltaire, "Sir Isaac Newton wrote his comment upon the Revelation to console mankind for the great superiority he had over them in other respects.") William Whiston, Newton's successor as professor of mathematics at Cambridge, produced several influential prophecy books. In Restoration England, across the social and intellectual spectrum, prophecy continued to be a serious matter.[52]

But in the altered political climate of the day, prophecy no longer impinged so directly on current events. Talk of Antichrist and the New Jerusalem, ubiquitous a few years before, almost vanished; apocalyptic speculation, Christopher Hill suggests, represented an unwelcome reminder of the recent violence and social upheavals. A genteel prophecy expositor of 1664 apologized for even mentioning Antichrist, "of which the breath of the rude and ignorant vulgar usually smells as strong as of onions and garlic." John Bunyan criticized writers who had "predicted the time of the downfall of Antichrist, to the shame of them and their brethren." As Hill concludes, "Once the revolutionary decades had shown how very radical the quest for Antichrist could become, conservatives began to draw back from the attempt to identify him at all."[53]

Post-Restoration English prophecy writers focused less on the immediate scene than on matters of hermeneutic interpretation and details of their last-days timetables. From this period one can discern in embryo the two theories of Christ's return that would eventually be designated premillennial and postmillennial. Adherents of the former view held that in the last days, conditions on earth would steadily worsen, culminating in a crescendo of disasters, both natural and spiritual. Only an eschatological event wholly outside history—the Second Coming—would end these horrors and establish God's Kingdom on Earth. As earlier anticipations of an immediate Millennium collapsed, this bleaker view found influential exponents among English prophecy expositors who, buttressing their interpretations with current theories in physics and astronomy, offered naturalistic explanations for the end-time cataclysm. In *The Sacred Theory of the Earth* (1681) Thomas Burnet, the master of Charterhouse (a London benevolent and educational institution), speculated that the last days would see terrible drought, "a veil drawn over the Face of the Sun," and volcanoes and earthquakes producing on earth "a Disposition everywhere to break into open Flames." At this point, "Particles of Fire"—atoms under enormous pressure at the earth's molten core—would burst forth in a universal conflagration. (A good Protestant, Burnet anticipated the first outbreak in Rome.) The destruction would be awful: "The Cities and the Towns, and all the Works of Man's hands, will burn like Stubble before the Wind." [54]

Sir Isaac Newton's *Principia Mathematica* (1687) undermined Burnet's scientific assumptions, but not the larger effort to invoke science in defense of prophecy. In 1682 Edmund Halley had calculated the orbit of the comet bearing his name and predicted its next appearance for 1758 or 1759. Drawing on Halley's work, William Whiston's *Vindication of the New Theory of the Earth* (1696) argued that a comet's close passage had caused Noah's flood, and that the earth's prophesied destruction by fire would be by the same means. Whiston showed much ingenuity, as James Davidson notes, in "bringing in a comet every time he needed to get his scenario over a rough spot." [55]

Perry Miller, in a brilliant 1950 essay, "The End of the World," pinpointed the problem with this approach: if earth's final end is to be by wholly natural means, can this dénouement still be considered a divine judgment? Whiston's end-time drama, Miller noted, included no Second Coming, no Last Judgment—only the comet-induced conflagration. "Do flames that arise from natural fissions of matter give quite as much satisfaction to the mind as those that rain arbitrarily from Heaven?" Miller asked, then answered his own rhetorical question: "When the end of the world was a descent from Heaven, it was also a Judgment; if it becomes more and more a contrivance, it has less and less to do with good and evil . . . Catastrophe, by and for itself, is not enough." [56]

The same dilemma confronted late-twentieth-century prophecy writers whose end-time scenarios—bristling with knowing discussions of the neutron bomb, ozone depletion, the greenhouse effect, and other hazards—seemed very different from earlier accounts of God's own wrath descending on wicked humanity. Whatever its troubling eschatological implications, the science-based premillennialism of Burnet, Whiston, and others proved highly influential on both sides of the Atlantic.

The more hopeful *post*millennial view found champions as well, particularly among religious liberals who anticipated the gradual diffusion of Christianity until the Millennium almost imperceptibly became a reality. The Second Coming and other end-time events would occur only at the end of this thousand-year interval of peace and harmony. In *A Paraphrase and Commentary on the New Testament* (1703), the proto-Unitarian Daniel Whitby, rector of Saint Edmund's Church, Salisbury, challenged those who foresaw a bleak prophetic destiny for mankind. Whitby's more sanguine prospect envisioned steadily improving conditions with the spread of Protestantism and Christian morals. New editions of Whitby's hopeful work appeared through the mid-nineteenth century.[57]

Prophetic Speculation in Early America

Post-1945 prophecy writers who discussed—usually in sepulchral tones—America's prophetic destiny were merely the latest participants in a discourse that had been under way for nearly four centuries. From the early seventeenth century through the late eighteenth, the entire span of American colonial history was marked by speculation about America's role in God's plan. That the colonizing venture began at a time of intense apocalyptic awareness in England meant that it, like everything else in these years, took on an aura of eschatological meaning. In *General Considerations for Planting New England* (1629), John White urged his countrymen to support the undertaking as "a bulwark . . . against the Kingdom of Antichrist which the Jesuits labour to rear up in all quarters of the world." Puritan leader John Davenport found early reports from New England so moving that (according to Cotton Mather) they "brought into his Mind the New Heaven, and the New Earth, wherein dwells Righteousness."[58]

The Puritans who migrated to Massachusetts fully shared the eschatological hopes of those who stayed behind. John Cotton, minister of Boston's First Church, often preached on prophecy and wrote a commentary on Revelation. Addressing a public thanksgiving service after the execution of Charles I, Cotton took as his text the passage in Revelation describing the Beast's defeat. After extensive historical and scriptural study, he predicted the final end of Antichrist's power in 1655.[59]

As millennial expectations in England receded after 1660, American Puritans increasingly found prophetic meaning in their own history. This "Americanization of the apocalyptic tradition," as Stephen Stein calls it, is central to our story. Proclaiming the Lord's "great

Interest in this Land," Boston minister Increase Mather in 1676 speculated about America's prophetic destiny as a forerunner, or "type," of the New Jerusalem. Boston political leader Samuel Sewall, writing in 1697, shared Mather's conviction that America might be "the seat of the Divine Metropolis" in the Millennium. From such cosmic visions down to the most mundane events, New England prophecy writers proved as adept as those of Old England at finding apocalyptic meaning in current events. The bloodshed of King Philip's War (1675–1676), which pitted colonists against Indians, Mather suggested, was foretold in the red horse of the Apocalypse.[60]

Increase Mather's son Cotton (1663–1728), as Robert Middlekauff notes, "inaugurated an era of apocalyptical expectation in America that did not lose its force until after the American Revolution." He frequently expounded eschatological themes in his sermons at Boston's First Church, devoured the works of Joseph Mede and other English expositors, devoted many pages to prophecy in his unpublished Bible commentary, and often took up the subject in his diary. (One entry recorded a dream of a millennial meeting between Moses, Abraham, David, and himself.) His sermon "Things To Be Look'd For" (1691) found portents of the Second Coming in local and world events and, after calculations involving the Ottoman Empire and the revocation of the Edict of Nantes, tentatively predicted the end in 1697. Developing a theme prominent in twentieth-century prophecy writing, Mather further proclaimed that Christ's kingdom would bring economic justice, social harmony, and the downfall of dishonest merchants and politicians.[61] From its memorable opening, "I WRITE the *Wonders* of the CHRISTIAN RELIGION, flying from the Depravations of *Europe,* to the *American Strand,*" apocalypticism pervades Mather's ecclesiastical history of New England, *Magnalia Christi Americana* (1702). The work's aim, he added, was to "Report the *Wonderful Displays* of [God's] Infinite Power, Wisdom, Goodness, and Faithfulness, wherewith His Divine Providence hath *Irradiated* an *Indian Wilderness."* Mather bristled at Mede's conjecture that American Indians (or, worse still, *"Indianize[d]"* colonists) might constitute the demonic army that would rebel against Christ at the end of the Millennium. "I that am an American," he stoutly declared in "Problema Theologicum" (1703), "must needs be Lothe to allow all *America* still unto the Devils possession, when our Lord shall possess all the rest of the world."[62]

Indeed, Mather in his more exalted moments had little doubt about the location of the New Jerusalem. New England, he insisted in the *Magnalia* (echoing his father), would provide not only a bulwark against Antichrist but possibly be "the Spot of *Earth,* which the God of Heaven *Spied out*" as the capital of the millennial kingdom. "Many Arguments . . . perswade us," he added in a 1709 sermon, "that our glorious LORD, will have an Holy city in AMERICA, a *City,* the Street whereof will be *Pure* Gold." As New England's spiritual condition deteriorated, however, Mather's prophetic hopes dimmed. Perhaps, he speculated sadly in 1726, New England had already "done the most that it was intended for." [63]

To rouse sinners, Mather stressed the nearness of the end. "All that has been *foretold . . .* as what must come to pass before the *Coming . . . ,*" he wrote shortly before his death, "is, as far as we understand, Fulfill'd: I say ALL FULFILL'D!" (Nearly three centuries later, prophecy writers were reaching the same conclusion.) Mather was also an inveterate date setter. When 1697 passed quietly, he fixed on 1736; later, adopting a timetable proposed by Whiston, he settled on 1716, a year he spent in an agony of anticipation. [64]

Mather's potent brew of eschatology, patriotism, and date setting was not universally admired, particularly in the early eighteenth century as rationalism advanced and apocalypticism faded. The prophet Ezekiel made plain that the New Jerusalem could not be in America, insisted a minister in Hatfield, Massachusetts; it must be in Judea. Liberals such as Mather's younger contemporary Benjamin Colman, of Boston's Brattle Street Church, warned against becoming "too *Curious* and *Positive*" in linking prophecy to current events. Another critic in 1721 cautioned against apocalyptic pronouncements that could arouse "whole Hords of the Vulgar." [65]

With the Great Awakening, however, apocalyptic speculation again surged to the fore. In some quarters the religious revival that swept the colonies in the early 1740s sparked end-time expectations comparable to those in England a century earlier. "The *Millennium* is begun," proclaimed Boston minister John Moorehead; "Christ dwells with Men on Earth." In 1743 some seventy New England ministers signed a manifesto hailing the Awakening as a sign that the Kingdom of God was at hand. Others, slightly more cautious, viewed the revival as "an earnest of what God will do towards the close of the Gospel day." [66]

Jonathan Edwards (1703–1758), pastor of a Congregational church in Northampton, Massachusetts, that experienced a revival as early as 1734–1735, offered the fullest discussion of the Awakening's eschatological meaning. If not quite "the greatest [American] artist of the apocalypse" (Perry Miller's exuberant phrase), Edwards was certainly much interested in prophecy. He began a journal on the subject ("Notes on the Apocalypse") at the age of twenty, and in a 1739 sermon series issued posthumously as *A History of the Work of Redemption* he offered various reflections on prophecy. Although Edwards occasionally speculated in his notebooks and private letters about the prophetic meaning of comets and current events, and even about the date of Antichrist's fall (he was drawn to Samuel Sewall's belief that the year 2000 might bring the Millennium), he avoided Cotton Mather's propensity for public date setting. "I am far from pretending to determine the time when the reign of Antichrist began," he observed in his 1739 sermon, "a point . . . so much controverted among divines and expositors."[67]

But Edwards *did* believe the Millennium was approaching: the Reformation represented the Fifth Vial of Revelation, and the world was now in the period of the Sixth Vial—the last before the end. Through revival, prayer, and missionary effort, the prophesied Age of Grace would dawn. Edwards' millennial expectations peaked in *Some Thoughts Concerning the Present Revival of Religion in New-England* (1742), written as the Awakening crested. The revival, he wrote, appeared to be "the dawning, or at least a prelude, of that glorious work of God, so often foretold in Scripture, which in the progress and issue of it, shall renew the world of mankind." Further, he added, echoing generations of New England Puritans: "Many things . . . make it probable that this work will begin in America." Edwards was thus in the postmillennial tradition of Daniel Whitby: the earth will ultimately be destroyed, he taught (following Burnet and Whiston), "by fire from heaven, or by fire breaking out of the bowels of the earth, or both," but only *after* the Millennium and the saints' removal to heaven, "there being no further use for it." Further, as Nathan Hatch has argued, in placing the Great Awakening at the center of his prophetic scenario, Edwards helped transform postmillennialism "into a dynamic paradigm to explain current events"—a transformation that would influence American understanding of the Revolution in the next generation.[68]

The French and Indian War (1754–1763) spawned a large body of extremely sanguinary prophetic writing, with the French Catholic enemy cast as Antichrist. Presbyterian leader Samuel Davies identified the struggle with the French as "the grand decisive conflict between the Lamb and the beast." A Rhode Island minister characterized the Gallic enemy as the "Offspring of that *Scarlet Whore, that Mother of Harlots, who is justly the Abomination of the Earth.*" The French surrender of Canada in 1760 inspired Samuel Langdon of Portsmouth, New Hampshire, to quote Revelation 18: "*Babylon the great is fallen, is fallen!*" [69] This eschatologizing of the imperial struggle between France and Great Britain influenced the course of prophetic belief in the late eighteenth century and beyond. While Edwards and others during the Great Awakening had interpreted America's *spiritual* history apocalyptically, viewing the Millennium as a product of the gradual spread of Christianity, expositors of the late 1750s and early 1760s typically explained God's prophetic plan in political and military terms, as nearly synonymous with British interests in North America. By 1760, Hatch writes, few New England ministers drew any clear distinction "between the Kingdom of God and the goals of their own political community." [70] This shift would be profoundly important in determining prophetic interpretations of the American Revolution.

With the struggle for independence, patriot prophecy writers reenacted the familiar process of adapting their end-time scenarios to current events, and vied in identifying contemporary British leaders as Antichrist. The fact that the hated Lord Bute came from a Scottish island, declared a Providence orator in 1766, clearly marked him as "the Beast from the sea" of John's Apocalypse. A pamphleteer, describing the Stamp Act as a prelude to Antichrist's reign as described in Revelation, advised his readers to refuse all documents bearing the hated stamp, "lest by touching any paper with this impression, you receive the mark of the beast." By 1773 King George himself, like Charles I 150 years earlier, was being portrayed as Antichrist. Inevitably, someone calculated that in both Greek and Hebrew the words "Royal Supremacy in Great Britain" totaled—666. [71]

The independence movement also revived the belief of the Mathers and of Jonathan Edwards that America might be the seat of Christ's millennial kingdom. But what had been formulated in religious terms now took on a secular cast, as prophecy speculation—already politicized during the French and Indian War—oriented itself around the revolutionary cause, laying the groundwork for what Hatch felicitously calls the era of "civil millennialism." In "A Poem on the Rising Glory of America," delivered to their Princeton graduating class in 1771, Philip Freneau and Hugh Henry Brackinridge looked to the day when the New Jerusalem would "grace our happy earth, perhaps this land." An independent American nation, declared Ebenezer Baldwin in 1776, would be "the principal seat of that glorious Kingdom, which Christ shall erect upon the Earth in the latter Days." [72] Revolution and liberty, rather than revival, now became the high road to the blessed future foreseen by the biblical apocalypticists.

With symbolic appropriateness, Jonathan Edwards' grandson Timothy Dwight most fully elaborated this secular vision of the Revolution's prophetic significance. Dwight's 1771 poem "America," written when he was a nineteen-year-old Yale student, contains the kernel of his civil millennialism:

> O Land supremely blest! to thee 'tis given,
> To taste the choicest joys of bounteous heaven;
> Thy rising Glory shall expand its rays,
> And lands and times unknown rehearse thine endless praise.

Five years later, speaking at Yale three weeks after the Declaration of Independence, the now twenty-four-year-old Dwight fully eschatologized the stirring events of the day. In America, he said, history would reach its climax in the fulfillment of "that remarkable Jewish tradition" of a thousand years of "peace, purity, and felicity." Ushered in by Yale-trained lawyers, physicians, and other professionals, the star-spangled Millennium, he speculated (echoing Samuel Sewall, whose ideas had intrigued his grandfather), would probably begin about the year 2000. In the soaring apocalyptic language of the prophet Isaiah, Dwight hailed the emerging nation: "Arise, shine, for thy light is come." [73]

Thus, while the pamphleteers examined by Bernard Bailyn and J. G. A. Pocock debated the nuances of republican ideology, others, in an age when most Americans still found the Bible central to understanding current events, defined the conflict in different terms. What, if anything, did prophecy belief contribute to revolutionary ideology? While James Davidson argues that "millennial thought reflected rather than influenced political ideology," one could also suggest a more complex interaction in which the prophecy writers, if not prime shapers of political ideology, added a vital yeasty ingredient that helped transform a constitutional crisis into a popular movement. Whether, as Ruth Bloch claims, apocalypticism was "basic to the formation of American revolutionary ideology," she is certainly correct to suggest a "reciprocal, dynamic relationship" between the two, with apocalypticism adding "another—and to many a deeper—layer of meaning to the crisis." When Thomas Paine early in 1776 proclaimed, "We have it in our power to begin the world over again," he was tacitly drawing upon centuries of millennialist thinking about political events.[74]

The shifting fortunes of the Revolutionary War itself invited further prophetic reflection. Timothy Dwight interpreted the collapse of Burgoyne's invasion from Canada in the wilds of northern New York in October 1777 as a fulfillment of Joel's prophecy of invaders from the north whom God would drive into "a land barren and desolate." The Reverend David Tappan of Massachusetts saw Cornwallis' surrender in 1781 as "a principal link" in the fulfillment of "Scripture prophecies relative to the *millennial state*" when America would attain "a greater height of perfection and glory than the world has yet seen." Dwight, too, viewed the victory as a big step toward the Millennium, whose beginnings he again placed near the year 2000. Just as God gave the Jews Palestine as part of His divine plan, Dwight argued in *The Conquest of Canaan* (1785), He would give all North America to the new nation in the final fulfillment of that plan: "Here Empire's last, and brightest throne shall rise; / And Peace, and Right, and Freedom, greet the skies."[75]

Dwight's allusion to Jewish history touched on a central intellectual strategy by which Americans defined their place in prophecy: the argument that Old Testament Israel was the *type* of America; America, the *antitype* of Israel. This typological hermeneutic—perfected by generations of Puritan ministers—pervades the sermons of the revolutionary and early national periods. "There is no one (I trust)," observed a Connecticut minister in 1777, "whose mind is not at once struck with the description of Israel as being a most perfect resemblance of these American colonies." Abiel Abbot of Haverhill, Massachusetts, elaborated the analogy in minute detail in a 1799 sermon, citing, for example, the parallelism between God's destruction of Israel's enemies in ancient Palestine and the plague that killed many New England Indians just before the Pilgrims' arrival.[76]

Of course, the America/Israel equation had a darker side as well, in that Israel had suffered grievously for its sins. But overall, the positive theme prevailed: the United States, as God's favored nation in the last days, would prosper just as the Israelites had flourished when they walked in God's ways. "God hath graciously patronized our cause, and taken us under his special care, as he did his ancient covenant people," declared a New Hampshire minister in 1788. Abiel Abbot, pronouncing the United States "nearer to a parallel with Ancient Israel, than any other nation upon the globe," pointed to the nation's prosperity, piety, and admirable Constitution as evidences of God's favor.[77]

The 180-odd years from the first English settlements to the ratification of the Constitution thus represented a cycle of American history in which successive generations interpreted their collective experience in generally hopeful, "postmillennialist" terms: specially favored of God, the New World would play a central role in bringing on the Millennium. Christ's return would crown a long period of growing Christian influence and diminishing tyranny—a process in which America would figure prominently.

But the bleaker *pre*millennial position, which looked for the Millennium only after a dark interval of wars, wickedness, persecution, and natural disasters, had forceful advocates as well, including (despite their view of America's eschatological role) Increase and Cotton Mather. Increase wrote of the earth's coming destruction by fire, and cited scriptures proving that the saints would "be *caught up into the Air*" beforehand, thereby escaping the final conflagration—an early formulation of the Rapture doctrine more fully elaborated in the nineteenth century. Cotton criticized prophecy writers whose theme was "*Happy Times* to arrive"; he graphically pictured the destruction to precede the Second Coming, as God in "an all-devouring rage" unleashed "a terrible *Conflagration*" annihilating all evidence of human endeavor.[78]

This vein of prophetic interpretation provided a somber counterpoint to the more hopeful strand in colonial-era religious thought. As early as 1662, Michael Wigglesworth's verse epic *The Day of Doom* memorably pictured the Second Coming and Last Judgment as lightning-bolt eschatological events, with no reassuring hint of gradual betterment or an intervening Millennium. In *The Certainty and Suddenness of Christ's Coming* (1716), Samuel Sewall's son Joseph foresaw a "Day of Universal Doom, when in a literal sense, the Elements shall melt with fervent heat."[79]

Even the colonial prophecy writers usually labeled postmillennial introduced "premillennial" themes. (Indeed, as James Davidson and Ruth Bloch both remind us, to force a stark premillennial/postmillennial polarity obscures many nuances.) The "postmillennialist" Jonathan Edwards, for example, while sometimes writing hopefully of Christianity's advance on all fronts, could also—as in his sermon "Sinners in the Hands of an Angry God"—picture the terrors of divine wrath in terms worthy of any premillennialist. Edwards and other eighteenth-century "postmillennialists," Davidson argues, generally embraced an "afflictive model of progress" in which advance comes only after trials, setbacks, and suffering; they could thus simultaneously hail the approaching Millennium and gloomily foresee wickedness, persecution, and turmoil ahead. Postmillennialists were not necessarily dewy-eyed optimists.[80]

A proto-premillennialist eschatology clearly influenced popular thought in colonial America. When an earthquake struck Boston in 1755, a contemporary reported that "many Persons jump'd out of their Beds, and ran immediately into the Streets, while others sprung to the Windows, trembling, and seeing their Neighbors as it were naked; *shrieked with Apprehension of its being the Day of Judgment,* and some tho't they heard the LAST TRUMP sounding, and cry'd out for Mercy." Four years later, a Boston printer reissued *The Strange and Wonderful Predictions of Mr. Christopher Love,* the alleged work of an English radical executed by Cromwell. A sensational, date-setting work loosely grounded in biblical apocalyptic, it predicted earthquakes and wars in the 1750s, the rise of Antichrist in 1761, and the final end in 1763. Another big seller in the colonies, Richard Clarke's book *The Prophetic Numbers of Daniel and John Calculated* (1759), forecast the end by 1766 at the latest.[81]

As the euphoria induced by the British defeat and the ratification of the Constitution faded, this gloomier strand of prophetic interpretation revived—Elhanan Winchester's *Lectures on the Prophecies That Remain to Be Fulfilled* (1795) is illustrative. Prophecy writers dwelt on the spread of sinfulness and religious infidelity. And as the politically inspired millennialism of the revolutionary era diminished, American prophecy writing—like that in post-Restoration England—also became more cautious, more concerned with textual analysis, and less absorbed with the present. The familiar figures of the Pope and the Turk replaced the British in Antichrist speculation. Benjamin Foster's *Dissertation on the Seventy Weeks of Daniel* (1787) offered detailed chronological calculations proving that the Book of Daniel precisely fore-told Jewish history through Jesus' resurrection, and that the Bible could therefore be trusted as a guide to end-time events.[82] As the eigh-teenth century closed, Nathan Hatch writes, New England ministers "vacillated between an attitude of hope inspired by the achievements of American liberty and a sense of foreboding occasioned by the spread of national vice." Whatever its form, the eschatological vision was never long absent from colonial and revolutionary America. "Handed down from generation to generation," Stephen Stein notes, it illuminated the underlying meaning of events that many Americans found compelling as they "struggled to understand themselves, their responsibilities, and their place in history."[83]

As we reflect on this far-too-hasty review of apocalypticism over a seventeen-hundred-year span of Western history, certain themes emerge that may enhance our understanding of later prophetic belief. Bearing in mind the special significance the prophecies attach to cer-tain numbers, let me briefly mention seven.

First, one is struck not only by the durability of apocalyptic be-lief, but also by its enormous adaptability. From second-century Asia Minor to eighteenth-century America, in vastly different historical circumstances, interpreters found vastly different meanings in the prophecies. Indeed, one revolutionary-era American minister saw this adaptability as their great strength. After all, he wrote, these revela-tions had been given "for the instruction, support, and consolation of God's saints, in the wars and conflicts they might have with their ene-mies, in every age and period of time."[84] He did not explore the im-plications of this pragmatic view: if the prophecies can be applied with equal validity to *any* historical situation, what becomes of their status as a divinely inspired foretelling of *specific* events?

Second, apocalyptic belief, given the right circumstances, can serve radical ends. From the Taborites and the early Anabaptists to the English radicals of the 1640s and the American revolutionaries of the 1770s, the prophetic scriptures have provided conceptual guidance and emotional succor to groups challenging the established order. As we turn to the post-1945 era, we shall again encounter prophecy writ-ers who, while conservative in their overt social and political views, nevertheless retained, in the interstices of their prophetic systems, echoes of apocalypticism's subversive heritage.

Third, in the American colonial period, religious and secular themes increasingly intermingled in popular eschatological writings from the Great Awakening to the Revolution. As we shall see, this tradition of politicized prophetic belief remains vigorously alive in the late-twentieth-century United States.

Fourth, prophecy belief has a history and an organic integrity of its own; while obviously colored by current events, it is not merely a "reflection" of other realities. At many critical junctures in Western history, apocalyptic cosmologies have functioned dynamically, helping to mold political and social ideology and thus influencing the course of events. This too will be useful to remember as we seek to understand the social meaning of post-1945 prophetic belief.

Fifth, the welter of interpretive approaches, and their complex interactions, underscore the difficulty of charting a straightforward evolution of prophetic belief systems. One approach will flourish and then wane, to be replaced by another, or by an interval when prophecy interest recedes. But then, under different circumstances, the picture changes: apocalypticism again looms large; long-dormant interpretive approaches take on new vitality. In assessing the importance of the prophetic mode of historical understanding in post-1945 American popular thought, we would do well to remain alert to this remarkable persistence—sometimes in latent, half-recognized, or much altered form—of the ancient beliefs whose history we have sketched in this chapter.

A sixth, related observation suggested by a historical retrospective of this kind, particularly if one undertakes it (as I did) after an immersion in late-twentieth-century popular prophecy writing, is the remarkable continuity of basic themes and preoccupations. Concern with America's destiny, the Jews' prophetic role, Antichrist's identity, the precise sequence of end-time events; anticipations of Antichrist's rule in current economic and political trends; the vision of a world far different from the present one—all these components of contemporary prophetic speculation have deep roots in the past. Interest in the prophetic significance of powerful Islamic leaders, from Saladin in the twelfth century to the Ottoman Turks in the sixteenth to Saddam Hussein in the twentieth, has been another constant. Specifics change; underlying thematic structures remain.

Seventh and last: one is, of course, struck by discontinuities as well. The most obvious, perhaps, is in the intellectual standing of the expositors of prophecy belief. In earlier eras, the interpretation of prophecy challenged the intellectual leaders of successive ages. From the nineteenth century on, and certainly by the late twentieth century, this was no longer the case. Prophecy remains of absorbing interest to millions of Americans, but those who expound the prophetic scriptures are no longer the era's intellectual or even theological leaders. It is not to disparage the ingenuity or earnestness of the television evangelists and paperback writers who are today's principal prophecy expositors to observe that they hardly bear comparison to Irenaeus, Origen, Augustine, Joachim, Hildegard, Mede, Milton, Newton, the Mathers, Edwards, and Dwight—intellectuals all. Fully to explore the reasons for that profound shift, however, would involve nothing less than writing an intellectual history of the modern world.

3   The Premillennial Strand

P rophetic belief, a continuing motif in American thought from the early nineteenth century through World War II, periodically flared to even greater levels of intensity. Viewing current events through the lens of biblical apocalyptic, evangelicals produced a rich body of eschatological interpretation over this long span of time. In the antebellum years, prophecy writing and popular millenarian movements reflected the era's reformist, perfectionist, and expansively nationalistic spirit. As the nineteenth century wore on, however, a more somber version of premillennialism—deeply skeptical about reform and indeed about the entire contemporary social and intellectual order—challenged liberal Protestantism's hopeful affirmations. Largely forgotten today, these Gilded Age prophecy writers helped shape the ideological climate of their day.

In the early decades of the twentieth century, the emergence of fundamentalism, the Depression, and two world wars all stimulated prophetic speculation. The year 1945 found prophecy belief strongly entrenched in American popular religion, where it formed the groundwork for an outpouring of apocalyptic conjecture in the post-war years. This long cycle of prophetic interpretation, illustrating yet again the protean quality of the biblical apocalypses and their applicability to very different historical situations, provides a valuable doorway to the world of post-1945 prophecy writing that will be our focus in succeeding chapters.

Prophecy in Antebellum America

The hopeful, reformist interpretation of Bible prophecy formulated as early as 1703 by Daniel Whitby, and embraced in different forms by various eighteenth-century American ministers, writers, and polemicists, won broad support in the antebellum United States, appealing not only to liberal religionists but to many evangelicals as well. An implicit postmillennialism underlay not only the utopian experiments of this era before the Civil War but also the crusades for social betterment—temperance, prison reform, the abolition of slavery, and so forth—that pervaded the North, including the evangelical churches. (Among rationalist theologians at Harvard Divinity School and other leading seminaries, prophetic interpretation of any kind ceased to be of much interest. The long downward slide of prophecy belief on the intellectual scale was accelerating.)[1]

But premillennialism remained alive even in these optimistic, expansive years. The leaders of the revivals that swept the frontier and many eastern cities all preached the Lord's return. The Disciples of Christ (Campbellite) Church, founded by revivalist Alexander Campbell in 1827, embraced the imminent Second Coming as a central tenet. Indeed, Campbell called his periodical the *Millennial Harbinger.*[2]

The one manifestation of American prophetic belief known to all, the Millerite excitement of the 1830s and early 1840s, unfolded in a premillennialist milieu. Like many Americans of his day, an upstate New York farmer and Baptist layman named William Miller (1782–1849) found biblical prophecy absorbing. Witnessing the battle of Plattsburgh during the War of 1812, he ascribed the U.S. victory to divine intervention. Later, after long biblical study, he concluded that the Second Coming would occur "about the year 1843." (He derived this date from Dan. 8:14: "Unto two thousand and three hundred days; then shall the sanctuary be cleansed." Making the usual day = year transposition, and starting from 458 B.C.—when Artaxerxes I of Persia authorized the exiled Jewish priest Ezra to rebuild the Temple in Jerusalem—Miller arrived at 1843.) From the early 1830s on, Miller crisscrossed the North expounding his theory.[3]

Utilizing tracts, prophecy conferences, and tent services; periodicals with titles such as *The Midnight Cry* and *Signs of the Times;* and colorful illustrated charts with menageries of lions, bears, and dragons from the Book of Daniel, the movement won followers across New England, upstate New York, the upper Midwest, and as far away as England. When 1843 came and went, some younger Millerites settled on a new and specific date: October 22, 1844. As summer gave way to fall that year, committed Millerites lived in keen anticipation. The passage of the appointed day left an aftermath of profound disappointment. "Our fondest hopes and expectations were blasted, and such a spirit of weeping came over us as I never experienced before," one Millerite recalled. "We wept, and wept, till the day dawn."[4]

For all its notoriety, Millerism remains in some respects a byway in the history of prophetic belief in America. Miller's timetable involved an archaic historicist approach that would fade out almost entirely after 1844. Further, with occasional exceptions, subsequent prophecy writers avoided the lure of date setting, citing Jesus' warnings, "Of that day and hour knoweth no man" (Matt. 24:36) and "It is not for you to know the times or the seasons, which the Father hath put in his own power" (Acts 1:7). Indeed, Millerism's principal long-term significance, apart from spawning the Seventh-day Adventist Church, has been as the definitive example of the perils of date setting. The rise of dispensational premillennialism, to which we turn in a moment, was in part a response to the Millerite fiasco.

Despite its atypicality, the Millerite excitement underscores the pervasiveness of apocalyptic belief in antebellum America. Avowed Millerites numbered perhaps fifty thousand, but countless thousands more took Miller seriously without formally "joining" the amorphous movement. John Humphrey Noyes, for example, founder of the Oneida perfectionist community, once characterized his outlook in the early 1830s this way: "My heart was fixed on the Millennium, and I resolved to live or die for it." Millerism enlisted a cross-section of the population in northeastern America—including many of the middle class. As David Rowe observes, "Millerites are not fascinating because they were so different from everyone else but because they were so like their neighbors." [5]

The movement also sheds light on the relation between apocalyptic belief and social thought, a central concern of this book. Many leaders were veterans of a variety of reforms, including antislavery, temperance, and other causes. Miller's key lieutenant, Boston minister Joshua Himes, was a friend of William Lloyd Garrison and an avowed abolitionist. To be sure, earthbound concerns faded as the predicted date approached. But many Millerites saw no contradiction in working for reform while awaiting the end. Angelina Grimké Weld, simultaneously an abolitionist, women's-rights advocate, and avid Millerite, wrote to her sister in 1845:

> I fully believe in the downfall of every Earthly throne and the overthrow of every political government—the annihilation of every Ecclesiastical Establishment and the dissolution of every sect and party . . . But I am calm, hopeful, happy, for I see arising out of their ruins the Everlasting kingdom of God. [6]

Such passages remind us not to draw too sharp a distinction between a pessimistic, passive *pre*millennialism and an optimistic, activist *post*-millennialism. Later in the nineteenth century, as factories and immigrant slums proliferated, some leading premillennialists did pronounce reform effort worthless—a bleak attitude that would survive and even intensify in the twentieth century. Yet when the climate is favorable, premillennialism can certainly accommodate the hopeful view that the imminence of the Second Coming dictates not social withdrawal, but redoubled effort to battle sin in its many guises, social as well as personal, as the end approaches.

At heart, however, Millerism must be understood in religious terms. The teachings of "Father Miller" appealed to thousands of evangelicals convinced that biblical apocalyptic, rightly interpreted, could pierce the veil of the future. Further, Miller's message promoted conversion. At a time when both the Second Great Awakening and Charles G. Finney's urban revival campaigns had faded, Millerite evangelists proved remarkably effective at stirring revival embers into flame.[7]

Other characteristics of Millerism provide further clues to its appeal—clues that also shed light on the persistence of prophecy belief in post-1945 American culture. Miller, himself possessing little formal education, insisted that *anyone* could interpret the prophecies. Indeed, he urged others to check his system against their own calculations. Just as the Jacksonians claimed that any (white male) citizen could perform the duties of government, so the Millerites insisted that untutored believers could unravel the apocalyptic mysteries. Millerism heralded the full democratization of prophetic belief in the United States. Like their late-twentieth-century successors, the Millerites, as we have seen, used every available means of mass communication—visual aids, tent evangelism, high-speed printing presses—to spread their message. Established ministers were sharply critical, recognizing the movement as a threat to their status as privileged expounders of sacred truth.[8]

While open to all, prophecy interpretation had its rules. No wild-eyed fanatic, Miller stressed the systematic nature of his method and the rationality of his conclusions. Prophecy study, he insisted, was precisely analogous to science's probing of nature's secrets. At a time when numeracy was increasingly becoming a culturally valued skill disseminated through the population by almanacs and by the public schools, Miller and his followers applied this proficiency to elucidation of the numerological mysteries of the Book of Daniel.[9]

Both themes, the democratic inclusiveness and the rationalistic aura of the enterprise, would remain prominent in the post-1945 prophecy subculture.

While Millerism rose and fell, the civic millennialism of the revolutionary era continued to flourish, saturating antebellum political rhetoric. In the expansionist 1850s, several minister-patriots offered elaborate scenarios of America's prophetic destiny. In 1854 Samuel Davies Baldwin, a Methodist minister and president of Soule College, a Methodist school for young women in Murfreesboro, Tennessee, published a 480-page book arguing that the Bible's prophetic references to "Israel" really meant the United States. The tide of immigrants pouring into America, he said, fulfilled the prophecy that in the last days people from many nations would gather in "Israel." Rejecting the idea of a literal restoration of ancient Israel as "absurd, fanatical, and repugnant to Scripture, as well as to common sense," Baldwin elaborately demonstrated that the timetable presented in the Book of Daniel, misunderstood by the Millerites, actually foretold the interval between the cessation of temple sacrifice in Jerusalem in 68 A.D., and *July 4, 1776!* Citing Ezekiel 38, Baldwin predicted an invasion of the United States by a Russian-led European alliance that would be promptly annihilated: "How dreadful the fray when the thrones [of Russia and its allies] shall be cast down by our republic!" Its foes destroyed, the United States—the "Christian Israel"—would achieve "an importance and sublimity absolutely overwhelming" and exercise "Dominion over the Whole World." [10]

Baldwin's prophetic scenario was popularized by another Tennessee Methodist minister, the wonderfully named Fountain Pitts. On February 22, 1857 (Washington's Birthday), by invitation of "several members of Congress," Pitts delivered in the U.S. Capitol a day-long sermon on America's prophetic destiny. Word of his morning discourse spread rapidly through Washington, and the afternoon audience jammed the Capitol to overflowing. Pitts, indeed, was no ordinary man. As an obituary tribute tells us:

> His head was large, and his intellectual powers, in many respects, were of the highest order, and he was highly gifted as a speaker. His voice was full, clear, and musical; his enunciation

distinct; his manner was deliberate, grave, solemn, and persuasive . . . Although his mind was of a poetical cast, with a rich
fancy and brilliant imagination, yet he was never carried off into
extreme views or doubtful theories.[11]

Disavowing "Millerism, and all that class of fanatical fancies
[that] have deluded misguided thousands," the eloquent Pitts elaborated Baldwin's exegesis. He, too, found the Declaration of Independence foretold in Daniel. A journalist who took notes on the discourse
summed up his chronology:

> The United States arose at the end of 1290 symbolic days from
> the destruction of Jerusalem; . . . Daniel's 70 weeks being equal
> to 603 years and 129 days of solar time, according to the eclipses
> of the sun . . . , so that if 70 symbolic weeks equaled 600 years
> and 129 days, 1290 symbolic days reached from the burning of
> the temple on the 189th day of the year 68 A.D. to the 4th of
> July, 1776 . . . Making the starting-point at the occasion of the
> daily sacrifice, which happened, according to astronomy, at
> sunrise, three minutes past five o'clock A.M. on the day the
> temple was burnt, the 1290 days run out at a quarter to three
> o'clock P.M., on the 4th day of July, 1776; and, from the best
> sources of information, the Declaration of Independence was
> proclaimed at that hour on the glorious Fourth.[12]

Buttressing his related argument that the United States was the divinely ordained fifth kingdom of King Nebuchadnezzar's dream, Pitts
quoted George Berkeley's famous poem with its echoes of Daniel's
sacred chronology:

> Westward the star of empire makes its way;
>   The first four acts already passed,
> The fifth shall close the drama with the day:
>   Time's noblest offspring is the last.[13]

Still following Baldwin, Pitts identified virtuous America as the
prophetic Israel. Certainly wickedness abounded, he conceded, "but
bad as we are, . . . we are the very best people on the face of the earth."
Geographical details match as well: references in Ezekiel to a nation
lying between two seas clearly fit the United States better than Palestine. All in all, Pitts concluded, prophecy offered "almost a daguerrotype portraiture" of the United States.[14]

Pitts, too, foresaw an invasion of republican America by monarchical England and Russia. The Meshech and Tubal of Ezekiel 38, he said (anticipating scores of Cold War prophecy writers), were Moscow and Tobolsk. The ensuing Armageddon battle, fought in the Valley of the Mississippi, would be horrendous: "These ascending powers, like two towering clouds culminating in the heavens, surcharged with electric ruin, will shock the world with their collision, and bathe the world in blood." But the United States would prevail with God's help and would lead the world into a millennial age when "commerce and trade, agriculture and manufactures, science and art" would flourish, and humanity would know "but one kind of civil government . . . , Republicanism, and but one religion . . . , Christianity." [15]

Pitts's scenario captured the mood of 1857—expansive, assertive, yet troubled by deepening sectional conflict. (Within four years, war indeed did overtake America, although not the one Pitts envisioned.) The "America as Israel" theme—derived from late-eighteenth-century New England prophecy writers, and a variant of "British-Israel" theories current at this time—obviously appealed to national vanity. A long and respectful summary of Pitts's sermon appeared in the *National Intelligencer,* a leading Washington newspaper. The full text, published in 1859, went through several editions. "The work . . . will, we have no doubt, soon be issued by the hundred thousand," the publisher predicted. [16]

Another popularizer, one J. P. Philpott, offered more evidence for the "America as Israel" thesis in an 1864 work issued by the Southern Methodist Publishing House. Joseph's son Manasseh had thirteen children, Philpott pointed out—obviously a type of the thirteen colonies. Further, five of Manasseh's offspring were female—*and five of the thirteen colonies had female names!* [17] The expansive view of America's prophetic destiny expounded by Baldwin, Pitts, Philpott, and many others proved long-lived. By the end of the twentieth century, however, as we shall see, a far darker vision had largely supplanted it.

John Darby and the Rise of Dispensationalism

While patriotic popularizers found a glorious destiny for the United States in prophecy, evangelical ministers and Bible scholars (and soon a great many ordinary believers) responded to a very different interpretive approach, which originated in Great Britain in the 1820s. The key figures were Edward Irving, Henry Drummond, and John

Darby. Irving, minister of a Scotch Presbyterian chapel in London in the early 1820s, won a following for his charismatic preaching, sharp social criticism, and proclamations of Christ's imminent return. He elaborated his eschatological views in an 1828 Edinburgh lecture series on John's Apocalypse. Excommunicated by the London presbytery in 1830 for heresy (he taught that Jesus' earthly nature was sinful), Irving continued to preach until his death in 1834—winning further notoriety by encouraging glossolalia ("speaking in tongues") as one of the "signs and wonders" foretold by Jesus as a harbinger of the last days.[18]

In 1835 Irving's followers organized the Catholic Apostolic Church, led by twelve apostles, of whom at least one was expected to be alive at the Second Coming. (When the last of the original twelve died at an advanced age in 1901, the sect died out.) Among Irving's converts was Henry Drummond, wealthy London banker and Tory member of Parliament. A founder and financial backer of the Catholic Apostolic Church, Drummond for several years beginning in 1826 sponsored annual prophecy conferences at his estate in Surrey. The prophetic interest stimulated by Drummond and the Irvingites helped spread premillennial beliefs in the United States.[19]

Even more important on the American scene was John Nelson Darby (1800–1882), the nephew of Henry Darby, a naval commander who fought with Admiral Horatio Nelson in the battle of the Nile in 1798. Ordained in the (Protestant) Church of Ireland in 1825, Darby soon withdrew in opposition to its hierarchism and its links to the Crown. He joined a new sect, the Brethren, that rejected state ties and all organizational structure beyond the congregational level. When the sect split in the 1840s, he emerged as leader of the stricter faction, the Plymouth Brethren, or Darbyites.[20]

Influential far beyond his immediate circle, Darby wrote and preached extensively, and from 1837 to the end of his life toured regularly outside the British Isles, including—from 1859 on—in the United States.[21] A key figure in the resurgence and reorientation of premillennialism in late-nineteenth-century America, he is particularly identified with *dispensationalism,* a distinct form of prophecy interpretation that won many evangelical adherents.

Darby taught that God has dealt with mankind in a series of epochs, or dispensations—in each of which the means of salvation differed. While Bible prophecy reveals much about past and future dispensations, it is silent on the present one, the Church Age. (The

"Great Parenthesis," some called it.) One cycle of prophesied events ended with Jesus' crucifixion; the next will begin with the *Rapture*—the moment when all believers will rise to meet Christ in the air. Once the prophetic clock starts ticking again with the Rapture, the final sequence of events will unfold with dismaying rapidity for those left behind, beginning with the seven-year rule of Antichrist and the Apostate Church, the so-called *Tribulation* (Matt. 24:21), of which the second half will be sheer hell. (Rejecting both Augustine's historicist approach and the day = year theory of earlier interpreters, Darby held that the 1,260 days of the Beast's rule prophesied in Daniel meant just that: a future period of 1,260 days, or three and one-half years.) The Tribulation will end with the *Battle of Armageddon,* when Christ, the saints, and the heavenly host return to earth and defeat Antichrist and his army. Next will come the *Millennium,* Christ's thousand-year rule on earth; a final, doomed uprising by Satan; the resurrection of the dead; and history's final event, the Last Judgment.[22]

In a sense, Darby's system contained nothing new. His focus on the future fulfillment of prophecy followed the eschatology of the early Christians. Premillennialism had been an option for Protestant evangelicals since Joseph Mede's day, while rudimentary forms of "dispensationalism" go back at least as far as Joachim of Fiore. Even Rapture doctrine, as we have seen, can be found in the writings of earlier interpreters, including Increase Mather. But Darby wove these diverse strands into a tight and cohesive system that he buttressed at every point by copious biblical proof texts, then tirelessly promoted through his writings and preaching tours.[23]

What was Darby's appeal to American evangelicals? No doubt the anti-institutional bias of the Plymouth Brethren, a major theme in Darby's prophecy writings, found fertile soil in nineteenth-century America, where laissez-faire ideology abounded. Further, since the Rapture's precise timing remains hidden (though by observing "the signs of the times" one may be sure it is near), dispensationalism avoided the reef of date setting on which Millerism had foundered. Rejecting the historicist approach of matching world events since Jesus' time with specific prophecies, Darby firmly placed apocalyptic fulfillment either in the pre-Christian era or in the eschatological future. Like Mede, he sought to incorporate *all* the prophecies into a single interpretive system, rather than belaboring one or two verses, as the Millerites and other interpreters tended to do.

Dismissing all theories of England or America as the "New Is-rael," Darby assigned a distinct end-time role to the Jews. Indeed, he saw two prophetic tracks—one for Jews, one for Gentiles—and this approach became dispensationalism's most distinctive and controver-sial feature. Sometime soon, he taught, fulfilling the prophecies of Israel's restoration, God's chosen people would reestablish a nation in their ancient homeland and rebuild the Temple. At long last, after ter-rible persecution during Antichrist's reign, a surviving remnant of Jews would embrace their long-rejected Messiah.[24] Darby was far from alone in teaching a Jewish return to Palestine, but in placing this event at the heart of his dispensational system, he had a profound long-term influence.

Dispensationalism arrived at a time of mounting evangelical con-cern over challenges to the Bible's divinely inspired status by liberal theologians in the United States and by historical-critical scholars in Germany. The formation of the Evangelical Alliance in England in 1846 and of an American branch in 1867 signaled the rising uneasi-ness. At the founding convention in London, the eight hundred dele-gates adopted a credal statement explicitly affirming the Bible's inspi-ration and authority.[25] Many embattled evangelicals thus welcomed Darby's strong emphasis on biblical authority and his literal reading of the prophetic texts.

Darby's indefatigable promotion of dispensationalism, rein-forced by many other ministers and writers, stimulated a surge of premillennial interest at midcentury. Elhanan Winchester's 1795 premillennial lectures were reprinted in 1851 in response to "consid-erable demand." Edward Hitchcock, Amherst College geologist and evangelical tract writer, in 1851 offered evidence from science that "in a very short time—far shorter than we imagine—all the scenes of fu-turity will be to us a thrilling reality!" A series of premillennial popu-larizations by the Scottish minister John Cumming, including *Signs of the Times* (1854), enjoyed great success in the United States.[26]

The Last Times (1856), by the Reverend Joseph Seiss, was perhaps an effort to capitalize on the popularity of Cumming's work of two years before. It presented the premillennialist message in vivid, arrest-ing prose. Two years after Thoreau's *Walden* had portrayed nature as a manifestation of the divine and a source of moral knowledge, Seiss offered a very different picture of a hostile and malignant nature that expressed God's mounting anger:

> This world is a disjointed and dilapidated fabric . . . Cold, storms, earthquakes, volcanoes, barren fields, pestilential airs, smiting sunshine, tearing briars, and noxious things, combine in the terrific accusation against man, and . . . his unholy deeds. What was created to minister to our joy has become a disorderly servant, as if indignant to obey a convict sovereign.[27]

And society was equally out of joint. Like post-1945 prophecy writers, Seiss culled abundant evidence from contemporary periodicals to prove that crime and wrongdoing were increasing, social institutions collapsing, and ancient belief systems crumbling. The world had entered a "startling and critical" stage foreshadowing the end:

> All society, everywhere, with its politics, its philosophy, and its religion, is in a perturbed condition . . . The stream of earthly things is overflowing its old banks, and spreading out in every direction, in wild, disordered, ungovernable, and overwhelming volume. Old systems and modes of thought and belief, which have stood for ages, are everywhere tottering . . . That "the world to come" is . . . a vast improvement upon the present scene of things, will be inferred on all hands without argument.[28]

In 1863, as the Civil War raged, Seiss insisted in a new edition of his work that the intervening seven years had only deepened his conviction that the world was sinking into the final abyss of wickedness immediately preceding the end.[29] As the nineteenth century wore on, while some celebrated the nation's technological advances and wrote of inevitable human evolution toward perfection, the dark forebodings of the premillennialists became ever more insistent.

Premillennialism from the Civil War to World War I

Amid the convulsive social transformations of the years from Appomattox to World War I, Darby's version of premillennial prophecy belief gained many adherents among American evangelicals who found this system a valuable if sobering source of meaning. Darby made at least six U.S. tours between 1859 and 1877, winning many prominent ministers and laypersons, especially Baptists and Presbyterians, to dispensationalism.[30]

Another influential British prophecy writer in these years was Sir

Robert Anderson (1841–1918), longtime chief of criminal investigation in London's Scotland Yard. (The Jack the Ripper case was among those handled by Anderson.) An adherent of the Plymouth Brethren and an avid prophecy scholar, Anderson "tracked down myths and religious error, arrested and exposed it, with the same skill and courage that he displayed when he tracked down criminals."[31] In *The Coming Prince* (1884), which won an immediate U.S. audience, Anderson marshaled scores of Bible texts, vast historical erudition, Hebrew-calendar data, and even a letter from the royal astronomer at Greenwich, to buttress his prophetic interpretation. He contended that the reference in Daniel 9:25 to the sixty-nine "weeks" between "the going forth of the commandment to restore and to build Jerusalem" and the coming of "Messiah the Prince" in fact (making the usual day = year assumption) referred to a period of 483 years ($69 \times 7 = 483$) and foretold *to the day* the interval between Artaxerxes' famous order to Ezra and Jesus' triumphal entry into Jerusalem. If prophecy so precisely foretold a known historical occurrence, Anderson triumphantly concluded, surely it could be trusted to predict events still in the future. (But not their precise dates: as a Darbyite, Anderson harshly criticized date setters who had degraded Bible prophecy "to the level of the predictions of astrologers, to the confusion and grief of faithful hearts, and the amusement of the world.") Any who doubted the Second Coming, Anderson declared, had "no claim whatever to the name of Christian." *The Coming Prince* went through eleven editions in England and America, including one as recently as 1986, and at the close of the twentieth century was still respectfully cited in prophecy circles.[32]

Among late-nineteenth-century American premillennialists, James Brookes and William Blackstone loom large. Brookes, a St. Louis Presbyterian minister, was an avid Darbyite whose *Maranatha: or, The Lord Cometh* (1870) long remained in print. Blackstone, a prominent Chicago real-estate entrepreneur, evangelical layman, and prophecy devotee, wrote the dispensationalist *Jesus Is Coming* (1878), which also had a wide readership. Subsidized by wealthy sympathizers, a 1908 reissue was distributed to several hundred thousand religious leaders.[33]

A series of prophecy conferences organized by Brookes and others, beginning in 1875 at Niagara-on-the-Lake, Ontario, sustained the growing movement. An 1878 conference at New York's Holy Trinity

Episcopal Church attracted many prominent premillennialists and gained respectful media attention. The *New York Tribune* issued the conference sermons in an "extra" printed in fifty thousand copies. The published papers, edited by Nathaniel West (a Presbyterian clergyman from Cincinnati), began with the "Pre-Millennian Creed" of John Charles Ryle, the Anglican bishop of Liverpool and a strong evangelical. History, Ryle held, was rapidly moving toward its climax: Jesus Christ's "real, literal, personal bodily coming." The period immediately before this event, he went on, would see unprecedented wickedness and unbelief. Since only divine intervention could fundamentally affect the human condition, Ryle warned believers to "expect as little as possible from churches, or governments, under the present dispensation."[34] The conference resolutions echoed these themes, affirming the Bible's absolute authority, the certainty of Christ's return "at any moment," and the millennium only *after* the Second Coming. The resolutions were adopted, West noted, not merely by vote of the delegates, but also by "the vast audience voluntarily rising *en masse* to its feet—a magnificent spectacle not soon to be forgotten."[35]

The Gilded Age revivalist Dwight L. Moody preached Christ's imminent Second Coming, as did hundreds of now-forgotten evangelists like Methodist itinerant Leander Munhall (1843–1934), a premillennialist who averaged two sermons a day for over fifty years, reaching an estimated 17 million souls. A network of Bible schools, many of which also conducted active publication programs—Chicago's Moody Bible Institute, William Bell Riley's Northwestern Bible and Missionary Training School in Minneapolis, the Bible Institute of Los Angeles, or BIOLA, and some fifty others—spread the premillennial word far and wide. So did magazines such as *Prophetic Times, The King's Business,* James Brookes's *The Truth,* Charles Trumbull's *Sunday School Times,* and Arno Gaebelein's *Our Hope.* By 1900, dispensationalism had become a bedrock doctrine for vast numbers of conservative Protestants.[36]

Prophecy interest also flourished in the Seventh-day Adventist Church, which survived the stigma of its Millerite origins to become an important premillennialist denomination, and the Watchtower Bible and Tract Society (Jehovah's Witnesses), founded in 1884 by Charles Taze Russell. In his *Watchtower* magazine and his book *Millennial Dawn* (1886), Russell emulated William Miller in expounding his own idiosyncratic historicist interpretation of Daniel and Revelation, including a predicted end of the world in 1914. The outbreak of war in that year gave a strong stimulus to "Russellism." The rise of modern American pentecostalism, usually dated from a revival in Los Angeles in 1906, further stimulated premillennial belief, since pentecostalists, like Edward Irving earlier, viewed their distinctive practices, especially glossolalia and divine healing, as signs of the last days. Wrote one leader in 1908, " 'Jesus is coming soon' is the message that the Holy Ghost is speaking today through nearly everyone that receives the baptism with the Holy Ghost." The Assemblies of God Church (founded in 1914), the leading pentecostal denomination, is still in the 1990s a mighty fortress of premillennial belief.[37]

The rise of premillennialism paralleled the fundamentalist movement in U.S. evangelicalism. Disturbed by Darwinism, liberal theology, the reformist Social Gospel, and historical-critical Bible scholarship—an alarming congeries of trends they lumped together as "Modernism"—evangelicals in the late nineteenth and early twentieth centuries sought to systematize and protect long-held beliefs. The movement crested with the founding of the World's Christian Fundamentals Association in 1919 and publication of *The Fundamentals: A Testimony of Truth* (1910–1915), twelve brief manifestos sent free (thanks to the support of wealthy patrons) to some 3 million U.S. Protestant leaders. In *The Fundamentals* evangelical scholars set forth what they viewed as the core of the Christian faith, including biblical inerrancy and Jesus' virgin birth, resurrection, and physical return to earth. Proof of fulfilled prophecy, such as that offered by Anderson, seemed powerful ammunition in the battle for the fundamentals. As Reuben Torrey of the Bible Institute of Los Angeles put it, prophecy represented "the ultimate antidote for all infidelity and the impregnable bulwark against liberalism and false cults."[38]

Premillennialism obviously diverged sharply from what is usually seen as the dominant strand of social and religious thought in these years. Brookes readily conceded that premillennialism "clouds some of the fairest prospects, and scatters to the wind some of the most fondly cherished expectations of the Church and the world." Even at the risk of being thought to have "diseased mind[s]," he went on, premillennialists would continue to oppose the natural tendency "to think well of ourselves, . . . and to point with triumph to the glorious car of human progress as it moves across the face of the earth, carrying light and liberty to the nations." A prophecy chart of the day echoed the point: "Each dispensation . . . end[s] in failure . . . The natural tendency of mankind is to degenerate." Moody summarized in the simplest possible terms: "I don't find any place where God says the world is to grow better and better . . . I find that the earth is to grow worse and worse." [39]

In making their case, premillennialists matched the most vehement radicals in describing capitalism's human toll and conditions in the industrial city. Wrote Brookes, "The respectable people who attend preaching do not seem to know that they are sauntering in their gay clothes to the house of God over a slumbering volcano." [40] "Law-breaking corporations . . . and iniquitous business combines" controlled America, declared another premillennialist in 1892, "a Plutocracy having been substituted for Democracy." He went on to quote James 5:1–7, a stinging polemic against the rich embedded within an apocalyptic vision of the last days and of Christ's return:

> Go to now, ye rich men, weep and howl for your miseries that shall come upon you.
> Your riches are corrupted, and your garments are motheaten.
> Your gold and silver is cankered; and the rust of them shall be a witness against you, and shall eat your flesh as it were fire. Ye have heaped treasure together for the last days.
> Behold, the hire of the laborers who have reaped down your fields, which is of you kept back by fraud, crieth: and the cries of them which have reaped are entered into the ears of the Lord of Sabaoth.
> Ye have lived in pleasure on the earth, and have been wanton; ye have nourished your hearts, as in a day of slaughter.
> Ye have condemned and killed the just; and he doth not resist you.
> Be patient, therefore, brethren, unto the coming of the Lord.

"If these verses do not speak of today, with the rich becoming richer, by dishonest methods; and the poor poorer," this author concluded, "to what age do they belong?" [41]

Such criticisms surfaced not only in the prophecy writing of the turbulent, depression-ridden 1890s, but also in the prosperous, reform-minded Progressive era. For example, anticapitalist rhetoric pervades Isaac Haldeman's premillennialist work *The Signs of the Times* (1910). "Commerce is becoming a universal kingdom," he wrote; "a sign that the Coming of the Lord draweth nigh." To Haldeman, pastor of Manhattan's First Baptist Church, the Babylon of Revelation was a city much like New York—a center of "congested wealth," "a whirlpool of mad and maddening excess," "the most beautiful and the most wanton of cities"—and a metropolis marked for destruction.[42]

These late-nineteenth- and early-twentieth-century prophecy writers similarly rejected the prevailing view that science and technology assured human betterment. Despite the "irresistible charm about the very word *science,* which ministers to the self-conceit of the human heart," wrote Brookes, "important discoveries and wonderful inventions" would not halt humanity's downfall. Even with "rapid transit, chemical analysis, and progressive aviation," agreed Haldeman, "the world, like the deluded rower in his fated skiff, is drawing nearer and nearer to the swirling whirlpool of destruction."[43]

While premillennialists agreed with reformers who deplored conditions in industrial America, they also dismissed most secular proposals to *ameliorate* those conditions. Programs of social and economic betterment by human means were at best misguided and at worst inspired by the devil. Reform movements, labor activism, and what Brookes called "the fell spirit of Socialism" merely underscored the prophesied social crisis ahead. Some interpreters even saw union-made labels as the Mark of the Beast. In short, premillennialists viewed reform in the same way they viewed the conditions that spawned it: as another sign of the times. God's plan was unfolding at its own pace, irrespective of human striving or the babble of reform, wrote Brookes, and Christians should "keep aloof from the whole defiling scene." Modern society was like a shipwreck, said Moody in his vivid way—individual survivors might be rescued, but the vessel itself was beyond hope. Only the Lord's return, agreed Torrey in 1913—the high noon of progressivism—would resolve the "political and social and commercial problems that now vex us."[44]

Deftly incorporating contemporary currents of thought into their work, premillennialists offered a vision of Utopia to match Edward Bellamy's—but one resulting from a cataclysmic eschatological event, not gradual social evolution. "The storm will be brief," wrote Torrey, "and beyond the storm there is a golden day, such as philosophers and poets never dreamed of." And they offered scriptural grounds for their position: the attack on economic exploitation in the passage from the Book of James quoted above, for example, ends with a call for *patience*—only Christ's coming offers hope. Jesus and the apostles were not reformers, noted a premillennial leader, so Christians ought "not attempt in this age the work which Christ has re-served for the next." [45]

This reading of Scripture, coupled with dispensationalists' deep anti-institutional bias—recall Bishop Ryle's "Pre-Millennian Creed": "Expect as little as possible from . . . governments"—shaped premil-lennialism to its core, making it a functional equivalent of the antigov-ernment, antireform ideology of laissez-faire advocates such as Wil-liam Graham Sumner. As we shall see, a similar juxtaposition of sharp social criticism and skepticism about all efforts at betterment contin-ued to characterize late-twentieth-century premillennial writings.

To consistent premillennialists, democracy itself was simply an-other sign of the secular order's malaise. "It is an age of mobs," wrote Sir Robert Anderson: as the prophecies revealed, democratic excess would lead to anarchy, paving the way for Antichrist. The statue's crumbling clay feet in Nebuchadnezzar's dream, wrote another ex-positor in 1892 (as strikes and agrarian protest swept the nation), fore-told the modern uprising of the masses—"ignorant, superstitious, suspicious, and uncontrolled." [46]

Most premillennialists also firmly rejected Charles Darwin's theory of evolution, not only because it challenged their reading of Genesis, but because the belief in progress associated with it ran counter to their vision of steadily worsening conditions as the end approached. They could not have differed more with Darwin's affir-mation that after "long-continued slow progress . . . , man in the dis-tant future will be a far more perfect creature than he is now." [47]

Premillennialists also dismissed theological works such as Shailer Matthews' *Social Teaching of Jesus* (1897) and Walter Rauschenbusch's *Christianity and the Social Crisis* (1907), which foresaw society's grad-ual redemption through Christian social action. The effort to "Chris-tianize men by bettering their physical and social state," wrote Halde-man, denied prophetic truth. With all their lofty talk of human progress, he went on, Rauschenbusch and other Social Gospel advo-cates actually personified the end-time apostasy foretold in Scripture. The man-made Utopia of liberal theologians, agreed another writer, was simply "the devil's cunning scheme for bringing in a mock mil-lennium without Christ." [48]

The Social Gospel advocates, of course, vigorously fought back. Harris Franklin Rall, a Methodist theologian at Garrett Bible Institute in Evanston, Illinois, in 1914 dismissed early Christian apocalypticism as a Jewish carryover that had faded as the Church had realized that the Kingdom would come not by an eschatological lightning bolt but "by gradual moral and spiritual development." The premillennialists' "historical pessimism," declared Rauschenbusch, a professor at Rochester Theological Seminary, was "a dead weight against any effort to mobilize the moral forces of Christianity to share in the modern social movement." [49]

While dismissing social reform, premillennialists strongly endorsed missionary work. Mankind's collective doom was certain, but *individuals* could escape. Quoting Jesus' words "And this gospel of the kingdom shall be preached in all the world for a witness unto all nations; and then shall the end come" (Matt. 24:14), they viewed evangelism as central to the unfolding end-time plan. Far from "paralyzing . . . missionary effort," wrote Nathaniel West in 1879, premillennial belief was "one of the mightiest incentives to earnestness in preaching the Gospel to every creature, until He comes"—"not to make the world better," but "to save the people out of [the world]." [50]

All these themes came together in the work of Cyrus Scofield (1843–1921), a towering figure in twentieth-century premillennialism. A Tennessean dogged by scandal, heavy drinking, and marital problems in his early years, Scofield fought as a Confederate in the Civil War, practiced law in Kansas, and hastily left that state in 1877 (abandoning a wife and two children) amid accusations that he had stolen political contributions to Senator John Ingalls, a former partner. (No one who knew Scofield's early life, Ingalls later observed, could "doubt the efficacy of the scheme of Christian salvation.") Jailed in St. Louis in 1879 on forgery charges, Scofield experienced religious conversion in prison and fell under the influence of James Brookes, the Darbyite dispensationalist. In 1882 he became pastor of Dallas' First Congregational Church. (The following year, his wife back in Kansas filed for divorce on grounds of desertion.) In Dallas Scofield also edited a monthly magazine, *The Believer,* and conducted a Bible correspondence course. In 1895 he joined the faculty of Moody's Northfield Bible School in Massachusetts. After 1902 he devoted his full time to speaking tours, Bible research and writing, and an annual summer Bible conference on Long Island. [51]

Scofield's continuing reputation rests on his Reference Bible (1909), which more than any other single work solidified the premillennial movement. Between 1909 and 1967, according to the publisher, Oxford University Press, sales certainly surpassed 5 million copies and may have exceeded 10 million. A 1967 revision sold an additional 2.5 million copies by 1990. For more than eighty years the Scofield Reference Bible has been a major conduit for disseminating premillennial dispensationalism throughout the world. One scholar has called it "perhaps the most important single document in all fundamentalist literature." A doggerel variant of a familiar gospel song testifies to this influence: "My hope is built on nothing less / Than Scofield's Notes and Moody Press."[52]

Unlike most commentators, Scofield combined his notes and the biblical text on the same page, so the former took on much the same authority as the latter; readers often could not remember whether they had encountered a particular thought in the notes or in the text. Scofield skillfully wove through his commentary the Darbyite dispensational scenario. Reflecting a premillennialist consensus, he predicted the Jews' return to Palestine in the last days and identified the Gog of Ezekiel 38 as Russia. A gifted stylist, he gave Darby's "beautiful system" (as he called it) remarkable unity and capaciousness. "The thought and word of God," he wrote, "have ever an inner and vaster content than appears upon the surface."[53]

Scofield perceptively sensed apocalypticism's roots in the longing for a better world, and in his Reference Bible and works such as *What Do the Prophets Say?* (1918) he acknowledged the power of that aspiration:

> There is a deathless thing in the heart of humanity: . . . the belief that there must yet be for humanity on this earth . . . a corporate, ordered life, a life not for a few fortunate and powerful ones, but a life for all which shall be rich in truth, justice, power and love . . . The race, after all, is one; and it is a kind of corporate logic which keeps the hope of a golden age alive in the universal human mind.

But only the Second Coming could translate hope into reality:

> "Optimists" patter of peace when there is no peace, and will not see that the evils from which the philosophers would save us are as old as the race . . . Every method whereby the race has sought to realize the deathless vision has been tried to the dregs, and has failed . . . The futility of the ideal commonwealths of Plato and the others is precisely the futility of all

superficial optimism—the notion that for the common good, men are going to give up ambition, greed, and pride . . . [But] that which . . . has sought expression in the Utopias, stands boldly forth in Scripture as a revealed purpose of God.[54]

Utopia will come in the Kingdom Age (his term for the Millennium), not in this dispensation. Like all premillennialists, Scofield held a grim view of society's prospects: not betterment by imperceptible degrees, but degeneration and sudden devastation. The age would end, he wrote,

> not as some would have us believe, by the gradual process of evolution, lifting the race higher and higher until it passes, by insensible gradations, into a state of blessedness and peace, but in sudden and awful ruin . . . I am very tired of pulpit laudations of human nature. When I turn to God's book I find no single commendatory word regarding it.[55]

Human nature is contemptible; every human institution is fatally flawed. A profound suspicion of all organizations, civil and religious, pervades Scofield's work. "The predicted future of the visible church is apostasy," he insisted, dwelling on the absolute distinction between the true believers who will vanish at the Rapture and the "professed Christians" who fill the churches and will flock to Antichrist's banner during the Tribulation.[56]

"This is a layman's age," Scofield wrote—and the observation is a key to his popularity.[57] Like William Miller, he believed that anyone could interpret prophecy; book learning and theological training were unnecessary and probably a hindrance. He himself, though highly intelligent, had little formal education, and his Reference Bible, which confidently explained obscure texts while remaining accessible to ordinary laypersons, had strong grassroots appeal.

In stressing premillennialism's importance in the pre–World War I years, one must maintain perspective. Social Gospelers such as Walter Rauschenbusch unquestionably spoke for a large constituency in the moderate to liberal sectors of American Protestantism. A 1919 survey of two hundred thirty-six theology professors at twenty-eight seminaries of eight major denominations found only seven avowed premillennialists.[58] But despite the pervasiveness of the "liberal" (allegorical, reformist, historical-critical, "postmillennial") reading of the prophecies, one must give premillennialism its due. From the Civil

War to World War I, while liberal religious leaders spoke optimisti-
cally of Christianizing the social order, premillennialists offered a
bleak view of the human prospect in general and U.S. society in particular, and looked to the Second Coming as mankind's only hope.
While eschatological interest declined in some mainstream denominations and premillennialism nearly vanished from the leading seminaries, it flourished at the grassroots level, fed by a shadowy but powerful network of itinerant evangelists, prophecy conferences, Bible
schools, books, and magazines—and Scofield Bibles.

Nor did premillennialism in the 1865–1920 years appeal solely to
the poor and disaffected; it also found support among the middle
classes, the well-to-do, and even the elite. The signers of an 1891 memorial to President Benjamin Harrison written by premillennialist
William Blackstone and urging support for a Jewish homeland in Palestine included Cyrus McCormick, J. P. Morgan, and John D. Rockefeller. Two Los Angeles oilmen, Lyman and Milton Stewart, financed
the publication and distribution of *The Fundamentals*. Chicago
department-store owner John Pirie hosted Cyrus Scofield's annual
Bible conferences at Sea Cliff, Pirie's estate on Long Island. The head
of the Quaker Oats Company, Henry Crowell, chaired the board of
trustees of the Moody Bible Institute. Large middle-class Baptist and
Presbyterian churches in New York, St. Louis, Boston, Cincinnati,
Minneapolis, and many other cities were bastions of premillennialism
in these years. As Ian Rennie has written, dispensationalism attracted
some of the most outstanding evangelicals of the day—and some of
the wealthiest.[59] Whatever else may be said of it, belief in an imminent
Second Coming, in punishment of the wicked, and in a Millennium
when the injustices of the present age will be set right, cannot be dismissed—in the Middle Ages, in the pre–World War I era, or in the late
twentieth century—as merely the desperate creed of the disinherited.

Toward the Present: Prophecy Belief from World War I through 1945

In the three decades that began in 1914, crises at home and abroad gave
a tremendous impetus to premillennialism. The first, of course, was
the outbreak of war in Europe. The guns of August 1914 riveted
prophecy believers' attention. "War! War!! War!!!" proclaimed a pentecostal journal. "The Nations of Europe Battle and Unconsciously

Prepare the Way for the Return of the Lord Jesus." A Niagara of books, articles, and pamphlets speculated about the war's meaning and likely outcome in the light of prophecy. Five thousand people jammed a Philadelphia prophecy conference early in 1918, and more thousands attended a second one at Chicago's Moody Bible Institute in 1919. As Timothy Weber writes, "Though times were tragic, things were never better for American premillennialism." [60]

Prophecy books yellow with age appeared in hastily updated versions. "The War has apparently created an increased interest in the prophecies of Daniel," observed the elderly Sir Robert Anderson in a new edition of *The Coming Prince.* " 'Armageddon' has now become a household word," commented another author in a 1915 reissue of an earlier prophecy book. Reflecting in 1918 on the "remarkable recrudescence of the Millennial hope," a professor at Oberlin's School of Theology wrote, "A universal nervousness has seized society . . . One manifestation of this is the greatly quickened expectation of the speedy coming of the Lord. The interpreters of prophecy are . . . [making] *rapid progress.*" [61]

The premillennial message of inevitable decline seemed frighteningly apt after 1914. Taking note of worsening conditions in Europe as the war dragged on, Reuben Torrey observed almost smugly, "The darker the night gets, the lighter my heart gets." Further, the conflict appeared to hasten the end-time geopolitical alignment prophecy writers had long anticipated. If a defeated Germany lost its lands west of the Rhine, and the Allied alliance continued in peacetime, wrote Arno Gaebelein in 1914, the latter could lead to "the predicted revival of the great confederacy of Europe"—the ten-nation revived Roman Empire ruled by Antichrist supposedly foretold in the Book of Daniel. "PROPHECY CHANGING THE MAP OF EUROPE" proclaimed a 1918 prophecy textbook by James Gray of Moody Bible Institute. [62]

Events affecting the Middle East roused prophecy writers to a still higher pitch of expectancy. On November 2, 1917, in a letter to Lord James Rothschild, British Foreign Secretary Arthur Balfour wrote, "His Majesty's government view with favour the establishment in Palestine of a national home for the Jewish people." That December, as Ottoman power collapsed, Field Marshal Edmund Allenby captured Jerusalem without firing a shot. For premillennialists, the long-anticipated Jewish restoration to Palestine seemed suddenly a distinct possibility. When Allenby took Jerusalem, Cyrus Scofield wrote to a friend, "Now for the first time we have a real prophetic sign." The Reverend A. B. Simpson, a leading premillennialist and founder of the Christian and Missionary Alliance Church, wept as he read the Balfour Declaration to his congregation.[63]

Wartime events in Russia, too, bore their freight of prophetic meaning. Prophecy writers had long been divided over the identity of the northern power that, according to Ezekiel, would invade Israel in the last days; some favored Turkey, some Russia. The 1917 Russian Revolution, in conjunction with the Ottoman collapse, tilted the balance decisively in Russia's favor—where it would long remain. Writing during Aleksandr Kerensky's brief ascendancy, James Gray welcomed Russia's "new-found freedom" but added somberly that on the basis of his reading of prophecy he would feel no surprise if it proved shortlived.[64]

With remarkable precision, then, the events of 1914–1918 seemed to produce the global configuration foretold in prophecy. Indeed, nearly every theme of post-1945 prophecy interpretation emerged in this brief interval. The Cold War, the creation of Israel in 1948, and the formation of the European Common Market simply reinforced world trends already taking shape by 1918. (The exceptions were the advent of thermonuclear weapons, which suggested how the prophesied end-time holocaust might occur, and the rise of global television and computers, which clarified how Antichrist could impose his worldwide political and economic dictatorship.)

Premillennialists remained unmoved by Woodrow Wilson's exalted war rhetoric. Pronounced Scofield in 1918, "The prophetic Word . . . [gives] not the least warrant for the expectation that the nations engaged in the present gigantic struggle will or can make a permanent peace." Even if a United States of the World did emerge from the war, he warned, it would simply prepare the way for Antichrist's rule. The failure of the Versailles peace conference was another step on the prophetic timetable, believers held; the League of Nations, simply another example of humankind's misplaced hopes. The League would not prevent "the most awful universal war that this old world has ever seen," predicted Reuben Torrey; another writer, speculating that "religio-political reformers" would exploit the League for their own purposes, reiterated the essential premillennialist truth: "The kingdom of Christ will not be established through absorption of earthly kingdoms, but after their sudden and violent overthrow."[65]

Liberal theologians resisted the premillennialists' interpretation of the war's meaning. Those who insisted that "conditions shall grow constantly worse as the hour of impending doom approaches," declared Shirley Jackson Case, professor of church history at the University of Chicago, "readily [play] into the hands of all enemies of social and political reform."[66]

Case's critique of premillennialism revealed much about his own worldview. In the spirit of William James, he granted that premillennialism met "a wide range of human needs"—providing hope in time of crisis, escape from social ills, and "a vehicle of fancy, enabling the native curiosity of the human mind to construct for itself marvelous pictures of the unknown future." He conceded, too, that "certain biblical writers expected a catastrophic end of the world" and that the allegorizing approach of Origen and Augustine had departed sharply from the apocalyptic outlook of the earliest Christian believers.[67]

Having made these concessions, Case went on the attack. The premillennialists distorted Scripture even more egregiously than their liberal opponents, he insisted, with their proof-text approach and their assumption that "every ancient worthy shared their own state of mind . . . , without the slightest regard for the author's own immediate experiences and problems." Prophecy interpreters who found the railroad in the Book of Nahum obviously ignored historical context, but "the true premillennialist can perform this feat of fancy with the ease of a professional acrobat, at the same time solemnly affirming that he stands upon the solid rock of Scripture."[68]

Attacking the premillennial view that "each hour in the world's history must be darker than the one that came before," Case ringingly affirmed his belief in inevitable progress through scientific advance:

> It is sheer nonsense to talk dolefully about the gradual deterioration of society to a student of history . . . The actual course of human development from prehistoric times down to the present . . . exhibits one long process of evolving struggle by which humanity as a whole rises constantly higher in the scale of civilization and attainment, bettering its condition from time to time through its greater skill and industry. Viewed in the long perspective of the ages, man's career has been one of actual ascent. Instead of growing worse, the world is found to be growing constantly better . . .
>
> Scientific knowledge leaves no room for the retention of primitive fancies regarding a cataclysmic end of the world . . . Modern scientific thinking is fundamentally optimistic in its

outlook upon the world's future . . . The ills of life are to be cured by a gradual process of remedial treatment rather than by sudden annihilation." [69]

If we disregard their respective intellectual methods, was it the pre-millennialists or the Shirley Jackson Cases of the American religious scene who offered the more clear-eyed reading of the war's meaning?

Unfazed by such attacks, premillennialists insisted that the war confirmed their worldview. In 1919 William Pettingill of the Philadel-phia School of the Bible offered a final assessment of the conflict: "It is a great thing to know that everything is going on according to God's schedule . . . We are not surprised at the present collapse of civiliza-tion; the Word of God told us all about it." [70]

Prophecy interest waned in the 1920s as wartime excitements faded, and fundamentalism came under attack. The liberal *Christian Century* in 1926 confidently discussed "Vanishing Fundamentalism." The World's Christian Fundamentals Association survived, but "Modernists" like Harry Emerson Fosdick, Shailer Matthews, and Edward Mortimer Chapman became increasingly assertive. Fosdick in *The Modern Use of the Bible* (1924) again interpreted the biblical apocalypses as allegories of a just social order. Matthews, formulating a modernist "Affirmation of Faith" in 1924, proposed an alternative to the fundamentalists' insistence on a literal Second Coming and Last Judgment: "I believe in the ultimate triumph of love and justice be-cause I believe in the God revealed in Jesus Christ." Chapman's *A Mod-ernist and His Creed* (1926) found "pathos and appeal" in premillenni-alists' apocalyptic hopes, but roundly criticized their aversion to reform and their belief that only through the divinely ordained de-struction of the present order could a just society be achieved. In treat-ing the books of Daniel, Ezekiel, and Revelation, the *Abingdon Bible Commentary* of 1929, a major scholarly endeavor of liberal Protestant-ism, adopted an historical-critical approach and a mildly amused tone. The commentator on Ezekiel, for example, flippantly observed of its apocalyptic section, "These very difficult and obscure chapters raise many problems too intricate for discussion here, a loss the less serious in that few of them have been solved." [71]

Even among fundamentalists, the Second Coming took second place in the 1920s to the battle over evolution most memorably waged at the 1925 Scopes "Monkey Trial" in Dayton, Tennessee. A promi-nent figure in the evolution controversy, William Jennings Bryan, ignored eschatology altogether in his 1924 summary of the fundamentals, *Shall Christianity Remain Christian?*[72]

But as historians of American religion now emphasize, conservative evangelical faith was far from moribund in the 1920s. In a complex process of "withdrawal and regrouping" described by George Marsden, fundamentalists left mainstream denominations for smaller sects or independent congregations. Prewar fundamentalist leaders like William Bell Riley not only remained active but were joined by others such as John Roach Straton, a premillennialist who led New York's Calvary Baptist Church from 1918 to 1929. As Joel Carpenter reminds us, a "thriving network" of institutions and periodicals sustained fundamentalism in these years. Existing evangelical Bible schools flourished and new ones were founded, such as Dallas Theological Seminary (1924) and Westminster Theological Seminary of Philadelphia (1929)—the latter started by J. Gresham Machen (author of the 1923 fundamentalist manifesto *Christianity and Liberalism*) and three colleagues who left Princeton Theological Seminary in a dispute with "inclusivists" who wanted all varieties of theology, including liberalism, represented at the school.[73]

In this volatile religious setting prophecy belief, if less visible, remained alive and well. The prophecy magazines mentioned earlier appeared regularly; older expositors such as James Gray and Arno Gaebelein continued to write, teach, and preach. Oswald Smith, a popular Toronto minister with a strong interest in prophecy, drew large audiences and published several books in the 1920s. In *The Antichrist* (1923) Arthur Pink speculated that the prophesied rebuilding of Babylon would be much facilitated by the projected Euphrates Valley Railway. A celebrity recruit to the cause was the erstwhile British suffragist Christabel Pankhurst. "Those days of the suffrage campaign were the days of political childhood," wrote Pankhurst in 1924. "Now is the time . . . to abandon the childish, nay foolish dreams of a human-made Utopia, and in its stead hold fast, rejoicing, to the certainty that the Lord cometh."[74]

The tempo of prophecy interest quickened in the 1930s. Sermons on prophecy attracted large crowds, and scores of prophecy books and pamphlets appeared, some by interpreters who would enjoy long careers: Wilbur Smith of Moody Bible Institute; Harry Ironside, a member of the Plymouth Brethren who served as pastor of Chicago's Moody Memorial Church; and Donald Grey Barnhouse of Philadelphia, who edited the prophecy journal *Revelation* and conducted a weekly religious program on CBS Radio. Barnhouse was not alone in using radio to spread the prophetic word. By 1930 evangelical programs filled the airwaves, including those on Moody Bible Institute's powerful station, WMBI. Charles Fuller's California-based "Old-Fashioned Revival Hour," a program "saturated with the truth of Christ's near return" (according to one admirer), was heard on 456 stations by the 1940s.[75]

The 1930s also gave rise to a genre that continues to flourish, the prophecy novel. A 1937 novel described the impact of the Rapture on a typical American city, where the righteous have suddenly vanished, leaving the ungodly behind. A committee is appointed to investigate the mass disappearances. Recalling that a recently deceased mother and child were buried together, the committee opens the grave to see if the Rapture has reached the dead as well as the living:

> The excavation showed that the body of the child had slipped from the downy casket and only a few lacy garments were left. The body of the devoted mother reposed there with empty arms . . . , never again to embrace her lovely child . . .
>
> "I guess the Bible is infallible," said one committeeman.
>
> "It looks that way," agreed another.[76]

The author describes Antichrist's barbarity in very graphic detail: people who refuse the Mark of the Beast at "Branding Stations" are stripped, sprayed with sulfuric acid, and decapitated. In one scene Antichrist takes time from ruling the world to order the killing of the pet dog and canary of a little boy who has offended him. The author's concern for animals emerges, too, in the observation that after the Rapture "many pets were found dead, shut in the houses of the departing saints."[77]

Just as earlier writers found the railroad in prophecy, those of the 1930s noted the eschatological significance of air travel and television. One interpreted Ezekiel 38:16 ("And thou shalt come up against my people of Israel, as a cloud to cover the land") as foretelling an aerial bombing attack. To another commentator the "cloud" suggested parachutes. (In the 1950s, it would become a "cloud" of ICBMs.) A 1936 writer, discussing the prophecy that Christ's return would be witnessed by the whole earth, commented, "In the past, we have had to fall back on the explanation that it does not necessarily mean that all should see the Lord coming in the clouds of heaven at the same time, but now we know that by Television, that beatific sight can be seen the world over at one and the same moment." [78]

As in the Gilded Age, some anticapitalist themes surfaced in Depression-era prophecy treatises. "God hates Big Business [and the] spirit of commercialism," proclaimed one writer, because both catered to "the unholy desires of the flesh." A rebuilt Babylon would function as the world's "commercial center" in the last days, and its destruction would be "quick and complete and terrible." "Every class," irrespective of "wealth or fortuitous circumstances," Donald Grey Barnhouse stressed, would appear at the Last Judgment. The doomed Babylon of John's Apocalypse, he went on, referring his readers to "the great prophecy against capitalism in the epistle of James," symbolized "the whole idea of commerce." [79]

But, again, prophecy writers viewed efforts to *resolve* the economic crisis much as they viewed the crisis itself: as evidence of the vanity of all secular human endeavor, and of the accuracy of the end-time prophecies. Discussing "The Church and Politics" in 1931, Barnhouse struck the familiar premillennial theme: the Bible gave Christians no mandate "to go out and crusade for political righteousness." During the 1932 presidential campaign, a pentecostal journal asked: "What can we do to arrest the downward current? Nothing! It is too late to patch up this old world . . . Our objective is to get men ready for the next age." [80]

Prophecy writers' responses to the New Deal ranged from skepticism to outright hostility. To Louis Bauman, a Los Angeles minister and well-known prophecy interpreter, the blue eagle of the NRA (National Recovery Administration) suggested the Mark of the Beast. Arno Gaebelein, in a litany of end-time signs, mentioned "the so-called New Deal, with its colossal failures" and the "radical, communistic tendencies" of FDR's brain trust. The unionization campaign of the 1930s struck many prophecy writers as equally ominous. Gaebelein pointedly described Antichrist's economic rule as "the great trades-union to which all will have to belong on pain of death." [81] While counseling aloofness from politics, in short, prophecy writers of the 1930s constantly espoused views that had obvious conservative, anti–New Deal political implications—a paradox found in post-1945 prophecy writing as well.

The rise of fascist dictatorships and military regimes in Europe and Japan, and especially of a rabidly anti-Semitic regime in Germany, captured prophecy writers' attention as they scanned the horizon for events of eschatological significance. While the prophetic interpretation of the Holocaust is complex, most prophecy writers of the 1930s and early 1940s, citing God's promise to Abraham "And I will bless them that bless thee, and curse him that curseth thee" (Gen. 12:3), taught that Hitler's anti-Semitism sealed his doom. "It may be postponed longer than we expect," one argued, "but God's Word cannot fail!" [82]

Some popularizers saw Hitler as Antichrist, pointing out that if A is given the value 100, B 101, C 102, and so on, then the name "Hitler" adds up to 666. Others found prophetic forecasts of a U.S. role in the German dictator's overthrow. The reference in Ezekiel 38 to "the merchants of Tarshish, with the young lions thereof," they argued, meant Great Britain and its present or former colonies, including the United States. "It is good to know," observed one in 1940, that in the end-time conflict "the great English-speaking nations" would be on God's side. [83]

The favored candidate for Antichrist, however, was not Adolf Hitler but Benito Mussolini. The fact that Mussolini ruled in Rome and in 1929 signed a concordat with the Pope (the Protestants' prime candidate for Antichrist since the sixteenth century) seemed to fit him for the role of the end-time figure who would lead a restored Roman Empire. Toronto's Oswald Smith, citing Mussolini's "well-known . . . intention" to revive the Roman Empire, pinpointed him in 1926 as "a foreshadowing at least of the coming super-man." The *Sunday School Times* speculated about the Italian dictator's prophetic destiny up to the moment of his death. Another writer pointed to the fasces, the symbol of Italian fascism, on the U.S. dime introduced early in the twentieth century, as a preparation for Antichrist's world rule. [84]

Most interpreters cautiously refrained from identifying Mussolini absolutely as Antichrist, at the same time marshaling all the evidence leading to that conclusion. Gaebelein's formulation was typical: "Will this man, known for his ambition to be Europe's great dictator, develop into the final dictator? This is a question which only God can answer." The pastor of New York's First Baptist Church, writing in 1938, similarly hedged his bets: "I am not prepared to say Stalin, Hitler, or Mussolini is the Beast, but I have no hesitation in saying they are his forerunners and are beating the trail for him to come upon the scene. Mussolini, above them all, bears the earmarks."[85]

Prophecy writers of the 1930s also found evidence of Russia's growing eschatological significance. The 1939 Nazi-Soviet pact briefly galvanized prophecy interpreters, many of whom held that Gog's ally Gomer, mentioned in Ezekiel 38, referred to Germany. "Students of prophecy have long awaited the day when this alliance would come to pass," proclaimed one writer.[86]

Turning to Asia, many interpreters cited the reference in Revelation 16:12 to an invasion by "the kings of the east" just before Armageddon as a prophecy of the rise of Japan or "all the dark-skinned peoples—the nations of India, of China, of Japan, of the Mongolian hordes." Warned Harry Ironside in 1938: "The tocsin of doom is sounding. The yellow peril becomes more and more ominous. The preparation of the day of the Lord goes on apace."[87]

Prophecy writers of the 1930s also viewed the darkening international situation more broadly, as evidence of history's downward trajectory. Yet again, wrote Arno Gaebelein in 1937, world events were confounding religious liberals, who saw the biblical apocalypses as allegories of humanity's upward march. In fact, he wrote, "the sun of our age is setting, the evening is here. The prophecies relating to our age-ending are rapidly approaching their fulfillment." On the brink of World War II, Harry Rimmer was already looking beyond it. "No matter how bad this present war may be," he wrote in 1940, "there will be another after it, more terrible in its consequences than any conflict in history." The Christian's task, Rimmer went on, echoing Dwight L. Moody half a century earlier, was "not to make a warless world, and bring universal peace, [but] to save out of the wreck of this age such individuals as may be persuaded to turn to Christ and be saved."[88]

Two books captured the mood of prophecy believers as the 1930s ended. In *The Eleventh "Hour"* Arthur Brown saw the Depression and "the incessant unrest of nations in turmoil" as signs of a gathering global crisis "in politics, industry, finance, and morals." "Everywhere intense dread clutches at the hearts of men and women . . . Civilization drifts rapidly toward the precipice—men sense impending dissolution and stand helpless and impotent, overcome by the dread of threatening calamity. Governments and legislatures, science and philosophy, confess failure."[89]

In *History's Crowded Climax* Arthur Maxwell, editor of *Signs of the Times,* a Seventh-day Adventist prophecy magazine, offered an equally somber view:

> Suddenly, in the midst of the brilliant civilization of the twentieth century, all the worst attributes of humanity have come to the front; all the most evil passions have been unleashed; all the evil spirits some thought were exorcized centuries ago have returned sevenfold, more loathsome and diabolical than of old.
>
> All the strange and terrible developments of these tremendous times . . . are indeed but a further indication that we are in the midst of the crowning crisis of the ages.[90]

Like their apocalyptic predecessors, both authors found the situation shimmering with eschatological promise. As Maxwell put it:

> With wars raging all about us, with civilization threatened with complete destruction, with all the world plunged once more into the utmost confusion, it is a great consolation to reflect that there are some things which will definitely outlast all earthly conflicts . . . However dark and forbidding the world situation may appear—and it is surely dark enough today—God still rules in heaven . . . , quietly and patiently working out His eternal purpose.[91]

On the eve of war, the premillennial worldview won at least qualified support from an unexpected source: theologian Reinhold Niebuhr. A Social Gospel advocate in the 1920s, Niebuhr in 1940 observed that while biblical apocalyptic and its picture of "human history as moving toward a climax in which evil becomes more and more naked and unashamed" had been dismissed by liberal theologians, perhaps it was time for a second look: "Taken seriously, though not literally, these various apocalyptic visions point to an interpretation of history in which there is no suggestion of a progressive triumph of good over evil, but rather a gradual sharpening of the distinction between good and evil."[92] In light of world conditions, Niebuhr suggested, premillennialism at least merited respectful attention.

During the war itself, some prophecy writers continued to view enemy leaders as potential candidates for Antichrist and to find an Allied victory foretold in the Bible. Wrote one popularizer in 1942:

> Hitler's defeat appears certain because his course is contrary to Scripture. History is against him. Every man's hand in the con-

quered and allied countries is against him. God is against him for his treatment of His ancient people. The Prophetic Word is against him, and all these forces combined will bring him down in defeat.[93]

Others, however—the more consistent premillennialists—stood apart from the conflict. Hopes for the United Nations and a peaceful postwar era would soon be dashed, proclaimed the editor of the premillennialist *Christian Digest* in 1942:

> The Bible contradicts such a utopian dream . . . Uncle Sam will be no match for the Antichrist . . . [The] present cruel dictatorships are but the precursors of the most brutal, bloody, dictatorship the world has ever seen . . . This is not to be the last war. Present horrors are but the spawn to produce still more terrible anguish . . . The worst is yet to appear.[94]

At a 1943 prophecy conference in New York City, John Bradbury, editor of the Baptist *Watchman-Examiner,* pictured the war as a vast exercise in futility, and postwar peace planning as a vain chimera:

> The peace of the Prince of Peace is not the result of man-made, earth-bound processes . . . A wealth of Scripture indicates that nations will not voluntarily submit to His rule. If one wishes a reason for Armageddon, there it is. Only Jesus Christ the Lord will be able to make the nations disarm and dwell together in righteousness and peace.
>
> The Christian Church has a far more important duty than to bless military banners, christen battleships, sing "praise the Lord and pass the ammunition" . . . When the fires have ceased to burn and the tyrants are caged, it will be all too plain that this tremendous effort has all the earmarks of an expediency. We shall still be faced with a world conditioned to revolt against the moral law of God and to refuse the sovereign rule of our Lord Jesus Christ.[95]

To Howard Ferrin of Providence Bible Institute, speaking at the same conference, the struggle represented yet another blow to the "faith in human achievement and world progress" that had underlain the Social Gospel's praiseworthy but vain dream of abolishing war abroad and class conflict at home. So long as nations and social groups "struggle heartily and ruthlessly among themselves for breathing space," he said, war and class conflict would continue; only Christ's return would bring true harmony. "We know that many will despise us . . . ," Ferrin acknowledged, "but we confess that the history of mankind and present world conditions have disillusioned us concerning world peace . . . through human effort." [96]

As the war raged on, prophecy writers found compelling empirical validation of their unfashionable but remarkably tenacious vision of human destiny. When the conflict ended in searing atomic flashes that obliterated two cities, that apocalyptic reading of the war's meaning seemed even more fully confirmed.

II

Key Themes after World War II

4 *The Atomic Bomb and Nuclear War*

F rom Christianity's earliest days, biblical images of earth's convulsive final cataclysm both awed and challenged prophetic interpreters. "This our city will be burned with fire from heaven," Christian warns his family in John Bunyan's *Pilgrim's Progress* (1678). A nineteenth-century American prophecy work vividly pictured a planet trembling on the brink of disintegration:

> Modern science . . . teaches that this globe is an enormous "terrestrial bombshell" . . . , its hidden interior . . . an intensely heated mass in a condition of molten fluidity, agitated, restless, and rolling its fiery waves hither and thither age after age, incessantly seeking with a terrible expressive power an outlet to diffuse its igneous elements over the surface and into the atmosphere. On this thin, rocky film, or outer surface, dwells a fallen, sinful, and dying race of mortals . . . Is it any wonder that thinking, sober people have from the earliest ages looked for a final, awful convulsion and burning day?[1]

Down to 1945, prophecy interpreters typically envisioned this "burning day" in naturalistic terms—earthquakes, comets, volcanic eruptions—or as an eschatological event beyond human understanding. One writer, for example, simply attributed the destruction at Armageddon to "the all-consuming 'breath of God'" and did not speculate further.[2]

With the coming of the atomic bomb, everything changed: it seemed that man himself had, in the throes of war, stumbled on the means of his own prophesied doom. Beginning in autumn 1945, a chorus of preachers, Bible scholars, and paperback writers insisted that the Scriptures not only foretold atomic weapons, but also their eventual cataclysmic use. This chapter explores the nuclear theme in postwar prophecy belief and reflects on its role in shaping attitudes and influencing policy.

First Assessments

President Harry Truman's August 1945 announcements of the atomic destruction of Hiroshima and Nagasaki triggered a torrent of apocalyptic pronouncements, many of them explicitly biblical. "Atomic Energy for War: New Beast of Apocalypse," headlined the *Philadelphia Inquirer*. William Laurence of the *New York Times* titled the final section of his history of the Manhattan Project "Armageddon."[3] Countless commentators quoted II Peter 3:10: "The heavens shall pass away with a great noise, and the elements shall melt with fervent heat, the earth also and the works that are therein shall be burned up."

A popular culture steeped in prophecy quickly enveloped the bomb in an aura of biblical imagery. A 1945 country-music hit, Fred Kirby's "Atomic Power," evoking images of brimstone fire raining down from heaven and describing atomic energy as "given by the mighty hand of God," tapped directly into this reservoir of grassroots end-time belief. Even Truman, in the privacy of his diary, responded in biblical terms to the first A-bomb test in New Mexico: "It may be the fire destruction prophesied in the Euphrates Valley Era, after Noah and his fabulous Ark."[4]

Post-Hiroshima theologians, too, displayed a quickened interest in eschatology. In an influential 1941 essay, the German theologian Rudolph Bultmann had written: "The parousia [Second Coming] of Christ never took place as the New Testament expected. History did not come to an end, and as every schoolboy knows, it will continue to run its course." Accordingly, Bultmann insisted, eschatology must be demythologized and shifted from the future to the present—the moment when each person confronts the claims of the Gospel.[5]

Close kin to Jean-Paul Sartre's existentialism, Bultmann's individualistic, "demythologized" eschatology enjoyed a postwar vogue in the pulpits and seminaries of mainstream U.S. Protestantism. But even in the liberal churches, many recognized its lack of a social and temporal dimension. The atomic threat, they sensed, demanded an eschatology that said something about history, not just about individual spiritual life. Four years after Bultmann's assertion of what "every schoolboy" knew, Hiroshima had thrown the assurance of history's continuity radically into question. In the atomic era, an Anglican cleric commented in October 1945, "the biblical declaration that the end of the world will come suddenly is driven home to us with fresh

meaning." An American theologian made the same point in the liberal
Christian Century:

> A function of Christians is to make preparation for world's end.
> For generations this fundamental aspect of the Christian faith
> has been ignored or relegated to the subconscious. But now
> eschatology confounds us at the very center of consciousness
> . . . We need to consider the meaning of first century eschatol-
> ogy for our scientific era and the role of Christians as they face
> the threat offered by the atomic bomb.[6]

The post-Hiroshima theological crisis would eventually be fully
articulated in Klaus Koch's 1970 work, *The Rediscovery of Apocalyptic.*
Meanwhile, as an evangelical leader observed in 1948, "the atomic
bomb seems to be persuading some who delighted in ridiculing those
who had earnestly tried to interpret the eschatological portions of the
Word of God in a sober way, to recognize that this earth may be nigh
to a disaster . . . more terrible than was ever depicted by any modern
student of prophecy." The bomb hardly set off a stampede to premillennialism among mainstream theologians; still, as John A. T. Robinson noted in 1950, it impelled many to look afresh at biblical apocalyptic in a manner that helped shape postwar religious thought.[7]

At the level of popular religious belief, the bomb's impact was
immediate and dramatic. In contrast to the secular press, where pleasure at its apparent role in ending the war counterbalanced fears about
the future, prophecy writers from the first adopted an unrelievedly
somber tone. "It is the devil who caused man to devote his highest
and most successful potencies to the discovery of those things by
which man destroys his fellows," commented E. Schuyler English,
associate editor of *Our Hope,* "and no greater weapon has ever been
devised than this one, the A-bomb." The ultimate cataclysm foretold
in the Bible, English went on, sounded "singularly similar in its effects
to those of the atom bomb." *Moody Monthly* agreed: "The Bible is
ahead of science again," it said; an atomic blast offered an "exact picture" of the burning and melting depicted in II Peter 3:10.[8]

Philadelphia's Donald Grey Barnhouse, prophecy writer and radio preacher, explored the bomb's prophetic significance in his *Eternity* magazine of December 1945. Citing the *New York Herald Tribune*'s
cautious editorial hope that global holocaust might yet be avoided,
Barnhouse declared somberly: "It is already too late. The threads of

inevitability have been caught in the mesh of the hidden gears of history and the divine plan moves toward the inexorable fulfillment." Civilization, he went on, was a truck careening downhill with no brakes.[9]

Barnhouse displayed great ingenuity in finding biblical allusions to atomic energy. He suggested that Zechariah's question "For who hath despised the day of small things?" foretold the importance of the atom. The same prophet's prevision of a day when there would be "no hire for man, nor any hire for beast," he speculated, forecast mass unemployment as atomic energy transformed the economy.[10]

Weighing the prospects of atomic war, Barnhouse diverged sharply from the self-congratulatory mood of a nation flushed with victory. The bomb, he said, had given fresh plausibility to a speculation he had long entertained: that New York City was the "Babylon" whose obliteration "in one hour" was foretold in Revelation. With atomic power, not only New York but all the nation's great cities could be instantly wiped out. "The destruction of the United States . . . is certainly consistent with the nature of God," Barnhouse declared implacably; the nation had sinned and faced "terrible judgment." Barnhouse's calm in contemplating mass slaughter reflected his conviction that believers faced a happier destiny. "If atomic bombs fall upon our cities," he wrote, a few weeks into the nuclear age, "we shall be in heaven the next second."[11]

Of postwar prophecy writers who combed not only the Bible but also the interpretive literature of the past for anticipations of the atomic bomb, the most indefatigable was surely Wilbur M. Smith (1894–1976). The son of a prosperous Midwest apple grower, Smith (after failing to get into Dartmouth) in 1913 enrolled at Moody Bible Institute, where his father served on the board. A 1914 prophecy conference addressed by luminaries such as Cyrus Scofield and James Gray (Moody's president) awakened Smith's lifelong interest in this subject. Some newspapers scoffed at the conference, Smith later recalled, but with the outbreak of war a few months later, their tone changed. In 1938, after sixteen years as a Presbyterian pastor, Smith returned to Moody to teach. In 1947 he joined the newly founded Fuller Theological Seminary in Pasadena, California. A prolific writer, conference speaker, and editor of an annual volume of aids for Sunday school teachers, Smith was not only America's best-known prophecy expounder of the early postwar era, but also the most erudite; with a library of twenty-five thousand volumes, he was sometimes called "Christianity's No. 1 Bookworm."[12]

The atomic bomb immediately caught Smith's attention. Like many others, he preached on II Peter 3:10—"the passage that was in everyone's mind"—after Hiroshima, and in November 1945 produced a booklet, "This Atomic Age and the Word of God," that sold fifty thousand copies and was condensed in the January 1946 *Reader's Digest*. His much-expanded book of the same title appeared in 1948.[13]

In the manner of prophecy writers from time immemorial, Smith strove for a tone of up-to-the-minute contemporaneity. The Greek word *luo* in II Peter 3:11, translated as "dissolved" in the King James Version ("Seeing then that all these things shall be dissolved . . ."), he suggested, in fact meant to *unfasten* or *release* and thus explicitly foretold "the principle involved in nuclear fission." God may have destroyed Sodom and Gomorrah with nuclear power, he speculated, foreshadowing the judgment now confronting all humanity. Smith scoured the press for doomsday pronouncements by scientists. "The very phrases that were formerly used by Bible students and laughed at by the world," he observed, "are now being used by our outstanding thinkers without any reference to the Scriptures and without any knowledge of prophetic truth." Documenting the somber mood, he cited the clock of the *Bulletin of the Atomic Scientists*, poised a few minutes before midnight, and a *Collier's* article by physicist Harold Urey entitled "I'm a Frightened Man." Never in history, he said, had Jesus' prophecy of men's hearts failing them for fear been more clearly fulfilled.[14]

While activist scientists evoked the horrors of atomic war to rally support for world government or the Acheson-Lilienthal atomic-energy control plan, prophecy writers such as Smith marshaled the rhetoric of terror to underscore the hopelessness of humanity's situation as the end approached. The bomb, said Smith, forced nonbelievers to consider seriously the claims of Bible prophecy. The fear aroused by the prospect of atomic annihilation, he asserted, had produced a sharp reversal in thinking about the Second Coming and end-time events. Like Barnhouse, Smith rejected world government as a panacea. Without God's blessing, he warned, world government would lead only to global tyranny under Antichrist. The international atomic-energy control agency envisioned by the Acheson-Lilienthal plan, he said, could turn out to be the vehicle for the rise of the demonic end-time ruler.[15]

Combing his prophecy library for anticipations of the bomb, Smith cited Burnet's *Sacred Theory of the Earth,* Adam Clarke's 1837 Bible commentary, a treatise by Edward Hitchcock, and other works that to the eye of faith did indeed seem strikingly prescient. For example, John Cumming, the Scottish prophecy writer of the 1850s, expounded II Peter 3:10 in these words: "At that day, we infer that the air shall become one sheet of flame, clasping the earth in its burning bosom . . . The whole earth, from its loftiest hill to the depth of its deepest mine, will be penetrated by fire. The tainted air shall thus be purged. It is predestined to this."[16]

Gleefully, Smith quoted fatuous comments by pre-1914 liberal theologians hailing the imminent advent of the Kingdom of God through human effort. The atomic bomb, he said, should finally quash all such "foolish dreams." Far more on target, he suggested, was Bishop Ryle, the Anglican evangelical, who as early as 1883 had written: "The last days of the earth shall be its worst days. The last war shall be the most fearful and terrible war that ever desolated the earth." Smith reflected on the contrast between the world of 1948 and the "bright, warm, unclouded days" of his youth, when "a sort of general conviction [prevailed] that we were on the verge of a millennium" and "the idea of atoms was only a theory in our textbook of physics." The bomb, he insisted, radically challenged not only the notion of inevitable progress, but also cyclical theories of history in which renewal follows degeneration and collapse. History's "great, awful climax" was at hand, he proclaimed, "and every act and plan and invention of godless men can only hasten that day."[17]

One of the more interesting early efforts to link the atomic bomb to the tradition of prophetic interpretation came not from the evangelical ranks, but from Harvard's Perry Miller, the intellectual historian of American Puritanism. In "The End of the World," the 1950 essay discussed in Chapter 2, Miller noted the similarities between post-Hiroshima doomsday rhetoric and the work of Thomas Burnet and other late-seventeenth-century prophecy writers whose end-time scenarios had incorporated current scientific thinking. But the ubiquitous intimations of doom in contemporary secular discourse, Miller suggested, while superficially similar, in fact differed radically from those of earlier writers for whom the coming cataclysm had profound eschatological meaning. The nuclear end that seemed all too possible after 1945 lacked such a framework. In an era when "the very concept of a future becomes meaningless," Miller suggested, the sense that history had meaning—and that America had a special role in history—might finally atrophy and die.[18]

Miller's distinction between a theologically rooted apocalypticism and a merely rhetorical one grafted upon an essentially secular worldview was important; but for many evangelical ministers, revivalists, and prophecy popularizers, not to mention millions of grassroots believers, the intellectual distance between 1650 and 1950 was narrower than Miller might have imagined. Numerous early postwar prophecy writers viewed atomic war as "apocalyptic" not in some metaphorical sense, but quite literally. For them, the bomb and the global holocaust it portended brought infinitely closer the fulfillment of a divine plan formulated before the dawn of time.

While some writers discussed the bomb's prophetic significance in general terms, others readily applied biblical prophecies of Earth's final destruction—now so dramatically reinforced—to specific public-policy issues. Wilbur Smith, for example, despite government propaganda to the contrary, suggested that civil defense in the atomic age was futile, in view of the warning in Revelation that "the caves and rocks of the mountains" would provide no protection in the last days.[19]

Many writers echoed Smith in dismissing proposals for the international control of atomic energy, and indeed all efforts to reduce the risk of atomic war, as further manifestations of the vain hope that humanity could avoid catastrophe through its own efforts. All plans for controlling the atom would fail, one author proclaimed in November 1945, "and the nations will be destroyed, because God's word declares it." William Ayer of New York's Calvary Baptist Church, heard regularly on sixteen radio stations, echoed this pessimism. "The emerging peace program is not God's program," he proclaimed as the United Nations debated the Acheson-Lilienthal proposal, "but only a variation of man's international plans, which always come to naught." The UN itself was "doomed to failure," agreed Donald Grey Barnhouse in 1951; the stark marble monolith that was its New York headquarters might well serve as the smoldering city's tombstone.[20]

Even those who deplored the post-Hiroshima explosion of

prophecy interest as simplistic could not ignore its intensity. In 1949 Henry Sloane Coffin of Union Theological Seminary, a bastion of liberalism, lamented that mainstream Protestantism's neglect of eschatology had left the field to "sensational propagandists" and "mushrooming cultists," who found blueprints of the future in Daniel and Revelation and promised their followers easy escape from the coming cataclysm. The liberal *Baptist Courier* lashed out at "cults that preach the doom of the present evil order by a sudden intervention of God." Like Communism, it said, "this doctrine thrives on darkness and distress." [21]

In response, the *Sunday School Times* pointed out that the heightened receptivity of the "plain people" to an eschatology that taught a convulsive end to human history ought not be surprising, since the experience of recent decades had so utterly discredited "the dream of a better world" long preached by "the Modernists." [22] In a world shadowed by nuclear fear, premillennialism had taken a vigorous new lease on life.

The 1950s and 1960s

Reflecting a broader trend in U.S. culture, prophecy writers devoted somewhat less attention to the bomb in the fifties and sixties. [23] But even this "lull" was relative. Wilbur Smith, who was in a position to know, commented in 1953 on the prophecy books "pouring from the presses," many of which dealt with the atomic bomb. Despite Washington's efforts to allay nuclear fear, prophecy writers saw no silver lining. "Today the whole world lives in fear of annihilation," declared the manifesto of a 1952 prophecy conference in New York City, and several speakers elaborated the point. Implicitly dismissing government propaganda touting the atom's peacetime uses, one speaker insisted on "the dreadful implications of modern atomic science." Another cited the environmental damage inflicted by U.S. atomic tests in the Pacific, described in David Bradley's *No Place to Hide* (1948), as a sign of the approaching end. [24]

Beginning in the mid-1950s with anxiety about radioactive fallout from U.S. and Soviet hydrogen-bomb tests, and continuing until the Limited Nuclear Test Ban Treaty of 1963, a second wave of nuclear fear and political activism swept the nation. Prophecy writers' attention to the bomb mirrored this trend. "At no time in past history has the universal situation of the human race been so desperate as it is today," wrote the author of a 1955 prophecy work. "Dread of a third world war hangs heavily on the hearts of men." Echoed another author in 1956, "The dread reality of guided missiles and nuclear weapons," had stimulated "a new and vital interest" in end-time prophecies.[25]

In the early 1960s, as fallout fears intensified, President Kennedy proposed a crash program of shelter construction and sparred with Nikita Khrushchev over Berlin and Soviet missiles in Cuba. Prophecy writers both fed and exploited the rising tension. A 1960 *Moody Monthly* article cited the arms race as a major contributor to a climate of terror comparable to the biblical picture of the last days. Given the world situation, wrote J. Dwight Pentecost of Dallas Theological Seminary in 1961, the war prophesied in Ezekiel could break out at any time. America's vaunted scientific prowess, these writers insisted, offered no hope in this hour of crisis. Far from advancing human well-being, declared one in 1962, modern science, in burdening the world with thermonuclear bombs and ICBMs, had only deepened the mood of "bewilderment and fear for what lies ahead."[26]

These authors interlaced their discussions of the nuclear threat with a stock set of proof texts: the vision of a melting earth in II Peter; the crescendo of catastrophes in John's Apocalypse; the all-consuming conflagration and terrifying astronomical events woven through the Book of Joel's three short chapters ("O Lord, to thee will I cry; for the fire hath devoured the pastures of the wilderness, and the flame hath burned all the trees of the field . . . The sun shall be turned into darkness, and the moon into blood, before the great and the terrible day of the Lord come"); and the prophet Zechariah's terrifying description of Jehovah's judgment on Israel's enemies (a description strikingly similar to John Hersey's account of Japanese atomic-bomb victims in his 1946 bestseller, *Hiroshima*):

> And this shall be the plague wherewith the Lord will smite all the people that have fought against Jerusalem; Their flesh shall consume away while they stand upon their feet, and their eyes shall consume away in their holes, and their tongue shall consume away in their mouth.[27]

Since the days of the Millerites with their colorful charts, prophecy popularizers had used visual aids to good effect. This tradition continued in the 1950s and 1960s, as photographs of mushroom clouds and ICBMs adorned many articles. "ROCKETS AND MISSILES IN THE SPACE AGE THREATEN WORLD DESTRUCTION" declared a photo caption in a 1960 *Moody Monthly* article on "Prophetic Patterns in the World Today." In the late 1950s, anticipating the extensive use of films, TV, and videocassettes by prophecy popularizers, Moody Bible Institute's "Sermons from Science" series distributed to church and youth groups a film, *God of the Atom,* that offered a dollop of popularized physics, discussed the effects of nuclear war, and postulated that Bible prophecy foretold the whole process. [28]

One of the most influential interpreters of this period was M. R. DeHaan of Grand Rapids, whose "Radio Bible Class" aired on five hundred stations, including the Mutual and ABC networks. In broadcasts and books of the early 1960s, DeHaan often discussed the nuclear threat. "Hanging over the heads of the nations," he wrote in 1962, "is the dire, horrible fear that at any moment some trigger-happy despot will . . . drop a missile that would set the world on fire." Demonstrating the skill of prophecy writers at incorporating new developments in their scenarios, DeHaan discussed the neutron bomb, "technology's deadliest weapon," with its capacity to destroy life without harming physical structures. Elaborating a passage from Jesus' "Little Apocalypse" as recorded in Mark's Gospel, DeHaan proclaimed, "This present age will close with a time of peril and war and destruction so great, what with our atomic weapons and supersonic missiles, that God must halt the holocaust, or man would utterly destroy himself." [29]

Prophecy conferences helped believers place the deepening nuclear threat in biblical context. A speaker at a 1956 gathering in New York City quoted Zechariah's account of human flesh "consum[ing] away," and asked: "Did you ever wonder how it could be fulfilled? Well, the atomic bomb, the hydrogen bomb, and the cobalt bomb have made real this passage of Scripture." The arms race, he went on, was "the training ground for Armageddon." Added John Walvoord at a 1961 Los Angeles prophecy conference, "The Bible plainly forecasts the coming of yet another great war . . . eclips[ing] anything that the world has ever seen before." [30]

Given this conviction, prophecy writers dismissed Washington's message of peace through strength, survival through civil defense, and Utopia through peacetime use of atomic energy. Whatever the soothing rhetoric, they insisted, the nuclear arms race obviously represented a giant step toward Armageddon. "No shelter . . . can protect us from the bombs being perfected today," declared DeHaan in 1962. "The only way *out* is *up*." [31]

Like their Gilded Age predecessors who had dismissed reforms aimed at ameliorating the social toll of industrialization, these writers equally scorned activists who *opposed* the government's nuclear policies. The test-ban and arms-control movements they saw as yet another futile effort to alter history's foreordained course. One 1957 author warned, "Let no man be deceived by the idea that the banning of atomic weapons, or even the reduction of conventional armaments, will ensure peace." DeHaan agreed: "Our hope does not lie in peace treaties [or] . . . human means of organization," he wrote in 1962, as the test-ban talks inched forward; only the Second Coming would end the nuclear threat. [32]

Prophecy writers of the late 1950s and early 1960s continued to point to the nuclear threat as compelling evidence for the inerrancy and divine inspiration of the apocalyptic passages in the Scriptures. As one put it: "The holocaust of atomic war would fulfill the prophecies . . . The Bible and science go right down the line together on the forecasting of future events for earth." Nuclear weapons not only confirmed Earth's doom in a general way; they also suggested the precise means by which it would be accomplished:

> The words used by Joel and Peter centuries ago could well have been a description of an atomic explosion on a gigantic scale; the great rushing sound as the huge pillar of smoke ascends and breaks out into a tremendous mushroom formation, the blazing fire and blood-red cloud, the fission of atoms and disintegration of elements—the whole picture of nuclear horrors was painted in vivid but restrained language by the Biblical writers centuries ago. [33]

Following the lead of Barnhouse and others, these writers pointed out how readily the prophesied end-time ruler could use nuclear terror to dominate the world. Los Angeles minister J. Vernon McGee asked rhetorically in 1961: "When [Antichrist] is sitting there with his finger on the button, what will the nations of the world do? They will do exactly what he wants them to do! He will be an absolute dictator." [34]

As they updated the premillennial scenario with images of nuclear war, prophecy writers maintained a tone of calm assurance. All is foretold; if the prophetic plan is understood, one need feel no alarm. A major source of nuclear fear, suggested Walvoord in 1955, lay in people's failure to heed the Bible, "the only Book in the world which will tell us accurately and without error concerning future events." Writing in 1957, amid deepening anxiety about radioactive fallout, another interpreter made the same reassuring point: "Wars and disasters may come and go; atom bombs may pose their threat of universal annihilation . . . But these things are recognized as part of the great design of the God of Israel."[35]

The narratives of horror ended formulaically: the Christian would escape. One writer, after a particularly gruesome recital of the disasters facing humankind, went on: "But let us turn our face from that dreadful scene, and be reminded that the redeemed of God . . . shall not be on the earth at that time." Despite the ubiquitous fear of nuclear war, observed Dwight Pentecost in 1961, "the child of God who is acquainted with the prophetic Scriptures rests in assurance because he has before him God's own blueprint." And what did this blueprint tell the believer? Before the final crisis "you and I . . . will have been translated into the presence of our Lord and Savior Jesus Christ." M. R. DeHaan agreed: "One of these days [the Rapture] is really, actually going to happen . . . The darker the days become, the more glorious this blessed hope shines in our lives."[36]

The world's doom was sealed, but individuals might still be snatched as brands from the burning. After describing the grim nuclear prospect and the Christian's blessed hope, the prophecy writers always concluded with the ancient, ever-urgent theme: accept Christ today, and escape the holocaust that could break over the earth at any moment. As one reminded his readers, updating Jonathan Edwards' spider dangling over a flame: "Only the touch of a button stands between you and eternity at every moment of every day."[37]

The Seventies and Beyond

Hal Lindsey's bestsellers of the 1970s, *The Late Great Planet Earth* and *There's a New World Coming,* contributed nothing new to an already well-established framework of premillennialist nuclear-war interpretation. (Indeed, his fellow students at Dallas Theological Seminary complained that Lindsey had simply repackaged his lecture notes!)

Lindsey presented the familiar doctrine in chatty prose embellished with trendy phrases—Antichrist as "The Weirdo Beast," the Rapture as "The Ultimate Trip," and so on. Utilizing contemporary strategic terminology as he wove the biblical apocalypses into a narrative of the coming holocaust (which he labeled "World War III"), he enhanced the up-to-the-minute aura of his books with maps bearing captions such as "Phase I: Pan-Arabic Assault" and "Phase II: Russian Counter-attack [and] Amphibious Assault." [38]

Assuming that all scriptural allusions to fiery destruction and mass suffering foreshadowed nuclear war, Lindsey (usually with a qualifying phrase such as "quite possibly" or "may very well be") relentlessly turned the Bible into a manual of atomic-age combat: Zechariah's image of human flesh consuming away portrays "exactly what happens to those who are in a thermonuclear blast"; "fire and brimstone" means tactical nuclear weapons; the falling stars and stinging locusts of Revelation are warheads fired from space platforms and Cobra helicopters spraying nerve gas; the scorching heat and awful sores mentioned in Revelation describe the effects of radiation as observed at Hiroshima and Nagasaki. [39] For page after mind-numbing page, Lindsey systematically went through the apocalyptic scriptures, mechanically transcribing every phrase and image into the vocabulary of Pentagon strategists.

The biblical writers, said Lindsey patronizingly, had been unable to decipher their own visions. "After all," he wrote, "how could God transmit the thought of a nuclear catastrophe to someone living in the year A.D. 90!" The "hail and fire, mixed with blood" of Revelation 8, he says, are clearly missiles as they appeared "to John's eyes, unsophisticated as to ICBM's." Similarly, John's image of horses with lion-like heads and fire pouring from their mouths was his feeble effort to describe "some kind of mobilized ballistic missile launcher." [40]

Lindsey paraded his insider's knowledge of current events and scientific developments. "Recently as I was studying about nuclear weapons," begins a typical passage,

> I discovered that science has perfected a cobalt bomb—one of the most lethal weapons known to man. A cobalt bomb is made by placing a shield of cobalt 59 metal around a hydrogen bomb. By this comparatively simple operation the destructive capacity of the hydrogen bomb is doubled. More significantly, however,

the radioactive contamination . . . is tremendous. Scientists have dubbed it "the dirty bomb" because of its fallout. This is what I believe may be pictured in Revelation 6:12.[41]

Lindsey described the end–time holocaust with unholy zest, hypnotically piling catastrophe upon catastrophe: "multiplied millions" of soldiers are incinerated; civilian casualties mount into the billions amid nuclear horrors including a "quadrillion megaton explosion"; mass poisoning results as water turns to blood ("There's going to be a big run on Coca-Cola, but even this will give out after a while!"). Reflecting on all this, Michael Barkun has perceptively observed:

> As the exclamation points march forward, it becomes clear that Lindsey finds these prospects enormously attractive. His prose pants on with scarcely a word of sympathy for the hundreds of millions killed or maimed. For him, the tribulation is grand, cosmic theatre, the ultimate Hollywood spectacle.[42]

Not only secular critics, but many from the religious world (even evangelicals), dealt harshly with Lindsey's imaginative flights. One dismissed his "science fiction fantasy" as "a farrago of nonsense." A seminary student called him "the Geraldo Rivera of the Christian world." A British Baptist leader wrote dismissively: "This is obviously 'popular' stuff which makes exciting reading for those who may be inclined that way. But I for one find it difficult in the extreme to give any credence whatsoever to such a literalistic and pseudo-scientific approach to scripture." Nevertheless, by embedding nuclear war in a framework of foreordained meaning, Lindsey struck a note that resonated with millions of Americans. "Bible-believing Christians have become extremely sensitive to the apocalyptic prophecies," observed *Christianity Today* in 1973, as the Lindsey phenomenon surged on.[43]

The prophecy books that proliferated in the 1970s and 1980s emulated Lindsey in making nuclear war a centerpiece of their scenarios. "Billions will perish in the coming cataclysm," wrote Merrill Unger (yet another Dallas Seminary faculty member) in *Beyond the Crystal Ball,* adding that while the approaching judgment would ultimately be God's doing, "on the natural plane, H-bombs and the latest thermonuclear weapons will play a large part." John Phillips in *Only the Bible Can Foretell the Future,* after describing the potential effects of a thermonuclear attack on the eastern United States ("The entire East Coast, from Portland, Maine, to Norfolk, Virginia, and up to 150 miles inland, would become a lake of fire") concluded somberly, "Truly, the dawning of the atomic age is of great prophetic significance."[44]

Among the post-1970 prophecy popularizers who proclaimed a coming nuclear war, few reached a larger audience than evangelist Jack Van Impe of Royal Oak, Michigan, whose weekly broadcasts appeared on more than ninety UHF channels, the Trinity Broadcasting religious network, forty-three U.S. radio stations, and internationally on Trans-World Radio. Van Impe also promulgated his end-time interpretations in short, easy-to-read paperbacks with titles such as *Signs of the Times, The Coming War with Russia,* and *11:59 and Counting.* Describing a visit to Hiroshima, he foresaw much worse in "the near future" as "a holocaust of fire" unleashed "atomic devastation beyond comprehension." Bible quotations studded Van Impe's apocalyptic predictions, including not only the familiar ones from Revelation, Zechariah, and II Peter ("as clear a definition of atomic warfare as is contained in any library"), but also more obscure selections from Joel, Zephaniah, Malachi, and this from Ezekiel:

> The flaming flame shall not be quenched, and all faces from the south to the north shall be burned therein.
> And all flesh shall see that I the Lord have kindled it: it shall not be quenched.[45]

Striving to outdo one another, the post-Lindsey popularizers produced ever more sensational prose and tortuous interpretations. Jeremiah's phrase "make bright the arrows," suggested one, described the launching of a nuclear missile. Another triumphantly unearthed a cryptic phrase from Habakkuk—"for they shall heap dust and take it"—as an obvious prophecy of radioactive fallout. In *Project for Survival* Leon Bates employed italics, capitals, and home-made drawings to convey his message that "NUCLEAR WAR IS PROBABLE" and "could come at any time!" "The death count . . . will be almost UNBELIEVABLE," he cried. Expounding Ezekiel 39, Bates hypothesized that the seven-month delay in burying the dead after Gog's invasion of Israel would be a "cooling off period" because of radioactive contamination from the corpses.[46]

To keep their apocalyptic scenarios timely (and perhaps to gain

an edge in a highly competitive field), these writers also emulated
Lindsey in citing the latest developments in nuclear technology. "An
entire country's targets could be hit simultaneously by releasing a
SWARM of . . . Cruise missiles," wrote the breathless Leon Bates; "this
is a major development in modern warfare, *just in time for the TRIBU-
LATION!*" A writer of the 1980s, discussing Antichrist's feat of calling
down fire from the skies (Rev. 13:13), described a satellite device allegedly under development by the Soviets that could "at any given
moment . . . trigger the release of a laser beam flame which could
descend in an apocalyptic flash on a predetermined target."[47]

This decades-long effort to find prophetic intimations of mankind's nuclear fate helps one understand the excitement set off by Edgar Whisenant's 2-million-copy bestseller, *88 Reasons Why the Rapture
Will Be in 1988.* Willing to boldly go where no man (or not many) had
gone before, Whisenant set his dates without the usual safety net of
hedges and qualifications. The fact that Jesus said no man can know
the *day* or the *hour* of the Second Coming, he logically pointed out,
does not mean we cannot know the month or the year. Marshaling
elaborate and highly ingenious prophetic evidence, he dated the Rapture between September 11 and 13, 1988, the Jewish holiday of Rosh
Hashana. World War III, he went on, would begin three weeks later
with Russia's invasion of Israel at sunset on October 3, 1988—precisely 70 years, 364 days, and 23 hours after "the birth of Communism" in Russia on October 4, 1917—and end one hour later with
Russia's annihilation. (Ps. 90:10—"The days of our years are three-
score years and ten"—he argued, foretold the lifespan of Communism, whereas Rev. 18:10 prophesied its destruction "in one hour.")
This divinely ordained holocaust, he predicted, echoing many other
prophecy writers, would produce nuclear winter, mass starvation,
radioactive water, and mountains of unburied bodies.[48]

Few prophecy writers followed Whisenant's venture into date
setting, but many did go beyond general predictions of global thermonuclear war to speculate about the form it would take, and the
nations that would be involved.

Scenarios of Nuclear War

As prophecy writers reflected on the end-time cataclysm foretold in
Scripture, some tried to work out the precise details. Although, as

two 1974 authors admitted in a rare confession of uncertainty, it is often "not quite clear who fights with whom about what," [49] many made the effort. Their divergent interpretations, while puzzling to the uninitiated, illuminate the complex ways prophetic belief influenced perceptions of reality—and, specifically, perceptions of our nuclear future.

One troublesome issue was whether the prophesied cataclysm would in fact be a nuclear *war,* as usually understood, or a divine intervention in which God would punish mankind, possibly by nuclear means. In contrast to Lindsey's detailed nuclear scenarios of World War III, other writers stressed the transcendent character of the eschatological fulfillment. Merrill Unger, for example, while not excluding nuclear conflict from his end-time scenario, emphasized that the devastation portrayed in Revelation might well be a direct "outpouring of God's wrath" upon humanity. Herbert Vander Lugt, research director for the "Radio Bible Hour," explicitly criticized Lindsey on this point in 1983, arguing that the biblical apocalypses do not foretell a human war, but rather "supernatural judgments from heaven." (The Jehovah's Witnesses similarly hold that the Bible foretells punishment of wicked humanity by God himself.) The Revelation passage in which Christ slays his enemies at Armageddon with a sword that "proceeded out of his mouth," Walvoord noted, hardly suggests nuclear war. Even Van Impe conceded that "God does not need man's modern inventions" to work his will. [50]

Some resolved the dilemma by positing *two* nuclear-related eschatological events: World War III and *then* God's destruction of the earth. In *11:59 and Counting,* for example, Van Impe in 1983 hypothesized a thermonuclear conflict during the Tribulation, followed, after the Millennium, by God's nuclear annihilation of the world in preparation for the New Heaven and the New Earth. Proponents stressed this theory's hopeful aspect: although World War III would be devastating, many would survive since, as Unger noted: "If mankind succeeded in exterminating itself, there would be no one . . . over whom [Christ] could reign [during the Millennium]. In such a case, God's prophetic program would collapse." Even if a billion people were to die in World War III, another writer pointed out, "there would be a couple [of] billion others left." This scenario is what Tim LaHaye had in mind in 1972 as he reassured those gripped by nuclear fear: "Let me put you at ease immediately. Although this world will be destroyed some day (and perhaps by a giant nuclear explosion . . .), it will not be accomplished by man, but by God himself." Harold Lindsell, a former editor of the evangelical journal *Christianity Today,* elaborated this point in 1984: "The Bible clearly states that . . . when [Christ] comes, millions or billions of people will still be on this planet . . . Annihilation of all life is a threat which cannot become a reality." As for the earth's prophesied "melt[ing] with fervent heat," he went on, "no people will be here on earth when this takes place; all will have been judged and assigned either to [heaven or to hell]." Warnings of universal annihilation in nuclear war, Lindsell concluded, reflected "either a misunderstanding of the Bible or a lack of biblical knowledge." [51]

Those who sought nuclear allusions in the prophecies faced another problem: the apocalypticists' visions involved weapons of their own day—spears, bows and arrows, mounted warriors, and the like. Some writers, faithful in their literalism, argued that precisely these weapons will be used in the final battle. Walvoord, for example, noting that the wooden weapons described in Ezekiel 39 are burned as kindling by the people of Israel after the invading army's destruction, commented, "If these are symbols, it would be difficult to burn symbols." [52]

Those who held this position offered ingenious explanations of why bows and arrows would be the weapons of choice in history's final war. Richard DeHaan (the son and successor of M. R. DeHaan) suggested in 1968 that as disarmament talks proceeded, only such low-tech weapons could be produced undetected. In *Apocalypse Next* William Goetz warned that the Soviets, with 70 percent of the world's horses, would fall back on horsepower as the oil crisis worsened. Goetz also reported Russian research on a new superstrong wood product, lignostone, ideal for making weapons that could escape radar detection. Another writer, striving for contemporaneity while remaining faithful to biblical literalism, speculated that the final war would involve "highly sophisticated" nuclear-tipped arrows and spears "for close-up fighting." [53]

But most prophecy writers, for all their insistence on inerrancy, freely followed Hal Lindsey in transmuting swords and chariots into modern-day nuclear weaponry. As S. Maxwell Coder explained in *The Final Chapter,* elucidating a passage in Ezekiel:

Hebrew is a language of word pictures . . . The word for "arrow" means a piercing missile, and the word for "bow" means a launching device for such a missile . . . If we use the word pictures instead of what was meant in ancient times, the verse [Ezek. 39:3] translates, "And I will smite thy launcher out of thy left hand, and will cause thy missiles to fall out of thy right hand" . . . The word pictures can describe modern weapons just as accurately as they described those in use twenty-five hundred years ago.[54]

Despite the troubling similarity of this "word-picture" hermeneutic to the allegorizing of liberal theologians, there were obvious evangelistic (and market?) advantages, enabling fundamentalist popularizers freely to "translate" biblical language into vivid nuclear-war scenarios. Proponents rationalized this technique as did Lindsey: the language of Daniel, Ezekiel, and Revelation represents the writers' feeble efforts to verbalize visions of twentieth-century weaponry that utterly baffled them. As one writer put it, Ezekiel "could only use the language and vocabulary available to him. He could not mention missiles and tanks when the terms had not yet been coined . . . He was simply directed by the Spirit of God to describe a future battle in the popular terms of his day . . . Certainly, centuries of military techniques will not be discarded when they are desperately needed."[55]

Which nations would be involved in the coming holocaust? While many prophecy writers, as we shall see in Chapter 5, tied their nuclear-war predictions to forecasts of Russia's destruction in the course of an invasion of Israel, most proceeded cautiously in discussing the precise nature and source of that destruction. In *What's This World Coming To?* (1970), discussing Gog's destruction as foretold in Ezekiel, Ray Stedman wrote: "It is apparent from this description that God himself will assume the prerogative in dealing with the Russian threat. Whether it will involve nuclear warfare, or be purely a natural disaster, is difficult to determine."[56] David Webber of the popular "Southwest Radio Church" program was similarly cagey about specifics in interpreting Ezekiel 38–39: "The miraculous intervention of God could be by an earthquake or by a nuclear mistake by the Russians," he wrote in 1979. "If a ballistic missile were to fall short of its intended target it could destroy millions of Russians." Doug Clark, in *Shockwaves of Armageddon* (1982), perhaps came closest to identifying the "fire" that incinerates the land of Magog in Ezekiel 39: "Could this . . . be European and American nuclear power destroying the Soviet Union? Certainly it could. God uses earthly as well as heavenly powers to do his will." [57]

But nuclear war did not figure in these prophecy popularizations solely in an anti-Soviet context. Whatever its specific cause, the final conflict would soon engulf the entire globe. As a speaker at a 1970 prophecy conference put it, "The very idea of a coming cataclysmic judgment that will destroy the nations seems preposterous; yet for those . . . acquainted with the prophetic word, there resides the conviction that the dissolution of the present world order must be near." James Boice, a Philadelphia Presbyterian minister and Barnhouse's successor on the "Bible Study Hour," explicating Ezekiel 38 and 39 in 1984, foresaw "a general exchange of nuclear missiles" in a "horribly destructive war" engulfing every nation, including "the United States, Great Britain, Japan, China, and other world powers." [58]

The most precise list of the nations facing destruction appeared in Jack Van Impe's *Signs of the Times*. Noting the Revelation prophecy that a third of the globe will be consumed by fire and citing *Life's Pictorial Atlas of the World,* Van Impe calculated one-third of the earth's land mass as 18,963,194 square miles. He next listed the area of the nations he believed destined for annihilation: Israel, the "Persian Empire (including West Pakistan)," Ethiopia, Libya, the Soviet Union, the Warsaw Pact nations; the ten nations of Western Europe ruled by Antichrist, and the United States. The total? *Precisely* 18,963,194 square miles! "How much more proof is needed," he concluded triumphantly; "to convince the lost that Christ's return is very near[?]" [59]

As Van Impe's calculations suggest, the United States fared poorly in most of these narratives of nuclear destruction. Indeed, we shall see in Chapter 7 that most late-twentieth-century prophecy writers, after chronicling America's decline into wickedness and apostasy, sadly concluded that it would share the judgment foretold for the nations as a whole. For many, this prognosis meant nuclear destruction. As early as 1945, Donald Grey Barnhouse had warned of the atomic destruction of New York and other U.S. cities, and the theme ran through the next forty-five years of prophetic writing. The United States will either ally with Antichrist, declared one writer in 1974, and thus face direct annihilation, or be a "helpless casualty of global thermonuclear effects." A 1985 author expressed the prevailing view with particular starkness: America, the latter-day Babylon whose doom is foretold in Revelation, "is going to be destroyed by fire! Sudden destruction is coming and few will escape . . . A hydrogen holocaust will engulf America—and this nation will be no more." [60]

In a variant of the debate discussed above, some popularizers foresaw America's nuclear judgment coming directly from God, others from human intermediaries—usually the Soviet Union. "Russia possesses enough hydrogen bombs . . . to devastate America," wrote Roy Hicks, a pentecostal prophecy writer and speaker, in 1982. "Of course, this must be in the knowledge and timing of the Lord, but her threats to bury us cannot be ignored." [61]

Certain common themes emerge in these various speculations. First, one is struck by the pervasive sense of inevitability. God's plan for mankind, established before the world began, is unalterable. As a chapter title in one book put it, the drift toward nuclear Armageddon is "A TREND THAT CANNOT BE REVERSED." These works abound with fatalistic pronouncements: "It is only a matter of time . . . , [a] nuclear holocaust is coming"; "Our world is in a death-dive. We have peaked and now we're plunging rapidly to the end"; and other similar sentiments. [62]

Second, nuclear war, while horrendous, will also be the means to a beneficent and even glorious outcome. "If God permits men to use atomic warfare," Merrill Unger wrote, "it will be to accomplish His purpose and to glorify His name." Robert Gromacki, an Idaho Baptist minister and church-college professor, observed in 1970:

> Although Armageddon will be an awesome and terrifying experience for the world, it should be welcomed by the child of God as the day of vindication of our holy and sovereign Creator. Many beneficial results will be produced by this great battle . . . What then should be the believer's attitude to the destruction of the world by fire? First of all, he should welcome it and pray for its nearness. [63]

David Wilkerson, an Assemblies of God minister and pentecostalist leader, elaborated:

> Are we so blind, so earthbound, that we want God to keep us alive physically, only to live in a contaminated, hostile environment? Why can't we see that a holocaust can only dissolve this

earthly body; but that very dissolving brings us into a celestial one. It will be instant glory. How can we who are already dead to the world be adversely affected by a holocaust? As for me, I died to the world—its pleasures, its pains, its destruction—so that a meltdown simply brings me into the fullness of an inheritance I already possess in measure . . . To me, going home to Jesus in a sudden fiery holocaust *is* an escape from God's wrath. How can it be wrath when He takes me by the hand and leads me to paradise? God's chosen can look at every disaster right in its fury and declare: "Nothing can move me; I am safe in the palm of his hand."

A 1972 prophecy writer made the point in a corporate rather than an individual context. A divinely ordained nuclear holocaust, he wrote, could be God's means "to end human history and start a clean new chapter." [64]

Finally, as we have seen, this hopefulness found further grounding in the assurance that Christians will escape Earth's ultimate crisis by way of the Rapture. One writer put it exuberantly in 1967: "Thank God, I will get a view of the Battle of Armageddon from the grandstand seats of the heavens. All who are born again will see the Battle of Armageddon, but it will be from the skies." Wrote another author in 1977: "The world has one great war yet to endure . . . The slaughter that will take place is too frightening to imagine. Just be thankful that you're not going to be around!" This escapist theme was deeply rooted in premillennialist thought. As early as 1854, discussing Earth's final holocaust, John Cumming wrote, "When this great flame shall wrap the earth, those that are united in the Lord shall not be scathed; they shall be sheltered under [the Lord's] outstretched pinions." [65]

Obviously, then, prophecy writers viewed nuclear holocaust from a unique vantage point. They described its horror as graphically as any antinuclear activist, but not as a *possible* historical outcome to be avoided at all costs. For them it was the *probable* form of Earth's divinely ordained end. *Escape* had an individual meaning, but not a corporate, social meaning: hope lay only in accepting Christ and holding oneself in readiness for the Rapture. In the secular world, the possibility of thermonuclear war tended to be either psychologically numbing or politically energizing, as people transformed anxiety into action. For prophecy writers it served different functions: spurring missionary effort, promising future judgment, and validating the pre-millennial belief system and the Bible itself.

Three Nuclear-Age Prophecy Interpreters

Politics penetrated even the hermetic world of prophecy popularizers, generating subtle shifts in the treatment of nuclear war. Such shifts occurred in particularly interesting ways in the pronouncements of three politically active late-twentieth-century evangelical leaders: Jerry Falwell, Pat Robertson, and Billy Graham.

Falwell, prince of the electronic church, New Right leader, and confidant of President Ronald Reagan, offered a succession of prophetic pronouncements on nuclear war in the 1970s and 1980s. Most echoed the familiar post-1945 premillennialist theme: nuclear destruction is prophesied and inevitable. In a 1980 pamphlet, "Armageddon and the Coming War with Russia," complete with mushroom-cloud cover, Falwell described the final holocaust to follow Russia's invasion of Israel. "All hell will break out" at this time, he told an interviewer in 1981, paraphrasing Ezekiel 39; "blood shall flow in the streets up to the bridles of the horses." "The Tribulation will result in such bloodshed and destruction that any war up to that time will seem insignificant," he told his "Old-Time Gospel Hour" audience in 1983. Falwell's grim descriptions of Armageddon took on special resonance when, on tours of Israel, he preached from the actual prophesied site of the battle at Megiddo, near Haifa. "God only knows how many human beings will be wiped out in that battle," he reiterated in his *Fundamentalist Journal* in 1988, "but they *will* be wiped out." Believers will escape the approaching horror, however: "If you are saved, you will never go through one hour, not one moment of the Tribulation." [66]

With Falwell's growing political involvement, he periodically qualified the view that nuclear war was inevitable, imminent, and (for most human beings) inescapable. In 1983, for example, he endorsed the position that the final holocaust would come only *after* the Millennium, as God used nuclear power "to destroy the present universe" and make way for the New Heaven and New Earth. Therefore, he said reassuringly, "We don't need to go to bed at night wondering if someone's going to push the button and destroy the planet between now and sunrise." Falwell even suggested that same year that Americans could influence their nuclear destiny, not only individually through conversion but collectively through diplomacy. Washington had a duty "to negotiate for peace with the Soviet Union and other nations," he said; "we have a human responsibility to do all we can to seek sensible arms controls . . . and so forth."[67] In thus finding Earth's nuclear annihilation foretold in the Bible while simultaneously hinting that the end might be long delayed and even that politics could make a difference, Falwell hewed to a central post-Hiroshima premillennial theme while preserving the role in Reagan-era conservative politics that he so obviously valued.

Pat Robertson, a U.S. senator's son who experienced a religious conversion in 1956 and went on to found the Christian Broadcasting Network, revealed a similar tension between the stark premillennial view of nuclear war and the lure of politics. In the late 1970s and early 1980s he, like Falwell, often foretold a nuclear war triggered by Russia's invasion of Israel. Israel's 1967 capture of Jerusalem's Old City, he wrote in 1980, had set the stage for Antichrist's reign and the final battle, Armageddon. Venturing into date setting, he predicted the ultimate holocaust by 1982 and became increasingly apocalyptic as that year wore on. "The onrush of events toward the end of the year may see the world in flames," he wrote in February. "I guarantee you by the fall of 1982 there is going to be a judgment on the world," he added in a May broadcast.[68]

But when 1982 passed—and as the White House beckoned—Robertson backpedaled from doomsday predictions. In 1985 he told the *Wall Street Journal* that he no longer anticipated nuclear war or history's end in the near future. "There is no way I feel I'm going to help the Lord bring the world to an end," he added elsewhere; "God doesn't want to incinerate the world . . . [Armageddon] is an act of God Almighty that has nothing to do with human abilities whatsoever." In fact, already in his 1982 book *The Secret Kingdom* deep fissures had emerged in Robertson's eschatology, as he both embraced the standard premillennial position and espoused a breathtakingly optimistic postmillennialism. Through Christ, he proclaimed, we can enjoy the Millennium here and now. "There *can* be peace; there *can* be plenty; there *can* be freedom." Citing God's grant of earthly "dominion" to Adam and Eve, Robertson urged Christians to "assume the authority, power, and dominion that God intends for men to exercise over the rest of creation."[69] This so-called dominion theology, an interesting minor strand in contemporary fundamentalist eschatology explored more fully here in a later chapter, eased Robertson's transition to a stance more politically acceptable. To no avail: his 1988 presidential campaign collapsed as voters remained leery despite his reassurances, and he returned to the more congenial arena of TV evangelism.

Even more interesting, because less obviously motivated by political ambition, was the eschatological evolution of Billy Graham, who burst on the revivalistic scene in 1949 and remained influential into the 1990s. While his sermons and books did not heavily emphasize prophecy, Graham clearly embraced premillennialism. Christ's kingdom would arise from the ruins of earthly institutions, he proclaimed in *World Aflame* (1965): "Secular history . . . is doomed . . . The whole world is hurtling toward a war greater than anything known before." Acknowledging his debt to Wilbur Smith, Graham speculated that the melting elements and "fervent heat" of II Peter referred to atomic fission, as God used nuclear means for Earth's "purification." [70]

In the early 1980s, however, social issues loomed larger in Graham's sermons. In Moscow in 1982, he called the nuclear arms race "a moral and spiritual issue that must concern us all" and offered a five-point disarmament program culminating in a ban on all nuclear, biochemical, and laser weapons. To evangelicals unsettled by this new activist emphasis, he described himself as a man "in process" still exploring "the deeper . . . implications of [his] faith." [71] Graham's *Approaching Hoofbeats* (1983) offered a fascinating picture of this evolution, as it vacillated between social meliorism and classic premillennial fatalism. The "hoofbeats" of the title were those of the four horses of the Apocalypse, conventionally taken to represent famine, pestilence, war, and death. Discussing each "horse" in the allegorical fashion favored by theological liberals, Graham addressed issues such as Third World poverty, disease, and overpopulation; drought and famine; environmental hazards; and the arms race. Vividly evoking the horrors of modern war, he insisted that one cannot "sit silently by" in the face of the threat; the red horse "rides in warning to effect positive change." Jesus blessed the peacemakers, and Christians must work to slow the arms race and avoid nuclear war. Alone among Cold War premillennialists, Graham confessed that he should have done more to address issues of world peace and social justice. [72]

Yet the classic premillennial outlook too shaped *Approaching Hoofbeats*. History's final movements ("perhaps just ahead"), Graham wrote, will see "nuclear conflagrations, biological holocausts and chemical apocalypses rolling over the earth, bringing man to the edge of the precipice. History will 'bottom out' in the battle of Armageddon." Struggling to resolve the book's eschatological schizophrenia, he argued that while prophecy is sure, God may *delay* foreordained events in response to human effort. Therefore, we must never lapse into passivity in the face of issues such as the nuclear threat. Still, *whatever* we do, "ultimate peace" will come only when Christ reigns on earth.[73]

In a nationally televised sermon in 1990, Graham, now in his early seventies, still vacillated between premillennial orthodoxy and his newly awakened social conscience. Addressing the question "Are the Last Days Almost Here?" Graham insisted that they are. "We've become so technological and so wicked at the same time, that we have been on the verge of destroying our world. But . . . God is going to step in and not allow us to have an atomic war." How will God accomplish this purpose? He will "cleanse the earth by fire" just as He "cleansed" it by flood in Noah's day! The implication was not reassuring: like the American troops who burned the Vietnam village in order to save it, God will destroy the earth to prevent wicked mankind from blowing it up. (Or, as one critic of the premillennial nuclear scenario put it, "God so loved the world that he sent it World War III.")[74]

At the same time, echoes of Graham's flirtation in the early 1980s with social activism survived at least vestigially in this 1990 sermon: the arms race was "a spiritual and moral problem," he declared, and whatever humanity's ultimate destiny, Christians must speak out against it. The confusing message reflected the ambivalence of a man of conscience deeply rooted in one intellectual and theological tradition seeking to accommodate himself to another, very different one. Graham went perhaps as far as one could in adapting premillennialism to an ethic of social engagement with the nuclear threat and other issues of global import.

Prophetic Belief and Nuclear Policy

Thus far, our analysis has been textual, focusing on the pronouncements of preachers and prophecy writers. Is it possible to contextualize this evidence and assess its influence, if any, on U.S. nuclear policy? The question is difficult, the evidence sketchy. Hal Lindsey insisted that the impact was direct and dramatic. He described earnest prophecy discussions with newspaper publishers, government officials, and military strategists. When he spoke at the American Air War College, "virtually the entire school turned out, including many officers accompanied by their wives." At the Pentagon, "hundreds . . . jam[med] the room" with more crowding outside.[75] If we move beyond such self-serving anecdotal evidence, two lines of analysis suggest themselves: the direct influence of premillennialist dogma on policymakers, and the more amorphous role of end-time belief in shaping public attitudes on issues of war and peace.

The direct influence of prophecy belief on nuclear decision making surfaced as an issue in the 1980s as the eschatological interests of several Reagan-administration officials became known. Secretary of Defense Caspar Weinberger, asked about the subject in 1982, replied, "I have read the Book of Revelation and yes, I believe the world is going to end—by an act of God, I hope—but every day I think that time is running out." Interior Secretary–designate James Watt, questioned at his confirmation hearing about preserving the environment for future generations, forthrightly replied, "I do not know how many future generations we can count on before the Lord returns." Reagan's Surgeon General, C. Everett Koop, attended a 1971 prophecy conference in Jerusalem and reported on it for a leading premillennial journal.[76]

The most sensational scenario, of course, was the election of a president who believed that nuclear war was inevitable and set out to help God bring it about. In *Kingdoms in Conflict* (1987), born-again Christian Charles Colson, a former Nixon advisor, offered a fictional account of just such a situation. Colson's "President Hopkins," an amalgam of Pat Robertson and Jerry Falwell, spends his spare moments in the Oval Office reading Ezekiel and telephoning premillennialist faculty members at "Mid-South Seminary." He defiantly tells critics, "I ran my campaign on the Bible, and I intend to run this nation on the Bible." Hopkins arranges the clandestine demolition of the Dome of the Rock, an Islamic shrine in Jerusalem, to make way for the prophesied rebuilding of the Jewish Temple, despite (or because of) the warnings of his theological advisors that this action will set the stage for Armageddon. As Colson's account ends, CBN is playing

"The Battle Hymn of the Republic" while the Dome of the Rock crumbles into ruin.[77]

For a time in the 1980s, such a scenario seemed eerily plausible. Ronald Reagan's abiding interest in prophecy, dating from his youthful immersion in the theology of the Christian ("Campbellite") Church, deepened in the 1960s and 1970s through contacts with Billy Graham, Hollywood minister Donn Moomaw, born-again entertainer Pat Boone, and other prophecy believers. "Apparently never in history," then-governor Reagan told *Christian Life* magazine in 1968, "have so many of the prophecies come true in such a relatively short time." *The Late Great Planet Earth* strengthened Reagan's prophecy belief, and at a 1971 political dinner in Sacramento shortly after a leftist coup in Libya (a nation mentioned in Ezekiel as one of Israel's invaders), Reagan observed somberly:

> That's a sign that the day of Armageddon isn't far off . . . Everything is falling into place. It can't be long now. Ezekiel says that fire and brimstone will be rained upon the enemies of God's people. That must mean that they'll be destroyed by nuclear weapons.[78]

During the White House years Reagan's prophecy interests continued. In 1983 he told a lobbyist for Israel:

> You know, I turn back to your ancient prophets in the Old Testament and the signs foretelling Armageddon, and I find myself wondering if we're the generation that's going to see that come about. I don't know if you've noted any of those prophecies lately, but believe me, they certainly describe the times we're going through.[79]

Asked about the subject by newsman Marvin Kalb in one of the 1984 presidential debates with Walter Mondale (as Nancy groaned "Oh, no" off camera), Reagan acknowledged a "philosophical" interest in Armageddon, and noted that "a number of theologians" believed "the prophecies are coming together that portend that." But no one knew, he insisted (echoing Falwell and others), whether "Armageddon is 1,000 years away or the day after tomorrow." In any event, Reagan concluded, he had "never seriously warned and said we must plan according to Armageddon." The issue faded in the late 1980s, as improved East-West relations eased nuclear-war fears. Reagan's successor, George Bush, while proclaiming himself a born-again Christian ("I'm a clear-cut affirmative to that"), did not, so far as one could tell, interest himself deeply in the arcana of eschatology.[80]

But for a time in the mid-eighties, the politics of prophecy elicited intense public discussion. The *New York Times* worried that "Armageddonist" advisors might subtly influence nuclear policy, and one hundred prominent religious leaders urged Reagan to disavow the dogma that nuclear holocaust is foreordained in the Bible. Such beliefs could lead to "historical fatalism," they cautioned, and prove self-fulfilling. People for the American Way, a liberal lobbying group, warned of the "disdain for peace" implicit in Armageddon belief. Wrote columnist Hunter S. Thompson in 1987: "The president is very keen on the Book of Revelation. I love it for the sharp and terrible power of the language, but Dutch really believes it." After quoting a particularly lurid passage from Revelation, Thompson went on:

> A lot of acid freaks have been taken away in white jackets with extremely long sleeves for seeing things like that, but the visions normally don't last for more than 72 hours. Reagan, though, has believed in the coming of these hideous "four beasts with six wings and full of eyes within" for something like 72 years.[81]

Even some evangelicals expressed uneasiness about having a premillennialist in the Oval Office. An editor of *Sojourners,* the voice of a small but articulate band of evangelical social activists, warned of the politicization of prophecy:

> The popular link between nuclear weapons and portions of apocalyptic scripture began as an innocent, if biblically shaky, attempt by simple people of faith to make some sense out of a new and horrifying evil . . . But the linking of "our" weapons and "God's" plan became a part of presidential rhetoric, and frighteningly it has provided the one thing our military planners have always lacked—a religious justification for nuclear weapons.[82]

On the other hand, evangelicals active in New Right politics denied that premillenial belief implied advocacy of nuclear war. Only a "small minority" of evangelicals, contended Harold Lindsell in 1984, opposed efforts to prevent nuclear holocaust as contrary to God's prophetic plan. Two Falwell associates, Ed Dobson and Ed Hindson, writing in the conservative journal *Policy Review* in 1986, insisted on

God's sole responsibility for prophetic fulfillment. "A lot of talk about speeding up the apocalypse would be stopped," they complained, "if more people understood that prophecy cannot be altered." But despite such reassurances, nagging worries persisted that apocalyptic belief might inspire some future president or military leader to try, in Michael Barkun's nice phrase, "to make the inevitable, paradoxically, even more certain."[83]

And what of the second question: How did nearly half a century of books, articles, cassettes, films, and sermons finding nuclear war foreshadowed in prophecy shape the larger climate of public opinion? Few studies of nuclear attitudes include religious belief as a variable, but the limited data available do pinpoint prophetic belief as an important and neglected factor. In a 1984 Yankelovich poll, for example, 39 percent of the respondents said that biblical prophecies of Earth's destruction by fire referred to nuclear war, with 25 percent convinced that God would spare them personally from the coming holocaust. Danny Collum, the *Sojourners* editor, recalled the large urban Southern Baptist church he had attended as a youth in the late 1960s and early 1970s as full of "lay, self-taught 'prophecy experts' who regularly turned Sunday School classes into seminars on the 'signs' of our apocalyptic nuclear times." The pastor of a Dallas-area Baptist church observed in 1989 that many of his parishioners professed little concern about the nuclear threat; they believed either that God would never permit nuclear war, or that if it did come, it would be as "part of God's sovereign plan which cannot be altered."[84]

Although the Falwell spokesmen writing in *Policy Review* found no nuclear-policy significance in premillennialism, the insistence of countless postwar prophecy writers on the futility of efforts to limit the arms race or to ease Cold War tensions had obvious policy implications. As one author declared flatly in 1970, disarmament "will never be achieved this side of the millennium." Another in 1972 found some antinuclear campaigners "very subversive" and under communist influence. "Arms Control Agreements Always Fail," proclaimed a third in 1978, as negotiations on the ill-fated SALT II treaty crept forward. In *The Late Great Planet Earth* Lindsey warned that Antichrist would delude the world with promises of peace. The prophetic scriptures, he told *Eternity* in 1977, underscored the need for America to maintain "a strong military posture" and the readiness to use its military might.[85]

With the politicization of fundamentalism in the 1980s, such pronouncements increased. Via TV and mass-market paperbacks, prophecy writers commented on nuclear-policy issues from a conservative, promilitary perspective. Earlier writers had rejected official propaganda portraying the nation's growing nuclear arsenal as a guarantor of peace and stressed that America would not escape the end-time holocaust. These themes did not wholly disappear in the 1980s, but many prophecy writers, increasingly mobilized into the ranks of the New Right, now treated God's prophetic plan and Reagan's military buildup as indistinguishable. Lindsey's 1981 bestseller, *The 1980s: Countdown to Armageddon,* was even more blatantly political than his earlier works. Rabidly nationalistic and virulently anti-Soviet (with charts showing the Russians' alleged nuclear superiority), *Countdown* insisted that the "Bible supports building a powerful military force," including more nuclear missiles, and urged readers to make themselves heard politically.[86] A book more in tune with the beefed-up military spending and anti-Soviet rhetoric of the early Reagan presidency is hard to imagine.

A strident chorus of prophecy writers—characterized by one critic as "the court prophets"—supported the weapons buildup of the 1980s and dismissed peace activism as at best "superficial window dressing" masking history's inexorable march to Armageddon. Falwell in 1983 lashed out at the movement for a freeze on the production and deployment of nuclear weapons as a "suicidal effort to force our country into . . . unilateral disarmament" and assure the victory of communism. Proclaimed James Robison, the premillennialist television preacher who delivered an invocation at the 1984 Republican National Convention: "Any teaching of peace prior to [Christ's] return is heresy . . . It's against the Word of God; it's Antichrist." In a 1985 novel about the end times, Antichrist wins a world following by espousing nuclear disarmament.[87]

Even Harold Lindsell, while denying that prophecy believers pined for nuclear war and insisting that all "reasonable men, including Christians, should try to prevent any use of nuclear bombs . . . and wars of any kind around the globe," undercut this apparently forthright statement by insisting on the inevitability of end-time wars as "part of God's plan." Belying his conciliatory tone, Lindsell denounced peace activists for "helping the enemy," attacked the nuclear freeze campaign as KGB-inspired, implicitly endorsed Reagan's Star

Wars proposal, and approvingly cited Edward Teller's debunking of the "myths" about the devastating effects of nuclear war.[88]

Unquestionably this wave of blatantly political commentary on nuclear issues by prophecy popularizers helped shape the political culture, as millions of Americans absorbed supposedly Bible-based teachings that proclaimed history's imminent and catastrophic end. As Robert Jewett of Garrett Theological Seminary observed in 1984, Ronald Reagan's musings on prophecy, like his reflections on other matters, were "uncannily close to the public pulse." Despite some interpreters' efforts to distinguish nuclear war from the eschatological events portrayed in Revelation, such hermeneutic subtleties escaped many grassroots prophecy believers for whom, as the 1984 Yankelovich survey revealed, "Armageddon" and "World War III" were virtually indistinguishable. Many cultural observers outside the premillennial camp expressed fears that Armageddon theology would hasten the holocaust its proponents saw as foreordained. As a British churchman put it, "One rather frightening by-product of this process of [prophetic] interpretation is that it is so easy to *create* the very situation which is being described, so that the interpretation . . . brings about its own fulfillment."[89]

My own sense is that the connection between grassroots prophecy belief and nuclear-weapons policy, while real, was subterranean and indirect. Few post-1945 prophecy believers consciously sought to bring on Armageddon as quickly as possible. Rather, convinced that the Bible foretells the end and secure in the knowledge that believers will be spared, they tended toward passive acquiescence in the nuclear-arms race and Cold War confrontation. As Stephen O'Leary has argued, "The real issue is not . . . whether some born-again believer is going to get his hands on the button that could destroy all of us, but on the way this interpretation of end-time prophecy conditions all our expectations . . . , [making nuclear war seem] a perverse fulfillment of divine destiny." The assimilation of nuclear holocaust into the comfortably familiar premillennial scenario, agreed a young Southern Baptist minister critical of the prophetic views prevalent in his denomination, "encourage[s] social and political complacency." It "may lead to exciting preaching, attract a large following, and even pad the prophet's pocketbook," he concludes, but it "falls far short of responsible biblical interpretation."[90]

In the early postwar period, prophetic interpretations of inevitable atomic war led to skepticism not only about efforts to diminish the nuclear threat, but also about official rationalizations of the nuclear-arms race as a guarantor of peace. To a slight degree, this attitude was apparent into the 1980s. A 1984 prophecy expositor, for example, interpreted the breaking of the seals in the Book of Revelation (antecedent to a series of horrible afflictions for humankind) as a foretelling of "the destructive power of militarism." The vast firepower available to modern nation-states, he said, invoking an image of the demonic familiar to prophecy believers, "is why [they] can so easily become beastly"—hardly a ringing endorsement of U.S. nuclear-weapons policies.[91] But such critical assessments were rare in the politicized prophecy writings of the Reagan years.

One might argue that the prophecy popularizers, in compelling some readers not avidly political to confront the reality of nuclear war, unwittingly served the antinuclear cause. This function seems at best minor and peripheral. Indeed, not only premillennialism's theology but also its vocabulary was more anesthetizing than energizing. In contrast to the rhetorical strategies of antinuclear activists, who translated the abstract calculus of nuclear war into gripping accounts of emotional trauma, radiation's medical effects, and the devastation a missile attack would bring to specific cities, the "nuclear war" of the prophecy writers had, with rare exceptions, little tangible reality or affective power. They spoke of billions killed, of cities obliterated, of oceans poisoned, of "a bloodbath of astounding proportions,"[92] but the prose remained curiously inert. One reacts in much the same way as to King Saul's smiting of the Amalekites in I Samuel. Did the Amalekites bleed and moan? Did Amalekite children cry for their mothers?

The seventeenth-century biblical language retained by many prophecy writers—armies "perish," God "slays" or "chastises" his enemies—further emasculated the prose. The distancing from reality built into the language of nuclear strategists noted by Robert Jay Lifton, Carol Cohn, and others has its counterpart in the prophetic literature.[93] The theology may insist on the terrible literalness of these "inerrant" prophecies, but the rhetoric is mythic, a fairy tale domesticated through many tellings. The "billions of dead" are not flesh-and-blood human beings with families, hopes, and aspirations; they are eschatological zombies, signposts marking another stage in a sequence of familiar events.

Premillennialism's fundamental structure, as well as its rhetoric, encouraged skepticism toward efforts to reduce the U.S.-Soviet nuclear competition. *Nations* are central to biblical prophecy. Of the Bible's 480-odd references to "nation" and "nations," some 70 are found in the books of Daniel, Ezekiel, and Revelation. During the Tribulation, Antichrist rules "all . . . nations." At Armageddon, where "the kings of the earth and of the whole world" gather, Jesus Christ returns "to smite the nations; and . . . rule them with a rod of iron." In the Millennium, Christ governs "all people, nations, and languages." In the prophecies, in short, *nations* remain intact to the end of history and beyond. Discussion of "the nations" pervaded the writings of John Darby, Cyrus Scofield, and subsequent interpreters. Wrote Doug Clark in *Shockwaves of Armageddon,* after describing the national rivalries that will worsen as the end nears: "Is this the plan of God? If you believe that the powers that be are ordained of God (Romans 13:1), and if you believe that prophecy must be fulfilled in order to bring about the return of Christ, then this must be of God." Conversely, in the grammar of premillennialism, all forms of political organization beyond the national level were associated with Antichrist—and thus deeply suspect. Prophecy evangelist Hilton Sutton drew laughter and applause in his 1988 appearance in Madison, Wisconsin, when he jeered at "the United Nothing in New York." [94] Premillennial belief thus emphasized the centrality of national power calculations in discussions of nuclear policy; encouraged the view that nuclear-weapons competition among nations is a natural expression of the divine order of things; and deepened suspicion of any individual, organization, or movement seeking to address the issue from a supranational or global perspective.

How many U.S. premillennialists acquiesced in a long series of governmental decisions that pushed the nuclear-arms race to new levels of menace, in the belief that the entire process was a foreordained inevitability? How many did *not* become involved in the late-1940s effort toward international atomic-energy control, the test-ban movement of the 1950s, or the nuclear-weapons freeze campaign of the early 1980s, in the conviction that such efforts were doomed to failure, and indeed ran counter to God's plan for mankind? If national conflict must go on to the end of time, and if nuclear cataclysm awaits us at the last turning of history's long path, then are not efforts to deviate from that course pointless and perhaps even impious? Believers' energies, the logic of premillennialism makes evident, are better spent in winning souls for Christ than in trying to shape world events.

Explaining premillennialism to *Policy Review* readers in 1986, Falwell aides Dobson and Hindson argued that only a "relatively small group" of "extreme fundamentalists" had "given up on the world" because of their eschatology and become "complacent about evils such as nuclear proliferation." How could Falwell support Reagan's Strategic Defense Initiative, they asked, if he thought no human effort could influence our nuclear fate?[95]

Certainly it would be unwise to offer sweeping generalizations about all premillennialists, or to posit a crude cause-and-effect relationship between this belief system and an automatic acceptance of the inevitability of nuclear holocaust. Yet the implications of premillennial doctrine, as well as the empirical evidence of public-opinion data and a mass of popular prophecy writing, suggests that the links between premillennialism and nuclear attitudes were stronger and more unsettling than Dobson and Hindson wished to concede.

Gordon Kaufman of Harvard Divinity School spoke to this issue in his 1982 presidential address to the American Academy of Religion. To find in prophecy the message that nuclear holocaust represents "the ultimate expression of God's sovereignty over history," he said, "is not only an ultimate evasion of our responsibility as human beings; it is demonically to invoke the divine will as a justification for that very evasion." To teach that nuclear cataclysm is inevitable (or, conversely, impossible because God would not permit it), he went on, means "cutting the nerve of human responsibility." In an age of nuclear menace and a witches' brew of environmental hazards, he concluded, "traditional images of divine providential care have become not only outmoded, they have become misleading and dangerous, and must be thoroughly reworked."[96]

A similar perspective informed *Blessed Assurance,* A. G. Mojtabai's 1986 report on nuclear attitudes in Amarillo, home of the Pantex Corporation, a hydrogen-bomb assembly plant. Mojtabai quickly discovered that the worldview of Pantex workers and Amarillans generally was inseparable from their fundamentalist religious beliefs—an interpenetration of the mundane and the sacred summed up in an Amarillo advertising sign:

JESUS CHRIST IS KING OF KINGS
ALTERNATORS STARTED

Time and again in her interviews Mojtabai found variations on a single core belief: God controls history; nuclear war, if it occurs, will not result from human action or inaction, but from God's prophetic plan. And, of course, believers will be spared whatever terrors lie ahead. One resident put it: "There's a possibility of nuclear war, but if it comes, it's because God allowed it. I believe as a Christian I'm ready to go home at any time—the world stinks." The Reverend Charles Jones, pastor of Amarillo's 2,600-member Second Baptist Church, echoed the point: "Some day we may blow ourselves up with all the bombs . . . But I still believe God's going to be in control . . . If He chooses to use nuclear war, then who am I to argue with that?" In complex and subtle ways, Mojtabai came to realize, premillennial doctrine enabled men and women abetting the nuclear-arms race in the most direct way imaginable to distance themselves emotionally from the implications of their work. Amarillo represented in microcosm vast stretches of the American religious and cultural landscape. Mojtabai concluded:

> The danger is not limited to possible actions by individuals in government or foreign policy positions, or working in nuclear weapons plants and launch sites, who might consider themselves instruments of Providence and decide to help the millennium along. It lurks everywhere, and deeply, in the habits of mind and heart of innumerable ordinary citizens who vote for those who help make policy.[97]

Passivity, whatever its theological underpinnings, is also a political stance. Insofar as prophecy belief influenced citizens to avoid confronting nuclear issues in the Cold War era, it had direct political implications—implications that became explicit in the 1980s. "As the fundamentalists moved into the partisan political arena," Collum noted in 1986, "they brought their theories about nuclear war and the endtime along with them"[98]—theories that saw a certain inevitability to the military buildup and heightening of Cold War tension in the early Reagan era. In these years the premillennial eschatology that had saturated grassroots religious culture for decades converged with a larger rightward thrust in American life in a synergistic process that, for a time at least, transformed the political landscape.

But has not Armageddon become passé? With the apparent end of the Cold War as the 1990s begin, global nuclear conflict seems a nightmare from which the world has blessedly awakened. Certainly the convulsive changes in the Soviet Union and Eastern Europe have had profound implications for prophecy belief, as we shall explore in later chapters. But given the durability of the ancient cosmology, and the resourcefulness of prophecy writers in adapting their scenarios to shifting events—not to mention the continued risk of nuclear confrontation, particularly in the volatile (and prophetically significant) Middle East—this theme seems likely to continue to figure prominently among those invoked by prophecy writers in documenting humankind's bleak prospects. Like frugal homemakers, they learned over the centuries to recycle their basic themes. The genre grows by accretion—rarely abandoning a theme, simply adding new ones as world conditions change. Certainly a motif as powerful as the melting of the earth with fervent heat is unlikely to vanish entirely from the repertoire of prophetic themes. Should history take a more menacing turn (and who would confidently predict that it will not?), premillennialist images of a foreordained cataclysm will be available to make sense of events, and offer a paradoxical reassurance, as men and women peer into the mists of an opaque and frightening future.

5 Ezekiel as the First Cold Warrior

og will come from the north. For millions of Americans in the decades after World War II, the Soviet Union loomed not merely as a Marxist society committed to an alien political and economic system, or even as an expansive power bent on world domination. Beyond all this, for many evangelicals and fundamentalists, Russia was the nation whose prophesied invasion of Israel would trigger a global cataclysm of horrendous proportions—a cataclysm that would leave the Soviet Union a smoldering ruin. For prophecy believers, the Cold War posed not merely military, diplomatic, and ideological challenges—it was quite literally a struggle with a power singled out by God for a demonic end-time role.

Gog, Magog, and the King of the North

Various biblical passages provide the basis for finding Russia in prophecy, including allusions to "the king of the north" (as in Dan. 11:15); to the north as a source of danger (for instance, "Out of the north an evil shall break forth upon all the inhabitants of the land"—Jer. 1:14); and specifically to a mysterious northern ruler named Gog. The best-known of these passages, Ezekiel 38, details Gog's invasion of Israel:

> And the word of the Lord came unto me, saying,
> Son of man, set thy face against Gog, the land of Magog, the chief prince of Meshech and Tubal, and prophesy against him.
> And say, Thus saith the Lord God; Behold, I am against thee, O Gog, the chief prince of Meshech and Tubal:
> And I will turn thee back, and put hooks into thy jaws, and I will bring thee forth, and all thine army, horses, and horsemen, all of them clothed with all sorts of armour, even a great company with bucklers and shields, all of them handling swords:
> Persia, Ethiopia, and Libya with them; all of them with shield and helmet:
> Gomer, and all his bands; the house of Togarmah of the north quarters, and all his bands: and many people with thee . . .

> And thou shalt come from thy place out of the north parts, thou, and many people with thee, all of them riding upon horses, a great company and a mighty army.[1]

The Book of Revelation picks up this motif, as Gog and Magog join in Satan's final rebellion against God at the end of the Millennium.[2]

Who is Gog, and how does all of this prophecy involve the Soviet Union? As so often in the study of apocalyptic belief, a long running start is advisable. Magog appears in Genesis (together with Gomer, Tubal, and Meshech) as a grandson of Noah, but this fact sheds little light on the Ezekiel reference. In the first century A.D., the Jewish historian Flavius Josephus identified Gog with "the Scythians," by then a generic term for various feared peoples of the north. By the late fourth century, according to Saint Jerome, the "Gog = Scythians" equation had been widely accepted by the Jews.[3]

From the beginning of Christian prophetic exegesis, Gog's identity puzzled theologians and lay interpreters alike. Augustine viewed the term as representing all unbelievers. Joachim of Fiore, as well as various medieval cartographers, saw Gog and Magog as tribes from beyond the Caucasus that would invade at the end of time. With the rise of Islam, and specifically of the Ottoman Turks in the late thirteenth century, Gog came to be firmly identified with this aggressive and much-feared power. For centuries nearly all English and Continental prophecy writers wove the Ottoman Empire into their end-time scenarios, some hopefully interpreting the drying up of the Euphrates River in Revelation as symbolic of the Ottomans' eventual decline.[4]

The Turk-as-Gog theme figured prominently in American prophecy writing of the colonial and early national periods. The seventeenth-century poet Anne Bradstreet wove it into one of her verses; Elhanan Winchester in 1788 identified the attacking armies of Ezekiel 38 as all the Islamic nations combined, and Gog as "the Grand Turk." As late as 1919, a U.S. interpreter still identified Turkey as "the king of the north." In Greece the hated Turks continue to this day to be associated with Gog.[5]

But the Turks never won unanimous support as Gog. Sir Robert Anderson had no love for the Ottomans—"a clique of Pachas who, ghoul-like, fatten on the misery around them"—and welcomed their decline as "a blessing to suffering humanity." But to view Turkey as vital to God's eternal plan, wrote Anderson in 1884, was "the merest trifling with the solemn language of Scripture, and an outrage on common sense."[6]

Meanwhile, a new contender for the role of Gog had emerged: Russia. The first fateful linking of the two remains obscure; an 1834 British prophecy writer, identifying Russia as "the king of the north" of Daniel 11, quoted a still earlier author who, in reaching the same conclusion, had written, "Russia has not yet attained the maturity of her strength . . . Who is able to predict her future greatness, or to tell how far her limits may yet extend?"[7]

Those who found Russia in Ezekiel 38 rested their case in part on the phrase "chief prince" in verse 3, a translation of the Hebrew *nesi rosh*. The editors of the 1611 King James Bible rendered "rosh" as "chief," but later scholars argued that it was a proper name and that the phrase should be translated "prince of Rosh." The eighteenth-century British churchman and Bible scholar William Lowth, for example, took this position in his multivolume *Commentary on the Prophets* (1714–1725). (In fact, the case for "prince of Rosh" is strong: the Septuagint translation of the Old Testament from Hebrew to Greek, prepared in Alexandria in the third century B.C., treats "Rosh" as a proper name, as do the English and American revised versions of the Bible published in 1880 and 1890.)[8]

The German Hebraicist Wilhelm Gesenius (1786–1842), professor of theology at the University of Halle in Prussia, played a key role in the process by which Gog came to be identified as Russia. Gesenius, whose Old Testament lexicon of 1828 long stood as a standard reference work, viewed "Rosh" not only as a proper name but as an early form of the word "Russia." In another step that would prove highly influential for prophecy interpretation, he also claimed that "Meshech" and "Tubal" were present-day Moscow and the Siberian city of Tobolsk. The historian Dwight Wilson has suggested that the surge of Prussian patriotism following the Treaty of Tilsit (1807), by which Napoleon and Alexander I of Russia sharply reduced Prussia's territory and autonomy, created a congenial political environment in Germany for prophetic interpretations casting Russia in a sinister role.[9]

Soon translated into English (a U.S. edition appeared in 1836), Gesenius' lexicon influenced the early dispensationalists. John Darby identified Gog as Russia in his writings and lecture tours. "In the present day," he declared in 1840, "we may observe Russia extending her power exactly over the nations who will be found under Gog."[10]

The Crimean War (1853–1856), which pitted Russia against England and other countries for dominance in southeastern Europe, stimulated interest in Russia's role in prophecy. John Cumming's book *The End* (1855), a big seller in the United States, popularized the Gog = Russia connection. In the last days, declared Cumming (the nineteenth-century Hal Lindsey), Russia would "burst forth, overcome all resistance, [and] march to Palestine," only to "perish ultimately . . . amid tremendous scenes." The Americans Samuel Baldwin and Fountain Pitts, as we saw in Chapter 3, also viewed Russia as the invader from the north in their sermons and writings of the 1850s, although they identified the United States, rather than Israel, as the target of attack.[11]

In the late nineteenth century this interpretation won broad support on both sides of the Atlantic. Ezekiel 38 "is supposed to be the earliest historical allusion to the people afterwards known as the Russians," wrote the Reverend Henry Cowles of Oberlin College in 1867. "The Russian policy . . . of steady aggression, not only in Europe but in Asia," noted an 1888 author, foreshadowed the attack prophesied in the Bible. Even more explicitly, an 1892 writer found Russia's "armed interference and aggression" in eastern Europe and in Afghanistan clear evidence that the end-time invasion was imminent.[12]

Meanwhile, with the rise of historical-critical Bible scholarship, the identification of Russia as Gog had come under attack. Ezekiel was poetry, not history or eschatology, argued Ernst Hengstenberg, professor of theology at Berlin, in a commentary published in English in 1869. Specifically rejecting Gesenius' Rosh = Russia theory, Hengstenberg observed, "The poor Russians have been here very unjustly arranged among the enemies of God's people." The annotator of a college-study edition of the Bible published in England in 1892 accepted the "prince of Rosh" translation but added, "Of course, any connection between the name and Russia is to be rejected."[13]

At the grassroots level, the vague similarity of "Rosh" and "Russia," "Meshech" and "Moscow," not to mention the undeniable geographic fact that Russia lay north of Palestine, gave the theory a commonsense appeal. By the early twentieth century Russia's end-time role had become a staple of premillennialist writing. Arno Gaebelein, for example, often discussed it in his prophecy magazine, *Our Hope.* Russia's move southward "cannot be far off," Gaebelein wrote in 1916. Belief in Russia's end-time invasion of the Holy Land, observed Cyrus

Scofield the same year, was "well-nigh universally held." Scofield himself contributed mightily to this unanimity. His 1909 Reference Bible, following Darby, said of Ezekiel 38, "That the primary reference is to the northern (European) powers, headed up by Russia, all agree." [14]

In Czarist days the *reason* for this invasion remained obscure. Ezekiel provides little help, describing Gog's motives this way:

> To take a spoil, and to take a prey; to turn thine hand upon the desolate places that are now inhabited, and upon the people that are gathered out of the nations, which have gotten cattle and goods, that dwell in the midst of the land. [15]

Some writers simply attributed the invasion to God's will and sought no further explanation. Indeed, the biblical text does imply a divinely ordained action that Gog is helpless to resist: "And I will . . . put hooks into thy jaws, and I will bring thee forth." Perhaps troubled by the bald determinism of this image, most writers tried to explain Russia's invasion in rational terms. One pre-1918 author suggested that because so many Russian pilgrims visited Holy Land shrines, "there is no land under the sun [Russia] would [more] like to possess." Scofield, citing Czarist pogroms, speculated that the attack would arise from Russian anti-Semitism. [16]

When the Bolsheviks seized power in October 1918 and the new regime repudiated Christianity and espoused atheism, history and prophecy seemed to converge; the identification of Russia as Gog took a powerful new lease on life. A 1919 prophecy writer saw "THE BOLSHEVIST GERM" as an unequivocal sign of the last days. Articles with titles such as "The Red Menace" and "When Russia's Bear Meets Judah's Lion," which combined apocalyptic foreboding about Russia's Mideast invasion and communism's spread to the United States, filled prophecy journals of the interwar years. [17] And Soviet atheism provided a more compelling motive for the assault: a nation that denied God would naturally seek to destroy God's chosen people.

With fresh motivation, prophecy writers of the interwar years combed both the Bible and the newspapers for evidence of Russia's end-time role. Donald Grey Barnhouse, for example, argued that Nahum 2:3—"The shield of his mighty men is made red"—foretold the day when "a 'red' army" would invade Palestine. A 1936 writer speculated that Russia might invade Palestine in order to seize an oil pipeline newly completed to the port of Haifa. While speculative detail proliferated, most writers agreed on the key point: Bible prophecy pinpointed the Soviet Union. "Satan is mobilizing for the last battle of this age," noted a 1934 author; "he has indeed established his head-quarters in Moscow." [18]

Even during the World War II years of U.S.-Soviet alliance, prophecy writers continued to identify Russia as Gog. A 1944 work discussed *The Red Terror and Bible Prophecy*. Examining *Russian Events in the Light of Bible Prophecy* in 1942, Louis Bauman summed up his thesis in chapter titles such as "Gog's War on God," "Gog's Invasion of Israel's Land," and "Any American or British Alliance with Gog Is Abnormal." [19] After a century of interpretation identifying Russia as the demonic end-time power, premillennialist prophecy writers entered the postwar era.

Russia and Prophecy in the Cold War

From 1945 to the early 1990s, scores of prophecy popularizers endorsed and embellished the ancient belief that Russia will attack Israel in the last days. The war had scarcely ended when one proclaimed that the forthcoming Soviet invasion would make Pearl Harbor "look like child's play." In 1947, a moment of flux in U.S. views of Moscow, *Christian Life* made its position crystal clear: "One thing certain, according to God's Word, is that one day—perhaps in the near future—Russia will strike." [20]

As the Cold War settled in, prophecy writers, like their Crimean War predecessors, issued a stream of pronouncements on Russia's end-time role. "The spotlight of prophecy . . . cast[s] its all-revealing rays upon *Russia,*" declared one in 1954, "that sinister nation . . . so persistently in the limelight at the present time." That Soviet aggression would soon engulf the world in war ought not surprise believers, he said. "Centuries ago it was foretold that Russia would gain her allies by craftily swallowing them up under the pretense of 'guarding' them. Today we see this very thing happening as she overcomes one defenseless people after another in the assumed role of 'protector'!" [21]

These authors emphasized the historical roots of their focus on Russia. Endlessly they cited Gesenius, Bishop Lowth, Scofield, and other pre-1945 writers; quoted "able and learned ethnologists and geographers"; and otherwise invoked the venerable hermeneutic tradition identifying Russia as Gog and linking "Rosh," "Meshech," and "Tubal," to modern Soviet place names. Wilbur Smith in 1952 traced the word "Russia" to Proclus, a fifth-century patriarch of Constantinople who, in a sermon against the Huns, had recalled Ezekiel's prophecy of northern invaders led by the prince of Rosh. By the ninth century, Smith went on, Byzantine writers and officials, following Proclus, routinely called the lands to the north "Rucia." Eventually the Russians themselves adopted the name. Concluded Smith solemnly, "And so this nation, so determined to remove from its people the very belief in God, has branded upon her . . . a name . . . derived from a prophecy in God's Word."[22]

S. Maxwell Coder, vice president of Moody Bible Institute, rehearsed Smith's argument in a 1963 address on "The Future of Russia," which he later published in *Moody Monthly* and eventually incorporated in his 1984 book, *The Final Chapter.* (Like other writers, prophecy expounders recycle their material.) Tracing the history of the word "Rosh" in various Bible translations and its alleged evolution into "Russia" in medieval Constantinople, Coder, echoing Smith, affirmed, "The name is branded upon that godless nation as though God wanted the whole world to know that this is the people He has foredoomed to perish upon the mountains of Israel before He sets up His kingdom."[23] The New Scofield Reference Bible of 1967 (which had sold 2.5 million copies by 1990), retained Scofield's original identification of Gog as Russia.

Prophecy writers also marshaled the geographic evidence for the Gog = Russia link: not only is the Soviet Union north of Israel, but the longitudes of Moscow and Jerusalem are almost precisely the same. Lindsey and other writers noted that the Hebrew term in Ezekiel translated as "north" in the King James Version appears as "uttermost north" or "far north" in other translations, pointing even more inescapably to distant Russia. "On the basis of geography alone," wrote John Walvoord in the *Fundamentalist Journal* in 1984, "it seems quite clear that the only nation which could possibly be referred to as coming from the far north would be the nation Russia."[24]

In finding Russia in prophecy, these writers insisted, they were not simply echoing Cold War rhetoric but following a long hermeneutic tradition. The focus on Russia was "not the conclusion of prophetic opportunists," insisted Jack Van Impe in 1979; it arose from well-established interpretive principles. "My belief that Ezekiel 38 and

39 depict a coming disaster for the Soviet Union and her allies does not stem from a feeling of animosity," added Herbert Vander Lugt in 1983; "I don't think these chapters make good sense when interpreted in any other way." [25]

These protestations had some validity: the Gog = Russia theory long antedated the Cold War. But as this interpretation evolved after 1945, it took on an intense political coloration and a highly contemporary aura, as popularizers wove current events into their scenarios. "In view of Ezekiel's prediction," wrote Milton Lindberg of the American Messianic Fellowship soon after the war, "it is thrilling to learn that in World War II Russia strengthened her hold upon both Turkey and Persia." Russia's domination of East Germany and China (widely viewed as key players in the end-time drama), added Coder in 1963, "surely mean[s] that the stage is being set for the earth-shaking events of the last days." Articles in the secular press that seemed to confirm Ezekiel's prophetic scenario, such as Joseph Alsop's "Russia's Menacing New Challenge in the Middle East" (*Reader's Digest,* August 1970), received heavy attention. [26]

The novelty of popularizers such as Lindsey lay not in incorporating Russia into their prophetic scheme—prophecy writers had been doing that for a century—but in the ingenuity of their updated scenarios, as they vied to infuse the familiar recital of end-time events with an aura of evening-news timeliness. So overwhelming was Russia's military superiority, wrote David Webber in 1979, that Leonid Brezhnev or "his immediate successor" might at any moment attack Israel. The 1980 Soviet intervention in Afghanistan, proclaimed a prophecy writer that year, was clearly the beginning of the end-time invasion foretold in Ezekiel 38. [27]

A 1981 writer, finding prophetic significance in the installation of a Marxist government in Ethiopia, added that the overthrow of the pro-U.S. Shah of Iran had opened the door for an alliance between "fanatic Muslims and . . . atheistic Soviets," united in their hatred of Israel. [28] Such events, marveled the authors of a 1987 update of *The Coming Russian Invasion of Israel,* proved that the Soviet Union and other nations mentioned in prophecy were "moving inexorably toward their great moment of destiny" and underscored Ezekiel's divine inspiration in foreseeing that "roving bands of virtual cave people" would one day become a great nation, Russia. [29] While the prophecy expounders avidly cataloged every sign of Russia's aggressive intent, particularly toward its southern neighbors, they ignored or explained away evidence that did *not* fit the scenario or ran counter to it, such as the Soviet *withdrawal* from Afghanistan or the rabid anticommunism of Iran's Shiite Muslim rulers.

The prophecy popularizers of the 1970s and 1980s discussed Russia's destiny in forms calculated for mass appeal. Hal Lindsey's books, uniformly anti-Soviet, featured catchy chapter titles such as "Russia Is A Gog" and "The Bear Moves Southward" as well as pages of charts showing Moscow's alleged military superiority. While the TV ministries of Jerry Falwell, Pat Robertson, and Jimmy Swaggart, all of whom emphasized the Soviet Union's end-time role, attracted much attention, these electronic-church superstars were not alone. "Pastor Chuck" Smith, founder of a network of West Coast churches linked to his Calvary Chapel, for example, reached a national audience via some 125 radio stations and nearly 20 television channels, and further disseminated his prophetic message—in which Moscow's imminent attack on Israel figured prominently—via paperbacks, films, and audio and video cassettes.[30]

Jack Van Impe endlessly discussed Russia's end-time role. "The latest CIA and British intelligence reports concerning the Soviet Union . . . are very grim," he proclaimed in *11:59 and Counting;* "Russia is preparing for war." Van Impe offered his sermon "The Coming War with Russia" on videocassette; his 1975 TV special "The Middle East, World War III, and Christ's Return," won an Angel, the most coveted award of religious broadcasters.[31] Via TV, radio, paperbacks, cassettes, and local "prophecy conferences," scores of obscure expositors spread the word of Moscow's prophesied future.

So hackneyed had this scenario become by the 1980s that its proponents hardly bothered with the geographic and linguistic evidence marshaled by earlier writers. Ezekiel 38 offered "an exact description of Russia," declared Hilton Sutton the same year, as though noting a self-evident fact. William Goetz, whose *Apocalypse Next* went through many editions in the 1980s, similarly assumed, with minimal documentation, Russia's invasion of Israel: "It is not a question of *if,* but *when."*[32]

To be sure, this scenario had its critics. Bible scholars who did not embrace the fundamentalist approach to Scripture continued to reject readings that linked Ezekiel 38–39, and the other apocalyptic texts, to modern-day trends and events. The fall of the "imaginary king" Gog and his allies, said the *Westminster Study Edition of the Bible* (1948), symbolized the ultimate triumph of righteousness. The 1965 *Oxford Annotated Bible,* discussing Ezekiel 38, speculated that Gog was probably "a grandiose surrogate for Babylon" and linked "Meschech" and "Tubal" with now-vanished Assyrian cities. It cautioned, however, that "though people and places in apocalyptic literature can often be identified, they are part of the literary equipment and should rarely be taken literally." [33]

Liberal or "mainstream" books about Bible prophecy aimed at general readers similarly advised a symbolic approach. "Connect[ing] biblical prophecies with modern events" required "the greatest caution," noted a Presbyterian theologian in 1982; the apocalypticists foresaw a final struggle between good and evil, he said, but "how this is to work out in history, we are not explicitly told." Gog and the others mentioned in Ezekiel "represent distant people in distant places," declared another author in 1984 and warned against identifying them with present-day nations. The function of apocalyptic texts is "to tell us how to live in the present," he went on (adopting Rudolph Bultmann's view of eschatology), "not to satisfy our curiosity about the future." [34]

Even evangelical prophecy writers occasionally cautioned against fitting these texts to specific current events. "When we find ourselves digging in the prophetic literature for some obscure point," warned Morris Inch, a Bible professor at Wheaton College, an evangelical school in Illinois, "we have almost certainly excavated beyond its intended purpose." The author of Ezekiel used a familiar historical reality of his day, the marauding Scythians and other warrior bands of the north, Inch suggested, to impart a spiritual truth: the menace and danger God's people will always confront in a sinful world. That underlying message, he concluded, would "live on in prophecy when the Scythians (and perhaps the Russians as well) have ceased to be." [35]

Such allegorizing, rare at best in premillennial circles, could hardly compete in marketplace appeal with sensationalized books that found the fate of America's Cold War enemy encoded in the apocalyptic language of Ezekiel. The scholars who viewed the prophecies as assemblages of historic, mythic, and poetic material, and applied to them the same historical-critical methods used in studying noncanonical works, carried weight in liberal seminaries and mainstream churches. Their approach, nonetheless, did not penetrate very deeply that stratum of American evangelicalism where millions of believers, Scofield Bible in one hand and *The Late Great Planet Earth* in the other, had no doubt about the identity of "the prince of Rosh."

At his now-famous 1971 dinner with California legislators, prophecy student Ronald Reagan concisely summed up his view of Russia's end-time role:

> Ezekiel tells us that Gog, the nation that will lead all of the other powers of darkness against Israel, will come out of the north. Biblical scholars have been saying for generations that Gog must be Russia. What other powerful nation is to the north of Israel? None. But it didn't seem to make sense before the Russian revolution, when Russia was a Christian country. Now it does, now that Russia has become communistic and atheistic, now that Russia has set itself against God. Now it fits the de-scription of Gog perfectly.

As the flaming cherries-jubilee dessert bathed the darkened dining room in an eerie glow, Reagan offered a chain of evidence—the crea-tion of the State of Israel in 1948, the recent leftist coup in Libya—to drive home his conclusion: "For the first time ever, everything is in place for the battle of Armageddon and the second coming of Christ." Twelve years later, addressing the National Association of Evangeli-cals, now-President Reagan offered a shorthand version of this same worldview, describing the Soviet Union as an "evil empire" and "the focus of evil in the modern world." [36] Some took this as a speechwrit-er's hyperbole—raw meat for an audience predisposed to view the world in theological terms. Those who understood the depth of Rea-gan's prophecy beliefs realized that the phrases had a quite precise meaning. And those familiar with the stream of apocalyptic teaching about Russia that had coursed through American popular religion for well over a century recognized that the President was far from alone in his beliefs.

Fleshing Out the Scenario

Although Cold War prophecy writers drew on a very old interpretive tradition in identifying Russia as Gog, they elaborated and updated this tradition in important ways. Specifically, they analyzed the Soviet Union's motives for invading Israel in terms that reflected contemporary geopolitical realities and Cold War ideological preoccupations. They also discussed in revealing detail the nations, peoples, and races destined to share Gog's fate.

As we have seen, the *motive* behind Russia's anticipated invasion of Israel had long vexed prophecy interpreters. After the Bolshevik Revolution, with Moscow's official embrace of atheism, the picture became clearer; but Cold War writers, while always mentioning Russian godlessness, sought other explanations as well. Some emphasized Russia's desire for Israel's mineral wealth and natural resources. "In the last days," wrote Harry Ironside in 1949, the Soviet leaders would "look with covetous eyes upon the great developments going on in the land of Palestine, and . . . determine that Russia must have her part of the wealth." Specifically, many writers focused on the Dead Sea, arguing, as did Harry Rimmer in 1946, that its "rich harvest of chemicals," including potash, magnesium chloride, and sodium chloride, would provoke Moscow's greed. "Like some mystical Fort Knox," wrote Merrill Unger in 1973, this salt lake on the border of Israel and Jordan had been storing up mineral resources for millennia, preparing for its eschatological role. (Indeed, as I realized a few years ago in the gift shop of Tel Aviv Airport, the Israelis are already cashing in on this gold mine with a line of cosmetics made from Dead Sea minerals.) By common consent, prophecy writers put an exact price tag on this treasure trove of Dead Sea mineral wealth: $1.2 trillion. Ignoring inflation, they repeated this figure decade after decade—another small example of the genre's deep conservatism. Jack Van Impe upped the estimate to $2 trillion in 1983, but $1.2 trillion remained the favored sum.[37]

Other writers, noting Israel's agricultural productivity, suggested that the Soviet Union's chronic food shortages would trigger the fateful invasion. Salem Kirban's 1968 prophecy work, *Guide to Survival,* argued that Russia's food needs would become desperate as the prophesied famines of Revelation unfolded; the authors of *The Coming Russian Invasion of Israel,* updating their work in 1987, linked the coming famine to the Chernobyl nuclear-power disaster.[38]

In the seventies and eighties many writers portrayed Russia's move against Israel as part of a larger strategy for cornering oil from the Middle East. The era of OPEC (Organization of Petroleum Exporting Countries) and soaring gas prices saw a spate of prophecy books with titles such as *Arabs, Oil, and Energy.* In 1974 John Walvoord and his son collaborated on *Armageddon, Oil, and the Middle East Crisis*—which, we have seen, sold 750,000 copies in English and twelve foreign-language editions. Jerry Falwell in 1979 put a contemporary spin on Ezekiel 38:12: "If one but removes the first two letters from this word 'spoil,' he soon realizes what Russia will really be after—obviously, oil." Chuck Smith's 1978 prophecy film, *Future Survival,* predicted that oil shortages could trigger a Soviet Mideast invasion at any time; Doug Clark's *Shockwaves of Armageddon* described "the coming oil war" in detail and reiterated Falwell's hermeneutic breakthrough in finding "oil" embedded in "spoil." [39]

Other Cold War popularizers, picking up on an idea advanced by Cyrus Scofield years before, pointed to Russian anti-Semitism as a motive for the upcoming invasion. Lindsey in *The Late Great Planet Earth,* while largely ignoring the problem of motivation as he elaborated the military and strategic details of the eschatological conflicts ahead, mentioned in passing Moscow's desire "to utterly destroy the Jewish people." [40]

Most authors offered not just one explanation for Russia's invasion but a smorgasbord of motives. Tim LaHaye, for example, cited Soviet anti-Semitism, a desire for plunder, and, ultimately, "God's sovereign will." Lindsey in 1981 supplemented the anti-Semitism theme with a geopolitical rationale: "Throughout its history, the single most consistent motive of the Soviet Union's military invasions has been the acquisition of warm-water ports for its merchant and naval fleets. Recently, the importance of oil has made the Persian Gulf and the Middle East even more attractive to the Russians." Jack Van Impe, while emphasizing the fundamental role of divine foreordination, also noted the practical considerations that would shape Moscow's calculations: "The Russians . . . will be pleased to cooperate in the conquest of Israel, knowing that when their military forces overrun the Middle East they will control all the wealth there, including the Arab oil." [41]

Along with the geopolitics of Russia's prophesied aggression against Israel, prophecy writers explored the eschatological meaning of communism. The fear of Russia that was gripping the United States should turn Americans to the Bible, wrote John Walvoord in 1955, "the one Book in all the world which tells us the future of Communism. If you want the inside story on Communism, turn to the inside of your Bible." Cold War prophecy writing bristled with somber warnings against the Soviet Union's Marxist leaders, described by Harry Ironside in 1949 as "a thoroughly atheistic group . . . opposed to everything in the way of divine revelation and the recognition of spiritual realities." A speaker at the 1952 New York City prophecy conference noted that while "the devil has too much intelligence to be a Communist," Satan was "using Communism to arrange the political map of the world to suit his own devilish purposes." [42]

Several writers found communist aggression foretold by the prophet Habakkuk:

> O Lord, how long shall I cry, and thou wilt not hear! even cry out unto thee of violence, and thou wilt not save!
> Why dost thou shew me iniquity, and cause me to behold grievance? for spoiling and violence are before me: and there are that raise up strife and contention . . .
> For lo, I raise up the Chaldeans, that bitter and hasty nation, which shall march through the breadth of the land, to possess the dwellingplaces that are not their's . . .
> They shall come all for violence: their faces shall sup up as the east wind, and they shall gather the captivity as the sand.
> And they shall scoff at the kings, and the princes shall be a scorn unto them: they shall deride every strong hold. [43]

Discussing "Habakkuk in the Nuclear Age" in 1963, Wheaton College president V. Raymond Edman found the above passage an explicit preview of "the horrendous cancer of communism." Arthur Bloomfield argued that the "Chaldeans" of the passage referred not to the ancient people of southern Babylonia but figuratively to the Soviet Union. Concluded Bloomfield, "It would be difficult to put into words, even today, a more accurate or concise statement of what happens when Communist gangsters take over a country." The ultimate Soviet threat, John Walvoord argued, was less military than ideological. "More than just an economic theory," he declared, communism was "a movement built upon blasphemy against God" that clearly anticipated the demonic world religion of the Tribulation. Following the logic of this interpretation, the Toronto evangelist John Wesley White in 1981 focused on Marxist ideology as the probable reason for Russia's foreordained ruin. After describing Gog's utter destruction, White commented: "A theological bleeding heart might protest, claiming that the God of love would never permit this to happen to the Soviets. In fact, it's because He is a God of grace that He would likely so act, since unchecked communism simply continues to propagate and inflict its atheism on increasing millions." [44]

Weaving menacing developments at home and abroad into their eschatology, prophecy writers linked predictions of Russia's invasion of Israel with warnings against domestic leftists, liberals, and secular humanists who were preparing the way for Antichrist by their contempt for religion, morality, and traditional values. From this broader perspective, Russia's attack on Israel—"an outpost of democracy standing directly in the way of the communist expansion," as a prophecy work of the mid-1970s put it—became only an episode in a much larger sequence of end-time events. [45]

Nor would Russia be alone. Ezekiel speaks of an alliance of kingdoms, and Cold War prophecy writers worked strenuously to identify its members. Of the five nations mentioned in Ezekiel 38, the identity of "Persia" (Iran) and "Libya" seemed clear. But "Ethiopia" was problematic, while the other two had no obvious contemporary analogues: "Gomer, and all his bands; the house of Togarmah of the north quarters, and all his bands." Togarmah remained a puzzle (though Lindsey linked it to "modern Southern Russia"). But in the nineteenth century the scholarly Gesenius and the popularizer Cumming both identified Gomer as Germany, and later writers followed their lead. Having interpreted the 1918 Brest-Litovsk treaty as a prelude to the Gog-Gomer alliance, prophecy writers, as we saw in Chapter 3, greeted the 1939 Nazi-Soviet pact calmly and even exultantly. [46]

With the division of Germany in 1945, some prophecy writers discerned an aspect of the Gomer = Germany equation they had earlier missed: *West* Germany lay within the old Roman Empire and thus would be part of Antichrist's domain, while Soviet-dominated *East* Germany was "definitely identifiable" as Gog's ally Gomer. Most popularizers, however, did not insist strongly on "Gomer's" precise boundaries. To Lindsey, Gomer represented "a part of the vast area of modern Eastern Europe" under Soviet domination; other authors lumped Gomer and Togarmah together as the "Iron Curtain countries." [47]

Filling out the roster of Gog's allies, prophecy writers turned to the books of Daniel and Revelation. In 1963 S. Maxwell Coder identified "the king of the south" mentioned in Daniel 11 as "a confederacy of African nations with Egypt as the leader." Robert Gromacki in

1970 speculated that this southern power would be "either the Muslim, Pan-Arab alliance led by Egypt, the nationalistic Black African peoples, or both of them." Others viewed Daniel's "king of the south" and Ezekiel's "Ethiopia" as a reference to Africa as a whole. (This interpretation, too, had a long pedigree: Gesenius suggested that "Ethiopia"—the King James translation of the Hebrew "Cush"—more properly referred to a vast region of Africa than to the modern nation of that name.) The Organization of African Unity, founded at Addis Ababa in 1963, various prophecy writers suggested, foreshadowed the southern component of Gog's alliance. "Many of the African nations will be united and allied with the Russians in the invasion of Israel," declared Lindsey in his brisk and assured fashion; "[Africa] will become converted to Communism."[48]

The Kings of the East

The prophecy in Revelation of the drying up of the Euphrates River to make way for "the kings of the east" and "two hundred thousand thousand" mounted warriors was another challenge for biblical interpreters. A 1982 writer found significance in Syria's construction of a dam on the Euphrates that could drain the river "at the flick of a switch." During World War II, as we have seen, the "kings of the east" passage provoked thoughts of Japan. But with Japan's defeat and China's fall to Mao Zedong's communists in 1949, prophecy writers focused on China instead. During the 1950s they portrayed the Sino-Soviet alliance as prefiguring the coming association of Gog and "the kings of the east." A Chinese boast, reported in *Time* magazine, that Beijing could assemble an army of 200 million—the precise figure mentioned in Revelation—attracted much comment.[49]

Many saw the breakup of the Sino-Soviet alliance at the end of the 1950s as a temporary deviation from an alignment foretold in prophecy. Despite their differences, said Lindsey in 1970, both nations still shared a common goal: "total world conquest for Communism." Beijing's cultivation of Washington, Lindsey added in 1977, was "one of the most clever political maneuvers to date." The author of *Red China in Prophecy* deplored President Nixon's rapprochement with China as a "tragic miscalculation" on the scale of King Jehoshaphat's alliance with wicked King Ahab.[50]

Often, however, the discussion slipped away from the ideological plane to an older, deeper level, as explications of "the kings of the east" lapsed into discussions of an undifferentiated tide of "200 million Asiatics" surging westward. Robert Gromacki in 1970 pictured Armageddon as a "climactic struggle between two diametrically opposed worlds of race, color, and creed" pitting "the white segment of the world's civilization" against "the yellow, Oriental peoples of Red China and her neighbors." Echoed Doug Clark in 1982, "They hate the white man now in Communist China." China's "economic adultery with Western nations" would last only "until they can rise and snuff us out," he went on; the "motivating factor" behind Armageddon would be "Oriental hatred of Occidental power in the world." [51]

As Japan's economic challenge to the West grew more intimidating, prophecy writers again ranked that country among "the kings of the east." As early as 1962, John Walvoord listed Japan's resurgence with "the rising might of Red China" and "the growing force of nationalism in India" as developments that would soon bring an Asiatic army to the banks of the Euphrates. Japan would "go about her peaceful pursuits in accord with the decrees of the Western democracies until the Rapture," predicted a California religious broadcaster in 1968, then would join the other eastern powers in attacking the West. Merrill Unger, discussing the World War II defeat of Admiral Yamamoto in the Battle of the Coral Sea, wrote in 1973: "Plainly, divine providence was at work. The time was not yet ripe for God to loosen the restraint imposed upon Asiatic peoples." That restraint would soon end as "a huge Oriental army, equipped with nuclear weapons" become "a scourge in God's hands" to punish the wicked. [52]

The racist subtext of these views emerged with particular clarity in a 1974 Moody Press prophecy book by a Kentucky Baptist minister:

> Western Europe has always dreaded an invasion of Asiatics whose sheer numbers could inundate them. America also dreads a conflict with the raw hordes of Orientals apart from the protection of nuclear arms. Their numbers are awesome. Like the plague of locusts described in the first chapter of Joel, these people, if we did not have the deterrent of nuclear weapons, could swarm over the western world and deluge it with the sheer weight of their numbers. This seems to happen at the close of the tribulation. [53]

Salem Kirban's 1970 novel, *666,* evoked the scene as Beijing's masters harangued Chinese troops about to move westward:

> "We will conquer all of Asia, we will conquer the Middle East, we will conquer Africa. Tomorrow 200 MILLION warriors will march. We will not be stopped until the whole world kneels at our feet. We will be victorious." The ovation was spontaneous and tremendous as the citizens raised their familiar Red Book and shouted . . . "VICTORY VICTORY VICTORY!" [54]

Fear and loathing of Asians pervade Hal Lindsey's work. He titled a chapter of *The Late Great Planet Earth* "The Yellow Peril" and described with zest how the "vast hordes of the Orient," probably united under the "Red Chinese war machine," would meet their doom. *The 1980s: Countdown to Armageddon* (1981) exuded even more open hostility to China. From the Korean War (in which Lindsey fought), when President Truman rejected General MacArthur's advice to use the atomic bomb against China, down to the rapprochement of the 1970s, Lindsey saw the United States as being repeatedly tricked into helping the Chinese "prepare for their role in the last awful war." [55] Here again is the fundamental dilemma of those who use prophecy to pronounce on public-policy issues: if all is foreordained, how can one criticize nations or individuals—even a Truman or a Nixon—for playing their assigned roles in God's unfolding plan?

In summary, among the many demonic forces foreordained to shape history's course in the last days, communistic Russia and its allies, the Arabs and the darker-skinned peoples of Africa and Asia, loomed large. Liberals and secular humanists might prattle of international understanding, racial harmony, and global cooperation, but prophecy popularizers knew better: danger lurked in foreign nations and alien peoples; in God's good time, those dangers would coalesce in a cataclysm of global upheaval.

The Manner of Gog's Destruction

After describing Israel's invasion by Gog and his allies, Ezekiel goes on to present a chilling vision of the attackers' destruction:

> And it shall come to pass at the same time when Gog shall come against the land of Israel, saith the Lord God, that my fury shall come up in my face.

> For in my jealousy and in the fire of my wrath have I spoken, Surely
> in that day there shall be a great shaking in the land of Israel . . .
> And I will plead against him with pestilence and with blood; and I
> will rain upon him, and upon his bands, and upon the many
> people that are with him, and overflowing rain, and great hail-
> stones, fire and brimstone . . .
> Therefore, thou son of man, prophesy against Gog, and say, Thus
> saith the Lord God; behold, I am against thee, O Gog, the chief
> prince of Meshech and Tubal:
> And I will turn thee back, and leave but the sixth part of thee, and
> will cause thee to come up from the north parts, and will bring
> thee upon the mountains of Israel . . .
> Thou shalt fall upon the mountains of Israel, thou, and all thy bands,
> and the people that is with thee: I will give thee unto the raven-
> ous birds of every sort, and to the beasts of the field to be de-
> voured . . .
> And I will send a fire on Magog, and among them that dwell care-
> lessly in the isles, and they shall know that I am the Lord.[56]

The vision continues: the burial of bodies takes seven months; the
stench reaches far out to sea; the burning of the invaders' weapons
occupies seven years. Birds and beasts gorge on the putrefying flesh:
"And ye shall eat fat till ye be full, and drink blood till ye be drunken
. . . Thus ye shall be filled at my table with horses and chariots, with
mighty men, and with all men of war, saith the Lord God."[57] The
prophet Joel, writing in the early fourth century B.C., spoke too of
Gog's destruction:

> But I will remove far off from you the northern army, and will drive
> him into a land barren and desolate, with his face toward the east
> sea, and his hinder parts toward the utmost sea, and his stink shall
> come up, and his ill savor shall come up.[58]

Early Cold War prophecy interpreters did not shrink from applying these grim passages to the Soviet Union and its allies. Ezekiel's
prophesied judgment on "Gog and all his hordes," wrote Louis Talbot
in 1948, foretold Russia's "irrevocable doom." A 1958 prophecy book
devoted eight pages to Ezekiel 38–39 under the caption "The Destruction of the Russian Confederacy."[59]

As tensions waxed and waned, the coming Russian bloodbath on
the plains of Israel remained a staple of premillennial teaching. Coder
in 1963 described Russia's "complete ruin" and contemplated "the

blessed results for the whole world when this godless power is finally forever destroyed." Richard DeHaan, discussing the prophecy that the burial of the dead invaders will take seven months, calculated in 1968 that "one million people, each burying two corpses a day, would in the 180 working days of seven months, dispose of 360 million men." Clearly, DeHaan concluded, the body count from Russia's "supernatural and crushing defeat" will be staggering. Kirban's novel *666* vividly pictured the Soviet army's final moments:

> The scene . . . was not a pleasant one for tender stomachs. Sores erupting over the skin of the Russian soldiers; running open sores that generated welts of puffed up flesh. The hot sun combined with the unquenchable fires made the flesh burn. The crazed horses were trampling on man and beast. The crazed army was pitted man against man, dying on their brother's sword, becoming victims to their brother's bullets.[60]

Noting the prophesied fire on Magog ("the land of Gog"), many writers foresaw the destruction not only of Russia's armies but of the nation itself. The author of a blood-drenched 1972 work summed up his account of Russia's invasion this way: "I have come to the conclusion that all of the people of the Northern Confederacy will be killed."[61]

Prophecy writers distinguished the destruction of Gog from the Battle of Armageddon, in which Christ destroys Antichrist's armies. As one put it, "The Russian invasion of Israel, in all its horror and devastation, will be only a curtain raiser" to Armageddon. Fitting Russia's demise into the dispensational timetable, most writers placed it halfway through the seven-year Tribulation period, just before Antichrist's brief period of world domination. "With Russia out of the way," wrote Walvoord, "the head of the revived Roman Empire . . . will be able to proclaim himself as dictator of the whole world."[62]

Prophecy writers eagerly sought empirical confirmation of Russia's eschatological destiny. For example, David Webber, commenting in 1979 on the birds that will gorge on Russian corpses, quoted another writer: "A new breed of vulture has appeared in Israel, a breed never seen before. These vultures are multiplying at three times the normal rate in Israel. This is a sign of the end time." A 1985 writer reported that when he queried his Israeli tour guide on this point, the man replied: "You have surely asked the right person. I belong to the Bird Watching Society of Israel. What you heard is certainly true. We cannot explain it, but for the first time in history, those birds are increasing enormously." [63]

The preoccupation with Russia's prophesied annihilation that crested in the 1970s and early 1980s was distinguishable from the many decades of premillennial interpretation that preceded it by its dogmatic certitude and urgency of tone. "Russia is in trouble," proclaimed Hilton Sutton in 1982; "she is set up like the ten pins on a bowling alley." The Soviet Union's "ultimate judgment" could come at any moment, Pat Robertson declared in 1982. [64]

On Russia's prophetic destiny, America's best-known premillennialist of the Reagan years, Jerry Falwell, was only one voice among many. The Soviets would one day strike Israel, he said in 1981, and be "totally destroyed." Once five-sixths of the Russian army had been obliterated in fulfillment of Ezekiel's prophecies, he added in a 1983 broadcast, "the Communist threat will cease forever." [65]

Some prophecy writers, reading literally Ezekiel's images of a supernatural punishment employing natural elements—fire, hailstones, and the like—ascribed Russia's devastation to God's direct action. Wrote one in 1957: "We [Americans] have had the idea for several years that we will have to fight [the Soviet Union] sooner or later. This prophecy of God should get us straight. God handles Russia himself, in his own way, without the help of a single nation." Tim LaHaye, writing in 1972, agreed: "Almighty God is going to destroy Russia's massive armies by his supernatural power. Furthermore, he will send a fire on the homeland of Magog, or Russia . . . Russia will be almost entirely destroyed." (This event, he said, would produce "a tremendous harvest of souls.") In a variant of this interpretation, Arthur Bloomfield argued that *Antichrist* would destroy the Soviet Union, his only rival for world domination. "When Antichrist gets through with Russia," Bloomfield wrote in 1975, "she will not be any threat to the world." [66]

Other writers, linking Gog's destruction to the nuclear-war theme, offered scenarios that employed human agency more directly and reflected Cold War power alignments. Before the Russians met their end, a speaker at the 1961 Los Angeles prophecy conference speculated, God might use them "as an instrument of judgment upon others." Russia's Middle East invasion, wrote Charles Taylor in *The Destiny of America,* will be "synchronized with an all-out CBW [chemical-biological warfare] and thermonuclear bombardment of the

U.S.A." LaHaye in 1984 discussed Russia's attack on Israel, a U.S. ally, as part of a larger strategy for defeating the United States itself. "Israel is the Achilles heel to the Soviets' design for world supremacy," LaHaye argued; "before they can suppress the world with their totalitarian ideology they must first knock out the United States, and to do that, they must first remove Israel."[67]

How will the United States react to all this? Some interpreters cited a cryptic passage in Ezekiel's account of Gog's invasion to argue that America will only weakly protest the Soviet assault on Israel:

> Sheba, and Dedan, and the merchants of Tarshish, with all the young lions thereof, shall say unto thee [that is, Gog], Art thou come to take a spoil? hast thou gathered thy company to take a prey? to carry away silver and gold, to take away cattle and goods, to take a great spoil?[68]

One venerable interpretation of this puzzling verse, as we have seen, holds that "Tarshish" refers to Great Britain and "the young lions" to its former colonies, including the United States. Whatever their identity, their role at this climactic moment indeed seems less than forceful. As Chuck Smith glossed this passage in 1978, the nations mentioned therein ("which could conceivably include the United States") merely complain, "Russia, what are you doing: it isn't right for you to attack this little nation!" Another writer speculated that the United States would fall so far behind Russia in the arms race that at the critical moment "all America will do, or be able to do, is to lodge an innocuous protest."[69]

Many popularizers, however, envisioned a more militant U.S. role as the events of Ezekiel 38–39 unfold. As one put it in 1956, God could use America and other powers as a "rod" to destroy the attacking Soviets. Charles Taylor, discussing Ezekiel 39, predicted in 1980 that while the United States would suffer hideously in the Soviet missile assault, "the computerized response of the Western powers . . . will be colossal and horrendous." A 1985 author found a prophetic role for America in Daniel 11:30: "For the ships of Chittim shall come against him." Noting that both the British and American Mediterranean fleets used bases in Cyprus (the biblical Chittim), he argued that the Royal Navy and the U.S. Sixth Fleet would defend Israel when Russia invaded.[70]

All interpreters who foresaw a U.S. role in Russia's destruction insisted that the United States would not *initiate* the attack. As Taylor wrote: "America will not strike first, but it WILL be ready to retaliate unmercifully at a moment's notice . . . Then will come to pass the fulfillment of Ezekiel 39:6 wherein America, as a weapon of God's indignation, will 'send a fire on Magog' (Russia)." Some went to tortuous lengths to underscore American blamelessness in Russia's annihilation, even if U.S. missiles were involved. Hilton Sutton, for example, proposed a complex scenario for the fulfillment of Ezekiel 38–39: Moscow launches a first strike against the United States as part of its invasion of Israel. The prophesied earthquakes and great hailstones drive the missiles off course, and they detonate over Russia itself. Meanwhile, Western monitoring devices sense the Soviet launches, and the retaliatory attack begins: "The United States will send her ICBMs on their way to Russian targets. Europe will strike its powerful nuclear blow, and in only one single day, the war will begin and end . . . [leaving] Russia totally wiped out." Russians who do not die at once, he speculated, will succumb to nuclear winter, the global cooling resulting from all-out thermonuclear war—a phenomenon that in Sutton's view will affect only communists.[71]

Many prophecy writers, however, avoided specific scenarios of Russia's demise. Even Pat Robertson, who (for a time) so confidently predicted the precise year of Russia's destruction, hedged on its means: the annihilation portrayed in Ezekiel, he wrote in 1982, "could of course be a vision of nuclear bombing. But it may also be the direct, miraculous intervention of God." Whatever the means, scores of Cold-War-era prophecy writers agreed on the fundamental point made by David Webber in 1986: "Russia will be largely wiped out." Whether the Soviet Union is destroyed by missiles or divine intervention, wrote Ray Stedman in 1970, "it is quite clear that the earth will never be governed from Moscow."[72]

What, finally, is the public-policy significance of all this speculation about Gog, Magog, Meshech, Tubal, the kings of the south, and the kings of the east? Why should those who do not share these interests concern themselves with such arcana?

In the first place, of course, this material is firmly embedded in the belief system of millions of Americans, and thus on its own terms merits attention from students of religious belief and popular ideology. Further, these ideas unquestionably helped shape U.S. Cold War attitudes—supplying theological reinforcement for the rigidly hostile view of the Soviet Union that pervaded American culture for several postwar decades; encouraging a highly schematic view of world power alignments; and enabling millions of prophecy believers to contemplate with equanimity and even anticipation the prospect of a fiery holocaust in which a vast portion of the human race (dematerialized under the mysterious rubric "Gog") will be incinerated.

In unraveling the details of premillennial eschatology, then, we must keep the larger picture in view: from the end of World War II to the closing years of the twentieth century, scores of prophecy writers, in books selling millions of copies, as well as TV and radio preachers reaching more millions of individuals, taught that Russia's destruction is explicitly foretold in a sacred text most Americans revere as divinely inspired. We cannot fully understand Cold War politics and culture without close attention to this religious component. National opinion surveys in the mid-1980s revealed that a quarter of Americans viewed the U.S.-Soviet conflict in theological terms, and over half endorsed Reagan's view of the Soviet Union as an "evil empire." George Gallup, Jr., and Jim Castelli, summing up various polling data in 1989, reported that "white evangelical Protestants are the most suspicious religious group [in America] when it comes to dealing with the Soviets." When asked, for example, whether trust or suspicion of the Soviets posed the greater risk to peace, 54 percent of white evangelicals viewed *trust* as the greater threat, as contrasted to the 43 percent of white nonevangelicals who chose this option.[73] Statistics such as these underscore the public ramifications of the private religious beliefs explored in this chapter.

These beliefs also reduced the complex and diverse societies of Africa, Asia, and the Middle East to walk-on roles as allies of Gog in God's great end-time drama. Further, the deeply nationalistic structure of the dispensational system affected believers' attitudes not only toward the nuclear threat but also toward the configuration of the Cold War world. The conviction that the nation-state is divinely ordained and will endure to the end of time encouraged a static view of the international order—including the bimodal polarities of the post–World War II decades—and intensified suspicion of any efforts to modify that order.

Still, one must be careful not to view postwar prophecy belief as merely a theological rationalization of Cold War ideology that exalted virtuous America, demonized the wicked communists, and gloated over Russia's approaching doom. Some writers approximated this stereotype, but most also took a highly critical view of the United

States, even foretelling *America's* end-time destruction as well. Jack Van Impe, who yielded to none in the bloodthirstiness of his account of God's judgment on the "godless communistic monstrosity," preached that the United States, too, will be "crushed" when God's final judgment falls on wicked humanity.[74] The premillennial world-view is not wholly reducible to the contours of any secular political ideology. But the strand that derives from Ezekiel 38–39, with its implacable account of Gog's fate, has implications that are chilling indeed.

Gog and Glasnost

How did the transformations in the Soviet Union and Eastern Europe at the close of the 1980s affect prophecy belief? Did the end of the Cold War fatally undermine a prophetic scenario in which the Soviet Union had for so long played a prominent role? Probably not, but certain adjustments and adaptations seemed likely.

In previous periods of thaw, prophecy writers vehemently resisted any diminution of Cold War conflict that might challenge their view of the foreordained end-time alignments. We have already seen the sharp criticism directed at Nixon's rapprochement with China, putative leader of the kings of the east in the last-days scenario. The warnings sounded even more insistently at any hint of improved relations with Gog itself, the Soviet Union. Throughout the Cold War, prophecy writers cautioned that a sure sign of Antichrist's rise would be false promises of peace. Temporary improvements in world relations would in no way alter God's "definite program" for the last days, warned J. Dwight Pentecost in 1971. "Russia is bent on world domination," another writer reminded believers in 1975. " 'Détente' has been and is being used by them to this end." [75]

As the political activism of fundamentalists increased in the late 1970s and early 1980s, so did the warnings of prophecy writers against efforts to moderate Cold War tensions. "The crescendo of peace rhetoric" in the world, wrote Jack Van Impe, "is but a sign of end-time destruction, the harbinger of history's bloodiest hour." Moscow's "fog-screen" of conciliatory gestures, agreed another author, could not affect the prophetic timetable. "No human negotiations or peace demonstrations," asserted still another, would influence the predetermined course of events.[76] With their heavy ideological investment in the bipolar postwar world—a mirror of their bipolar moral world—premillennial prophecy writers vehemently resisted threats to that configuration.

With striking unanimity these writers dismissed the reforms of Mikhail Gorbachev and the improved U.S.-Soviet relations of the late 1980s and early 1990s. These were not the next act of the script they were following! An older generation of premillennialists had resisted the optimism of the pre–World War I era, and their late-twentieth-century successors did not shrink from a similarly unfashionable position. The improved world climate was "probably just a temporary thing," speculated J. Dwight Pentecost in a 1989 interview; despite glasnost, he said, prophecy interest was increasing. "Sometime soon, Russia WILL invade Israel and the Middle East!" declared Jack Van Impe's newsletter in October 1991. "Gorbachev is still a committed Marxist," pointed out prophecy writer Louis Goldberg. "Given the right set of circumstances, those things that we preach prophetically could very quickly come into play."[77]

The durable Salem Kirban warned in 1989 that U.S. assistance to the Soviet economy would only hasten Russia's invasion of Israel. Glasnost, he cautioned, was merely a ruse of the Soviets "to get more Western technology and financial investments" to pursue their sinister goals. As for Moscow's efforts to patch up relations with Beijing, "those who know Bible prophecy realize this alliance brings us one step closer to the seven-year Tribulation Period!"

Another veteran popularizer, Charles Taylor, writing in his *Bible Prophecy News,* warned of "Gorbachev's dubious design," quoted conservative columnist Jeane Kirkpatrick on the continuing Soviet threat, and ended with an uncompromising reiteration of the familiar theme, "WAKE UP AMERICA! THE SOVIETS ARE GOING TO ATTACK THE U.S.A.—SOON!" In 1990 he reiterated, "Do not be fooled by Gorbachev."[78]

Another prominent prophecy writer and lecturer, James Mc-Keever, founder of Omega Ministries in Medford, Oregon, adopted a similarly skeptical tone in his monthly *End-Times News Digest.* Glasnost, he warned, was "a KGB-inspired campaign to soften Western resolve against Communism . . . As they do periodically, the communists are waving the peace flag in order to gain concessions from the West. But once all those concessions are in place, we believe the conflict will resume." As Cold War certitudes crumbled, McKeever grew increasingly shrill in warning of "The Great Soviet Deception" and describing how "Gorbachev and his brilliant KGB script writers" were loosening their grip on Eastern Europe merely as a tactic to destroy NATO. "DESPITE BULLSNOST, SOVIET TANK PRODUCTION SOARS," McKeever headlined one such story. Tim LaHaye took a different tack, arguing that glasnost was in fact prophesied. Since Ezekiel makes clear that Russia's invasion will come when "Israel dwelleth safely," LaHaye suggested, U.S.-Soviet détente, particularly if it reduced Mideast tension, could promote the very sense of false security prophesied to precede the Soviet attack.[79]

In assessing Gorbachev himself, prophecy writers quoted scriptures suggesting that Antichrist will not initially be a blatantly evil figure, but instead a warm, charismatic leader promising peace. In *Gorbachev! Has the Real Antichrist Come?* Robert Faid not only noted the numerical equivalent of "Mikhail S. Gorbachev" in Russian (1,332, or 666 × 2), but also the Soviet leader's appealing manner and message of peace—characteristics of Antichrist in the early phases of his career.[80]

Prophecy popularizers making the circuit of fundamentalist and pentecostal churches similarly railed against weakening Cold War tensions. In his August 1988 appearance in Madison, Hilton Sutton offered the classic premillennialist reading of Ezekiel 38–39: Russia is Gog; the East European satellites are Gomer; Russia will invade Israel and face divine retribution; and so on. And this scenario will be orchestrated, Sutton insisted (updating the script), by Mikhail Gorbachev, "the prince of Rosh." To be sure, he conceded, Gorbachev and his fashionable wife *seem* attractive and nonthreatening. ("Raisa dresses in the latest Gucci fashions. You can't afford them, but his wife wears Gucci fashions from Italy.") But this only makes him more dangerous: "Gorbachev is no different from any of the ones before him . . . In him you find Karl Marx, Lenin, Stalin, Khrushchev, Brezhnev. He is a combination of them all."[81]

Evangelist Paul Olson of Minneapolis developed the same themes in a November 1989 sermon, "When Russia Attacks Israel," before a packed audience at another of Madison's large pentecostal churches. Recounting yet again the familiar narrative drawn from Ezekiel and citing his thirty-three visits to Israel, Olson grandly proclaimed, "Every Jewish person in Israel today believes that this prophecy refers to the Soviet Union." Intent on strangling the West's economy by controlling its oil, he said, Moscow will first move against

Israel, the Mideast's one nuclear power. Honoring its treaty obligations, the United States will come to Israel's aid with missiles from its Trident submarine fleet, provoking a general thermonuclear war. The populations of all major U.S. cities could be wiped out by the Russians within fifteen minutes, Olson warned, while the Soviet urban population in their underground shelters would survive. ("The Bible is telling us there's going to be a war . . . The only hope that you and I have left in this world is the hope of Jesus Christ.") But God will step in: battered by hundred-pound hailstones and sheets of fire from on high, the Soviet troops will turn on one another. ("God's got a little button on his computer up there called 'the Crazy Button.' God doesn't need any England, France, or United States to mete out His judgment on Russia. All He needs is the natural elements.") The prophesied end-time alignment is shaping up, Olson continued: Ethiopia is no longer ruled "by a cute little fellow called Haile Selassie" but by communists loyal to Moscow. ("The Soviets are stockpiling arms in Ethiopia today. All America does is feed her starving children.") Iran and Gog's other allies will soon fall in line as we see prophecy fulfilled "right before our very eyes." The appearance of diminished tensions, Olson insisted, could not change history's foreordained trajectory. On Gorbachev, he quoted Andrei Gromyko: "Behind that winsome smile are teeth of iron." As for glasnost, Olson cited the warning in Jeremiah 6:14 (much invoked by premillennialists when world conditions improve) against those who cry "peace, peace, when there is no peace." Soviet leaders came and went; the essential point remained: "Communism was born in hell. Communism was created by Satan." [82]

To move from the world of *Time* magazine, "All Things Considered," "The McNeil-Lehrer Report," and the *New York Times* to the world of Salem Kirban, James McKeever, Hilton Sutton, and Paul Olson is to experience intense culture shock. It is to confront a worldview that would have sounded familiar to Wilbur Smith or Donald Grey Barnhouse in 1950, and, in general outline, to Cyrus Scofield in 1920 or John Darby in 1840. To witness the crowds contemporary prophecy speakers attract, the earnestness with which their message is received, and the avidity with which their books and cassette sermons are snapped up, is to understand not only the pervasiveness of premillennial ideology but also its power.

Given the durability of premillennialism, and specifically its interpretation of Ezekiel 38–39, the core group of prophecy believers could well be the last sector of American society to finally concede that the Cold War is over—a concession that will force upon them the painful process of restructuring an entire belief system. In view of the prophecy writers' resourcefulness and long experience at adapting to changing realities, however, this restructuring will probably be successfully accomplished. Some may continue to claim that despite appearances, Russia will ultimately fulfill its prophetic destiny and invade Israel. Others may retreat to the safer and more cautious position that while the prophecies are certain in broad outline, details such as Gog's identity remain hidden to us. Or perhaps a more radical shift will occur, and another power altogether will emerge as Gog: perhaps Syria, which unquestionably lies north of Israel and certainly is hostile to the Jewish nation; or, if one shifts the compass slightly to the northeast, Iraq.

If, on the other hand, the Cold War thaw proves illusory, premillennialists will be the first to say "We told you so." In any event, Russia has enjoyed a very long run as Gog, and during the most recent decades of that run millions of Americans have been reinforced in their Cold War fears by apocalyptic pronouncements written in a strange tongue in a faraway land more than twenty-five hundred years ago. When prophetic interpretations of world realities converge with those of secular opinion molders in government and the media, the result can be an ideological groundswell of enormous power.

6   *The Final Chastisement of the Chosen*

Israel and the Jews loom large in post–World War II American prophecy popularizations. Complex and deeply paradoxical, the treatment of these interwoven topics merits careful exploration. What writers have had to say on these subjects has influenced millions of Americans' perception of events in the Middle East—and of their Jewish fellow citizens. In the premillennial system the Jews enjoy a privileged niche. But they also face future horrors worse than anything yet encountered in millennia of suffering and persecution.

As with so much else in the ancient and deeply conservative belief system we are exploring, what contemporary prophecy writers have to say about the Jews is firmly rooted in interpretive traditions stretching back over the centuries. To lay the groundwork, then, it will be useful to look briefly again at earlier eras of prophecy belief before we turn to the complex and fascinating ways modern-day prophecy popularizers treat the Jews and their destiny.

The Long Shadow of the Jews

Just as they have debated the meaning of Gog and the kings of the east, theologians from the dawn of Christianity have pondered the Bible's prophetic references to the Jews and Israel. Saint Augustine saw them as allegorical allusions to the Church; the Jew qua Jew had no eschatological role. This approach became Catholic doctrine, and remained so. But another line of interpretation foresaw a distinct prophetic destiny for the Jews, including their end-time conversion. As early as the middle of the fourth century the Tibertine Oracle, the first of the so-called Sibylline Oracles popular in medieval Europe, prophesied the Jews' eventual turn to Christ.[1]

In medieval Europe the extermination of Jews who refused conversion was often linked with the recovery of the Holy Land from the infidels as divinely sanctioned undertakings. Popular and scholarly interpretations of prophesies about the fate of unbelieving Jews, as well as mystery plays portraying Antichrist as a Jew, combined with larger social and economic changes to fuel anti-Semitic outbreaks of murderous intensity.[2]

The link between prophecy belief and hatred of the Jews is not simply a matter of what Norman Cohn has called "the popular demonology" of medieval Europe's lower ranks. As Marjorie Reeves and, more recently, Heiko Oberman have shown, the upsurge of anti-Semitism in the late Middle Ages relates as well to the eschatological ideas of theologians and biblical scholars. Reeves and Oberman point specifically to the pseudo-Joachian prophetic writings that inundated late medieval Europe. Joachim of Fiore, in his work *Adversus Judaeos* (Against the Jews), argued that while all Jews will be converted at "the day of the Lord," *before* that time they will follow Antichrist, bringing terrible suffering upon themselves and the whole world. Joachim urged conversion of the Jews before Antichrist could lead them astray. In the pseudo-Joachian literature, the emphasis on conversion faded, whereas the link between the Jews and Antichrist loomed larger. Some interpreters echoed the theme of the mystery plays—that Antichrist would *be* a Jew. The fifteenth-century writer Jacobus Perez of Valencia, for example, took this position in his vituperative *Tractatus contra Judaeos* (Treatise against the Jews).[3]

By the mid-sixteenth century this theme had sunk deep roots in both Protestant and Catholic thought. Pope Paul IV established Rome's Jewish ghetto in 1555 to facilitate conversion efforts. Martin Luther in his 1543 *Von den Juden und ihren Lugen* (Concerning the Jews and their lies) wrote that if the Jews were to convert, "we will be glad to forgive them; if not, we should not tolerate and suffer them."[4]

While post-Reformation Lutheran and Reformed (Calvinist) theologians generally adhered to the view of Saint Augustine (and John Calvin) that the prophecies relating to Israel found fulfillment in Christian history, the English Puritans, influenced by dissenting Continental theologians such as Johann Alsted, took literally the biblical prophecies of Israel's restoration and looked to the Jews' eventual conversion. Joseph Mede argued that in the last days the Jews would embrace Christianity and return to Judea to share in Christ's millennial kingdom. This belief became almost universal among Puritan theologians and lay leaders. Oliver Cromwell mentioned it in a 1653 address to Parliament. John Napier's popular 1594 work, *A Pleine Discoverie of the Whole Revelation of St. John,* taught it, as did Sir Henry Finch's book *The World's Great Restauration; or, The Calling of the Jews* (1621).[5]

The New England Puritans carried this doctrine to America as part of their intellectual baggage. Attracted by the idea of an American New Jerusalem, as we have seen, they also embraced the notion of the Jews' distinct eschatological destiny. Increase Mather in *The Mystery of Israel's Salvation Explained and Applyed* (1669)—a work much cited by twentieth-century popularizers—taught that the Jews, after turning to Christ, would be "brought into their own land again" and found "the most glorious nation in the whole world." Decades later, in 1709, the aged patriarch published a sermon on *The Future Conversion of the Jewish Nation* and seized on a report that hundreds of Hamburg Jews had converted. When "Jew and Gentile to one worship go," wrote Anne Bradstreet, "dayes of happiness and rest" would follow.[6]

This theme faded in the early 1700s but revived strongly toward the end of the century with works such as Joseph Eyre's *Observations upon the Prophecies Relating to the Restoration of the Jews* (1771). As Mayir Vereté has shown, the French Revolution and its challenge to papal power brought a surge of eschatological writing in England in the 1790s, with the restoration of the Jews a major motif. This theme was central, for example, in works such as James Bicheno's *Signs of the Times* (1792) and Joseph Priestley's *Present State of Europe Compared with Ancient Prophecies* (1794). Ruth Bloch has explored the American echo of this wave of prophecy interest, including the theme of Jewish restoration. In the 1790s a New Jersey Presbyterian minister prepared houses and a wharf in New Haven for the Jews—who, he believed, would shortly embark for Palestine. "The return of the Jews to their own land is certain," declared Elhanan Winchester in 1800. Nor did this expectation grip only prophecy specialists. "I really wish the Jews again in Judea, an independent nation," wrote ex-President John Adams toward the end of his life.[7]

John Darby, building on this exegetical tradition, placed the Jews at the heart of his dispensational system. When they rejected Christ, he taught, God set them aside and launched the Church Age. But at the Rapture, the prophetic clock would resume ticking. Returning to center stage, the Jews would establish a nation in Palestine where, after terrible persecution, the surviving remnant would hail Christ as Messiah upon his return at Armageddon.[8]

This belief won support in high places. The Jews' return to Palestine, argued Lord Anthony Ashley Cooper, Earl of Shaftesbury, in 1839, must occur before the Second Coming. Through Shaftesbury's influence, Great Britain opened a consulate in Jerusalem. The consul, a devout evangelical, was instructed to look out especially for the interests of the nearly ten thousand Jews living in Palestine under Ottoman rule. Linking prophecy belief with strategic calculations, a Colonial Office official argued in 1845 that a Jewish nation in Palestine under British protection would "place [England] in a commanding position in the Levant . . . to overawe our enemies and, if necessary, to repel their advance." [9]

The popularizer John Cumming discussed "The Jew: His Ruin and Restoration" in his books of the 1850s, and many other writers of the middle and late nineteenth century echoed the theme. An 1863 expositor, conceding that some might be upset by the Jews' "enviable place" in God's plan, quickly added: "Shall we bend and modify the word of God to make it harmonize with our whims and jealousies? Are we to explain away the positive statements of revelation because they disagree with our tastes and conflict with our vanity and pride? Away with such unworthy feelings upon a subject like this!" [10]

To be sure, other approaches competed in the arena of nineteenth-century prophecy writing. Some interpreters continued to see the Church as the "Israel" of biblical prophecy; others gave this theme a more patriotic twist. In an 1804 poem that would become Britain's national hymn, William Blake invoked prophetic imagery to express his vision of England's future greatness:

> I shall not cease from mental fight,
> Nor shall my sword sleep in my hand,
> Till we have built Jerusalem,
> In England's green and pleasant land. [11]

Long before, some interpreters had offered a literal version of Blake's vision, teaching that the Jews of Bible times had migrated across Europe to ancient Britain. As one exponent of this theory wrote in 1723, "Unless the ten tribes [of Israel] have flown into the air, or have plunged into the center of the earth, they must be sought for in the north and west, and in the British Isles." Promoted by an eccentric British naval officer named Richard Brothers (1757–1824) and others, "British-Israel" theories attracted a small following. [12] In the United States, meanwhile, as we have seen (and shall explore further in Chapter 7), some nineteenth-century interpreters carried on in the tradition of Jonathan Edwards and other colonial-era expositors who placed the Millennium in the New World, not in ancient Palestine.

Darby and the dispensationalists turned the prophetic spotlight on the Jews, where hundreds of subsequent expounders kept it tightly focused. The promised restoration to Palestine loomed large in the U.S. prophecy conferences held between 1878 and 1918, and in the influential books of Robert Anderson of Scotland Yard and the Reverend James Brookes of St. Louis. The Ottoman Empire's collapse, wrote Anderson, would open the door for the Jews' restoration to Palestine, a key part of the prophetic plan. Brookes foresaw the Jews' "literal return . . . to their ancient land"—a land given them by "absolutely unconditional" divine grant. Cyrus Scofield followed this well-worn path. "Israel regathered from all nations, restored to her own land and converted," he declared in his 1909 Reference Bible, "is yet to have her greatest earthly exaltation and glory." In another work he proclaimed, "Upon the sacred soil of Palestine God has decreed the reconstitution of the nation of Israel." [13]

This facet of dispensationalist belief spurred missionary activity among the Jews, since most prophecy writers held (at least prior to 1948) that conversion must precede nationhood. As a Scottish cleric put it in 1840, urging missionary work among the Jews to hasten prophetic fulfillment, "Israel, as a people, shall be saved—the only question may be *when?*" [14]

The role of prophecy belief in stimulating missionary effort emerges clearly in the careers of Arno Gaebelein, the German-immigrant editor of *Our Hope* magazine, and William Blackstone, the Chicago businessman and prophecy writer. Gaebelein, with his patriarchial beard and flawless Yiddish, proselytized among New York's Jewish immigrants from the 1880s through the end of the century. Blackstone in 1887 helped start the Chicago Hebrew Mission (later the American Messianic Fellowship), which by 1906 boasted a staff of twenty-three. Among those active in the Chicago Hebrew Mission was Milton Lindberg, a prophecy writer and speaker active from the 1930s to the 1960s. Another group, the American Board of Missions to the Jews, regularly sponsored prophecy conferences throughout the 1940s and 1950s. These groups prized the rare Jewish convert (Louis Meyer of the Chicago Hebrew Mission, for example) as evidence that the prophesied end-time conversion process was beginning. [15]

In America as in England, prophetic belief about the Jews had political implications. Indeed, nineteenth-century prophecy believers on both sides of the Atlantic helped lay the intellectual groundwork for the Zionist movement, officially launched by Theodore Herzl at the 1897 World Zionist Congress in Basel. Again, the careers of Gaebelein and Blackstone are illustrative. Gaebelein tirelessly promoted a Jewish return to Palestine in *Our Hope,* at prophecy conferences, and in evangelical pulpits nationwide. "The time may soon be here, sooner than we think," he wrote in 1894, "when the world shall behold the Jewish state." This theme figured prominently, too, in Blackstone's frequently reprinted *Jesus Is Coming* of 1878.[16]

In 1891, six years before Herzl's Basel conference, Blackstone presented to President Benjamin Harrison a memorial urging U.S. support for a Jewish homeland in Palestine, partly on humanitarian grounds (persecuted Russian Jews were pouring into Ellis Island), but also to conform to "God's distribution of nations" and "to further the purposes of God concerning His ancient people." Palestine is the Jews' "inalienable possession, from which they were expelled by force," declared the memorial, citing Bible prophecy. "Let us now restore them to the land of which they were so cruelly despoiled by our Roman ancestors." Signed by over four hundred well-known public figures of the day drawn from the ranks of national politics, industry, and finance, Blackstone's memorial influenced official and popular perceptions of Mideast politics at the turn of the century. The secularism of Herzl and the other early Jewish Zionists disappointed premillennialists—Blackstone sent Herzl an Old Testament with key prophecies marked—but, in general, prophecy believers welcomed the movement as a step toward prophetic fulfillment. "Of all the signs of our times," Gaebelein declared in 1900, Zionism was "the most startling."[17]

As we saw in Chapter 3, prophecy believers ecstatically greeted Great Britain's 1917 Balfour Declaration, which formally endorsed "the establishment in Palestine of a national home for the Jewish people." Calling the document "the beginning of a series of events that are destined to establish God's kingdom here upon earth," a 1918 writer exclaimed: "The Jews and the land of Palestine are like charts to the mariner. As we study the prophecies concerning 'the people' and 'the land' we hold the key to the mysteries of God's plan and purposes for the world."[18]

Through the interwar years, prophecy believers kept their eyes fixed on Palestine. *The Remarkable Jew* (1928) by Leonard Sale-Harrison (an Australian evangelist and prophecy writer popular in

America) sold over two hundred thousand copies. "One may as well attempt to destroy the solar system as . . . to hinder God's plan for his people," declared Louis Bauman, a Los Angeles minister and prophecy writer, in 1934. When Zionist leader David Ben Gurion in 1937 defiantly told the British Royal Commission on Palestine "The Bible is our mandate," prophecy believers breathed a heartfelt amen. "Palestine belongs to the Jews, not by mandate from the League of Nations, nor from any country, but from God," declared one in 1940; "the Title Deeds are recorded in His Book."[19]

We shall in a moment explore the response of prophecy writers to the Nazi holocaust, but suffice it to say here that during World War II the Jews' prophetic destiny remained a matter of intense interest. "The Jews are God's index finger when it comes to prophecy," declared the editor of the *Christian Digest* in 1942; "the Jew is indestructible." Speakers at the 1943 New York City prophecy conference looked to the postwar era with tense expectancy. "We all know that the day is coming when Israel is to be restored to the Land of Promise to enjoy what God has covenanted she should have," declared one. A conference on "Prophecy and the Jew" at Winona Lake, Indiana, in the summer of 1945 attracted, the organizers reported, "thousands of friends of the cause."[20]

Prophecy Fulfilled

When the Jewish National Council proclaimed Israel a nation on May 14, 1948, prophecy believers responded with intense emotion, tempered by the gratified awareness that they had known all along that this event would take place. A teacher at the Bible Institute of Los Angeles in a radio address called the announcement "the greatest piece of prophetic news that we have had in the twentieth century." In Alabama a mother exhorted her young children to remember the date as "the most significant event since Jesus Christ was born." With Israel again a nation, she told them, Jesus could come at any moment.[21]

The sense of living in times of enormous prophetic import sharpened with the passing years. "The valley of dry bones, the arid land, the stony hills, and the swampy marshes [of Israel] are coming to life," exulted a *Moody Monthly* writer in 1950; "God's clock has struck." Israel's rebirth, suggested William Culberson of Moody Bible Institute in 1960 was "the most striking of all the signs" that the Rapture could occur at any instant.[22]

The Six-Day War of 1967, especially Israel's recapture of the Old City of Jerusalem on June 8, 1967, apparently confirming centuries of prophetic speculation, stirred another tremendous wave of excitement and an outpouring of prophecy writing. Pat Robertson, breaking ground for his Christian Broadcasting Network headquarters when the news arrived, saw it as "a direct sign from God" forever linking his destiny and Israel's. "The events of recent months," declared John Walvoord that October, "climaxed one of the most remarkable fulfillments of biblical prophecy since the destruction of Jerusalem in A.D. 70." [23]

As though by design, the long-awaited New Scofield Reference Bible appeared almost simultaneously with the momentous event. The vast sales of Lindsey's *Late Great Planet Earth,* published three years later, underscored the intensity of this surging interest. "The hands on Israel's prophecy clock leaped forward on June 8, 1967," proclaimed Tim LaHaye in *The Beginning of the End,* another best-selling popularization from the early seventies. *His Land,* a 1970 Billy Graham film about Israel's destiny, attracted large audiences. Since 1967, wrote Hilton Sutton in the early 1980s, "Bible prophecy has come into its own." [24]

Shortly after the Israelis retook the Old City, Carl Henry, editor of the evangelical *Christianity Today,* announced a prophecy conference in Jerusalem. The 1971 event proved a stunning success, drawing fifteen hundred delegates from thirty-two nations. Prime Minister David Ben-Gurion greeted the delegates. The Jerusalem Symphony, pop singer Anita Bryant, the Metropolitan Opera's Jerome Hines, and the choir of California's Azuza Pacific University provided the music. In addition to Henry, speakers included the venerable Wilbur Smith; the Reverend W. A. Criswell of Dallas' fifteen-thousand-member First Baptist Church; officials from the National Association of Evangelicals, Youth for Christ, and Inter-Varsity Christian Fellowship; and prophecy scholars from Dallas Theological Seminary, Talbot Theological Seminary in Los Angeles, and Gordon-Conwell Divinity School in Massachusetts. Nearly all stressed the eschatological significance of Israel's national rebirth and the recapture of the Old City. As future Surgeon General C. Everett Koop noted, differences over detail faded as delegates agreed on the key point—"the soon return of the Lord." [25]

In succeeding decades the drama of modern Israel remained a

centerpiece of prophecy popularizations. The nation's founding posed "an inexplicable enigma apart from [God's] promises and power," claimed one writer in 1978; "Israel, plainly and simply, exists because God decreed she should." Israel and prophecy went together like lox and bagels, wrote Louis Goldberg of Moody Bible Institute. "What is Israel without prophecy? It would have no meaning."[26]

However they expressed it—"All prophetic truth revolves around the Jews"; "The Jew is God's timeclock"; Israel is "the only nation on earth to have its history written in advance"—post-1948 popularizers pointed to Israel as both a validation of prophecy and (as Jerry Falwell put it) "the single greatest sign indicating the imminent return of Jesus Christ." Since Jesus' ascension, Falwell went on, "the most important date we should remember is May 14, 1948." In the 1970s and 1980s, a stream of tour groups led by Falwell and other premillennialists descended on Tel Aviv Airport. Chuck Smith even cordoned off a portion of the Jordan River, where he baptized his followers.[27]

What biblical texts underlay this rock-solid belief in Israel's prophetic destiny? After citing prophesies of the unfaithful Jews' dispersion "from the one end of the earth even unto the other" (Deut. 28:64), premillennialists quoted passages such as this one from Jeremiah, foretelling a time of restoration and blessedness for the scattered people:

> Behold, I will gather them out of all countries, whither I have driven them in mine anger, and in my fury, and in great wrath; and I will bring them again unto this place, and I will cause them to dwell safely.[28]

The prophet Isaiah supplied another much-quoted text: "And [the Lord] shall set up an ensign for the nations, and shall assemble the outcasts of Israel, and gather together the dispersed of Judah from the four corners of the earth."[29] While historical-critical scholars, and Catholic and Reformed theologians, interpreted such passages as reflecting the prophets' own concerns and hopes, or allegorized them as calls to righteous living,[30] premillennialists read them as divinely revealed prophecies of the Jews' physical return to Palestine and their literal creation of a new nation.

In the New Testament, a key passage occurs in Matthew 24, where Jesus, discussing the last days, tells his disciples:

> Now learn a parable of the fig tree; When his branch is yet tender,
> and putteth forth leaves, ye know that summer is nigh:
> So likewise ye, when ye shall see all these things, know that it is near,
> even at the doors.
> Verily I say unto you, This generation shall not pass, till all these
> things be fulfilled.[31]

To premillennialists, the budding fig tree (like Ezekiel's vision of dry bones springing to life) foretold Israel's national rebirth.[32]

Indeed, some found in the parable a clue to the precise timing of the end. Dating the beginning of "this generation" to 1948 and the founding of modern Israel, and further assuming that a biblical "generation" is forty years (and that the Rapture will occur seven years before the Second Coming), some ingenious popularizers predicted the Rapture for 1981 (1948 + 40 − 7 = 1981). Skirting perilously close to date setting, Lindsey suggested in 1970 that "within forty years or so" after 1948, all the end-time prophecies would be fulfilled. Others, placing the fig tree's "budding" in June 1967, speculated that the Rapture might occur in the portentous year 2000. David Webber, assuming a generation of seventy rather than forty years, and viewing the 1917 Balfour Declaration as the fig tree's budding, hinted in 1979 that 1987 "could be a very important year on God's prophetic calendar."[33]

The California TV preacher and prophecy writer Charles Taylor, an inveterate date setter, successively predicted the Rapture in 1976, 1980, 1988, 1989, and 1992, based on different calculations involving modern Israel's history. ("This could be THE YEAR!" Taylor exclaimed in 1989, announcing a Rosh Hashanah tour to Israel. "*If we need our return tickets,*" he told readers of his *Bible Prophecy News,* the group could relive the trip's highlights on the flight back. To a historian who wrote just as he departed for Israel, Taylor replied hastily that he would answer more fully when they met in Heaven.) Such date setting reinforced the conviction that Israel represented an end-time sign of the first importance and that "God's timepiece," as Webber put it, was "rapidly ticking off the remaining seconds."[34]

Becoming more specific, one writer found the 1967 war and Israel's recapture of Jerusalem foretold in Zechariah:

> And in that day will I make the governors of Judah . . . like a torch
> of fire in a sheaf; and they shall devour all the people round about,

on the right hand and on the left; and Jerusalem shall be inhabited again in her own place, even in Jerusalem.[35]

To another, a verse in Jeremiah ("And the measuring line shall yet go forth . . . upon the hill Gareb, and shall compass about to Goath") prophesied modern Jerusalem's urban expansion and the building of the King David Hotel and the YMCA outside the Old City's walls in the 1920s. Still another triumphantly cited a passage in Zephaniah ("For then will I turn to the people a pure language, that they may all call upon the name of the Lord, to serve him with one consent") as a prophecy of Israel's revival of Hebrew as the national language.[36] Late-twentieth-century prophecy popularizations bristled with such scriptural citations, convincing believers that the Bible does indeed provide an amazingly detailed prophetic guide to Israel's recent history—and its future.

Not all prophecy writers agreed. Reformed (Calvinist) theologians continued to argue that God's promises to "Israel" and "my people" encompassed all believers. The founding of a nation-state called Israel, they insisted, whatever its historic significance, had no eschatological import. The prophecies speak of Israel's *repenting,* one pointed out in 1959, adding: "The Jews who on May 14, 1948, established the state of Israel had not repented." Added another Reformed theologian in 1978: "The New Testament church is the fulfillment of Old Testament Israel . . . To suggest that God has in mind a separate future for Israel . . . is like putting the scaffolding back up after the building has been finished." Israel *once* enjoyed God's special favor, a Dutch Calvinist scholar told the 1971 Jerusalem prophecy conference, but would regain it only by accepting Jesus as Messiah. George Ladd in 1978 rejected "the popular Dispensational position that Israel is the 'clock of prophecy.'" Modern Israel *might* have prophetic significance, he wrote, "but the New Testament sheds no light on this problem."[37]

Various sectarian movements, too, espoused prophetic scenarios that bypassed Israel. Herbert W. Armstrong's Worldwide Church of God adhered to a version of British Israelism. The "vital key" to God's plan, wrote Armstrong in 1967, "is the identity of the United States and the British peoples in biblical prophecy." Some racist, violence-prone fringe groups such as the Aryan Nation and the Posse Comitatus also embraced versions of British Israelism. The Seventh-day Adventists and Jehovah's Witnesses denied Israel a special prophetic role. The latter asserted that the 144,000 sealed "servants of God" drawn from "all the tribes of the children of Israel" (Rev. 7:3,4), whom dispensationalists identified as Jews converted during the Tribulation, would be the early converts to their own sect.[38]

Even some premillennialists expressed muted uneasiness at the claim that Israel's political emergence in 1948 and forcible expansion in 1967 were prophetic fulfillments. Prior to 1948, most held that the Jews' national restoration would *follow* their acceptance of Christ at the Second Coming. Some even dismissed political Zionism as a prophetic dead end. Gaebelein, for example, quickly became disillusioned. "What the Jews are doing today is an infidel movement which will land them in the darkest night," warned *Our Hope* magazine in 1920; only the Second Coming would bring Israel's "true restoration and blessing." Cautioned Donald Grey Barnhouse in 1945: "Rifles will not give [the Jews] the land of their fathers. The promises which were made to Abraham will be fulfilled to the last letter, but the land will come to Israel in a way which shall bring the glory to God." The Reverend William Ayer of New York's Calvary Baptist Church, a prominent radio preacher, agreed. "The Jew is going back to his land in unbelief," Ayer declared in 1947; "Little is being accomplished toward the fulfillment of God's prophecied plan . . . The Jew cannot have his land permanently until he has his Messiah."[39]

Such arguments largely vanished after 1948, however, as premillennialists gave the State of Israel increasingly uncritical support. Gentile Christians were Abraham's "spiritual seed," John Walvoord argued in his influential 1962 work, *Israel in Prophecy;* but the Jews, his physical seed, were heirs to all the prophecies directed to Israel. To apply these promises to the Church, declared another author in 1988, made hash of the prophecies that Christ's millennial kingdom would be based in Jerusalem "with national Israel restored to its place of supremacy over the nations." It also rendered meaningless "one of the greatest events in the history of the world—the return of the Jewish people to their own land and the rebirth of Israel in 1948."[40]

As for the claim that the Jews' true national restoration would come *after* they accept Christ, John Walvoord developed what would become the accepted premillennial view. In *Israel in Prophecy* Walvoord conceded that only those Jews who trust in God (and who, presumably, accept Jesus as Messiah), and who thereby become part of Abraham's "spiritual seed" as well as his "physical seed," would "enter into the future millennial kingdom." In his address at the 1971

Jerusalem prophecy conference, Walvoord nevertheless insisted that the Jews' return to their land and the creation of the State of Israel in 1948 was a crucial first stage in God's plan for his people. "The prophetic Word pictures Israel as a nation forever," he emphasized. "Of the many aspects of prophecy relating to Israel, none is more pointed than the promise of the land."[41]

Despite rival interpretive traditions and occasional dissent within the premillennial camp, the understanding of Israel's prophetic destiny described in this chapter saturated postwar U.S. evangelicalism. The popularizers' colorful version of the premillennial scenario, which infused the daily headlines from the Middle East with urgent prophetic import, demonstrated far more market appeal than quibbles over whether the Jews had returned in "belief" or "unbelief," or subtle distinctions between "national Israel" and "spiritual Israel." While the theologians debated, the Hal Lindseys sold millions of paperbacks.

Apart from Jews, white evangelical Protestants are Israel's firmest backers in America. In 1987, 37 percent of this group described themselves as "strongly pro-Israel," in contrast to the 20 percent of non-evangelical Protestants who chose this option.[42] An ancient tradition of prophecy belief that sees a restored Jewish nation as essential to God's plan for human history is one key foundation stone of this solid support.

The Next Stage

The years 1948 and 1967, while important milestones, hardly fulfilled Israel's prophetic destiny. Premillennialists foresaw a nation of vastly larger boundaries, and the rebuilding of the Jewish Temple on its ancient site. Both beliefs had profound implications.

God Himself, premillennialists held, defined Israel's boundaries when he promised Abraham, "Unto thy seed have I given this land, from the river of Egypt unto the great river, the river Euphrates" (Gen. 15:18). The believer in biblical inerrancy, Walvoord wrote, could reach "only one possible conclusion—that is, that Israel in some future time will possess their promised land, including the entire area described in Genesis 15." John Darby interpreted the Nile-to-the-Euphrates passage literally. Later dispensationalists echoed his view, describing the future Jewish nation, as Dwight Wilson notes, in terms exceeding "even the wildest Zionist dreams." If expanded to "the ancient scriptural limits," William Blackstone's 1891 memorial to President Harrison noted, a Jewish homeland could absorb millions of Jews.[43]

As Israel moved toward nationhood, prophecy writers continued to envision its boundaries in sweeping terms. Declared one in 1947:

> The Jews will eventually be given not a partitioned Palestine, but the whole of the land, and ultimately the whole of Trans-Jordan as well. This may sound fantastic, yet I dare to assert it on the authority of One . . . whose revealed Word can never fail . . . The title deeds from the original Owner of the earth naming the Jews as legal owners of Palestine are still extant in millions of Bibles the world around.[44]

Israel's expansion to its biblical bounds quickly became an article of faith for prophecy writers. "Israel must yet possess the entire land as Jehovah has promised," agreed Lewis Sperry Chafer in 1948. "How it may be brought to pass cannot be foreseen, but that it will be . . . is as certain as the oath of Jehovah can make it." Added a 1956 author: "We are accustomed to thinking of Palestine as a little strip of land between the Jordan River and the Mediterranean Sea. However, look at Genesis 15:18 and see what God included in His gift to Abraham. This land was once occupied by Israel during the reign of Solomon, and all of it God has preserved for His people against the day when He gathers them back to their homeland."[45]

Some writers foresaw this territorial aggrandizement in the Millennium, not the present age. Only at the Second Coming, wrote Edgar James of Moody Bible Institute, would Israel "be completely restored to the land." John Walvoord and Dwight Pentecost, when queried on the point, agreed that Israel's vast geographic expansion would come in the millennial age. Opinion differed, too, about the "river of Egypt." While most writers identified it as the Nile, some, including Walvoord, favored the Wadi-el-Arish, a stream in the eastern Sinai.[46] Others questioned the meaning of "thy seed" in the Genesis passage. Since Abraham fathered not only Isaac by his wife, Sarah, but also Ishmael, founder of the Arab peoples, by his handmaiden, Hagar, some held that the Abrahamic covenant covered Arabs as well. Most, however, rejected this view. As Milton Lindberg wrote, citing another Genesis passage: "[The Jews] 'title deed' to the entire land is secure . . . Arabs are also descendants of Abraham; but to Abraham, God said: 'In Isaac [not Ishmael] shall thy seed be called.' "[47]

Such nuances vanished as one entered the realm of television evangelists and paperback popularizers. There the message became starkly simple: Israel would expand enormously—not only in the hereafter, but in the present age. As one writer put it in 1974, "Israel is invincible, because it is flowing in the tide of divine prophecy." Soon, predicted another in 1981, Israel would grow to 180,000 square miles, over twenty times its 1948 size.[48]

In *The Last Word on the Middle East* (1982), the English pentecostalist Derek Prince, a favorite on the U.S. prophecy circuit, commented on a passage from Isaiah ("They will swoop down on the slopes of Philistia to the west; together they will plunder the people to the east. They will lay hands on Edom and Moab, and the Ammonites will be subject to them"): "I am not making any predictions [always the warning of a prediction to come], but the Bible seems to indicate that instead of the Palestinians taking over the West Bank, the Israelis will in due course establish some kind of governmental control over the East Bank." Tim LaHaye in 1984, illustrating his point that "the Jews today occupy only a small portion of what God intended for them to enjoy," superimposed "God's Original Land Grant to Israel" on a map of the modern Middle East; it showed Israel absorbing all of Lebanon, part of Saudi Arabia, and most of Jordan, Syria, and Iraq. Other writers foresaw Israel's expansion to absorb "all of the Arabian Peninsula" or "the oil-rich gulf states."[49]

Even when authors confined their territorial predictions to the Millennium, the amplitude of their vision tended to obscure the eschatological caveat. A 1955 writer, after detailing Israel's precise Nile-to-Euphrates boundaries in "earth's Golden Age," concluded: "This is real estate, actual . . . land on the surface of the earth. This is Israel, the nation, reoccupying its land in the future."[50]

The popularizers fleshed out their scenarios with "microprophecies" of specific events. One, for example, found Israel's control of the West Bank foretold in Jeremiah 31:5: "Thou shalt yet plant vines upon the mountains of Samaria." Another discerned the Jews' future ownership of the Mideast's oil fields in God's promise to the tribe of Asher, recorded in Deuteronomy: "Let Asher be blessed with children; let him be acceptable to his brethren, and let him dip his foot in oil."[51]

Instructed by scores of prophecy expositors, many Americans became convinced that God himself set modern Israel's boundaries three thousand years ago. As a Nebraska real-estate man observed on a pilgrimage to Israel in 1985: "The Arabs have to leave this land, because the land belongs only to the Jews. God gave all of this land to the Jews."[52]

Prophecy writers also foresaw the rebuilding of the Jewish Temple in Jerusalem, destroyed by the Romans in 70 A.D. Drawing on various biblical passages, they held that as the Tribulation begins, Antichrist will encourage the Jews to resume Temple worship. After three and a half years, however, he will set up his own image in the Temple. Christ will destroy this desecrated Temple at the Second Coming and erect a new one for his millennial reign. The key text (interpreted according to the day = year convention) is Daniel 9:27:

> And he [Antichrist] shall confirm the convenant with many for one week: and in the midst of the week he shall cause the sacrifice and the oblation to cease, and for the overspreading of abominations he shall make it desolate, even until the consummation, and that determined shall be poured upon the desolate.

In a parallel New Testament passage, Saint Paul proclaimed that before Christ's return "the son of perdition" will sit "in the temple of God, shewing himself that he is God." Concluding that these passages imply the existence of a Temple as the Tribulation *begins,* dispensationalist writers foresaw its rebuilding in the present age.[53]

Like most elements of the dispensational system, this one has a long history. Already in the early nineteenth century, prophecy writers were predicting the Temple's rebuilding. They noted with interest the passage in Benjamin Disraeli's 1832 novel *Alroy,* in which the Jewish hero declares: "You ask me what I wish: my answer is the Land of Promise. You ask me what I wish: my answer is Jerusalem. You ask me what I wish: my answer is the Temple."[54]

Such anticipations soared after 1948. Wilbur Smith, writing in 1949 of Jerusalem's age-old lure, could have been describing its fascination for prophecy believers as well:

> It is as though underneath its ancient walls and buildings a powerful magnet was placed, drawing people to it, century after century, until the city was destroyed in 70 A.D.; then the current of the magnet was turned off, only to be turned on again during the crusades, turned off again for six hundred years, and now more powerful currents seem to flow through this unseen magnet than since the Day of Pentecost.

Until recently, Smith continued, the idea of a restored Temple had seemed absurd. But in 1949, with the Israelis poised on the Old City's outskirts, it seemed "not ridiculous, but inevitable." By the 1950s, with this ultimate prophetic fulfillment seemingly so close, Smith could barely restrain his impatience: "Why the Jews do not go in and take that city, I do not know."[55] Prophecy-conference speakers and prophecy magazines such as *Moody Monthly* and *The Kings' Business* offered similar eager speculations in these years.[56]

After the 1967 war such forecasts multiplied. "The Temple will be rebuilt," exulted a 1968 writer; "Israel has the will, access to the means, and now the site." At the 1971 Jerusalem prophecy conference several speakers, including Charles Feinberg of Talbot Theological Seminary in Los Angeles, placed the rebuilding of the Temple next on the prophetic timetable. (Feinberg, a key figure in postwar prophecy circles, was an Orthodox Jew converted to Christianity in 1930. After study at Dallas Theological Seminary, he earned a Ph.D. in archaeology and Semitic languages from Johns Hopkins University.)[57]

A rare premillennial dissenter was George Ladd of Fuller Theological Seminary in Pasadena. In a 1978 challenge to the standard Darby-Scofield scenario, Ladd quoted the New Testament's characterization of Jewish ritual as "a shadow of good things to come, and not the very image of the things," to buttress his argument that prophecies of revived Temple worship should be read typologically, as anticipations of Christianity, rather than literally. Similarly, Ladd contended, passages describing the Temple's desecration were not to be taken literally but as a way of expressing Antichrist's general attempt to usurp God in the last days.[58]

Again, the popularizers showed little interest in such hermeneutic subtleties. Through paperbacks and the audiovisual media, including a heavily promoted 1983 film, *The Temple,* they confidently peddled their message: a new Temple will arise, probably very soon.[59]

Furthermore, they avidly reported every scrap of evidence that seemed to support this prediction, including excavations at Qumran by U.S. prophecy believer Vendyl Jones (inspiration for the *Indiana Jones* adventure movies of the 1980s) in search of the Ark of the Covenant and the vials of oil and red-heifer ashes used in Temple purification rites. They publicized the activities of Rabbi Yisrael Ariel's Temple Institute in Jerusalem, which prepared robes and furnishings for the rebuilt Temple, and Gershon Salomon's Temple Mount Faithful, ultra-Orthodox Jerusalem Jews who trained rabbis in the ancient rituals (including animal sacrifice), scoured the world for red heifers, conducted prayers on Temple Mount, and periodically sought to lay a cornerstone for the new Temple. Reports that Israel was stockpiling Indiana limestone for the future Temple circulated among prophecy believers in the 1970s. (Patiently denying the tale, Radio Israel answered queries by pointing out that Israel's one abundant natural resource is *stone,* so even if a rebuilt Temple were planned, imported limestone would hardly be necessary!)[60]

A major roadblock lay in the way of a restored Temple, however: since the seventh century, the Temple Mount site (known to Muslims as Haram al-Sharif, or Noble Sanctuary) has been occupied by the Mosque of Omar (the so-called Dome of the Rock), marking the spot where Mohammed ascended to heaven, and by Al Aksa Mosque, dating from the eighth century. As early as 1884 Robert Anderson recognized that rebuilding the Temple logically required eliminating the Mosque of Omar. The *Sunday School Times* suggested hopefully in 1919 that the mosque might simply be "transformed into a temple."[61]

After 1967 this arcane debate became more urgent. Some writers placed the earlier Temple site at a distance from the Mosque of Omar and argued that it could be rebuilt without disturbing the mosque. Most, however, assumed that the mosque must go. As one observed, "God is sensitive to the exact location of the Temple." Many quoted the reply of the Israeli historian Israel Eldad, reported in *Time* in 1967. When asked how the Temple could be rebuilt on an Islamic site sacred to millions, he responded: "Who knows? Perhaps there will be an earthquake."[62]

Eldad's "earthquake" rumbled through post-1967 prophecy expositions. Some writers foresaw direct divine intervention. "Perhaps God will act to clear the site," a 1973 book speculated. Others anticipated more mundane means. A 1930 writer had conjectured that a bomb could solve the Dome-of-the-Rock problem "in a few minutes," and in succeeding years many others toyed with the same idea. Louis Goldberg suggested in 1982 that in a future Arab-Israeli war "a surface-to-surface missile could be fired from the Syrian or Jordanian side which might unintentionally hit the mosque and destroy it." In Salem Kirban's prophecy novel *666,* Antichrist zaps the mosque with his ruby laser ring. (The Temple Mount Faithful proposed still another option: transport the Dome of the Rock stone by stone to Mecca.) American prophecy writers avidly reported the efforts by Jewish zealots in 1981 and again in 1984 to blow up the Mosque of Omar.[63]

In their obsession with the rebuilding of the Temple, these prophecy popularizers ignored the fact that most Israelis rejected the whole notion. Epithets like "a bunch of nuts" and "dangerous lunatics" routinely dotted Israeli press accounts of groups like the Temple Mount Faithful. (My Jerusalem tour guide, a student at Haifa University, observed in 1990 that any tampering with Haram al-Sharif would set off an Islamic holy war, and added, "The best thing that ever happened to us was when we stopped sacrificing cows and started reading the Book.")[64]

The intense emotions surrounding this issue boiled over in October 1990 when the Temple Mount Faithful announced plans to lay a cornerstone for the Temple, on Temple Mount, during the Jewish holiday week of Succoth. On the appointed day, crowds of Palestinian Arabs gathered protectively around Haram al-Sharif. Some pitched rocks at Jews praying at the Western Wall (the only remaining section of the earlier Temple, and Judaism's most sacred spot). Israeli police, at first driven back, returned some time later (when the rock throwing had stopped) and raked the crowd with automatic weapons fire, leaving 125 wounded and 21 dead, including a seventy-one-year-old man, a forty-year-old woman, and a fifteen-year-old boy.[65]

Warnings that the destruction of Haram al-Sharif would unleash a holy war carried scant weight with premillennialists, who already foresaw horrendous conflict in Israel's future. The precise means by which Temple Mount would be cleared they dismissed as a minor detail. Ray Stedman wrote in 1970 that how the Israelis "surmount the problem of rebuilding a temple on the place now occupied by an Arab holy place is anyone's guess. But rebuild it they shall, for as Jesus said . . . , 'The Scriptures cannot be broken.'" A new Temple, agreed John Wesley White in 1980, "is an absolute necessity for the completion of the prophetic picture."[66] As Mideast conflict ebbed and flowed, and as yet more blood seeped into the saturated stones of Temple Mount, this ancient and alluring prospect, with all its potential for folly and catastrophe, continued to shimmer on the pages of countless popular works of prophetic interpretation.

What about Ishmael?

An uneasy question hovered over all discussions of Israel's prophetic destiny: what about the millions of Arabs inhabiting the lands granted Abraham by divine decree? Since Mohammed and Islam were for centuries identified with Antichrist or Gog, prophecy writers from the medieval era on viewed the Arab world with suspicion.[67] John Darby set the tone for modern premillennialists as early as 1840: "The first thing, then, which the Lord will do, will be to purify His land (the land which belongs to the Jews) of the Tyrians, the Philistines, the Sidonians—of all the wicked, in short, from the Nile to the Euphrates." In the 1850s the popularizer John Cumming discussed "The Moslem and His End" as a sign of the last days. Although the Balfour Declaration mentioned "the civil and religious rights of existing non-Jewish communities in Palestine," prophecy believers who hailed this document displayed, as Dwight Wilson notes, "a total lack of awareness" of the indigenous Arab population. Indeed, Wilson finds a "general anti-Arab disposition" in interwar premillennial writings.[68]

This hostility continued as a Jewish state moved closer to realization. A 1946 popularizer wrote of "the rabble Moslem hordes" resisting the Jewish restoration. A 1947 *Moody Monthly* author wistfully traced the problem to its source: "Had Sarah believed God, there would have been no Palestine problem today. Had she not given her slave girl, Hagar, to Abraham, there would have been no Arabs." In 1948 Lewis Sperry Chafer wrote:

> When Israel first entered the land from Egypt, they were given instructions to "drive out" the inhabitants and were given power to do so. They have no such instructions or power to clear the land today of the children of Ishmael; yet that very thing may occur in the end.[69]

An anti-Arab bias colored much post-1948 prophecy writing. As we saw in Chapter 5, many authors assumed Arab complicity in Russia's invasion of Israel. Others speculated that the Arabs would use their control of oil to enforce Antichrist's global economic order during the Tribulation. "The Arab world is an Antichrist-world," one asserted.[70]

In addressing Mideast issues specifically, most prophecy writers either ignored the Arabs or treated them as an obstacle to be removed.

While portraying Jewish nationalism as a "divine call back to the Holy Land," writes Dwight Wilson, they presented Arab nationalism as "a sinister demonic force." Some even suggested that God favored Jewish over Arab agriculture: "[When Jews] are in possession of the land, it prospers," wrote one; "when they are absent from the land, it withers and is only good for keeping goats."[71]

The consensus was clear: prophetic imperatives required the eventual elimination of the Arabs not only from Temple Mount, but from most of the Middle East. The scriptural basis of this view was both inferential—they stood in the way of God's promises to the Jews—and explicit. Wilbur Smith in 1967 cited God's curse on "mount Seir" (which he took as a reference to modern-day Arabs) recorded in Ezekiel:

> Thus saith the Lord God; Behold, O mount Seir, I am against thee, and I will stretch out mine hand against thee, and I will make thee most desolate.
>
> I will lay thy cities waste, and thou shalt be desolate, and thou shalt know that I am the Lord.
>
> Because thou hast had a perpetual hatred, and hast shed the blood of the children of Israel by the force of the sword in the time of their calamity, in the time that their iniquity had an end:
>
> Therefore, as I live, saith the Lord God, I will prepare thee unto blood, and blood shall pursue thee: sith [since] thou has not hated blood, even blood shall pursue thee.[72]

Israel's triumph in the 1967 war, observed Smith, confirmed "the truthfulness of this ancient prophecy." Commented another writer that year, "The Old Testament prophets make it abundantly plain . . . that judgment will fall upon the Arab people . . . , the Arab will be swept out of the land and . . . Israel will be reestablished there."[73]

Such grim forecasts proliferated in the ensuing years. "God will in His own good time cast out the sons of Ishmael, despite all their devisings and intrigues, and will settle the sons of Isaac," wrote Charles Feinberg in 1968. When Christ rules on earth, "Edom will be gone forever," predicted S. Maxwell Coder in 1984, "along with other Arab nations which have sought to destroy the chosen people of God." Perhaps bluntest of all was Arthur Bloomfield:

> When all the Jews return at once under the power of God, and in complete fulfillment of the prophecies . . . , Arab power will be destroyed . . . God says he will lay the land of the Arabs

waste and it will be desolate . . . This may seem like a severe punishment; but the provocation is going to be very great. The terms of the covenant must be carried out to the letter: "I will curse him that curseth thee." [74]

A few authors sympathized with the Arabs' plight while insisting on its inevitability. A 1951 *Moody Monthly* writer, though reiterating God's vast land grant to the Jews, described the "pitiable" sufferings of the Palestinian refugees and conceded that "we cannot expect unredeemed Arabs, or any unsaved people, to look at this whole thing in the light of Scripture." A 1980s popularizer called the Palestinian situation "a tragedy," but one "apparently in keeping with the prophetic foresight." "God loves the Arabs as well as the Jews," observed John Walvoord in 1989, but insisted that God's promises to the Jews remain unalterable. Those who "resent that are not fighting me," he added; "they're fighting the Bible." [75]

A handful of prophecy writers deplored the genre's anti-Arab tone and criticized Israel's policies. Of the Palestinian refugees, Donald Grey Barnhouse wrote in 1949, "Israel must remember that there are promises to Ishmael as well as to Isaac, and they will drink a bitter cup if they continue in their cruel and heartless way." In a 1967 manifesto reaffirming Israel's high prophetic destiny, the Bible Institute of Los Angeles included a good word for the Arabs:

> God's purpose for the Arab world includes promises of national enlargement and blessing. They along with all Gentiles are the objects of God's love and of the proclamation of His grace. Therefore, we acknowledge our indebtedness to them, as to all nations, and desire to contribute to their spiritual, social, and material needs. [76]

A delegate to the 1971 Jerusalem prophecy conference emphasized that God's restoration of the Jews to Palestine "does not exempt Israel any more than her neighbors from full answerability to justice and judgment." Belief in the Jews' preordained destiny, wrote Harold Lindsell in 1984, ought not blind one to "the plight of the Arabs who have been forcibly removed from homes and villages they have occupied for hundreds of years." [77]

But such qualifications were rare. More typically, prophecy writers provided an eschatological rationale for anti-Arab prejudice. However unwittingly, premillennialist popularizers over the decades contributed to the anti-Arab biases and stereotypes that pervaded U.S. mass culture.

Over the years, the premillennial perspective induced feelings of fatalism toward Mideast peace initiatives or efforts to moderate the region's ancient enmities. A 1978 popularizer dismissed as futile the "hesitant, bargaining peace arrangement we are seeing today in the Middle East"; only in the Millennium would Arab-Israeli conflict cease. Invoking a similar sense of divine fatality, the Lebanese Christian diplomat Charles Malik wrote in *Foreign Affairs* in 1952, "To dismiss the present conflict between the children of Isaac and the children of Ishmael . . . as just another ordinary politico-economic struggle, is to have no sense whatever for the awful and holy and ultimate in history." [78] Whatever the value of such a perspective for one's historical sensibility, its effect on the impulse toward diplomacy and peacemaking can be enervating. If God is on Israel's side, what point has compromise or negotiation? If Jew and Arab are foreordained to "perpetual hatred" (as Wilbur Smith put it), why make any effort to diminish that hostility?

Policy Implications

In the decades since 1948, as we have seen, prophecy believers formed a bulwark of support for Israel. As one put it in 1975, as long as God used Israel as an instrument of prophetic fulfillment, "I can do no other as his servant than stand with him whatever the cost." Jerry Falwell made the same point: "Theologically, any Christian has to support Israel, simply because Jesus said to"; and "If we fail to protect Israel, we will cease to be important to God." Addressing a 1985 conference of rabbis, Falwell denied that his pro-Israel politics arose from his eschatology, but for him and many others the link is clear. Warned Hal Lindsey in 1981, "If the U.S. ever turns its back on Israel, we will no longer exist as a nation." Jews should realize, observed Tim LaHaye in 1984, that "Bible-believing, pre-millennialist Christians are Israel's best friends." [79]

Over the years, premillennialists gave Israel largely uncritical support. In 1965, rejecting United Nations and United States policy, one popularizer wrote: "Any attempt to divide the land of Palestine is contrary to God's word, for it has been set aside by God as the exclusive home for Israel. A great error on the part of the nations has been to partition the Promised Land." [80]

From Israel's perspective this backing grew more important as other support diminished. When Israel was founded, the National Council of Churches and other liberal Protestant voices warmly backed the new nation. (So did evangelicals, but their pronouncements received less attention.) As time passed, however, liberal Protestantism grew increasingly critical, displaying what many Jews felt to be (in the words of the historian Hertzel Fishman) a "persistently hostile attitude" toward "Jewish national and ethnic interests." The mutual disenchantment intensified after the Six-Day War in 1967, when Israel occupied not only Jerusalem's Old City but also the West Bank and the Gaza Strip. [81]

While liberal Protestant leaders expressed growing reservations about Israel's policies, evangelicals and especially premillennial writers hailed the 1967 expansion as a dramatic prophetic fulfillment. A few expressed caution—"The State of Israel is not relieved of its obligation to act responsibly in the community of nations even though the secret purpose of God may be brought to fruition through its actions," wrote Charles Ryrie of Dallas Theological Seminary—but such qualifications were rare. [82]

As liberal Protestant support eroded, Israel played its fundamentalist card. Privately ridiculing premillennialist readings of prophecy as those of a six-year-old child, they recognized an important political bloc and dealt with it accordingly. Not only did David Ben-Gurion welcome the 1971 Jerusalem prophecy conference, but his government provided the hall. Israel's UN ambassador, Chaim Herzog, gave an interview for the film version of *The Late Great Planet Earth*. In the 1970s and 1980s, Holy Land tours led by televangelists and prophecy writers such as Falwell and Oral Roberts received red-carpet treatment, including briefings from top Israeli officials such as Defense Minister Moshe Arens. On one occasion Prime Minister Menachem Begin met with a delegation of some sixty U.S. evangelical leaders. "I have personally discussed the Ezekiel 38 passage with . . . Begin," boasted one prophecy writer in 1982, "and I know that Rev. Hilton Sutton has met with Begin's advisors, shown them films, and done a presentation for them on the Gog and Magog (Russia) passage." Another told of eleven meetings with his "old friend" Begin, including a late-night get-together at New York's Waldorf-Astoria Hotel in 1984, attended by officials of the National Association of Religious Broadcasters and the National Association of Evangelicals, and the wife of Texas oilman Clint Murchison, Jr., among others, the day before Begin met with President Reagan.[83]

The Israeli-premillennialist nexus, sealed by the former's *Realpolitik* and the latter's prophecy beliefs, certainly figured in Israel's political calculations during this period. Shortly after the 1967 war, Yona Malachy of the Israeli Department of Religious Affairs, in America to study fundamentalist attitudes toward Israel, urged the Bible Institute of Los Angeles (BIOLA), a major center of prophecy study, to take a stronger pro-Israel stand. BIOLA responded with a manifesto that, while noting Arab interests, emphasized Israel's eschatological role and suggested that "recent developments in the Middle East may be preparing the way for these great prophetic events. The true people of God should not be found in league with those who oppose the will and work of God for Israel."[84]

Another manifestation of the post-1967 realignment was Christians Concerned for Israel (later the National Christian Leadership Conference for Israel). Among the executive committee members in 1990 was prophecy writer Hilton Sutton. To achieve its goal of "educat[ing] the American public, and especially the Christians, in the political and religious significance of the close relationship between the United States and Israel," NCLCI organized rallies, conferences, pilgrimages to Israel, and letter-writing campaigns to legislators and editors. "God's irrevocable covenant with the Jewish people," it asserted in a 1990 statement, "has never been withdrawn or transferred to any other people." Any attempt to internationalize Jerusalem "is wrong and futile," the statement went on, "and ignores biblical and historical reality."[85]

Some U.S. Jews defended on pragmatic grounds Israel's courting of fundamentalist support. Wrote Nathan Perlmutter, director of the Anti-Defamation League, in 1982: "Jews can live with all the domestic priorities of the Christian Right on which liberal Jews differ so radically, because none of these concerns is as important as Israel." While liberal Protestantism had embraced the Palestinian cause, Perlmutter added in 1985, fundamentalists were "respectful, even downright reverential toward Jews" and gave Israel "wholehearted, uncritical admiration." Jews should revise "smug assumptions" about fundamentalists loosely derived from Sinclair Lewis, he said, and recognize them as strong supporters of Israel. Irving Kristol, in a 1984 *Commentary* article, similarly urged Jews to overcome the assumption that fundamentalism meant anti-Semitism and recognize that modern fundamentalists were "unequivocally pro-Israel." With "anti-Israel sentiment. . . distinctly on the rise," he went on, fundamentalist support could "in the near future, turn out to be decisive for the very existence of the Jewish state." Meanwhile, similar views had emerged from the far right of Israeli politics. Rabbi Meir Kahane, founder of the violence-prone Jewish Defense League and advocate of the expulsion of Arabs from Israel, in 1975 praised evangelical Christian prophecy believers for their "total and unconditional" support of Israel.[86]

Israel's wooing of U.S. fundamentalists paid off handsomely; numerous prophecy writers portrayed Israel as the key to God's end-time plan and supported the Jewish state on a wide range of policy issues. "There is something going on in Israel," exulted Oral Roberts after a trip to Israel paid for by the Israeli government, and interviews with high government officials.

> It is of eternal consequence, and the spiritual significance of that something leaps in my blood like a flame. God's ancient people are carving out an empire . . . That's what the Bible told us they would do. The meaning of this in terms of a coming great world revival and the Second Coming of Jesus has thrilled me to the very fibre and core of my being.

The 1970 Billy Graham film, *His Land,* dramatizing the premillennial view of Israel, aroused criticism as thinly veiled propaganda for current Israeli policies and for its anti-Arab stereotypes. A Calvin College professor, writing from the Reformed theological tradition, attacked the film's premise "that modern Palestine is God's own special piece of real estate."[87]

Lindsey and other prophecy writers identified themselves with Israel's most expansionist political elements. Some praised Israel's 1982 invasion of Lebanon (which led to massacres in Palestinian refugee camps) as a means of prophetic fulfillment. Declared one premillennialist soon after: "It was a sacred war . . . It was right out of the Old Testament and confirms biblical prophecy." David Lewis, chairman of the board of directors of the Assemblies of God Church and a founder of the National Christian Leadership Conference for Israel, argued in *Magog 1982 Canceled* that Israel's action in Lebanon had delayed the Russian invasion foretold in Ezekiel, and thus temporarily postponed the end of the world. NCLCI itself organized a pro-Israel White House demonstration and ran a large advertisement in the *New York Times* defending Israel's actions and dismissing reports of heavy civilian casualties in Lebanon as "highly exaggerated." Among the 104 signers were several prominent premillennialists, including David Lewis, Jerry Falwell, and NCLCI board member Hilton Sutton. (On the hustings, Sutton claimed that flying saucers are celestial craft flown by Israel's guardian angels. UFO sightings increase dramatically, he asserted in his 1988 Madison appearance, whenever Israel goes to war.)[88]

When Prime Minister Yitzhak Shamir visited Los Angeles in 1988, prominent Jews such as actor Richard Dreyfuss attacked his hard-line position on the Palestinian issue. By contrast, a delegation of evangelical ministers greeted him enthusiastically, insisting on the perfect harmony between biblical prophecy and Likud Party policies. "We support you and we love you, Mr. Prime Minister," said the group's leader. Responded Shamir emotionally: "Your arguments are brilliant . . . Your devotion to our country will become a strong arm in our arsenal of defense."[89]

Acting on their prophetic beliefs, some U.S. premillennialists gave moral and financial support to Israel's West Bank settlement program, to the Temple rebuilding project, and even to fringe groups plotting to demolish the Mosque of Omar. Particularly active in the Temple-rebuilding cause, according to writer Grace Halsell, were oilman Terry Reisenhoover; the ubiquitous Hilton Sutton; James De-Loach of Houston's Second Baptist Church; and Bobi Hromas, wife of a TRW Corporation executive (and daughter of an Assemblies of God minister). Charles Colson's fictional 1983 scenario of the outbreak of World War III, in which U.S. prophecy believers encourage and finance Israeli zealots who blow up the Dome of the Rock, had a kernel of fact at its core.[90]

We have seen that prophecy writers discounted diplomatic efforts for a negotiated peace in the Middle East. As one put it as early as 1950, Israel's territorial claims reflected God's will and thus transcended politics: regardless of UN resolutions, other nations' interests, or "the ebb and flow of conflict between Arab and Jew," he wrote, "this matter was settled centuries ago." With diplomacy irrelevant, its practitioners became suspect. During Secretary of State Henry Kissinger's Mideast shuttle diplomacy of the early 1970s, some prophecy writers pegged him as Antichrist, the end-time figure who will initially present himself as a man of peace.[91]

The dismissal of Mideast peace efforts by prophecy writers, and their conviction that Israel's territorial expansion is foreordained, aroused the ire of groups from the liberal lobby People for the American Way to the peace-minded evangelical magazine *Sojourners;* nothing was more likely to undermine Mideast peace initiatives, said the latter in 1977, "than the belief that God has a vested interest in the amount of real estate controlled by the state of Israel."[92] Such criticism had scant effect, however. Jerry Falwell spoke for mainstream premillennialist thought when he proclaimed at the signing of the Camp David accords between Israel and Egypt in 1979: "In spite of the rosy and utterly unrealistic expectations by our government, this treaty will not be a lasting treaty . . . You and I know that there's not going to be any real peace in the Middle East until the Lord Jesus sits down upon the throne of David in Jerusalem."[93]

Probably more important than prophecy writers' pronouncements on specific Mideast issues was the cumulative effect of premillennialist teaching. Via TV and radio sermons, paperback books, audiovisual productions, and articles in the religious press, the word ceaselessly went out in the decades after 1948: Israel's history (like all history, only more so) is best understood from the perspective of Bible prophecy—a perspective from which the clashes of nations and the hatreds of peoples are eternally determined, and beyond human influence or control.

The Darker Side of the Picture

Early in 1990, at Jerusalem's Yad Vashem Holocaust Memorial, amid searing photographs and relics of the Nazi death camps, a Nigerian Christian professor from Ibadan University murmured to me, "Surely when the Jews see how they've been persecuted, they must realize their mistake in not accepting Christ." My African acquaintance was far from alone in her view. While premillennialists foresee a bright future for Israel, terrible events lie ahead as well. The Jews, long punished by God for their sinfulness, face a final horrendous ordeal during the Tribulation. Only after this "winnowing" will the survivors at last accept Jesus as Messiah. If we are fully to understand prophetic belief about the Jews, these somber and disturbing themes demand attention.

Talk of persecution ahead for the Jews pervaded Anglo-American prophecy writing from the seventeenth century on. One finds it in Increase Mather and in Samuel Hopkins' *Treatise on the Millennium* (1793).[94] During the Tribulation, John Darby taught, Antichrist will slaughter two-thirds of the Jews regathered in Palestine. This endlessly repeated figure derives from Zechariah: "And it shall come to pass, that in all the land, saith the Lord, two parts therein shall be cut off and die; but the third shall be left therein."[95]

In the last days, wrote James Brookes in 1870, "an unequalled visitation of wrath" would fall on the Jews, "a people still so inveterate in their prejudices, and so obstinate in their rejecting the Messiah." At the 1878 New York City prophecy conference, a Philadelphia Reformed Episcopal bishop, discussing the Jews' return to Palestine, observed, "The object of their gathering is ultimately their conversion, but primarily their chastisement and suffering." William Blackstone is said to have hidden a cache of New Testaments at Petra (in present-day Jordan) where, according to a passage in Revelation, Jews fleeing the end-time persecution will seek refuge.[96]

In the early twentieth century, Cyrus Scofield portrayed both Antichrist and Gog as participants in a "mad attempt to exterminate the remnant of Israel." Before the Jews' "glorious future," argued Arthur Pink in *The Antichrist* (1923), they would atone for the "murder of Christ" with unparalleled suffering, as Antichrist tried "to banish Israel from the earth." In permitting this persecution, explained another 1920s writer, God would not seek to destroy the Jews, but to "chasten them as a father would a wayward child."[97]

Prophecy writers of the 1930s and early 1940s generally treated Nazi persecution of the Jews as a sad but wholly foreseeable instance of God's effort to correct his recalcitrant people, and a foretaste of worse ahead. The prophesied punishment of the Jews for "deliberate, persistent, and continued apostasy," wrote the editor of the *Sunday School Times* in 1937, was being "fulfilled with poignant fidelity . . . in Germany today." The Jews' "wail of distress is heard even now," wrote Arno Gaebelein that same year, but "greater troubles are gathering for them and the storm will break when [Antichrist] appears." A 1942 prophecy expositor observed calmly, "The recent Jewish persecutions in Germany and elsewhere were all foretold in God's Holy Word thousands of years ago"; Nazi assaults on Jews, he added, would pale in comparison to the mass slaughter during Antichrist's reign.[98]

As Israel proclaimed its independence in 1948, a Canadian prophecy writer foresaw an "awful massacre" ahead; "much suffering awaits Israel," agreed the *Sunday School Times* somberly. In the July 1951 issue of *Moody Monthly,* one writer cautioned that the Jews' return to Palestine in unbelief would bring only "sorrow, suffering, disappointment, and death," while another applied to the new nation a grim prophecy from Hosea: "They shall fall by the sword: their infants shall be dashed in pieces, and their women with child shall be ripped up." Added Paul Alderman in 1954: "Much-beloved, but persistently disobedient, the Christ-rejecting nation must . . . drink the cup of God's wrath to the last drop—even to the point of apparent destruction and extermination . . . The Lord God will, as heretofore, also use human instruments in His scourging of His wandering people." [99]

As Israel's continued "apostasy" became unavoidably apparent, such warnings increased. Having failed to show "repentance and faith in Jesus Christ," declared the editor of *Prophetic Word* in 1960, the Jews of Israel faced "certain disaster." As the people who crucified Jesus, added a 1962 writer (invoking the principle of corporate guilt that pervaded this literature), the Jews would soon "reap the dreadful harvest of their evil sowing." Six million Jews died at Hitler's hands, observed a prophecy-conference speaker in 1963, but their "greatest sorrow is yet to come." Citing an often-quoted passage from Jeremiah, this speaker foresaw "the time of Jacob's trouble" ahead for the Jews. Ultimately Israel's suffering would yield to a glorious destiny, but first, dreadful events loomed on the prophetic calendar. [100] These writers offered their forecasts sorrowfully, but few questioned their inevitability.

John Walvoord, in *Israel in Prophecy* and other writings, elaborated the hermeneutics of this belief. While the Jews will ultimately reign with Christ and possess all the land promised to Abraham, Walvoord argued, this favored people was also, paradoxically, "destined for suffering . . . exceed[ing] that of any other nation of the world." Deuteronomy foretells the whole sad history:

> And ye shall be left few in number, whereas ye were as the stars of heaven for multitude; because thou wouldest not obey the voice of the Lord thy God.
> And it shall come to pass, that as the Lord rejoiced over you to do you good, and to multiply you; so the Lord will rejoice over you to destroy you, and to bring you to nought; and ye shall be plucked from off the land whither thou goest to possess it.

> And the Lord shall scatter thee among all people, from the one end of the earth even unto the other, and there thou shalt serve other gods, which neither thou nor thy fathers have known, even wood and stone.
>
> And among these nations shalt thou find no ease, neither shall the sole of thy foot have rest: but the Lord shall give thee there a trembling heart, and failing of eyes, and sorrow of mind:
>
> And thy life shall hang in doubt before thee; and thou shalt fear day and night, and shalt have none assurance of thy life:
>
> In the morning thou shalt say, Would God it were even! and at even thou shalt say, Would God it were morning! for the fear of thine heart wherewith thou shalt fear, and for the sight of thine eyes which thou shalt see. [101]

Not only in the days of Babylon and Rome, said Walvoord in 1962, but through all history, this grim prophecy has been and shall be fulfilled:

> Israel is destined to have a particular time of suffering which will eclipse any thing that it has known in the past . . . Heart-rending as it may be to contemplate, the people of Israel who are returning to their ancient land are placing themselves within the vortex of this future whirlwind which will destroy the majority of those living in the land of Palestine. The searching and refining fire of divine judgment will produce in Israel that which is not there now, an attitude of true repentance and eager anticipation of the coming of their Messiah. [102]

With proof texts from Deuteronomy, Jeremiah, Daniel, Zechariah, Matthew, and Revelation, Walvoord offered the following detailed timetable of end-time events as they impinge on the Jews. As Antichrist's seven-year rule begins, he helps Israel rebuild the Temple and defends the nation against its enemies, and many Jews hail him as Messiah. But midway through the Tribulation, when he sets up his own image in the Temple ("the abomination that maketh desolate"— Dan. 12:11), many horrified Jews realize their error and reject his claims. Indeed, 144,000 men drawn from the twelve tribes of Israel proclaim Christ to the world and suffer martyrdom. As Antichrist unleashes "a bloodbath of astounding proportions," Jews die in ghastly numbers. A few find refuge in the rocks of Petra, but only a remnant survive at the Second Coming to acclaim the true Messiah. [103]

Scores of late-twentieth-century popularizers repeated and embellished this basic scenario. One, discussing Antichrist's initial treaty with Israel, noted, "What he gets from the Jews no one knows, though it is fairly certain that money figures in this move some-where." Others, reviving an ancient interpretive tradition based on Daniel 11:37 ("Neither shall he regard the God of his fathers"), con-tended that Antichrist *himself* will be a Jew. (Lindsey, with his usual freewheeling approach, foresaw *two* Beasts: one Gentile, claiming to be God; the other Jewish, the "False Prophet," masquerading as the Messiah.)[104]

The 1967 recapture of Jerusalem, while hailed as a stunning pro-phetic fulfillment, also brought Israel's final holocaust ominously closer. Wilbur Smith, warning that year of "terror and tragedy" ahead for the Jews, quoted the ominous words of Zechariah—"For I will gather all nations against Jerusalem to battle; and the city shall be taken, and the houses rifled, and the women ravished." During the Tribulation, agreed Merrill Unger, the Jews will face "the greatest crisis of anguish they have ever endured in their long history of suf-fering." [105]

As usual, Hal Lindsey offered a slangy, juiced-up pastiche of fa-miliar beliefs. In a section of *The Late Great Planet Earth* wittily en-titled "God's Woodshed," Lindsey traced God's "disciplinary action" against the Jews from Babylonian and Roman days to its culmination under Antichrist, when Israel will endure "unparalleled catastrophe" and "a numberless multitude" of Jews will die, including the 144,000 witnesses for Christ ("144,000 Jewish Billy Grahams"). Lindsey inter-preted Revelation 12:14, in which a woman menaced by "a great red dragon" sprouts "two wings of a great eagle" and flies into the wilder-ness, as U.S. Air Force jets transporting Jews beyond Antichrist's clutches.[106]

Though without Lindsey's imaginative flair, subsequent popular-izers shared his view of the Jews' dark prospects. "Things are going to get worse—much worse—before they get better," declared a 1975 author discussing "Israel's Coming Day of Calamity." S. Maxwell Coder, citing Zechariah's prophecy that "two parts . . . shall be cut off and die," foresaw "the worst persecution of the Jews known to history" during the Tribulation.[107]

Prophecy writers portrayed this coming holocaust as the means to a good outcome: Israel's salvation and future glory. Walvoord, cit-ing the Deuteronomy passage quoted above—"the Lord will rejoice over you to destroy you"—argued that God's punishments of the Jews are in reality "demonstrations of His love" in drawing a "godly remnant" back to the fold. Paul Lee Tan made the same point in *The Interpretation of Prophecy*:

> The tribulation will definitely be a part of Israel's sorrowful and tragic history . . . The unbelief and failures of Israel are pruned and punished through the unparalleled fires of the tribulation. The Jewish remnant entering the millennium at the end of the tribulation will thus have been purified for the kingdom.

(This "remnant," scoffed Shirley Jackson Case in 1918, "will be like a couple of legs or a piece of ear recovered by a shepherd after the lion has preyed upon his flock.") While the Jews' prophetic fate "has had its ups and downs," a 1987 work observed, ultimately it will prove "a profound blessing and privilege" in "finally restoring much chastened Israel to its God." [108]

Jews will not be the only victims during the Tribulation. *All* who miss the Rapture will endure agonies as the earth reels under God's lash. Gentiles as well as Jews who resist Antichrist face martyrdom. But the Jews' fate will be uniquely grim. Israel will be "the focal point of the coming judgments," observed Charles Taylor, and those judgments will continue until "the wicked ones and the wicked ways thereof are purged out of her." [109]

As one seeks the precise source of Israel's final ordeal, a telling ambiguity arises. Taken as a whole, the genre sees Jews as victims of *both* God's loving judgment *and* Satan's hatred. While some writers say God will unleash the invasion foretold in Ezekiel 38 to punish the Jews for *worshiping* Antichrist, others view it as Satan's revenge for their *refusal* to bow down to the Beast! A speaker at a 1956 prophecy conference developed the latter theme in discussing Gog's invasion:

> Blood will flow up to the horses' bridles, and the people of Israel will be right in the midst of the sea of blood, about to be engulfed in it. All the fury of hell will be poured out upon them. Satan has never forgiven them for the fact that . . . Christ . . . is of Judah's seed, and the Antichrist will be consumed with indignation against them because of their refusal to pay him divine homage. [110]

This ambiguity goes very deep. One finds it even in a careful expositor such as Walvoord, who in *Israel in Prophecy* portrayed the

Jews both as the objects of "special Satanic attack" because they are God's chosen ones and of God's wrath for their unbelief. Dwight Pentecost similarly pictured the Jews' end-time suffering as coming from God, because they "wilfully and knowingly rejected Jesus Christ as their Savior and Sovereign," and also from Satan, who will persuade his earthly allies "to unleash their fury against the land of Israel." [111] The Jews, in short, face the ultimate catch-22: whether they reject or accept Christ in the last days, powerful supernatural and human foes will try to wipe them out. (The premillennialist, of course, would point out that Tribulation-era Jews who profess Christ and die for their faith will soon be resurrected to a glorious reward, while those who die in unbelief enjoy no such hope.)

What is the moral status of those whose deeds contribute to God's "chastisement" of the Jews? After all, Hitler in *Mein Kampf* justified his actions on theological grounds: "I believe today that I am acting in the sense of the Almighty Creator. By warding off the Jews, I am fighting for the Lord's work." Prophecy writers who addressed the issue vehemently rejected any such blasphemous conclusion. While human actions may further the prophetic plan, they argued, these actions are nevertheless subject to judgment if they violate moral law. Cyrus Scofield took this position in discussing past and future persecution of the Jews, and most of his successors agreed. In 1937, as Hitler's anti-Jewish campaign raged, one author observed, "While God has permitted anti-Semitism to be the rod of correction upon His ancient people, the fact remains that for those who participate in this persecution, there are no more burning warnings in the Word of God." This was consistent with a long-standing exegetical tradition. As a prophecy writer of 1794 had put it, in commenting on the role of the atheistic French Revolution in weakening the papacy, "God often accomplishes his purposes by his enemies." [112]

In contemplating the way evil individuals and evil means can further the divine purpose, prophecy writers cited passages from II Chronicles, in which a wrathful God incites the Chaldeans to slaughter the Jews for their wickedness, and from Jeremiah, where God calls the pagan ruler Nebuchadnezzar "my servant" for attacking the wayward Israelites. In the same fashion, argued a 1973 author, God will use Antichrist as "the instrument for bringing [the Jews] to a proper attitude of humility for accepting Christ as their Messiah-Deliverer." History, especially twentieth-century history, makes no sense, observed Derek Prince in 1982, "until we realize that God is prepared to let terrible things happen in order to accomplish His purpose with one particular nation: Israel . . . God permits those He loves to pass through suffering, because the end result is of infinite value in His sight; and it cannot be achieved in any other way." [113]

Among the prophecy writers to wrestle with this issue was Louis Goldberg of Moody Bible Institute. "It is a chilling prospect to talk about a future crisis and catastrophe for Israel in view of all the Jewish people have already experienced," wrote Goldberg (himself a Christian of Jewish background) in 1982. Nevertheless, he proceeded to set forth the familiar premillennial scenario involving a coming Jewish holocaust and the extermination of two-thirds of Israel's population. Who will be responsible? Here Goldberg, like most prophecy writers, equivocates. "The carnage and destruction" will be "in exact accordance with Satan's desires"—but it will *also* be God's work "in preparing His people to identify the Messiah." Ultimately, one comes back to the fact of foreordination: "Israel can never escape its . . . divine rendezvous." In conversation, Goldberg distinguished between direct will and permissive will: God sometimes allows human agents such as Judas (who in betraying Jesus advanced the plan of salvation) to do evil things, but these actions, even when they further the prophetic timetable, remain evil, and will be punished. [114]

Many of these complex and troubling themes coalesced in the retrospective comments of prophecy writers on the Nazi era. Terrible as it was, the argument went, the Holocaust furthered God's plan for the Jews. First, it was yet another in a long series of chastisements. Jack Van Impe in *Israel's Final Holocaust* (1979) wrote feelingly of the Jews' suffering under Hitler, yet saw it as a direct consequence of their spiritual blindness:

> The Jews missed their Messiah. He walked among them and they did not recognize Him . . . Following the rejection of their Messiah and the dispersion after the destruction of Jerusalem, the Jews entered upon their longest period of suffering and persecution. Sixty years after the leveling of Jerusalem . . . , a sizable number of Jews [attempted] to return to their land, but this abortive move was doomed to failure and more than one-half million were massacred . . . In taking the long look at history, one sees that the Jews had been steadily marching toward Hitler's ovens ever since the fall of their beloved city in A.D. 70. [115]

The Holocaust also helped drive the Jews back to the Promised Land. "All that Hitler accomplished by his European-wide persecution may be summed up in one sentence," wrote Harry Rimmer in 1946: "He accelerated the return of Israel to Palestine."[116]

Yet once the return to the land is complete, the "chastisement" that flared in Hitler's Germany will surge to a new crescendo of horror. Adopting the typological interpretive mode familiar in Christian exegesis, prophecy writers saw the Holocaust of the 1930s as a foreshadowing of future events, and Hitler, while not himself Antichrist, as the latest in a long parade of evil figures, going back to Antiochus Ephiphanes, who anticipate the Evil One. Antichrist's persecution, said Lindsey, would make Hitler and his ilk "look like Girl Scouts weaving a daisy chain." Wrote Arthur Bloomfield:

> It took a Hitler to turn the Jews toward Palestine. It will take a greater Hitler to turn them to God . . . Antichrist's persecution will be much more terrible than Hitler's. Hitler used gas chambers; he got rid of six million Jews, but Antichrist's purpose will be to do away with all Jews of all nations. That many Jews cannot be driven into gas chambers, but they could be driven into Egypt. Egypt has great deserts where Jews could be sent to die and their bones would not clutter up good ground.

A 1982 writer summarized matters concisely: "As much as Israel wants to avoid a repeat of the tragedies experienced in those Nazi concentration camps, another holocaust is inevitable."[117]

But almost without exception, these same writers viewed Hitler, despite his prophetic role, as a moral monster who suffered divine retribution for his evil deeds. Lewis Sperry Chafer wrote in 1948 that "Jehovah may chasten His people and even use the nations to that end, but invariably judgment falls on those who afflict Israel." God's promise to Abraham, "I will . . . curse him that curseth thee," Chafer continued, "has never failed in its fulfillment, nor will it fail to the end of human history on the earth."[118]

We have wandered into difficult theological terrain, yet these issues lie at the heart of the premillennial view of Israel. Amid the general end-time horrors, Jews face a special and terrible fate. As Dwight Pentecost candidly responded when asked in 1989 if the approaching Jewish holocaust could be avoided, "Prophetically, the only thing that could prevent it is Israel's repentance."[119]

We have seen that Israeli politicians and some U.S. Jewish leaders welcomed the support of premillennialists. Irving Kristol, commenting in 1984 on the specific case of a fundamentalist leader who claimed that God does not hear Jewish prayers, wrote: "Why should Jews care about the theology of a fundamentalist preacher . . . ? What do such theological abstractions matter as against the mundane fact that this same preacher is vigorously pro-Israel?" [120] Contemplating the river of Jewish blood oozing its crimson way through these "theological abstractions," one may well ask whether turning a blind eye to one of premillennialism's core doctrines is not a very high price to pay for the premillennialists' admittedly enthusiastic backing of Israel.

Prophecy and Prejudice

We noted earlier the complex links between apocalyptic belief and anti-Semitism in medieval Europe. An obvious question arises: does premillennial prophecy belief, too, encourage anti-Semitism? Historians have offered sharply divergent answers. In the half-century from 1875 to 1925, Timothy Weber argues, premillennialists were "fierce opponents of anti-Semitism in any form." In *Zionism within Early American Fundamentalism* (1979), David Rausch painted a consistently positive picture of fundamentalists propelled by their eschatology toward philo-Semitic and pro-Israel positions. Challenging historian Martin Marty and others, Rausch argued that fundamentalists, far from espousing anti-Semitism, have been "ardent supporters of Israel and the Jewish heritage." He cited evidence such as the 1976 proclamation by eleven leading fundamentalists characterizing the Holocaust as "a racist act" perpetrated by "the enemies of God." Concluded Rausch, "The more Fundamentalist in theology that one is, the more pro-Jewish one becomes." [121]

Certainly Rausch was correct to challenge the "scratch a fundamentalist, find an anti-Semite" canard, and to emphasize the philo-Semitic component of fundamentalist thought. Yet he largely ignored the open anti-Semitism espoused by some fundamentalists in the twenties and thirties, and their receptivity to crude anti-Jewish propaganda such as *The Protocols of the Elders of Zion*. As for pre-1945 prophecy writers specifically, some condemned anti-Semitism, others indulged in it. Anti-Semitic stereotypes may be found, for example, in the influential *Signs of the Times* (1910) by Isaac Haldeman, pastor of the First Baptist Church of New York City. "As a nation, [the Jews] crucified their king," wrote Haldeman, "and the nations have crucified them." Faced with universal contempt, he went on, Jews "seemed to fawn, to yield, took advantage of their foes, cheated when they could, and lied themselves out of threatened danger." Wherever they settle, Haldeman continued, Jews "bear upon them the mark and stamp of the alien." Except in Palestine, the Jew "is out of place. He is in everybody's way . . . He needs to go back to his own land." Arthur Pink, in a work published in 1923 (and reprinted as recently as 1988), contended that the "mercenary spirit [of] the covetous Hebrews" had held them back from Zionism, but as they saw Palestine's commercial potential, they would return. Also in 1923 the editor of the *Sunday School Times,* discussing the Jews' prophesied restoration to their ancient land, asked rhetorically, "What will 'little old New York' do then, with all its Jewish bankers and merchants missing, together with their silver and their gold?" The notorious fundamentalist anti-Semite Gerald Winrod predicted in a 1933 prophecy work that Mussolini, who he thought might be Antichrist, would endorse the Jews' "international program" as prelude to an alliance with them. "There is something that binds Benito Mussolini to Jewry," Winrod noted darkly; "what is it?" [122]

Zondervan Publishing Company (later Hal Lindsey's publisher) in 1942 issued a prophecy work tinged with anti-Semitism. Some representative passages convey its flavor:

> God may be permitting Satan to use a Hitler, Goebels [*sic*] or a Stalin to chasten His People and thus make them discontented in their wealth and prosperity . . . The Hebrew has grown up in his commercialism . . . The world of commerce is linked up with him . . . We are living in the day of a godless Commercialism, in which the Jew is the dominating factor . . . The Jew is gradually being forced to go back to his promised land. He is not wanted in very many lands.

The author, a Pennsylvania Methodist minister, the book's jacket reported, was "in constant demand as a prophetic lecturer" and attracted large audiences wherever he spoke. [123]

Nor did David Rausch address the way premillennial belief encouraged a passive view of anti-Semitic outbreaks as foreordained "chastisements" or "corrections." Furthermore, the "philo-Semitism" he emphasized was of a special variety. Prized for their role in biblical times and their high place in Christ's millennial kingdom, Jews in their present "unbelieving" state were viewed far more ambivalently. They had a glorious past and future; only the present posed problems. At a 1918 Los Angeles Zionist rally, William Blackstone urged Jews either to convert to Christianity or to embrace Zionism; the one unavailable option was acceptance as non-Zionist American Jews. Citing God's denunciation of exiled Jews who take their ease in alien lands, Blackstone warned that Jewish "assimilationists [who] wish to remain in the various nations enjoying their social, political, and commercial advantages" faced dire consequences.[124]

Dwight Wilson's *Armageddon Now! The Premillenarian Response to Russia and Israel since 1917* (1977) offered a different perspective. An Assemblies of God minister, Wilson not only documented blatant anti-Semitism in pre-1945 prophecy writing, but also argued a more subtle point: those who believe that the Jews face endless chastening and persecution for their collective guilt in rejecting and crucifying Jesus, even if they are not openly anti-Semitic, are more inclined to "expect the phenomenon of anti-Semitism and tolerate it matter-of-factly." Viewing anti-Semitism less as a social problem than as a prophetic sign, Wilson suggests, premillennialists

> expected and condoned anti-Semitic behavior because it was prophesied by Jesus. Their consent (even though given while spewing pro-Zionism out the other side of their mouths) makes them blameworthy with regard to American as well as Nazi and Soviet anti-Semitism. Neither as a body nor as individuals has their cry against such inhumanity been more than a whimper.[125]

Timothy Weber, while denying that the early premillennialists were anti-Semitic, similarly notes the "ironic ambivalence" of prophecy believers who simultaneously honored the Jews as God's chosen people and foresaw a terrible fate for them in the Tribulation.[126]

A few early postwar prophecy writers conveyed a tone of anti-Semitism and Jewish stereotyping. One in 1945 saw "International Jewry," with its grip on world finance, as the forerunner of Antichrist's economic order. "Like a serpent crawling through the centuries," he proclaimed, Jews had fought Christianity at every turn. When all Jews return to Palestine, wrote Harry Rimmer in 1946, "you can have three guesses as to where the wealth of the world will then be." Even some who *condemned* anti-Semitism did so in ways that reinforced old prejudices. Just because Jews "are under a curse and rejected by Jehovah," noted one scrupulous author in 1947, this fact did not "justify any degree of antisemitism." Another early postwar writer, urging pity rather than hatred, observed: "The Jews are spiritually blind and many of their irritating acts are committed in blindness. We do not persecute the blind because they bump into us; rather, we take them by the arm and lead them." [127]

Open anti-Jewish innuendo soon faded, however, often to be replaced by denunciation of anti-Semitism, especially from prophecy writers involved in Jewish missionary work. The 1945 prophecy conference sponsored by the American Association for Jewish Evangelism (AAJE) denounced anti-Semitism as "a movement conceived by Satan" that was both "unChristian" and "utterly unAmerican." At the 1956 conference, Frank Gaebelein (son of veteran prophecy writer Arno Gaebelein) criticized historian Arnold Toynbee's derogatory comments about Judaism. As time passed, prophecy popularizers routinely denounced anti-Semitism. Jack Van Impe called it "a cancer that seems never to heal." Hal Lindsey spoke of "the insane flames of hatred and slaughter" directed against the Jews throughout history. In his *Road to Holocaust* (1989) Lindsey explicitly rejected all anti-Semitic versions of prophecy belief. [128]

Before concluding that anti-Semitism vanished from postwar premillennialism, we need to explore the question a bit more. Darby and Scofield, we have seen, distinguished sharply between God's plan for the Church and for the Jews. Thus, at the heart of dispensationalism lies the assumption that Jews are essentially and eternally *different*. The view of "the Jew" is not necessarily hostile, but he is always *separate*, a figure whose special traits and destiny arouse endless speculation. As a prophecy writer of the 1940s put it: "Unique in origin, the Jew is equally unique in racial purity . . . We cannot assimilate and absorb the Jew. *He remains a Jew.*" This theme pervades postwar prophecy exposition. The Jew is "the blueprint to guide the student of Scripture so that we can know God's next move," asserted a 1965 author, and, as such, "peculiarly different because God made him different." [129]

The Jew's cosmic *otherness* in the premillennial system encouraged subtle stereotyping that, if not consciously "anti-Semitic," nevertheless shaped perceptions of what one popularizer called "that

Strange People, the Jews." At the 1952 Winona Lake prophecy conference, Hyman Appleman (a popular Jewish Christian evangelist of the
day) discussed the Jews' dominance of the movie industry and other
realms of American life, to underscore the urgency of converting
them.

> The Jews are a brilliant people, energetic, ambitious. If these
> [traits] are not directed in the way of Christ and Christianity,
> they are extremely dangerous. We have to Christianize them or
> they will paganize us . . . I am still a Jew. I am proud of my
> people . . . However, we must not be blinded to their possibil-
> ities for evil.[130]

Tim LaHaye linked "world Jewry" by a circuitous process to dangerous contemporary trends that portended the end:

> One wishes that all Jewish idealists would recognize that the
> secular humanist cause which they actively champion provides
> a philosophical haven for Communists and other anti-Semitics
> that will eventually undermine their purpose. It is hoped that
> one day world Jewry will realize that Bible-believing, premil-
> lennialist Christians are Israel's best friends.[131]

"Why are the Jews so maligned and hated when they are so productive
and helpful?" asked television evangelist Jack Van Impe in *Israel's Final
Holocaust.* "There can be but one explanation—the fulfillment of
prophecy." Citing various Deuteronomy passages that pronounced
dire judgment on the Lord's unfaithful people, Van Impe continued:

> The Jew finds himself in a difficult situation. He is a blessing,
> yet a byword. He is a treasure, yet he experiences great trouble.
> He is a contributor, yet he causes conflict wherever he goes. In
> short, although the material gains brought by Jews are desired,
> the Jew himself is unwanted . . . Their skill in handling money
> has often brought them grief.[132]

In allusive and indirect ways, the discussion of Jews by postwar
prophecy writers often managed to focus on their wealth and commercial skill, or otherwise invoke familiar stereotypes. The "Babylon" whose destruction is foretold in Revelation 18, commented
Chuck Smith in 1977, is represented in the modern world by a
"monolithic commercial system" centered in Wall Street. And, Smith
added, "God is calling His people, the nation of the Jews, to come out

of this commercial system." S. Maxwell Coder found Jewish prosperity foretold in Deuteronomy 8:18: "Remember the Lord thy God: for it is he that giveth thee power to get wealth." Through Antichrist's persecution, said Merrill Unger, "the Jewish people will be transformed from their unbelieving, scheming Jacob role to their regenerated character as Israel, a prince with God." The Reverend Paul Olson of Minneapolis, explaining in 1989 why the United States would have to retaliate when the Soviet Union invaded Israel, declared: "There's too many Jews in this country, with too much influence and power, [for America not to respond]. The most powerful lobby in America today is the Jewish lobby." [133]

Far from viewing the Jews' alleged control of politics, commerce, finance, and entertainment in classic anti-Semitic fashion as sinister, postwar prophecy writers professed to *welcome* it as a key to the divine favor enjoyed by America—a fulfillment of God's promise to Abraham: "And I will bless them that bless thee, and curse him that curseth thee." U.S. support of Israel, wrote Lindsey, "is one of the reasons we've survived as a nation." The power of the "Jewish lobby" is a *good thing,* Paul Olson went on—it proves that America has blessed the Jews, and will be blessed in return. "If there ever has been a nation that could claim that blessing, it is the United States," wrote Arthur Bloomfield in 1975; "the Jews have prospered in this country from the very beginning." Explaining why the United States would survive the end-time conflict foretold by Ezekiel, Doug Clark in 1982 quoted the "I will bless them that bless thee" promise and went on in a burst of staccato paragraphs:

> The United States and Canada have afforded millions of Jews a home and a place to rise to the highest of positions in power, politics, and money.

> They are in every industry and lead the nation in many areas, including the entertainment industry of Beverly Hills and Hollywood.

> Every communications medium has on its corporate board some American Jews. They abound in the medical world of North America, as well as in education, government, and you name it!

> God has to keep His Word. We have been a friend to the Jew, whether we were right on other issues or not! [134]

In addition to placing Jews in a distinct eschatological category, premillennialists, as we have seen, echoed the Gospel of Matthew in teaching the collective guilt of the Jews for Jesus' death ("Then answered all the people, and said, His blood be on us, and on our children") and viewed the long history of pogroms and anti-Semitic outbreaks as God's punishment for that ancient deed. "Of course, all the world is guilty of piercing the Son of God," wrote Ray Stedman in 1970, "but the Jews were particular instruments in that respect." For this reason, observed Louis Bauman in 1952, anti-Semitism, though deplorable, would "grow worse and worse" until the Tribulation, when "the nations will gather to deliver to the remnant of Israel the coup de grace." Hal Lindsey, even as he deplored the "insane flames" of Jew hatred, quoted prophetic scripture to show that persecution will reach "its most feverish pitch" in the end times. [135]

The prophesied pattern of Jewish persecution will culminate in the last days, agreed Jack Van Impe in *Israel's Final Holocaust,* when a "wave of anti-Semitism will sweep the earth." Reiterating the dual explanation that pervaded prophecy writers' discussions of Jewish suffering, Van Impe portrayed this final holocaust both as an expression of God's will and as "motivated by Satan and promoted by the Antichrist." Returning to the paradox in 1983, Van Impe tried to square God's love of His chosen people with their horrendous fate:

> [God] allowed Jews to write both the Old and New Testaments
> . . . He also chose a Jewish virgin as the vehicle through which
> He brought His Son, the Lord Jesus Christ, into the world. Oh,
> how Jehovah God loves the Jew! Still, he will permit Satan one
> last attempt to murder every Jew upon the face of the earth . . .
> [But] God will remain on the side of His ancient people. He
> still loves them. [136]

Even the 1976 denunciation of the Holocaust that David Rausch cites to prove that premillennialists are free of anti-Semitism suggests the ambiguities embedded in their view of the Jews. While a "racist act," the statement said, the Holocaust was also a "part of Israel's sacred history." In fact, insofar as it hastened the creation of the State of Israel, it offered "proof that the covenant of God with His people had not been broken." [137]

To understand American attitudes toward the Jews and toward Israel, one must attend carefully to the nuances and subtexts of popular prophecy belief. Premillennialism is a complex system; it is *not* merely a theological mask for Jew hatred. Indeed, it incorporates many philo-Semitic elements. Yet important structural components of this ideology encourage an obsessive preoccupation with the Jews as a people eternally set apart, about whom sweeping generalizations can be made with the sanction of biblical authority. Premillennialism also incorporates a view of Jewish history that, while not condoning anti-Semitic outbreaks, sees them as foreordained and inevitable. Israel in this scheme is, as we have already seen, "the only nation on earth to have its history written in advance."[138] For prophecy believers, the most tragic chapter of that history still lies ahead. And no human effort can prevent that blood-soaked chapter from unfolding as God has ordained, at a time of God's own choosing.

7   *The United States in Prophecy*

U ncle Sam, with all his might, will be no match for
Antichrist." [1] When the editor of the *Christian Digest* wrote
these words in 1942, he was both reaffirming a basic
premillennial tenet and anticipating a theme that would loom large in
the next half-century of prophecy writing. Prophecy interpretation
historically has provided a capacious framework for moral critiques of
the writers' own societies, and the post-1945 popularizers carried on
this tradition. Despite the flag-waving of some premillennialist television preachers, this belief system cannot be dismissed as simply a
theological rationalization of a pro-American political ideology.
Deeply skeptical of *all* human societies and *all* economic and political
systems, post–World War II popular eschatologists offered a bleak
view of the United States and its destiny. The rising ooze of wickedness, materialism, and secularism inundating the West, and particularly contemporary America, they argued, offered further compelling
evidence that the end was near.

Reprise: Early Visions of America's Millennial Destiny

The somber view of the United States promulgated by postwar
prophecy writers contrasted starkly with the outlook of earlier times,
when many religious and (ostensibly) secular writers had discerned a
bright destiny for America, the New Israel. Indeed, Christopher Columbus himself, an avid prophecy student, wrote toward the end of
his life, "God made me the messenger of the new heaven and the new
earth of which he spoke in the Apocalypse of St. John after having
spoken of it through the mouth of Isaiah; and he showed me the spot
where to find it." [2]

As we saw in Chapter 2, millennial anticipation often gripped
colonial-era intellectuals. In 1653 Edward Johnson, an early chronicler
of New England history, addressed his fellow colonists: "For your full
assurance, know this is the place where the Lord will create a new

Heaven and a new earth . . . , new Churches and a new Common-wealth together." Through the voyages of discovery and Christianity's spread to the New World, Jonathan Edwards told his Northampton flock in 1739, God had prepared the way "for the future glorious times of the church, when Satan's kingdom shall be overthrown throughout the whole habitable globe, on every side, and on all continents." Three years later, as revival fires burned brightly, Edwards described America as the land where God could "begin a new world in a spiritual respect, when he creates the *new heavens* and *new earth*." [3]

To be sure, warnings of the need for repentance tempered such anticipations. The earlier millennial vision contained much of what Perry Miller called the jeremiad. And premillennialism, which viewed all human societies skeptically and looked to Israel, not America, as the key to the prophetic plan, was a force in American thought from the time of the earliest settlements. As Darby's premillennial dispensationalism became an increasingly important strand of U.S. prophecy writing, belief in America's special millennial destiny diminished accordingly.

Nevertheless, through much of American history, especially until the Civil War, the conviction that God had assigned a special role to America exerted a powerful appeal. The New England Puritans in their more hopeful moods, and eighteenth-century churchmen such as Edwards, envisioned that role as mainly spiritual: through prayer, piety, and evangelism, New World believers would help bring about universal revival and Christ's millennial reign. By the late eighteenth century, as we saw in Chapter 3, the vision incorporated a civic component as well: freed of British rule and championing liberty and justice, the new nation would inaugurate an era of religious *and civic* purity. Though diluted theologically, the apocalyptic component in this broadened view of America's mission remained powerful. The simultaneous spread of the Gospel and of republican principles, speculated a minister in 1797, would ultimately bring the world to the Millennium. As Nathan Hatch puts it, revolutionary-era ministers "extended the canopy of religious meaning so that even the cause of liberty became sacred. The cycles of republican history and the linear perspective of Christian eschatology became indivisible." This potent blend of sacred and secular prophetic expectation, he suggests, represented "the first substantively new eschatology since the Reformation." [4]

Belief in America's sacred destiny extended far beyond the pulpit. John Adams in a 1765 diary entry described the European settlement of America as "the opening of a grand scene and design in Providence for the illumination of the ignorant and the emancipation of the slavish part of mankind all over the earth." [5] In the Declaration of Independence and the Constitution, Adams' generation created the sacred texts of a civil religion that sanctified American republicanism and gave it cosmic significance. The motto enscribed on the new nation's currency, NOVUS ORDO SECLORUM, with the momentous date 1776, was not chosen lightly.

This religio-civic millennialism, despite competing interpretive approaches, saturated American thought well into the nineteenth century and beyond. One finds it not only in the works of Samuel Baldwin, J. P. Philpott, and the ineffable Fountain Pitts, who enthralled Washington with his flights of prophetic speculation in 1859, but also in Lyman Beecher's 1835 tract, *A Plea for the West,* which urged winning the vast interior for Christ and for republicanism. As Alexis de Tocqueville observed in the 1830s, American religious and political values were so intertwined as to be inseparable. [6]

Eschatological expectations that had once been "largely the preserve of gentlemen and scholars," Hatch observes, seeped into popular religion in the early nineteenth century. Amid democratizing movements in both the political and ecclesiastical worlds, "Americans of all ranks sensed that events of truly apocalyptic significance were unfolding before their eyes." Declared two early leaders of the Christian (Disciples of Christ) Church, a denomination gestated in the frontier revivals of 1801–1803, "We confidently thought that the Millennium was just at hand, and that a glorious church would soon be formed; we thought, also, that we had found [its] very plan." An early nineteenth-century gospel song expressed the same conviction: "The great reform is drawing near, / Long look'd for soone will come / The time will move both earth and sea, / Just like a glorious Jubilee." [7]

The United States as a political entity figured centrally in all these expectations. Elias Smith, a New England Jeffersonian, itinerant evangelist, and dabbler in prophecy, in 1808 argued that not only the religious awakening but also the American and French revolutions had laid the groundwork for the glorious end-time age foretold in the Bible. An 1846 writer in *The United States Magazine and Democratic*

Review expressed the prevailing impulse in these years to transcend mundane politics and articulate a loftier vision of the nation's destiny: "There is a moral sense—a soul in the state, which longs for something more than the tariffs, the bank, and the bankrupt bills of a temporizing present; which looks for some celestial beacon to direct the course of popular movement through the eternal future!" For many, millennial (or, more precisely, *post*millennial) belief supplied that framework of meaning. One finds versions of it across the spectrum of antebellum cultural expression, from revival hymns to Herman Melville's *White Jacket* (1850): "We Americans are the peculiar, chosen people—the Israel of our time; we bear the ark of the liberties of the world . . . God has predestined, mankind expects, great things from our race; and great things we feel in our souls." [8]

Beginning in the 1830s, the Mormons offered their distinctive version of America's millennial role. In the *Book of Mormon* (1830) the books called I and II Nephi told of Columbus, who "went forth upon the many waters" to a promised land—"a land of liberty" whose well-being became the Lord's special concern:

> And I will fortify this land against all other nations.
> And he that fighteth against Zion shall perish, saith God.

The Book of Ether, another part of the *Book of Mormon,* further elaborated God's special favor to the new Zion, "a choice land above all other lands, a chosen land of the Lord," a land that would be the site of the New Jerusalem. "Zion will be built upon this continent," proclaimed an early Mormon doctrinal statement. Mormon leader Parley Pratt in 1855 listed "the discovery of America" along with the railroad, the telegraph, and other mechanical advances as "preparatory steps" for the gathering of the New Zion. [9]

As Ernest Lee Tuveson has convincingly argued, belief in America's millennial role reached its apogee just before and during the Civil War. The historical popularizer Benson Lossing wrote to a friend in April 1862:

> I have had unswerving faith in three beings, in connection with the Rebellion, namely, General McClellan, President Lincoln, and the Lord of Hosts. I have believed, from the beginning, that the hand of the Almighty was to be put forth at this time, so tangibly in the chastisement, strengthening, and purification of

this nation, that the most stupid and skeptical observer must perceive God in the history of our day.[10]

Harriet Beecher Stowe's *Uncle Tom's Cabin,* Julia Ward Howe's "Battle Hymn of the Republic" (a work saturated in biblical apocalyptic), and Abraham Lincoln's Second Inaugural Address, with its richness of scriptural allusion and its brooding meditation on God's purposes in history, distilled the conviction that the nation's history had a sacred meaning transcending the mundane world of political maneuvering and battlefield encounters. "Mine eyes have seen the glory of the coming of the Lord . . ."

In the late nineteenth and early twentieth centuries, as the nation grappled with the stresses of industrialization, and as premillennialism won adherents among evangelical leaders, some continued to affirm the earlier confidence in America's millennial role. Social-gospel ministers redefined that role as the struggle for tenement reform, child-labor laws, and railroad regulation. "Here upon these plains, the problems of history are to be solved," Washington Gladden told a small-town Ohio audience in 1890. "Here, if anywhere, is to rise that city of God, the New Jerusalem, whose glories are to fill the earth." Expansionists took a different tack, combining postmillennial rhetoric, imperial dreams, technological pride, and assumptions of racial superiority into a jingoistic version of America's divinely ordained role. In the United States, proclaimed the Reverend Josiah Strong in *Our Country: Its Possible Future and Its Present Crisis* (1886), "God is training the Anglo-Saxon race for its mission." [11]

American secular millennialism enjoyed a final efflorescence, Tuveson argues, in the exalted rhetoric with which Woodrow Wilson expressed the nation's war aims in 1917, and in Wilson's doomed campaign to bring the United States into the League of Nations. In October 1919, just before his devastating stroke, Wilson spoke movingly of the young men who had died in France, and he called on Americans to accept "the moral obligation that rests upon us not to go back on those boys, but to see the thing through . . . , and make good their redemption of the world. For nothing less depends upon this decision, nothing less than the liberation and salvation of the world." [12]

But the social upheavals of the Gilded Age and the early twentieth century, followed by the shock of World War I, the disillusioned and hedonistic 1920s, and then the battering of the Great Depression, made it increasingly difficult to sustain the old confidence in America's role as midwife to the Millennium. By 1937 Arno Gaebelein was describing the United States as a once-virtuous society fast succumbing to Satan; "the powers of darkness are rushing in," he sadly concluded.[13] In the post-1945 decades, the old synthesis collapsed altogether. While many themes in prophetic belief exhibited remarkable continuity over the generations, the view of America's destiny shifted dramatically. Politicians still occasionally mouthed the old platitudes ("This is the greatest nation God ever put on this earth"—vice-presidential candidate Dan Quayle, August 1988),[14] but prophecy writers exhibited a very different mood. Echoes of the older, more hopeful view could still be heard, but the prevailing note was dark indeed.

A Premillennial Portrait of Modern America

For an American to plow through the hundreds of popular prophecy books published since 1945 is an unsettling experience. From these works emerges a picture of a nation mired in wickedness and trembling on the brink of chaos—a nation whose destiny is as grim as it is certain.

While some writers found specific biblical allusions to the United States, most relied on general scriptural discussions of the end times, such as Jesus' preview of mankind's final stage, recorded in the Gospel of Luke:

> As it was in the days of Noe, so shall it be also in the days of the Son of man.
> They did eat, they drank, they married wives, they were given in marriage, until the day that Noe entered into the ark, and the flood came, and destroyed them all.
> Likewise also as it was in the days of Lot; they did eat, they drank, they bought, and they sold, they planted, they builded;
> But the same day that Lot went out of Sodom it rained fire and brimstone from heaven, and destroyed them all.
> Even thus shall it be in the day when the Son of man is revealed.

In the version of this sermon in the Gospel of Matthew, Jesus explicitly instructs believers to observe social trends carefully for signs of the end and concludes somberly: "Therefore be ye also ready: for in such an hour as ye think not the Son of man cometh."[15] Passages such

as these sent prophecy writers back to the accounts in Genesis of
Noah's Flood and the destruction of Sodom and Gomorrah—periods
of wickedness, impiety, sensual indulgence, and sexual immorality
distressingly similar, they contended, to conditions in contemporary
America.

Wilbur Smith in 1949 found a mirror of postwar American society in the catalog of end-time evils set forth in II Timothy:

> In the last days perilous times shall come.
> For men shall be lovers of their own selves, covetous, boasters,
> proud, blasphemers, disobedient to parents, unthankful, unholy.
> Without natural affection, trucebreakers, false accusers, incontinent,
> fierce, despisers of those that are good,
> Traitors, heady, highminded, lovers of pleasures more than lovers
> of God;
> Having a form of godliness, but denying the power thereof: from
> such turn away.
> For of this sort are they which creep into houses, and lead captive
> silly women laden with sins, led away with divers lusts,
> Ever learning, and never able to come to the knowledge of the
> truth.[16]

In their comments on the United States, prophecy writers also
invoked the destruction of wicked Babylon foretold in Revelation and
elsewhere in the Bible. A 1979 prophecy work drew a detailed comparison between modern America and Babylon: like the ancient kingdom on the Euphrates, the United States too possessed great military
power, boasted of its "technical, scientific" achievements, sheltered an
"apostate world church movement" (the World Council of Churches),
and encouraged "loose morals and defiance of God's laws" worldwide
through its movies and TV programs. Clearly, the authors concluded,
America would have "a prominent role in preparing the world for the
last Babylonian system."[17] Building on these and other biblical descriptions of end-time wickedness, writers constructed their profile of
a nation far gone in evil and debauchery.

Doleful recitals of human sinfulness as evidence of the last days
have, of course, long been a staple of prophecy writing. In 250 A.D.,
Cyprian, Tertullian's successor as bishop of Carthage, wrote:

> Who cannot see that the world is already in its decline, and no
> longer has the strength and vigor of former times? There is no
> need to invoke Scripture authority to prove it. The world tells

> its own tale and in its general decadence bears adequate witness
> that it is approaching its end . . . There is less innocence in the
> courts, less justice in the judges, less concord between friends,
> less artistic sincerity, less moral strictness.[18]

Martin Luther preached that conditions in early-sixteenth-century
Germany (including the "commercial operations" that were "encir-
cling and swallowing up the world") precisely matched Jesus' description of the end times, and concluded that "the day of judgment is not
far off." In 1756, concluding a series of sermons on the end-time signs
(including earthquakes), Jonathan Mayhew of Massachusetts wrote,
"There has probably been no age or period of the world, wherein
events have more nearly corresponded to this prophetic description,
than the present."[19] Despite the formulaic nature of prophecy writers'
jeremiads, the particular themes emphasized in different time periods
can be instructive. In making their case for the imminence of the Rapture, post–World War II premillennialists singled out those features of
contemporary American life they found especially unsettling.

The rising tide of sexual immorality rolled across many, many
pages. Arno Gaebelein in the 1930s had noted the alarming increase in
condom sales, and postwar prophecy writers endlessly deplored similar evidence of rampant sexuality. Tim LaHaye warned in 1972 of "an
avalanche of pornographic filth." Wrote Jack Van Impe in 1979:
"Swingers are the rage of the day. They get together for a supper bash
and end up exchanging their mates for a night of glorified orgies.
How low can humans go?" Sex magazines and X-rated movies are
everywhere, he went on; "savages are roaming the streets raping and
sodomizing victims"—a reminder that "earth's goriest, blood-soaked
hour" would soon strike.[20]

Abortion figured prominently among the end-time signs in
prophecy writing of the 1970s and 1980s. "In addition to the killing of
people on our streets," observed a 1988 author, "we now tolerate the
most terrible of all crimes—the murder of the unborn . . . The blood
of innocent children is on the hands of an unrepentant generation. Can
judgment be far behind?" Venereal disease, genital herpes, and AIDS
made their successive appearance as evidences of sexual decay.[21]

Warnings of moral collapse led naturally to discussions of popular
music. In *The Days of Noah,* a 1963 prophecy work, M. R. DeHaan
found jazz, swing, and "tin-pan tabulations which defy all effort at

description" so full of "squeaks and squawks and empty groans and baby talk and monkey moans [that] we read of people going almost completely crazy under [their] spell." The rise of rock and roll provided a rich field for such criticism. Backward masking, the process by which rock groups allegedly recorded lewd and blasphemous messages and then inserted them backward in their songs, particularly fascinated prophecy writers, relating as it did not only to their concerns about raging immorality, but also to the obsession with conspiracies that we shall explore in Chapter 8. [22]

The changing status of women offered further evidence of social disintegration. Muted in the domestic 1950s, this theme surfaced frequently thereafter as women sought careers and a revived feminist movement captured public attention. DeHaan linked the rising divorce rate and other signs of moral breakdown to "women leaving their homes and children to enter factories and shops and offices." A 1981 writer blamed TV's portrayal of "weak fathers [and] dominant mothers" for the spread of secular humanism. The proposed Equal Rights Amendment, he went on, reflected the false belief "that mere men and women can decide what is good and evil without regard to divine directives." Mourned the pentecostal prophecy speaker Roy Hicks, "Homes and marriages are no longer considered sacred . . . women take to the streets to strike for equality with men, even if it means going to war and fighting to show their equality." The true aim of the women's movement, agreed Dave Hunt, was not equality but matriarchy—a demonic inversion of the God-ordained social order. James McKeever's *End-Times News Digest* in 1990 described the environmental movement and radical feminism as a twin-pronged plot to revive witchcraft and displace Father God with Mother Nature. [23]

The so-called New Age movement, with its interest in meditation, Eastern religions, and a vaguely pantheistic harmony with nature, preoccupied post-1970 prophecy writers as well. Dave Hunt devoted an entire book to *The New Age Movement in Prophecy*. He speculated that this movement in its many guises—the Montessori system, Waldorf schools, Freudianism, Indian gurus, the human potential movement, secular humanism, biofeedback, radical feminism, planetary consciousness—could be "part of a cosmic conspiracy to install the Antichrist." When the end comes, he said, "millions of New Agers in thousands of network groups around the world will be sincerely implementing Antichrist's programs in the name of peace, brotherhood, and love." Prophecy writers cited a 1972 *Time* cover story on Satanism, astrology, and other occult fads as confirmation that the last days were at hand.[24]

Quoting scriptures that foretell an end-time upsurge in "unnatural affections," prophecy writers reacted vehemently to the greater openness of homosexuality in post-1970 U.S. culture. Citing the rising tide of "sodomy, homosexuality and Lesbianism," Boston evangelical leader Harold John Ockenga declared at the 1971 Jerusalem prophecy conference: "Between 1965 and 1970 the moral dam gave way and . . . the resulting flood has played havoc with civilization . . . Certain groups could hardly go any lower; they meet every day one of the many details predicted for the last days of this age." The reason God destroyed Sodom, Wilbur Smith reminded the same gathering, "was nothing else but homosexuality." Many writers cited a cryptic phrase in the Book of Daniel describing the coming Evil One ("Neither shall he regard . . . the desire of women") to argue that Antichrist himself will be homosexual.[25]

The most gripping images of America as Sodom appeared in the much-reprinted prophecy books of the Assemblies of God evangelist David Wilkerson. In contrast to most prophecy interpreters, Wilkerson in *The Vision* reported verbatim communications from God foretelling a coming "moral landslide" of "nudity, perversion, and a flood of filth." Television networks will show bare-breasted women; churches will feature nude dancing; "wild, roving mobs of homosexual men" will attack unsuspecting victims openly on the streets.[26] Wilkerson, now speaking in his own voice, returned to the fray in *Set the Trumpet to Thy Mouth* (1985) with a long recital of all-pervasive wickedness:

> God is going to judge America for its violence, its crimes, its backslidings, its murdering of millions of babies, its flaunting of homosexuality and sadomasochism, its corruption, its drunkenness and drug abuse, its form of godliness without power, its lukewarmness toward Christ, its rampant divorce and adultery, its lewd pornography, its child molestation, its cheatings, its robbings, its dirty movies, and its occult practices . . . . America today is one great holocaust party, with millions drunk, high, shaking their fist at God, daring him to send the bombs.[27]

While early-nineteenth-century commentators had viewed

America's prosperity as confirmation of God's favor, post-1945 pre-millennialists saw the nation's wealth and consumer abundance as yet another ominous end-time sign. The same America fighting godless communism abroad "denies God and glories in materialism" at home, declared a speaker at a 1961 prophecy conference. Rich America was "concerned about cars, college, cottages, and crabgrass, not about conversion," proclaimed an alliterative writer in 1970. The nation's "comfortable, affluent, high standard of living," he went on, enabled Satan "to lull people into spiritual insensitivity." Tim LaHaye in *The Beginning of the End* (1972) saw the rise of "monumental fortunes" and the proliferation of "the pleasure-seeking rich" as evidence of America's approaching doom.[28]

The more favorable the economic indicators, prophecy writers suggested, the more ominous the eschatological meaning. Indeed, although most popularizers foresaw an economic collapse just before Antichrist's rise (see Chapter 8), a few anticipated an end-time economic boom. "A careful examination of the Biblical description of the 'last days,'" concluded a 1983 writer, revealed that an interval of "unprecedented peace and prosperity" would lead directly to the final holocaust. The last days would see unparalleled affluence and "a mad round of materialism and pleasure seeking," agreed the authors of *Prosperity in the End Time*. Sodom, they noted, basked in great wealth just before its incineration. The computer boom, the knowledge explosion, and military spending fueled by the prophesied end-time wars would all contribute to the feverish prosperity of America's final days. Rising income and a surging Gross National Product all too easily diverted attention from the truly important: "Hypnotized by affluence, the world continues its binge of eating and drinking, buying and selling, planting and building, as it did in the days of Noah and Lot . . . But God's prophetic clock keeps ticking."[29]

While nineteenth-century writers of a postmillennial bent had praised *education* as a counterweight to immorality and apostasy, post–World War II expositors typically treated the schools as part of the problem, not part of the solution. Wilbur Smith in 1949 saw America's "Godless, Bibleless, Christless secular education" as clearing the path for Antichrist, and similar fears eddied through scores of subsequent prophecy works. Many writers, quoting a prophecy in Daniel that "knowledge shall be increased" in the last days, treated educational advances as simply another end-time portent.[30]

On this point, the prophecy popularizers reinforced fundamen-

talism's broader indictment of contemporary education. Salem Kirban's prophecy novel *666* included the following Tribulation-era exchange between a young woman and her father:

> "Dad, when did religion start falling apart? I mean, when
> did people start turning away from Christ and developing their
> own theology?"
> "That's a hard question to answer, Faye," George replied.
> "Some say it started in the late 1800s and in the early 1900s.
> Perhaps the most marked change occurred way back in 1968–
> 69 almost coinciding with the then-famous campus revolts." [31]

Tim LaHaye, prophecy writer, TV evangelist, and later head of
the Washington-based American Coalition for Traditional Values, offered a particularly alarming survey of U.S. education. The younger
generation—"the confused 'Age of Aquarius'"—he wrote, was falling prey to the "scoffers" and sophisticated unbelievers "on the facul-
ties of tax-supported colleges." He went on, "The most intellectually
trained members of our culture," in propagating "Darwinism and
evolution, Marxism and socialism, Freudianism and liberalism," had
spawned "the most lawless generation of young people in all of history." When divine judgment falls on Russia, LaHaye declared, the
consuming fire would also seek out Moscow's U.S. sympathizers,
including "the Communists on the university campus." In ferreting
out subversives in the classroom and elsewhere, he declared, "the
F.B.I. may someday get help from an unexpected source—
Almighty God." [32]

America's vaunted scientific accomplishments further deepened
prophecy expositors' sense of spreading apostasy. Ray Stedman offered a typical formulation of the premillennialist view: "The day is
coming, Jesus says, when the triumph of the scientific method, as we
know it today, will bring man to confirm himself in the deadly delu-
sion that he is his own god, and does not need any other." Advocates
of solving society's problems through "the scientific methods of observation, experiment, and logic," he said, were peddling the same
false message of human self-sufficiency. And Stedman's reading of
prophecy told him that the problem would only worsen: "Doubtless
a mad science, like the Sorcerer's Apprentice, will go blithely on,
mixing evil potions and conjuring up still more fearful forces of un-
controllable, murderous power." [33]

Prophecy writers saw in modern science mankind's most recent effort to become as gods—the boast of Antichrist. With advances in fields from nuclear weaponry to gene control, wrote Roy Hicks, soon "there will be nothing that man cannot do unless God stops him." Confronted with "surging human brilliance . . . , God [will] have to take action."[34]

Prophecy popularizers subjected America's technological prowess to the same scathing analysis. While employing every technological means available to disseminate their message, from videocassettes to communications satellites to computerized high-speed printing presses, they saw technology's prophetic significance as wholly ominous. Television, predictably, they portrayed as corrosive of morality and a prelude to Antichrist's global thought control. David Wilkerson's apocalyptic discussion of TV—"that speaking idol"—offered in intensified form a theme common to scores of prophecy works: "Satan has taken full possession of secular television . . . Demonic principalities and powers are now in full control . . . , including the horrible erotic commercials . . . Television . . . is the mouth of hell, swallowing multitudes of our precious children."[35]

Supersonic air travel, the interstate highway system, and other transportation advances simply confirmed Daniel's prophecy that in the last days "many shall run to and fro." The space program reminded Jack Van Impe of Jeremiah's prophecy that "though Babylon should mount up to heaven," its destruction was sure. The planting of a U.S. flag on the moon, he added, fullfilled Jesus' words that the last days would see "signs in the sun, and in the moon." M. R. DeHaan, discussing *Coming Events in Prophecy* in 1962 as the National Aeronautics and Space Administration rushed to put an American on the moon, dismissed the space race as "open defiance of God's plan" as plainly conveyed in Psalm 115: "The heaven, even the heavens, are the Lord's: but the earth hath he given to the children of men." Generalizing from this example, DeHaan drove home the familiar premillennial argument:

> After centuries and millenniums of our flaunted civilization, and boasting of human progress, with its advance in education and reform, [and] scientific evolution, the heart of man has not been improved one bit . . . The more educated a sinner is, the more dangerous he becomes . . . Nowhere in the entire Bible is there a single verse to support the contention that this world

will become better and better until at last by the efforts of man in the field of education, science, and the preaching of a watered-down, social "gospel," man will finally learn his lesson and the age will climax in a great worldwide revival, and then wars will be abolished, and the nations live in peace. *No! No!* My friend, the Bible knows nothing of such a program! Instead the Bible teaches without exception that the world will grow worse and worse.[36]

Such themes, of course, had preoccupied evangelical writers for centuries. New England's Puritan ministers had perfected the jeremiad, with its stylized lamentations about the spread of immorality and irreligion. But for these late-twentieth-century prophecy writers, the nation's wickedness and apostasy functioned as *signs* of the end-time moral collapse foretold in Scripture. Events and trends rich in prophetic meaning abounded; one had only to identify and interpret them. As Ray Stedman put it, "If we could learn to read life rightly, almost everything is a sign." No hint of moral declension escaped the notice of these devout semiologists. A 1947 writer discussed that year's New York City newspaper strike as one of the "Unmistakable Signs of Our Times." A 1982 author cited the rise in overdue library books as one of many evidences of the approaching end.[37]

These authors described America's apostasy regretfully, conceding that things had once been very different. In some early postwar prophecy writings, the longing for the soaring civic millennialism that had nearly vanished from cultural discourse—the sense of the magnitude of the nation's betrayal of its once-bright promise—became almost palpable.[38] John Walvoord, discussing "America in Prophecy" at the height of the Vietnam War, offered a somber view of the nation's past, present, and future:

> History has many records of great nations which have risen to unusual power and influence only to decline because of internal corruption or international complications. It may well be that the United States of America is today at the zenith of its power much as Babylon was in the sixth century B.C. prior to its sudden downfall at the hands of the Medes and Persians . . . God has offered unusual benefits to the United States both in a material and religious way, but they have been used with such profligacy that ultimate divine judgment may be expected.[39]

During the troubled 1970s, as Watergate, the Vietnam War's bitter finale, and successive energy crises jolted the nation, a sense of divine displeasure obsessed prophecy writers. The United States had "fallen away into a quagmire of wickedness and lasciviousness, immorality and debauchery, deceitfulness and false religions," observed Charles Taylor in *The Destiny of America,* and for this it must suffer. "Perhaps no nation in history has had a greater opportunity than America to realize a social and political utopia, if such were attainable," wrote Merrill Unger in 1973. Lyndon Johnson's early years as president had propelled this lofty effort to "a grand crescendo," Unger added, but despite Johnson's attempts to achieve a Great Society, human wickedness had reasserted itself, as the Bible said it would. Another 1970s popularizer made the point aphoristically: "America has ceased to be good—she will cease to be great." [40]

Despite their political activism in the 1980s, prophecy writers felt a deepened sense of national decline in these years. America faced a "clear and imminent danger," Hal Lindsey warned in 1981: "THE CRISIS OF INTERNAL DECAY." Although its "foundations and roots were anchored in God and the Bible," agreed Jack Van Impe in 1983, "America . . . is on the decline, and may soon suffer horrendous judgment." [41]

This cosmic drama of a once-favored but now-apostate people hurtling to ruin became almost hypnotic in its repetition. "God . . . set [America] in a good land and blessed its founding fathers," wrote David Wilkerson in 1985; "but evil has become so great, disobedience so widespread, God has declared, 'I will pluck it up, pull it down, destroy it, as it seemeth good to me.'" John Walvoord, reflecting in 1989 on America's prophetic role, reiterated the views he had taught for decades: the nation had once figured importantly in God's plan as a sponsor of missionary endeavor and friend of the Jews; indeed, this role explained its years of power, prosperity, and well-being. But the century's end saw conditions growing steadily worse; after the Rapture, with all Christian influence removed, the United States will "go down like a stone." [42]

Pat Robertson grappled throughout the 1980s with the issue of America's prophetic destiny. *The Secret Kingdom* (1982), ostensibly a work of postmillennial optimism proclaiming the right of believers to assert "dominion" over the earth, opened with a brief chapter that encapsulated the bleaker premillennialist view of American history. Robertson described an evening when he had stood near Cape Henry, where the James River and Chesapeake Bay join the Atlantic, reflecting on the piety of Virginia's first English colonists, who had planted a cross in the sand and dedicated the land to God. From these beginnings "grew the most prosperous nation in humanity's history. Unparalleled freedom and creativity burst upon the earth." But then Robertson's reverie, like that of Nick Carraway at the end of F. Scott Fitzgerald's *Great Gatsby*, darkened:

> As I surveyed that historical site and looked eastward at the Atlantic beneath that dazzling moon, I was gripped by the renewed realization that a dread disease had fastened itself upon the lands sending forth our forefathers. As I turned westward toward my car, my mind's eye swept across the huge country that lay before me. And I mourned more deeply because the same sickness was fastening itself upon my land, the new world so sincerely dedicated to God three hundred and seventy-five years ago.[43]

Robertson elaborated this interpretive schema—pious beginnings followed by a long decline—in two documents of 1986: his book *America's Dates with Destiny* and the manifesto that launched his 1988 presidential campaign, "A New Vision for America." As Stephen O'Leary and M. W. McFarland have observed, Robertson in these works offered a *Heilsgeschichte,* or salvation-history, of America, in which discovery and settlement, Declaration of Independence, Revolution, and Constitution all function as sacred events and texts.[44]

But, as in the Puritan jeremiads on which these works are patterned, Robertson balanced his vision of America's divine origins with a recital of its fall. Offering a familiar catalog of sins, from drug addiction to sexual immorality, he pinpointed one source of the infection—the public schools:

> We have permitted during the past twenty-five years an assault on our faith and values that would have been unthinkable to past generations of Americans. We have taken virtually all mention of God from our classrooms and textbooks . . . We have taken the Holy Bible from our young and replaced it with the thoughts of Charles Darwin, Karl Marx, Sigmund Freud, and John Dewey.[45]

As one might expect of a prophecy expounder turned presidential candidate, particularly one with a basically hopeful and activist temperament, Robertson ended his *Heilsgeschichte* on an upbeat note.

If Americans would only once again choose virtuous leaders—himself, for example—the downward spiral could be reversed and divine favor regained.[46] But few prophecy popularizers embraced Robertson's politicized postmillennialism. They shared his sense of America's decline into apostasy and wickedness, but not his hope of restoration this side of the Second Coming.

Expressions such as those we have quoted from Graham, Van Impe, LaHaye, and Walvoord—as well as Robertson in his darker moods—could be multiplied many times over from the works of contemporary popularizers. Their verdict on late-twentieth-century America, though full of sorrow and regret, was harsh: the nation had fallen into apostasy and grievous sin, and the situation was worsening with every passing hour. The judgment was all the more implacable because postwar America stood in such tragic contrast to the spiritual promise and millennial hope it had once embodied. As Walvoord observed in 1967, "The question no longer is whether America deserves judgment, but rather why divine judgment has been so long withheld from a nation which has enjoyed so much of God's bounty."[47]

The Coming Judgment

While America's sinfulness offered a generalized sign of the end, it also pointed specifically to a time of judgment; for in the dispensational scheme *nations* as well as individuals must face God. As Charles Taylor wrote in 1972, nations, like individuals, have free will, but "*God fore-knew America's choice as a nation, and He sealed its destiny in accordance therewith.*" Forebodings about America's end-time destiny filled many pages of post-1945 U.S. prophecy writing. Even though the general prognosis was bleak, no firm consensus on detail emerged. Indeed, uncertainty and ambivalence characterized postwar discussion of America's prophetic destiny, hinting at emotional unease in the hearts of prophecy writers who also saw themselves as patriotic Americans.[48]

In a few works, the older view of America's special prophetic destiny survived vestigially as a hope that God would shelter the United States from the full force of His end-time wrath. Jerry Falwell at least conditionally embraced this expectation: "If God is on our side, no matter how militarily superior the Soviet Union is, they could never touch us. God would miraculously protect America." Arthur Bloomfield in 1975 reserved a sheltered niche for the United States in his scenario: "I do not believe [Antichrist] will destroy America . . . Unless I am very misled, I believe the United States will almost have to be the principal location of the tribulation saints." [49] The patriotic Hilton Sutton, in his 1988 Madison appearance, similarly insisted that America would continue to enjoy God's blessing. Declared Sutton: "I absolutely refute . . . anyone that prophesies the destruction of the United States." [50]

Much more cautiously, S. Dwight Coder of the Moody Bible Institute also suggested that America might enjoy special end-time treatment. "If any nation now on the earth is going to exist in eternity," he wrote in 1973, "nations such as America, from which missionaries . . . have gone in large numbers, with the faithful support and prayers of countless Christians, may be expected to be there." Added Coder in 1984, "The Lord is going to judge America some day, but we are justified in hoping our country will be spared and that Americans will share the joy of the [millennial] kingdom." [51]

In the same exculpatory vein, other writers saw America's Tribulation-era difficulties arising from the massive losses it would experience at the Rapture. Though sadly fallen, noted one in 1974, the United States

> still has a larger percentage of born-again believers in its population than any other important country. When Jesus comes for his own, thousands of responsible leaders in government, industry, education, religion, the arts, and the professions will be removed. With these leaders taken to meet the Lord in the air, the structure of government, industry, education, the arts, and the professions will be so weakened that it will reduce the United States to an impotent and prostrated nation. [52]

John Wesley White, making the same point some years later, cited a Gallup poll showing that 52 percent of Americans claimed to be born again, and reflected on the catastrophic effects if half the nation's population were suddenly to disappear. Even if America had only half the number of believers the polls showed, commented a 1983 author, "the rapture would put this country into a state of total chaos and collapse." [53]

As we have seen, the search for hopeful allusions to the United States in prophecy led some commentators to Ezekiel 38:13, in which "the merchants of Tarshish, with all the young lions thereof" question Gog's attack on Israel: "Art thou come to take a spoil? hast thou gathered thy company to take a prey?" Many nineteenth-century British writers took this passage to heart. An 1877 commentator, while confessing that he had "no time to work out the subject," expressed the "fervent hope" that Tarshish "may prove to be the navy of England, and the young lions the bravest sons of her merchant princes." To American expositors the "young lions" suggested Britain's former colonies, including the United States. A few postwar writers continued this interpretive tradition. Doug Clark, for example, found the United States in the "young lions" passage, and drew from it a broad and inspiring meaning:

> God planned for America to be the end-time nation so strong as to ensure that the Biblical prophecies would be carried out by this human instrument of the Lord . . . America was born of God, Who knew He would use her expertise for His own ultimate glory as well as for the good of the world.[54]

Most writers rejected this interpretation of Ezekiel 38:13—or found it at best, as one said, "rather tenuous." Pat Robertson concluded in 1982 that the passage could only tentatively be linked to the United States and was in any case unclear in its implications, since Tarshish and the "young lions" apparently do little but ineffectually question Gog's attack.[55]

Other writers seeking a hopeful prophetic message combined the older view of America as a chosen land with the more recent darker outlook by arguing that the United States (like Israel) would be severely chastised for its sins, but would emerge intact. For example, Charles Taylor (an oracular writer with a penchant for italics and capital letters) agreed with other commentators that America had "*sinned grievously*" and was "MARKED FOR JUDGMENT," but insisted that it would be purified by its chastening ordeal and survive into the Millennium. Though it would be "greatly affected" by thermonuclear attack when the Soviet Union invaded Israel, Taylor argued, the United States would not be totally wiped out. Rather, after being "*purged and punished,*" America "SHALL ULTIMATELY BE DELIVERED . . . *and find* PEACE."[56] Doug Clark, citing U.S. support for Israel and the Jews, and America's worldwide evangelism and humanitarianism, asked rhetorically in 1982: "Would God allow a godless, Christless, Communistic power guilty of inhuman butchery to conquer and destroy the last bastion of Christianity? No." Nevertheless, after the usual catalog of American sinfulness, Clark concluded that even though the United States would not be "totally destroyed" in the coming nuclear war, it might well be "hurt badly" in punishment for its wickedness.[57]

A few dissented or tried to soften the verdict, yet most post-1945 prophecy popularizers foresaw America's imminent destruction or drastic decline as recompense for its wickedness and unbelief. This theme, central to the Puritan jeremiad and present in premillennial writings from the mid-nineteenth century on as a muted counterpoint to more hopeful views of America's destiny, loomed large after 1945. Within weeks of the end of World War II, as America still basked in the glow of victory, Donald Grey Barnhouse pronounced harsh judgment on the postwar spiritual and moral climate:

> The United States has departed a-whoring after strange gods . . . We have come to a fitful peace by means of the crushing might of our industrial power. Today, like the anti-Christ to come, there are many in our country who worship "the god of forces" (Dan. 11:38). The greed of the labor unions, the lust of Hollywood, the debauchery of the masses cry to high Heaven for judgment. *Life* magazine writes a full page editorial against the menace of the gambling at race tracks where the nation is frittering almost two billion dollars in a year . . . [A] warning alert [was recently] sent out to the hotels, restaurants and night clubs of the land to stock up very heavily, for Thanksgiving, Christmas and New Year's would be the greatest "social season" in the history of America. They call it social season; we call it debauch.
>
> The starving nations of the world, with lips too dry to drool, look hungrily at our prosperity, and growl in surly fashion at our proud boasts of power.

Punishment must come soon, Barnhouse wrote grimly. "It is certainly consistent with the nature of God to move toward the destruction of the United States of America." The terrible retribution of Armageddon, he warned, would descend upon America as upon all apostate nations.[58]

Barnhouse's apocalyptic vision of looming destruction was reiterated by scores of prophecy writers in the ensuing decades. "The world is covered with the ashes of nations which have repudiated

God," declared Louis Talbot in 1952; "America will be no exception." Jack Van Impe, writing twenty-seven years later, echoed the point. "America will undoubtedly be part and parcel of [the] suffering in the days ahead," he proclaimed and drove home the point by including the United States on his chart showing the one-third of the population that, according to Revelation, would die in the Tribulation.[59]

Like Taylor, some linked America's destruction to Gog's invasion of Israel. Wrote Lindsey in *The Late Great Planet Earth,* "It is quite possible that Ezekiel was referring to the U.S. in part when he said: 'I will send fire—upon those who dwell securely in the coastlands . . .' The Hebrew word translated as "coastlands," Lindsey claimed, actually meant "continents" and "designated the great Gentile civilizations across the seas."[60]

Other popularizers found America's doom foretold in Isaiah:

> Woe to the land shadowing with wings, which is beyond the rivers of Ethiopia:
> That sendeth ambassadors by the sea, even in vessels of bulrushes upon the waters, saying, Go, ye swift messengers, to a nation scattered and peeled, to a people terrible from their beginning hitherto; a nation meted out and trodden down, whose land the rivers have spoiled![61]

Carrying on an interpretive tradition dating to the early nineteenth century, postwar prophecy writers displayed great ingenuity in finding the United States in these cryptic verses: "shadowing with wings," they said, could apply to the American eagle or to the U.S. aircraft industry; "peeled" to clean-shaven men (the U.S. Army was the first to distribute razors to its troops, one interpreter claimed); and "meted out and trodden down" to Washington's comprehensive geographic surveys. "Terrible" could also be translated "awesome," they claimed; "spoiled" by rivers could mean "nourished" by rivers, and so on. The entire passage, Jack Van Impe concluded in 1983, "amazingly resembles modern America."[62]

Writers applied these verses to the United States in full awareness that they foretold the *destruction* of the land "shadowed with wings." After the opening judgment of "woe," the chapter proceeds through a series of memorable images to describe a rich, fertile land left sere and desolate:

> For afore the harvest, when the bud is perfect, and the sour grape is

> ripening in the flower, he shall both cut off the sprigs with pruning hooks, and take away and cut down the branches.
>
> They shall be left together unto the fowls of the mountains, and to the beasts of the earth: and the fowls shall summer upon them, and all the beasts of the earth shall winter upon them.[63]

Concluded one writer after linking this and other apocalyptic passages to America: "The forecast for the USA is gloomy . . . We see from these verses that the USA will survive, but it would appear that very few people will be left alive. Does this mean that nearly all of our 230,000,000 people will be killed? It would appear so."[64]

Others saw America's demise, as well as its wickedness, prefigured in the "Babylon" whose destruction "in one hour" is prophesied in Revelation. In *Set the Trumpet to Thy Mouth,* David Wilkerson offered a nightmarish vision of the moment "the Modern Babylon" vanishes:

> America is going to be destroyed by fire! Sudden destruction is coming and few will escape. Unexpectedly, and in one hour, a hydrogen holocaust will engulf America—and this nation will be no more . . . In one hour it will all be gone! The stock market will burn—with all the buildings, the investments. The skyscrapers will melt; the fire of divine vengeance will turn cities into polluted wildernesses . . . Make no mistake about it. God's word clearly warns a great dissolving will happen.[65]

A. G. Mojtabai, offering a rare glimpse of prophecy preaching at the grassroots level, reports a 1982 sermon in which an Amarillo pentecostal minister, Royce Elms, pictured wasteful, self-indulgent America as "the end-time economic Babylon" described in Revelation 18. Quoting verse 7, Elms made a crucial substitution: "How much *America* hath glorified herself, and lived deliciously, so much torment and sorrow give her . . ." "Deliciously! Deliciously!" he repeated, savoring the unexpected adverb:

> Is there anybody else in the world that has lived as deliciously as the United States of America? Listen to this: We have 5½ percent of the population, but out of all the money in the world that's spent on food, we spend 60 percent of it. For she hath *lived deliciously* . . .
>
> Last year we spent eighty-four billion dollars on food for the USA. Twenty-one billion was spent on recreation. Forty-

seven billion on gambling. Eleven billion on alcohol. Eight billion on tobacco. Seven billion was spent on pets alone last year. And two hundred and ten million of that was spent on dog food. Yet we pat ourselves on the back and we declare that we are a godly nation, that we are a God-fearing people, that our nation loves God, and we send out all the missionaries throughout the world. But, friend, we better wake up to the fact that we are also the wickedest nation on earth.

And just as wicked America fits the Babylon profile, so it will suffer the fate foretold for Babylon: "You say, Brother Elms, are you talking about nuclear holocaust for the USA? Do you mean to tell me that we are going to be the victim of a terrifying nuclear attack? Absolutely! It is ordained in God's word beyond any shadow of a doubt." [66]

Not all writers found explicit scriptural forecasts of America's end. "No specific mention of the United States or any other country in North America or South America can be found in the Bible," declared Walvoord flatly in 1967. LaHaye, while acknowledging Americans' "tendency to think of our country as a nation of destiny," agreed in 1984 that the Scriptures are silent on the subject of the United States. [67]

Even authors who failed to find the United States in prophecy offered a dismal prognosis based on the Bible's numerous references to the end-time fate of "the nations" or "all the kingdoms of the world," on the logical assumption that these categories included the United States. These wicked kingdoms would assemble at Armageddon, according to Revelation, and be destroyed by Jesus Christ. [68] Whatever their interpretive approach, in short, most postwar prophecy writers foresaw horrendous eschatological prospects for apostate America.

Democracy, Capitalism, and Prophetic Judgment

Other popularizers, only slightly less apocalyptically, foresaw political and economic collapse in America's near future. Neither democracy nor the free-enterprise system will count for much, they insisted, when history's final hour strikes. Dismissive of all human political constructs, prophecy writers did not exempt democracy; government of the people, by the people, and for the people enjoyed no privileged standing in their eyes. Indeed, suspicion of democracy has long been part of the premillennial worldview. In the visionary 1830 utterances of Margaret MacDonald, a young Scotswoman from whom John Darby is said to have taken the idea of the Rapture, one finds: "It was first the awful state of the land that was pressed upon me. I saw the blindness and infatuation of the people to be very great. I felt the cry of Liberty just to be the hiss of the serpent, to drown them in perdition."[69]

This theme—"the cry of Liberty" as "the hiss of the serpent"—pervaded nineteenth-century and early-twentieth-century premillennial writings. Democracy was simply a way station to Antichrist's dictatorship, declared Sir Robert Anderson in 1884: "First the revolution; then the *plebiscite;* then the despot." The Populist movement and labor unrest of the 1890s foreshadowed the final collapse of human government prophesied in the Book of Daniel, warned an 1892 writer; with the masses in turmoil, he went on, "what can we anticipate but dissension and uproar?" Isaac Haldeman, upholding the same position in 1910 at the height of the Progressive-era campaigns for expanding democracy through women's suffrage, the direct election of senators, and the like, offered a labored interpretation of King Nebuchadnezzar's famous dream by which democracy became the final stage of government before Antichrist's rise:

> We must measure final things by the image [in Dan. 2]. The image has a two-fold process of fulfillment; from the head to the feet—from the feet to the head. So far [history] has been going down from the head to the feet. We are undoubtedly in the region or the beginning of the region of the clay. The Antichrist can come only when the prophecy starts backward or upward from the feet to the head. As the clay is the basic element (and that is the people), then the iron (the autocratic) element can come in only after the clay has come to the front.[70]

As Timothy Weber has noted, turn-of-the-century premillennialists viewed democracy as essentially "sinful man's ultimate attempt to have things his own way," and thus as simply another sign of end-time degeneracy.[71]

A similar skepticism pervaded post-1945 prophecy writings. In the early postwar era, when Cold War intellectuals celebrated American democracy as the antithesis of totalitarianism, premillennialists remained aloof. They condemned communism, but did not simultaneously embrace the other side in the ideological struggle. "God's ideal government is not a democracy," declared Oswald Smith in 1948, "but an absolute monarchy . . . with Jesus Christ as the monarch." A speaker at the 1956 New York City prophecy conference genuflected to the conventional pieties of Cold War political discourse, but ultimately affirmed premillennial doctrine: "Now, I thank God for democracy . . . [and] for all the blessings that are mine as a citizen of the United States of America. But you and I know full well that neither democracy nor dictatorship is God's final answer for the time in which we are living." Another expositor, writing the following year, included no such qualifications: "Democracy . . . , the philosophy of rule by the people, offers no hope for the fulfillment of Christ's prayer: 'Thy kingdom come, thy will be done in earth, as it is in heaven.'" The prophecy believer, he went on, "has no reason to consider the pros and cons of the question of the preservation of the American union . . . Democracy is not ordained of God to be the ultimate ideal of human government."[72]

In the years that followed, although some politicized premillennialists ostentatiously embraced the secular political order, the skeptical note remained strong. "Democracy and liberation, carried to distorted extremes, end in despotism," declared one; in excess, he went on, democracy "can produce the social chemistry ideal for the rise of a dictator." Many authors, following Haldeman's 1910 interpretation of Nebuchadnezzar's dream, argued that the statue's clay feet (as well as the sea from which the Beast emerges in Rev. 13) represented democracy run amok. Chuck Smith in 1978 foresaw the imminent demise of "man's futile efforts to govern himself." "Most forms of government have only been able to endure for about 200 years before totally disintegrating," Smith added in 1984, as America was in the midst of a series of bicentennial observances. He continued:

> Just about every form of government that can be conceived in the human mind, city kingdoms, monarchy, democracy, communism . . . , has ultimately deteriorated. Man cannot govern himself without greed and corruption setting in.[73]

Smith spoke for a host of postwar premillennialists for whom democracy was only the latest in a series of doomed attempts at self-government by a fallen human race.

Holding little brief for democracy, post-1945 prophecy writers exhibited even less enthusiasm for consumer capitalism. While a few such as Lindsey endorsed the U.S. economic system uncritically, most (as we shall note more fully in Chapter 8) foresaw an end-time economic crisis paralleling the political collapse. Karl Marx erred in believing that a just social order could be achieved within history, observed a 1957 writer, but he was "basically correct in his indictment of capitalism . . . Capitalism has never voluntarily given up any of the evils of the profit system, and this constitutes a valid basis for distrusting it . . . God's will is that the profit system be judged and destroyed." And it *would* be destroyed, this author continued, with "a violence beyond that [en]visioned by Marx." Any economic system that encouraged a big corporation to spend $35,000 on a dog-food commercial, said Salem Kirban in 1968, was ripe for punishment. David Wilkerson in 1974 quoted verbatim some grim and remarkably explicit economic news communicated to him by God in a vision: "The auto industry is going to be hurt badly. Makers of recreational vehicles are going to get hit very hard. Appliance inventories will pile up, and sales will fall off drastically." Antichrist's rule, Wilkerson warned, was "just a world depression away." [74]

Criticisms of U.S. capitalism and warnings of economic collapse continued unabated in the 1980s, despite the enthusiasm of some prominent fundamentalists for the Reagan movement. Doug Clark's *Shockwaves of Armageddon* foresaw a frightful end-time fiscal crisis: "Business will fail; the stock market will collapse; the government will go bankrupt. The nation will go hungry, with jobless millions ready for any kind of an answer." In the midst of this upheaval, Clark suggested, the United States would plunge into war to secure its oil resources. [75]

Capitalism encouraged "hedonistic love of pleasure and selfish lust for money, possessions, and power," proclaimed another author, and for this reason capitalism would "eventually lose its battle with Communism." S. Maxwell Coder, quoting the prophet Joel—"Turn ye even to me with all your heart, and with fasting, and with weeping, and with mourning"—wrote in 1984: "An affluent generation long free from affliction knows nothing of such words. But here they are . . . Our nation will experience the worst time of distress and affliction it has ever known." [76]

Whatever the specific scenario, nearly all prophecy interpreters from the end of World War II through the 1980s foresaw a weakened America sinking fast as the end drew nearer. "Look quickly, because the United States of America seems doomed as a world power," wrote one in 1972. Only "wishful thinking," said Walvoord in 1989, could lead anyone to find hope for the United States in the prophetic scriptures.[77]

All the central themes, as well as the ambivalence, of postwar prophecy treatment of the United States were evident in Hal Lindsey's numerous popularizations. At times a jingoistic superpatriot, Lindsey preached a vehement anticommunist stance; called for a massive U.S. military buildup; and fulsomely praised the free-enterprise system that had rewarded him so lavishly. Yet intimations of national catastrophe hovered over Lindsey's writings as well. His suggestion in *The Late Great Planet Earth* that God may incinerate the United States when He destroys the Soviet Union, and his speculations about America's coming economic collapse illustrate the apprehension beneath the surface bombast. Discussing the destruction of "the cities of the nations" foretold in Revelation, he did not exclude America's urban centers. "Imagine, cities like London, Paris, Tokyo, New York, Los Angeles, Chicago—obliterated!" Writing in the turbulent late 1960s, Lindsey saw the conditions that would lead to America's collapse already shaping up:

> The United States will not hold its present position of leadership in the western world . . . Internal political chaos caused by student rebellions and Communist subversion will begin to erode the economy of our nation. Lack of moral principle by citizens and leaders will so weaken law and order that a state of anarchy will finally result.[78]

The United States will "lose its role as the leader of the West" when Antichrist arises, Lindsey added in 1973, and, as part of that godless dictator's empire, it will perish at Armageddon.[79]

In 1981, as the Reagan era began, Lindsey the militant patriot reemerged. In *The 1980s: Countdown to Armageddon,* the most strident of his books, he called for a redoubled campaign to destroy communism, a massive nuclear buildup to overtake the Soviets, an aggressive defense of capitalism to silence its domestic detractors, and a mobilization of opinion against internal moral rot and the welfare state. "If some critical and difficult choices are made by the American people

right now, it is possible to see the U.S. remain a world power," he proclaimed. "The Bible supports building a powerful military force. And
the Bible is telling the U.S. to become strong again."[80] Listing the
reasons "why the U.S. has been preserved as a free country" (the
prayers of millions of believers, support for missionary activity, favorable treatment of the Jews and Israel, and so forth) Lindsey concluded,
"I believe that America will survive this perilous situation and endure
until the Lord comes to evacuate His people."[81]

Lindsey's message was confused and contradictory, saved from
total incoherence by the doctrine of the Rapture. (The United States
will survive and may even remain mighty until the Lord comes for the
saints, but it faces collapse and ultimate destruction during the Tribulation.) While urging aggressive action to restore American greatness,
Lindsey also preached the usual premillennial dogma: history is in
God's hands; human effort is in vain; all the Gentile nations of the
earth face doom when Christ returns. To be simultaneously a consistent premillennialist and a Cold War ideologue was not an easy task.

Like Lindsey, many postwar premillennialist writers linked their
predictions of America's decline to the belief that the United States
will eventually be dominated by Antichrist's ten-nation revived Roman Empire—the demonic world power that, according to the dispensational scenario, will emerge during the Tribulation. Antichrist's
domain, argued an editor of *Our Hope* magazine in 1945, while centered in the old Roman Empire, will extend to the Western Hemi-
sphere as well. "Our peoples, our laws, our customs, our culture, our
language are all the projection and the continuation of the old Roman
Empire," said a speaker at the 1961 Los Angeles prophecy conference.
"The United States will be a part of this ten-toed, ten-horned federation, under the authority of the Beast."[82]

As European economic cooperation gained momentum with the
founding of the Common Market in 1967, America's eventual absorption by the new economic and political colossus arising in the region
once controlled by the Caesars seemed increasingly plausible. "It is
probable that the United States will be in some form of alliance with
the Roman ruler," speculated Walvoord in 1967. "In this event," he
went on, "it should be clear that the United States will be in a subor-
dinate role and no longer the great international power that it is today." When Antichrist arises on the world scene, wrote S. Maxwell
Coder in 1973, the United States "will be among the nations yielding

allegiance." The passage in Revelation describing Antichrist's power over "all kindreds, and tongues, and nations," added Coder in 1984, pointed to the end of American influence in international affairs.[83] A few writers demurred,[84] but most agreed in linking America's fate to Antichrist and concluded somberly that both would fall together on the plains of Megiddo.

From the earliest days of European exploration, in cautious speculations or in soaring panegyrics, countless prophecy writers encouraged belief in America's special destiny. This conviction eroded after the Civil War, and following World War II it practically vanished. With rare exceptions, postwar eschatologists, even the most freewheeling popularizers, no longer embraced the view that the United States enjoyed a special, favored place in God's plan—indeed, quite the reverse.

This radical shift did not occur without anxious soul-searching. As Doug Clark wrote in *Shockwaves of Armageddon,* after outlining America's coming economic and moral collapse:

> Naturally, this leaves us with somewhat mixed emotions if we are both patriotic and Christian.
>
> But patriotism must never take the place of God's highest plan and will for men. We are not citizens of this world . . . if we have been transformed by the regenerating power of Christ in salvation. We are citizens of heaven, from whence we look for the coming of the Lord.

In earlier times, Clark went on, God *had* used the United States for His purposes—as recently as World War II, American power had helped defeat Satan's agent Hitler—but America's most-favored-nation status had ended forever. The nation had sunk into apostasy and faced God's righteous wrath. The prophecy believer, even though a loyal American, must bow to the divine will: "As we look at the whole world objectively and realize that the greatest event, the most blessed epoch that could change this world completely, would be the coming of the Lord Jesus Christ, then it is easier to accept what is happening."[85] Nations rise and fall—democratic, capitalistic America no less than the vanished autocracies of ages past. God's eternal plan remains.

8 *Antichrist, 666, and the Mark of the Beast*

What is coming is but the unfolding . . . of movements and processes
already at work in human society. The future has already begun.
—Ray Stedman, 1986

Along with nuclear war, the Soviet threat, Mideast conflicts, and
contemporary wickedness, post-1945 prophecy popularizers
addressed another level of modern reality: sweeping historical
trends that pointed to a demonic order ahead. Radicals seeking
evidence of grassroots disaffection with the structure of modern society have ignored a rich potential source—the torrent of skeptical commentary by premillennialists, whose array of prophetic "signs" included social, economic, and technological processes so broad as to be
almost coterminous with modernity itself. Collectively these authors
offered a strikingly comprehensive critique of contemporary mass society as dehumanizing and dangerously centralized.

Worse lay ahead. After the Rapture, prophecy writers taught, all
these dangerous trends would coalesce into a demonic world order
that would erase the last vestiges of individual autonomy. George Orwell and Aldous Huxley may have written with more literary panache
and intellectual power, but neither presented his dystopic vision more
fervently than did the authors of dozens of postwar prophecy books.

Chaos and Consolidation: A Bimodal View of Contemporary Society

A superficially contradictory view of the modern order emerged in
post-1945 prophecy popularizations. These writers saw disintegration
on every side, with multiple threats to family cohesion, traditional
hierarchies, economic structures, and, indeed, society itself. Simultaneously, however, they discerned a frightening new order on the horizon that would be consolidated, standardized, and dominated by
impersonal global structures. Taken together, perhaps more radically

than any one author realized, these discussions challenged modernity to the core and revealed a profound sense of apprehension about the emerging world system.

But before this new world order could fully take shape, the old order would collapse. Much writing about the Rapture focused not on the joys of the redeemed, but on the catastrophe their disappearance would unleash as disintegrative processes already under way reached a crescendo. Some books evoked the mass disorders triggered by the Rapture with photographs, drawings, and paintings of bursting graves, crashing planes, and cars careening out of control. Others created vivid word pictures:

> A chaotic rubble will result as many of the Christians "caught up" shall be taken from positions of traffic control, industrial production control, and from all walks of life: many of them taken while driving their cars, or even while piloting aircraft— and crashes of all sorts will occur. Communications will be disrupted; . . . police and fire control will also be very greatly affected.[1]

Leon Bates in his characteristic staccato style offered a harrowing account:

> It may be a typical, normal day, when suddenly AIRPLANES MAY CRASH all over the world . . . due to the mysterious disappearance of BOTH THE PILOT AND CO-PILOT. Many air traffic controllers, radar operators and other people essential for flight operations will also be gone.

> It will be no safer on the highways. Thousands of cars will suddenly be left DRIVERLESS. It will happen "*in the twinkling of an eye*" so there simply WILL NOT BE TIME to stop and park the cars . . .

> Traffic jams on expressways and turnpikes may be GIGANTIC! Bridges may be blocked. Fire trucks, police and ambulances may have great difficulty responding due to missing crew members, the tremendous number of collisions and the unbelievable traffic tieups.

> Telephone circuits may be jammed by the flood of attempted calls. CB radio transmissions may be so covered up they will be almost useless to summon aid, especially in the large cities.

> The panic and terror WILL BE WORLDWIDE![2]

Such accounts, endlessly duplicated, telescoped into a single imagined moment the broader fear of social collapse pervading these works.

Family disruption emerged not only in descriptions of the Rapture, but also in discussions of the end-time signs that would become manifest *before* the Rapture. Long a staple of prophecy writing, as Timothy Weber has noted, this theme loomed especially large after 1970. "The number-one youth problem of the future will be *hatred of parents*," declared David Wilkerson in 1974; "[it] is spreading like a cancer." Reacting to the unrest of the 1960s, he went on: "The radicals of the near future will be . . . totally alienated from father and mother . . . We face undeclared war in our homes." After the Rapture, wrote Merrill Unger in 1973, "rebellious teenagers who despised their Christian parents, will find at last they are 'free' of parental restraint, as both father and mother are nowhere to be found." Leon Bates proclaimed: "Many families will be SPLIT UP—FOREVER! . . . Unsaved TEENAGERS may come home from a night of sin and find their saved parents GONE . . . HOW HORRIBLE it will be for LOVED ONES left on the earth." [3]

James McKeever in 1989 contrasted modern laxity toward rebellious youth with Old Testament days when "God commanded the people to stone to death any juvenile delinquent (any son who would not obey his father)." In an upbeat variation of this theme, a pentecostal prophecy writer, citing Acts 16:31 ("Believe on the Lord Jesus Christ, and thou shalt be saved, *and thy house*"), argued that believers' unsaved family members would be taken in the Rapture as well. He reassured those with unsaved spouses, "Get on your knees and thank God . . . you will see your mate in heaven." [4]

Shattered families abound in fictional and visual representations of the Rapture. In one early prophecy novel, a young man left behind laments to his sister: "The only reason you and I are here is because we didn't listen to mother." *Raptured,* a 1950 novel, featured several families broken up by eschatology—usually a saintly wife or "silver-haired mother" is taken, with husband and grown children left behind. In one Rapture painting, the lawnmower-pushing suburban husband gapes in wonder as his aproned wife soars over the clothesline to meet Jesus. (And recall the comic book about the Rapture in which all the babies in a maternity ward suddenly vanish.) [5]

Like Henry Adams and other late-nineteenth-century writers,

these authors foresaw an ill-defined but horrendous social crisis ahead. A 1950 writer interpreted "the sea and the waves roaring" mentioned in Jesus' list of end-time signs as "the roaring of the unstable and restless masses." John Walvoord in 1967 pictured a world "moving faster and faster like a colossal machine out of control whose very power and momentum inevitably will plunge it into ultimate disaster." Echoed a 1978 writer: "Civilization is on a collision course with destiny, and the pace is increasing at a frightening rate of speed . . . It is only a matter of time before our accepted form of civilization is derailed completely."[6]

Cataclysmic imagery pervaded these discussions of social trends. The disordered cosmos of Revelation—darkened sun, bloody moon, falling stars—said Donald Grey Barnhouse in 1945, symbolized a time "when all human government will be broken down," leaving only chaos. "The world today is like a bomb with a lighted fuse," declared a 1974 author; "it is only a matter of time before the bomb is ignited and a global upheaval takes place." Intimations of imminent collapse emerged, too, in a prophetic work otherwise very different from those considered in this book, Daniel Berrigan's *Nightmare of God* (1983), an interpretation of John's Apocalypse. Commenting on its present-day relevance, Berrigan wrote in his telegraphic style: "We ponder the Bible, we look around us. A sense, an atmosphere, makes itself felt: . . . something wrong, awry, the world off kilter . . . , a social illness. Break up; nothing holding; an ominous sense of remote tragedy nearing, impending, a shadow over life, a bad dream at high noon."[7]

In discussing the post-Rapture world, prophecy writers projected into the future their amorphous fears of today's unsettling trends. "CHAOS WILL BE ON EVERY HAND," proclaimed Charles Taylor. "Marauders, anarchists, and opportunists will be armed and dangerous." Advising Californians who miss the Rapture to move east of the San Andreas Fault, he added, "If you have a gun, take it with you, plus a good supply of ammunition." The Tribulation era, said a 1981 book, will seethe with "anarchistic guerrilla terrorism and rampant crime." Others quoted the prophet Isaiah's gripping vision of social cataclysm: "In the city is left desolation, and the gate is smitten with destruction . . . The earth shall reel to and fro like a drunkard." A character in a 1986 fictional account of the last days offered a different image to convey this sense of a once-vigorous organic system in a state of terminal collapse: "I feel like a physician watching the vital signs on a dying patient." [8]

The eighteenth-century British theologian William Paley pointed out in a famous analogy that if you discovered an intricate, beautifully functioning timepiece in your path, you would assume that someone had made it; in the same way, Paley went on, the complex and harmonious workings of the natural world proclaimed the existence of a Creator. Premillennialists turned the metaphor inside out: the world's increasing *dis*order validated God's plan as revealed in the Bible. "Like a bad watch," as one put it, inverting Paley, "the world will steadily deteriorate until it stops ticking." [9]

Images of social upheaval pervaded Dan Betzer's 1985 novel of the Tribulation, *Beast*. After describing the Rapture ("MILLIONS DISAPPEAR WORLDWIDE; JESUS CHRIST SAID TO BE RESPONSIBLE"—*New York Times*), Betzer presents a nightmarish picture of urban collapse. A scene anticipatory of Tom Wolfe's *Bonfire of the Vanities* describes a woman's impressions as she drives through New York City: "She could see cars overturned and on fire. Trash littered the streets. Shop windows had been smashed and the merchandise inside stolen. It was like a scene from hell, she thought to herself. There didn't seem to be any restraint left anywhere." Attacked by a howling mob, the pregnant young woman is gang-raped and left for dead. "The world has just blown up, that's all," reflects another character, " and without even one bomb being dropped." Commented Betzer: "Some great restraining hand had been lifted from the earth. The delicate veneer that kept mankind from the laws of the jungle had been jostled by an accident of cosmic proportions and the ooze of primitive man was escaping." [10]

As in *Beast,* scenarios of disintegration often focused on the city. M. R. DeHaan, noting the feverish urbanization just before the Flood, underscored "the dangers of city life—morally and spiritually—dangers utterly unknown in rural districts." This commonplace of American social thought—rural nostalgia, suspicion of the city—remained vigorously alive in the prophecy genre, a final repository for many social attitudes as they faded from the larger arena of public discourse. Discussing "What to Do if You Miss the Rapture," a 1981 popularizer advised: "Get Out of the Big City. Go to the country and hide out." New York City, speculated Jack Van Impe in 1983, would probably be Antichrist's capital. [11]

In Salem Kirban's prophecy novel *666,* urban sprawl proceeded to its logical culmination after the Rapture:

The United States was now made up of six cities . . . What once were Indianapolis and Fort Wayne, Dayton, St. Louis, and Minneapolis were now called CHICAGO. City after city had been merged into this Midwest conglomerate . . . PHILADELPHIA had swallowed up Harrisburg, Pittsburgh, Scranton and Williamsport. NEW YORK CITY extended as far north as Portland, Maine. LOS ANGELES went as far east as Denver. One patch of farm land remained. The state of Kansas was declared farm area. Topeka and Wichita were leveled to make the complete state a farm oasis. The rest of the United States was basically the six major cities.[12]

The mayor of NEW YORK CITY sums up conditions: "Some still think of New York as a Dream City, but I believe a more appropriate word would be 'nightmare.' Three-fourths of our population is on welfare. We haven't seen the sun in weeks!" When the mayor challenges Antichrist for power, Antichrist poisons the polluted cloud blanketing the elephantine metropolis, killing its entire population.[13]

DeHaan's evocation of an idyllic preurban world appeared in fictional form in Betzer's *Beast* as a harried TV mogul, frantically coping with the urban chaos of the last days, indulged in a brief reverie: "He dreamed of childhood days, of tossing a hooked worm into the shallows of Half Moon Lake and yelling in delight as a bullhead smacked the boat. He dreamed of gentle breezes blowing across the plains from the Missouri River and of laughter at the family table. It was a million years ago."[14]

Images of destroyed cities pervaded many scenarios of the end, as in Barnhouse's 1945 speculation that New York City might be the "Babylon" whose end is prophesied in Revelation, and Lindsey's catalog of great cities facing obliteration. In the same vein, Taylor declared in 1980 that while the United States would survive, "American cities soon will burn."[15]

Antiurban themes were especially prominent in the writings of the minority of premillennialists who held that the Rapture would occur *after,* rather than before, the Tribulation, and whose works abounded in back-to-the-land survivalist themes. James McKeever's *End-Times News Digest,* for example, blended discussion of end-time signs with tips on dietary fiber, freeze-dried greens, and solid-waste disposal. McKeever in 1989 advised his readers to get rid of their lawns and flower beds and plant vegetables instead, and then "preserve and can the harvest . . . , like our forefathers did." [16]

Along with a fragmenting *social* fabric loomed equally dangerous *political* trends. Suspicion of government pervaded this literature. While deifying the Founding Fathers, these authors generally viewed modern-day politicians as power-mad charlatans. America's public officials were preparing the way for Antichrist, asserted Kirban in 1968, by "casting a veil of illusion over the populace and lulling them into a slumber from which they will awake too late." Echoing New Left radicals whom he elsewhere denounced, Kirban noted that Lyndon Johnson had used the Gulf of Tonkin resolution to bypass the Constitution and concentrate more power in the presidency. "Men in high places are grabbing for unprecedented powers," agreed David Wilkerson in his 1974 survey of end-time political trends. [17]

Indeed, a radical suspicion of *all* earthly power pervaded these works. New Testament scholars note the contrast between the fiercely antiauthoritarian thrust of John's Apocalypse, written under the lash of Roman persecution, and Saint Paul's advice of a few decades earlier that Christians should respect the powers that be. Post-1945 prophecy interpreters followed John rather than Paul on this point. Again illuminating is Berrigan's *Nightmare of God,* written in a Washington jail after the Jesuit activist's arrest for trying to dig a grave on the White House lawn to protest U.S. militarism. [18]

"The book of Revelation ought to be burned, it is positively subversive!" exclaimed Berrigan, with its "horrific, phantasmagoric" images evoking the plight not only of the early Church "combating for its very soul with the imperial state," but also of contemporary believers who find themselves citizens of a militarized nation-state. Passages that to fundamentalist interpreters pointed to the Soviet Union suggested to Berrigan *American* power spreading malevolently over the world. The plague of locusts becomes U.S. helicopters ravaging Vietnam; wicked Babylon, "whose very stones ooze with the sweat and blood of victims," becomes the Pentagon; the eagle—"ravenous, carnivorous, rockets in claw and [with] a preternatural skill at smelling out living creatures"—turns into a "symbol of the United States Air Force" and the nation it serves. [19]

Offering a reading of John's Apocalypse as present-minded as Hal

Lindsey's, Berrigan ridiculed the "learned exegesis" of academic interpreters: "To most scholars of the Bible, the crimes of the U.S. Air
Force are forever beside the point. Thus does crime multiply and
scholarship rot." Revelation serves best, he argued, as "an antidote
. . . to the immense inflation of political rhetoric" by the modern corporate state. No rhetorical slouch himself, he continued:

> The corporate state wastes the earth, dislocates minds, corrupts
> all areas of science, in its expanding military and economic ad-
> venturism . . . Bellicose, selfish, self-deluded, icy, absurdly
> resolute—behold the Rome of the Book of Revelation. Behold
> also America? . . . What is left for humans, what is left for
> Christians to do? We must resist the state.[20]

Although "the housebroken Christian imagination has all but
given up on . . . [the] difficult, even outrageous images" of Revelation, Berrigan insisted, they deserve as much attention as the symbols
by which the modern state justifies itself. In Revelation, he concludes,
"a nightmare is in progress . . . We are well advised, for the sake of
soul and sanity, to listen—and to grow silent."[21]

Incorporating only the meagerest eschatological dimension and
urging open resistance to the secular order rather than preparation for
the imminent return of Jesus Christ, Berrigan's work diverged radically from that of premillennialist expositors. Yet his view of a sinister, ever-encroaching state and his repudiation of the secular order—
"a rampage of modern horrors"—echoed that of the premillennialists.
Two examples from many illustrate the point.

At the 1971 Jerusalem prophecy conference, James Houston,
principal of Vancouver's Regent College, found in prophecies of the
judgment of nations a scriptural basis for radically questioning the
presumptions of the state. "Apart from the rule of God," he said,
"the nation is really a myth that mankind perpetuates." Romans 13,
advising due respect for secular authority, and Revelation 13, portraying the state as monstrous, he said, set the parameters of a Christian
view of civil power: not to be renounced, but not to be "accepted
uncritically as the norm of final authority." Echoing the Reinhold
Niebuhr of *Moral Man and Immoral Society* (1932), and anticipating
Berrigan by a decade, Houston warned against "false patriotism" and
the temptation of "deifying our own state" as simply forms of "exaggerated self-interest."

In the same vein, prophecy writer A. Bekley Michelson in 1984 emphasized the skeptical view of government in the apocalypses of both Daniel and Revelation: in the former, the bear with three ribs protruding from its teeth offers "a vivid picture of a government consuming and devouring other nations," while the other fierce beasts suggest how "human government controls the people of the world by sheer force"; in Revelation, he went on, the rampaging Beast and Great Harlot symbolize the readiness of governments to destroy all "who get in the way of their purposes." While both apocalypses show "the important roles that government plays in human affairs," Michelson observed, they also offer "a divine alternative" to earthly power and make clear that "constant vigilance is absolutely essential for God's people, no matter where they live." [22]

The end-time trends discerned by prophecy writers involved not only the growth of the state but a far more insidious convergence of power involving all realms of modern life. The postwar Protestant ecumenical movement, for example, struck them as another clear sign of the end-time consolidation foretold in Scripture. A 1945 address by John D. Rockefeller, Jr., urging Protestant leaders to forget denominational differences and work for "the kingdom of God on earth" roused Donald Grey Barnhouse to thunderous denunciation: here in embryo was the prophesied apostate church! In succeeding years the World Council of Churches (1948) and its U.S. counterpart, the National Council of Churches, figured prominently in premillennial demonology. The ecumenical movement seemed doubly sinister, symbolizing both liberal Protestantism's drift from orthodoxy *and* the process of global consolidation. A speaker at the 1952 New York City prophecy conference, anticipating a common theme in postwar prophecy writing, predicted the eventual merger of the World Council of Churches and the Roman Catholic Church. John Walvoord, surveying the spreading apostasy of the mainstream denominations with their "great cathedrals" and "pomp and ceremony," and the growing "movement toward a world church," concluded in 1964, "Never before in the history of the church has there been more evidence that the end of the age is at hand." [23]

In the 1970s and 1980s, as evangelicalism thrived and the more liberal denominations faltered, attacks on the ecumenical movement intensified. Lindsey in *The Late Great Planet Earth* discussed the "mergers of denominations into 'religious conglomerates'" as an end-time sign; so bureaucratized were "the standard-brand denominations," he charged, that ordinary members had no voice in their policies. In their "ecumenical mania," predicted Merrill Unger, liberal Protestantism's leaders would soon propose a "superchurch" that would try to swallow all Christianity. Chuck Smith warned of counterfeit churches with their "elaborate structures, elaborate organizations, and elaborate rituals . . . pandering to the rich and exclusive classes."[24]

The postwar system of international finance and commerce impressed prophecy writers as another key end-time sign. Hardly a new theme, this motif had been embedded in prophecy writing since Martin Luther's day or earlier. A 1937 writer found business consolidation foretold—and denounced—in Isaiah: "Woe unto them that join house to house, that lay field to field, till there be no place, that they may be placed alone in the midst of the earth!"[25] The rise of "gigantic combinations and trusts," observed still another prewar author, would soon climax in "Babylonian confusion."[26]

After World War II, however, this venerable theme took on new vitality. The emerging global economy, scores of writers over the decades insisted, anticipated Antichrist's world system. Thanks to new electronic technologies, observed a 1982 writer, "the prophecy of total economic control has for the first time in history become a possibility." The Teamsters' grip on the U.S. food supply, said another author, offered a foretaste of the coming dictatorship.[27]

This foreordained economic consolidation, prophecy writers warned, was crushing the individual as it unfolded. Wrote Chuck Smith in 1977:

> As we look at this monolithic commercial system which has controlled the world and today controls our lives, we realize that the policies of nations are formed by and for commercial interests' sake. More and more our lives are being manipulated by schemes such as planned shortages so that these forces can gain more money . . . [and] power. We are victims, and we are helpless to do anything about it.
>
> These men play chess with the lives of the people of the world.[28]

Madison Avenue's "clever advertising schemes," Smith went on, echoing Vance Packard and many other postwar critics of the hidden role of advertisers in shaping behavior, served the manipulators' interests by numbing the consumers' will:

> They make you feel that you're not a complete or total person unless you use that particular deodorant. You can't truly obtain full manhood unless you use that particular cologne. The whole system is based upon creating a fictitious need in your mind . . . [for] the luxuries, the ease, and the soft things of life.[29]

Social-control experts, wrote Ray Stedman in 1970, were perfecting sophisticated techniques to turn the masses into mindless consumers, preparing them for Antichrist's rule: "It is not only the Marxists who think man needs remaking, but also the scientists of the West who propose to turn man from a human being with an unpredictable will and an unmanageable conscience into a robot or a marionette, a compliant human vegetable."[30]

Going beyond generalities, writers pointed to specific organizations behind the new global order. Updating earlier authors who had focused on the League of Nations, many pinpointed the United Nations as the forerunner of the prophesied world state. If not a proto–world government itself, Walvoord argued in 1964, the UN was playing a key prophetic role by eroding national loyalty and indoctrinating the masses in globalism. A 1979 work called attention to the miracle recorded in the Gospel of John, in which Peter, following Jesus' instructions, catches 153 fish—*the precise membership of the United Nations, excluding Israel!* This passage foretold, he suggested, the UN's destruction at Armageddon.[31]

But the United Nations was only the iceberg's tip. Wilbur Smith told the 1971 Jerusalem prophecy conference that the *Encyclopedia of Organizations* listed more than 320 bodies whose names began with "World." In *11:59 And Counting* Jack Van Impe listed three pages of international agencies to show that "a new world order is on the horizon." The World Bank, the International Monetary Fund, the Federal Reserve Board, the Council on Foreign Relations, the European Common Market, and the Society for Worldwide Interbank Telecommunications (SWIFT), with those old standbys the "international bankers" and even "the Rothschilds," received special attention. From the complex interplay of such forces, prophecy popularizers agreed, would emerge "a World State, based on collectivism, the planned economy, the regimentation of the individual, and a political and religious dictatorship."[32]

As early as 1910 Isaac Haldeman had identified Esperanto as a plot to promote globalism, and with similar thoroughness post-1945 prophecy writers exposed the many tentacles of the internationalist conspiracy. "Extremely rich world leaders in industry, banking, media, and politics," wrote one in 1979, had formed a "satanic plot . . . to thwart the plan of God for mankind" and were bringing the world "close to the Bible's predicted Tribulation period." "Stretching from Washington to London, Paris, Bonn, Moscow, and Tokyo," added another in 1983, a "mysterious web of intrigue" linked the world's richest families. UFOs, he speculated, were "psychologically programming us for some ultimate deception that is too horrible even to imagine as yet." The space program, he warned, was a scheme to promote global thinking. (Still another observant writer noted that the three astronauts of the 1968 Apollo 8 space mission—Lovell, Anders, and Borman—each had six-letter names: *666!*) Various authors dismissed the energy crisis of the 1970s as a fraud concocted to hasten the world state. The Council on Foreign Relations (or "the Gang of 2,300"), said a 1986 popularizer, had "more political influence than 50 million born-again Christians." Salem Kirban in 1989 traced both the Federal Reserve Board and the Council on Foreign Relations to the machinations of Woodrow Wilson's elusive advisor Edward M. House. Promoting a cassette called "The Great Conspiracy," Kirban declared: "Events in history are no accident. They are a conspiracy orchestrated by Satan himself."[33]

From the mid-1970s on, prophecy writers lavished special attention on the Trilateral Commission. Started in 1972 by banker David Rockefeller and Zbigniew Brzezinski, an international-affairs specialist at Columbia University, the commission sought to strengthen ties among the economic, political, and intellectual elites of the United States, Europe, and Japan. To broaden the organization's southern base, Rockefeller and Brzezinski in 1973 recruited Georgia's former governor Jimmy Carter. Upon Carter's election as President in 1976, Brzezinski became national security advisor, and other Trilateralists took high positions in the administration.[34]

The Trilateral Commission fit the prophecy writers' conspiratorial outlook perfectly—here was the sanctum sanctorum of the shadowy network of groups seeking global control; a key tool (as Lindsey put it) of "the western world's most powerful bankers, media leaders, scholars, and government officials bent on radically changing the world in which we live." The Trilateralists, he said, had indoctrinated Carter and then used their media influence to propel him into the White House. The editors of *Time,* the *New York Times,* the *Wall Street Journal,* the *Los Angeles Times,* and the *Washington Post* all had Trilateral Commission links, Lindsey charged, and the Council on Foreign Relations was its political arm. (Except for James F. Byrnes, Lindsey noted, every secretary of state since 1944 had belonged to the Council on Foreign Relations.) The emergence of a secretive group bent on making "changes of global significance . . . with no public consultation, no debate, no election," Lindsey concluded, was "setting the stage for the political-economic one-world system the Bible predicts for the last days." Salem Kirban, updating the story in 1989, noted that President George Bush and Secretary of State James Baker III both had ties to the Trilateral Commission and to the Council on Foreign Relations.[35]

Some writers focused so obsessively on these topics that the genre at its edges shaded off into the murky realm of money cranks and conspiracy fanatics. In *Criminal Politics: The Magazine of Trilateral Politics,* launched in 1975, Lawrence Patterson of Cincinnati offered a monthly exposé of the machinations of "Zionist–Trilats," whose influence he found everywhere. "David Rockefeller and his friends . . . run the drug cartel from their luxury suites in mid-Manhattan," he asserted; President Bush was the "Puppet of the International Bankers" and of "Zionists" like Alan Greenspan of the Federal Reserve Board, Canadian whiskey baron Edgar Bronfman, and South African diamond magnate Harry Oppenheimer. Even some pretended conservatives, he warned, "have merely covered their pointed ears and sharp teeth with a sheep's fleece." In addition to his magazine, Patterson ran seminars, peddled advice via a telephone message service ($1,200 per year to subscribers), and charged $850 per hour as a consultant. But apart from a monthly Bible verse, his magazine did not have a strong eschatological or even religious component. Rather than conversion, he emphasized gold and Swiss banks as the paths to security.[36]

But the belief that a demonic world order lies ahead, and that its beginnings may be discerned in contemporary world trends, was not confined to a handful of cranks. Central to dispensationalism, it figured prominently in paperback popularizations selling hundreds of thousands and even millions of copies. The global economy's complexity could leave ordinary citizens "completely bewildered," M. R. DeHaan noted in 1963, but prophecy revealed the larger pattern behind intricate developments and shadowy maneuverings, replacing confusion with coherence.[37]

The preoccupation with global conspiracy in post-1970s prophecy writings resembled in interesting ways the perspective of 1960s New Left theorists, who also saw powerful economic interests working in hidden ways. Indeed, at the 1971 Jerusalem prophecy conference, Samuel Wolgemuth, the head of Youth for Christ, drew explicit connections between the teachings of prophecy and the younger generation's "fear of becoming just another IBM number in the middle of the vast impersonal technological society."[38]

The differences, of course, were profound. While the New Left urged resistance to capitalism's hegemony, prophecy writers viewed the evolving world system as divinely ordained—an essential prelude, in fact, to Christ's millennial reign. After discussing the coming global order, a 1978 prophecy book concluded, "After 1000 hours of research into the predicament of modern man, your present authors join those who recognize that humanly speaking there is no hope."[39] One could understand the prophetic meaning of the emerging world order, but one could do nothing to alter its course.

If the Trilateral Commission epitomized the Great Conspiracy's institutional side, the *computer* embodied its technological dimension. From the 1960s on, prophecy popularizers invariably wove computers into their scenarios. Here at last was the precise *means* by which Antichrist's forerunners would achieve their aims. "Our computerized society, where we are all 'numbered' from birth to death," wrote Lindsey, foreshadowed the even-more-absolute social control prophesied for the future. "The fact that records on millions of people are available at the push of the proper buttons is a disturbing thought if wicked men come into power," agreed Jack Van Impe. "Nothing since the creation of Adam has changed the life of man and the world economy in such a brief span," declared David Webber and Noah Hutchings: "the computer commands the working, buying, and selling of every individual, every business, and every governmental department," and within a decade will "control mankind's total being."[40]

Combined with credit cards, money machines, communications satellites, laser-read price markings, and other electronic wizardry, wrote William Goetz in *Apocalypse Next,* computers would soon make possible a global system able "to dictate that every man, woman, and child in the world lives, works, buys and sells under a system of code marks and numbers." Very soon, he said, "Mr. and Mrs. Jones, your average citizens," will live in a "cashless, paperless society where money will move instantaneously and invisibly through a central joint operational center." Advertising campaigns such as American Telephone and Telegraph's 1990 "ONE WORLD/ONE CARD" promotion deepened prophecy believers' conviction that the new global order was indeed at hand.[41]

The computer-driven new system threatened privacy, autonomy, even the very concept of individual consciousness. Indeed, the new technologies not only made possible the control of man by machine, but blurred the line between the two. As Van Impe put it: "Computers seem almost human. They have memories. They solve difficult problems. They even speak." The computer of the future, said Goetz, "will be, in effect, a living entity." Soon, predicted Webber and Hutchings, the insolent computer will invade even the most intimate realms. "It is rapidly becoming possible for everyone to have his own omnipresent guide and counselor, the friendly talking computer . . . Inasmuch as men and women are finding it increasingly difficult to experience fulfillment in each other, computerized robots are being designed that will be everything a man or woman may want. Order to exact specifications."[42]

Prophecy writers combed the media for social-control applications of the new technologies. The laser tattooing of cattle had dire implications for the future, warned Leon Bates in 1979. Experiments in monitoring an entire room through a single tiny lens suggested to Goetz "a George Orwell 1984 scenario, in which it is impossible to escape the eye of Big Brother."[43] Pat Robertson and others wrote of microchip computers that could be implanted in the body to facilitate "the economic control of the world's population." Webber and Hutchings reported a *Ramparts* magazine article describing a device analogous to a heart pacemaker that could both sense and control human behavior. Their conclusion seemed amply justified: "All is not well for the Christian in Computerland."[44]

Prophecy writers (again echoing many critics on the left) also betrayed a profound suspicion of the mass media, especially television, for its capacity to weaken the will and feed the masses standardized ideas. "That our press lies, manipulates, and distorts the truth should be obvious to any thinking person," wrote James McKeever in 1988. Media professionals "who smugly report 'the news' but who actually conceal the truth from us," clearly presaged the end, observed another 1980s prophecy popularizer. "We are, in effect, being lied to every day by God-playing newscasters [and] media-minded manipulators." [45]

Just as conspiracy theories obsessed some prophecy writers, computers and other electronic gadgetry so mesmerized others that their books broke free of any coherent eschatology and became barely distinguishable from third-rate science fiction. As one author wrote breathlessly, "We are heading to a faceless society controlled by a master computer." The authors of another work declared excitedly: "Big Brother is watching you. You'd better believe it. That computer is right behind you." But an anxious preoccupation with the social implications of the new technology swept the genre from the 1960s on, with the computer as a central metaphor for disturbing large-scale social trends. Sensing among Americans "an instinctive fear of the awesome power of electronic control" (as David Hunt perceptively observed in 1983), prophecy writers updated their ancient message with knowledgeable disquisitions on lasers, microchips, transponders, and fiber optics. [46]

Underlying these interrelated nightmares of social collapse and absolute social control were profound anxieties about the erosion of human relationships and of individual autonomy under the battering of technosocial developments. As Salem Kirban declared in 1977, "Whoever can control the computer can control human life!" A 1978 work proclaimed, "The tentacles of a mindless controlling force are attempting to take over from Almighty God . . . The computer is set to destroy man's personality while so logically offering him ease of function and financial security." For Chuck Smith the electronic economy symbolized a larger assault on individuality. Only a few remote tribes remained "totally independent of the world system" with its credit cards and computers, he warned. "We're being mentally conditioned to by-pass money as a medium of exchange . . . Soon we'll completely forget about buying and selling with cash." These fears surfaced quite apart from considerations of patriotism or Cold War ideology. Indeed, many writers saw the U.S. and Soviet systems converging into identical patterns of manipulation and control. [47]

Though refracted through a premillennial lens, and with certain features luridly highlighted, the world evoked by these writers was a recognizable one. In this world the seemingly antithetical processes of disintegration and regimentation move forward simultaneously. As traditional structures (family, church, the cash economy) erode, a new global order thrusts itself into every realm of life, forcing the masses into lockstep conformity. The age of science and the machine, reflected Wilbur Smith in 1948, meant "the suppression of personality" and ultimately the concentration of all power in a single center. Whether one saw the menace emanating from "science," computers, the media, international bankers, apostate religious leaders, manipulative politicians, or all of the above, the result was the same: a standardized world ruled by the all-powerful computer inexorably reshaping humanity to its demands. As Webber and Hutchings put it in 1986, "The average person today is like a man caught in a nightmare, hoping that he wakes before he plunges over a precipice into oblivion." When the new order takes shape, declared a 1978 prophecy book, "our whole way of life will be changed . . . Mr. Private Citizen will be captured in a net with ramifications that are frightening and even monstrous." [48]

As early as 1944, Lewis Sperry Chafer had foreseen "a vast world system" dominating "all parts of human life and activity," and this theme sounded with growing insistence in postwar prophecy writing. "Huge combines in the world of industry, commerce, banking, and agriculture," predicted a 1958 writer, "will deliver the control of mankind, first, to a few powerful individuals, and finally to the control of one man." [49] Dispensational premillennialism, in short, provided a vocabulary for articulating an uneasiness many felt in the face of disorienting economic and technological change.

In verbalizing their social apprehension in the idiom of conspiracy, prophecy writers were very much in the American tradition. Whether the villains were Anglican bishops, Masons, Catholics, Jews, the trusts, or the Reds, Americans since colonial days had often found powerful and sinister forces thwarting a virtuous citizenry. In 1914 Walter Lippmann perceptively wrote of the way such theories can suffuse the monotonies of everyday life "with an alert and tingling sense of labyrinthine evil." [50]

But if conspiracy thinking has been endemic in American history, twentieth-century evangelicals, with their acute sense of alienation from the mainstream culture, were particularly susceptible to it.

Deeply skeptical of the modern order, James Davison Hunter pointed out, evangelicals found plausible the idea that cohesive and powerful forces—whether called the New Class or secular humanists—control the levers of power in politics, the media, and the world of electronic information processing.[51] Premillennialism, with its conviction that a single powerful figure would soon rule the world, obviously reinforced such a conspiratorial worldview and drove it to a pitch of high intensity.

The conspiracy thinking endemic in postwar prophecy popularizations was brilliantly parodied in a sequence in *True Stories,* David Byrnes's surreal 1986 film of life in the mythic Texas town of Virgil. As a choir repetitively chants "Puzzling Evidence" in the background, a stemwinding preacher warns of conspiracy on every hand, weaving together the death of Elvis, Kennedy's assassination, the Trilateral Commission, the Council on Foreign Relations, movie immorality, ABC, CBS, NBC, *Time, Newsweek,* credit cards, and the "fact" that people tend to run out of Kleenex, paper towels, and toilet paper at the same time. "What is the link?" he asks portentously as a giant TV screen in the background projects images of robots, automated production, skyscrapers, smiling politicians, stacks of gold bullion, and rows of standardized supermarket products.

Some describe this conspiracy-saturated end-time scenario as "paranoid," but does the label further our understanding? When a single individual becomes convinced that his or her life is controlled by an all-powerful conspiracy, psychiatrists have little hesitation in speaking of paranoia. But when such a worldview comes embedded within a system of religious belief embraced by millions and regularly elaborated and "documented" in books selling hundreds of thousands and even millions of copies, most psychiatrists shy away from applying clinical labels drawn from the vocabulary of mental illness. They point out the critical differences between individual and shared belief systems, as well as the difficulty of defining a belief system as "delusional," particularly one whose individual empirical components are for the most part drawn from the world of experience shared with the larger society. In these circumstances the clinicians tend to turn the problem over to the social psychologists, the political scientists, and the intellectual historians to make of it what they will.[52]

As always, the prophecy writers who formulated this conspiratorial view of the modern age balanced their grim vision with a message of reassurance: the changes transforming the world, unsettling as they appear, are in reality stepping stones to Christ's kingdom. As one put it in 1957, "The violent overthrow of civilization as we know it . . . will not be a tragedy but a blessing."[53] But while the joys of the millennial age remained shadowy, immediate trends loomed all too concretely as omens of the fast-approaching age when they would reach their culmination: the brief but terrible rule of the Beast, the Man of Sin, Antichrist.

The Reign of Antichrist

The theological foundation for these wide-ranging reflections on contemporary global developments was the doctrine of *Antichrist*—the evil figure who will arise after the Rapture and rule for seven years (the Tribulation) before his defeat at Armageddon. Fulfilling his fore-ordained role, as we saw in Chapter 6, he will sign a pact with Israel, break it, desecrate the rebuilt Temple, proclaim himself Messiah, and horribly persecute those Jews (and Gentiles) who resist his blasphemous claims.

This scenario derives from long-established interpretive conventions involving passages in Daniel, Revelation, and elsewhere. The Book of Daniel foretells Antichrist and his kingdom, popularizers teach, in the statue described in Nebuchadnezzar's dream; in the "little horn" that sprouts from the Beast; and in the allusion to "the prince that shall come." In Revelation, he appears in chapters 13 and 17 as a seven-headed beast and a beast that emerges from the sea, "make[s] war with the saints," performs "great wonders," and gains power "over all kindreds, and tongues, and nations." Jesus' warning about end-time "false Christs" as recorded in Mark 13:22, and Saint Paul's allusion in II Thessalonians to a "man of sin" who will arise before Christ's return, further buttress Antichrist belief. The actual word (Greek *antichristos*) occurs only in I and II John, but these verses do not loom large in prophecy exposition since they refer to a generalized evil already present on earth (for example, "This is that spirit of antichrist, whereof ye have heard that it should come and even now already is it in the world") rather than to a specific individual. The seven-year term of Antichrist's rule, with emphasis on the final three and one-half years, derives primarily from Daniel 9, where the Beast "confirm[s] the convenant with many for one week" but "in the midst of the week" halts Temple worship and spreads desolation, and from Revelation 13, where the Beast holds power for "forty and two months." Specific beliefs about Antichrist's defiling of the Temple are based on allusions in Daniel to "the abomination that makes desolate" and to Jesus' reference to the Temple's desecration in the "Little Apocalypse" of Mark 13.[54]

From these brief and cryptic references evolved a vast body of belief and legend that took many forms throughout Christianity's two-thousand-year history. Antichrist loomed large for the patristic writers as persecution intermittently ravaged the Church. Justin Martyr in the second century foresaw Antichrist's appearance just before the Second Coming. Irenaeus, warning against efforts to identify Antichrist, nevertheless noted the omission of the tribe of Dan from a listing of the tribes of Israel in Revelation 7 and surmised that Antichrist would be a Jew of that tribe. Cyprian, bishop of Carthage, reassured the faithful shortly before his martyrdom in 258 A.D.: "Antichrist is coming, but above him comes Christ also. The enemy goeth above and rageth, but immediately the Lord follows to avenge our sufferings and our wounds." Saint Augustine in several passages of *The City of God* affirmed that Antichrist would be a specific individual but, in keeping with his antieschatological approach to prophecy, avoided further speculation about Antichrist's identity or the time of his coming and emphasized instead the spiritual application of the term as symbolic of the forces of evil in the world. In the Middle Ages, as we have seen, prophecy interpreters identified various Islamic leaders, including Saladin, as the Man of Sin, while at the popular level, belief that Antichrist would be a Jew contributed to periodic rampages against European jewry.[55]

In the nineteenth century, historical-critical biblical scholars traced Antichrist belief to ancient Mideast myths of a dragon who would fight the Creator-God, interpreted the Daniel passages as veiled allusions to Antiochus Epiphanes, and linked the Beast and Great Harlot of Revelation to Nero and the cult of emperor worship. Evangelical interpreters, however, particularly dispensationalists, strongly endorsed the view that a literal Antichrist would emerge in the last days. Antiochus and Nero, they argued, were but *types* of the Beast to come.[56]

No Antichrist tradition has a more ancient lineage than that pointing to the Pope. As early as the fourth century, Hilary, bishop of

Poitiers, taught that Antichrist would arise from within the Church, and some pseudo-Joachian writers elaborated this theme. A series of medieval dissenters, including the French Waldensians, the English followers of John Wycliffe, and the Bohemian adherents of Jan Hus, denounced the Pope as the Beast or his consort the Great Harlot, drunk with the blood of saints and martyrs. The leaders of the Protestant Reformation, for all their differences, agreed on this point. In England the Westminster Confession (1646) formally enshrined the Antichrist = Pope equation; four years earlier, a fellow of the Royal Society had mathematically linked the papacy to 666, the Beast's number as recorded in Revelation. On the flyleaf of a 1612 German world history an unknown amateur gematraist of the past added the numerical values of "RÖMISCHER PAPST" (Roman Pope) to total 666.[57]

By the late nineteenth and early twentieth centuries, some prophecy writers were rejecting this conventional identification of Antichrist. Sir Robert Anderson called it a superficial reading of the prophetic texts, while James Gray of Moody Bible Institute included a section explaining "Why the Pope Is Not the Antichrist" in a 1918 prophecy work. Though "a monstrous system of evil," said Arthur Pink in 1923, Catholicism fell short of biblical descriptions of Antichrist.[58]

Nevertheless, some postwar expositors still affirmed the ancient link. Prophecy speakers in the 1950s, luring crowds by promising to show a picture of Antichrist, projected a profile of Pope Pius XII on the screen. Shortly after John F. Kennedy's election in 1960, J. Dwight Pentecost declared:

> Romanism is the great harlot . . . According to Revelation 17, this politico-religious system is going to move behind the scenes to cause nations to federate. When this alliance takes place, Rome will be in control, dominating, dictating, and directing . . . In our country, we have elevated to our nation's highest office one whose primary allegiance must be to one who resides across the ocean.[59]

Lindsey in *The Late Great Planet Earth*, predicting that the Vatican would become "more involved in world politics, especially in proposals for bringing world peace and world-wide economic prosperity," strongly hinted at a Pope = Antichrist connection. Antichrist's apostate religious system would be based in the Vatican, wrote Dave Hunt in 1988. Chick Publications, a California producer of fundamentalist tracts and comic books, many in Spanish and many on prophecy themes, espoused a virulent anti-Catholicism and unqualifiedly portrayed the Pope as Antichrist. Few went as far as the Scots-Irish firebrand Ian Paisley, who denounced Pope John Paul II as Antichrist to his face when the pontiff addressed a Common Market gathering in Strasbourg in 1988, but this ancient tradition remained alive in postwar prophecy belief.[60]

Overall, however, the Vatican faded after 1945 as a target of Antichrist watchers. One writer candidly observed in 1972 that the identification had ceased to be persuasive "because the papacy is not a giant among the powers of the modern world. History has stripped the papacy of most of its power, so that it no longer functions as the cruel oppressor of mankind." Cold War ideology played a role as well, as the Vatican's stalwart anti-Communism enhanced its standing with fundamentalists. The Texas fundamentalist J. Frank Norris, a leading Pope-baiter in the 1920s, by the 1950s was praising Rome as a "Gibraltar against Communism." The papacy still played a supporting role in the Antichrist drama, but few any longer cast it as the star.[61]

Over the centuries Antichrist speculation ranged far beyond the Vatican. During the American Revolution, George III, the Earl of Bute, and John Burgoyne all enjoyed brief notoriety in this role. Napoleon was the early-nineteenth-century favorite: in Tolstoy's *War and Peace,* Pierre makes "*L'Empereur Napoléon*" add to 666; others calculated that Napoleon's name totaled 666 in Arabic if two letters were omitted. (This led the British historian Thomas Macaulay to demonstrate that *Parliament* was Antichrist, since its membership added up to 666 if one included various clerks and doorkeepers.) During World War II both Adolph Hitler and Benito Mussolini attracted the attention of Antichrist spotters.[62]

Post–World War II Antichrist speculation ranged from a resurrected Judas to Moshe Dayan, Anwar el-Sadat, King Juan Carlos of Spain, and the Korean religious figure Sun Myung Moon. In the early 1960s some prophecy writers claimed that John Kennedy had received 666 votes in the vice-presidential balloting at the 1956 Democratic convention; in a distant echo of the Nero redivivus myth, some in 1963 expected Kennedy to rise from his coffin, fulfilling the prophecy in Revelation that the Beast would miraculously recover from a deadly head wound. In the 1970s, speculation fixed on Henry Kissinger: his name in Hebrew added up to 111 (666 divided by 6); his Mideast shuttle diplomacy fulfilled Antichrist's role as a peacemaker; and he fit the tradition that Antichrist would be a Jew. (One writer, however, noted that Kissinger failed to fulfill the prophecy in the Book of Daniel that the Beast would not "regard the desire of women.")[63]

In the 1980s, some prophecy believers noted that each of Ronald Wilson Reagan's names had *six* letters: 6 + 6 + 6. (Perhaps aware of such speculation, Reagan in 1988 insisted that the street number of the California mansion given him by wealthy friends be changed from *666* to *668*.) And, as we have seen, one author made the case for Mikhail Gorbachev as Antichrist. In the early 1990s, Iraq's Saddam Hussein—inevitably—enjoyed his fifteen minutes of fame as a potential Antichrist. Most writers, however, avoided the "Name the Antichrist" game. John Walvoord cautioned that it brought prophecy belief into disrepute. A 1984 writer in *Eternity* urged believers not to become "so captivated with the 666 that they forget that an unsaved world is sick, sick, sick."[64]

The consensus was that Antichrist would be a European, as yet unknown, who would rule a ten-nation revived Roman Empire, then extend his domain worldwide. This scenario, said to have been first advanced by the third-century Roman theologian Hippolytus, derived from the Book of Daniel, in which Daniel interprets the five components of the statue in Nebuchadnezzar's dream—gold, silver, brass, iron, and iron mixed with clay—as five kingdoms. Prophecy writers from earliest times saw the first four of these kingdoms as the Babylonian, Media-Persian, Greek, and Roman empires, and the fifth, the iron and clay of the statue's feet, emerging from the fourth (the Roman Empire), as Antichrist's. The belief that Antichrist will rule a *ten-nation* kingdom derives from the Bible's explicit identification of the Beast's ten horns in Daniel 7 and Revelation 13 as *kings,* and from a reference in Daniel to the statue's *toes.* (Some nineteenth-century interpreters, pushing this line of interpretation to its limit, argued that Antichrist would rule five nations in the East and five in the West, corresponding to the statue's left and right feet.)[65]

Updating this scenario, post-1945 prophecy writers saw its fulfillment in the movement toward European unity. Recalling Donald Grey Barnhouse's 1931 declaration that a European federation was "an absolute certainty" in light of prophecy, they watched with rising excitement the establishment of the Western European Union in 1948 (the year that also saw the birth of modern Israel and the World Council of Churches); NATO in 1949; and the European Economic Community, or Common Market, in 1959. The signing of the 1957 Treaty of Rome, laying the groundwork for the Common Market, on Rome's Capitoline Hill, the very heart of the ancient Roman Empire, linked the modern movement to the prophetic scenario in a particularly telling way.[66]

All of this activity stirred tremendous interest in prophecy circles. "Europe is the very key to world history as it is unfolding at this present hour," proclaimed J. Vernon McGee at the 1961 Los Angeles prophecy conference. If one read the daily newspaper in the light of prophecy, added a 1967 prophecy-conference speaker, the imminent emergence of a "United States of Europe, yea, of the Western world [was] as inevitable as the incoming tide." The Roman Empire's reappearance in modern form, echoed Merrill Unger in 1973, "is one of the most astonishing and incredible aspects of Bible prophecy." John Walvoord in 1981 questioned this absolute identification of the Common Market with Daniel's vision, but on this point his was distinctly a minority voice.[67]

Prophecy writers watched eagerly as Common Market membership crept toward ten, and Greece's admission as the tenth nation on January 1, 1981, provoked intense excitement. "Wow! How many toes? How many horns?" exulted Jack Van Impe. Matters became confused as membership rose to twelve by the end of the 1980s, but expositors cited a passage in Daniel in which the "little horn" destroys three of the Beast's horns to suggest that membership would increase to thirteen, then drop back to ten by the time of the Tribulation.[68]

Together with the founding of Israel and other signs, the European unity movement strengthened prophecy belief in the post-1945 era. With the Common Market, said James Montgomery Boice in 1974, "a united Europe, fashioned along the lines of Daniel's prophecy, at last is beginning to emerge." As plans evolved for full integration of the European economies in 1992, and as a "United States of Europe" seemingly moved closer to reality, interest among prophecy writers quickened. "Quietly and unobtrusively," added another writer in 1986, "the old empire is being reborn. When the time comes, it will be ready to install a modern-day successor to Nero Caesar on the throne." In emphasizing Europe's role in Antichrist's rise, prophecy writers drew on a very old belief in American innocence in contrast to Old World decadence. Although much weakened after World War II, this conviction still influenced premillennial thinking. America might be sinking fast, but the final push into apostasy would come from beyond the seas. As McGee observed in 1961, "the European mentality is ready for [Antichrist], and you may be sure that he is coming." [69]

Based in Europe, Antichrist will hold the entire world in his grip. After helping God destroy the Soviet Union, wrote J. Dwight Pentecost in 1961, Antichrist's European federation "will rule over all the earth. There will be one world government, one world religion, one world dictator." "Antichrist, not the Kremlin, will be taking over planet Earth!" proclaimed Dave Hunt in 1983; "the Bible declares freely that a new one-world government is coming." [70]

Each component of Antichrist's global order—religious, political, and economic—attracted close scrutiny and became a means of articulating apprehensions about a wide variety of postwar trends. On the religious front, the Harlot that rides the Beast and terrorizes the saints in Revelation 17, long identified with the papacy, in post-1945 prophecy writing more often symbolized a broader apostate system. Rome was seen as *part* of this system, but liberal Protestantism and the World Council of Churches were central as well. The Harlot, wrote Walvoord, "describes not the Roman church alone, but all Christendom combined under the Roman banner in that future day." Hal Lindsey, while suspicious of Rome, also assigned leading roles to the World Council of Churches and "liberal Judaism" in the coming apostate church. "All of the man-made religious orders of this world are headed into one massive religious system," agreed Hilton Sutton in 1981. "The merging of major religions that you see going on today is but a forerunner of the one-world religion." [71]

Prophecy novels elaborated the theme. In Kirban's *666,* apostate Protestants and apostate Catholics unite just before the Rapture to form the "CHURCH OF THE WORLD." In Betzer's *Beast,* an urbane, liberal Protestant bishop who has grown rich on the royalties from a book ridiculing prophecy belief phones a TV newsman after the Rapture to inform him of the key biblical texts that explain what has happened, and then puts a bullet in his brain, falling dead on top of "some of his highly prized books." Another prophecy writer, imagining typical Rapture scenes, described an airport limousine full of "ultraliberal churchmen on their way to an ecumenical conclave" that crashes when the driver, a humble believer, is whisked off to the skies. [72]

As a political leader, prophecy writers agreed, Antichrist initially would seem not monstrous but appealing—"a brilliant man intellectually and a dynamic personality," as Walvoord put it in 1967. Lindsey described Antichrist's "superhuman psychic powers, brilliance, and strong personal magnetism," while James Boice endowed him with "the oratorical ability and youth of a Kennedy, the intelligence of an Einstein, the moral stature of a Gandhi, as well as the administrative and military ability of an Eisenhower or MacArthur." His role in apparently resolving the Arab-Israeli conflict, wrote another author, would solidify his reputation as "the brilliant diplomat who brought peace to a clamorous world." This theme, too, had extensive antecedents—as early as 1884 Sir Robert Anderson had written of Antichrist's "transcendent genius," and Isaac Haldeman in 1910 had portrayed him as a masterly soldier, statesman, orator, and financier.[73]

Building on a brief phrase in Daniel (repeated in Revelation) that describes the Beast as having "a mouth speaking great things," postwar prophecy writers turned him into a mass-communications genius—"an electrifying, spellbinding public speaker" who would "almost hypnotize people" with his "overpowering charisma." Above all, he would exploit television. For in the postwar era, TV dominated end-time scenarios, just as it did U.S. culture. When Antichrist proclaims his rule, wrote Billy Graham in 1965, "television cameras will no doubt be on the scene, and the news will be flashed around the world." Updating the speculation in 1984, Hilton Sutton envisioned Antichrist's announcement of his global destiny as "a worldwide press conference televised via satellite."[74]

We have seen that Antichrist was to rule a world already conditioned to succumb to his appeal. The "Hollywood-idol hysteria" of modern politics, observed one writer, clearly foreshadowed the day when a "magnetic leader" like Antichrist could win a worshipful following. In an age seduced by "the allure of the false, the glamour of the phony," agreed another, Antichrist's strategy was already prefigured by apostate religious leaders and others who exploited the mass media to influence the mass mind. The mania for rock stars, typified by the John Lennon cult, agreed John Wesley White in 1981, foreshadowed the rise of the Evil One. (When the Beatles' press agent was quoted as boasting, "They're completely antichrist," the report only confirmed what prophecy believers already knew.)[75]

In the aftershock of the Rapture, Dave Hunt predicted in 1983, people "will experience a new sense of oneness, of belonging to and needing one another." Seizing the moment, Antichrist will proclaim peace and brotherhood and assure a terrified world that "someone cares and is keeping track." The future world order, in short, is latent in the present. As John Wesley White put it, "Antichrist's tracks are today imprinting man's trail ahead; the yet unidentified beast seems to be treading through the murky night of human society." [76]

Prophecy novels underscored the Beast's insidious mass appeal. In Kirban's *666,* Antichrist—an Iraqi born at 6 P.M. on June 6 and hence named "666" by his mother, but known to the world as "Brother Bartholomew"—rises to power on a wave of revulsion against the political power of international capitalism and solidifies his rule by bringing Mideast peace and solving other world crises with "steel-like composure and firmness." All his reforms— the ten-day week, banning private automobiles, births by official permit only, substituting a single tattooed number for the many different numbers people must remember today, even grinding corpses into protein cakes to relieve world hunger—win wide support, thanks to his manipulative genius and hypnotic TV performances. [77]

In Betzer's *Beast,* Antichrist, one Jacques Catroux, though fathered by Satan at the instant of Hitler's death, initially appears as the brilliant and suave head of the European Economic Community. With movie-star good looks and "oozing charm," he easily convinces key Americans such as TV mogul Clayton Daniels to support a unified "Europamerica" with a merged economy and a single leader: himself. Only occasional whiffs of a dreadful stench and the strange forehead mark left by the forceps of a bungling obstetrician betray him. A bisexual who wears "tight Italian-made boots," Catroux, a kind of demonic James Bond, serves only the best brandy (Remy Martin) in his plush suite at New York's Helmsley Palace. When the Bible-believing U.S. President disappears in the Rapture, Vice President Barry Cane, a secular humanist who favors disarmament, takes his place. At an Oval Office meeting between Catroux and Cane, Satan himself appears and wins Cane's pledge of allegiance:

> Drawing on all his strength, Barry Cane reached up on tiptoes to reach Lucifer's face with his hands, pulling it down to him. He then kissed him fully on the mouth after which his new father held him tightly to himself. Now drawing back, Lucifer looked at his family, smiled benignly and spoke. "This has been

the greatest hour of my long, long life. I shall . . . soon . . . give you plans for peace. You shall bring peace to the world."[78]

Now the pawn of Satan and Antichrist, Cane serves out the three-year unexpired term of his predecessor and a four-year term of his own: the seven years of the Tribulation.

Television is central to Betzer's fictional scenario of the end. The loathsome Cane, he emphasizes, has "superb television skills." And after Catroux/Antichrist bids for mass support by performing a staged "resurrection" at the globally televised funeral of Clayton Daniel's wife (raped and apparently murdered by a mob in New York City), Satan critiques his performance:

> Remember this because it is vital—people want to believe. They want to see miracles. And if you plant the seed of a miracle in their hearts, they will make that seed grow into anything they want . . . Just as today, the image on television catapulted you to international acceptance, so you will use the image throughout these years. Make it say anything you want.[79]

But it was the *economic* dimension of Antichrist's rule that most stimulated the prophecy popularizers' descriptive powers. The revived Roman Empire would be "more along economic lines," a 1986 writer predicted, than "the old military pattern of the former Caesars."[80] Three short verses in Revelation, already noted in Chapter 1, constitute the key prophecy:

> And he causeth all, both small and great, rich and poor, free and bond, to receive a mark in their right hand, or in their foreheads:
> And that no man might buy or sell, save he that had the mark, or the name of the beast, or the number of his name.
> Here is wisdom. Let him that hath understanding count the number of the beast: for it is the number of a man; and his number is Six hundred threescore and six.[81]

From these tantalizing hints, post-1945 prophecy expositors erected a vast edifice of speculation centered on the fears discussed early in this chapter—global regimentation, international conspiracies, eroding individualism, and the rest. All the sinister trends of the late twentieth century, they suggested, would culminate under Antichrist. Using technologies already available, the Beast would control every human being—a situation the masses would gladly accept because of its superficial benefits. The author of one prophecy novel even envisioned the Mark of the Beast as a status symbol. "It's the most popular thing of the day," a follower of Antichrist tells a reluctant holdout; "you don't want to be behind the times." [82]

This economic control would be absolute: "If a person wants to buy a single shoestring or a pickle, it must be okayed by world headquarters." Access to essential services such as health care would be restricted to those bearing the Mark—most likely an invisible, laser-read number implanted in the body and instantly transmittable by satellite to a central computer facility. Thanks to such electronically implanted codes, wrote David Wilkerson, each person on earth would become a "walking credit card." [83]

Plastic cards loomed large in accounts of Antichrist's new order. "The credit-card buying of today dovetails so perfectly" with biblical prophecy, observed a 1978 writer, "it makes Revelation appear to be written very recently." Salem Kirban in 1987 described his conception of Antichrist's "Worldwide Money Card," its tiny microprocessor containing the holder's life history, voice print code, and face scan. One ingenious writer, noting that VI is the Roman numeral for 6; that the number 6 in classical Greek resembles the letter S; and "the possibility" that the Babylonian letter A bore the value 6, calculated that "six" in three ancient languages (that is, 6 + 6 + 6) spelled "visa"— a major modern credit-card system! [84]

The computer phobia evident in prophecy writers' discussions of present-day trends intensified when they wrote of Antichrist's reign. "One day soon . . . we will all be assigned computer numbers for life," wrote Lindsey in 1981. "The person who controls the main computer controls the world." In *Computers and the Beast of Revelation,* Webber and Hutchings not only explored the computer's insidious uses in contemporary society, but looked to the future when, in "precise fulfillment" of prophecy, computers will undergird Antichrist's rule. The prophet Joel, they contended, foretold computer-controlled robot warriors:

> They shall run like mighty men; they shall climb the wall like men of war; and they shall march every one on his ways, and they shall not break their ranks:
> Neither shall one thrust another; they shall walk every one in his path: And when they fall upon the sword, they shall not be wounded.

By computer and satellite, Webber and Hutchings went on, rehearsing a now-familiar scenario, Antichrist will substitute electronic exchange for money; assign everyone a number; and "dictate to every man, woman, and child that they must work, buy, and sell by using code marks and numbers." [85]

Several popularizers even suggested that Antichrist would *be* a computer. Employees at Common Market headquarters in Luxembourg, Lu Ann Bransby reported, had affectionately nicknamed the central computer "the Beast." "Antichrist will enslave and control earth's billions through a sophisticated computer fashioned in his likeness," wrote Van Impe in 1983, citing current research on a "biocomputer" implantable in the brain. "The 'being' of an individual so equipped would live in the computer part, not in the central nervous system," he went on, and such an implant could be readily shifted to a fresh host when the old one died. These possibilities, Van Impe concluded, had "unprecedented prophetic significance." Another ingenious writer calculated that if A is given the value 6; B, 12; C, 18, and so on, then one finds the following:

$$
\begin{array}{rcl}
\text{C} &=& 18 \\
\text{O} &=& 90 \\
\text{M} &=& 78 \\
\text{P} &=& 96 \\
\text{U} &=& 126 \\
\text{T} &=& 120 \\
\text{E} &=& 30 \\
\text{R} &=& 108 \\
\hline
 & & 666
\end{array}
$$

(By this formula, he further noted, "MARK OF BEAST" and "NEW YORK CITY" also total 666.)[86]

In monitoring their environment for end-time signs, prophecy believers did not overlook money—that ubiquitous symbol of the state's economic power. In the 1950s a $1,000 Canadian note in which a grinning Satan seemed visible in the sworls of Queen Elizabeth's hair caused such a stir that it was withdrawn and redesigned. In later years Salem Kirban was one of many writers to explore currency's prophetic significance. In 1987 he explained "HOW *UNIFIED* NEW WORLD MONEY SYSTEMS BRING US ONE STEP CLOSER TO THE AGE OF ANTICHRIST"; in 1989 he offered (for a $100 contribution) a "New Age Currency

Collector's Album" of several new European currencies, each with a "mysterious blank area" awaiting Antichrist's image. Kirban also publicized a new Australian ten-dollar bill featuring a hologram and an engraving of a strangely marked aboriginal. "The Trilateralists have been busy in Australia," he noted. When Washington implemented plans to embed electronic strips in currency, allegedly to foil counterfeiters and drug dealers, Kirban added, spy satellites "could beam right into your home *from outer space* and record how much money is in your home!" When the new money system was in place, Kirban predicted, "many more people will be taking Tylenol and Maalox!" [87]

Antichrist and the Death of the Individual

During Antichrist's short but horrific reign, prophecy popularizers teach, the shadowy but powerful global organizations already in existence will band together and employ the new technologies to achieve absolute hegemony, leaving individuals utterly impotent. Using a panoply of new electronic devices, as well as nuclear weapons, wrote John Walvoord in 1974, a dictator could "seize control of the world in a way that would have been impossible in any previous generation . . . The necessary ingredients for a world government are present for the first time in the history of civilization." [88]

Initially focused on creating a monolithic economic order, Antichrist's system would quickly penetrate every realm of life until it controlled mankind totally. Computer-linked satellites would monitor the thought of everyone on earth, "even to the point of getting them to worship some individual as God, or even influence their national allegiance." In Kirban's *666*, Antichrist, using sophisticated surveillance devices to pick up conversations and monitor brain waves, erases all human memory and implants a new consciousness in individual brains. [89]

No bolt from the blue, Antichrist's rule would evolve from trends already well advanced. "Some computer somewhere knows facts about each one of us," declared a 1983 work; "they are sure to be used by the final world dictator in his effort to totally control the commerce of the world." Shopping carts that broadcast product commercials, warned Kirban, were part of a vast web of "subliminal suggestion" preparing the way for the end-time system; so were corporate slogans like the Bank of America's "The Whole World Welcomes World Money," added John Wesley White. The Mark of the Beast, speculated another writer, will be "like a trademark on a prominent product." James McKeever ran a regular Big Brother column in his *End-Times News Digest* that reported on fingerprint scanners and other devices laying the groundwork for Antichrist's regime. Still another expositor illustrated her discussion of the Tribulation era with a photograph of a baby bearing on its forehead the vertical black stripes of the product bar code familiar to every shopper.[90]

Here again, prophecy writers combed the press for portents of the new order. They cited *Omni* on biocomputers; *Readers' Digest* on electronic money; and a 1973 *Senior Scholastic* cover showing a schoolgirl with a number tattooed on her forehead, illustrating an article on privacy. When the British science magazine *Nature* in 1990 proposed a "machine-readable tattoo" as an alternative to a wallet full of plastic, the idea came as no surprise to those familiar with contemporary prophecy speculation.[91] Indeed, in 1977 Chuck Smith had written: "Bankers are actually planning on getting rid of money and implementing a totally computerized monetary system . . . Already we're conditioned to buy with numbers." Antichrist would simply take the final step, he went on, proposing tattooed numbers, for example, as a way to stop credit-card theft: "It'll be a very easy way of identification. No one will be able to buy or sell without it, just as the Scripture said. We can see the whole thing shaping up."[92]

Another strategy of Antichrist's advance guard, prophecy writers claimed, was to insinuate the number 666 into public awareness. Where earlier 666 speculation had focused on individuals' names, late-twentieth-century prophecy writers more typically saw this number as a component of Antichrist's global *system*. To show how humankind was being softened up for Antichrist, the popularizers emphasized how frequently these three digits could already be found on products, financial forms, and corporate ads. Webber and Hutchings, for example, noted that the expanded zip code combined with the Social Security number equaled eighteen digits, or 6 + 6 + 6. Other authors included pages of advertisements, corporate logos, and labels for products ranging from shoes to shirts to floor covering in which the fateful digits figured, including an Apple computer priced at $666.66. Jack Van Impe's prophecy paperbacks of the 1970s and 1980s elaborately documented "the increasing use of '666' throughout the world"; he cited a beginning algebra text called *666 Jellybeans*. This "brainwashing movement" by powerful interests intent on making 666 "an intriguing and acceptable code for the hour when it becomes a compulsory number," he said, provided compelling evidence "that prophecy is on the move." [93]

The ubiquity of 666 speculation in prophecy popularizations invited satirical treatment. In "Backsliders' Tractor Pull," a 1990 pop-music parody, a ranting "radio preacher" warns that in high-school cafeterias the average number of vegetables served is *six* and the average age of the employees is *sixty-six:* 666! Here in "the devil's dining room of damnation," he proclaims in a quavering voice, the nation's unsuspecting youths are each day being served "family-size portions of the apocalypse." [94]

No prophecy writer devoted more attention to these matters than Mary Stewart Relfe, a wealthy Montgomery, Alabama, widow and real-estate developer whose *When Your Money Fails: The "666 System" Is Here* (1981) sold over 600,000 copies. Her mother's solemn homilies on prophecy so affected her as a girl, Relfe wrote, that awareness of the Second Coming "filtered to the nucleus of every cell of my being with such force that I could not pry myself from its grasp." Early in 1980, she wrote, Jesus appeared in her bedroom and told her to write a book on prophecy. Such a work, she believed, must explore new ground: "As surely as the re-establishment of the nation of Israel in 1948 became the FOCAL POINT of Prophecy Study in the past generation, so the '666 System,' the Cashless Commerce of the end time, as prophesied by John, has become the FOCUS of Prophecy Study in this generation." [95]

Acting on this conviction, Relfe explored the conspiracy by which Americans were being "quietly, subtly, and dangerously drawn into the electronic Money Society." Her book offered a dizzying pot-pourri of data about SWIFT, Social Security, the Chase Manhattan Bank, the gold standard, fiber optics, and the Rothschilds. Relfe discussed the "mystery buttons" * and # on Touchtone telephone dials; the dollar bill's sinister inscription *Novus Ordo Seclorum;* and elusive IRS refund checks, intended for future use but said to have been inadvertently mailed to a few taxpayers, bearing the instructions: "Do not cash this check unless the recipient has a number on either his right hand or his forehead." Soon, she predicted, the Common Market would assign numbers to everyone in the world and distribute credit cards with a three-digit international code—666. Pop musicians subtly propagandize for Antichrist, she warned, with lyrics such as "What the world needs now is love, sweet love." Quoting John Lennon's "I hope some day you'll join us, and the WORLD will be as ONE," she cried, "Oh, Nathan Hale, where are you?" [96]

In a sequel, *The New Money System 666* (1982), Relfe zeroed in on the Uniform Product Code (UPC), "the basic juggernaut in the Cashless Society." She spared nothing in her effort "to uncloak the conspiracy, and expose the evils of this System . . . in the light of Bible Prophecy." She claimed: "I proceeded to spend thousands of dollars on researching the origin and development of the Bar Code Marking System. Libraries were searched, new encyclopedias were purchased, titles in industrial publications gleaned, books procured, and finally a brand new Random House Unabridged Dictionary was obtained." But the inner workings of the UPC system remained impenetrable. This lack of information, she suspected, "had to be more than blatant omission!" Complicating her task, the masters of the UPC constantly introduced new patterns and sequences, "to assure its continued secrecy to the general public." Nevertheless, through elaborate computations that defy comprehension despite pages of charts, Relfe concluded, "THE ONLY NUMBER FOR WHICH THREE DIFFERENT BARS EXIST IS THE NUMBER '6'." Lapsing into verse, she reflected:

> The question comes to me,
> As I gaze at prophecy,
> Why all the Sixes?

Dismissing assurances by the Uniform Product Code Council that "there are no unidentified characters in the Symbol," she further speculated that the letters F and H, which appear with suspicious frequency on the codes, stand for "Forehead" and "Hand." (The ubiquitous peace symbol of the Sixties and the Chai pendant worn by many Jews might also foretell the Mark of the Beast, she parenthetically speculated.) [97]

Like other writers, Relfe found the conspiracy shockingly widespread: beyond the UPC lay "the Banking Industry, the Credit Card Companies, the Computer Manufacturers, the Scientists, and the Politicians who say that the salvation of mankind is dependent upon a New International Economic Order." Refuse credit cards, she advised; "pay with Cash or Checks as long as possible." (All the same, her advertisements for a variety of publications, including a Christian diet book called *Trim for Him,* welcomed MasterCard and Visa.)[98]

Soon, Relfe predicted, when supermarket checkout lasers add scanners for reading ID's implanted in the hand, and the various credit-card systems merge into a global one controlled by SWIFT, "the bankers [will] . . . at last get their heart's desire . . . , all the money of the world." Looming on the horizon is "total slavery for mankind, an absolute '1984,' a literal fulfillment of Revelation." Saddest of all, the United States, with its ubiquitous credit cards and bar coding, is "leading the world down the primrose path to the 'Mark of the Beast.' "[99]

Chaotic, endlessly gullible, nearly illiterate ("I preceived"; "My repetoire of recent information . . . was becoming engorged"; and so forth) and often hilariously naive (as in a serious discussion of TV cable systems that vaporize stray dogs), Relfe's books nevertheless gained coherence and even a certain power from the fear that pervaded them—fear of "an unseen, but powerful few"; fear of "an international network whose aim is . . . to dominate the political system of each country and the economy of the world"; fear, in a word, of Antichrist.[100] But coupled with the fear was a determination to unravel the conspiracy's inner workings. Relfe, in fact, exemplified the emotions and objectives that fueled the postwar prophecy enterprise. That her books became bestsellers reminds us again that even "marginal" voices, evocative though they may be of the supermarket tabloids, ought not be too quickly dismissed by those seeking to understand American popular thought as the twentieth century draws to a close.

The anticapitalist animus we have noted elsewhere pervaded these discussions of Antichrist's reign as well. James Barr in 1977 accused fundamentalists of uncritically embracing capitalism, but the literature of prophecy popularization does not support this generalization. Some writers, to be sure, extolled the free-enterprise system as central to God's prophetic plan. Others, uneasy at the radical implications of their own teaching, tried to soften its implications. "We do not believe it is a sin to use the convenient aspects of the new banking methods," said Webber and Hutchings in 1979. "As long as we are in the world we have to live by the world's economic standards to some extent." But these same authors firmly reiterated the basic premillennial doctrine: "the system now being instituted, or one very similar to it, will eventually be seized upon by the Antichrist and used for his diabolical purposes."[101]

For the proof texts justifying their anticapitalist pronouncements, these authors drew on the denunciation of the rich in the Book
of James and, even more, on the graphic account in Revelation of Babylon's fiery destruction as "the merchants of the earth weep and
mourn over her." Historically, most interpreters viewed this passage
as a prophecy of ancient Babylon's literal restoration (since it could
hardly be destroyed if it did not exist). By the 1930s, however, as we
saw in Chapter 3, doomed "Babylon" was more typically seen as em-
blematic of an economic *system*. The Revelation prophecy foretold the
destruction of "commercialism, industrialism, [and] capitalism . . . in
one sudden stroke," argued Donald Grey Barnhouse late in the decade. The "Babylon" of Revelation represented "Big Business, or
world-commerce," agreed a 1940 writer, and its prophesied end
would be "quick and complete and terrible." [102]

In the postwar period this symbolic interpretation emerged as the
preferred one. A few writers still foresaw the restoration of a literal
Babylon—and quickened with excitement at Saddam Hussein's grandiose plans for restoring the ancient city on the Euphrates—but most
did not. While Babylon might indeed be rebuilt and demolished in
fulfillment of prophecy, argued Lindsey in 1973, "Babylon" also symbolized "the whole Satanic world system, including all the Godless
commercialism and hedonistic worship of luxury and pleasure which
economic success permits." Babylon was "all governments and busi-
nesses" with their "wicked deals" and "evil machinations," proclaimed Doug Clark in 1982, "and God can't wait to destroy it all in
one hour." [103]

Such rhetoric is noteworthy in a genre often thought of as conservative, patriotic, and staunchly antiradical. That premillennialism
has produced some of the most outspoken denunciations of consumer
capitalism promulgated in America since 1945—albeit without the activist political agenda associated with the strikingly similar denunciations emanating from the left—warns us against too readily stereotyping or pigeonholing this protean and sometimes surprising belief
system.

To post–World War II prophecy writers, vast social and technological
forces were regimenting the masses like iron filings in the field of a
powerful magnet. Very soon, they predicted, a centralized global order would impose a totalitarianism almost unimaginable in its scope.
As early as 1948, Wilbur Smith had discerned a "growing sense of fear

and hopelessness" as "subtle currents of thought" prepared America and the world for Antichrist, and scores of subsequent prophecy writers reiterated the theme. Nightmares of zombie-like behavior pervade this literature. The Mark of the Beast, asserted one writer in 1955, "stands symbolically for conformity." [104]

Conformity, alienation, advancing corporate power, the degradation of politics, and the narcotizing effects of the mass media were, of course, the common coin of postwar social thought. What is noteworthy is that these themes should also have been so central in a belief system supposedly passive, acquiescent, and otherworldly, and that the ancient image of Antichrist proved capable of embodying and personifying so many highly charged contemporary concerns.

While these trends are foreordained and unavoidable in their aggregate effects, prophecy writers teach, the believer who interprets the Bible correctly has the key to their meaning and thus is armored against their menace. Be aware! Search the Scriptures, they exhort; maintain your guard while others succumb to the new order. As Hal Lindsey put it, "Don't be part of the vast crowd that will be deceived by the ingenious schemes of this coming world leader." [105] Guided by prophecy, the believer can resist the siren call of the depersonalizing new economic system, the hypnotic brainwashing of the media, and the deceptive appeal of political charlatans. In God's own time, the demonic world system that seems so irresistible today will vanish in a final, fiery cataclysm. Then will arise the *true* global leader and the *true* world order—Jesus Christ and his millennial reign.

III

The Enduring Apocalyptic Vision

9   *The Continuing Appeal of Prophecy Belief*

Over the centuries prophecy belief has remained a bedrock of American popular religion. Through decades of social change, technological innovation, and world upheaval, millions of Americans have clung to the conviction that the Bible offers a key to history and its final end. What underlies this remarkable tenacity of a belief system seemingly so alien to the secular, naturalistic mindset one associates with modernity? To the prophecy adherent, the answer is simple: these beliefs are true! The historian operating from a somewhat different frame of reference is inclined to look further.

Certainly the persistence of prophecy belief is related to the comparatively high level of evangelical faith and practice in the United States noted in the Prologue. From this perspective, the problem of explaining the endurance of these beliefs dissolves into the larger question of why evangelicalism has remained so vital on the American scene. If we acknowledge a foundation of evangelical faith as a precondition for prophecy belief, certain characteristics of these teachings, and specific ways they may serve the psychic needs of those who hold them, further illuminate their continuing attraction.

A Validation of Faith

The enduring appeal of prophecy belief for evangelicals testifies to its value as a quasi-empirical, "scientific" validation of their faith. In the eighteenth century, when natural theology found evidence for God in the order and symmetry of nature, prophecy belief harmonized well with prevailing religious thought and coexisted comfortably with some strands of Enlightenment ideology. As Nathan Hatch observes, "The study of prophecy offered rational men the opportunity to see God's plan unfold in history and produced tangible and coherent proof of religious doctrine."[1] With the erosion of natural theology under the corrosive effects of Darwinism and other nontheistic explanations of the physical order, prophecy remained a historicist alternative, providing evidence for God's oversight of the world in the order and symmetry of past, present, and future events.

Far from demanding a blind leap of faith, prophecy belief was presented as a logical inference from the evidence of prophecies already fulfilled. As Sir Isaac Newton wrote in the posthumously published *Observations upon the Prophecies of Daniel, and the Apocalypse of St. John* (1733), the central value of Bible prophecy is not that it enables one to foretell the future, but that its fulfillment offers "a convincing argument that the world is governed by providence." In the same spirit, nineteenth-century expositors explicitly portrayed their endeavor, at least by analogy, as a *science*. Prophecy interpretation is difficult, conceded one in 1856, but he added rhetorically, "Does the geologist cease to dig and bore into the bowels of the earth, or give over the study of its rocks and fossils, because he cannot find out all that lies hidden in its unknown center[?]" Dispensationalists, as George Marsden has noted, insisted that their methods paralleled those of the laboratory researcher. By Baconian, inductive techniques, one searched the apocalyptic scriptures, formulated a "hypothesis" about their meaning, then tested that hypothesis by examining history past and present.[2] (Needless to say, in the "science" of prophecy investigation, the empirical evidence always bore out the "hypothesis.")

Sir Robert Anderson's 1884 book, *The Coming Prince,* which elaborately proved that the Book of Daniel foretold the precise *day* of Jesus' triumphal entry into Jerusalem, was the classic demonstration of this technique. Anderson's tour de force dramatically enhanced the standing of prophecy study and seemed to offer, as one admirer exulted, "an unanswerable argument for the divine inspiration of the Bible." Anderson's work, this author continued, was "nothing less than a mathematical demonstration." Inspired by Anderson's example, early-twentieth-century writers pointed to more recent events as comparably impressive fulfillments. And, indeed, as Timothy Weber notes, the 1914–1918 war, the Balfour Declaration, the Soviet Union's break with the West, the Turks' departure from Palestine, and the collapse of the Austro-Hungarian Empire did indeed come "extremely close to the mark" in matching various dispensationalist scenarios. More recently, the pre–World War II writings of Harry Rimmer, including *The Coming War and the Rise of Russia* (1940), have been cited as examples of prophecy students' ability to "forecast future events with mind-boggling accuracy."[3]

The evidence of fulfilled prophecy, premillennialists argued, validated their enterprise, justified the belief that such fulfillments would continue, and buttressed the entire structure of evangelical faith. "If Prophecy were intelligently studied," Arno Gaebelein insisted, the denial of biblical inerrancy "could not flourish as it does, for Prophecy gives the clearest and most conclusive evidence that the Bible is the inspired and infallible Word of God." Fulfilled prophecy, agreed Milton Lindberg in 1930, "points unerringly to the divine origin of the Bible." Another author, writing as World War II raged, made the point with a literary flourish that distantly echoed the natural theologians: "History is not a dark and meaningless panorama of confusion . . . History is a sequel of events, coming out of the mold of Prophecy, which proves, as surely as the daffodil, the plan of a perfect order designed by the Almighty."[4]

For believers World War II provided further prophetic confirmation. Writing in 1942, William H. Boyer, an evangelical mission pastor in Dayton, Ohio, marveled that Jesus' prophecy of "nation . . . ris[ing] against nation, and kingdom against kingdom" was being fulfilled before his eyes, "as there are so many nations involved in war at this time."[5] As we have seen, a whole series of post-1945 events aroused prophecy students to a still higher pitch of expectancy. The atomic bomb, the establishment of the State of Israel, the World Council of Churches, the Common Market, the atheistic Soviet Union's emergence as a hostile world power, Israel's recapture of Jerusalem's Old City, the rise of a computer-based global economy—all were interpreted as explicit prophetic fulfillments, and thus as further compelling proof of biblical inerrancy. "The twentieth century," proclaimed Walvoord as early as 1952, even before the momentous events of 1967, "has witnessed the most significant array of prophecy being fulfilled of any century since the time of Christ."[6]

For prophecy to confirm the fundamentalist view of biblical inerrancy, its precise "fit" with historical reality had to be maintained—a feat that required constant adjustment and ingenuity. While the core structure of the premillennial scenario remained remarkably stable for 150 years, new events were continually elevated to the status of "prophetic fulfillments" or "end-time signs" while individuals or events that failed to live up to their expected role were quietly dropped: the

Soviet Union replaced the Ottoman Empire as the most likely candidate for Gog; a long parade of world figures succeeded each other as Antichrist possibilities; and the details of Antichrist's end-time system were repeatedly updated to incorporate the latest technological innovations, from railroads and the telegraph to computers and communications satellites. Although strict dispensationalists asserted that the present "Church Age" is a "great parenthesis" devoid of specific prophetic fulfillments, the writings of the popularizers were full of allusions to current events that fell under the rubric of *end-time signs* showing that the Rapture is near and that the power alignments prophesied for the Tribulation era are "already taking shape."

Some writers heightened the effect of contemporaneity by informally "translating" the King James text into modern terms, changing the bows and arrows of Ezekiel to missiles and missile launchers, for example. Chuck Smith repeatedly offered verbatim renderings of what appeared to be biblical prophecies but were in fact his own very loose paraphrases.[7] Hal Lindsey "quoted" the Revelation passage describing the world's amazed reaction to Antichrist—"Who is like unto the beast, and who is able to make war with him?"—but substituted "dictator" for "beast" to give a more contemporary ring.[8] Countless writers casually substituted "Russia" for "Gog" in discussing Ezekiel 38. Such pious linguistic tinkering further convinced readers that Bible prophecy is, indeed, strikingly timely. The historian, reading hundreds of prophecy books published over a two-hundred-year period, can readily see this process of inserting current events into an archaic belief system. The average believer, encountering the genre for the first time, may be stunned by the uncanny contemporaneity of the prophecies.

And, of course, the popularizers pointed not simply to one event, but to an array of examples—from AIDS to Common Market currency decisions—to show that the *trend* of history is following the course foretold thousands of years ago. To those predisposed to believe, specific prophecy fulfillments and the general tendency of world events offered convincing empirical validation not only of the premillennial system, but of evangelical faith itself.

Mediating Ancient Dilemmas

Prophecy belief offered a middle way between theological and practical antinomies long vexing in Christian thought. First, it finessed the ancient conflict of free will versus determinism (or Arminianism versus Calvinism, as early Protestants framed the debate) by embracing both positions.

On the one hand, they held, history's *overall course* is foreordained, or at least foreknown. The fate of nations and Earth's final destiny are fixed and unalterable. As David Wilkerson put it in 1974:

> Let depression or recession come . . . Let pollution and inflation come. Let there be wars and rumors of wars. Let the fabric of society disintegrate. Let mankind go to the drunken brink of disaster . . . The future is . . . under His control so we need not fear. God has it all preprogrammed. He knows the exact moment Christ will return. The final tribulation, the judgment, and the battle of Armageddon are all on His calendar.[9]

The determinist assumption underlying Wilkerson's comments is implicit in all premillennial scenarios. John Walvoord said in a 1989 interview:

> An omnipotent God . . . is not going to create a world He doesn't control to some extent . . . It is impossible to explain the prophetic history of the Bible without determinism. God determined that the Jews should be an important people. He determined where their land should be . . . It's rather obvious that if you're premillennial you believe in a divine providence that's guiding the world to an intelligent end.[10]

But within this deterministic system lies a realm of freedom: individuals do control their *personal* destiny. Sir Robert Anderson wrote in 1886 that "the surface currents of human responsibility and human guilt are unaffected by the changeless and deep lying tide of the foreknowledge and sovereignty of God." (But if *all* individuals, exercising their free will, became Christian, what would happen to the prophecies about nations and epochs? Was God the original probability theorist?) Post-1945 prophecy writers preserved this realm of freedom. As one put it, "God is not a cookie-cutter God, and He leads each one of us individually." Even Walvoord, for all his Calvinistic insistence on prophecy's deterministic implications, quickly added: "But the Bible also teaches human responsibility. We reap what we sow."[11]

Acting on this conviction, the popularizers ended their expositions of the apocalyptic texts with calls for repentance. "The prophe-

cies are coming to pass and . . . you are going to be left out of everything except the damnation for failing to believe," went a typical
formulation; but by confessing one's sins, one can gain redemption
and become an integral part of "God's thrilling plan for the ages." [12]

Prophecy writers also steered a middle course on a closely related
practical question of perennial concern to evangelicals: How ought the
believer whose hope lies in a future age relate to the present-day world
and its concerns? Should one plunge into secular politics and social
activism, or passively withdraw and await the unfolding of God's
plan?

Logically, the premillennial outlook seemed to imply passivity,
since society's evils and injustices merely bore out the prophesied degeneracy and wickedness of the present age. And, indeed, from John
Darby's day on, a vast body of premillennialist writing warned against
the lure of social activism. "The true mission of the church is not the
reformation of society," declared Cyrus Scofield at the height of the
Progressive Era. "What Christ did not do, the Apostles did not do.
Not one of them was a reformer." [13] Through the Depression and
World War II, prophecy writers emphasized the uselessness of human
efforts at social betterment: regardless of what governments and uplift
organizations might do, war, suffering, and conflict were bound to
grow worse.

This acquiescent viewpoint pervaded post–World War II prophecy popularizations as well, as they chronicled what Lindsey called
"modern man's countdown to extinction." If "God's timepiece for this
present age is rapidly ticking off the remaining seconds" (as a 1979
work put it), what is the point of battling social evils? "One who hon-
estly feels that Christ may come at any moment is not involved with
this world," declared Jack Van Impe. With a certain note of qualifica-
tion, John Walvoord agreed:

> Perhaps Christians are not as concerned about social, political,
> and moral conditions in the world as they should be; but . . . it
> is not God's purpose in our present age to have social justice or
> to have all the ills and problems of life removed now. God is not
> opposed to our doing what we can to alleviate the situation; but
> with the nature of man being such as it is, and the nature of
> Satan's activities being what they are . . . things are going to
> get worse and worse. There will be more oppression, more in-

justice, more persecution, more immorality as the age wears
on.[14]

Prophecy writers underscored the point with various arresting images. "God didn't send me to clean the fishbowl," observed Hal Lindsey; "he sent me to fish."[15] Others compared social reform to polish-
ing the brass fixtures on a sinking ocean liner.

Belief in the Rapture—"God's rescue of all true Christians from
this tortured earth"—further diluted the impetus to political activism.
The redeemed would watch history's climax from the skies. Quoting
Jesus' exhortation to believers to watch and pray, "that ye may be ac-
counted worthy to escape all these things that shall come to pass . . .,"
Hilton Sutton emphasized, "the key word here is *escape*." Agreed
Doug Clark, "It is such a marvelous comfort to Christians to know
that Jesus Christ is coming and that He will snatch us up and out of
this mundane sphere of living." John Darby had made the same point
as long ago as 1840: "Let us remember one thing . . . we Christians
are sheltered from the approaching storm."[16]

As we saw in Chapter 4, the escapist theme loomed especially
large when prophecy writers addressed issues of war and peace. Coming from a different source, the comment of the 1983 prophecy writer
who declared "I am not about to resign myself . . . to being destroyed
in a nuclear holocaust," would have been a prelude to a call for nuclear
disarmament. But this author made a quite different point: "I have
good reason for saying this, because I believe the rapture of the church
could take place at any moment." Herbert W. Armstrong's Worldwide
Church of God, despite its idiosyncratic eschatology, reflected the
broader premillennial view: "Man will *always* have war until a reshaping of his very nature comes about. Men, through their own efforts,
cannot bring peace to this earth."[17]

Unsurprisingly, such pronouncements opened premillennialists
to charges of passivity. An eschatolology that treats the Bible's apocalyptic scenes "as literal, datable events in history," wrote one critic in
1954, traps the believer "between a fixed past and a fixed datable future with no urge for present Christian action in love" and renders that
person vulnerable to a radical pessimism that sees the world "awaiting
complete destruction by a heavenly intervention." From such a perspective, said James Barr, Christ becomes less a loving savior than "a
kind of automaton or switch, whose actions introduce each new stage
of the apocalyptic sequence." A Lutheran critic, dismissing millenni-

alism as dubious theologically and "void of any significance for our salvation," found it nothing but "a concession to our own human impatience" and readiness to hand over to a supernatural power the laborious task of building a more just, more humane social order. In the same vein, the historian R. Laurence Moore has interpreted the entire course of U.S. fundamentalism as a process by which economically disadvantaged people who might otherwise have challenged the status quo were instead neutralized by their premillennial eschatology, so that their activist impulses, never robust, "grew weaker as the years passed." [18]

Yet the issue is not a simple one. When they addressed the matter, most premillennialists vigorously denied that their eschatology led them to a solipsistic withdrawal from the world around them. Many insisted, for example, that their beliefs *did* offer a broad scope for activism—*in the religious arena.* "It simply isn't true that premillennialists sit back and do nothing," John Walvoord asserted, citing their record of missionary activity. In making this point, Walvoord was in the tradition of Calvin, who had cautioned that awareness of God's control of history should not lead believers to "grow torpid, and become idle and slothful," but should stimulate them to prayer and religious effort. The early dispensationalists similarly presented their system as a tremendous spur to missionary effort. Darby wrote, after outlining his end-time scenario, "This is the evil which is coming, and the world ought to be warned of it, because some may be salutarily frightened at the thought, and led to consider the Word of God." Prophecy's primary value, agreed James Brookes in 1870, was "as a motive to repentance." [19]

Post-1945 writers found countless ways to express the conviction that while human civilization faces doom, individuals may still be rescued; believers must not sit with folded hands, but alert the lost to what lies ahead. "Our loved ones and friends . . . need a warning today," proclaimed Tim LaHaye; "God will thunder judgment upon this generation . . . It is high time we Christians recognize that we are in the warning business." [20] A 1974 prophecy paperback put it this way:

> Christians can relax, if we wish. The rapture will take us off this sinking ship, and we'll be spared further grief. But . . . we can do better than that . . . If believers can show the world a united, triumphant front in these troubled times, it may just cause some of the world to think. They may want to know why we are as we are, and we surely can tell them. [21]

Such exhortations were taken seriously. James Davison Hunter has documented the high priority evangelicals place on winning souls for Christ, not only through missionary effort but through individual witnessing, and the premillennial beliefs that most of them embrace reinforce this commitment.[22]

Beyond soul-winning, some postwar premillennialists, influenced by books such as Carl Henry's *Uneasy Conscience of Modern Fundamentalism,* became more engaged with social issues of the day.[23] In the 1970s this impulse grew into a wave of conservative political activism focused on a wide range of issues: abortion, pornography, the gay-rights movement, suggestive rock music, sex and violence on television, the need for a strong military, school prayer, the teaching of Creationism in the schools, "family values," and so on. Jerry Falwell's Moral Majority marched to the polls to support candidates who shared its agenda. A smaller group of evangelicals, oriented around the magazine *Sojourners* and the organization Evangelicals for Social Action, espoused peace and social-justice causes historically identified with liberal Protestantism. How does one explain this phenomenon, seemingly so at variance with the premillennialist worldview?

In the first place, not all premillennialists rushed into the political arena. Indeed, S. Maxwell Coder of Moody Bible Institute argued in 1989 that a *majority* did not. Politicized preachers like Falwell, he said, were "lone wolves," unrepresentative of grassroots premillennialism.[24] (By the early 1990s, the fundamentalists' flirtation with politics did, indeed, seem somewhat on the wane.)

Furthermore, the contradiction may be more apparent than real, since the spiritual and the secular realms obviously overlap. Insofar as the moral order the fundamentalists sought through political mobilization would be more conducive to winning souls to Christ, their political involvement could be justified as a legitimate extension of their evangelistic mandate and rationalized in premillennialist terms.

Premillennialists who campaigned for nuclear disarmament or environmental protection justified *their* position on the grounds that such issues were important *in the present age,* even though human society and the earth itself would ultimately fall under God's judgment. As one evangelical environmentalist analogized: "We know that our buildings won't last forever, but we still hire maintenance crews to paint them and wax the floors to increase their longevity. The earth is our home, and it needs proper upkeep, too." Billy Graham, as we have seen, invoked this line of argument in his 1983 book, *Approaching*

Hoofbeats. "As we approach our study of the four horsemen and their judgment," the veteran evangelist declared, "we must not feel that we are to do nothing to fight evil just because some day they will come with full and final force upon the earth." [25]

In assessing premillennialists' social views, one must bear in mind the truism that most human beings act from a complex tangle of motives, impulses, and values; absolute consistency is rare. The understanding of prophecy was *one* powerful influence shaping the outlook of premillennialists, but many other factors entered the equation as well. What one saw in practice was an amalgam of motivations and theological perspectives, rather than the unmodified application of premillennial eschatology to every decision and every issue. Louis Goldberg of Moody Bible Institute summed up this commonsense point when he observed in a 1989 interview: "My position is, yes, I'm interested in prophecy, but I never at the same time want to ignore the needs of the social arena . . . I preach the soon coming of the Lord, but at the same time we're left here for a purpose, to make an impact on society." [26]

Explaining premillennial eschatology to the perhaps somewhat bemused readers of the Heritage Foundation's *Policy Review* in 1986, Falwell associates Ed Dobson and Ed Hindson firmly denied that premillennialism foreclosed political engagement. Basing their argument on the Bible, they emphasized a point rarely made by the prophecy popularizers: there is more to Holy Writ than the books of Ezekiel, Daniel, and Revelation:

> Just as there are many Bible passages that describe the end times, there are scores of passages that outline Christian responsibilities in this world. We take both sets of passages seriously. The Bible says that we should be ready for the Second Coming and that we should be good citizens—the salt of the earth. We do not view those missions as contradictory or mutually exclusive. We will work to better the world because the Bible tells us to, and we will await Christ's return because the Scripture says it will happen.

Pointing to the Moral Majority's campaign for school prayer and against abortion and pornography, they insisted, "Our enthusiastic political involvement is proof that we are not among those evangelicals whose apocalyptic views are a pretext for this-worldly despair." [27]

Yet the paradox remained, and American premillennialists, heirs as well to a long national tradition of reformism, continued to struggle with it. Oregon prophecy writer James McKeever, for example, espoused an activist eschatology rooted in his belief (rare among premillennialists) that the Rapture would occur *after,* not before, the Tribulation. Christians should prepare now for that terrible seven-year period, McKeever taught, when believers will band together in strictly disciplined survivalist cadres—he called them variously Bondslaves, Overcomers, and the Omega Force—to wage "spiritual war" against Antichrist's supporters. In *The Rapture Book* (1987) McKeever included a sign-up form for Bondslave recruits, to whom he promised secret conferences not announced to the general public. McKeever's Bondslave pledge included a vow to God "to do absolutely anything You tell me to do, even if it goes against my knowledge of what is good." [28]

In the 1970s, reacting against the hesitancy of many premillennialists to enter the public arena, some evangelicals abandoned premillennialism altogether to embrace "Reconstruction" or "Dominion" theology, a kind of fundamentalist postmillennialism committed to achieving a Christianized world in the present age. Drawing on the work of theologian Rousas J. Rushdoony, Reconstructionists insisted that Christians must take seriously God's command to Adam and Eve to exercise "dominion" over the earth and "subdue" it. This meant, they argued, aggressive action to impose Christ's rule on the world now, *before* His return at Armageddon. While postmillennialists of an earlier day had focused on issues of social justice, the Reconstructionists were more preoccupied with imposing their own (they saw it as Christ's) stern morality on the world. (One leader, Jay Grimsted, founder of an organization called Coalition on Revival, proposed for starters the Christianization of Santa Clara and Orange counties in California.) In addition to Rushdoony and Grimsted, the movement's leaders included Gary North of Tyler, Texas (Rushdoony's son-in-law), and David Chilton, a California Presbyterian minister. Pat Robertson vacillated between premillennialism and a Reconstructionist or Dominion eschatology. Apart from electing candidates "firmly committed to no-nonsense Christian values," the Reconstructionists' strategy remained vague, but their long-term objective was clear: "Our goal is world dominion under Christ's lordship, a 'world takeover' if you will . . . We are the shapers of world history." [29]

The "dominion" envisioned by this school of prophecy interpreters included massive exploitation of the earth's natural resources and control of the weather by the saints. Pat Robertson won fame when a hurricane turned away from the East Coast after his prayerful intervention. James McKeever, on a more modest scale, successfully held off a threatened rainstorm at an outdoor wedding dedication service. This strand of prophecy belief, in short, resolved the conflict between God's ultimate sovereignty and the American impulse toward activism and social control by viewing certain favored individuals as direct instruments of the divine will. But premillennialists sharply criticized this outbreak of postmillennialism in the heart of the evangelical camp and it remained a minor strand in late-twentieth-century prophecy belief, volubly espoused by a few, but lacking broad grassroots support.[30]

Skeptical of the Reconstructionists' soaring vision, many premillennialists continued to view the political arena as a weak reed at best and a demonic deception at worst; activist impulses were far better employed in the spiritual realm (in evangelism, witnessing, intercessory prayer, and encouraging other believers). Not by chance did prophecy books invariably close with a call to repentance. While prophecy interpretation had the appeal of a jigsaw puzzle or an intellectual game, it was, for believers, a supremely serious game involving the eternal destiny of immortal souls. Even for the most activist-inclined American, here was challenge enough.

A Theology of the People

Postwar prophecy belief drew strength, too, from the heterodox and centrifugal energies of U.S. religious life—characteristics foreign visitors had commented on since at least the early nineteenth century. Anthony Trollope observed in 1862: "[Americans] are willing to have religion, as they are willing to have laws; but they choose to make it for themselves. They do not object to paying for it, but they like to have the handling of the article for which they pay." [31] Unrestrained by the inhibiting apparatus of a state church, this diversity continued to flourish in the pulpits, television airwaves, and paperback book marts of late-twentieth-century America, creating a rich loam in which prophecy belief could thrive.

Post-1945 prophecy popularizers were rarely trained theologians, denominational leaders, or settled ministers, but were freelance writers, evangelists, or TV preachers. Hal Lindsey, as we have seen, was a Mississippi River tugboat captain before he found Jesus, attended Dallas Theological Seminary, joined the Campus Crusade for Christ, and began to preach in the open air at UCLA and other Los Angeles–area schools. Mike Evans earned a black belt in karate before his 1966 conversion. Hilton Sutton, Salem Kirban, Jack Van Impe, Tim LaHaye, and many other expositors held no formal pastorates, but operated their "ministries" largely as personal enterprises. Van Impe, a precocious accordionist, performed with his father in Detroit-area clubs and contemplated a musical career before becoming a traveling evangelist. James McKeever, formerly an IBM economist, doubled as an investment counselor; Mary Stewart Relfe had extensive real-estate interests in Montgomery, Alabama; Thomas McCall, coauthor of *The Coming Russian Invasion of Israel,* was a TV scriptwriter and real-estate investment consultant.[32] These origins were all in the tradition of dispensationalism, many of whose pioneers—Sir Robert Anderson, William Blackstone, the great Scofield himself—had no formal theological credentials.

A striking number of post-1945 prophecy writers had backgrounds in science or engineering. Edgar Whisenant, author of *88 Reasons Why the Rapture Will Be in 1988,* was an electrical engineer and NASA scientist who became fascinated by prophecy; Leon Bates had a twenty-year career in electronics before founding the Bible Believers' Evangelistic Association; Robert Faid, author of *Gorbachev: Has the Real Antichrist Come?* was a nuclear engineer; Gerald Stanton, author of a 1956 Rapture study, was preparing for a career as a chemist with the Dupont Corporation when he decided to attend Dallas Seminary instead; another prophecy writer worked as an electrical engineer with General Motors before enrolling at Dallas. Texe Marrs, author and producer of prophecy books and videos (including *Satan's New Age Plan for a One World Order*), listed his background as "U.S. Air Force officer, professor of American defense policy and international affairs, and high tech consultant."[33] And the list goes on. Prophecy writing was not a pursuit that attracted settled ministers or trained theologians, but instead enthusiastic amateurs, firm in their evangelical faith, often trained in scientific and analytic (but not historical-critical) methods, and eager to share their interpretive deductions with the world. As we saw in the Prologue, prophecy belief was particularly strong in decentralized denominations such as the Southern Baptist Convention and the Assemblies of God; in pentecostalism's three hundred denominational varieties; and in independent churches that relied more on charismatic local leaders than on formal denominational ties.

Far from apologizing for their lack of credentials or denominational standing, these writers offered it as evidence for the trustworthiness of their message. The genre exuded suspicion of the mainstream Protestant establishment with its formal hierarchies. In the Great Awakening itinerant preachers had won adherents by denouncing the settled clergy, and post-1945 prophecy writers followed in their footsteps. Interpret prophecy for yourself, they advised; don't leave it to the ecclesiastical elite. In the end times, apostate religious leaders will mislead the people—and signs of such apostasy already abound. In novels such as Dan Betzer's *Beast,* the learned ministers of fashionable churches invariably express contempt for the Rapture, only to repent bitterly when the event actually occurs. Beware not only "false prophets" in the churches, one author cautioned, but "any who speak authoritatively—philosophers, professors, scientists, statesmen—those leaders of thought" who try to control mass opinion. Jack Van Impe, warning that "our seminaries are filled with apostates," made the same point: "Quit listening to clergymen and lay people who are too lazy to adequately study prophecy, and begin listening to God." Declared another expositor, explaining the nuances of his system: "You don't have to be a great theologian to figure this out. Or even a great mathematician. All you have to do is read the Scriptures and accept them for what they say." [34]

Skepticism toward authority—except, of course, the ultimate authority: God's revealed Word—has characterized prophecy believers for centuries. One in seventeenth-century England versified as follows:

> Thou shalt read the visions John had
> Not after the learned doctor's way;
> But thou shalt read them in plainness,
> And clear light of day . . .
>
> Thou shalt not run to Antichrist's libraries,
> To fetch from thence any skill
> To read the Revelation of Christ,
> But be with knowledge fill'd. [35]

Late-eighteenth-century American prophecy writers, Ruth Bloch notes, were often "lay writers without clear denominational preferences" and "tinged with populist anti-intellectualism." A western Massachusetts expositor, in a 1792 work, "reserved his harshest attacks for the learned and salaried ministers of the established church." In the end times, he proclaimed, churches "built on the sandy foundations of worldly wisdom, traditions of men, money, and liberal education will fall, and great will be the fall." [36]

In this spirit, and in emulation of John Nelson Darby, who left the Church of Ireland to join a dissenting sect, postwar prophecy popularizers stressed their lack of institutional ties and formal theological education—or, often, formal education of any kind. Scofield proclaimed the twentieth century "a layman's age," and his epigoni proved the shrewdness of his insight. In evangelical churches across the land, lay experts delighted in sparring with their pastors over obscure points in Daniel, Ezekiel, or Revelation. As early as 1938 a critic of premillennialism grumbled that "Sunday-school teachers and others who consider themselves illuminated by the Scofield Bible beyond their pastors, form a troublesome element." In the early 1960s, an evangelical minister complained of do-it-yourself eschatologists who were turning church board meetings "into an oral examination of the preacher to see how much he knows of the details of prophecy." [37]

Exploring "Evangelicalism as a Democratic Movement" in 1984, Nathan Hatch cited books such as *The Late Great Planet Earth* as evidence of evangelicals' continuing confidence "that truth is simple and open to all," and their tendency to play out even "the most serious and complex intellectual issues . . . before a popular audience." The strength of grassroots American religious movements, Hatch observed a few years later, "springs from their ability to communicate with people at the culture's edge and to give them a sense of personal access to knowledge, truth, and power." Prophecy popularizations of the second half of the twentieth century epitomized these characteristics. Simply written, often in large type with short paragraphs, they stressed the universal accessibility of prophetic truth. As the introduction to one work put it, "Mr. [Oswald] Smith . . . aims to be understood by the people, rather than to be praised by the scholars." Wilbur Smith, noting in 1952 the failure of intellectuals to foresee World War I, drew the moral: "My Christian friend, you may not ever be a member of a great academy of science, or of a faculty of a distinguished university . . . , but by a careful study of the Scriptures, you may know more of the days in which we live and the days to come than these great scholars knew." Prophetic understanding does not depend on creeds, confessions, or "ordinances of synods," insisted Lewis Sperry Chafer the same year; it is conveyed in "simple terms known to all."[38]

This theme pervaded postwar prophecy writing. "We need child-like, unsophisticated minds which are prepared to accept in the simplicity of faith whatever is written," observed a 1962 author; another promised to avoid "the fine points of theology" and "simply relate the facts concerning the Last Days so that the ordinary layman can understand." "There is no such thing as a difficult text," declared a Seventh-day Adventist minister at a 1990 prophecy seminar in Wisconsin; "when the puzzle is put together we'll all see the same thing." (The jigsaw puzzle analogy, a favorite of popularizers, suggested both prophecy's universal accessibility and the certainty that, rightly assembled, the texts will yield a single meaning apparent to all.)[39]

At the outer fringes of this genre were the photocopied expositions and self-published treatises in which obscure folk earnestly explained their theories. Joe Civelli of Pensacola offered a "50-page typewritten report on the Second Coming" for $5.00; another Floridian identifying himself only as "Ted," distributed a 333-page, densely packed typescript complete with 6,283 biblical references. "We are in the last generation," he began, "and this book proves it." John Shepherd of Martinsburg, West Virginia, urgently sent Mary Relfe a cassette tape on the prophetic meaning of the UPC codes; "God gave me the interpretation . . . ," he told her, "so I could give [it] to you, because you have the means of getting this out to the people." An Alabama man's interpretive system, distributed free to one and all, concluded disarmingly: "P.S. If these prophecies do not come to pass as I indicated, you will all know that I misunderstood the prophecy."[40]

Many of these writers told of the precise moment when God spoke to them. "In January 1980, while kneeling in prayer in my bedroom," Relfe related, "the Lord interrupted my praying, and spoke very clearly inwardly, 'You are to teach "Current Events as They Relate to Bible Prophecy."'" She at once organized a thirteen-week prophecy course, at the end of which came a second message: "The Lord 'quickened' to me that it was now time to write. But, it was not to be written scholarly, or even systematically . . . , it was to be oriented toward the lay person, the businessman, and the unchurched."

Similarly, Lu Ann Bransby described her response when God told *her* to write a prophecy book:

> I was very careful to remind God that I was somewhat limited, because I take care of my grand-baby eight hours a day and it is difficult to go places with a baby, diapers, and bottles.

> God understood my limitations; yet that didn't prevent Him from giving me a very big job!

> He was very specific when he said. . . *"Lu Ann, write a book on the last days before Christ returns! Make it brief! Make it easy to read and to understand!. . .*

> God instructed me to omit highly technical information about the seventy weeks of Daniel and the dispensational periods of time . . . "KEEP IT SIMPLE," God said.[41]

These books abounded in stories in which the prophecy believer confounds the expert. Mike Evans recorded a conversation with a former head of Air Force Intelligence: "As we talked I told him about Ezekiel's prophecies that Russia would invade the Middle East. He stared at me in amazement." Wrote another author: "Not too long ago, one of America's scientists said that if men continued experimenting with the hydrogen bomb, there might come a day when the heavens would be on fire. A Christian who attended the meeting showed the speaker the amazing verses in Peter's epistle, and the great man was astounded."[42]

Premillennialism, in short, gave its adherents not only the emotional benefits of being part of a shared network of belief, but also a privileged source of knowledge not dependent on elaborate study or formal academic training. Indeed, they believed an excess of brainpower could be a positive liability. Hilton Sutton reminded his prophecy audiences, "You cannot escape hell because you are vastly intellectual." Avoid Bible commentaries and "study the Word itself," he advised, and "the jigsaw puzzle of understood details" will fall into place.[43]

But as Hatch further observes, a religious movement that "measures the importance of an issue by its popular reception" pays a price for such a dilution of theological discourse: "Evangelical thinking, which once was razor-sharp and genuinely profound, now seems dull, rusty, even banal." Premillennialism's current state amply confirms this generalization. In the seventeenth century, as we have seen, prophecy speculation attracted some of the most powerful minds of the age—Milton, Newton, Leibniz, Napier, and, in America, the leaders of Puritan New England. In the late eighteenth century, American prophecy writers included not only obscure dissidents but also prominent graduates of Harvard, Yale, and Princeton. Samuel Langdon, a former president of Harvard, in 1791 produced a study of John's Apocalypse.[44]

Even when prophecy ceased to interest most intellectuals, it could still attract able individuals such as Hitchcock, Darby, Scofield, Gaebelein, and more recent expositors such as Donald Grey Barnhouse and Wilbur Smith—whose writings, though directed to a popular audience, displayed erudition, rhetorical subtlety, and a degree of sophistication. The allusions in a typical editorial in Barnhouse's prophecy magazine, *Eternity,* might range from the novelist Thomas Mann to the painter Bartolomé Murillo. Wilbur Smith's readers encountered diverse figures such as Georg Hegel, Pitirim Sorokin, Reinhold Niebuhr, and Eugene Rabinowitch, editor of the *Bulletin of the Atomic Scientists.*[45]

By the late twentieth century premillennialism no longer attracted expositors of even the Barnhouse or Smith caliber. (The rare exceptions—George Ladd of Fuller Seminary before his death in 1982, John Walvoord of Dallas Theological Seminary—only proved the rule.) As one writer conceded, to profess this belief was "to classify oneself in the category of the nonintellectuals and the simpleminded."[46] Living off the intellectual capital of the past, the interchangeable parade of popularizers continued, as though in a time warp, to expound a system of belief wholly cut off from the larger world of ideas and scholarship. Yet the paucity of intellectual substance and cultural depth proved no great liability, as premillennialism remained vastly popular at the grassroots level.

Despite the popularizers' strident populism and suspicion of authority, they exhibited a touching eagerness for intellectual respectability. The "visible anxiety" of the fundamentalists "to have learning on [their] side" pervaded this genre.[47] To some extent these writers tried to have it both ways, jeering at the learned while simultaneously invoking the prestige and name recognition of secular experts. Symbolizing this ambivalence, many writers, even as they derided academia, proudly styled themselves "Dr."—usually an honorary degree from a Bible college. (Mary Stewart Relfe did not respond to my inquiries about the source of the Ph.D. she listed after her name.) They endlessly cited "famous scientists" and "well-known experts" and peppered their work with knowing allusions to DNA, gene splicing, the neutron bomb, fluorocarbon pollution, laser technology, and computer electronics. Just as they manhandled the Bible, they quoted their authorities only in snippets as "proof texts" devoid of context, never engaging the ideas substantively. A Chuck Smith prophecy film began, "In the next hour you will be meeting with doctors, professors, scientists, world leaders, and Chuck Smith." Quasi-scientific sensationalists such as Immanuel Velikovsky, author of *Worlds in Collision* (1950), or the authors of *The Jupiter Effect,* a work that predicted catastrophic destruction from a 1982 planetary alignment, were as likely to be cited as more reputable scientists. Albert Einstein, Paul Harvey, the *New York Times, Reader's Digest,* and the *South Bay Daily Breeze* of Torrance, California (much quoted by "Dr." Charles R. Taylor), were on an equal plane in prophecyland. Indeed, these authors often cited each other as authorities: Salem Kirban cited J. Dwight Pentecost, Hal Lindsey quoted Harry Rimmer, Jack Van Impe invoked John Walvoord, and on and on. Inveterate name-droppers, they often got things slightly askew. "Manachem Begin once let me in on a hot story," confided Mike Evans; "I recently spoke to a member of the Senate Arms Race Committee," boasted Hal Lindsey. Illiteracies and howlers of various kinds abounded. Antichrist "will become worshipped," wrote Lindsey; Evans referred to the speed of an F15 jet as "mock 2.2"; another author alluded knowingly to the French novelist "Albert Camu." But, again, for millions of believers, none of this appeared to detract in the slightest from the appeal of the genre as a whole.[48]

Prophecy writing's populist appeal arose, too, from its vigorous, if selective and superficial, engagement with contemporary issues. Continually mining the headlines for end-time signs, the promulgators of this belief system addressed subjects of widespread concern, from communism and nuclear war to family disruption and the computer. Readers of these prophecy popularizations could recognize their own world and confront their own fears and anxieties, spread upon a vast canvas of eschatological meaning.

Harmony, Symmetry, and Meaning in History

Late-twentieth-century prophecy writers, like their predecessors, view history as predetermined. (Some qualify this perspective, arguing that the prophecies reveal God's *foreknowledge*, rather than *foreordination*, of the future. As one believer put it: "The Bible doesn't determine what's going to happen. It just tells what will happen." [49] Whatever the theological import of this nuance, functionally it seems a distinction without a difference.) What are the implications of this conviction that history represents the unfolding of a divine plan?

First, it reflects a profound dissatisfaction with "secular" versions of history. Without an eschatological goal, observed one writer, history is meaningless—a mere "stream of isolated atoms falling through a void." Nonbelievers, echoed another, watch "the conflict of forces [that] runs through the whole course of human history . . . without knowing anything about its origins, its issues, or its termination." In the absence of a transcendent dimension, agreed George Ladd, history becomes a "snarl of irrational and demonic threads . . . which men cannot weave into a meaningful and purposeful pattern." [50]

From this perspective, most historical scholarship seems pointless—a mere recital of facts, signifying nothing. "Few secular historians have any conception of the meaning and purpose of history," declared one author; "they may be able to record and systematize the characters and events which allegedly comprise its raw material, but they have little or no clue to their interpretation or significance." John Walvoord, interviewed in 1989, emphatically agreed: "In my studies . . . I found that the historians usually ended up with their hands up. They didn't have a satisfactory explanation of human history." Alva J. McClain, president of Grace College and Theological Seminary in Winona Lake, Indiana, expressed the same frustration: "[History] should have some proper goal. *It ought to go someplace . . .* There ought to be in history some worthy consummation of its long and arduous course." [51]

In an earlier era, when historians routinely wrote of God's controlling influence over events, this divergence between "secular" and "prophetic" history was much narrower. As Dorothy Ross has pointed out, a providential model of historical causation pervaded American historical writing throughout most of the nineteenth century. George Bancroft, America's best-known historian in the nineteenth century, repeatedly invoked God's directing hand in his multi-volume history of the United States. In the introduction to the first volume (1834), Bancroft spoke of his reliance on documentary sources and assured the reader: "I have applied, as I have proceeded, the principles of historical skepticism." Yet God in various guises operates as a causal force throughout the work. Describing the English theological disputes that led the first colonists to New England, Bancroft wrote:

> Who will venture to measure the consequences of actions by the apparent humility or the remoteness of their origin? The mysterious influence of that Power which enchains the destinies of states, overruling the decisions of sovereigns and the forethought of statesmen, often deduces the greatest events from the least commanding causes.

In a later volume, Bancroft dramatically juxtaposed the Treaty of Aix-la-Chapelle (1748), whereby Europe's rulers negotiated the end of the War of the Austrian Succession, with the fact that sixteen-year-old George Washington, already fatherless, was then living in obscurity in a remote outpost of the British Empire. But the divine view of history is not man's view:

> And yet God had selected not Kaunitz, nor Newcastle, not a monarch of the house of Hapsburg, nor of Hanover, but the Virginia stripling, to give an impulse to human affairs, and, as far as events can depend on an individual, had placed the rights and destinies of countless millions in the keeping of the widow's son.[52]

As long as "secular" historians wrote in this vein, believers in God's oversight of history had little cause for complaint. But as teleology and divine causation gradually disappeared from secular historical writing, prophecy writers filled the void. For many Americans, the latter offered a far more satisfying and persuasive rendering of history's meaning.

From the aimlessness of secular history, these writers turned with joy to the literature of apocalyptic, where the "stream of isolated atoms" could be seen to possess "symmetry and continuity," and what had lacked any meaning beyond itself took on transcendent significance. To quote Walvoord: "Human history from a biblical standpoint is the unfolding of God's attributes, His power, His wisdom, His grace, His righteousness . . . All of these are part of God's plan in history." From this vantage point, secular history's futile meanderings give way to an orderly, harmonious, and above all teleological pattern. As Alva J. McClain put it:

> If there is anything crystal clear in Biblical history, it is that the existence of our sinful race falls into periods of time (call them eras, ages, dispensations, or whatever you will) and that each age represents an advance over the preceding age, when looked at from the standpoint of what God is giving and doing for man . . . Thus to the old question "Is the world getting better or worse?" from one standpoint one might answer, "The *age* is getting worse, but the *course of history,* by the grace of God, is moving forward." [53]

The contrast between the two views could hardly be sharper. To the prophecy believer, observed one expositor, history is no mere "narrative of unrelated events . . . History is going somewhere, and its terminals are predetermined by a sovereign God." While to "our time-shaded perspective . . . history is as a speck of dust . . . ," added another, "from the divine point of view, we are moving through an orderly sequence of events which will in the end bring us to the culminating terminal where all things promised find fruition." [54]

Best of all, this pattern and goal can be *known*. In dark and uncertain times, observed William Culbertson, president of Moody Bible Institute, the believer understands "not only the nature of the approaching crisis, but its purpose, sequence, and outcome. All this is in his grasp because he has the prophetic message of the Bible." [55]

This mode of ordering past, present, and future history into a coherent whole offered both emotional and aesthetic rewards. In contrast to the agnosticism of most historians about history's larger pattern and meaning, prophecy believers viewed it as unified and majestically purposeful, with past, present, and future subtly interlinked. Chaos gave way to coherence; randomness, to meaning. A. G. Mojtabai has described dispensationalism as a "structuralist's dream . . . [that] reduces all of the Bible to a single basic plot." Indeed, this system sees not only the Bible but *history itself* as a unified whole—a single idea—extending from eternity to eternity. Chuck Smith in 1984 noted the symmetry of a "day of creation" balanced by a "day of termination." Significantly, the one "secular" historian postwar prophecy writers regularly cited was Arnold Toynbee, who, like them, sought history's grand themes and great recurring patterns.[56]

The premillennial view of history has profoundly shaped American evangelicalism's larger worldview. To evangelicals, writes George Marsden, "all that is significant about history can be found in the Bible. There, the pattern of history of all the coming ages was written in advance . . . Modern history is of interest only as it produces some facts that document the cultural decline predicted in the Bible." (This is not quite the whole story, since modern history is also of interest for the *specific* prophetic fulfillments it has brought, most notably relating to Israel.) From this perspective, Marsden continues, the study of history becomes "basically a matter of collecting and classifying facts that fit the biblically derived pattern." Epitomizing this general tendency, prophecy expositors have divided history horizontally into rigidly segmented epochs ("dispensations") and vertically into the confrontation of divine and demonic forces. As Walvoord observed, prophecy's underlying pattern exemplifies "the conflict between good and evil which is the basic Christian philosophy of history." Or, as Tim LaHaye put it in *The Beginning of the End,* "It is helpful to keep in mind that there are only two kinds of people on the earth: Christians, and unbelievers."[57]

The impulse to uncover coherence and overarching meaning in events has always been a central attraction of prophecy belief. Peter Brown writes of the "sense of wonder . . . [that] flood[s] into the language of Augustine as he speaks of the marvellous and perfectly ordered distribution of the ages." Without the insights afforded by prophecy, wrote Jonathan Edwards, history would seem a mere "jumble and confusion to us, because of the limitedness of our sight." Cyrus Scofield's enduring appeal lay not only in the clarity of his prose and the ingenuity of his interpretations, but in his sensitivity to the enterprise's aesthetic dimension. "There is a beautiful system in this gradualness of unfolding," Scofield wrote. "The past is seen to fall into periods, marked off by distinct limits, and distinguishable period from period, by something peculiar to each." Scofield invited his readers to share his awe at "the majestic, progressive order of the divine dealings of God with humanity, [and] the increasing purpose which runs through and links together the ages, from the beginning of life to the end of eternity."[58]

Another historiographical genre, the textbook, offers interesting similarities to prophecy exposition. Like the prophecy author, the textbook writer reduces the "jumble and confusion" of events to order by exercising great selectivity; emphasizing the arbitrary demarcations of decades and centuries; structuring chapters around a few basic themes; and designating larger time periods "ages" and "eras." Even a kind of dispensationalism prevails, as Western history advances by successive stages from feudalism to democracy, from the Age of Belief to the Age of Science. While textbook history unfolds in a deceptively rational fashion, as it does in the dispensationalists' writings, textbook authors notoriously lack the prophecy expositors' mantle of divine authority, and the order they create can never be more than provisional. Their efforts to shape history into meaningful patterns encounter at every point a raucous chorus of critics and second-guessers. Above all, they lack the certainty that their story is moving toward a denouement knowable in advance. Whereas textbook writers, like secular historians generally, avoid the teleological, speaking instead of "change" and "development," the prophecy writer sees history moving toward an *end.* "We must alert our loved ones to history's destiny," wrote the president of Fuller Theological Seminary in 1984. "They can learn nothing about this from history books or news media. History's most important lessons are not to be found there."[59]

Prophecy writers employed diverse metaphors to convey their sense of history's predestined course. Some drew analogies from nature. "The twentieth century is a stream," wrote Walvoord, "moving exactly in the pattern of the prophetic Word." Echoed Billy Graham, "We are caught up in a stream of history that is beyond our ability to control." Others, giving a more somber thrust to Augustine's music imagery, invoked the concert hall: "The music of life increases its tempo. Faster and faster move the hands of the players in the grim orchestral finale of human history." Still others compared the unfolding of history to the inevitability of natural processes. Events that prepared the way for prophetic fulfillments, wrote one, were "catalysts as in a chemical reaction, to set in motion a whole chain reaction of other events."[60]

The *theater,* however, provided the richest metaphorical lode. Cyrus Scofield wrote of "the immense drama of human history," and a 1936 expositor elaborated the thought: "The stage is being set for the close of the Times of the Gentiles. As the great actors in the terrible drama move to their predicted places they can be recognized by this programme of coming events." Similar imagery abounded in post-1945 prophecy writings. One author titled a chapter "The

Assembling of the Cast." Chuck Smith, describing the rewards of prophecy study, wrote: "It's as if we were backstage at a play feeling the drama and excitement just before the curtain rises for the final act. The director is positioning all the players and seeing that the props are all in order before he signals for the curtain to rise."[61]

The theater metaphor distances the audience from the action—raptured believers will watch from the skies. "The best seat for this particular play is in the balcony," commented one writer; another spoke of viewing history's last act "from the grandstand seats of the heavens." This metaphor also suggested a performance one can savor precisely *because* one knows the outcome. "A study of the prophetic Scriptures is like having the program of a grand play," wrote Hilton Sutton. "Act after act is being staged, leading to the grand finale. All nations are included and the whole story is excitingly dramatic." A 1979 prophecy work made the point even more explicitly: for the prophecy believer, "watching the events unfold is similar to viewing a play after having read a synopsis of the drama. We recognize the main characters and we are able to forecast many of the major twists in the plot. We are certain, in advance, of exactly how the story will end."[62] Unsettling global developments and tyrants strutting on the world stage thus become, in this reassuring view of history, mere "scenes" and "actors" in a drama whose script one holds in one's hands.

As so often in prophecy writing, this metaphor has been around a long time. John Wesley employed it in a 1774 "playbill" advertising "THE GREAT ASSIZE, OR DAY OF JUDGMENT" to be performed "at the Theatre of the UNIVERSE on the Eve of Time," in a playhouse consisting of a spacious gallery and a "Pit without bottom." Wesley's tract, with woodcuts of saints and sinners, angels and demons, heaven and hell, described the play's three acts, concluding "with an Oration by the Son of God . . . AFTER WHICH THE CURTAIN WILL DROP." The music, it added, "will consist chiefly of Cries, accompanied with Weeping, Wailing, Lamentation and Woe."[63]

This sense of history's underlying unity and overall trajectory was, of course, achieved at high cost, as events, trends, and possible eventualities—the complex texture of actual historical experience—were arbitrarily selected, shaped, and arranged to fit the prophetic scenario and perform their signifying function. But it was a price the premillennial expositors, and their millions of readers, appeared more than willing to pay. With secular historians no longer speaking the language of progress or portraying the majestic unfolding of a divine plan in history, prophecy popularizers took up the slack and found a vast audience in the process.

Turning toward the Millennium

One easily forgets, amid the forecasts of doom, that premillennialism is, at heart, a Utopian belief system. John's Apocalypse, for all its horrifying and blood-drenched images, closes with a soaring vision that has comforted believers and inspired artists, poets, and composers through the ages. "And God shall wipe away all tears from their eyes; and there shall be no more death, neither sorrow, nor crying, neither shall there be any more pain: for the former things are passed away." [64]

Dismissed by Origen and Augustine and rejected by the guardians of orthodoxy in the Catholic, Lutheran, and Reformed theological traditions, millennialism—that is, belief in Christ's future earthly reign when evil, injustice, and suffering will be eradicated from human experience—survived on the fringes of medieval Christian thought; flourished among Anabaptists, English Puritans, Pietists, and other early Protestant radicals; and from the days of John Darby formed a linchpin of the dispensational system. (The early dispensationalists preferred the term "Kingdom Age" to "Millennium.") Citing references in Revelation to the thousand years when Satan will be bound, premillennialists insisted that between Armageddon and the Last Judgment, Jesus Christ will rule on earth for precisely one thousand years. Cyrus Scofield, as we observed in Chapter 3, saw in the Millennium the realization of man's age-old dream of a transformed human order. "It is impossible to conceive to what heights of spiritual, intellectual, and physical perfection humanity will attain in this, its coming age of righteousness and peace," he wrote. [65]

Post-1945 expositors, quoting proof texts from Isaiah, Jeremiah, Joel, Amos, and Revelation, typically included a final section in their books (just before the call to repentance) describing the glories of the Millennium—that "new world in which peace and righteousness prevail," as Billy Graham characterized it in 1965. "This will be the golden age," proclaimed Doug Clark; "the age of Utopia that so many people have looked for, longed for, and through a variety of religious philosophies striven for." (The phrases "Utopia" and "golden age" recur over and over in these accounts.) [66]

When they turned to the Millennium, the fixation of these writers on wickedness, war, and conspiracy was transformed into an equally obsessive effort to evoke the perfect social order. The idealism that suffused the hopes of liberal theologians for gradual improvement of the human condition was focused by the premillennialists on Christ's earthly reign. In this concentrated, undiluted form, their idealism became almost euphoric in its exaltation. Rather than use a somewhat feeble light to illuminate vaguely an entire landscape, they directed a single powerful beam to one small spot, flooding it with dazzling brightness amid the surrounding blackness.

In describing the Millennium, they invoked a vision of an age as different from the present in every particular as one could imagine. John Wesley White wrote in 1981:

> The arrival of Christ as King will be the best news that a weary, exhausted, terror-ridden earth could ever hear. The beatings, the burnings, the tortures—all the pain and cruelty inflicted on people—will be banned. No more small babies with swollen bellies and discolored hair. No more terrified peasants afraid to plant rice because soldiers might come and take it away. No more hungry stomachs and slave labor camps. No more dysentery and malaria . . . No more of Satan's evil horrors.[67]

Economic justice will prevail. As early as 1710, in *Theopolis Americana,* Cotton Mather envisioned a millennial city where the Golden Rule would govern all business dealings—and this theme loomed large in post-1945 prophecy writing as well. "The kingdom of Christ will sweep away all economic conflict and will provide fair and enjoyable working conditions," wrote Jack Van Impe; "strikes by workers and oppression by employers will be unknown." Under Christ's dominion, agreed Chuck Smith, "the commercial exploitation of others, creating untold personal financial woes, will be gone forever." Louis Goldberg in 1982 explicitly contrasted present-day economic conditions with the era to come:

> It is staggering to contemplate the magnitude of social problems today. Cities employ social workers who struggle with a mountainous load of cases representing economic privation, conflicts with the law, losses poor people suffer because of unscrupulous entrepreneurs, and so on . . . The [millennial] kingdom, however, will rectify these depressing situations . . .

Every person, no matter who he is, will have equality before the law and will enjoy all the fruits of his labor. No one will be able to oppress his neighbor, and no special interest groups will oppress or enslave any peoples.

Here at last, Goldberg concluded, will come "the utopia that men have longed for but have not been able to accomplish with their man-made schemes."[68]

On the authority of the prophet Isaiah ("with righteousness shall he judge the poor"), John Walvoord offered assurance that in the Millennium even society's lowest ranks would enjoy equality and justice. Ethnic and racial minorities, benefiting from "government protection and greatly reduced crime," would especially benefit. Ostentatious waste and conspicuous consumption would cease. "The smooth and suave rich whose bank accounts grow fat at [the poor's] expense" would feel Christ's displeasure, predicted Goldberg. Under Christ's rule, when everyone receives "a just allotment, based on the individual's faithfulness or merit," added another writer, getting down to cases, "it would be difficult to imagine . . . a Caesar's Palace in Las Vegas paying Ann-Margaret [sic] $200,000 a week, Sammy Davis $225,000 weekly, and Frank Sinatra a million dollars annually."[69]

Oppressive economic conglomerates will be no more. "Everyone will be self-employed and will enjoy the full fruitage of his own labor," wrote M. R. DeHaan in 1962. "Every single inhabitant of the world in that age will be independent, own his own property and his own home, and provide for his own family in abundance." The Jehovah's Witnesses magazine Awake, discussing automated techniques for measuring workers' performance, observed in 1990, "We can be confident that in God's new world, there will be no room for such joy-robbing monitoring devices."[70]

Everyday existence will be richly fulfilling. The coming age, observed Billy Graham, "will be much like the present life, . . . but missing all the imperfections that have destroyed the full and true meaning of life." Christ's reign will not bring mere empty leisure, he went on, but "labor, adventure, excitement, employment, and engagement." This will be an age of "vibrant, pulsating life—not inertia, not entropy," added another author.[71]

Shattered relationships will be mended. As one writer put it, "Our Lord will have the happy ministry of reuniting broken families and friendships." "The aged will be treated with respect, and little children will laugh and frolic without fear," added Herbert Vander Lugt. A lonely God's "yearning for companionship" will be satisfied in the Millennium, suggested another author appealingly, when "the family of God" is together at last. Hal Lindsey reported that his wife, whose father died when she was a baby, could hardly wait to spend "the first thousand years or so curled up in her heavenly dad's lap, since she has never had that experience with an earthly father!" [72]

For those who leave loved ones behind forever at the Rapture, the community of saints will be a more-than-adequate surrogate family. As Lindsey wrote at the end of *The 1980s: Countdown to Armageddon,* "I sincerely hope to see all who read this book at the soon-coming 'family reunion.' "[73]

Above all, the Millennium will fulfill (in Walvoord's words) humankind's "agelong desire for peace among nations" and Isaiah's memorable visions of swords beaten into plowshares and lions and lambs lying down together. After history's endless wars, Antichrist's brutalities, Gog's invasion of Israel, and the holocaust of Armageddon, peace will at last descend on a battered, conflict-ridden earth, freeing for human betterment resources once wasted on war. An end to military spending, Walvoord went on, "will have a beneficial effect upon both the social and economic life of the world . . . This, coupled with absolute justice, . . . will establish a social and economic order far different from anything the world had ever experienced prior to the millennium." [74]

Christ's kingdom will have a specific geographic locus: "And I John saw the holy city, new Jerusalem, coming down from God out of heaven, prepared as a bride adorned for her husband." The Bible, which begins with a narrative of Utopia as a garden, ends with a vision of Utopia as a city. After the Tribulation with its nightmarish urban congestion, pollution, and random violence, the New Jerusalem will be a place of righteousness, beauty, and harmony—the city of mankind's dreams. All problems that plague today's suffering metropolises will be solved, even power shortages. "God has his own lighting system," wrote Chuck Smith; "no sun, no moon—just an iridescent glow from His glory throughout the whole city. There'll be no energy crisis in this city." When the Lord's own splendor illuminates the world, agreed Doug Clark, dangerous nuclear power and expensive Arab oil will both become superfluous. [75]

The generational bonds so often shattered by the conditions of modern urban life will be restored in this city of brotherly (and sisterly) love. "Within the walls, old men and women will watch boys and girls playing on wide 'streets,' which are literally broad places or parks," wrote S. Maxwell Coder. "It will be a holy city . . . in striking contrast with metropolitan centers today."[76]

Prophecy writers stressed the absolute break between the present age and the next. The new order will be entirely God's doing; human endeavor will count for nothing as Christ "take[s] care of the mess that man has made of his world." Indeed, as Chuck Smith emphasized, before the Millennium must come Armageddon, when "the systems of the world" will be "rooted out, pulled down, and destroyed." Not only institutions, but masses of evildoers must perish to make way for the coming era of blessedness. As Arthur Bloomfield put it, "The rubbish has to be cleaned up and burned before the garden can be planted."[77]

A key motif in this outpouring of writing about the Millennium is an emphasis on order and harmony, often explicitly contrasted with the *dis*order and *dis*harmony of contemporary social existence. The uncertainties, distractions, and unpleasant surprises of today's world will vanish. Everyone will have a role to fill in this "perfect environment where righteousness can settle down and be at home." With "no more starvation, wars, pollution, or wasted billions on armaments[,] the world shall be a virtual Garden of Eden, and men shall live in harmony." Indeed, "the universe itself will run more harmoniously than at any time since creation."[78]

Enforcing this unity and harmony will be Christ himself. As Scofield insisted, the "tranquility, blessedness, and peace" of the Kingdom Age will be possible only because "the government will be a theocracy" committed to "instant destruction of the insubordinate or rebellious." Scofield's post–World War II followers reiterated the point. Walvoord, citing the prophet Isaiah ("He shall smite the earth with the rod of his mouth, and with the breath of his lips shall he slay the wicked"), wrote in stark terms of the nature of Christ's reign: "The millennial rule of Christ . . . will be absolute in its authority and power; He [will be] supreme over the entire earth." Only thus, said Walvoord, could the "golden age" dreamed of by "social reformists through the ages" be realized.[79]

Electoral campaigns, televised presidential debates, and congressional wheeling-dealing will not loom large in the Millennium. The "new world order," Lindsey emphasized, will not be "devised by politicians or maneuvered by men." In contrast to all the failed schemes of human self-rule, including democracy, wrote Chuck Smith, Christ will introduce "a new form of government: a monarchy that will embrace the entire world . . . The Kingdom of God [will] cover the earth as the water covers the sea." These authors did not shrink from the implications of their belief. "Jesus will be an absolute dictator," wrote Herbert Vander Lugt; "He will displace one of our cherished freedoms—that of religion. He will not permit the practice or propagation of false religion in any form." [80]

The same authors who wrote with such apprehension of Antichrist's mind control described the identical characteristic of Christ's rule with reverence and awe. At the Last Judgment, said one, "no oral evidence will be required as in human courts; from the recesses of the individual's own memory the whole story will be revealed and flashed instantaneously before [Christ's] mind." [81] This genre, in short, betrayed a profound ambivalence toward authoritarian rule and social regimentation, revealing both deep anxiety about succumbing to spurious authority and an almost palpable longing for an authentic supreme leader who will at last lift the burden of responsibility from humanity's shoulders.

But Christ will need help in ruling the world. Faithful Christians, mocked and maligned in this age, will come into their own in the Millennium. "Have you ever been a king?" asks Paul Lee Tan in *Jesus Is Coming* (1982). "If not, do not despair. Someday you will be a king. You will reign with Christ over the millennial earth." Christ will rule with the "glorified saints" (the raptured ones who will return with him at Armageddon), asserted a 1973 writer, and as "the number of living saints increases . . . , the need for more rulers will grow; and, probably, before the millennium closes, all glorified saints will be needed." A 1974 author put the matter in the no-nonsense vocabulary of a motivational seminar as he described the "high 'management' openings for can-do Christians" that the Millennium will bring:

> Jesus is now silently recruiting those demonstrating capability as overcomers. He needs saints who develop success patterns in this present real-life testing ground . . . Many leaders will be needed to reign over cities, nations, territories and millennium

projects . . . Don't be surprised when, during the Kingdom Age, we find some little-known Christians reigning in positions of great honor and scope.[82]

Frustrated hopes and unrealized dreams will be gloriously fulfilled in the Millennium, as the thwarted and the exploited at last enjoy parity with the great of the earth. S. Maxwell Coder, writing of the saints' physical transformation, captured something of this psychological dimension as well: "Our new bodies will be incapable of ruin and decay. They will be glorious rather than dishonored and lacking in dignity, and powerful rather than weak."[83]

The hopeful impulses and visions of the good society that premillennialists sternly denied themselves in writing about the present age poured forth in riotous profusion as they strained to portray Christ's reign. Millennial belief, declared a prophecy-conference speaker in 1956, spoke to "the deathless urge in the heart of humanity for a better world" and the longing of men and women for "a corporate ordered life; a life not for the few powerful and fortunate, but for all a life that shall be rich in truth, justice, power and love." A 1973 author agreed: "In nobler moments, people have ideals in their minds which they would like to see realized. The millennium will see them brought to fruition." Often criticized as pessimists, premillennialists insisted that the opposite was true. "Every true believer is an optimistic futurist," agreed John Wesley White; "he is looking for Jesus Christ to come and set up His kingdom of peace and plenty."[84]

The soaring Utopian rhetoric of the prophecy popularizers' descriptions of the Millennium highlighted with harsh if unconscious clarity the depth of their rejection of the present order, and the intensity of their longing for a radically different form of society. At a time when nuclear war threatened, the Cold War rumbled on, materialism and self-indulgence seemed all-pervasive, and an impersonal, computerized economic order threatened human autonomy, the Millennium shimmered on the horizon as an alternative future—an age of peace, justice, and rich human fulfillment under the absolute but righteous rule of an all-wise leader.

10 *Apocalyptic Portents in a Post–Cold War World*

As the twentieth century enters its final decade and radical changes transform the familiar contours of the Cold War world, several key elements of the end-time scenario promulgated by scores of post-1945 prophecy writers seem in jeopardy.

First, the Soviet Union, featured for decades as the menacing northern power that would shortly invade Israel and suffer devastating divine retribution, has suddenly emerged as an enfeebled and fragmenting collection of squabbling, independence-minded republics and ethnic groups. Grappling with manifold crises at home, Soviet leader Mikhail Gorbachev pursued rapprochement with the West and eagerly collaborated in the dismantling of the Cold War.

At the same time, apprehension about global thermonuclear war, so urgent a few years before, has diminished almost to the vanishing point. As Cold War hostility fades and the superpowers negotiate deep slashes in their nuclear arsenals, fears of a world–destroying holocaust seem a bad dream. Some cassandras continue to warn of serious dangers, including the threat of regional proliferation, but in the popular mind nightmares of nuclear annihilation have largely faded. This trend, too, poses a challenge for prophecy popularizers, who have long woven images of nuclear war into their end-time scenarios.

Far from diminishing in the wake of these changes, in the early 1990s popular prophecy interest is surging to new heights. How has this happened? In the first place, of course, key elements of the end-time scenario remain intact: the Common Market; the rise of multinational corporations and a computerized global banking system; an increasingly depersonalized domestic economy; Israel's perennial struggles with its Arab enemies; the tide of human wickedness that in prophecyland never recedes, only swells higher.

Further, again demonstrating the chameleon-like (and phoenix-like) qualities of prophecy belief, popularizers have adapted their message to shifting world realities and emergent popular concerns. As this durable and protean belief system enters its third millennium, its popularizers have little difficulty absorbing minor blips on the radar screen of history such as the collapse of the Soviet menace, the demise of the Cold War, and the waning of the nuclear threat.

Reassessing Gog in an Age of Glasnost

In the short run, as we saw in Chapter 5, some prophecy writers clung to the Russian demon. After all, they pointed out, the Scriptures warn: "For when they shall say, Peace and safety; then sudden destruction cometh upon them." Jack Van Impe, who since 1953 had described "The Coming War with Russia" via TV, cassettes, paperbacks, and coast-to-coast evangelistic tours, insisted that despite glasnost the final conflict with Gog was nearer than ever. "These events only *underscore* the accuracy of the prophetic Word—not disprove it," he declared; "Russia's new role is the predicted final plan developing before our very eyes at breakneck speed. These shocking events are giant steps toward . . . WORLD WAR III and then, ARMAGEDDON." Salem Kirban's *Russia's Rise to Ruin* (1990) included a chapter entitled "The Trojan Horse Is Back: Russia's Design for Deception." The upsurge of Islamic fundamentalism in the Soviet Union, Kirban suggested, increased the likelihood of a Russian invasion of Israel.[1]

Other resourceful writers suggested, as the Cold War wound down, that the new era of superpower amity would in fact facilitate Antichrist's emergence. In *Global Peace and the Rise of Antichrist* (1990), Dave Hunt argued that "the well intentioned global peace initiatives of the Pope, Gorbachev, and President Bush" would lead directly to the prophesied end-time world order headed by the Beast. The *Omega-Letter,* a prophecy monthly based in Niagara Falls, New York, warned in 1991, "Combined with the unification of Europe, this new spirit of 'Glastnost' [*sic*] is paving the way for the political union that will exist in the last days."[2] War fears or peace hopes—it made little difference to the skilled prophecy interpreter. All could be fitted into the end-time scenario.

Encore for an Ancient Eschatological Actor

We have seen that Islam in its various guises—Saladin, "the Grand Turk," the Ottoman Empire—figured prominently in prophecy writing from the medieval era to World War I. As Ottoman power then finally collapsed, the Muslim world diminished as a focus of eschatological attention. During the Cold War, Russia largely replaced the Islamic nations in the end-time drama.

But even at the Cold War's height, prophecy writers always insisted that the Arab states would be *part* of Gog's end-time alliance. In the 1970s, as OPEC inaugurated a series of oil-price increases and Islamic fundamentalism flooded across the Middle East, prophecy writers restored this ancient enemy to a primary end-time role. Recall that John Walvoord's *Armageddon, Oil, and the Middle East Crisis* (1973) sold three-quarters of a million copies.

In 1979, as followers of the militant Shiite leader Ayatollah Ruhollah Khomeini overthrew the Shah of Iran, prophecy writers quickly explored the eschatological meaning of this event, their task eased by the fact that the Book of Ezekiel specifically mentions Persia as an ally of Gog. Lester Sumrall's *Holy War Jihad: The Destiny of Iran and the Moslem World* (1980) featured a menacing-looking Khomeini on the cover. Another 1980 popularizer called the Ayatollah "a demonically appearing forerunner of Antichrist." To be sure, the Shiites were as rabidly anti-Soviet as they were anti-American, but the popularizers suggested that their attitude would change as the final lineup of nations took shape. "Iran is virtually in the Soviet camp, or at least sufficiently so for Russia's purposes," wrote one in 1987. Striking a note that would have been familiar to Joachim of Fiore, Martin Luther, or Cotton Mather, James McKeever wrote in 1989: "The Muslims have declared war on the West, the United States, and especially the Christians . . . The Muslim faith . . . could turn out to be the 'beast system' . . . We will keep you posted."[3]

The invasion of Kuwait by Iraq's Saddam Hussein in August 1990 shifted attention from Tehran to Baghdad. In an era of satellite TV, 800 call-in phone numbers, and paperback books that could literally move from the authors' computer disks to bookstore shelves in a few days, technology enabled prophecy popularizers to incorporate new developments into their scenarios with dizzying speed—a fact dramatically demonstrated by the 1990–91 Persian Gulf crisis.

Soon after the Iraqi invasion, Salem Kirban, reproducing *New York Times* headlines about the attack, declared: "The nations of the world are drifting into their final formation of alliances for the Tribulation Period . . . *Overnight* the nations could be engulfed in World War 3!" McKeever devoted an issue of his *End-Times News Digest* to

Iraq's prophetic significance. Hilton Sutton, on his Prophecy Hotline, warned: "We know from Genesis . . . that Saddam Hussein is a wild man . . . We must pray for a divine intervention in the Middle East." (Sutton's allusion was to Gen. 16:12: "And [Ishmael] will be a wild man; his hand will be against every man, and every man's hand against him.") A U.S. defeat of Iraq, Hal Lindsey told a reporter, would incite the Arabs to the long-prophesied invasion of Israel, with the Russians joining in.[4]

The veteran prophecy writer Charles Taylor, having early in 1990 put "Public Enemy Saddam Hussein" on the cover of his *Bible Prophecy News,* in September offered a "vital new cassette": "WHEN THE ARABS ATTACK JERUSALEM." Citing Ezekiel, he described "the soon-to-come war wherein the Arab states, supported by Soviet and Warsaw Pact forces," would invade Israel and suffer destruction at God's hands. (The attack might be triggered by the Rapture, he conjectured—an event that would decimate U.S. military forces as well as Washington officialdom.)[5]

In common with most other popularizers, Taylor avoided labeling Saddam as Antichrist or Gog or predicting an imminent Armageddon, since the Darby-Scofield timetable holds that Antichrist and Gog will emerge only after the Rapture, while Armageddon must await the end of Antichrist's seven-year rule. But Taylor, along with Walvoord and others, saw these events as important preliminaries to the main events. "That which is transpiring is a shuffling of the nations to get them in proper position" for the conflict described in Ezekiel 38, Taylor wrote, and definitive evidence of the "wars and rumours of wars" that, according to Jesus' words in Matthew 24, will precede the end.[6]

The Persian Gulf War stimulated a swelling of eschatological interest across America. Twenty-five thousand turned out for a prophecy sermon by evangelist Greg Laurie in Orange, California. Billy Graham told a throng on Long Island that a full-scale Mideast war would be "far more sinister" than those in Korea or Vietnam because of the "spiritual forces at work." (Graham made the same point at the Kennebunkport, Maine, Episcopal church as vestryman George Bush sat in the congregation.) "These events are happening in that part of the world where history began," mused Graham, "and, the Bible says, where history as we know it, will some day end." In Dallas' gargantuan First Baptist Church, the Reverend Paige Patterson preached on

"Is Saddam Hussein the Antichrist?" (Reflecting the premillennial view that Antichrist will arise in Europe after the Rapture, he answered no.)[7]

In Cleveland, Minneapolis, and many other cities, thousands flocked to prophecy sermons by local ministers. Some expositors suggested that the "noisome and grievous sore[s]" mentioned in Revelation 16 could refer to an Iraqi chemical-weapons attack. When the Iraqis set fire to hundreds of Kuwaiti oil wells, luridly illuminating the night sky and blanketing the region in foul smoke, talk of "Armageddon" was on many lips. (As early as 1985, David Wilkerson had written, "Before the great holocaust there will be smaller holocausts—the oil fields of the middle east will be ablaze, and the smoke will rise night and day as a warning of the greater holocaust yet to come.") Others linked Saddam's massive release of oil in the Persian Gulf to prophecies of the seas turning to blood. "[The end] is definitely coming," a University of Minnesota graduate student told a reporter, adding: "It's freaky but it doesn't scare me, because I'm a Christian. It'll be other people who will suffer." A California woman with a son in the Persian Gulf told National Public Radio, "The Bible says you're going to have these wars, so you accept life for what it is." Another believer wrote a long, impassioned letter to *Time* magazine explaining that Saddam was the larger of the two horns of the ram mentioned in the eighth chapter of Daniel, and warning that the Tribulation would begin in January 1991.[8]

Bookstores reported booming sales of prophecy studies. "The more unstable the world gets, the more people look to these kinds of books," commented an Iowa City bookseller. "The way everything's going, it's not going to be too much longer," reflected a young clerk in a Christian bookstore in Texas; "I don't think I'm going to get old." In December 1990 John Walvoord's publisher rushed on the market with an update of *Armageddon, Oil, and the Middle East Crisis*. Within a few weeks a million copies were in print. "I have never seen this kind of interest in prophecy before," said the veteran prophecy expounder, "and I've been at it a long time." Sales of *The Late Great Planet Earth* soared. Bantam Books reported in October 1990 that Grant Jeffrey's *Armageddon—Appointment with Destiny* was its "hottest single religious title."[9]

By early 1991 a front-page *New York Times* story found prophecy interest in America at "fever pitch." John Walvoord appeared on

CNN, CBN, and CBS-TV and was interviewed on sixty-five radio stations across the nation to explain the meaning of the Persian Gulf crisis in the light of the Bible. (Commented a university-press editor after watching Walvoord on CBS, her first exposure to this strand of U.S. popular culture, "I must say he was impressive—very confident, and he didn't seem at all silly or strange.") From Boston to Los Angeles, newspapers devoted many inches of column to the nuances of the premillennial system. The Jews for Jesus organization placed full-page advertisements in the *New York Times,* the *Boston Globe,* and other major newspapers linking Saddam Hussein to Antichrist and urging readers to dial "900–4–MESSIAH" for more information. Country singer Johnny Cash released "Goin' by the Book," a song that interspersed statements by President Bush with doomsday lyrics. "The big one is definitely on the way," Cash told the *Los Angeles Times.*[10]

The Iraqi crisis focused attention on Revelation 18, which foretells the destruction of Babylon, Nebuchadnezzar's ancient capital on the Euphrates, sixty miles from Baghdad. While many popularizers interpreted the passage as symbolic of the demise of the global economic order as a whole, others interpreted it literally. Since Babylon could hardly be destroyed if it did not exist (the original city fell to ruin after 275 B.C., when the inhabitants were removed to the new city of Seleucia), Lindsey and others had for years called attention to Iraqi plans to rebuild it. After August 1990 such interest quickened. Charles Taylor offered his listeners a book and a cassette on *Saddam's Babylon the Great.* "That city in Iraq has to be rebuilt," he stated, "because THE BIBLE DECLARES IT." *The Rise of Babylon* (1991), by Charles Dyer of Dallas Theological Seminary, with Saddam's picture on the cover, quickly sold 300,000 copies.[11]

News reports whetted prophecy believers' interest. The *New York Times* noted that Saddam, a great admirer of Nebuchadnezzar, had poured vast resources into the project, including construction of a huge palace on the ruins of the ancient one—an edifice intended, many felt, as his own future residence. "Because Babylon was built in ancient times, and was a great city, it must be a great city again in the time of our new great leader, Saddam Hussein," said the project's chief archaeologist. Emphasizing Saddam's similarities to Nebuchadnezzar, his Iraqi admirers noted that the latter's empire had included modern Kuwait, Syria, Jordan, and Israel, and that he had conquered Jerusalem three times and carried many Jewish captives to Babylon.[12] All this provided grist for the mills of the prophecy writers.

With Iraq's defeat in the Gulf War this wave of prophecy interest has abated, and end-time belief has receded to its more accustomed position on the fringes of cultural awareness. But the episode demonstrated the latent power of this belief system, and how readily, in moments of crisis, it could move from the periphery to the center of American consciousness.

A Darkened Sun and Bloody Seas

Another ancient apocalyptic theme is assuming new prominence as the twentieth century winds down: the decay of the environment. The surge of concern about nuclear accidents, oil spills, global warming, the greenhouse effect, vanishing rain forests, and a host of other environmental issues strikes many prophecy writers as highly suggestive in view of the environmental motifs in biblical apocalyptic. The Book of Revelation, they point out, unfolds the ultimate ecological catastrophe as the seven seals are broken, the seven trumpets sounded, and the seven vials of wrath poured out: the sun grows as black as sackcloth and then becomes searingly hot, "scorch[ing] men with fire" and consuming all grass; the moon takes on a bloody cast; monstrous, scorpion–like locusts make human life a torment; people suffer from horrible sores; the oceans and rivers become "as the blood of a dead man," killing all sea creatures and poisoning the world's water supply; earthquakes tumble mountains into the sea, and giant hailstones pound the earth.[13]

Passages from the Old Testament, such as this one from the Book of Isaiah, have a disturbingly contemporary ring in the late twentieth century:

> Come near, ye nations, to hear; and hearken, ye people: let the earth hear, and all that is therein; the world, and all things that come forth of it.
> For the indignation of the LORD is upon all nations . . .
> And the streams thereof shall be turned into pitch, and the dust thereof into brimstone, and the land thereof shall become burning pitch.
> It shall not be quenched night nor day; the smoke thereof shall go up for ever: from generation to generation it shall lie waste; none shall pass through it for ever and ever.[14]

Beginning around 1970, prophecy writers increasingly linked such biblical forecasts of catastrophic upheavals in the natural order to the rising tempo of environmental concern. In Salem Kirban's prophecy novel *666*, Tribulation-era tourists visit a "Living Tree Exhibit." Environmental pollution and the population explosion, declared Kirban in another work, were creating "an irreversible trend toward the End Times." A speaker at the 1971 Jerusalem prophecy conference cited "disruption of both regional and global ecosystems" as a last-day sign. Charles Taylor, expounding Isaiah's dire prophecies regarding a nation "whose land the rivers have spoiled" suggested in 1972 that "the ecology reports currently available as to the 'spoiling' of the U.S. rivers and waterways by many forms of pollution" clearly linked the United States to this verse.[15]

Hal Lindsey, discussing the Tribulation in 1973, included a section, "Judgment on Vegetation," based on Revelation 8:7: "The first angel sounded, and there followed hail and fire mingled with blood, and they were cast upon the earth; and the third part of trees was burnt up, and all green grass was burnt up." The environmental consequences of these events, he suggested, would be catastrophic: "With this massive loss of vegetation will come soil erosion, floods, and mudslides. Air pollution will be immense; the smoke of the fire will fill the atmosphere, and the remaining vegetation will be unable to adequately absorb the hydrocarbons from automobiles and industry. Ecology will be thrown chaotically out of balance." The prophesied darkening of the sun, Lindsey went on, was already beginning:

> There have been days in some large cities of the world . . . when the pollution has been so bad that people have had to turn their car lights on for safety! Trees and vegetation have also been adversely affected by the persistent lack of sunlight. To this present man-made pollution add the pollution of . . . nuclear fallout . . . , and it's easy to see how one-third of all light will be diminished.[16]

Chuck Smith, discussing the prophesied end-time catastrophes in a 1977 work, found it "extremely interesting that scientists are now crying grave warnings concerning the ozone blanket around the earth." Today's water-pollution problems point to the Tribulation, Smith went on, when people will "turn on a spigot in their houses to get a drink and bloody water pours out." Smith's 1978 prophecy film, *Future Survival*, featured scientists learnedly discussing fluorocarbon gases and the ozone layer, the population explosion, pesticides, and new staphylococcus and virus strains. "All the pieces of the puzzle are coming together," Smith intoned. Added Jack Van Impe in 1979: "The sixth seal [of Revelation] pictures ecological upheavals that challenge description. Generations of pollution . . . may contribute to the chaos in nature pictured here."[17]

In the 1980s and early 1990s, this theme assumed even greater prominence in prophecy writing. The bibliography of Billy Graham's *Approaching Hoofbeats* contained only two or three books on prophecy and many on pollution, ecology, and world famine, as well as the nuclear threat. The "pestilences" prophesied by Jesus as a sign of the end, declared another 1983 work, "may . . . have to do with man's poisoning of his environment through massive industrialization." "Tampering with nature has produced some side effects that have just begun to haunt us," this book went on. "The plague will increase and become more serious." Even eschatological writers who rejected biblical literalism could not resist finding a sobering message for the present in Revelation's chronicle of environmental woe. One, for example, while describing the earthquakes, bloody seas, and darkened sun of Revelation as "typical apocalyptic effect[s]" that did not refer to literal events but rather enunciated a "universal principle of judgment," nevertheless asked rhetorically: "What about the pollution of the air, our fresh waters, the sea, and even the very soil from which our food is grown? Is this the way we are bringing God's judgment upon us?"[18]

As always, these writers demonstrated great ingenuity in giving the prophecies a contemporary twist. To David Wilkerson, the horrible sores mentioned in Revelation suggested skin cancers related to rising levels of solar radiation. "Revelation 16 actually describes effects now being attributed to the hole in the Ozone Layer," declared the *Omega-Letter* in 1991.[19]

Many writers saw the environmental crisis as a prelude to the rise of Antichrist; overwhelmed by ecological disasters, the world would turn to this charismatic leader. Soon, Lindsey predicted in 1977, humanity would face such massive environmental problems that only "a 'new world order' with some form of global government and world economic control" would offer hope. The *Omega-Letter* made the same point: "Environmental issues are pushing the planet closer to the World Government spoken of in the Bible." Going further, James McKeever in 1990 claimed that the *explicit,* though hidden, goal of environmental activists was a world government headed by Antichrist. Even their professed aim of protecting the environment challenged God's sovereignty, he went on, since the ecological crisis was plainly a divinely ordained sign of the end. Recalling the plagues God sent upon Egypt—turning the Nile to blood, killing the Egyptians' cattle, sending devouring locusts—McKeever drove home his point:

> Do you see God creating ecological and environmental disasters in Egypt? He certainly did. The will of God must be far, far preeminent over the concern for the environment or ecology.
>
> The same thing is going to occur in the future . . . God and Jesus are the ones who are in charge, and they are going to bring total disaster to the environment.[20]

Whereas McKeever viewed God as the direct cause of the catastrophes so memorably described in Revelation, most writers linked them to trends that resulted from human heedlessness. While this view linked prophecy to contemporary concerns, it also raised again, in different form, the dilemma Perry Miller had posed in 1950: if the ultimate environmental crisis occurs by natural means, in what sense does it represent divine judgment? In *Is This the Last Century?* David Webber and Noah Hutchings confronted this problem. To view the disasters foretold in Scripture as a consequence of human actions is not to deny God's power, they argued; God *may* perform miracles, but He also has "the liberty to use established scientific laws to accomplish His purposes if He so desires." In this instance, they suggested, God could use humankind's abuse of the environment as a means of prophetic fulfillment. In the same vein, commenting on the prophesied "death of world ecology," Lindsey wrote in 1973 that humanity would bring the catastrophe upon itself: "God simply steps back and removes His restraining influence from man, allowing him to do what comes naturally out of his sinful nature."[21]

While they vividly described Tribulation-era environmental horrors, prophecy writers also dwelt lovingly on the "new earth" foretold for the Millennium. This theme, too, harked back to a centuries-old interpretive tradition. In an early-nineteenth-century Bible commentary revered by generations of evangelicals, for example, the British cleric Adam Clarke declared, "The present earth, though destined to be burned up, will not be destroyed, but be renewed and refined, purged from all moral and natural imperfections and made the endless abode of blessed spirits." Edward Hitchcock of Amherst College, geologist and devout evangelical, in an 1840 geology textbook envisioned an earth "purified by the fires of the last day, and rising from the final ruin in renovated splendor." The description in II Peter of the earth "melt[ing] with fervent heat" did not portend its *destruction,* agreed an 1856 interpreter, but rather "a regeneration of the material world by fire, analogous to the regeneration of the natural man by the Holy Ghost." He continued: "The earth shall not pass away. It shall live on—survive its baptism of fire—. . . and come forth, minus its curse, to flourish with all its sister orbs forever in its Maker's smile." [22]

Premillennial leaders of the late nineteenth and early twentieth centuries similarly stressed the renewal of nature during Christ's earthly reign. "The earth will not be annihilated but renovated," commented James Brookes in 1870, "and remain as a chosen and honored theatre for the everlasting display of the glory of God in Christ." "The heavens and the earth will be brought into the closest fellowship," agreed an 1881 expositor; "the whole earth will become exceedingly fertile and fruitful beyond man's highest expectations." Cyrus Scofield wrote longingly in 1918 of the millennial age when nature will no longer be debased by man's "avarice, his ruthless use of her power, [and] his unequal distribution of her benefits." [23]

In the same vein, a 1969 author foresaw that in the Millennium "the new earth [will be] sealed forever against the entrance of anything that would defile, pollute, deceive, or destroy this paradise." Hal Lindsey, writing in 1973, gave his pen full rein:

> In order for man to inhabit the ravaged earth during the Millennium, it will first have to be restored by Jesus. That means that the whole animal and vegetable worlds will be at their highest state of development. Man won't have marred it with the refuse of his selfish activities. The sky will be bluer, the grass will be greener, the flowers will smell sweeter, the air will be cleaner, and man will be happier than he ever dreamed possible![24]

A 1988 author described the environmental transformation of the Millennium in phrases worn smooth by years of reiteration: "This globe has been polluted in a multitude of ways by the technology and selfishness of mankind. We are in an ecological crisis . . . One day a total change will take place; everything will be made *new. Our present phys-ical environment will pass away.*"[25]

The prophecy writers' post-1970 emphasis on environmental themes related in interesting ways to the wave of popularized caution-ary books on ecological topics that appeared in these years. By a nice symbolic appropriateness, Alvin Toffler's bestselling *Future Shock*—with its warnings of catastrophe ahead if various environmental, tech-nological, and demographic trends were allowed to proceed un-checked—appeared in 1970, the same year as Lindsey's *Late Great Planet Earth.* The ensuing years brought *The Eco-Spasm Report, The Closing Circle, The Promise of the Coming Dark Age,* and a spate of other books in a similar vein. Michael Barkun in a perceptive 1983 essay labeled this genre "secularized apocalyptic" and found it "as intense and as deeply felt" as the religious version:

> Couched in the idioms of social and political criticism, it evokes world destruction and transformation through ecologi-cal disaster, nuclear holocaust, and technological breakdown. The curious result is that two quite different bodies of apoca-lyptic literature flourish simultaneously. Based upon different premises and utilizing dissimilar styles of argument, they none-theless converge upon the belief that the accepted texture of re-ality is about to undergo a staggering transformation, in which long-established institutions and ways of life will be destroyed.

This ostensibly secular genre gained power from its resonance with, and structural similarity to, biblical apocalyptic, sometimes through explicitly religious language and imagery. As Barkun went on, these writers' "predictions of 'last things' generate[d] the feelings of awe that have always surrounded eschatology, even if in this case the predictions often [grew] out of computer modelling rather than Biblical proof-texts."[26]

Completing the symbiotic circle, prophecy popularizers end-lessly quoted the dire statistics of secular authors. "Men of science, men with Ph.Ds who are highly respected for their knowledge," wrote Chuck Smith in 1977, gave the earth only a few more decades if current ecological trends continued.[27]

But the two genres also differed sharply. The secular apocalypti-cists offered their litanies of doom as a stimulus to action. Even the grim Toffler concluded that a little time yet remained for humankind to avert disaster: "This is the supreme instant, the turning point in history at which man either vanquishes the processes of change or vanishes." The premillennialists, by contrast, drew from the same evidence the opposite conclusion: catastrophe looms, just as the Bible foretells, *and nothing can prevent it*. In the fictional segment that begins Mike Evans' book *The Return,* the giant computer of the "International Center for Multidisciplinary Analysis of the State of the World," after processing a mass of data on global environmental trends, confirms what premillennialists had long known: "There is apparently no way to avoid world disaster!"[28]

While their end-time scenarios increasingly incorporated an environmental component that could be linked rhetorically to current concerns, the prophecy writers as always distinguished sharply between man's role and God's. Conceding that the human race's brutal assaults on nature might contribute to the environmental horrors portrayed in Revelation, and to this extent play a role in prophetic fulfillment, they insisted that the millennial *renewal* of nature would be wholly God's doing. Except perhaps for the redeemed saints who would help Christ run things, human effort would have no role in this restoration. In their view of nature and its place in prophecy, premillennialists remained faithful to their larger sense of divine omnipotence and human powerlessness: apart from assuring our own salvation and trying to win others to Christ, we are helpless to shape history's course. A few evangelicals tried to harmonize premillennialism with an ethic of environmental activism, but the task was a difficult one.

In summary, as the 1990s began, the components of a partially restructured end-time scenario were falling into place, ready to take up the slack, as it were, left by the end of the Cold War and the decline of nuclear anxiety. This new scenario, supplementing age-old themes with warnings of ecological catastrophe and visions of a globe restored to Edenic purity, appears capable of sustaining prophecy belief far into the twenty-first century.

Attention focused, too, on the fast-approaching year 2000. Just as the arrival of the year 1000 A.D. had provoked intense end-time anticipation in medieval Europe, some prophecy popularizers, including Pat Robertson, suggested that the year 2000 might have prophetic significance. One writer, discussing God's "7000 year plan for mankind" and calculating the Creation at around 4000 B.C., speculated that the Millennium—the final thousand years of the seven thousand allotted to human history—would begin around the year 2000.[29]

James McKeever arrived at the year 2000 by a different intellectual route. Sacred history, he argued, appeared to be divided into two-thousand-year segments: two thousand years from Adam to Abraham; two thousand from Abraham to Jesus; and, possibly, two thousand from Jesus' first coming to His second coming. Hedging his predictions (as the shrewder prophecy writers always did), McKeever wrote: "We are not saying that Jesus will come back at the year 2000. We are saying if this parallel continues to hold, it is possible that Jesus will come back around the year 2000, plus or minus thirty years."[30] This, again, was a very old theme in prophecy exposition, going back at least to Joachim of Fiore, and in American history to Jonathan Edwards and Timothy Dwight, both of whom had viewed the year 2000 as eschatologically momentous.

Although "orthodox" dispensationalists did not focus on the calendar in this way (the Rapture will occur in God's good time, they taught, irrespective of human chronology), the beginning of a new millennium—though not *the* Millennium—did appear likely to intensify grassroots prophecy interest as the twentieth century wound down.

When all is said and done, we are confronted with the remarkable endurance of this ancient way of understanding the world. Prophecy belief, and specifically premillennialism, not only survived the "secular" twentieth century but exhibited vigorous signs of renewal as the century ended. Daniel Bell in 1960 compiled a grim list of devastating world events since 1930—global depression, the rise of fascism, World War II, the Holocaust, the perversion of the socialist ideal in the Soviet Union—and concluded: "For the radical intellectual who had articulated the revolutionary impulses of the past century and a half, all this has meant an end to chiliastic hopes, to millenarianism, to apocalyptic thinking—and to ideology. For ideology, which was once a road to action, has come to be a dead end."[31] Yet the same cycle of horrors that eroded secularized apocalyptic ideologies served to reenergize the original, religious version. All these dark events strengthened the premillennialist vision of worsening world conditions as the end approaches.

As the configuration of world power alignments and public concerns shifts at the end of the century, prophecy popularizers, like their predecessors over the centuries, are proving extremely resourceful at restructuring their scenario. Timothy Weber's 1977 prognostication still appears valid fifteen years later: "As long as premillennialists are able to fit current events into their system, there seems little doubt that they will be able to attract significant numbers of adherents."[32]

Nurtured by the dense network of colleges, seminaries, Bible schools, publishing houses, Christian bookstores, radio and television programs, and churches by the tens of thousands that sustain the vast subculture of late-twentieth-century U.S. evangelicalism, the conviction that God's plan for human history lies encrypted in ancient biblical texts remains very much alive as the century draws to its close. From pulpits, cassette tapes, orbiting communications satellites, and the pages of millions of paperbacks, the ancient cry rings out as it has for hundreds of years: "He Is Coming Soon."

NOTES

Prologue

1. Isa. 28:10.
2. George Gallup, Jr., and Jim Castelli, *The People's Religion: American Faith in the Nineties* (New York, Macmillan Publishing Co., 1989), pp. 4, 58, 61, 66; George H. Gallup, *The Gallup Poll: Public Opinion, 1980* (Wilmington, Del., Scholarly Resources, 1981), pp. 186–187.
3. Dwight Wilson, *Armageddon Now! The Premillenarian Response to Russia and Israel since 1917* (Grand Rapids, Baker Book House, 1977), p. 12.
4. Gallup and Castelli, *The People's Religion,* p. 60.
5. James Davison Hunter, *American Evangelicalism: Conservative Religion and the Quandary of Modernity* (New Brunswick, Rutgers University Press, 1983), p. 49; idem, *Evangelicalism: The Coming Generation* (Chicago, University of Chicago Press, 1987), p. 5; Gallup and Castelli, *The People's Religion,* p. 17 (Methodist and Presbyterian membership); George H. Gallup, Jr., and David Poling, *The Search for America's Faith* (Nashville, Abingdon Press, 1980), p. 133 ("strong tide"); Leonard I. Sweet, "The 1960s: The Crisis of Liberal Christianity and the Public Emergence of Evangelicalism," in George Marsden, ed., *Evangelicalism and Modern America* (Grand Rapids, Wm. B. Eerdman's Publishing Co., 1984), p. 43 ("dominant . . . force").
6. Gallup and Castelli, *The People's Religion,* pp. 14, 46.
7. Ibid., p. 17 (table 1.2); *Yearbook of American and Canadian Churches,* ed. Constant H. Jacquet, Jr. (Nashville, Abingdon Press, 1990), pp. 248, 250, 254; "Southern Baptists Pick Fundamentalist Head," *New York Times,* June 13, 1990, p. A15; "Baptists Espouse 'Inerrancy,'" *Wisconsin State Journal* [Madison] (June 23, 1990), 6A; Margaret Paloma, *The Charismatic Movement: Is There a New Pentecost?* (Boston, Twayne Publishers, 1982), esp. pp. 55–60; Edith Waldfogel Blumhofer, *The Assemblies of God: A Chapter in the Story of American Pentecostalism* (2 vols., Springfield, Mo., Gospel Publishing House, 1989).
8. Gallup and Castelli, *The People's Religion,* pp. 17, 92; M. James Penton, *Apocalypse Delayed: The Story of Jehovah's Witnesses* (Toronto, University of Toronto Press, 1985), esp. pp. 190–195; Jan Shipps, ed., *Mormonism: The Story of a New Religious Tradition* (Urbana, University of Illinois Press, 1985); Jonathan Butler and Ronald Numbers, "The Seventh-day Adventists," in Mircea Eliade, *The Encyclopedia of Religion* (New York,

Macmillan Publishing Co., 1986); Roy Branson, "Adventists between the Times: The Shift in the Church's Eschatology," *Spectrum,* 8 (Sept. 1976); Bruce R. McConkie, *The Millennial Messiah: The Second Coming of the Son of Man* (Salt Lake City, Deseret Books, 1982); Herbert W. Armstrong, *The United States and Britain in Prophecy* (n.p., Worldwide Church of God, 1967); "Armageddon—A War That Leads to True Peace," *Watchtower,* Feb. 15, 1985, pp. 5–7; Joseph Martin Hopkins, *The Armstrong Empire: A Look at the Worldwide Church of God* (Grand Rapids, Wm. B. Eerdman's Publishing Co., 1974); David O. Moberg, "Fundamentalists and Evangelicals in Society," in David F. Wells and John D. Woodridge, eds., *The Evangelicals: What They Believe, Who They Are, Where They Are Changing* (Nashville, Abingdon Press, 1975), p. 161.

9. Author interview with Babatunda A. Agiri (Department of History, University of Lagos), Jan. 10, 1990; *New York Times,* Oct. 12, 1988, p. 1 (as Pope John Paul II addresses the European Parliament in Strasbourg, the Reverend Ian Paisley attacks him as Antichrist); Christopher Hill, *Antichrist in Seventeenth-Century England* (London, Oxford University Press, 1971), p. 175 (inexplicably overlooking North America, Hill says, "Northern Ireland is one of the few places in the world where Antichrist is still alive today"); Joan Spielholz to author, Jan. 10, 1990 (Antichrist belief in Greece).

10. "Enlarged Summer TV Schedule," *Bible Prophecy News* (Charles R. Taylor), Apr.-May-June 1988, p. 12; Richard Ostling, "Evangelical Publishing and Broadcasting," in Marsden, *Evangelicalism and Modern America,* pp. 49, 52; David Webber and Noah Hutchings, *Computers and the Beast of Revelation* (Shreveport, La., Huntington House, 1986), back cover.

11. William Martin, "Waiting for the End," *Atlantic Monthly,* June 1982, p. 31; Hal Lindsey, *The 1980s: Countdown to Armageddon* (New York, Bantam Books, 1980), front cover and frontispiece; Hunter, *American Evangelicalism,* pp. 56–57; Timothy P. Weber, *Living in the Shadow of the Second Coming: American Premillennialism, 1875–1925* (New York, Oxford University Press, 1979), p. 4; "Prophets of Doom: We're a Leg Up on Armageddon," *Dallas Times Herald,* Sept. 8, 1990, p. 1 (quoting Hal Lindsey on current sales figures of *The Late Great Planet Earth*).

12. Salem Kirban, *Guide to Survival* (Huntington Valley, Pa., Salem Kirban, updated edition, 1978), front cover and title page; Doreen Frick (daughter of Salem Kirban) to author, Sept. 5, 1988; A. Donald Fredlund (publications coordinator, Christian Literature Crusade, Fort Washington, Pa.) to author, Dec. 5, 1988 (Billheimer statistics); author interview with John F. Walvoord, Aug. 8, 1989; "World Is Shaken, and Some Booksellers Rejoice," *New York Times,* Oct. 22, 1990, p. C10.

13. James H. McConkey, *The End of the Age* (Pittsburgh, Silver Publishing Co., 1964; orig. publ. 1918); Alfred H. Burton, *The Failure of Europe Politically and Religiously in the Light of Holy Scripture and Russia's Destiny in the Light of Prophecy* (Oak Park, Ill., Bible Truth Publishers, 7th ed., 1967; orig. publ. 1896); Julianne Booth, *Book of the New Testament for Children* (St. Louis, Concordia Publishing Co., 1981), p. 28; poem reprinted by permission.

14. Ray Walters, "Paperback Talk: Apocalypse," *New York Times Book Review,* Mar. 12, 1978, p. 45; author interview with David Rowe (Word Books), Dec. 26, 1990; "Harper and Row Adds Religious Book Unit," *New York Times,* July 14, 1988.

15. Hunter, *Evangelicalism,* p. 7.

16. "Revelation Seminars" advertisement, *Sacramento Bee,* Apr. 4, 1988; *Update Newswire Alert!* (Hilton Sutton newsletter), Aug. 1988, p. 3. I attended a Seventh-day Adventist–sponsored prophecy seminar at the Sheraton Inn and Conference Center, Madison, Wis., on Mar. 10, 1990.

17. Anis A. Sharrosh, *Jesus, Prophecy, and the Middle East* (Nashville, Thomas Nelson Publishers, 1981), p. 6; Salem Kirban, undated advertising material in author's files; Bible Believers' Evangelistic Association, undated catalog [1990] in author's files.

18. W. Warren Wagar, *Terminal Visions: The Literature of Last Things* (Bloomington, Indiana University Press, 1982), pp. 221–233 (quoted phrase p. 221). See also Frank Kermode, *The Sense of an Ending: Studies in the Theory of Literature* (London, Oxford University Press, 1967), and Lois Parkinson Zamora, *Writing the Apocalypse: Historical Vision in Contemporary U.S. and Latin American Fiction* (New York, Cambridge University Press, 1989).

19. K. E. Snow, "The Seventh Sign," *Entertainment Today* (Los Angeles), Apr. 8, 1988, p. 6; "At the New York Film Festival, the Spirit Is the Focus," *New York Times,* Sept. 20, 1991, pp. B1, B6 (*The Rapture*).

20. Greil Marcus, *Lipstick Traces: A Secret History of the Twentieth Century* (Cambridge, Mass., Harvard University Press, 1989), p. 1 (Sex Pistols); Jean Siberry, "Mimi on the Beach," *No Borders Here* cassette (Duke Street Records, 1984); "Nick Cave Issues Apocalyptic Storm Warnings," *Los Angeles Times,* Mar. 4, 1989, sec. V, p. 1; "Elvis Costello: The Believing Skeptic," Stephen Holden, "The Pop Life," *New York Times,* May 15, 1991, p. B3; Genesis (Phil Collins, Peter Gabriel, Michael Rutherford), "Apocalypse," *Foxtrot* record (Famous Charisma, 1972), lyrics on record jacket; Aphrodite's Child, *666* (Mercury Records, 1972, lyrics by Costas Ferris, music by Vangelis Papathanassiou). My thanks to Nick Hook for sharing with me his undergraduate research paper, "Let's Go to the Apocalypse: The Apocalyptic Idiom in Rock and Roll"

(Macalester College, 1991), which argues persuasively that while rock groups do not offer "a complete and definitive doctrine of apocalypticism," they make "frequent and blatant use of the apocalyptic idiom." See also, for general essays on the apocalyptic vision in secular culture, Lois Parkinson Zamora, ed., *The Apocalyptic Vision in America: Interdisciplinary Essays on Myth and Culture* (Bowling Green, Ohio, Bowling Green University Popular Press, 1982).

21. "Christian Pop Music Is Gathering Converts," *New York Times,* Dec. 1, 1987, p. 24.

22. *Sing Out,* 22, no. 2 (Mar.-Apr. 1973); "Chicagoland Gospel Fest," WGN-Chicago broadcast, Oct. 1, 1989 (Calvin Bridges); Bob Keating, "Head for the Hills," *Travel and Leisure,* June 1990, p. E10.

23. *Los Angeles Times,* Nov. 14, 1987 (San Pedro Oriental Rugs advertisement); "Amazing All-New Bible Prophecies," *National Examiner,* Aug. 4, 1987; "Just Discovered: New Bible Cures and Predictions," *Sun* (supermarket tabloid), June 27, 1989.

24. Richard Misrach, *Desert Cantos* (Albuquerque, University of New Mexico Press, 1987); "Robert Longo Challenges Image of Modern Times at MCA," *Daily Cardinal* (University of Wisconsin), Feb. 19, 1990, p. 4; Daniel Rosenfeld, "New Visions of the Apocalypse" (exhibit catalog, Providence, Museum of the Rhode Island School of Design [1988]), p. 2.

25. Wilbur M. Smith, introduction to Oswald J. Smith, *When the King Comes Back* (Wheaton, Ill., Sword of the Lord Publishers, [ca. 1953]), p. 3; Herman A. Hoyt, introduction to Elsa Raud, *Introduction to Prophecy* (Findlay, Ohio, Dunham Publishing Co., 1960), n.p.

26. Timothy P. Weber, *The Future Explored* (Wheaton, Ill., Victor Books, 1978), p. 9; Stanley A. Ellisen, *Biography of a Great Planet* (Wheaton, Ill., Tyndale House Publishers, 1975), p. 9; William Griffin, ed., *Endtime: The Doomsday Catalog* (New York, Collier Books, 1979), p. xviii; Martin, "Waiting for the End." See also Millard J. Erickson, *Contemporary Options in Eschatology: A Study of the Millennium* (Grand Rapids, Baker Book House, 1977), p. 140.

27. Gary Wilburn, "The Doomsday Chic," *Christianity Today,* 22 (Jan. 27, 1978); Samuel Allen Creed, "Hot-Line Prophecy," ibid., 25 (Dec. 11, 1981), 28; Bernard M. Archer, "Prophecy Panic!" *Eternity,* Jan. 1975, p. 49; Michael Barkun, "Divided Apocalypse: Thinking about the End in Contemporary America," *Soundings,* 66, no. 3 (Fall 1983), 257.

28. The Reverend Les Krober (Wenatchee Free Methodist Church, Wenatchee, Wash.), conversation with author, June 23, 1990.

29. R. Stephen Humphreys, conversation with author, Apr. 11, 1990; author interview with Kim Little, Nov. 5, 1990; William V. Trollinger to

author, Oct. 1, 1990; "Larry King's Open-Phone America," Cable News Network, Oct. 18, 1989.

30. Emily Rosenberg (Macalester College) to author, Jan. 29, 1990; "Horicon Chief Sends Back License Plate," *Horicon* [Wis.] *Reporter,* Feb. 15, 1990; Mark Pittenger to author, Aug. 22, 1989.

31. Leonard I. Sweet, "Millennialism in America: Recent Studies," *Theological Studies,* 40 (Sept. 1979), 531.

32. Gallup and Castelli, *The People's Religion,* pp. 26, 61; George Gallup, Jr., *The Gallup Poll: Public Opinion, 1986* (Wilmington, Del., Scholarly Resources, 1987), p. 236. A 1991 study found that over half the population of Mississippi, Alabama, and Georgia were Baptists, with nearly as high a proportion in other southern states, compared to 19 percent nationwide. "Portrait of Religion in U.S. Holds Dozens of Surprises," *New York Times,* Apr. 10, 1991, pp. 1, 11.

33. "Portrait of Religion in U.S.," pp. 1, 11; Gallup and Castelli, *The People's Religion,* p. 66.

34. Marlene Tufts, "Snatched Away before the Bomb: Rapture Believers in the 1980s," Ph.D. dissertation, University of Hawaii, 1985.

35. Hunter, *American Evangelicalism,* pp. 53 (quoted passage), 54; idem, *Evangelicalism: The Coming Generation,* p. 11; Moberg, "Fundamentalists and Evangelicals in Society," p. 149.

36. Gallup and Castelli, *The People's Religion,* pp. 58, 61, 63; Hunter, *American Evangelicalism,* pp. 50, 51, 58–60. Gallup and Castelli report (p. 61) that 44 percent of blacks and 29 percent of whites believe the Bible to be literally true.

37. Gallup and Castelli, *The People's Religion,* p. 265.

38. Marjorie Reeves, *The Influence of Prophecy in the Later Middle Ages: A Study in Joachimism* (Oxford, Clarendon Press, 1969), p. 508; Hill, *Antichrist in Seventeenth-Century England,* p. 159.

39. Timothy L. Smith, *Revivalism and Social Reform: American Protestantism on the Eve of the Civil War* (New York, Harper and Row, 1957); Marsden, *Evangelicalism and Modern America;* idem, *Fundamentalism and American Culture: The Shaping of Twentieth-Century Evangelicalism, 1870–1925* (New York, Oxford University Press, 1980); Ernest Sandeen, *The Roots of Fundamentalism: British and American Millenarianism, 1800–1930* (Chicago, University of Chicago Press, 1970); Robert Mapes Anderson, *Vision of the Disinherited: The Making of American Pentecostalism* (New York, Oxford University Press, 1979); Weber, *Living in the Shadow of the Second Coming;* Nathan O. Hatch, *The Democratization of American Christianity* (New Haven, Yale University Press, 1989), esp. pp. 210–219; Joel A. Carpenter, "From Fundamentalism to the New Evangelical Coalition," in Marsden, *Evangelicalism and Modern America,* pp. 3–16; idem,

"Fundamentalist Institutions and the Rise of Evangelical Protestantism, 1929–1942," *Church History,* 49 (Mar. 1980), 62–75; Mark A. Noll, *Between Faith and Criticism: Evangelical Scholarship and the Bible* (San Francisco, Harper and Row, 1987); R. Laurence Moore, *Religious Outsiders and the Making of Americans* (New York, Oxford University Press, 1986); William Vance Trollinger, Jr., *God's Empire: William Bell Riley and Midwestern Fundamentalism* (Madison, University of Wisconsin Press, 1990). The Institute for the Study of American Evangelicals at Wheaton College, Wheaton, Ill., with its publication and conference program, also is helping to compensate for this scholarly neglect.

40. Barkun has written "Divided Apocalypse"; *Disaster and the Millennium* (New Haven, Yale University Press, 1974), esp. chap. 6, pp. 166–211; "Racist Apocalypse: Millennialism on the Far Right," *American Studies,* 31 (1990), 121–140; and "Nuclear War and Millenarian Symbols: Premillennialists Confront the Bomb," paper presented at the annual meeting of the Society for the Scientific Study of Religion, Savannah, Oct. 25–27, 1985.

41. "Gorby the Antichrist," *Harper's Magazine,* Jan. 1990, pp. 24, 26; "The Day Before" (extract from Jerry Falwell sermon on the end of the world), ibid., July 1984, p. 17; "The Boom in Doom," *Newsweek,* Jan. 10, 1977, p. 49; "Reckoning with Armageddon," *New York Times* editorial, Oct. 25, 1984.

42. A. G. Mojtabai, *Blessed Assurance: At Home with the Bomb in Amarillo, Texas* (Boston, Houghton Mifflin Co., 1986); Grace Halsell, *Prophecy and Politics: Militant Evangelists on the Road to Nuclear War* (Westport, Conn., Lawrence Hill and Co., 1986).

43. Hill, *Antichrist in Seventeenth-Century England,* p. 177.

1. Origins of the Apocalyptic

1. Isidore Singer, ed., *The Jewish Encyclopedia,* I (New York, KTAV Publishing House, [1901]), 672 ("Apocalypse"); Paul J. Alexander, *The Byzantine Apocalyptic Tradition,* ed. and intro. Dorothy deF. Abrahamse (Berkeley, University of California Press, 1985); Bernard McGinn, "Early Apocalypticism: The Ongoing Debate," in C. A. Patrides and Joseph Wittreich, eds., *The Apocalypse in English Renaissance Thought and Literature* (Manchester, Manchester University Press, 1984), p. 13; John J. Collins, *The Apocalyptic Imagination: An Introduction to the Jewish Matrix of Christianity* (New York, Crossroads Publishing Co., 1984), pp. 14, 21–28, 80; T. F. Glasson, *The Revelation of John* (Cambridge, Cambridge University Press, 1965), p. 13; John M. Court, *Myth and History in the Book of Revelation* (London, SPCK, 1979), p. 124. See also,

for general discussions of the origins of the apocalyptic genre: Paul D. Hanson, *The Dawn of Apocalyptic* (Philadelphia, Fortress Press, 1975); Christopher Rowland, *The Open Heaven: A Study of Apocalyptic in Judaism and Early Christianity* (New York, Crossroads Publishing Co., 1982).

2. "Hesiod's Works and Days" in *Hesiod: The Homeric Hymns and Homerica* (Loeb Classical Library, Cambridge, Mass., Harvard University Press, 1914), pp. 11–17 (quoted passage p. 17); Collins, *Apocalyptic Imagination,* p. 74.

3. "An Oracular Dream Concerning Ashurbanipal," in James B. Pritchard, ed., *Ancient Near Eastern Texts Relating to the Old Testament* (Princeton, Princeton University Press, 1955), pp. 451–452.

4. Ruth H. Bloch, *Visionary Republic: Millennial Themes in American Thought, 1756–1800* (New York, Columbia University Press, 1985), p. xi; Singer, *Jewish Encyclopedia,* I, 673–674 ("Apocalypse"); David Noel Freedman, "The Flowering of Apocalyptic," *Journal for Theology and the Church,* 6 (1969), 166; Collins, *Apocalyptic Imagination,* pp. 2–8; Rowland, *Open Heaven,* p. 15.

5. Singer, *Jewish Encyclopedia,* I, 672 ("Apocalypse"); Collins, *Apocalyptic Imagination,* p. 30.

6. Hanson, *Dawn of Apocalyptic.* See also Collins, *Apocalyptic Imagination,* p. 19.

7. Collins, *Apocalyptic Imagination,* pp. 4 (quoted passage), 6, 30. For another (similar) definition, see Rowland, *Open Heaven,* p. 21.

8. Collins, *Apocalyptic Imagination,* pp. 18, 29; Freedman, "Flowering of Apocalyptic," p. 173; McGinn, "Early Apocalypticism," p. 15.

9. H. H. Ben-Sasson, ed., *A History of the Jewish People* (Cambridge, Mass., Harvard University Press, 1976), pp. 152–158.

10. Ibid., pp. 162–163; "'Why Will Ye Die, O House of Israel?': Introduction to Ezekiel," *The Westminster Study Edition of the Holy Bible* (Philadelphia, Westminster Press, 1948), pp. 1162–65.

11. G. A. Cooke, *A Critical and Exegetical Commentary on the Book of Ezekiel* (Edinburgh, T. and T. Clarke, 1936), p. 407.

12. Ben-Sasson, *History of the Jewish People,* pp. 202–210; Emil G. Kraeling, *Rand McNally Bible Atlas* (New York, Rand McNally and Co., 1956), p. 346; Singer, *Jewish Encyclopedia,* I, 80–81 ("Abomination of Desolation"), 634–635 ("Antiochus IV, Epiphanes"). H. H. Rowley, *The Relevance of Apocalyptic* (London, Athlone, 1944; reprinted Greenwood, S.C., Attic, 1980), emphasizes the role of the Book of Daniel in the emergence of apocalypse as a distinct genre.

13. Pritchard, *Ancient Near Eastern Texts Relating to the Old Testament,* p. 149; Shemaryahu Talmon, "Daniel," in Robert Alter and Frank Kermode,

eds., *The Literary Guide to the Bible* (Cambridge, Mass., Harvard University Press, 1987), p. 345; Collins, *Apocalyptic Imagination,* pp. 69, 80.

14. Collins, *Apocalyptic Imagination,* pp. 5, 68–92, passim; McGinn, "Early Apocalypticism," pp. 8–9; Freedman, "Flowering of Apocalyptic," p. 168.

15. Collins, *Apocalyptic Imagination,* pp. 78, 87.

16. Ibid., pp. 7, 70, 77, 88, 91; Rowland, *Open Heaven,* p. 13.

17. Collins, *Apocalyptic Imagination,* p. 90.

18. Dan. 11:33.

19. Ben-Sasson, *History of the Jewish People,* pp. 239–260, 296–303; Singer, *Jewish Encyclopedia,* I, 673–674 ("Apocalypse"); McGinn, "Early Apocalypticism," p. 9; Rowland, *Open Heaven,* p. 9; Collins, *Apocalyptic Imagination,* p. 29.

20. Ben-Sasson, *History of the Jewish People,* pp. 272–274; Moshe Pearlman, *The Dead Sea Scrolls in the Shrine of the Book* (Jerusalem, Israel Museum, 1988), pp. 26–30; Freedman, "Flowering of Apocalyptic," pp. 170–172; Rowland, *Open Heaven,* p. 16.

21. Pearlman, *The Dead Sea Scrolls,* pp. 50, 60; Freedman, "Flowering of Apocalyptic," pp. 166, 172; Klaus Koch, *The Rediscovery of Apocalyptic* (London, SCM Press, 1972), p. 20; Bernard McGinn to author, Oct. 30, 1991.

22. R. H. Charles, *Eschatology: The Doctrine of the Future in Israel, Judaism, and Christianity* (New York, Schocken Books, 1963; orig. publ. 1899); Freedman, "Flowering of Apocalyptic," p. 167. An early example of the historical-critical approach to biblical apocalyptic literature, cited by Collins in *Apocalyptic Imagination* (p. 2), is Friedrich Lücke, *Versuch einer vollständigen Einleitung in die Offenbarung Johannis und in die gesamte apokalyptische Literatur* (Bonn, Weber, 1832).

23. Koch, *Rediscovery of Apocalyptic;* Ernst Käsemann, "The Beginnings of Christian Theology," *Journal for Theology and the Church,* 6 (1969), 17–46 (quoted passage p. 40); McGinn, "Early Apocalypticism," pp. 17–31, esp. pp. 19, 30. See also Court, *Myth and History in the Book of Revelation,* p. 163; Collins, *Apocalyptic Imagination,* pp. 1, 206; Rowland, *Open Heaven,* p. 447.

24. I Thess. 5:1–11; II Thess. 2:1–12; Robert Jewett, *The Thessalonian Correspondence: Pauline Rhetoric and Millenarian Piety* (Philadelphia, Fortress Press, 1986), pp. 161–178; II Pet. 3:10; Rowland, *Open Heaven,* pp. 352, 386–392; McGinn, "Early Apocalypticism," p. 20; F. L. Cross, ed., *The Oxford Dictionary of the Christian Church* (London, Oxford University Press, 1957), p. 1051 ("Peter, Epistle of St."); *The Anchor Bible: The Epistles of James, Peter, and Jude,* intro., trans., and notes Bo Reicke (Garden City, N.Y., Doubleday & Co., 1964), p. 144 (90 A.D. dating of II Peter).

25. I John 2:18; Cross, *Oxford Dictionary of the Christian Church*, pp. 730–731 ("John, Epistles of St.").
26. Cross, *Oxford Dictionary of the Christian Church*, pp. 859–860 ("Mark, Gospel of St."); McGinn, "Early Apocalypticism," pp. 20–21.
27. Court, *Myth and History in the Book of Revelation*, p. 133; Rowland, *Open Heaven*, pp. 403–404; McGinn, "Early Apocalypticism," p. 22; Cross, *Oxford Dictionary of the Christian Church*, p. 414 ("Domitian, Titus Flavius"); Glasson, *Revelation of John*, pp. 8–9, 13.
28. Rev. 4:1. To avoid excessive annotation I have not provided a note for each biblical quotation in the following section. My summary parallels the sequence of the text of Revelation, with chapter references provided from time to time to help readers orient themselves.
29. Quoted in Bernard McGinn, "Revelation," in Alter and Kermode, *Literary Guide to the Bible*, p. 523.
30. Ibid., pp. 523–524; Glasson, *The Revelation of John*, p. 10, makes a similar point.
31. Court, *Myth and History in the Book of Revelation*, pp. 125–138, 164.
32. Cross, *Dictionary of the Christian Church*, p. 945 ("Nero, Claudius"); *The Annals of Tacitus*, XLIV (Loeb Classical Library, Tacitus IV, Cambridge, Mass., Harvard University Press, 1937), pp. 283–284; Glasson, *The Revelation of John*, pp. 6–9, 79; Court, *Myth and History in the Book of Revelation*, pp. 125–136; Rowland, *Open Heaven*, pp. 403–407; McGinn, "Early Apocalypticism," p. 28; Rev. 17:1,9; Rev. 18.
33. Court, *Myth and History in the Book of Revelation*, pp. 133–136; Rev. 13:3 ("And I saw one of his heads as it were wounded to death; and his deadly wound was healed: and all the world wondered after the beast"); Rev. 17:8,10.
34. *The Oxford Annotated Bible with the Apocrypha*, ed. Herbert G. May and Bruce M. Metzger (New York, Oxford University Press, 1965), p. 1503; Glasson, *The Revelation of John*, p. 83; Singer, *Jewish Encyclopedia*, V, 589–592 ("Gematria").
35. Adela Yarbro Collins, *The Combat Myth in the Book of Revelation* (Missoula, Mont., Scholars Press for *Harvard Theological Review*, 1976), pp. 2, 3. John Court adopts a somewhat similar position in *Myth and History in the Book of Revelation*, pp. 164–166, although he emphasizes more heavily the work's immediate historical context.
36. Court, *Myth and History in the Book of Revelation*, p. 164. On this point see also Collins, *Apocalyptic Imagination*, p. 18, and Rowland, *Open Heaven*, p. 27.
37. Court, *Myth and History in the Book of Revelation*, pp. 130, 153.
38. Walter Schmithals, *The Apocalyptic Movement: Introduction and Interpretation* (Nashville, Abingdon Press, 1975; trans. from the German orig. publ. 1973), p. 33; Ernest Lee Tuveson, "The Millenarian Structure of

The Communist Manifesto," in C. A. Patrides and Joseph Wittreich, eds., *The Apocalypse in English Renaissance Thought and Literature* (Manchester, Manchester University Press, 1984), pp. 323–341.

39. Schmithals, *Apocalyptic Movement,* chap. 3, pp. 50–67; Collins, *Apocalyptic Imagination,* pp. 11–14.

2. Rhythms of Prophecy Belief

1. Norman Cohn, *The Pursuit of the Millennium: Revolutionary Millenarians and Mystical Anarchists of the Middle Ages* (London, Temple Smith, rev. ed., 1970), p. 25; F. L. Cross, ed., *The Oxford Dictionary of the Christian Church* (London, Oxford University Press, 1958), pp. 918–919 ("Montanism"); Christopher Rowland, *The Open Heaven: A Study of Apocalyptic in Judaism and Early Christianity* (New York, Crossroads, 1982), pp. 392–396.

2. Cross, *Oxford Dictionary of the Christian Church,* pp. 918–919, 701–702 ("Irenaeus"), 1334–35 ("Tertullian, Quintus Septimius"), 1418–19 ("Victorinus, St."); W. H. C. Frend, *The Rise of Christianity* (Philadelphia, Fortress Press, 1984), pp. 244 (Irenaeus), 348–351 (Tertullian); *A Select Library of Nicene and Post-Nicene Fathers of the Christian Church, Second Series,* ed. Philip Schaff and Henry Wace (reprinted Grand Rapids, Wm. B. Eerdman's Publishing Co., 1982), I, 219n6 (Irenaeus and Montanism); Shirley Jackson Case, *The Millennial Hope: A Phase of War-Time Thinking* (Chicago, University of Chicago Press, 1918), pp. 162–167; Millard J. Erickson, *Contemporary Options in Eschatology: A Study of the Millennium* (Grand Rapids, Baker Book House, 1977), p. 95; Peter Toon, Introduction to Toon, ed., *Puritans, the Millennium, and the Future of Israel: Puritan Eschatology, 1600–1660* (Cambridge, James Clark and Co., 1970), p. 12 ("hallowed seventh day"); Johannes Quasten, *Patrology,* vol. 2, *The Ante-Nicene Literature after Irenaeus* (Utrecht, Spectrum Publishers, 1964), pp. 411–413 (Victorinus); *Apocalyptic Spirituality: Treatises and Letters of Lactantius, Adso of Montier-en-der, Joachim of Fiore, the Franciscan Spirituals, Savonarola,* trans. and intro. Bernard McGinn (New York, Paulist Press, 1979), 17–24 (Irenaeus and Lactantius), 25–80 (selections from Lactantius' *Divine Institutes*). Early-church historians often refer to millennialism as "chiliasm," after the Greek word for a thousand. For simplicity's sake, I use "millennialism" throughout.

3. Frend, *Rise of Christianity,* pp. 194–228; Cross, *Oxford Dictionary of the Christian Church,* pp. 564–565 ("Gnosticism"), 991–993 ("Origen"); Cohn, *Pursuit of the Millennium,* p. 290; Bernard McGinn, "Revelation," in Robert Alter and Frank Kermode, eds., *The Literary Guide to the Bible* (Cambridge, Mass., Harvard University Press, 1987), p. 530; Case,

Millennial Hope, pp. 172–178; Donald Guthrie, *The Relevance of John's Apocalypse* (Grand Rapids, Wm. B. Eerdman's Publishing Co., 1987), p. 13.

4. Joseph Wilson Trigg, *Origen: The Bible and Philosophy in the Third-Century Church* (Atlanta, John Knox Press, 1983), pp. 53–54; Case, *Millennial Hope,* p. 174 (Origen quote); Cross, *Oxford Dictionary of the Christian Church,* p. 992; Eusebius, *Church History,* chap. 8, in Schaff and Wace, *Select Library of Nicene and Post-Nicene Fathers,* I, 254–255.

5. Cross, *Dictionary of the Christian Church,* pp. 334–335 ("Constantine the Great").

6. Peter Brown, *Augustine of Hippo: A Biography* (Berkeley, University of California Press, 1969), pp. 303–325 (quoted phrases pp. 314, 319); Case, *Millennial Hope,* p. 182 ("community of unbelievers"); Toon, Introduction, pp. 14–17; McGinn, "Revelation," p. 528; Bernard McGinn, "Early Apocalypticism: The Ongoing Debate," in C. A. Patrides and Joseph Wittreich, eds., *The Apocalypse in English Renaissance Thought and Literature* (Manchester, Manchester University Press, 1984), pp. 28–29.

7. Brown, *Augustine of Hippo,* p. 315.

8. Ibid., pp. 317–318.

9. Toon, Introduction, pp. 14, 17; Quaston, *Patrology,* II, 411–412; Cohn, *Pursuit of the Millennium,* p. 29; McGinn, "Early Apocalypticism," p. 28; Katharine R. Firth, *The Apocalyptic Tradition in Reformation Britain, 1530–1645* (Oxford, Oxford University Press, 1979), p. 8.

10. Richard Erdoes, *A.D. 1000: Living on the Brink of the Apocalypse* (New York, Harper and Row, 1988); Cohn, *Pursuit of the Millennium,* p. 30. Although Cohn, whose purpose was to trace the ideological origins of Nazi ideology, overemphasizes the outer fringes of medieval apocalypticism, his work is carefully researched and, within its limits, useful.

11. Cross, *Oxford Dictionary of the Christian Church,* p. 935 ("Mystery Plays"). On the Sibylline oracles, see Christopher Rowland, *Open Heaven: A Study of Apocalyptic in Judaism and Early Christianity* (New York, Crossroads, 1982), p. 20; McGinn, *Apocalyptic Spirituality,* p. 21; Cohn, *Pursuit of the Millennium,* pp. 30–35; Marjorie Reeves, *The Influence of Prophecy in the Later Middle Ages: A Study in Joachimism* (Oxford, Clarendon Press, 1969), pp. 299–300. See also Bernard McGinn, *Visions of the End: Apocalyptic Traditions in the Middle Ages* (New York, Columbia University Press, 1979); idem, *Apocalyptic Spirituality,* pp. 1–16; idem, "Apocalypticism in the Middle Ages: An Historiographical Sketch," *Medieval Studies,* 37 (1975), 252–286; Richard K. Emmerson, *Antichrist in the Middle Ages: A Study of Medieval Apocalyptic Art and Literature* (Seattle, University of Washington Press, 1981); and Sylvia

Thrupp, ed., *Millennial Dreams in Action: Essays in Comparative Study* (The Hague, Mouton, 1962).

12. Barbara Newman, "Hildegard of Bingen: Visions and Validation," *Church History,* 54 (1985), 163–175; Kent Kraft, "The German Visionary: Hildegard of Bingen," in Katherina M. Wilson, ed., *Medieval Women Writers* (Athens, University of Georgia Press, 1984), pp. 109–130; Reeves, *Prophecy in the Later Middle Ages,* pp. 302 (quoted passage), 314–317.

13. *Illuminations of Hildegard of Bingen,* text by Hildegard of Bingen with commentary by Matthew Fox (Santa Fe, Bear and Co., 1985), p. 86; J. Paul Getty Museum, "Handbook of the Collections" (Malibu, Calif., J. Paul Getty Museum, 1986), p. 71; "The End of the World in Brilliant Technicolor," *New York Times,* May 26, 1991, p. H29 (Getty exhibit); Tony Campbell, *Early Maps* (New York, Abbeville Press, 1981), p. 10; J. B. Harley and David Woodward, eds., *Cartography in Prehistoric, Ancient, and Medieval Europe and the Mediterranean* (Chicago, University of Chicago Press), p. 333; *The Columbia Encyclopedia,* ed. William Bridgwater and Seymour Kurtz (New York, Columbia University Press, 1963), p. 608 ("Dürer, Albrecht"). My thanks to Michael Kammen for calling my attention to the Angers tapestries.

14. Reeves, *Prophecy in the Later Middle Ages,* pp. 6–8; Cohn, *Pursuit of the Millennium,* pp. 61–70; Alexander Shapiro, "Jews and Christians in the Period of the Crusades: A Commentary on the First Holocaust," *Journal of Ecumenical Studies,* 9 (1972), 725–749.

15. Christopher Hill, *Antichrist in Seventeenth-Century England* (London, Oxford University Press, 1971), p. 6; Cohn, *Pursuit of the Millennium,* p. 34.

16. Reeves, *Prophecy in the Later Middle Ages,* pp. 8, 16–27; McGinn, *Apocalyptic Spirituality,* pp. 97–112 (introductory essay on Joachim), and 113–148 (selections from Joachim's writings); Cohn, *Pursuit of the Millennium,* pp. 108–110; McGinn, "Revelation," pp. 528 (quoted passage), 532–534. See also Bernard McGinn, *The Calabrian Abbot: Joachim of Fiore in the History of Western Thought* (New York, Macmillan, 1985).

17. McGinn, "Revelation," p. 532; Reeves, *Prophecy in the Later Middle Ages,* pp. 28 (papal encouragement), 32–33 (condemnation by Fourth Lateran Council); Cohn, *Pursuit of the Millennium,* pp. 108–110.

18. Cohn, *Pursuit of the Millennium,* pp. 110–111; McGinn, *Apocalyptic Spirituality,* pp. 149–158 (introduction to Spiritual Franciscans, and focus on the year 1260, p. 152), 159–181 (excerpts from Spiritual Franciscans' writings). Reeves, *Prophecy in the Later Middle Ages,* pt. 2, pp. 133–292, discusses this process in detail.

19. McGinn, "Revelation," p. 533; Heiko A. Oberman, "The Stubborn Jews: Timing the Escalation of Antisemitism in Late Medieval Europe," Leo Baeck Institute, *Yearbook,* 34 (1989), xi–xxv.

20. Reeves, *Prophecy in the Later Middle Ages,* pp. 242–250 (quoted phrase p. 242); Cohn, *Pursuit of the Millennium,* p. 81.

21. Cohn, *Pursuit of the Millennium,* pp. 111–118; Reeves, *Prophecy in the Later Middle Ages,* pp. 104, 123–124, 126, 166, 307–313, 322 (on Antichrist).

22. Cohn, *Pursuit of the Millennium,* p. 117.

23. Ibid., pp. 119–126 (quoted passage p. 121).

24. Ibid., pp. 210–212; Cross, *Oxford Dictionary of the Christian Church,* pp. 1318–19 ("Taborites"). See also F. C. Heymann, *John Zizka and the Hussite Revolution* (Princeton, Princeton University Press, 1955) and Howard Kaminsky, *A History of the Hussite Revolution* (Berkeley, University of California Press, 1967).

25. Cohn, *Pursuit of the Millennium,* pp. 211–214 (quoted passage p. 211).

26. Ibid., pp. 212–222 (quoted passage p. 212); Case, *Millennial Hope,* p. 188.

27. Robert E. Lerner, "The Black Death and Western European Eschatological Mentalities," *American Historical Review,* 86 (June 1981), 533–552; Pauline Moffitt Watts, "Prophecy and Discovery: On the Spiritual Origins of Christopher Columbus's 'Enterprise of the Indies,'" ibid., 90 (Feb. 1985), 73–102 (quoted phrase p. 74); Toon, Introduction, p. 12 (Irenaeus' Antichrist teaching); McGinn, *Apocalyptic Spirituality,* pp. 11–12.

28. From a vast literature, useful points of entry are Roland H. Bainton, *Here I Stand: A Life of Martin Luther* (New York, Abingdon Press, 1950); Bernard Lohse, *Martin Luther: An Introduction to His Life and Writings* (Philadelphia, Fortress Press, 1986); A. G. Dickens and John M. Tonkin, *The Reformation in Historical Thought* (Cambridge, Mass., Harvard University Press, 1985); Peter J. Klassen, *The Reformation: Change and Stability* (St. Louis, Forum Press, 1980); Heiko O. Oberman, *Masters of the Reformation: The Emergence of a New Intellectual Climate in Europe* (Cambridge, Mass., Harvard University Press, 1981). A useful concise history of the Reformation is Felix Gilbert et al., *The Norton History of Modern Europe* (New York, W. W. Norton, 1970), pp. 126–175.

29. François Wendel, *Calvin: The Origins and Development of His Religious Thought,* trans. Philip Mairet (New York, Harper and Row, 1963); William J. Bouwsma, *John Calvin: A Sixteenth-Century Portrait* (New York, Oxford University Press, 1988); G. R. Potter, *Zwingli* (New York, Cambridge University Press, 1976); W. P. Stephens, *The Theology of*

Huldrych Zwingli (New York, Oxford University Press, 1986); Robert Kingdon, "Calvin, John," *Encyclopedia Britannica* (Chicago, Encyclopedia Britannica, 15th ed., 1974), IV, 671–676.

30. A. G. Dickens, *The English Reformation* (London, B. T. Botsford, 1964).

31. Peter Blickle, *The Revolution of 1525: The German Peasants' War from a New Perspective,* trans. Thomas A. Brady, Jr., and H. C. Erik Midelfort (Baltimore, Johns Hopkins University Press, 1981); Janos Bak, ed., *The German Peasant War of 1525* (London, F. Cass, 1976); Cohn, *Pursuit of the Millennium,* pp. 245–249, 254, 257; Gilbert et al., *Norton History of Modern Europe,* pp. 153–156.

32. Müntzer continues to attract the attention of historians; he was the subject of five new books in 1989 alone. See James M. Stayer, "Thomas Müntzer in 1989: A Review Essay," *Sixteenth-Century Journal,* 21, no. 4 (Winter 1990), 655–670, esp. pp. 667–669 on Müntzer's apocalypticism. On Müntzer's theology see also Gunter Vogel, *Thomas Müntzer* (Berlin, Dietz Verlag, 1989), and W[erner] P[ackull], "Müntzer, Thomas," in *The Mennonite Encyclopedia,* ed. Cornelius J. Dyck and Dennis D. Martin (Scottdale, Pa., Herald Press, 1990), V, 607–609. See also Cohn, *Pursuit of the Millennium,* pp. 235–250.

33. W[alter] K[lassen], "Apocalypticism," *Mennonite Encyclopedia,* V, 28–30, summarizes recent scholarship on Anabaptist apocalypticism and Joachian influences (quoted passages p. 29). See also, for Melchior Hoffmann entries, ibid., II, 778–785, and V, 384–385. For earlier studies see Harold S. Bender, "The Anabaptist Vision," *Church History,* 13 (Mar. 1944), 3–24, and Guy F. Hershberger, ed., *The Recovery of the Anabaptist Vision* (Scottdale, Pa., Herald Press, 1957), which contains a number of valuable essays. See also Cohn, *Pursuit of the Millennium,* pp. 252–254, 258–260; Cross, *Oxford Dictionary of the Christian Church,* pp. 46 ("Anabaptists"), 644 ("Hoffmann, Melchior").

34. James M. Stayer, "The Historical Discussion of Anabaptist Münster 450 Years Later," *Mennonite Quarterly Review,* 60 (July 1986), 261–288, esp. p. 263; *Mennonite Encyclopedia,* III, 777–783 ("Münster Anabaptists"); V, 606–607 ("Münster Anabaptists"); Cohn, *Pursuit of the Millennium,* pp. 250–262.

35. Cohn, *Pursuit of the Millennium,* pp. 262–279 (quoted passage p. 272).

36. Ibid., pp. 279–280.

37. Martin Luther, *Against the Robbing and Murdering Hordes of Peasants* (1525), *Works of Martin Luther* (Philadelphia, 1931), IV, 249; Cross, *Oxford History of the Christian Church,* pp. 1491–1492 ("Zwingli, Ulrich"); *The New Cambridge Modern History,* vol. 2, *The Reformation,* ed. G. R.

Elton (Cambridge, Cambridge University Press, 1958), p. 129 (Calvin's reaction). For later manifestations of Anabaptist radicalism see Gary K. Waite, "From Apocalyptic Crusaders to Anabaptist Terrorists; Anabaptist Radicalism after Münster, 1535–1544," *Archiv für Reformationsgeschichte,* 80 (1989), 173–192.

38. Firth, *Apocalyptic Tradition in Reformation Britain,* pp. 9–14; Toon, Introduction, p. 19; McGinn, "Revelation," p. 529; Walter Schmithals, *The Apocalyptic Movement: Introduction and Interpretation* (Nashville, Abingdon Press, 1975), p. 224; T. F. Glasson, *The Revelation of John* (Cambridge, Cambridge University Press, 1965), p. 6; Erickson, *Contemporary Options in Eschatology,* p. 76; John Calvin, *A Commentary on Daniel* (Edinburgh, Banner of Truth Trust, 1966; 1st Latin ed. 1561, 1st English ed. 1570), pp. 24–27. Of the "little horn" of Dan. 7:8, Calvin wrote: "Some twist this to mean the Pope, and others the Turk; but neither opinion seem to me probable . . . I have no doubt that *the little horn* relates to Julius Caesar and the other Caesars who succeeded him." *Commentary on Daniel,* pp. 26–27.

39. Firth, *Apocalyptic Tradition in Reformation Britain,* pp. 11, 13; Hill, *Antichrist in Seventeenth-Century England,* pp. 4 (Geneva Bible), 9, 18 (quoted passage); Gilbert et al., *Norton History of Modern Europe,* p. 168, reprints Melchior Lorch's 1545 woodcut of the Pope as a particularly loathsome Antichrist; Cross, *Oxford Dictionary of the Christian Church,* p. 169 ("Bible, English"). Calvin's most explicit identification of the Pope as Antichrist occurs in Book IV, 2.12 of the *Institutes:* "Daniel and Paul had predicted that Antichrist would sit in the temple of God. The head of that cursed and abominable kingdom, in the Western Church, we affirm to be the Pope." John Calvin, *On the Christian Faith: Selections from the Institutes, Commentaries, and Tracts,* ed. and intro. John T. McNeill (Indianapolis, Bobbs-Merrill Co., 1957), p. 104. My thanks to Robert Kingdon, as well as to Bernard McGinn, for helping to clarify my understanding of the reformers' views of Antichrist.

40. Firth, *Apocalyptic Tradition in Reformation Britain,* p. 11. For other references to Islam and the Turk in prophecy writing of this period see John M. Court, *Myth and History in the Book of Revelation* (London, SPCK, 1979), p. 11 (a 1547 commentary by a Louvain University professor); Toon, Introduction, pp. 19–20 (p. 19: "References to the Turkish Empire appear in virtually every Commentary on the Apocalypse of John which was produced by English Puritans, Independents, Presbyterians and Baptists"); idem, "The Latter-Day Glory," in ibid., p. 29; R. G. Clouse, "The Rebirth of Millenarianism," in ibid., p. 58.

41. Glasson, *Revelation of John,* p. 10; Court, *Myth and History in the Book of*

Revelation, pp. 8–9; Loraine Boettner, *The Millennium* (Grand Rapids, Baker Book House, 1957), p. 367; McGinn, "Revelation," p. 538. For interesting comments on the way visitations by the Virgin Mary have functioned in popular Roman Catholicism somewhat as prophecy belief has functioned in popular Protestantism, see Kenneth L. Woodward, "Going to See the Virgin Mary," *New York Times Book Review,* Aug. 11, 1991, p. 22.

42. Firth, *The Apocalyptic Tradition in Reformation Britain,* p. 11; Hill, *Antichrist in Seventeenth-Century England,* pp. 9–25, 28, 40.

43. Hill, *Antichrist in Seventeenth-Century England,* pp. 20, 25, 32 (quoted passage), 33, 185; McGinn, "Revelation," pp. 535–537, esp. p. 536 (Napier); Toon, "Latter-Day Glory," p. 25; Robert G. Clouse, "John Napier and Apocalyptic Thought," *Sixteenth-Century Journal,* 5 (1974), 105–114; *Oxford Companion to English Literature,* ed. Sir Paul Harvey (Oxford, Clarendon Press, 1967), pp. 774–775 ("Spenser, Edmund" entry, which also notes that Spenser's first published verse appeared in a 1569 pamphlet attacking the Pope as Antichrist); William Shakespeare, *King Henry V,* act II, sc. 3, *The Riverside Shakespeare,* ed. G. Blakemore Evans (Boston, Houghton Mifflin Co., 1974), p. 945. For a study of apocalypticism in Shakespeare's later plays, see Cynthia Marshall, *Last Things and Last Plays: Shakespearian Eschatology* (Carbondale, Southern Illinois University Press, 1991).

44. Richard Bauckham, *Tudor Apocalypse: Sixteenth-Century Apocalypticism, Millenarianism, and the English Reformation: From John Bale to John Foxe and Thomas Brightman* (Oxford, Sutton Courtenay Press, [1978?]), p. 11; Hill, *Antichrist in Seventeenth-Century England,* pp. 26 (quoted passage, italics added), 181–182; Clouse, "Rebirth of Millenarianism," pp. 42–45 (Alsted); Toon, Introduction, p. 19; Schmithals, *The Apocalyptic Movement,* p. 224.

45. Firth, *Apocalyptic Tradition in Reformation Britain,* p. 253; Hill, *Antichrist in Seventeenth-Century England,* chaps. 2–3 (pp. 41–145), traces the shift in English Antichrist thinking from the papacy to the domestic sphere; see esp. pp. 43, 53 (quoted passage); Alan Simpson, "Saints in Arms: English Puritanism as Political Utopianism," *Church History,* 23 (1954), 119–131.

46. Hill, *Antichrist in Seventeenth-Century England,* p. 68.

47. Ibid., pp. 66, 135–136.

48. Ibid., p. 61. Jonson also ridiculed prophecy belief in *The Alchemist* (1610), in which one churchman says that another "bears / The visible mark of the Beast in his forehead."

49. Firth, *Apocalyptic Tradition in Reformation Britain,* pp. 252–253; Hill, *Antichrist in Seventeenth-Century England,* pp. 80, 104 (1647 quote), 106

(quoted phrase). On Milton see Hill, ibid., pp. 30, 94, 105; Michael Fixler, *Milton and the Kingdoms of God* (London, Faber and Faber, 1964), pp. 76–106 (chap. 3, pt. 1; p. 102, quote from Milton's 1641 pamphlet *Of Reformation Touching Church Discipline in England*); Austin C. Dobbins, *Milton and the Book of Revelation: The Heavenly Cycle* (Tuscaloosa, University of Alabama Press, 1975), which interprets *Paradise Lost* as a commentary on John's Apocalypse.

50. Hill, *Antichrist in Seventeenth-Century England,* p. 27; McGinn, "Revelation," pp. 536–537; Clouse, "Rebirth of Millenarianism," pp. 56–65; James W. Davidson, *The Logic of Millennial Thought: Eighteenth-Century New England* (New Haven, Yale University Press, 1977), pp. 43–45.

51. Hill, *Antichrist in Seventeenth-Century England,* pp. 107 (Mary Cary quote, which alludes to Joel 2:28: "your sons and your daughters shall prophesy"), 122, 123; B. S. Capp, "Extreme Millenarianism," in Toon, *Puritans, the Millennium and the Future of Israel,* pp. 68–87, esp. pp. 71 (666 identification of Cromwell) and 70 (Aspinwall); Case, *Millennial Hope,* pp. 192–193.

52. Leon Festinger, Henry W. Riecken, Stanley Schachter, *When Prophecy Fails* (Minneapolis, University of Minnesota Press, 1956), p. 9; Robert Middlekauff, *The Mathers: Three Generations of Puritan Intellectuals, 1596–1728* (New York, Oxford University Press, 1971), p. 179; Capp, "Extreme Millenarianism," p. 71 (George Fox comment); McGinn, "Revelation," p. 537 (Voltaire quote); Cross, *Oxford Dictionary of the Christian Church,* p. 1454 ("Whiston, William"); Frank E. Manuel, *The Religion of Isaac Newton* (Oxford, Clarendon Press, 1974); I. B. Cohen, "Newton, Isaac," in Charles Coulston Gillespie, ed., *Dictionary of Scientific Biography* (New York, Charles Scribner's Sons, 1974), pp. 81–83 ("Alchemy, Prophecy, and Theology: Chronology and History"). See also Deborah M. Valenge, "Prophecy and Popular Literature in Eighteenth-Century England," *Journal of Ecclesiastical History,* 29 (1978), 75–92.

53. Hill, *Antichrist in Seventeenth-Century England,* pp. 146, 147 (Bunyan quote), 148 ("onions and garlic"), 158 (Hill quote).

54. Davidson, *Logic of Millennial Thought,* pp. 86–87 (quoted passage p. 87); Perry Miller, "The End of the World," in Miller, *Errand into the Wilderness* (New York, Harper Torchbooks, 1956), pp. 223–226 (quoted passage p. 224); Cross, *Oxford Dictionary of the Christian Church,* p. 268 ("Charterhouse").

55. Miller, "End of the World," pp. 226–230; Davidson, *Logic of Millennial Thought,* p. 87.

56. Miller, "End of the World," pp. 225, 231, 239.

57. Davidson, *Logic of Millennial Thought,* p. 141; Cross, *Oxford Dictionary*

of the Christian Church, p. 1454 ("Whitby, Daniel"); Ruth H. Bloch, *Visionary Republic: Millennial Themes in American Thought, 1756–1800* (New York, Cambridge University Press, 1985), p. 10.

58. Hill, *Antichrist in Seventeenth-Century England,* p. 69; Stephen J. Stein, "Transatlantic Extensions: Apocalyptic in Early New England," in Patrides and Wittreich, *Apocalypse in English Renaissance Thought and Literature,* p. 269 (Davenport quote).

59. Stein, "Transatlantic Extensions," pp. 269–271; J. F. Maclear, "New England and the Fifth Monarchy: The Quest for the Millennium in Early American Puritanism," *William and Mary Quarterly,* ser. 3, 32 (1975), 223–260.

60. Stein, "Transatlantic Extensions," pp. 273 (Stein quote), 274 (Mather quote and King Philip's War); Davidson, *Logic of Millennial Thought,* p. 67 (Sewall quote).

61. Middlekauff, *The Mathers,* pp. 323 (quote), 328, 330, 335, 336, 338; Stein, "Transatlantic Extensions," p. 277; Davidson, *Logic of Millennial Thought,* p. 13.

62. Stein, "Transatlantic Extensions," pp. 278 (*Magnalia* quoted), 281; Middlekauff, *The Mathers,* p. 342 ("Problema Theologicum" quote); Davidson, *Logic of Millennial Thought,* p. 54.

63. Stein, "Transatlantic Extensions," pp. 266 ("Spot of *Earth*" quote), 277 (1709 quote); Middlekauff, *The Mathers,* p. 349 (1726 quote).

64. Davidson, *Logic of Millennial Thought,* p. 62 ("all fulfill'd" quote); Middlekauff, *The Mathers,* pp. 342, 343, 346 (date setting).

65. Stein, "Transatlantic Extensions," p. 281 (Colman quote); Bloch, *Visionary Republic,* p. 13 ("whole Hords of the Vulgar" quote).

66. Stein, "Transatlantic Extensions," pp. 282 ("earnest" quote), 284 (Moorehead quote).

67. Ibid., p. 283; Davidson, *Logic of Millennial Thought,* pp. 16, 17, 152 (significance of year 2000); Miller, "End of the World," pp. 233–234 (quote re Edwards, p. 233); Bloch, *Visionary Republic,* p. 17.

68. Stein, "Transatlantic Extensions," p. 284 (Edwards' *Some Thoughts* quote); Miller, "End of the World," p. 235 ("fire from heaven" quote); Nathan O. Hatch, *The Sacred Cause of Liberty: Republican Thought and the Millennium in Revolutionary New England* (New Haven, Yale University Press, 1977), p. 31; Erickson, *Contemporary Options in Eschatology,* p. 61; Dietrich G. Buss, "Meeting of Heaven and Earth: A Survey and Analysis of the Literature on Millennialism in America, 1965–1985," *Fides et Historia,* 22 (Jan. 1988), 8–9. In the same vein, Edwards wrote in his 1739 sermon series "History of the Work of Redemption" that the spread of Christianity to America was one means "by which divine providence is preparing the way for the future glorious times of the church, when Satan's kingdom shall be overthrown throughout the

whole habitable globe, on every side, and on all its continents." Quoted in Ernest Lee Tuveson, *Redeemer Nation: The Idea of America's Millennial Role* (Chicago, University of Chicago Press, 1968), p. 100.

69. Bloch, *Visionary Republic,* pp. 23–42, passim (Davies quoted p. 40); Stein, "Transatlantic Extensions," p. 287 (*"Scarlet Whore"* quote); Hatch, *Sacred Cause of Liberty,* p. 42 (*"Babylon the great"* quote). See also Davidson, *Logic of Millennial Thought,* p. 204.

70. Hatch, *Sacred Cause of Liberty,* p. 43.

71. Davidson, *Logic of Millennial Thought,* pp. 237 (Lord Bute), 238 (Stamp Act warning); Bloch, *Visionary Republic,* p. 56 (666 allusion). See also Stein, "Transatlantic Extensions," pp. 288–289, and Ruth Bloch, "The Social and Political Base of Millennial Literature in Late-Eighteenth-Century America," *American Quarterly,* 40 (Sept. 1988), 378–396.

72. Bloch, *Visionary Republic,* p. 71 ("grace our happy earth" quote); Davidson, *Logic of Millennial Thought,* p. 248 (Baldwin quote); Hatch, *Sacred Cause of Liberty,* p. 53. See also Catherine L. Albanese, *Sons of the Fathers: The Civil Religion of the American Revolution* (Philadelphia, Temple University Press, 1976), and Christopher M. Beam, "Millennialism and American Nationalism, 1740–1800," *Journal of Presbyterian History,* 54 (1978), 182–199.

73. Tuveson, *Redeemer Nation,* p. 104 (quote from 1771 poem); Davidson, *Logic of Millennial Thought,* pp. 222–223 (1776 address); Stein, "Transatlantic Extensions," pp. 290–291 (1776 address).

74. Hatch, *Sacred Cause of Liberty,* p. 3; Davidson, *Logic of Millennial Thought,* p. 247; Bloch, *Visionary Republic,* pp. xiii, 53, 61.

75. Davidson, *Logic of Millennial Thought,* pp. 214 (Tappan), 237 (Dwight, 1777); Stein, "Transatlantic Extensions," p. 291 (Dwight, 1785); Tuveson, *Redeemer Nation,* p. 107.

76. Hatch, *Sacred Cause of Liberty,* p. 59; Abiel Abbot, *Traits of Resemblance in the People of the United States of America to Ancient Israel* (Haverhill, Mass., 1799), reprinted in *The American Republic and Ancient Israel* (New York, Arno Press, 1977).

77. Abbot, *Traits of Resemblance in the People of the United States of America to Ancient Israel,* p. 6; Samuel Langdon, *The Republic of the Israelites an Example to the American States* (Exeter, N.H., 1788), reprinted in *The American Republic and Ancient Israel,* p. 32.

78. Davidson, *Logic of Millennial Thought,* pp. 61 (Increase Mather), 13, 76 (Cotton Mather); Middlekauff, *The Mathers,* p. 328.

79. Stein, "Transatlantic Extensions," pp. 274–275 (Wigglesworth); Davidson, *Logic of Millennial Thought,* p. 39 (Sewall).

80. Davidson, *Logic of Millennial Thought,* pp. 75, 151 (quoted phrase), 260; Bloch, *Visionary Republic,* p. 18.

81. Thomas Prince, *An Improvement of the Doctrine of Earthquakes* (Boston,

1755), pp. 14, 16; quoted in Davidson, *Logic of Millennial Thought,* p. 107; ibid., p. 200 (Christopher Love); Bloch, *Visionary Republic,* pp. 24–28, 161–163.

82. Bloch, *Visionary Republic,* pp. 119–149 passim, esp. pp. 120–122, 131, 133, 145.

83. Hatch, *Sacred Cause of Liberty,* p. 160; Stein, "Transatlantic Extensions," pp. 286, 293.

84. Samuel Sherwood, *The Church's Flight into the Wilderness* (1776), quoted in Stein, "Transatlantic Extensions," p. 288.

3. The Premillennial Strand

1. James W. Davidson, *The Logic of Millennial Thought: Eighteenth-Century New England* (New Haven, Yale University Press, 1977), pp. 261, 269–270; Stephen D. O'Leary, "'Mine Eyes Have Seen the Glory': The Growth of Premillennial Apocalypticism in Nineteenth-Century America," unpublished, Department of Communication Studies, Northwestern University, 1987, pp. 2–10, on the "postmillennial" component of early-nineteenth-century revivalism; Perry Miller, "The End of the World," in Miller, *Errand into the Wilderness* (New York, Harper and Row, 1964), p. 235. For a taste of the exuberant millennial expectations that saturated early-nineteenth-century American evangelicalism, see William Walker's 1831 song "Millennium" in the classic shaped-note songbook *Original Sacred Harp: Denson Revision, 1971 Edition* (Kingsport, Tenn., Kingsport Press, 1971).

2. David Edwin Harrell, Jr., *Quest for a Christian America: The Disciples of Christ and American Society to 1866* (Nashville, Disciples of Christ Historical Society, 1966); Robert Richardson, *Memoirs of Alexander Campbell,* 2 vols. (Philadelphia, J. B. Lippincott and Co., 1868–1870); F. L. Cross, ed., *The Oxford Dictionary of the Christian Church* (London, Oxford University Press, 1957), p. 224 ("Campbell, Alexander"); Louis Billington, "The Millerite Adventists in Great Britain, 1840–1850," in Ronald L. Numbers and Jonathan M. Butler, eds., *The Disappointed: Millerism and Millenarianism in the Nineteenth Century* (Bloomington, Indiana University Press, 1987), p. 59 (*Millennial Harbinger* reference).

3. *Views of the Prophecies and Prophetic Chronology, Selected from Manuscripts of William Miller, with a Memoir of His Life* (Boston, Joshua V. Himes, 1842), pp. 11–12; Numbers and Butler, *The Disappointed,* p. xv; Wayne R. Judd, "William Miller: Disappointed Prophet," in ibid., pp. 18–35 (Battle of Plattsburgh, p. 18). See also Catherine L. Albanese, *American Religions and Religion* (Belmont, Calif., Wadsworth Publishing Co., 1981), pp. 145–146; J. F. C. Harrison, *The Second Coming: Popular Mil-*

lenarianism, 1780–1850 (New Brunswick, Rutgers University Press, 1979), pp. 192–203; Jonathan M. Butler, "Adventism and the American Experience," in Edwin Gaustad, ed., *The Rise of Adventism: Religion and Society in Mid-Nineteenth-Century America* (New York, Harper and Row, 1974); O'Leary, "'Mine Eyes Have Seen the Glory,' pp. 10–36; Ezra 7:12–26.

4. Numbers and Butler, *The Disappointed*, pp. xv, 215 (recollection of Hiram Edson); David L. Rowe, "Millerites: A Shadow Portrait," in ibid., pp. 2, 14; Jonathan M. Butler, "The Making of a New Order: Millerism and the Origins of Seventh-day Adventism," in ibid., p. 195 (charts); O'Leary, "'Mine Eyes Have Seen the Glory,'" p. 17.

5. Rowe, "Millerites," pp. 4, 7 (total who joined), 15 (Rowe quote); Michael Barkun, "'The Wind Sweeping over the Country': John Humphrey Noyes and the Rise of Millerism," in ibid., p. 157 (Noyes quote).

6. Ruth Alden Doan, "Millerism and Evangelical Culture," in Numbers and Butler, *The Disappointed*, pp. 121, 133; Ronald D. Graybill, "The Abolitionist-Millerite Connection," in ibid., pp. 140–150 (Angelina Grimké Weld to Sarah Grimké, Jan. 1845, quoted on p. 147); Butler, "The Making of a New Order," p. 193. See also R. Laurence Moore, *Religious Outsiders and the Making of Americans* (New York, Oxford University Press, 1986), pp. 131–134.

7. Judd, "William Miller," p. 31; Butler, "The Making of a New Order," pp. 191, 194–195.

8. David T. Arthur, "Joshua V. Himes and the Cause of Adventism," in Numbers and Butler, *The Disappointed*, pp. 46 (tents), 47 (opposition); Butler, "The Making of a New Order," p. 191 (comparison to Jacksonians).

9. See William Miller, "Rules of Interpretation" in Miller, *Views of the Prophecies and Prophetic Chronology*, pp. 20–21, quoted in O'Leary, "'Mine Eyes Have Seen the Glory,'" pp. 26–27; Judd, "William Miller," p. 17. James White, ed., *Sketches of the Christian Life and Public Labors of William Miller* (Battle Creek, Mich., Steam Press, 1875), pp. 287–289, provides a revealing colloquy between Miller and a skeptical minister, illustrating Miller's analytic approach to prophetic interpretation (quoted in O'Leary, pp. 27–28). Patricia Cline Cohen, *A Calculating People: The Spread of Numeracy in Early America* (Chicago, University of Chicago Press, 1982). My thanks to Mark Noll for calling my attention to the probable link between the spread of numeracy and the appeal of Miller's approach to prophecy interpretation.

10. S. D. Baldwin, *Armageddon; or, The Overthrow of Romanism and Monarchy; the Existence of the United States Foretold in the Bible, Its Future Greatness, Invasion by Allied Powers; Annihilation of Monarchy; Expansion*

into the Millennial Republic, and Its Dominion over the Whole World (Cincinnati, Applegate and Co., 1854), pp. 64, 67, 77–78, 80, 86–87 (July 4, 1776, foretold), 369; Mary Glenn Hearne (Nashville Public Library) to author, Jan. 28, 1991 (biographical information on Baldwin). For a thoughtful discussion of postmillenialism in nineteenth-century U.S. theological discourse see James H. Moorhead, "Between Progress and Apocalypse: A Reassessment of Millennialism in American Religious Thought, 1800–1880," *Journal of American History,* 71 (Dec. 1984), 524–542.

11. Cullen T. Carter, *History of the Tennessee Conference and a Brief Summary of the General Conferences of the Methodist Church from the Frontier in Middle Tennessee to the Present Time* (Nashville, Cullen T. Carter, 1948), pp. 189–190 (reprint of 1874 obituary); F. E. Pitts, *A Defence of Armageddon; or, Our Great Country Foretold in the Holy Scriptures* (Baltimore, J. W. Bull, 1859), title page.

12. Pitts, *Defence of Armageddon,* pp. 10, v–vii (*National Intelligencer,* Feb. 24, 1857, article; quoted passage p. vi).

13. Pitts, *Defence of Armageddon,* p. 34. Pitts substituted "star" for "course" in the first line.

14. Ibid., pp. 42 ("bad as we are"), 50, 60 ("daguerrotype").

15. Ibid., pp. 116, 103.

16. "To the American Public," ibid., p. iv.

17. J. P. Philpott, *The Kingdom of Israel* (Nashville, Southern Methodist Publishing House, 1883), preface to 1st ed., dated 1864, p. 3; preface to 2nd ed. [1883], pp. 6, 8, 115–127.

18. Dwight Wilson, *Armageddon Now! The Premillenarian Response to Russia and Israel since 1917* (Grand Rapids, Baker Book House, 1977), p. 21; Cross, *Oxford Dictionary of the Christian Church,* p. 702 ("Irving, Edward"); A[ndrew] L. Drummond, *Edward Irving and His Circle* (London, J. Clarke & Co., 1937); Barkun, "'The Wind Sweeping over the Country,' p. 163. Irving's premillennialism was influenced by a 1790 work by the Spanish Jesuit Manual de Lacunza y Diaz [pseud. J. J. Ben-Ezra], *La Venida del Mesias en gloria y majestad* (1790), which he translated and published in 1827 as *The Coming of the Messiah in Glory and Majesty*—Frederick A. Tatford, *God's Program of the Ages* (Grand Rapids, Kregel Publications, 1967), pp. 18–19, 61. See also Ian S. Rennie, "Nineteenth-Century Roots," in Carl Edwin Armerding and W. Ward Gasque, *Dreams, Visions, and Oracles: The Layman's Guide to Biblical Prophecy* (Grand Rapids, Baker Book House, 1977), pp. 49–50; Marjorie Reeves, *The Influence of Prophecy in the Later Middle Ages: A Study in Joachimism* (Oxford, Clarendon Press, 1969), p. 289. Reeves finds Joachian borrowings in Lacunza; she notes that Lacunza places the Millennium *after* the Second Coming and thus is "premillennial." It is fascinating to trace this

thread of interpretation from Joachim to Lacunza to Irving to Darby to Scofield to Lindsey and a whole host of contemporary popularizers.

19. Rennie, "Nineteenth-Century Roots," p. 50; Cross, *Oxford Dictionary of the Christian Church,* pp. 423 ("Drummond, Henry"), 251 ("Catholic Apostolic Church"); P[lato] E. Shaw, *The Catholic Apostolic Church, Sometimes Called Irvingites: A Historical Study* (New York, King's Crown Press, 1946); *Dictionary of National Biography,* vol. 6 (London, Oxford University Press, 1921), pp. 28–29 ("Drummond, Henry"); Shirley Jackson Case, *The Millennial Hope: A Phase of Wartime Thinking* (Chicago, University of Chicago Press, 1918), pp. 198–199; D. W. Bebbington, *Evangelicalism in Modern Britain: A History from the 1730s to the 1980s* (Winchester, Mass., Allen and Unwin, 1989).

20. Henry Pickering, *Chief Men among the Brethren* (London, Pickering and Inglis, 1961; first pub. 1918), pp. 11–15 (biography of Darby); Bebbington, *Evangelicalism in Modern Britain* (Plymouth Brethren and Darbyism); Cross, *Oxford Dictionary of the Christian Church,* p. 373 ("Darby, John Nelson"); Clarence B. Bass, *Backgrounds to Dispensationalism: Its Historical Genesis and Ecclesiastical Implications* (Grand Rapids, Baker Book House, 1977), pp. 49–51; Case, *Millennial Hope,* pp. 200–201; Jerry Falwell, ed., with Ed Dobson and Ed Hindson, *The Fundamentalist Phenomenon: The Resurgence of Conservative Christianity* (Garden City, N.Y., Doubleday and Co., 1981), pp. 47–48.

21. Pickering, *Chief Men among the Brethren,* pp. 11–15; Loraine Boettner, *The Millennium* (Grand Rapids, Baker Book House, 1957), p. 368; Ernest R. Sandeen, *The Roots of Fundamentalism: British and American Millenarianism, 1800–1930* (Chicago, University of Chicago Press, 1970), pp. 70–71; Dietrich G. Buss, "Meeting of Heaven and Earth: A Survey and Analysis of the Literature on Millennialism in America, 1965–1985," *Fides et Historia,* 22 (Jan. 1988), 15.

22. John N. Darby, *The Hopes of the Church of God in Connexion with the Destiny of the Jews and the Nations as Revealed in Prophecy* (trans. from the French, 2nd ed. London, 1842) and *Lectures on the Second Coming* (reprinted London, G. Morrish, 1909) presents his system in his own words. Summaries of dispensationalism are also found in Alexander Reese, *The Approaching Advent of Christ: An Examination of the Teaching of J. N. Darby* (London, Marshall, Morgan and Scott, 1937); Timothy P. Weber, *Living in the Shadow of the Second Coming: American Premillennialism, 1875–1925* (New York, Oxford University Press, 1979), pp. 18–23; Tatford, *God's Program of the Ages,* pp. 21–32; and Rennie, "Nineteenth-Century Roots," pp. 51–54. See also Charles T. Ryrie, *Dispensationalism Today* (Chicago, Moody Press, 1965), and John F. Walvoord, *The Rapture Question* (Findlay, Ohio, Dunham Publishing Co., 1957).

23. See Chapter 2 (on Joachim and Increase Mather). On pre-Darby for-

mulations of versions of dispensationalism—for example, Pierre Poiret, *L'Oeconomie Divine* (Amsterdam, 1687)—see Ryrie, *Dispensationalism Today,* pp. 67–76. Dave McPherson, *The Incredible Coverup* (Medford, Oreg., Omega Publications, 1975) offers a debunking account of Darby (pp. 31–32). He also reprints (pp. 152–154) an 1830 document by a fifteen-year-old Glasgow girl, Margaret Macdonald, citing revelations she received in a trance, from which Darby allegedly appropriated the doctrine of the Rapture.

24. Weber, *Living in the Shadow of the Second Coming,* pp. 17–18; Rennie, "Nineteenth-Century Roots," pp. 51, 52, 54.

25. Weber, *Living in the Shadow of the Second Coming,* p. 24; Cross, *Oxford Dictionary of the Christian Church,* pp. 477–478 ("Evangelical Alliance"); James Edwin Orr, *The Second Evangelical Awakening in Britain* (London, Marshall, Morgan, and Scott, 1949); John H. Gerstner, "The Theological Boundaries of Evangelical Faith," in David F. Wells and John D. Woodbridge, eds., *The Evangelicals: What They Believe, Who They Are, Where They Are Changing* (Nashville, Abingdon Press, 1975), p. 25.

26. Edward Hitchcock, "The Future Condition and Destiny of the Earth," lecture 11 in Hitchcock, *The Religion of Geology and Its Connected Sciences* (Boston, 1851), quoted in Joseph A. Seiss, *The Last Times and the Great Consummation: An Earnest Discussion of Momentous Events* (Philadelphia, Smith, English, and Co., 1856), p. 318; Wilson, *Armageddon Now!* p. 24; Elhanan Winchester, *A Course of Lectures on the Prophecies Which Remain to Be Fulfilled* (Cincinnati, Ed. Morgan and Co., 1851; reprint of 1788 work), p. iii; *Dictionary of National Biography* (London, Oxford University Press, 1921–1922), V, 297–298 ("Cumming, John").

27. Seiss, *The Last Times,* pp. 62, 63.

28. Ibid., pp. 10, 212.

29. Ibid., p. 4.

30. Rennie, "Nineteenth-Century Roots," pp. 57–58.

31. Warren W. Wiersbe, "Biographical Sketch," in Sir Robert Anderson, *The Coming Prince* (Grand Rapids, Kregel Publications, 1986; reprint of 1884 ed.), pp. 315–317 (quoted passage p. 317); Pickering, *Chief Men among the Brethren,* pp. 192–195.

32. Anderson, *Coming Prince,* passim (quoted passages pp. 3, 131); 124 (royal astronomer letter); xii–xiii (brief summary of the argument); iv (publishing history). For a contemporary popularization of Anderson's argument see Alva J. McClain, *Daniel's Prophecy of the Seventy Weeks* (Grand Rapids, Zondervan Publishing Co., 1969; reprint of 1940 ed.).

33. Wilson, *Armageddon Now!* p. 30; William Hyde and Howard L. Conrad, *Encyclopedia of the History of St. Louis* (New York, Southern History Co., 1899), p. 244 ("Brookes, James H."); Boettner, *The Millennium,* p. 368;

James H. Brookes, *Maranatha: or, The Lord Cometh* (New York, Fleming H. Revell, 10th ed., 1889); Beth N. Lindberg, "A God-Filled Life: The Story of William Eugene Blackstone" (n.p., n.d.)—my thanks to David C. Lindberg for lending me a copy of this tract; Rennie, "Nineteenth-Century Roots," p. 59.

34. Nathaniel West, ed., *Premillennial Essays of the Prophetic Conference Held at the Church of the Holy Trinity, New York City* (Chicago, Fleming H. Revell, 1879), pp. 6–9 (quoted passage from Bishop Ryle pp. 6–7); Rennie, "Nineteenth-Century Roots," p. 58; C. Allyn Russell, *Voices of American Fundamentalism: Seven Biographical Studies* (Philadelphia, Westminister Press, 1976), p. 17; Weber, *Living in the Shadow of the Second Coming,* p. 28. Useful general accounts include Sandeen, *Roots of Fundamentalism,* and George M. Marsden, *Fundamentalism and American Culture: The Shaping of Twentieth-Century Evangelicalism, 1870–1925* (New York, Oxford University Press, 1980).

35. West, *Premillennial Essays,* pp. 7–9 (quoted passage p. 9).

36. Weber, *Living in the Shadow of the Second Coming,* pp. 33–35, 80 (BIOLA); William Vance Trollinger, Jr., *God's Empire: William Bell Riley and Midwestern Fundamentalism* (Madison, University of Wisconsin Press, 1990), p. 84; David A. Rausch, "Arno C. Gaebelein (1861–1945): Fundamentalist Protestant Zionist," *American Jewish History* (Sept. 1978), 44, 55; Marsden, *Fundamentalism and American Culture,* pp. 32–39 (Moody), 71, 96; James F. Findlay, Jr., *Dwight L. Moody: American Evangelist, 1837–1899* (Chicago, University of Chicago Press, 1969); Rennie, "Nineteenth-Century Roots," p. 58; Leander W. Munhall, *The Lord's Return* (Grand Rapids, Kregel Publications, 8th ed., 1962; reprint of 1887[?] ed.), biographical information on jacket; James Davison Hunter, *American Evangelicalism: Conservative Religion and the Quandary of Modernity* (New Brunswick, Rutgers University Press, 1983), p. 27.

37. Moore, *Religious Outsiders and the Making of Americans,* pp. 130, 133, 136–138; Case, *Millennial Hope,* p. 203; M. James Penton, *Apocalypse Delayed: The Story of Jehovah's Witnesses* (Toronto, University of Toronto Press, 1985); Cross, *Oxford Dictionary of the Christian Church,* pp. 717 ("Jehovah's Witnesses"), 1189 ("Russell, Charles Taze"); Alan Rogerson, *Millions Now Living Will Never Die: A Study of the Jehovah's Witnesses* (London, Constable, 1969); Barbara Grizzuti Harrison, *Visions of Glory: A History and a Memory of Jehovah's Witnesses* (New York, Simon and Schuster, 1978); Robert Mapes Anderson, *Vision of the Disinherited: The Making of American Pentecostalism* (New York, Oxford University Press, 1979), chap. 3, pp. 47–78, 79 (quoted passage); Wilson, *Armageddon Now!* p. 37.

38. Marsden, *Fundamentalism and American Culture,* pp. 43–123, passim, esp.

pp. 118, 152; Russell, *Voices of American Fundamentalism,* pp. 17–18; Bernard Ramm, *After Fundamentalism: The Future of Evangelical Theology* (New York, Harper and Row, 1983), pp. 181–182; Erling Jorstad, *The Politics of Doomsday: Fundamentalism and the Far Right* (Nashville, Abingdon Press, 1970), pp. 21–23; Weber, *Living in the Shadow of the Second Coming,* p. 28 (Torrey quote). For a historical account from a fundamentalist perspective, see Falwell, *Fundamentalist Phenomenon,* chap. 4, pp. 78–107, esp. p. 80.

39. Brookes, *Maranatha,* p. 130; Sydney E. Ahlstrom, "From Puritanism to Evangelicalism: A Critical Perspective," in Wells and Woodbridge, *The Evangelicals,* p. 283 (Moody quote); Marsden, *Fundamentalism and American Culture,* p. 64 (prophecy chart quote). See also Isaac M. Haldeman, *The Signs of the Times* (New York, Charles C. Cook, 1914), p. 302.

40. Brookes, *Maranatha,* p. 381.

41. Beverley O. Kinnear, *Impending Judgments on the Earth* (New York, James Huggins, 1892), p. 15.

42. Haldeman, *Signs of the Times,* pp. 348, 353, 354, 361, 362; Marsden, *Fundamentalism and American Culture,* p. 125. On anticapitalist themes in the early pentecostalist movement, see Anderson, *Vision of the Disinherited,* pp. 109–110.

43. Brookes, *Maranatha,* pp. 130, 542; Haldeman, *Signs of the Times,* p. 302.

44. Brookes, *Maranatha,* p. 381 ("fell spirit of Socialism"); James H. Brookes, "Gentile Dominion," *Truth,* 6 (1880), 536, quoted in Weber, *Living in the Shadow of the Second Coming,* p. 93 ("the whole defiling scene"); ibid., pp. 86–87, 92–93, 95 (union labels), 101 (Torrey); Ahlstrom, "From Puritanism to Evangelicalism," p. 283; Reuben A. Torrey, *The Return of the Lord Jesus* (Los Angeles, Bible Institute of Los Angeles, 1913), pp. 7–8. See also D. T. Taylor, *The Coming Earthquake, and the Signs That Betoken Its Approach* (Boston, Scripture Tract Repository, 1870), p. 3, whose descriptions of approaching natural upheavals suggest anxiety about social upheavals as well; and Paul Clifford Wilt, "Premillennialism in America, 1865–1918, with Special Reference to Attitudes toward Social Reform" (Ph.D. dissertation, University of Chicago, 1976).

45. Torrey, *Return of the Lord Jesus,* pp. 7–8, quoted in Weber, *Living in the Shadow of the Second Coming,* p. 101; Cyrus I. Scofield, *Addresses on Prophecy* (New York, Arno C. Gaebelein, n.d.), p. 26.

46. Anderson, *Coming Prince,* p. 190; Kinnear, *Impending Judgments on the Earth,* p. 24. See also Isaac M. Haldeman's discussion of the clay feet of Daniel's statue as representing an age of mass society from which Antichrist will arise, quoted in James M. Gray, *A Text-Book on Prophecy* (New York, Fleming H. Revell, 1918), pp. 183–184.

47. Francis Darwin, *Charles Darwin: His Life* (New York, 1893), p. 65. Cf. Nathaniel West in 1880: "The beast is still unchanged in its heart, anti-Christian still, notwithstanding its Christian order, culture, and civilization," quoted in Boettner, *The Millennium*, p. 352.

48. Haldeman, *Signs of the Times*, p. 286; Harry A. Ironside, *Lectures on the Revelation* (Neptune, N.J., Loizeaux Bros., 1919), p. 103. Shailer Matthews was dean of the University of Chicago Divinity School. See also Hunter, *American Evangelicalism*, pp. 29–30.

49. Harris Franklin Rall, *New Testament History* (New York, Abingdon Press, 1914), p. 301, quoted in Weber, *Living in the Shadow of the Second Coming*, p. 39; Walter Rauschenbusch, *Christianity and the Social Crisis* (New York, Macmillan, 1907), pp. 202–203, quoted in ibid., p. 66; idem, *A Theology for the Social Gospel* (New York, Macmillan, 1917), p. 209. For a concise summary of the social-gospel ideology rejected by premillennialists, see "Christianity and Social Reform" and "The Church and Social Reform" in W. D. P. Bliss, ed., *The New Encyclopedia of Social Reform* (New York, Funk and Wagnalls, 1910), pp. 205–211, 212–221.

50. West, *Premillennial Essays*, pp. 9, 213; Weber, *Living in the Shadow of the Second Coming*, pp. 71–73.

51. Admiring biographical treatments that omit crucial details from Scofield's early life are Charles G. Trumbull, *The Life Story of C. I. Scofield* (New York, Oxford University Press, 1920); William A. BeVier, "C. I. Scofield: Dedicated and Determined," *Fundamentalist Journal*, 2 (Oct. 1983), 37–39, 56; and Falwell, *Fundamentalist Phenomenon*, p. 81. Boettner, *The Millennium*, pp. 367–369, offers a brief and factual sketch; a hostile, debunking account is given by Dave MacPherson, *The Great Rapture Hoax* (Fletcher, N.C., New Puritan Library, 1983), pp. 73–81 (Ingalls quote p. 81). A Dec. 8, 1883, Kansas court order granted Leontine Scofield a divorce from Cyrus I. Scofield, whom the court found guilty of "wilfull abandonment of the plaintiff for more than one year prior to the commencement of this action" (copy in author's possession).

52. Donald Kraus (Senior Editor, Bibles, Oxford University Press) to author, June 14, 1990; James Barr, *Fundamentalism* (Philadelphia, Westminster Press, 1977), p. 45 (quoted passage); Wilson, *Armageddon Now!* p. 15.

53. Cyrus I. Scofield, *What Do the Prophets Say?* (Philadelphia, Philadelphia School of the Bible, 1918), p. 161 ("thought and word of God" quote); Grace Halsell, *Prophecy and Politics: Militant Evangelists on the Road to Nuclear War* (Westport, Conn., Laurence Hill and Co., 1986), p. 7 ("beautiful system" quote); Boettner, *The Millennium*, p. 371; Weber,

Living in the Shadow of the Second Coming, p. 33; Wilson, *Armageddon Now!* pp. 15–17. For summaries of Scofield's dispensationalism see, in addition to his own works, G. Campbell Morgan, *God's Methods with Man* (New York, Fleming H. Revell, 1898), and Tatford, *God's Program of the Ages.*

54. Scofield, *What Do the Prophets Say?* pp. 159, 160, 161.

55. Scofield, *Addresses on Prophecy,* p. 91.

56. Scofield, *What Do the Prophets Say?* p. 121; Boettner, *The Millennium,* p. 351 ("apostasy" quote).

57. Quoted in Nathan O. Hatch, "Evangelicalism as a Democratic Movement," in George Marsden, ed., *Evangelicalism and Modern America* (Grand Rapids, Wm. B. Eerdman's Publishing Co., 1984), p. 78. See, on the same point, Ramm, *After Fundamentalism,* p. 185.

58. Weber, *Living in the Shadow of the Second Coming,* p. 32 (1919 survey); Ramm, *After Fundamentalism,* p. 183.

59. Marsden, *Fundamentalism and American Culture,* pp. 118–119, 144; Hertzel Fishman, *American Protestantism and a Jewish State* (Detroit, Wayne State University Press, 1973), pp. 19–20, 187; BeVier, "C. I. Scofield," p. 39; Weber, *Living in the Shadow of the Second Coming,* p. 100; Rennie, "Nineteenth-Century Roots," p. 56.

60. Anderson, *Vision of the Disinherited,* p. 202 ("War!" quote); Wilson, *Armageddon Now!* p. 45; Falwell, *Fundamentalist Phenomenon,* p. 81; Weber, *Living in the Shadow of the Second Coming,* p. 105.

61. Anderson, *Coming Prince,* p. viii (preface to 10th ed.); Henry Sully, *Is It Armageddon?* (London, Simpkin, Marshall, 1915; rev. of work orig. pub. 1904), p. 5; Kemper Fullerton, *Prophecy and Authority: A Study in the History of the Doctrine and Interpretation of Scripture* (New York, Macmillan, 1919), pp. x, xii (italics in original).

62. Wilson, *Armageddon Now!* p. 37 (Torrey); Weber, *Living in the Shadow of the Second Coming,* pp. 106–112 (Gaebelein quote p. 108); Gray, *Text-Book on Prophecy,* chap. 19 title.

63. Weber, *Living in the Shadow of the Second Coming,* p. 129; Charles G. Trumbull, *Prophecy's Light on Today* (New York, Fleming H. Revell, 1937), p. 67 (Scofield to Trumbull, Dec. 11, 1917); Wilson, *Armageddon Now!* pp. 37–46, 67 (A. B. Simpson).

64. Weber, *Living in the Shadow of the Second Coming,* pp. 106–112; Gray, *Text-Book on Prophecy,* p. 192. See also *World Peace in the Light of Prophecy* (Washington, D.C., *Review and Herald* Publishing Co., 1919), p. 17.

65. Scofield, *What Do the Prophets Say?* p. 18; Weber, *Living in the Shadow of the Second Coming,* p. 126 (Torrey); *World Peace in the Light of Prophecy,* pp. 50, 52.

66. Case, *Millennial Hope,* pp. v, vi. See also Wilson, *Armageddon Now!* p. 58; Marsden, *Fundamentalism and American Culture,* p. 146.

67. Case, *Millennial Hope,* pp. 207, 214–215.

68. Ibid., pp. 217, 218–219.

69. Ibid., pp. 235, 237–239.

70. Pettingill, quoted in Weber, *Living in the Shadow of the Second Coming,* p. 88.

71. Mark A. Noll, "Evangelicals and the Study of the Bible," in Marsden, *Evangelicalism and Modern America,* p. 104; "Vanishing Fundamentalism," *Christian Century,* 43 (June 24, 1926), 799; Millard J. Erickson, *Contemporary Options in Eschatology: A Study of the Millennium* (Grand Rapids, Baker Book House, 1977), pp. 19–20 (Fosdick); William R. Hutchison, *American Protestant Thought: The Liberal Era* (New York, Harper and Row, 1968), p. 95 (Matthews); Edward Mortimer Chapman, *A Modernist and His Creed* (Boston, Houghton Mifflin, 1926), pp. 326, 328, 329; *The Abingdon Bible Commentary,* ed. Frederick C. Eiselen, Edwin Lewis, and David G. Downey (New York, Abingdon Press, 1929), pp. 709ff. (W. Lansdel Wardle, "Ezekiel", quoted passage p. 741); 747ff. (Herbert H. Willett, "Daniel"); 1,316ff. (F. Bartram Clogg, "Revelation").

72. William Jennings Bryan, *Shall Christianity Remain Christian? Seven Questions in Dispute* (New York, Fleming H. Revell, 1924). My thanks to Michael L. Stine for calling this work to my attention.

73. Joel A. Carpenter, "From Fundamentalism to the New Evangelical Coalition," in Marsden, *Evangelicalism and Modern America,* pp. 3–4; Marsden, *Fundamentalism and American Culture,* pp. 193–195; Marsden, "From Fundamentalism to Evangelicalism: A History Analysis," in Wells and Woodbridge, *The Evangelicals,* p. 127 (quoted phrase); Falwell, *Fundamentalist Phenomenon,* p. 90; Russell, *Voices of American Fundamentalism,* pp. 47–78 (John Roach Straton), 135–161 (J. Gresham Machen); Richard Quebedeaux, *The Worldly Evangelicals* (San Francisco, Harper and Row, 1978), p. 31.

74. Oswald J. Smith, *The Dawn Is Breaking* (Grand Rapids, Zondervan Publishing Co., [1920s]); idem, *Is the Antichrist at Hand?* (Toronto, Tabernacle Publishers, 1926); Arthur W. Pink, *The Antichrist* (Grand Rapids, Kregel Publishers, 1988; orig. pub. 1923 by Bible Truth Depot, Swengel, Pa.), p. 234; Christabel Pankhurst, *Pressing Problems of the Closing Age* (London, Morgan and Scott, 1924), p. 43.

75. [Harry A. Ironside], *Four Golden Hours at Kingsway Hall, London, with Dr. Harry A. Ironside* (London, Marshall, Morgan, and Scott, 1939); Carpenter, "From Fundamentalism to the New Evangelical Coalition,"

pp. 10–11; Nathan O. Hatch, *The Democratization of American Christianity* (New Haven, Yale University Press, 1989), p. 217; Herbert Lockyear, *Cameos of Prophecy: Are These the Last Days?* (Grand Rapids, Zondervan Publishing Co., 1942), p. 112 (quoted passage).

76. Forrest Loman Oilar, *Be Thou Prepared, for Jesus Is Coming* (Boston, Meador Publishing Co., 1937), p. 110.

77. Ibid., pp. 100 (quoted passage), 177, 180, 184, 195–196.

78. Wilson, *Armageddon Now!* p. 112; Charles O. Benham, *Great Britain and the United States in Prophecy* (Joliet, Ill., National X-Ray Publications, 1942), p. 61 (parachutes); F. W. Pitt, *Coming Events Cast Their Shadows in the Air* (London, Marshall, Morgan, and Scott, 1936), p. 18 (television).

79. Arthur I. Brown, *The Eleventh "Hour"* (Findlay, Ohio, Fundamental Truth Publishers, 1940), p. 118; Donald Grey Barnhouse, *Revelation: An Expository Commentary* (Grand Rapids, Zondervan Publishing Co., 1971; orig. pub. *Revelation* magazine, 1941–42), pp. 140, 335, 339. See also Lewis Sperry Chafer, "The Coming Destruction of Ecclesiastical and Political Babylon," in John W. Bradbury, ed., *Light for the World's Darkness* (New York, Loizeaux Bros., 1944), pp. 54, 61, and Henry D. Houghton, *The New World Coming* (Toronto, Commonwealth Publishers, 1930), p. v.

80. Donald Grey Barnhouse, "The Church and Politics," *Revelation,* June 1931, p. 200, quoted in Carpenter, "From Fundamentalism to the New Evangelical Coalition," p. 8; "The Doom of Civilization," *Latter Rain Evangel,* July 1932, p. 3, quoted in Anderson, *Vision of the Disinherited,* pp. 199–200.

81. Louis S. Bauman, "The Blue Eagle and Our Duty as Christians," *Sunday School Times* (Sept. 16, 1933), 583–584, quoted in Carpenter, "From Fundamentalism to the New Evangelical Coalition," p. 9; Arno C. Gaebelein, *As It Was—So Shall It Be: Sunset and Sunrise: A Study of the First Age and Our Present Age* (New York, Our Hope, 1937), pp. 138, 143; Arno C. Gaebelein, *Meat in Due Season* (New York, Arno C. Gaebelein, n.d.), p. 155. See also Pitt, *Coming Events Cast Their Shadows in the Air,* p. 79; C. E. Robinson to Stanley H. Frodsham, circa Apr. 1941, quoted in Anderson, *Vision of the Disinherited,* p. 210.

82. Brown, *Eleventh "Hour,"* pp. 41, 43 (quoted passage).

83. F. S. Donn, *The Israel Way to Peace* (New York, Exposition Press, 1957), p. 103 (Hitler = 666); Timothy P. Weber, *The Future Explored* (Wheaton, Ill., Victor Books, 1978), p. 57 (Hitler as Antichrist); Brown, *Eleventh "Hour,"* p. 78 (quoted phrase); Clarence W. Boyer to author, Mar. 9. 1989.

84. Trumbull, *Prophecy's Light on Today,* pp. 98–99; Smith, *Is the Antichrist at Hand?* pp. 22, 65; Leonard Sale-Harrison, *The Resurrection of the Old Roman Empire* (1939), quoted in Robert G. Clouse, "The Danger of Mistaken Hopes," in Armerding and Gasque, *Dreams, Visions, and Oracles,* p. 35 (fasces design). For more allusions to Mussolini as Antichrist see Brown, *Eleventh "Hour,"* chap. 4; Gaebelein, *As It Was—So Shall It Be,* p. 128; Pitt, *Coming Events Cast Their Shadows in the Air,* p. 36; J. M. Ritchie, *Prophetic Highlights* (New York, Fleming H. Revell, 1935), p. 17; and George D. Beckwith, *God's Prophetic Plan through the Ages* (Grand Rapids, Zondervan Publishing Co., 1942), p. 103.

85. Gaebelein, *As It Was—So Shall It Be,* p. 175; W. H. Rogers, *"The End from the Beginning": A Panorama of Prophecy: or, History, the Mold of Prediction* (New York, Arno C. Gaebelein, 1938), p. 204.

86. *Evangel* (Assemblies of God periodical), Sept. 16, 1939, p. 9, quoted in Wilson, *Armageddon Now!* p. 117. See also Brown, *Eleventh "Hour,"* pp. 77, 155; Louis S. Bauman, "Russia and Armageddon," *King's Business,* 29 (Sept. 1938), 286, quoted in Wilson, *Armageddon Now!* p. 119.

87. Brown, *Eleventh "Hour,"* p. 156; Louis T. Talbot, *King's Business,* 23 (Oct. 1932), 424 ("dark-skinned peoples") quoted in Wilson, *Armageddon Now!* p. 119; Harry A. Ironside, "The Kings of the East," *King's Business,* 29 (Jan. 1938), p. 9, quoted in ibid. See also James M. Boice, "Are We Nearing the Last Holocaust?" *Eternity,* Dec. 1972, p. 59, on World War II discussions of Japan and "the kings of the East."

88. Gaebelein, *As It Was—So Shall It Be,* p. 128; Harry Rimmer, *The Coming War and the Rise of Russia* (Grand Rapids, Wm. B. Eerdman's Publishing Co., 1940), pp. 29, 85.

89. Brown, *Eleventh "Hour,"* pp. 23, 28, 146.

90. Arthur S. Maxwell, *History's Crowded Climax: Prophecy Speaks to Our Time* (Mountain View, Calif., Pacific Press Publishing Assn., 1940), pp. 13, 24.

91. Ibid., pp. 33, 122.

92. Reinhold Niebuhr, *Europe's Catastrophe and the Christian Faith* (London, Nisbet, 1940), pp. 35–36, quoted in Wilbur M. Smith, *This Atomic Age and the World of God* (Boston, W. A. Wilde Co., 1948), p. 219.

93. James F. Spink, *Will Hitler Obtain World Domination?* (New York, Loizeaux Bros., 1942), p. 24.

94. Lockyear, *Cameos of Prophecy,* pp. 66, 67, 71.

95. John Bradbury, "The Peace of the Prince of Peace," in Bradbury, *Light for the World's Darkness,* pp. 69–70.

96. Howard W. Ferrin, "Why Cannot Man Bring in Permanent Peace?", in Bradbury, *Light for the World's Darkness,* p. 111, 112, 114, 117. Harry

James Hager, "Armageddon in the Making—Some Hints to Postwar Planners," in ibid., pp. 120–129, makes the same point.

4. The Atomic Bomb and Nuclear War

1. John Bunyan, *The Pilgrim's Progress,* ed. and intro. Roger Sharrock (Baltimore, Penguin Books, 1965; orig. publ. 1678), p. 39; D. T. Taylor, *The Coming Earthquake, and the Signs That Betoken Its Approach* (Boston, Scriptural Tract Repository, 1870), p. 3.
2. Arthur I. Brown, *The Eleventh "Hour"* (Findlay, Ohio, Fundamental Truth Publishers, 1940), p. 91.
3. Wilbur M. Smith, *This Atomic Age and the Word of God* (Boston, W. A. Wilde Co., 1948), pp. 45, 52.
4. Paul Boyer, *By the Bomb's Early Light: American Thought and Culture at the Dawn of the Atomic Age* (New York, Pantheon Books, 1985), p. 25; idem, "'Some Sort of Peace': President Truman, the American People, and the Atomic Bomb," in Michael J. Lacey, ed., *The Truman Presidency* (Cambridge, Cambridge University Press, 1989), p. 193.
5. Rudolph Bultmann, "The New Testament and Mythology" (1941), quoted in Klaus Koch, *The Rediscovery of Apocalyptic* (London, SCM Press, 1972), p. 66. Zachary Hayes, *What Are They Saying about the End of the World?* (New York, Paulist Press, 1983), p. 7, offers a useful brief summary of Bultmann's eschatology and the similar views expressed by theologian C. H. Dodd in *The Parables of the Kingdom* (London, Nisbet, 1941).
6. Smith, *This Atomic Age and the Word of God,* p. 161 (quoted passage); Wesner Fallaw, "Atomic Apocalypse," *Christian Century,* Sept. 25, 1946, p. 1146.
7. Smith, *This Atomic Age and the Word of God,* p. 55; John A. T. Robinson, *In the End God* (New York, Harper and Row, rev. ed. 1968; orig. publ. 1950), pp. 27–30. See also Jim Garrison, *The Darkness of God: Theology after Hiroshima* (Grand Rapids, Wm. B. Eerdman's Publishing Co., 1982).
8. E. Schuyler English, *The Shifting of the Scenes* (New York, Our Hope, 1945), p. 41; Donald J. Holbrook, "What about the Atomic Bomb?" *Moody Monthly,* Nov. 1945.
9. Donald Grey Barnhouse, "Tomorrow: Current Events in the Light of the Bible," *Revelation,* Dec. 1945, pp. 505, 534; *Eternity,* Aug. 1952, p. 1.
10. Barnhouse, "Tomorrow," pp. 505, 534 (citations to Zech. 4:10, 8:10).
11. Ibid., pp. 535–536, 537.
12. Wilbur M. Smith, "World Crises and the Prophetic Scriptures," *Moody*

Monthly, June 1950, p. 679 (1914 prophecy conference); Bernard R. DeRemer, "Wilbur M. Smith: Christianity's No. 1 Bookworm," *Fundamentalist Journal* (May 1987), 55–56; Wilbur M. Smith, *Before I Forget* (Chicago, Moody Press, 1971).

13. Smith, *This Atomic Age and the Word of God,* p. 16.

14. Ibid., pp. 11, 132, 271, 291, 309; chap. 15, pp. 271–282.

15. Ibid., pp. 55, 160–161, 209–210, 217; idem, "The Bible, the Book for This Hour of World Crisis," *Sunday School Times,* 90 (Nov. 6, 1948), 969.

16. Smith, *This Atomic Age and the Word of God,* pp. 146–152 (quoted passage p. 152).

17. Ibid., pp. 256–257, 261 (Ryle quote); idem, "The Bible, the Book for This Hour of World Crisis," p. 968 (Smith's personal recollections).

18. Perry Miller, "The End of the World," in Miller, *Errand into the Wilderness* (New York, Harper Torchbooks, 1956), pp. 217 (quoted phrase), 239.

19. Smith, *This Atomic Age and the Word of God,* chap. 14, pp. 266–270. The biblical reference is to Rev. 6:15–17. Jonathan Schell, *The Fate of the Earth* (New York, Alfred A. Knopf, 1982), p. 127, makes a similar point.

20. English, *The Shifting of the Scenes,* p. 36; William Ward Ayer, *What Goes On Here!* (Grand Rapids, Zondervan Publishing Co., 1947), p. 81; Donald Grey Barnhouse, "Tomorrow: Current Events in the Light of the Bible: 1950," *Eternity,* Jan. 1951, p. 46.

21. Coffin and *Baptist Courier* quoted in "An Attack on Expositors of Revelation," *Sunday School Times,* 91 (Apr. 9, 1949), 326–327, 340.

22. Ibid., p. 340.

23. Boyer, *By the Bomb's Early Light,* pp. 291–351 passim.

24. Wilbur M. Smith, introduction, in Oswald J. Smith, *When the King Comes Back* (Wheaton, Ill., Sword of the Lord Publishers, 1953), p. 3; John W. Bradbury, ed., *Hastening the Day of God: Prophetic Messages from the International Congress on Prophecy in Calvary Baptist Church, New York City, November 9–16, 1952* (Wheaton, Ill., Van Kampen Press, 1953), pp. 11–12 (manifesto), 38 (Alva J. McClain, "Significant Signs of the Times"; "modern atomic science" quote), 42–43 (William Culbertson, "Are the Times of the Gentiles Drawing to a Close?").

25. Kenneth S. Wuest, *Prophetic Light in the Present Darkness* (Grand Rapids, Wm. B. Eerdman's Publishing Co., 1955), p. 11; Gerald B. Stanton, *Kept from the Hour: A Systematic Study of the Rapture in Bible Prophecy* (Grand Rapids, Zondervan Publishing Co., 1956), p. 12; Boyer, *By the Bomb's Early Light,* pp. 352–355. See also John F. Walvoord, *The Return of the Lord* (Findlay, Ohio, Dunham Publishing Co., 1955), pp. 6, 9.

26. Arthur W. Kac, "Prophetic Patterns in the World Today," *Moody Monthly,* May 1960, pp. 26, 27; J. Dwight Pentecost, *Prophecy for Today* (Grand Rapids, Zondervan Publishing Co., 1961), p. 113; J. Barton Payne, *The Imminent Appearing of Christ* (Grand Rapids, Wm. B. Eerdman's Publishing Co., 1962), p. 160.

27. Joel 1:19, 2:31; Zech. 14:12.

28. Kac, "Prophetic Patterns in the World Today," p. 26; Alden A. Gannett, "Where Is the Promise of His Coming?" in Charles Lee Feinberg, ed., *Prophecy and the Seventies* (Chicago, Moody Press, 1971), p. 47 (*God of the Atom* reference); telephone interview with Cecile Timari (Moody Film Rental), June 12, 1990; Cecile Timari to author, June 19, 1990.

29. M. R. DeHaan, *Coming Events in Prophecy* (Grand Rapids, Zondervan Publishing Co., 1962), pp. 103, 106, 119; idem, *The Days of Noah* (Grand Rapids, Zondervan Publishing Co., 1963), p. 73.

30. W. R. Wallace, "Shadows of Armageddon," in William Culbertson and Herman B. Centz, eds., *Understanding the Times: Prophetic Messages Delivered at the Second International Congress on Prophecy, New York City* (Grand Rapids, Zondervan Publishing Co., 1956), pp. 187–188, 189; John F. Walvoord, "The Crisis of This Present Hour," in *The Prophetic Word in Crisis Days* (Findlay, Ohio, Dunham Publishing Co., 1961), p. 15. This work includes addresses given at a 1961 prophecy conference at the Church of the Open Door, Los Angeles.

31. DeHaan, *Coming Events in Prophecy,* pp. 103, 119–120.

32. F. S. Donn, *The Israel Way to Peace* (New York, Exposition Press, 1957), p. 155; DeHaan, *Coming Events in Prophecy,* pp. 109, 146.

33. James Reid, *God, the Atom, and the Universe* (Grand Rapids, Zondervan Publishing Co., 1968), pp. 160, 165; Frederick A. Tatford, *God's Program of the Ages* (Grand Rapids, Kregel Publications, 1967), p. 138.

34. J. Vernon McGee, "The Prophetic Word and Europe," in *The Prophetic Word in Crisis Days,* p. 93.

35. Walvoord, *Return of the Lord,* p. 18; Donn, *The Israel Way to Peace,* p. 68.

36. Dale Crowley, *The Soon Coming of Our Lord* (New York, Loizeaux Brothers, 1958), p. 40; Pentecost, *Prophecy for Today,* pp. 18, 113. See also DeHaan, *Days of Noah,* p. 123; idem, *Coming Events in Prophecy,* p. 151.

37. Charles R. Taylor, *The Destiny of America* (Van Nuys, Calif., Time-Light Publishers, 1972), p. 9.

38. Hal Lindsey, *The Late Great Planet Earth* (New York, Bantam Books, 1973), pp. 124, 135, 144; Garry Friesen, "A Return Visit," *Moody Monthly,* May 1988, p. 31 (on Lindsey).

39. Lindsey, *Late Great Planet Earth,* pp. 149, 163, 164; idem, *There's a New World Coming: A Prophetic Odyssey* (Santa Ana, Calif., Vision House Publishers, 1973), pp. 110, 138–139, 217; Rev. 6:13, 9:10, 16:2.

40. Lindsey, *There's a New World Coming,* pp. 23, 130, 131, 132, 141.

41. Ibid., p. 110.

42. Michael Barkun, "Nuclear War and Millenarian Symbols: Premillennialists Confront the Bomb," paper given before the Society for the Scientific Study of Religion, Oct. 1985, p. 24 (quoted by permission); Lindsey, *There's a New World Coming,* pp. 219, 226, 227, 287. For a published version of Barkun's insightful paper (not including the passage cited, however), see Michael Barkun, "The Language of Apocalypse: Premillennialists and Nuclear War," in Marshall W. Fishwick and Ray E. Browne, eds., *The God Pumpers: Religion in the Electronic Age* (Bowling Green, Ohio, Bowling Green State University Popular Press, 1987), pp. 159–173.

43. James Barr, *Fundamentalism* (Philadelphia, Westminster Press, 1977), pp. 206, 207; D. S. Russell, *Apocalyptic Ancient and Modern* (Philadelphia, Fortress Press, 1978), p. 64; Michael L. Stine, Garrett Theological Seminary, Evanston, Ill., independent reading course, Spring 1989, report on Hal Lindsey; Peter Beyerhaus, "The Perils of Prosperity," *Christianity Today* (Feb. 16, 1973), 58.

44. Merrill F. Unger, *Beyond the Crystal Ball* (Chicago, Moody Press, 1973), pp. 100, 106, see also 112–113; John Phillips, *Only the Bible Can Foretell the Future* (Wheaton, Ill., Harold Shaw Publishers, 1975), pp. 106, 113.

45. Ezek. 20:47–48; Jack Van Impe, *Signs of the Times* (Royal Oak, Mich., Jack Van Impe Ministries, 1979), pp. 68–69; idem, *11:59 and Counting* (Royal Oak, Mich., Jack Van Impe Ministries, 1983), p. 143; "They Call Him the Walking Bible," *Perhaps Today* (Jack Van Impe Ministries magazine), May/June 1988, pp. 2–9, 18–21.

46. Arthur E. Bloomfield, *How to Recognize the Antichrist* (Minneapolis, Bethany Fellowship, 1975), p. 109; Hab. 1:10 ("heap dust and take it"); A. G. Mojtabai, *Blessed Assurance: At Home with the Bomb in Amarillo, Texas* (Boston, Houghton Mifflin Co., 1986), p. 179; Jer. 51:11 ("make bright the arrows"); Leon Bates, *Project for Survival* (Dallas, Bible Believers' Evangelistic Assn., 1977), pp. 111, 113, 145.

47. Bates, *Project for Survival,* p. 181; John Wesley White, *The Coming World Dictator* (Minneapolis, Bethany House, 1981), p. 63.

48. Edgar C. Whisenant, *88 Reasons Why the Rapture Will Be in 1988: New Expanded Edition* (Nashville, World Bible Society, 1988), pp. 3, 36, 56.

49. Thomas S. McCall and Zola Levitt, *The Coming Russian Invasion of Israel* (Chicago, Moody Press, 1974), p. 54.

50. Unger, *Beyond the Crystal Ball,* p. 115; Herbert Vander Lugt, *There's a New Day Coming!* (Eugene, Oreg., Harvest House Publishers, 1983), pp. 56–57; author interview with John Walvoord, Aug. 8, 1989; Van Impe, *Signs of the Times,* p. 66.

51. Van Impe, *11:59 and Counting,* pp. 71–73; Unger, *Beyond the Crystal*

Ball, p. 113; Paul Lee Tan, *Jesus Is Coming* (Rockville, Md., Assurance Publishers, 1982), p. 57 ("But what a world to be left in!" Tan added); Tim LaHaye, *The Beginning of the End* (Wheaton, Ill., Tyndale House Publishers, 1972), p. 9; Harold Lindsell, *The Armageddon Spectre* (Westchester, Ill., Crossway Books, 1984), pp. 16, 18.

52. John F. Walvoord, *The Nations in Prophecy* (Grand Rapids, Zondervan Publishing Co., 1967), reprinted in Walvoord, *The Nations, Israel, and the Church in Prophecy* (Grand Rapids, Zondervan Publishing Co., 1988), p. 115.

53. Richard W. DeHaan, *Israel and the Nations in Prophecy* (Grand Rapids, Zondervan Publishing House, 1968), pp. 140–141; William R. Goetz, *Apocalypse Next: Updated* (Cathedral City, Calif., Horizon House Publishers, 1981), pp. 149, 150, 151–152; Salem Kirban, *666* (Wheaton, Ill., Tyndale House, 1970), p. 136.

54. S. Maxwell Coder, *The Final Chapter: Understanding What the Bible Says about the Last Pages of Human History* (Wheaton, Ill., Tyndale House Publishers), pp. 97–98.

55. Robert Glenn Gromacki, *Are These the Last Days?* (Old Tappan, N.J., Fleming H. Revell, 1970), p. 128. The same point is made in Vander Lugt, *There's a New Day Coming,* p. 41; LaHaye, *The Beginning of the End,* p. 174; and James Montgomery Boice, *The Last and Future World* (Grand Rapids, Zondervan Publishing Co., 1974), p. 110.

56. Ray C. Stedman, *What's This World Coming To?* (Ventura, Calif., Regal Books, 2nd ed., 1986), pp. 72, 74.

57. David Webber and Noah Hutchings, *Is This the Last Century?* (Nashville, Thomas Nelson, 1979), p. 93; Doug Clark, *Shockwaves of Armageddon* (Eugene, Oreg., Harvest Books, 1982), p. 91.

58. Charles H. Stevens, "The Last Gentile World Ruler," in Feinberg, *Prophecy and the Seventies,* p. 238; Boice, *Last and Future World,* pp. 110, 112, 127.

59. Van Impe, *Signs of the Times,* pp. 73–74. The same argument is made by Charles R. Taylor in *The Destiny of America,* pp. 60–62.

60. McCall and Levitt, *Coming Russian Invasion of Israel,* p. 54; David Wilkerson, *Set the Trumpet to Thy Mouth* (Lindale, Tex., World Challenge, 1985), p. 1.

61. Roy Hicks, *Another Look at the Rapture* (Tulsa, Harrison House, 1982), p. 103. See also Carl G. Johnson, *Prophecy Made Plain for Times like These* (Chicago, Moody Press, 1972), p. 59.

62. Clifford Wilson and John Weldon, *1980s: Decade of Shock* (San Diego, Master Books, 1978), p. 78; Dave Hunt, *Peace, Prosperity, and the Coming Holocaust* (Eugene, Oreg., Harvest House Publishers, 1983), p. 224; Chuck Smith, *The Final Curtain* (Costa Mesa, Calif., Word for Today, 1984), p. 63.

63. Unger, *Beyond the Crystal Ball,* p. 115; Gromacki, *Are These the Last Days?* pp. 100, 152.

64. David Wilkerson, *Set the Trumpet to Thy Mouth* (Lindale, Tex., World Challenge, 1985), pp. 16, 17; Bill McKee, *Orbit of Ashes: Jesus Is Coming* (Wheaton, Ill., Tyndale House, 1972), p. 38. See also David Edwin Harrell, Jr., *All Things Are Possible: The Healing and Charismatic Revivals in Modern America* (Bloomington, Indiana University Press, 1975), pp. 186–187 (on Wilkerson); Roy E. Laurin, "Israel and the End of History," in Culbertson and Centz, *Understanding the Times,* p. 236; and Steven Kull, "Nuclear Arms and the Desire for World Destruction," *Political Psychology,* 4, no. 3 (1983), 563–591. Kull argues that the "present trend toward a nuclear holocaust" may be rooted in an "unconscious attraction to world destruction" linked in turn to "a symbolic or archetypal process of death and rebirth" (p. 563). In some respects the prophecy writers who link the Battle of Armageddon and the Millennium fit this model, although the historical rootedness of their belief system ought not be ignored.

65. Carl McIntire, *Christian Beacon,* June 24, 1965, p. 5, quoted in Erling Jorstad, *The Politics of Doomsday: Fundamentalists of the Far Right* (Nashville, Abingdon Press, 1970), p. 33; Chuck Smith, *What the World Is Coming To* (Costa Mesa, Calif., Word for Today, 1977), p. 134; John Cumming, *Voices of Today* (London, 1854), quoted in Smith, *This Atomic Age and the Word of God,* p. 153.

66. Robert Scheer interview with Falwell, *Los Angeles Times,* March 4, 1981, quoted in Grace Halsell, *Prophecy and Politics: Militant Evangelists on the Road to Nuclear War* (Westport, Conn., Lawrence Hill and Co., 1986), pp. 34–35; Jerry Falwell, *Nuclear War and the Second Coming of Jesus Christ* (Lynchburg, Va., "Old Time Gospel Hour," 1983); Jerry Falwell, "The Twenty-First Century and the End of the World," *Fundamentalist Journal* (May 1988), 11; Jerry Falwell, "Nuclear War and the Second Coming of Jesus Christ," cassette tape, 1983, quoted in Barkun, "Nuclear War and Millenarian Symbols," p. 10.

67. Falwell cassette tape, "Nuclear War and the Second Coming of Jesus Christ," and booklet *Nuclear War and the Second Coming of Jesus Christ,* pp. 2–3, both quoted in Barkun, "Nuclear War and Millenarian Symbols," pp. 9–10, 11.

68. Pat Robertson, *700 Club Newsletter,* Feb.-Mar. 1980, quoted in Stephen O'Leary and M. W. McFarland, "The Political Use of Mythic Discourse: Prophetic Interpretation in Pat Robertson's Presidential Campaign," typescript, p. 12—a revised version of this paper appeared in *Quarterly Journal of Speech,* 75 (Nov. 1989), 433–452; Robertson, *Perspective* (newsletter; Feb. 1982), quoted in David Allen Lewis, *Magog 1982 Cancelled* (Harrison, Ark., New Leaf Press, 1982), p. 7; Robertson,

"Israel: The Key to U.S. Security!" "700 Club" broadcast, May 19, 1982, quoted in Danny Collum, "Armageddon Theology as a Threat to Peace," *Faith and Mission,* Fall 1986, p. 63; David Edwin Harrell, Jr., *Pat Robertson: A Personal, Religious, and Political Portrait* (San Francisco, Harper and Row, 1987).

69. Harrell, *Pat Robertson,* pp. 149, 150, 151; Pat Robertson with Bob Slosser, *The Secret Kingdom* (New York, Bantam Books, 1984; orig. publ. 1982), pp. 46, 222.

70. Billy Graham, *World Aflame* (New York, Penguin Books, 1967; orig. publ. 1965), pp. 165, 191.

71. Billy Graham, *Approaching Hoofbeats: The Four Horsemen of the Apocalypse* (Waco, Tex., Word Books, 1983), pp. 133–139 (Moscow quote p. 134), 144 ("in process" quote).

72. Ibid., p. 122, 124, 132, 182.

73. Ibid., pp. 74, 146 ("ultimate peace"), 220–221 ("nuclear conflagrations").

74. Billy Graham, "Are the Last Days Almost Here?" telecast sermon from Little Rock, Mar. 5, 1990; Yehezkel Landau, "The President and the Bible: What Do the Prophets Say to Our Time?" *Christianity and Crisis,* Dec. 12, 1983, p. 475, quoting "a devout Catholic friend."

75. Hal Lindsey, *The 1980s: Countdown to Armageddon* (New York, Bantam Books, 1981), pp. 5–6.

76. Robert Scheer, *With Enough Shovels: Reagan, Bush, and Nuclear War* (New York, Random House, 1982), p. xi (Weinberger); Halsell, *Prophecy and Politics,* p. 8 (Watt); C. Everett Koop, "Prophecy Conference Meets in Jerusalem," *Eternity,* Aug. 1971, p. 23. Responding to a query about his remarks, Caspar Weinberger wrote to the author on June 25, 1990, "In the news conference you refer to, in response to a question as to whether I believed in the Bible, I merely answered that I did."

77. Charles Colson, with Ellen Santilli Vaughn, *Kingdoms in Conflict* (New York, William Morrow Co., 1987), "Prologue—March 24, 1998," pp. 12–40 (quoted passage p. 16).

78. Collum, "Armageddon Theology as a Threat to Peace," p. 61 (quoting Reagan from May 1968 *Christian Life* interview); James Mills, "The Serious Implications of a 1971 Conversation with Ronald Reagan: A Footnote to Current History," *San Diego Magazine,* Aug. 1985, p. 141.

79. Wolf Blitzer, *Jerusalem Post,* Oct. 28, 1983, quoted in Landau, "The President and the Bible," p. 474.

80. *New York Times,* Oct. 23, 1984, p. A28; "The Personal Testimony of George Bush: Have You Been Born Again?" *Update Newswire Alert* (Hilton Sutton newsletter), Aug. 1988, p. 2; Ed Dobson and Ed Hindson, "Apocalypse Now? What Fundamentalists Believe about the End of the World," *Policy Review,* 38 (Fall 1986), p. 16.

81. "Reckoning with Armageddon," editorial, *New York Times,* Oct. 25, 1984; Collum, "Armageddon Theology as a Threat to Peace," p. 63; Harrell, *Pat Robertson,* p. 148; Hunter S. Thompson, "As the Worm Turns," *Los Angeles Times,* Oct. 29, 1987.

82. Collum, "Armageddon Theology as a Threat to Peace," pp. 63–64.

83. Lindsell, *Armageddon Spectre,* p. 17; Dobson and Hindson, "Apocalypse Now?" p. 22; Michael Barkun, "Nuclear Weapons and Millennial Expectations," lecture at Northwestern University, Feb. 25, 1989.

84. Halsell, *Prophecy and Politics,* p. 10; Barkun, "Nuclear Weapons and Millennial Expectations"; Collum, "Armageddon Theology as a Threat to Peace," p. 56; Eddie F. Carder, "An Examination of the Dispensational Incorporation of Nuclear War into an Eschatological Frame of Reference with Special Reference to the Approaches of Jerry Falwell and Hal Lindsey," unpublished, Southwestern Baptist Theological Seminary, Fort Worth, 1989, p. 1. My thanks to the Reverend Mr. Carder for sending me a copy of this paper. See also Daniel Yankelovich and John Doble, "The Public Mood: Nuclear Weapons and the U.S.S.R.," *Foreign Affairs,* 63 (Fall 1984), 40–41.

85. Gromacki, *Are These the Last Days?* p. 104; Taylor, *Destiny of America,* p. 54; Wilson and Weldon, *1980s: Decade of Shock,* p. 82; "The Great Cosmic Countdown: Hal Lindsey on the Future," *Eternity,* Jan. 1977, p. 21.

86. Lindsey, *1980s: Countdown to Armageddon,* pp. 70–71, 77–86, 149 (quoted passage), 157.

87. Peter Stiglin, "Apocalyptic Theology and the Right," *Witness,* Oct. 1986, p. 7 ("court prophets"); Tom Sine, "Bring Down the Final Curtain," *Sojourners,* June–July 1984, p. 13 (Falwell); Jerry Falwell, "Nuclear War and the Second Coming of Jesus Christ," cassette tape; Collum, "Armageddon Theology as a Threat to Peace," p. 60 (Falwell); Halsell, *Prophecy and Politics,* p. 15 (Robison); Dan Betzer, *The Beast: A Novel of the Future World Dictator* (Lafayette, La., Prescott Press, 1985), p. 168. See also Smith, *The Final Curtain,* p. 9.

88. Lindsell, *Armageddon Spectre,* pp. 17, 19, 80, 98, 99, 120.

89. Robert Jewett, "Coming to Terms with the Boom Doom," *Quarterly Review,* 4, no. 3 (Fall 1984), p. 9; Russell, *Apocalyptic Ancient and Modern,* p. 64.

90. Stephen D. O'Leary, "Justice and Judgment in Competing Interpretations of Apocalyptic Texts: Modern Fundamentalism vs. the Social Gospel and the Theology of Liberation," paper delivered at the 1988 annual meeting of the Speech Communication Association, New Orleans, p. 4, quoted by permission; Carder, "Examination of the Dispensational Incorporation of Nuclear War," pp. 6, 7. See also Mojtabai, *Blessed Assurance,* p. 164, and A. G. Mojtabai, "Fundamentalism and Nuclear

Threat," in *Nuclear "Normality": The Ethics of Annihilation; A Conference Hosted by the Center on Violence and Human Survival and the Academy of Humanities and Sciences of the City University of New York* (New York, Center on Violence and Human Survival, [1990]), pp. 39–50.

91. A. Berkley Michelson, *Daniel and Revelation: Riddles or Realities?* (Nashville, Thomas Nelson Publishers, 1984), p. 149.

92. John F. Walvoord and John E. Walvoord, *Armageddon, Oil, and the Middle East Crisis: What the Bible Says about the Future of the Middle East and the End of Western Civilization* (Grand Rapids, Zondervan Publishing Co., 1974), p. 72. For a study suggesting the pervasiveness of abstract images of nuclear war, see Susan T. Fiske, Felicia Pratto, and Mark A. Pavelchak, "Citizens' Images of Nuclear War; Content and Consequences," *Journal of Social Issues,* 39, no. 1 (1983), 41–65.

93. Robert Jay Lifton, *Death in Life: Survivors of Hiroshima* (New York, Basic Books, 1967), and subsequent works; Carol Cohn, "Sex and Death in the Rational World of Defense Intellectuals," *Signs,* Summer 1987, pp. 687–718.

94. Clark, *Shockwaves of Armageddon,* p. 21; Hilton Sutton, Shalom Christian Center, Madison, Wis., Aug. 20, 1988; James Strong, *Exhaustive Concordance of the Bible* (New York, Abingdon Press, 1965), pp. 708–709 ("nation" and "nations" references); Rev. 16:4, 18:3, 19:15; Dan. 7:14.

95. Dobson and Hindson, "Apocalypse Now?" p. 16.

96. Gordon D. Kaufman, "Nuclear Eschatology and the Study of Religion," *Bulletin of the Harvard Divinity School* (Feb.-Mar. 1983), 6–10 (quoted passages p. 8).

97. Mojtabai, *Blessed Assurance,* pp. 90, 95 ("the world stinks"), 157–158 (Jones), 164.

98. Collum, "Armageddon Theology as a Threat to Peace," p. 59.

5. Ezekiel as the First Cold Warrior

1. Ezek. 38:1–6,15.

2. Rev. 20:8.

3. Gen. 10:2; Isidore Singer, ed., *The Jewish Encyclopedia* (New York, KTAV Publishing House, [1901]), VI, 19–20 ("Gog and Magog"); Patrick Fairbairn, *An Exposition of Ezekiel* (Grand Rapids, Zondervan Publishing House, 1960; reprint of undated nineteenth-century work), p. 415.

4. Peter Toon, "Introduction," in Toon, ed., *Puritans, the Millennium, and the Future of Israel* (Cambridge, James Clarke and Co., 1970), pp. 16 (Augustine), 19–20 (Turks); Marjorie Reeves, *The Influence of Prophecy in the Later Middle Ages: A Study in Joachimism* (Oxford, Clarendon

Press, 1969), p. 305; Norman Cohn, *The Pursuit of the Millennium: Revolutionary Millenarians and Mystical Anarchists of the Middle Ages* (London, Temple Smith, rev. ed., 1970), p. 236; Wilbur M. Smith, "Eastern Kings and Preparation for Armageddon," *Sunday School Times,* 90, no. 52 (Dec. 25, 1948), 1155 (prophetic interpretations of Euphrates River passage); Ruth H. Bloch, *Visionary Republic: Millennial Themes in American Thought, 1756–1800* (New York, Cambridge University Press, 1985), p. 120; Rev. 16:12 (Euphrates).

5. Stephen J. Stein, "Transatlantic Extensions: Apocalyptic in Early New England," in C. A. Patrides and Joseph Wittreich, eds., *The Apocalypse in English Renaissance Thought and Literature* (Manchester, Manchester University Press, 1984), p. 272 (Bradstreet); Bloch, *Visionary Republic,* p. 145; Elhanan Winchester, *A Course of Lectures on the Prophecies Which Remain to Be Fulfilled* (Cincinnati, E. Morgan and Co., 1851; reprint of 1788 work), pp. 114, 118; Robert Anderson, *The Coming Prince* (Grand Rapids, Kregel Publications, 1957; reprint of 1884 work), p. 142; *World Peace in the Light of Prophecy* (Washington, D.C., *Review and Herald* Publishing Assn., 1919), p. 83; Mary N. Layoun (Department of Comparative Literature, University of Wisconsin) to author, Mar. 13, 1990 (Antichrist belief in contemporary Greece).

6. Anderson, *Coming Prince,* p. 143.

7. M. Habershon, *A Dissertation on the Prophetic Scriptures, Chiefly Those of a Chronological Character; Shewing Their Aspect on the Present Times, and on the Destinies of the Jewish Nation* (London, James Nisbet, 1834), p. 79.

8. Francis Brown, S. R. Driver, and Charles A. Briggs, *A Hebrew and English Lexicon of the Old Testament* (Oxford, Clarendon Press, 1959), p. 912; John N. Darby, *Lectures on the Second Coming* (London, G. Morrish, 1909), p. 183; *Dictionary of National Biography* (London, Oxford University Press, 1921–1922), XII, 216–217 ("Lowth, William"); S. Maxwell Coder, *The Final Chapter: Understanding What the Bible Says about the Last Pages of Human History* (Wheaton, Ill., Tyndale House Publishers, 1984), p. 91.

9. Heinrich Friedrich Wilhelm Gesenius, *Hebräisches und chaldäisches Handwörterbuch über das Alte Testament* (Leipzig, 1828); Singer, *Jewish Encyclopedia,* V, 643 ("Gesenius, Heinrich Friedrich Wilhelm"); *Encyclopedia Britannica* (New York, Encyclopedia Britannica Co., 11th ed., 1910), XI, 909 ("Gesenius, Heinrich Friedrich Wilhelm"); David L. Cooper, *When Gog's Armies Meet the Almighty* (Los Angeles, Bible Research Society, 4th ed., 1970), p. 11; Dwight Wilson, *Armageddon Now! The Premillenarian Response to Russia and Israel since 1917* (Grand Rapids, Baker Book House, 1977), p. 152.

10. *A Hebrew and English Lexicon of the Old Testament, Translated from the*

Latin of William Gesenius by Edward Robinson (Boston, 1836); Darby, *Lectures on the Second Coming*, p. 183; idem, *The Hopes of the Church of God in Connexion with the Destiny of the Jews and the Nations as Revealed in Prophecy: Eleven Lectures Delivered in Geneva in 1840* (London, 1842; 2nd ed.), p. 64 (quoted passage).

11. James M. Gray, *A Text-Book on Prophecy* (New York, Fleming H. Revell, 1918), p. 165 (citing an 1855 tract by Benjamin Wills Newton predicting Russia's defeat in the Crimean War on the basis of biblical prophecy); Wilson, *Armageddon Now!* pp. 14, 26 (Cumming quote); *Dictionary of National Biography*, V, 297–298 ("Cumming, John").

12. Henry Cowles, *Ezekiel and Daniel with Notes, Critical, Explanatory, and Practical* (New York, D. Appleton and Co., 1875; copyright 1867), p. 219; article by Walter Scott in *Prophetic News and Israel's Watch*, June 1888, quoted in Wilbur M. Smith, "The Testimony of Bible Prophecy," *Moody Monthly*, Sept. 1949, p. 15; Beverley O. Kinnear, *Impending Judgments on the Earth* (New York, James Huggins, 1892), p. 2. For further examples of nineteenth-century references to Russia's role in prophecy see Edward Hoare, *Palestine and Russia* (London, Hatchards, 1877; reprinted London, 1918), p. 1; A. Whitman, *Prophecy Opened: Illustrating the Character of God, as Shown in His Providential and Gracious Administration on Earth* (Carthage, Mo., Advance Book and Job Printing House, 1874), p. 477; and Fairbairn, *Exposition of Ezekiel*, p. 415.

13. E. W. Hengstenberg, *The Prophecies of the Prophet Ezekiel Elucidated* (Edinburgh, T. and T. Clarke, 1869), pp. 331, 333 (quoted passage; added Hengstenberg [p. 332]: "Of Gog, Ezekiel only knows"); A. B. Davidson, *The Book of the Prophet Ezekiel with Notes and Introduction* (Cambridge, Cambridge University Press, 1892), p. 275.

14. A. C. Gaebelein, in *Our Hope*, Aug. 1916, quoted in Wilson, *Armageddon Now!* p. 37; New Scofield Reference Bible (New York, Oxford University Press, 1967), pp. 881–882. See also Gaebelein, *Hath God Cast Away His People?* (New York, Gospel Publishing House, 1905), pp. 231–232, 240.

15. Ezek. 38:12.

16. Hoare, *Palestine and Russia*, p. 1; Wilson, *Armageddon Now!* p. 16 (Scofield).

17. *World Peace in the Light of Prophecy*, p. 17; Joel A. Carpenter, "From Fundamentalism to the New Evangelical Coalition," in George Marsden, ed., *Evangelicalism and Modern America* (Grand Rapids, Wm. B. Eerdman's Publishing Co., 1984), p. 178n34, citing anticommunist articles in pre–World War II prophecy journals.

18. Donald Grey Barnhouse, *Revelation: An Expository Commentary* (Grand Rapids, Zondervan Publishing House, 1971; reprint of editorials in *Revelation*, 1939–1942), p. 362; F. W. Pitt, *Coming Events Cast Their Shadows*

in the Air (London, Marshall, Morgan, and Scott, 1936), p. 70; *Evangel* (Assemblies of God periodical), Aug. 4, 1934, p. 7, quoted in Wilson, *Armageddon Now!* p. 110. See also ibid., pp. 110–117, passim; Arthur I. Brown, *The Eleventh "Hour"* (Findlay, Ohio, Fundamental Truth Publishing Co., 1940), p. 155; and Robert G. Clouse, "The Danger of Mistaken Hopes," in Carl E. Armerding and W. Ward Gasque, eds., *Dreams, Visions, and Oracles: The Layman's Guide to Biblical Prophecy* (Grand Rapids, Baker Book House, 1977), p. 33.

19. Dan Gilbert, *The Red Terror and Bible Prophecy* (1944), cited in Wilson, *Armageddon Now!* p. 149; Louis S. Bauman, *Russian Events in the Light of Bible Prophecy* (New York, Fleming H. Revell, 1942), chaps. 8, 10, 21.

20. Charles O. Benham, *101 Roadsigns to Our Next Pearl Harbor and Armageddon* (Washington, D.C., *National Forecast Magazine,* 1945), p. 7; Merril T. MacPherson, "Russia in the News and Prophecy," *Christian Life,* 2 (Nov. 1947), 28, cited in Wilson, *Armageddon Now!* p. 152. See also, in the same vein, Arthur I. Brown, *I Will Come Again* (Findlay, Ohio, Fundamental Truth Publishing Co., 1947), p. 71.

21. Paul R. Alderman, Jr., *The Unfolding of the Ages: Prophecy Fulfilled, Prophecy Being Fulfilled, Prophecy to Be Fulfilled* (Grand Rapids, Zondervan Publishing Co., 1954), pp. 103, 105.

22. Ibid., p. 104; Wilbur M. Smith, *World Crises and the Prophetic Scriptures* (Chicago, Moody Press, 1952), pp. 248–251 (quoted passage pp. 250–251); F. L. Cross, ed., *Oxford Dictionary of the Christian Church* (London, Oxford University Press, 1957), p. 1110 ("Proclus, St."); *The Oxford English Dictionary* (Oxford, Clarendon Press, 1933), VIII, 925, says the word "Russia" in its Russian form "appears to have been adapted from Byzantine Greek." Scores, and probably hundreds, of postwar prophecy writers made the Rosh = Russia connection, usually citing Gesenius, Bishop Loth, Scofield, or all three. For a representative sampling see Herbert Vander Lugt, *There's a New Day Coming!* (Eugene, Oreg., Harvest House, 1983), p. 35; Jack Van Impe with Roger F. Campbell, *Israel's Final Holocaust* (Nashville, Thomas Nelson Publishers, 1979), pp. 132–133; Thomas S. McCall and Zola Levitt, *Coming Russian Invasion of Israel: Updated* (Chicago, Moody Press, 1987), p. 28; Alderman, *Unfolding of the Ages,* p. 104; Tom Westwood, *Palestine: The World's Last Battleground* (Redlands, Calif., Bible Treasury Hour, 1968), p. 31; Walter K. Price, *The Coming Antichrist* (Chicago, Moody Press, 1974), p. 184.

23. S. Maxwell Coder, "The Future of Russia," in Charles Lee Feinberg, ed., *Focus on Prophecy* (New York, Fleming H. Revell, 1964), pp. 77–91; idem, "The Future of Russia—Part I," *Moody Monthly,* Sept. 1963, pp. 24–25, 73–75 (quoted passage p. 74); idem, *Final Chapter,* chap. 8, pp. 91–100, esp. pp. 91–92.

24. John F. Walvoord, "Russia, King of the North—Part I," *Fundamentalist*

Journal, Jan. 1984, pp. 35–38 (quoted passage p. 37). See also, for "far north" argument, Hal Lindsey, *The Late Great Planet Earth* (New York, Bantam Books, 1973), p. 54; James Montgomery Boice, *The Last and Future World* (Grand Rapids, Zondervan Publishing Co., 1974), p. 105. Jer. 25:26 speaks of "all the kings of the north, far and near." See also Dan. 11:40, Joel 2:20, Jer. 25:9.

25. Van Impe and Campbell, *Israel's Final Holocaust,* p. 133; Vander Lugt, *There's a New Day Coming,* p. 33.

26. Milton B. Lindberg, *The Jew and Modern Israel in the Light of Prophecy* (Chicago, Moody Press, 1930; rev. Archie A. MacKinney, 1969), p. 60; S. Maxwell Coder, "The Future of Russia—Part II," *Moody Monthly,* Oct. 1963, p. 58; Carl G. Johnson, *Prophecy Made Plain for Times like These* (Chicago, Moody Press, 1972), p. 151 (Alsop article). As with many prophecy works, the dating of specific passages in Lindberg's book is difficult because it went through a number of editions and revisions. The quoted passage appears to date from the early postwar period.

27. David Webber and Noah Hutchings, *Is This the Last Century?* (Nashville, Thomas Nelson Publishers, 1979), p. 95; Wim Malgo, *Russia's Last Invasion* (Columbia, S.C., Midnight Call, 1980), cover statement.

28. John Wesley White, *The Coming World Dictator* (Minneapolis, Bethany House Publishers, 1981), p. 82.

29. McCall and Levitt, *Coming Russian Invasion of Israel,* pp. 9, 17. See also Lindsey, *Late Great Planet Earth,* pp. 56, 57, 146; Lindberg, *Jew and Modern Israel,* p. 59; and Hal Lindsey, *The 1980s: Countdown to Armageddon* (New York, Bantam Books, 1981), p. xi.

30. Lindsey, *Late Great Planet Earth,* chap. 5; idem, *The 1980s,* chap. 6, pp. 70–74 (charts); Chuck Smith, *Future Survival* (Costa Mesa, Calif., Word for Today, 1978), p. 92.

31. Jack Van Impe, *11:59 and Counting* (Royal Oak, Mich., Jack Van Impe Ministries, 1983), p. 25; *Perhaps Today* (Van Impe magazine), Nov./ Dec. 1988, pp. 22–23; "Profile: Jack and Rexella Van Impe Living Out the Word of God" (brochure, 1988), [p. 3]; Van Impe product order form, 1988 ("The Coming War with Russia" cassette); "They Call Him the Walking Bible," *Perhaps Today,* May/June 1988, pp. 9, 19.

32. Hilton Sutton, *World War III: God's Conquest of Israel* (Tulsa, Harrison House, 4th ed., 1982), p. 26; William R. Goetz, *Apocalypse Next: Updated* (Cathedral City, Calif., Horizon Books, 1981), pp. 126–134 (quoted passage p. 126). See also, for undocumented assertion that Russia's destruction is foretold, Elwood McQuaid, *It Is No Dream! Bible Prophecy: Fact or Fanaticism?* (West Collingwood, N.J., Spearhead Press, 1978), p. 213; and Rick Yohn, *What Every Christian Should Know about*

Bible Prophecy (Eugene, Oreg., Harvest House Publishers, 1982), n.p., "The Great Holocaust."

33. *The Westminster Study Edition of the Holy Bible* (Philadelphia, Westminster Press, 1948), p. 1219, general comment on Ezek. 38–39 and specific comment on Ezek. 38:2 (quoted phrase); Herbert G. May and Bruce M. Metzger, eds., *The Oxford Annotated Bible with Apocrypha* (New York, Oxford University Press, 1965), pp. 1049–50 (quoted phrase p. 1050).

34. William Sanford LaSor, *The Truth about Armageddon: What the Bible Says about the End Times* (New York, Harper and Row, 1982), pp. 146, 147; A. Bekley Michelson, *Daniel and Revelation: Riddles or Realities?* (Nashville, Thomas Nelson Publishers, 1984), pp. 207, 227.

35. Morris A. Inch, *Understanding Bible Prophecy* (New York, Harper and Row, 1977), pp. 26, 99.

36. James Mills, "The Serious Implications of a 1971 Conversation with Ronald Reagan," *San Diego Magazine,* Aug. 1985, pp. 140, 141; Ronald Reagan, "Address to the National Association of Evangelicals, March 8, 1983," in Paul Boyer, ed., *Reagan as President: Contemporary Views of the Man, His Politics, and His Policies* (Chicago, Ivan R. Dee, 1990), pp. 165–169.

37. Harry A. Ironside, *Expository Notes on Ezekiel the Prophet* (Neptune, N.J., Loizeaux Bros., 1949), p. 267; Harry Rimmer, *The Shadow of Coming Events* (Grand Rapids, Wm. B. Eerdman's Publishing Co., 1946), pp. 42–44 (quoted phrase p. 44); Merrill F. Unger, *Beyond the Crystal Ball* (Chicago, Moody Press, 1973), p. 89. See also Dale Crowley, *The Soon Coming of Our Lord* (New York, Loizeaux Bros. 1958), p. 62; Goetz, *Apocalypse Next,* p. 148; J. Dwight Pentecost, *Prophecy for Today* (Grand Rapids, Zondervan Publishing Co., 1961), p. 109. For precise value of Dead Sea minerals: Salem Kirban, *Guide to Survival* (Huntington Valley, Pa., Salem Kirban, 1978; rev. of 1968 work), p. 189; Paul Lee Tan, *Jesus Is Coming* (Rockville, Md., Assurance Publishers, 1982), p. 55; Van Impe, *11:59 and Counting,* p. 138.

38. Kirban, *Guide to Survival,* p. 189; McCall and Levitt, *Coming Russian Invasion of Israel,* p. 88.

39. John F. Walvoord with John E. Walvoord, *Armageddon, Oil, and the Middle East Crisis: What the Bible Says about the Future of the Middle East and the End of Western Civilization* (Grand Rapids, Zondervan Publishing Co., 1974); author interview with John F. Walvoord, Aug. 18, 1989; Grace Halsell, *Prophecy and Politics: Militant Evangelists on the Road to Nuclear War* (Westport, Conn., Lawrence Hill and Co., 1986), p. 33 (Falwell); Smith, *Future Survival,* p. 12; Doug Clark, *Shockwaves of Armageddon* (Eugene, Oreg., Harvest Books, 1982), p. 37.

40. Lindsey, *Late Great Planet Earth,* p. 149.

41. Tim LaHaye, *The Coming Peace in the Middle East* (Grand Rapids, Zondervan Publishing Co., 1984), p. 125–126; Lindsey, *The 1980s,* p. 13; Van Impe, *Israel's Final Holocaust,* p. 135.

42. John F. Walvoord, "What Is the Future of Communism?" *Eternity,* Mar. 1955, p. 14; Ironside, *Expository Notes on Ezekiel,* p. 266; Alva J. McClain, "Significant Signs of the Times," in John W. Bradbury, ed., *Hastening the Day of the Lord: Prophetic Messages from the International Congress on Prophecy in Calvary Baptist Church, New York City, November 9–16, 1952* (Wheaton, Ill., Van Kampen Press, 1953), p. 33.

43. Hab. 1:2–3,6,9–10.

44. V. Raymond Edman, "Habakkuk in the Nuclear Age," in Charles Lee Feinberg, ed., *Focus on Prophecy* (New York, Fleming H. Revell, 1964), p. 120; Arthur E. Bloomfield, *How to Recognize the Antichrist* (Minneapolis, Bethany Fellowship, 1975), p. 103; Walvoord, "What Is the Future of Communism?" pp. 14 (quoted phrase), 44. See also, for Walvoord's views on communism, idem, *The Return of the Lord* (Findlay, Ohio, Dunham Publishing Co., 1955), p. 132; idem, "Is the End of the Age at Hand?" in Feinberg, *Focus on Prophecy,* p. 175; and idem, *The Nations, Israel, and the Church in Prophecy* (Grand Rapids, Zondervan Publishing Co., 1988), p. 118; White, *Coming World Dictator,* p. 28.

45. McCall and Levitt, *Coming Russian Invasion of Israel,* p. 36.

46. Lindsey, *Late Great Planet Earth,* p. 59; Wilson, *Armageddon Now!* pp. 27, 50, 117; Brown, *Eleventh "Hour,"* p. 77. See also David L. Cooper, *When Gog's Armies Meet the Almighty* (Los Angeles, Biblical Research Society, 1970; reprint of 1940 ed.), pp. 11, 12, 13, 15.

47. Alderman, *Unfolding of the Ages,* p. 106; Lindsey, *Late Great Planet Earth,* p. 58; McCall and Levitt, *Coming Russian Invasion of Israel,* p. 30. See also Arthur I. Brown, *I Will Come Again* (Findlay, Ohio, Fundamental Truth Publishing Co., 1947), p. 70 ("Gomer, undoubtedly, is Germany"); Coder, *Final Chapter,* p. 93.

48. Coder, "The Future of Nations," in Feinberg, *Focus on Prophecy,* p. 107; Robert Glenn Gromacki, *Are These the Last Days?* (Old Tappan, N.J., Fleming H. Revell, 1970), p. 127; Lindsey, *Late Great Planet Earth,* pp. 56 (Gesenius), 57 (quoted passage); McCall and Levitt, *Coming Russian Invasion of Israel,* p. 30 (OAU).

49. Rev. 9:14–16, 16:12; Dan. 11:44; Boice, *Last and Future World,* pp. 108–109; Herman A. Hoyt, "The Crisis of This Present Hour," in *The Prophetic Word in Crisis Days* (Findlay, Ohio, Dunham Publishing Co., 1961), p. 35; Wilson, *Armageddon Now!* pp. 159–160; La Sor, *Truth about Armageddon,* p. 135; James Montgomery Boice, "Are We Nearing the Last Days?" *Eternity,* Dec. 1972, p. 59; Tan, *Jesus Is Coming,* p. 60 (quoted phrase).

50. Lindsey, *Late Great Planet Earth,* p. 73; Hal Lindsey with C. C. Carlson, *The Terminal Generation* (New York, Bantam Books, 1977), p. 56; Gordon Lindsay, *Red China in Prophecy* (Dallas, Christ for the Nations, 1972), front cover, pp. 3, 8.

51. Pentecost, *Prophecy for Today,* p. 122; Coder, "The Future of Russia—Part I," p. 75; Gromacki, *Are These the Last Days?* pp. 98, 126, 127; Clark, *Shockwaves of Armageddon,* pp. 45, 157.

52. John F. Walvoord, *Israel in Prophecy* (Grand Rapids, Zondervan Publishing Co., 1962), p. 129; Tom Westwood, *Palestine: The World's Last Battleground* (Redlands, Calif., Bible Treasury Hour, 1968), p. 35; Unger, *Beyond the Crystal Ball,* pp. 99, 100, 113. See also Charles Lea, *World Events in the Light of God's Word* (New York, Comet Press, 1959), p. 43; Hilton Sutton, *Revelation: God's Grand Finale* (Tulsa, Harrison House, 1984), p. 112.

53. Walter K. Price, *The Coming Antichrist* (Chicago, Moody Press, 1974), p. 197.

54. Salem Kirban, *666* (Wheaton, Ill., Tyndale House, 1970), pp. 234–235.

55. Lindsey, *Late Great Planet Earth,* pp. 70, 151; idem, *The 1980s,* pp. 90–96 (quoted passage p. 96).

56. Ezek. 38:18–19,22; 39:1–2,4,6.

57. Ezek. 39:19–20.

58. Joel 2:20.

59. Louis S. Talbot, "Palestine, Russia, and Ezekiel 38," *King's Business,* 39 (Jan. 1948), 13, in Wilson, *Armageddon Now!* p. 152; Dale Crowley, *The Soon Coming of Our Lord* (New York, Loizeaux Brothers, 1958), chap. 7, pp. 57–65. See also McClain, "Significant Signs of the Times," p. 35.

60. Coder, "The Future of Russia," in Feinberg, *Focus on Prophecy,* p. 78; Richard W. DeHaan, *Israel and the Nations in Prophecy* (Grand Rapids, Zondervan Publishing Co., 1968), pp. 80 (quoted passage), 143; Kirban, *666,* p. 134. See also Coder, *Final Chapter,* p. 96.

61. Johnson, *Prophecy Made Plain for Times like These,* p. 161.

62. McCall and Levitt, *Coming Russian Invasion of Israel,* p. 48; John F. Walvoord, *The Return of the Lord* (Findlay, Ohio, Dunham Publishing Co., 1955), p. 140. See also Kirban, *Guide to Survival,* p. 256; Smith, *Future Survival,* p. 20; Unger, *Beyond the Crystal Ball,* p. 79; Sutton, *World War III,* pp. 36–37. For a slightly different scenario see S. Franklin Logsdon, *Profiles of Prophecy* (Grand Rapids, Zondervan Publishing Co., 1970), p. 33.

63. Webber and Hutchings, *Is This the Last Century?* p. 16; Ivor Powell, *What in the World Will Happen Next?* (Grand Rapids, Kregel Publications, 1985), p. 131.

64. Sutton, *World War III,* p. 30; Halsell, *Prophecy and Politics,* p. 16 (quoting

Pat Robertson broadcast, Jan. 9, 1982). See also Hal Lindsey, *There's a New World Coming* (Santa Ana, Calif., Vision House Publishers, 1973), p. 224, and Smith, *Future Survival*, p. 16.

65. Falwell interview with Robert Scheer, *Los Angeles Times*, Mar. 4, 1981, quoted in Halsell, *Prophecy and Politics*, p. 34; Falwell 1983 broadcast, ibid., p. 35. See also Jerry Falwell, "The Twenty-First Century and the End of the World," *Fundamentalist Journal*, May 1988, p. 11: "God himself will effect a smashing defeat upon this godless government."

66. Lea, *World Events in the Light of God's Word*, p. 32; Tim LaHaye, *The Beginning of the End* (Wheaton, Ill., Tyndale House Publishers, 1972), p. 77; Bloomfield, *How to Recognize the Antichrist*, pp. 80–81, 137. See also Smith, *Future Survival*, p. 20; idem, *The Final Curtain* (Costa Mesa, Calif., Word for Today, 1984), p. 31; Pentecost, *Prophecy for Today*, pp. 110, 112; Coder, "The Future of Israel—Part I," *Moody Monthly*, Sept. 1963, p. 57 ("[Prophecy] ascribes the overthrow of the northern armies to God, and to God alone"); Kirban, *Guide to Survival*, p. 206; Unger, *Beyond the Crystal Ball*, p. 94; and John F. Walvoord, "The Prophetic Word and Russia," in *The Prophetic Word in Crisis Days* (Findlay, Ohio, Dunham Publishing Co., 1961), p. 118. Commenting on Ezek. 38–39, Walvoord says, "It is God himself who destroys this army."

67. Paul R. Bauman, "The Crisis of the Present Hour," *Prophetic Word in Crisis Days*, p. 58; Charles R. Taylor, *The Destiny of America* (Van Nuys, Calif., Time-Light Publishers, 1972), p. 236; LaHaye, *Coming Peace in the Middle East*, pp. 127, 167 (quoted passage). See also McCall and Levitt, *Coming Russian Invasion of Israel*, p. 40; Charles R. Taylor, *Those Who Remain, 1980 Edition* (Orange, Calif., Today in Bible Prophecy, 1980), p. 9; Van Impe, *11:59 and Counting*, p. 195; Roy Hicks, *Another Look at the Rapture* (Tulsa, Harrison House, 1982), pp. 103–104.

68. Ezek. 38:13.

69. Smith, *Future Survival*, p. 8; Unger, *Beyond the Crystal Ball*, p. 90.

70. Charles E. Pont, *The World's Collision* (Boston, W. A. Wilde Co., 1956), p. 133; Taylor, *Those Who Remain*, p. 28; Powell, *What in the World Will Happen Next?* pp. 118–119.

71. Taylor, *Destiny of America*, p. 225; Hilton Sutton, prophecy sermon, Shalom Christian Center, Madison, Wis., Aug. 20, 1988; Sutton, *World War III*, pp. 83–88 (quoted passage pp. 87–88).

72. Ray C. Stedman, *What's This World Coming To?* (Ventura, Calif., Regal Books, 1970; 2nd ed. 1986), p. 74; Webber and Hutchings, *Is This the Last Century?* p. 93; Pat Robertson with Bob Slosser, *The Secret Kingdom* (New York, Bantam Books, 1982), p. 214. See also, for similar ambivalence, Alderman, *Unfolding of the Ages*, p. 107, and Willard Cantelon, *New Money or None?* (Plainfield, N.J., Logos International, 1979), p. 178.

73. Daniel Yankelovich, "The Public Mood: Nuclear Weapons and the U.S.S.R," *Foreign Affairs,* 63 (Fall 1984), 40; Choichiro Yatani and Dana Bramel, "Trends in U.S. Public Opinion about the Soviet Union," *Journal of Social Issues,* 45 (Summer 1989), 13–32; George Gallup, Jr., and Jim Castelli, *The People's Religion: American Faith in the Nineties* (New York, Macmillan Publishing Co., 1989), pp. 211, 213.

74. Van Impe, *11:59 and Counting,* p. 195.

75. J. Dwight Pentecost, *Will Man Survive? Prophecy You Can Understand* (Chicago, Moody Press, 1971), p. 113; Lance Lambert, *Battle for Israel* (Wheaton, Ill., Tyndale House Publishers, 1975; rev. British ed. Eastbourne, Kingsway Publications, 1976), p. 62.

76. Van Impe and Campbell, *Israel's Final Holocaust,* p. 114; Malgo, *Russia's Last Invasion,* p. 9; White, *Coming World Dictator,* p. 116.

77. Author interview with J. Dwight Pentecost, July 13, 1989; *Lighting New Fires* (Jack Van Impe publication), Oct. 1991, [p. 3]; author interview with Louis Goldberg, Feb. 23, 1989.

78. *Salem Kirban's Prophetic Insights,* 1 [1989], pp. 11, 17; *Bible Prophecy News,* Apr.-May-June 1988, pp. 4–5; ibid., Jan.-Feb.-Mar. 1990, p. 6.

79. *End-Time News Digest,* Mar. 1989, p. 12; Sept. 1989, p. 15; Mar. 1990, pp. 1, 3; Apr. 1990, p. 11; May 1990, p. 15; LaHaye, *Coming Peace in the Middle East,* pp. 99–107.

80. Robert W. Faid, *Gorbachev! Has the Real Antichrist Come?* (Tulsa, Victory House Publishers, 1988).

81. Hilton Sutton, prophecy sermon, Shalom Christian Center, Madison, Wis., Aug. 20, 1988.

82. Paul Olson, prophecy sermon, Madison Gospel Tabernacle, Madison, Wis., Nov. 1, 1989.

6. The Final Chastisement of the Chosen

1. Grace Halsell, *Prophecy and Politics: Militant Evangelists on the Road to Nuclear War* (Westport, Conn., Lawrence Hill and Co., 1986), p. 134; Bernard Ramm, *After Fundamentalism: The Future of Evangelical Theology* (New York, Harper and Row, 1983), pp. 185–186, 189; Marjorie Reeves, *The Influence of Prophecy in the Later Middle Ages: A Study in Joachimism* (Oxford, Clarendon Press, 1969), p. 299.

2. Norman Cohn, *The Pursuit of the Millennium: Revolutionary Millenarians and Mystical Anarchists of the Middle Ages* (London, Temple Smith, rev. ed., 1970), pp. 68–69, 76–79, 86; Walter K. Price, *The Coming Antichrist* (Chicago, Moody Press, 1974), p. 22.

3. Heiko O. Oberman, "The Stubborn Jews: Timing the Escalation of Antisemitism in Late Medieval Europe," Leo Baeck Institute, *Yearbook,* 34 (1989), introduction, xi–xxv, esp. pp. xxi–xxv (quoted phrase

p. xxv); Cohn, *Pursuit of the Millennium,* pp. 76 (quoted phrase), 77; Reeves, *Influence of Prophecy in the Later Middle Ages,* pp. 6, 27, 80–81, 515.

4. Oberman, "Stubborn Jews," pp. xv, xvii (Luther quoted).

5. Ramm, *After Fundamentalism,* p. 189; Peter Toon, "The Latter-Day Glory," pp. 24, 25, 30–32, and "The Question of Jewish Immigration," pp. 115–125, esp. pp. 115, 120, 121, in Toon, ed., *Puritans, the Millennium, and the Future of Israel: Puritan Eschatology, 1600–1660* (Cambridge, James Clarke and Co., 1970). See also Ruth H. Bloch, *Visionary Republic: Millennial Themes in American Thought, 1756–1800* (New York, Cambridge University Press, 1985), p. 8; James W. Davidson, *The Logic of Millennial Thought: Eighteenth-Century New England* (New Haven, Yale University Press, 1977), p. 53 (Mede). For a comprehensive treatment, see Mayir Vereté, "The Restoration of the Jews in English Protestant Thought, 1790–1840," *Middle Eastern Studies,* 8 (Jan. 1972), 3–50. Despite the dates in the title, much of this essay focuses on the seventeenth century.

6. Hertzel Fishman, *American Protestantism and a Jewish State* (Detroit, Wayne State University Press, 1973), pp. 15–16; Toon, "Latter-Day Glory," pp. 34–35; Stephen J. Stein, "Transatlantic Extensions, Apocalyptic in Early New England," in C. A. Patrides and Joseph Wittreich, eds., *The Apocalypse in English Renaissance Thought and Literature* (Manchester, Manchester University Press, 1984), pp. 272 (Bradstreet), 274, 295n38; Dwight Wilson, *Armageddon Now! The Premillenarian Response to Russia and Israel since 1917* (Grand Rapids, Baker Book House, 1977), pp. 17–18 (Mather quoted); Wilbur M. Smith, *World Crises and the Prophetic Scriptures* (Chicago, Moody Press, 1952), p. 186 (Mather).

7. Vereté, "The Restoration of the Jews in English Protestant Thought," esp. pp. 3–13, 20–24, 37–42; Bloch, *Visionary Republic,* p. 140; Wilbur M. Smith, *Israeli-Arab Conflict and the Bible* (Glendale, Calif., Regal Books, 1967), p. 52 (Winchester); Fishman, *American Protestantism and a Jewish State,* p. 18 (Adams). See also Peter Grose, *Israel in the Mind of America* (New York, Alfred A. Knopf, 1983), p. 9.

8. John N. Darby, *The Hopes of the Church of God in Connexion with the Destiny of the Jews and the Nations as Revealed in Prophecy: Eleven Lectures Delivered in Geneva in 1840* (London, 2nd ed., 1842), pp. 49, 92, 102; Timothy P. Weber, *Living in the Shadow of the Second Coming: American Premillennialism, 1875–1925* (New York, Oxford University Press, 1979), pp. 17–22.

9. Halsell, *Prophecy and Politics,* pp. 135–137 (quoted passage p. 137). See also Vereté, "The Restoration of the Jews in English Protestant Thought," pp. 39–42.

10. Wilson, *Armageddon Now!* p. 24 (Cumming); Joseph A. Seiss, *The Last Times and the Great Consummation: An Earnest Discussion of Momentous Events* (Philadelphia, Smith, English and Co., 1863), p. 185. "The restoration of the literal Israel," wrote the Reverend William Ramsey in *Messiah's Reign; or, The Future Blessedness of the Church and the World* (Philadelphia, Joseph M. Wilson, 1857), pp. 47–48, "is a fixed fact in the plans and purposes of God." See also Isaac P. Labagh, *Twelve Lectures on the Great Events of Unfulfilled Prophecy Which Still Await Their Accomplishment and Are Approaching Their Fulfillment* (New York, 1859), p. vi; Wilson, *Armageddon Now!* p. 21.

11. Fishman, *American Protestantism and a Jewish State,* p. 16; F. L. Cross, ed., *The Oxford Dictionary of the Christian Church* (London, Oxford University Press, 1958), pp. 176–177 ("Blake, William").

12. Harry Benjamin Gray, "Eschatology of the Millennial Cults," Th.D. dissertation, Dallas Theological Seminary, 1956, pp. 10–74 (British-Israelism), esp. p. 11 (Brothers); Vereté, "The Restoration of the Jews in English Protestant Thought," pp. 8–9 (Brothers); Arno C. Gaebelein, *World Prospects* (New York, *Our Hope* Publication Office, 1934), p. 85 (quoting a 1723 work by "Dr. Abbadie"—most probably the well-known Swiss Protestant divine Jakob Abbadie (1654?-1727). *Encyclopedia Brittanica* (New York, Encyclopedia Britannica Co., 11th ed., 1910), I, 9 ("Abbadie, Jakob"). For a brief treatment of the origins of British Israelism, and an extended discussion of its manifestations in contemporary right-wing extremist movements in the United States, see Michael Barkun, "Racist Apocalypse: Millennialism on the Far Right," *American Studies,* 31 (1990), 121–140, esp. pp. 122–124.

13. David A. Rausch, *Zionism within Early American Fundamentalism, 1878–1918: A Convergence of Two Traditions* (New York, Edwin Mellen Press, 1979), chap. 4, pp. 79–146; Robert Anderson, *The Coming Prince* (Grand Rapids, Kregel Publications, 1986; reprint of 1884 work), pp. 149–150, 165–167; James M. Brookes, *Maranatha: or, The Lord Cometh* (New York, Fleming H. Revell, 1889), pp. 17, 396, and chap. 19, pp. 389 ff., passim; Wilson, *Armageddon Now!* p. 15 (Scofield Reference Bible quoted); C. I. Scofield, *Addresses on Prophecy* (New York, Arno C. Gaebelein, n.d.), p. 57. The restoration of the Jews also figured in *The Fundamentals,* the codification of evangelical doctrine published between 1910 and 1915 (Rausch, *Zionism within Early American Fundamentalism,* p. 291). See also Yaakov Ariel, *On Behalf of Israel: American Fundamentalist Attitudes toward Jews, Judaism, and Zionism, 1865–1945* (Brooklyn, Carlson Publishing Co., 1991); Walter Scott, *Future Events: With Numerous Prophetic Details* (London, Alfred Holness, 1881), p. 46.

14. Patrick Fairbairn, *The Prophetic Prospects of the Jews,* intro. Albertus Pie-

ters (Grand Rapids, Wm. B. Eerdman's Publishing Co., 1930; reprint of 1838–1839 sermon series), p. 26.

15. David A. Rausch, "Arno C. Gaebelein (1861–1945): Fundamentalist Protestant Zionist," *American Jewish History* (Sept. 1978), 43–55, esp. pp. 44, 55; David C. Lindberg (son of Milton Lindberg) to author, Feb. 21, 1991; John W. Bradbury, ed., *Light for the World's Darkness* (New York, Loizeaux Brothers, 1944; report of prophecy conference sponsored by American Board of Missions to the Jews); Beth A. Lindberg, "A God-Filled Life: The Story of William Eugene Blackstone" (n.p., n.d.); Weber, *Living in the Shadow of the Second Coming*, pp. 138, 142; Fishman, *American Protestantism and a Jewish State*, pp. 19–20; Rausch, *Zionism within Early American Fundamentalism*, pp. 295–307. Another missionary society with prophecy interests was Philadelphia's Friends of Israel Missionary and Relief Society, whose general secretary, Victor Buksbazen, was a Jewish Christian. See Victor Buksbazen, "The Miracle of Israel: A Land Comes to Life," *Moody Monthly*, June 1950, pp. 677–678ff.

16. A. C. Gaebelein, "Jewish Societies for the Colonization of Palestine," *Our Hope*, 1 (July 1894), 13–14, quoted in Rausch, "Arno C. Gaebelein," p. 45; Rausch, *Zionism within Early American Fundamentalism*, pp. 262–269 (Blackstone); Lindberg, "A God-Filled Life"; Fishman, *American Protestantism and a Jewish State*, p. 19. See also Ariel, *On Behalf of Israel*, which treats both Gaebelein and Blackstone in depth, and Evyatar Friesel, "The Balfour Declaration in Historical Perspective" (Kaplan Centre for Jewish Studies and Research, University of Cape Town, 1988), p. 4.

17. Weber, *Living in the Shadow of the Second Coming*, pp. 138–139; Fishman, *American Protestantism and a Jewish State*, p. 20 (Blackstone memorial quoted); Lindberg, "A God-Filled Life"; Grose, *Israel in the Mind of America*, pp. 36–37; Halsell, *Prophecy and Politics*, p. 139 (U.S. consul quoted); Arno C. Gaebelein, "The Fourth Zionistic Congress: The Most Startling Sign of Our Times," *Our Hope*, 7 (Sept. 1900), 72, quoted in Rausch, "Arno C. Gaebelein," p. 50.

18. E. L. Langston, *Great Britain, Palestine, Russia, and the Jews* (London, Charles J. Thynne, 1918), pp. 24, 26. See also James M. Gray, *A Text-Book on Prophecy* (New York, Fleming H. Revell, 1918), p. 46; Rausch, *Zionism within Early American Fundamentalism*, pp. 267–268; and Wilbur M. Smith, *The Israeli-Arab Conflict and the Bible* (Van Nuys, Calif., Regal Books, 1967), pp. 149–151 (bibliography listing early prophecy works dealing with the Jewish restoration).

19. Robert G. Clouse, "The Danger of Mistaken Hopes," in Carl E. Armerding and W. Ward Gasque, eds., *Dreams, Visions, and Oracles: The*

Layman's Guide to Biblical Prophecy (Grand Rapids, Baker Book House, 1977), p. 33 (Sale-Harrison); Louis S. Bauman in *Evangel,* Mar. 3, 1934, p. 5, quoted in Wilson, *Armageddon Now!* p. 89; Smith, *Israeli-Arab Conflict and the Bible,* p. 46 (Ben-Gurion); Arthur I. Brown, *The Eleventh "Hour"* (Findlay, Ohio, Fundamental Truth Publishers, 1940), p. 32. See also Keith L. Brooks, *The Jews and the Passion for Palestine in the Light of Prophecy* (Grand Rapids, Zondervan Publishing Co., 1937), preface; W. H. Rogers, *The End from the Beginning: A Panorama of Prophecy* (New York, Arno C. Gaebelein, 1938), p. 97.

20. Herbert Lockyear, *Cameos of Prophecy: Are These the Last Days?* (Grand Rapids, Zondervan Publishing Co., 1942), p. 98; R. S. Beal, "The Kings of the Kingdom," and Albert Lindsey, Jr., "The Church and the Jews; What the Church Will Have to Do for the Jew in the Postwar Period," in Bradbury, *Light for the World's Darkness,* pp. 90 (quoted passage), 203; John W. Bradbury, "To the Jew First," in Bradbury, ed., *Israel's Restoration: A Series of Lectures by Bible Expositors Interested in the Evangelization of the Jews* (New York, Iverson-Ford Associates, [1952]), p. 11 (report on 1945 conference).

21. William W. Orr of the Bible Institute of Los Angeles, quoted in Wilson, *Armageddon Now!* p. 132; Mary Stewart Relfe, *When Your Money Fails: The "666" System Is Here* (Montgomery, Ala., Ministries, Inc., 1981), p. 62.

22. Buksbazen, "The Miracle of Israel," p. 677; William Culbertson, "Could the Rapture Be Today?" *Moody Monthly,* May 1960, p. 14. See also George T. B. Davis, *Israel Returns Home, According to Prophecy* (Philadelphia, Million Testament League, 1950), pp. 113, 115; Paul R. Alderman, Jr., *The Unfolding of the Ages* (Grand Rapids, Zondervan Publishing Co., 1954), p. 109.

23. Wilson, *Armageddon Now!* p. 213; David Edwin Harrell, Jr., *Pat Robertson: A Personal, Religious, and Political Portrait* (San Francisco, Harper and Row, 1987), p. 146; John F. Walvoord, "The Amazing Rise of Israel," *Moody Monthly,* Oct. 1967, p. 22.

24. Tim LaHaye, *The Beginning of the End* (Wheaton, Ill., Tyndale House Publishers, 1972), p. 50; Rausch, *Zionism within Early American Fundamentalism,* p. 339 (*His Land*); Hilton Sutton, *World War III: God's Conquest of Russia* (Tulsa, Harrison House, 1982), front matter.

25. Carl F. H. Henry, ed., *Prophecy in the Making* (Carol Stream, Ill., Creation House, 1971), pp. 9, 15, 91, 167, 185, 215, 243, 289, 325; C. Everett Koop, "Prophecy Conference Meets in Jerusalem," *Eternity,* Aug. 1971, p. 25.

26. Elwood McQuaid, *It Is No Dream! Bible Prophecy: Fact or Fanaticism?* (West Collingwood, N.J., Spearhead Press, 1978), front matter; Louis

Goldberg, *Turbulence over the Middle East* (Neptune, N.J., Loizeaux Brothers, 1982), p. 16.

27. Jerry Falwell, "The Twenty-First Century and the End of the World," *Fundamentalist Journal,* May 1988, p. 10; Halsell, *Prophecy and Politics,* pp. 23, 60–61, 73, 81, 122–123. The three phrases quoted at the beginning of the paragraph are from Jack Van Impe with Roger F. Campbell, *Israel's Final Holocaust* (Nashville, Thomas Nelson Co., 1979), p. 9; A. G. Mojtabai, *Blessed Assurance: At Home with the Bomb in Amarillo, Texas* (Boston, Houghton Mifflin Co., 1986), p. 157 (quoting W. A. Criswell); and S. Maxwell Coder, *The Final Chapter: Understanding What the Bible Says about the Last Days of Human History* (Wheaton, Ill., Tyndale House Publishers, 1984), p. 16.

28. Jer. 32:37.

29. Isa. 11:12. See also Deut. 30:5, Zeph. 2:1–2; Isa. 43:5–6; Jer. 23:7–8, 31:35, 33:7; Ezek. 37.

30. See, for example, Anthony A. Hoekema, *The Bible and the Future* (Grand Rapids, William B. Eerdman's Publishing Co., 1979), p. 208.

31. Matt. 24:32–34.

32. See, for instance, Hal Lindsey, *The Late Great Planet Earth* (New York, Bantam Books, 1973), p. 43.

33. Ibid.; Wim Malgo, *Russia's Last Invasion* (Columbia, S.C., Midnight Call, 1980), p. 59; David Webber and Noah Hutchings, *Is This the Last Century?* (Nashville, Thomas Nelson, 1979), pp. 45–47 (quoted phrase p. 47).

34. Charles R. Taylor, *Get All Excited—Jesus Is Coming Soon* (Redondo Beach, Calif., Today in Bible Prophecy, 1975), pp. 89, 93; idem, *Those Who Remain: 1980 Edition* (Orange, Calif., Today in Bible Prophecy, 1980), pp. 70, 71; *Bible Prophecy News,* Apr.-May-June 1989, p. 7 (emphasis added); Charles R. Taylor to author, n.d. [Sept. 1988]; Charles R. Taylor to "Beloved Partners in Christ," May 20, 1991 ("I see no possibility for the delay of the rapture of the church beyond [September 1992]"); Webber and Hutchings, *Is This the Last Century?* p. 51.

35. Webber and Hutchings, *Is This the Last Century?* p. 53, quoting Zech. 12:6. See also Zech. 12:9: "And it shall come to pass in that day, that I will seek to destroy all the nations that come against Jerusalem."

36. Charles Lea, *World Events in the Light of God's Word* (New York, Comet Press, 1959), p. 4, quoting Jer. 31:39; Alderman, *Unfolding of the Ages,* p. 108, quoting Zeph. 3:9.

37. William Hendrickson, *The Bible on the Life Hereafter* (Grand Rapids, Baker Book House, 1959), p. 144 ("Jews . . . had not repented"); Hoekema, *Bible and the Future,* pp. 194n, 197, 201; Herman Ridderbos, "The Future of Israel—View I," in Henry, *Prophecy in the Making,* pp. 313–

322; George Eldon Ladd, *The Last Things: Eschatology for Laymen* (Grand Rapids, Wm. B. Eerdman's Publishing Co., 1978), p. 27. For the Reformed (Calvinist) theological view that God's covenant with Abraham was transferred to the Christian Church with the coming of Christ, see also Louis Berkhof, *Principles of Biblical Interpretation* (Grand Rapids, Baker Book House, 1966); Albertus Pieters, *The Seed of Abraham* (Grand Rapids, Wm. B. Eerdman's Publishing Co., 1950); and Herman Hoeksema, *Reformed Dogmatics* (Grand Rapids, Reformed Free Publishing Assn., 1966). For a Mennonite statement of this position see Chester K. Lehman, *The Fulfillment of Prophecy* (Scottdale, Pa., Mennonite Publishing Co., 1950).

38. Herbert W. Armstrong, *The United States and Britain in Prophecy* (Pasadena, Calif., Worldwide Church of God, 1980), p. xi; Michael Barkun, "Millenarian Aspects of 'White Supremacist' Movements," paper delivered at the American Political Science Association annual meeting, Washington, D.C., Sept. 1988; Wilson, *Armageddon Now!* p. 12; "The Last Days—A Time of Harvest," *Watchtower,* Jan. 1, 1988, p. 11.

39. Wilson, *Armageddon Now!* pp. 47 (quoting *Our Hope*), 134; Donald Grey Barnhouse, "Tomorrow—Current Events in the Light of the Bible, 1945," *Revelation,* Jan. 1945, p. 11; William Ward Ayer, *What Goes On Here!* (Grand Rapids, Zondervan Publishing Co., 1947), p. 113. See also E. Schuyler English, *The Shifting of the Scenes* (New York, 1945), p. 29; Harry A. Ironside, *The Lamp of Prophecy: or, Signs of the Times* (Grand Rapids, Zondervan Publishing Co., 1940), p. 91; Russell Bradley Jones, *The Things Which Shall Be Hereafter* (Nashville, Broadman Press, 1947), pp. 67–72.

40. John F. Walvoord, *Israel in Prophecy* (Grand Rapids, Zondervan Publishing Co., 1962), reprinted in Walvoord, *The Nations, Israel, and the Church in Prophecy* (Grand Rapids, Zondervan Publishing Co., 1988), pp. 37 (quoted passage), 31 (citation of works by J. Dwight Pentecost, Charles Feinberg, Alva J. McClain, and Lewis Sperry Chafer taking the same view); Dave Hunt, *Whatever Happened to Heaven?* (Eugene, Oreg., Harvest House Publishers, 1988), pp. 246, 250. See also Warren W. Wiesbe, *Be Ready* (Wheaton, Ill., Victor Books, 1979), p. 141.

41. Walvoord, *Israel in Prophecy,* pp. 36–38; idem, "The Future of Israel— View II," in Henry, *Prophecy in the Making,* pp. 333, 338. See also Rausch, *Zionism within Early American Fundamentalism,* p. 15 (on Walvoord); Coder, *Final Chapter,* pp. 22–24, 138.

42. George Gallup, Jr., and Jim Castelli, *The People's Religion: American Faith in the Nineties* (New York, Macmillan Publishing Co., 1989), pp. 209, 210. See also Steven R. David, "Bosom of Abraham: America's Enduring Affection for Israel," *Policy Review,* 55 (Winter 1991), 57–

59, esp. p. 59; and William E. Schmidt, "Americans' Support for Israel: Solid, But Not the Rock It Was," *New York Times,* July 9, 1990, pp. 1, A9.

43. Walvoord, *Israel in Prophecy,* p. 76; Darby, *The Hopes of the Church of God,* p. 102; Wilson, *Armageddon Now!* p. 46; Weber, *Living in the Shadow of the Second Coming,* p. 139 (Blackstone). See also Scott, *Future Events,* p. 78.

44. T. De Courcy Rayner, "Hidden Hands in Palestine," *Moody Monthly,* Dec. 1947, pp. 264, 284. See also Aaron J. Kligerman, "Palestine—Jewish Homeland," ibid., Dec. 1946, p. 248.

45. Lewis Sperry Chafer, "Why I Believe the Lord's Coming Is Near," *Sunday School Times,* 90 (Apr. 17, 1948), 344; W. R. Wallace, "Shadows of Armageddon," in William Culbertson and Herman B. Centz, eds., *Understanding the Times: Prophetic Messages Delivered at the Second International Congress on Prophecy, New York City* (Grand Rapids, Zondervan Publishing Co., 1956), pp. 186–187. See also Roy E. Laurin, "Israel and the End of History," ibid., p. 239 ("The title deed to this land was granted by Jehovah, and it is irrevocable").

46. Edgar C. James, *Arabs, Oil, and Energy* (Chicago, Moody Press, 1977), p. 84; author interviews with John F. Walvoord (Aug. 8, 1989) and Dwight Pentecost (July 13, 1989); Rausch, *Zionism within Early American Fundamentalism,* pp. 73–74 ("river of Egypt" debate). See also McQuaid, *It Is No Dream!* p. 247.

47. Anis A. Shorrosh, *Jesus, Prophecy, and the Middle East* (Nashville, Thomas Nelson Publishing Co., 1981), p. 54; Milton B. Lindberg, *The Jew and Modern Israel in the Light of Prophecy* (Chicago, Moody Press, 1930; rev. Archie A. MacKinney, 1969), p. 84 (interpolations in original). Lindberg's biblical reference was to Gen. 21:12. See also Gen. 17:21: "But my covenant will I establish with Isaac. . ."

48. David Wilkerson, *The Vision* (New York, Pyramid Books, 1974), p. 98; Shorrosh, *Jesus, Prophecy, and the Middle East,* p. 61.

49. Derek Prince, *The Last Word on the Middle East* (Grand Rapids, Zondervan Publishing Co., 1982), pp. 60–61. The Bible passage is Isa. 11:14, New International Version (North American edition). Tim LaHaye, *The Coming Peace in the Middle East* (Grand Rapids, Zondervan Publishing Co., 1984), p. 26; James, *Arabs, Oil, and Energy,* p. 80; Coder, *Final Chapter,* p. 33. On Derek Prince see David Edwin Harrell, Jr., *All Things Are Possible: The Healing and Charismatic Revivals in Modern America* (Bloomington, Indiana University Press, 1975), pp. 184–185.

50. Kenneth S. Wuest, *Prophetic Light in the Present Darkness* (Grand Rapids, Wm. B. Eerdman's Publishing Co., 1955), pp. 112–113, 120. See also Charles C. Ryrie, *The Final Countdown* (Wheaton, Ill., Victor Books, 1982), p. 47.

51. Robert H. Eisenman, *If I Forget You, O Jerusalem: A Handbook of Zionist Prophecy* (Fountain Valley, Calif., Yahwist Press, 1978), p. 29; James, *Arabs, Oil, and Energy,* p. 91; Deut. 33:24.
52. Halsell, *Prophecy and Politics,* p. 87.
53. The passage quoted is II Thess. 2:3–4. See also Matt. 24:15–31 and Dan. 12:11, 22:31. See also Smith, *Israeli-Arab Conflict,* p. 110.
54. Wilbur M. Smith, "The Centrality of Jerusalem in Prophecy," *Sunday School Times* (Feb. 19, 1949), 153–154.
55. Ibid., pp. 152, 153; idem, *Israeli-Arab Conflict,* p. 99.
56. Walter L. Wilson, "Thoughts from Ezekiel 37," in John W. Bradbury, ed., *Hastening the Day of God: Prophetic Messages from the International Congress on Prophecy in Calvary Baptist Church, New York City, November 9–16, 1952* (Wheaton, Ill., Van Kampen Press, 1953), p. 188; Carl Armerding, "The Sign of the Time of the End," *Moody Monthly,* July 1951, p. 721; Wilson, *Armageddon Now!* p. 167 (citing article from *King's Business,* Mar. 1952, p. 7).
57. Arnold T. Olson, *Inside Jerusalem: City of Destiny* (Glendale, Calif., Regal Books, 1968), p. 133; Charles Lee Feinberg, "The Rebuilding of the Temple," in Henry, *Prophecy in the Making,* pp. 91ff. See also James Montgomery Boice, *The Last and Future World* (Grand Rapids, Zondervan Publishing Co., 1974), pp. 91–92; Thomas S. McCall and Zola Levitt, *Satan in the Sanctuary* (Chicago, Moody Press, 1973), pp. 17–18; Lindsey, *Late Great Planet Earth,* p. 140; Falwell, "The Twenty-First Century and the End of the World"; David Hocking, *The Coming World Leader: Understanding the Book of Revelation* (Portland, Oreg., Multnomah Press, 1988), p. 179.
58. Ladd, *Last Things,* pp. 25, 66. The biblical passage cited is from Heb. 10:1.
59. McCall and Levitt, *Satan in the Sanctuary,* p. 4 (*The Temple*); Raymond L. Cox, "Time for the Temple?" *Eternity,* Jan. 1968, pp. 17–18; Malcolm Couch, "When Will the Jews Rebuild the Temple?" *Moody Monthly,* Dec. 1973, pp. 34–35, 86 (Couch was producer of *The Temple*); Wilson, *Armageddon Now!* p. 200.
60. Among the many discussions of Temple-rebuilding projects in Israel, both factual and rumored, see John Wesley White, *The Coming World Dictator* (Minneapolis, Bethany House Publishers, 1981), p. 90; Doug Clark, *Shockwaves of Armageddon* (Eugene, Oreg., Harvest Books, 1982), p. 39; McCall and Levitt, *Satan in the Sanctuary,* pp. 17–18; LaHaye, *Beginning of the End,* pp. 55–56; "Ashes of the Red Heifer," *Bible Prophecy News* Apr.-May-June 1988, p. 10; "Rabbis Expect to Rebuild Temple," ibid., Apr.-May-June 1989, p. 5; "Rebuild Herod's Temple? A Few Israelis Hope," *New York Times,* Apr. 9, 1989, p. 9 (Rabbi Yisrael Ariel and the Temple Institute).

The *Jerusalem Post* has published many articles on this subject. See, for example, "Unsung Texan Hero of Qumran," Mar. 9, 1989, p. 5; "Vendyl Jones and the Treasures of the Temple," May 28, 1989, p. 5; "On the Trail of the Holy Cow," Aug. 6, 1989, p. 5; "Engineers of Armageddon," Oct. 17, 1989, p. 4 (Gershon Salomon and the Temple Mount Faithful); "Assault on the Mount," Nov. 3, 1989, p. 12; "Rabbi Eliahu in Search of the Unsullied Beast," Dec. 13, 1989, p. 1; "Clash Connected to Faithful," Apr. 13, 1990, p. 2; "Faithful Put Actions into Words," May 25, 1990, p. 5.

Also helpful were author interviews with Benjamin Beit-Hallahmi (Department of Sociology, Haifa University), Jan. 9, 1990, and Yishai Eldar (Senior Editor, Israel Radio), Jan. 6, 1990. For a discussion of Jewish messianic movements, Jewish Jehovah's Witnesses, and Jewish evangelical Christians ("Messianic Jews") in contemporary Israel, see Beit-Hallahmi, *Despair and Deliverance: Private Salvation in Contemporary Israel* (Albany, State University of New York Press, 1991). My thanks to Professor Beit-Hallahmi for sharing this work with me in manuscript.

61. Anderson, *Coming Prince,* p. 168; William L. Pettingill, *God's Prophecies for Plain People* (Wilmington, Del., Just a Word, 1923; reprint of articles published in *Sunday School Times* in 1919), p. 60.

62. McCall and Levitt, *Satan in the Sanctuary,* p. 25 (quoted phrase); author interview with S. Maxwell Coder, Mar. 13, 1989; Couch, "When Will the Jews Rebuild Their Temple?" argued that the original Temple was fifty yards from the present Mosque of Omar; Wilson, *Armageddon Now!* p. 200. For similar arguments, see Edgar C. Whisenant, *88 Reasons Why the Rapture Will Be in 1988* (Nashville, World Bible Society, 1988), p. 27. For a few of the many writers to quote Israel Eldad's "earthquake" comment (originally reported in "Should the Temple Be Rebuilt?" *Time,* June 30, 1967), see McCall and Levitt, *Satan in the Sanctuary,* p. 17; Boice, *Last and Future World,* p. 92; Hal Lindsey, *There's a New World Coming* (Santa Ana, Calif., Vision House Publishers, 1973), p. 159; idem, *Late Great Planet Earth,* p. 46; LaHaye, *Beginning of the End,* p. 58; William R. Goetz, *Apocalypse Next: Updated* (Cathedral City, Calif., Horizon House Publishers, 1987), p. 188.

63. McCall and Levitt, *Satan in the Sanctuary,* p. 18; "Will the Temple Soon Be Rebuilt?" *Evangel,* Feb. 1, 1930, pp. 4–5, quoted in Wilson, *Armageddon Now!* p. 74; Goldberg, *Turbulence over the Middle East,* p. 191; Salem Kirban, *666* (Wheaton, Ill., Tyndale House, 1970), pp. 120–121; "Assault on the Mount," *Jerusalem Post,* Nov. 3, 1989, p. 12 ("Divine inspiration and modern technology, [Gershon] Salomon contends, will allow both mosques to be transported from Jerusalem to Mecca, intact"). See also Clark, *Shockwaves of Armageddon,* p. 39.

64. "Assault on the Mount," *Jerusalem Post;* "Rebuild Herod's Temple? A Few Israelis Hope," *New York Times,* Apr. 9, 1989, p. 9; "[Mayor Teddy] Kollek Hopes 'Faithful' Group Won't Bring Catastrophe as Other False Messiahs Have Done," *Jerusalem Post,* Oct. 17, 1989, p. 1; author interviews with Benjamin Beit-Hallahmi and Yishai Eldar.

65. Joel Brinkley, "Death in Jerusalem: How Passions and Violence Produced Tragedy," *New York Times,* Oct. 15, 1990, pp. 1, 6.

66. Ray C. Stedman, *What's This World Coming To?* (Ventura, Calif., Regal Books, 1970; 2nd ed. 1986), p. 39; White, *Coming World Dictator,* p. 89.

67. See Chapter 2.

68. Darby, *Hopes of the Church,* p. 102; Wilson, *Armageddon Now!* pp. 24, 40, 42 (Balfour Declaration), 71.

69. Harry Rimmer, *The Shadow of Coming Events* (Grand Rapids, Wm. B. Eerdman's Publishing Co., 1946), p. 37; Raynor, "Hidden Hands in Palestine," p. 265; Chafer, "Why I Believe the Lord's Coming Is Near," p. 344.

70. Guy Duty, *Escape from the Coming Tribulation* (Minneapolis, Bethany Fellowship, 1975), p. 126. See also Smith, *Israeli-Arab Conflict,* pp. 80–85; Hal Lindsey, *The 1980s: Countdown to Armageddon* (New York, Bantam Books, 1981), p. 54; idem, *Late Great Planet Earth,* p. 62; idem, *There's a New World Coming,* p. 223; Van Impe with Campbell, *Israel's Final Holocaust,* p. 135; Webber and Hutchings, *Is This the Last Century?* p. 96.

71. Wilson, *Armageddon Now!* 172; Webber and Hutchings, *Is This the Last Century?* p. 57. See also Buksbazen, "The Miracles of Israel," p. 678.

72. Smith, *Israeli-Arab Conflict,* pp. 84–85, quoting Ezek. 35:3–6.

73. Smith, *Israeli-Arab Conflict,* p. 85; Frederick A. Tatford, *God's Program of the Ages* (Grand Rapids, Kregel Publications, 1967), p. 89.

74. Charles L. Feinberg, "Isaac and Ishmael," *King's Business,* 58 (July 1968), 23, quoted in Wilson, *Armageddon Now!* p. 201; Coder, *Final Chapter,* p. 29; Arthur Bloomfield, *Before the Last Battle: Armageddon* (Minneapolis, Bethany House Publishers, 1971), p. 65. See also Thomas S. McCall and Zola Levitt, *The Coming Russian Invasion of Israel: Updated* (Chicago, Moody Press, 1987), p. 37.

75. Coulson Shepherd, "The Unholy Holy Land," *Moody Monthly,* July 1951, pp. 718, 762; Goetz, *Apocalypse Next: Updated,* p. 294; author interview with John F. Walvoord, Aug. 8, 1989. See also William Sanford La Sor, *The Truth about Armageddon: What the Bible Says about the End Times* (New York, Harper and Row, 1982), p. 46 ("I am not anti-Arab. However Edom (= Esau) comes in for some rather rough treatment in the Bible"); and Lance Lambert, *Battle for Israel* (Eastbourne, England, Kingsway Publications, 1975), p. 19 ("To those who would

charge me with being anti-Arab, let me say that I count many Arabs among my dearest friends").

76. Wilson, *Armageddon Now!* pp. 140 (Barnhouse), 195 (BIOLA proclamation).

77. Robert Walker, "Introduction," in Henry, *Prophecy in the Making*, p. 12; Harold Lindsell, *The Armageddon Spectre* (Westchester, Ill., Crossways Books, 1984), p. 2. See also Ralph Martin, *The Return of the Lord* (Ann Arbor, Servant Books, 1983), p. 44.

78. Smith, *Israeli-Arab Conflict*, front matter; Zola Levitt, *The Cairo Connection: Egypt in Prophecy* (Irvine, Calif., Harvest House Publishers, 1978), p. 125; Charles H. Malik, "The Near East: The Search for Truth," *Foreign Affairs*, 30 (Jan. 1952), 245.

79. Lambert, *Battle for Israel*, p. 110; Peter Stiglin, "Apocalyptic Theology and the Right," *Witness*, Oct. 1986, p. 9 (Falwell); Halsell, *Prophecy and Politics*, pp. 66, 74 (Falwell); Erling Jorstad, *The New Christian Right, 1981–1988: Prospects for the Post-Reagan Decade* (Lewiston, N.Y., E. Mellen Press, 1987), p. 158; Hal Lindsey, *The 1980s: Countdown to Armageddon,* quoted in Nathan Perlmutter, "Jews and Fundamentalists," *Reconstructionist*, 51 (Dec. 1985), 22; LaHaye, *Coming Peace in the Middle East*, p. 63. See also George Otis, *The Ghost of Hagar* (Van Nuys, Calif., Time-Light Books, 1974), pp. 47, 61 ("We Christians believe in fighting for God's people, the Jews, as well as praying for them"); McQuaid, *It Is No Dream!* p. 75 ("No group of human beings stand more firmly alongside Israelis than do evangelical Christians"); James Barr, *Fundamentalism* (Philadelphia, Westminster Press, 1977), pp. 118–119.

80. Lehman Strauss, *God's Plan for the Future* (Grand Rapids, Zondervan Publishing Co., 1965), p. 152.

81. Fishman, *American Protestantism and a Jewish State*, pp. 178–179; Halsell, *Prophecy and Politics*, pp. 147–154.

82. Charles C. Ryrie, "Perspective on Palestine," *Christianity Today*, 13 (May 23, 1969), 8; Halsell, *Prophecy and Politics*, pp. 152–154.

83. Author interview with Yishai Eldar, Jan. 6, 1990; Henry, *Prophecy in the Making*, pp. 9, 151; Lindsey, *The 1980s*, p. [35] (Herzog); Halsell, *Prophecy and Politics*, pp. 60–61, 73, 81; Oral Roberts, *The Drama of the End Time* (Tulsa, Oral Roberts, 1963), pp. 82–84; David Allen Lewis, *Magog 1982 Canceled* (Harrison, Ark., New Leaf Press, 1982), pp. 9 (quoted passages; parentheses in original), 33; Mike Evans, *The Return* (Nashville, Thomas Nelson Publishers, 1986), pp. 185–186. See also Merill Simon, *Jerry Falwell and the Jews* (Middle Village, N.Y., Jonathan David Publishers, 1984).

84. Wilson, *Armageddon Now!* p. 194 (BIOLA statement); Yona Malachy,

American Fundamentalism and Israel: The Relation of Fundamentalist Churches to Zionism and the State of Israel (Jerusalem, Hebrew University of Jerusalem, 1978).

85. Franklin H. Littell, "Present at the Creation," *Honor the Promise* (NCLCI newsletter), Winter 1989–90, p. 2; "A Christian Affirmation on Jerusalem," ibid., Fall 1990, pp. 1, 2; NCLCI promotional brochure, n.d. (summary of activities).

From 1945 on, to be sure, first the Zionist leaders and then the officials of the new Israeli nation had couched their claims in terms that would appeal to Christians. As former Israeli foreign minister Abba Eban has recalled, "We knew we were basically appealing to a Christian world for whom the biblical story was familiar and attractive, and we played it to the hilt"—quoted in Thomas L. Friedman, *From Beirut to Jerusalem* (New York, Doubleday Anchor Books, 1990), p. 438. After 1967, this generalized catering to Christian sensibilities tended to be more specifically targeted to Protestant fundamentalists.

86. Nathan Perlmutter and Ruth Ann Perlmutter, *The Real Anti-Semitism in America* (New York, Arbor House, 1982), quoted in Halsell, *Prophecy and Politics,* p. 155; Nathan Perlmutter, "Jews and Fundamentalists," *Reconstructionist,* 51, no. 3 (Dec. 1985), 20–23, quoted passages pp. 21, 23; Irving Kristol, "The Political Dilemma of American Jews," *Commentary,* 78 (July 1984), 25; Meir Kahane in *Jewish Press,* Brooklyn, N.Y., Jan. 24, 1975, quoted in Hal Lindsey with C. C. Carlson, *The Terminal Generation* (New York, Bantam Books, 1977), p. 50. See also Charles B. Strozier and Ayla Kohn, "The Ambiguous Image of the Jew in the Minds of Christian Fundamentalists," John Jay College of Criminal Justice, City University of New York, 1989.

87. Roberts, *Drama of the End Time,* pp. 82–84, quoted in Wilson, *Armageddon Now!* pp. 192, 193; Bert DeVries, "'His Land' and History," *Reformed Journal* (Apr. 1971), 10–11.

88. "Christians in Solidarity with Israel," NCLCI ad, *New York Times,* Aug. 1, 1982; Halsell, *Prophecy and Politics,* p. 61; Lewis, *Magog 1982 Canceled,* pp. 44; Hilton Sutton, prophecy sermon, Shalom Christian Center, Madison, Wis., Aug. 20, 1988. See also "Christians Speak Out for Israel," *New York Times,* Jan. 21, 1991, p. 17.

89. "Shamir: Israel Leader Defends Stand," *Los Angeles Times,* Mar. 19, 1988, pp. 1, 4 (quoted passages).

90. Halsell, *Prophecy and Politics,* pp. 9–10, 96, 170, 173; Charles Colson with Ellen Santilli Vaughn, *Kingdoms in Conflict* (New York, William Morrow, 1987), pp. 12–40.

91. Douglas Ober, *The Great World Crisis* (Wheaton, Ill., Van Kampen

Press, 1950), p. 72; Shorrosh, *Jesus, Prophecy, and the Middle East,* p. 104; Raymond L. Cox, "Will the Real Antichrist Please Stand Up!" *Eternity,* May 1974, p. 15.

92. Harrell, *Pat Robertson,* p. 148 (People for the American Way); *Sojourners,* Mar. 1977 editorial, quoted in Rausch, *Zionism within Early American Fundamentalism,* p. 10.

93. Danny Collum, "Armageddon Theology as a Threat to Peace," *Faith and Mission,* Fall 1986, p. 60.

94. Smith, *Israeli-Arab Conflict,* p. 51 (Mather); Bloch, *Visionary Republic,* p. 146 (Hopkins).

95. Darby, *Hopes of the Church of God,* p. 92; Zech. 13:8.

96. Brookes, *Maranatha,* p. 243; W. R. Nicholson, "The Gathering of Israel," in Nathaniel West, ed., *Second Coming of Christ: Premillennial Essays of the Prophetic Conference Held in the Church of the Holy Trinity, New York City* (Chicago, Fleming H. Revell, 1879), p. 232; Price, *Coming Antichrist,* pp. 189–190 (Blackstone).

97. Wilson, *Armageddon Now!* p. 16 (Scofield); Arthur W. Pink, *The Antichrist* (Grand Rapids, Kregel Publications, 1988; reprint of 1923 work), pp. 106, 293; E. M. Milligan, *Is the Kingdom Age at Hand?* (New York, George H. Doran, 1924), p. 209. See also Langston, *Great Britain, Palestine, Russia, and the Jews,* p. 30; *King's Business,* 12 (June 1921), 575, for predictions of the destruction of two-thirds of all Jews (Wilson, *Armageddon Now!* p. 77).

98. Charles G. Trumbull, *Prophecy's Light on Today* (New York, Fleming H. Revell, 1937), p. 71; Arno C. Gaebelein, *As It Was—So Shall It Be* (New York, Our Hope, 1937), p. 162; J. M. Ritchie, *Prophetic Highlights* (New York, Fleming H. Revell, 1935), p. 46; Perry F. Haines, *The End from the Beginning* (Grand Rapids, Zondervan Publishing Co., 1942), p. 17. See also David F. Cooper, *When Gog's Armies Meet the Almighty* (Los Angeles, Bible Research Society, 1970; reprint of 1940 work), pp. 76, 95, 102.

99. Oswald J. Smith, *The Voice of Prophecy* (London, Marshall, Morgan, and Scott, 1948), p. 33; George T. B. Davis, "Regathering Israel—A Modern Miracle," *Sunday School Times,* 91 (Mar. 19, 1949), 252; Shepherd, "The Unholy Holy Land," p. 763; Armerding, "The Sign of the Time of the End," p. 744 (quoting Hos. 13:16); Alderman, *Unfolding of the Ages,* pp. 111, 112. For more in the same vein from the 1950s see Howard W. Ferrin, "World-Wide Crisis and the Lord's Return," in Bradbury, *Hastening the Day of God,* p. 75; Dale Crowley, *The Soon Coming of Our Lord* (New York, Loizeaux Brothers, 1958), p. 53; Lea, *World Events in the Light of God's Word,* p. 43; J. Dwight Pentecost, "The Prophetic Word and Europe," in *The Prophetic Word in Crisis Days* (Findlay, Ohio, Dun-

ham Publishing Co., 1961), p. 96; Charles L. Feinberg, "The Future of Israel," *Moody Monthly,* Oct. 1958, p. 28; F. S. Donn, *The Israel Way to Peace* (New York, Exposition Press, 1957), p. 123.

100. Elsa Raud, *Introduction to Prophecy* (Findlay, Ohio, Dunham Publishing Co., 1960), p. 206 (Raud was editor of the journal *Prophetic Word*); E. W. Rogers, *Concerning the Future* (Chicago, Moody Press, 1962), p. 101; Charles H. Stevens, "Israel in the Tribulation," in Charles L. Feinberg, ed., *Focus on Prophecy* (New York, Fleming H. Revell, 1964), pp. 33–44 (quoted phrases pp. 35, 44); Jer. 30:7 ("the time of Jacob's trouble").

101. Deut. 28:62–67; Walvoord, *Israel in Prophecy,* pp. 101, 104.

102. Walvoord, *Israel in Prophecy,* pp. 107, 113–114.

103. Ibid., pp. 97–99, 107–112; John F. Walvoord with John E. Walvoord, *Armageddon, Oil, and the Middle East Crisis: What the Bible Says about the Future of the Middle East and the End of Western Civilization* (Grand Rapids, Zondervan Publishing Co., 1974), p. 72 ("bloodbath of astounding proportions"); author interview with John F. Walvoord, Aug. 8, 1989.

104. Herman A. Hoyt, *The End Times* (Chicago, Moody Press, 1969), p. 128 (Hoyt was president of Grace College and Grace Theological Seminary, Winona Lake, Ind.). On Antichrist as a Jew, see Shorrosh, *Jesus, Prophecy, and the Middle East,* p. 104; Lu Ann Bransby, *The Impending Hour* (Oklahoma City, Impending Hour, [1981]), p. 61; Cox, "Will the Real Antichrist Please Stand Up!" p. 17; Lindsey, *There's a New World Coming,* pp. 103, 180, 192; Scott, *Future Events,* p. 49; Pink, *The Antichrist,* p. 31; Arno Gaebelein, *Meat in Due Season* (New York, Arno Gaebelein, n.d.), p. 150. On the impending Jewish holocaust, see also Lea, *World Events in the Light of God's Word,* pp. 3–13; J. Dwight Pentecost, *Prophecy for Today* (Grand Rapids, Zondervan Publishing Co., 1961), chap. 5, pp. 55ff.; idem, *Will Man Survive?* (Chicago, Moody Press, 1971), pp. 75, 112–113; Robert Glenn Gromacki, *Are These the Last Days?* (Old Tappan, N.J., Fleming H. Revell, 1970), pp. 84, 137–138; Tatford, *God's Program of the Ages,* p. 88; Charles R. Taylor, *The Destiny of America* (Van Nuys, Calif., Time-Light Publishers, 1972), p. 19; Clark, *Shockwaves of Armageddon,* p. 42; Paul Lee Tan, *The Interpretation of Prophecy* (Rockville, Md., Assurance Publishers, 1974), p. 347.

105. Smith, *Israeli-Arab Conflict,* pp. 34–35; Zech. 14:2; Merrill F. Unger, *Beyond the Crystal Ball* (Chicago, Moody Press, 1973), p. 107.

106. Lindsey, *Late Great Planet Earth,* chap. 4, pp. 32–47 (quoted phrases pp. 35, 45); idem, *There's a New World Coming,* pp. 123, 178–179.

107. Stanley A. Ellison, *Biography of a Great Planet* (Wheaton, Ill., Tyndale House Publishers, 1975), p. 147; Coder, *Final Chapter,* p. 20.

108. Walvoord, *Israel in Prophecy,* pp. 103–104; Paul Lee Tan, *The Interpretation of Prophecy* (Rockville, Md., Assurance Publishers, 1974), pp. 347–

348; Shirley Jackson Case, *The Millennial Hope: A Phase of Wartime Thinking* (Chicago, University of Chicago Press, 1918), p. 57; McCall and Levitt, *Coming Russian Invasion of Israel,* pp. 22, 40. See also Clark, *Shockwaves of Armageddon,* pp. 134–136, 185; R. H. Lindsey, "History and the Jews," in H. Leo Eddleman, ed., *Last Things: A Symposium of Prophetic Messages* (Grand Rapids, Zondervan Publishing Co., 1969), p. 53; Stedman, *What's This World Coming To?* p. 105.

109. Taylor, *Destiny of America,* pp. 19, 20. See also Lindberg, *The Jew and Modern Israel,* pp. 38, 62; McQuaid, *It Is No Dream!* p. 230; Unger, *Beyond the Crystal Ball,* p. 107; and, for an emphasis on the worldwide nature of the Tribulation sufferings, E. Schuyler English, "The Church on Earth," in Charles Lee Feinberg, ed., *Prophetic Truth Unfolding Today* (Westwood, N.J., Fleming H. Revell, 1968), p. 34.

110. W. R. Wallace, "Shadows of Armageddon," in Culberson and Centz, *Understanding the Times,* p. 187. See also Pentecost, *Prophecy for Today,* p. 57.

111. Walvoord, *Israel in Prophecy,* pp. 101–104 (quoted passage p. 101); Pentecost, *Will Man Survive?* pp. 75, 135. See also McQuaid, *It Is No Dream!* pp. 229–230.

112. "Quote from 'Mein Kampf' Ignites Furor at Dartmouth," *New York Times,* Oct. 2, 1990; Wilson, *Armageddon Now!* pp. 15–16 (Scofield); Brooks, *Jews and the Passion for Palestine in the Light of Prophecy,* p. 42; William Linn, *Discourses on the Signs of the Times* (New York, 1794), p. 17, quoted in Davidson, *The Logic of Millennial Thought,* p. 296. See also Arthur I. Brown, *The Eleventh "Hour"* (Findlay, Ohio, Fundamental Truth Publishing Co., 1940), p. 41; Trumbull, *Prophecy's Light on Today,* p. 81; James F. Spink, *Will Hitler Obtain World Domination?* (New York, Loizeaux Brothers, 1942), p. 24.

113. Leon J. Wood, *The Bible and Future Events* (Grand Rapids, Zondervan Publishing Co., 1973), p. 123; Prince, *Last Word on the Middle East,* p. 64; II Chron. 36:16–17; Jer. 27:6. See also McCall and Levitt, *Satan in the Sanctuary,* pp. 56–61; Alderman, *Unfolding of the Ages,* p. 111.

114. Goldberg, *Turbulence over the Middle East,* pp. 180, 200, 204, 205, 243; author interview with Louis Goldberg, Feb. 23, 1989.

115. Van Impe, *Israel's Final Holocaust,* pp. 38, 50, 51. For an interesting recent article germane to this issue, see Yaakov Ariel, "Jewish Suffering and Christian Salvation: The Evangelical-Fundamentalist Holocaust Memoirs," *Holocaust and Genocide Studies,* 6 (1991), 63–78, esp. p. 76.

116. Harry Rimmer, *The Shadow of Coming Events* (Grand Rapids, Wm. B. Eerdman's Publishing Co., 1946), p. 63. Among the many post-1945 authors making the same point, see Lambert, *Battle for Israel,* p. 101; Bloomfield, *Before the Last Battle,* p. 63; Clark, *Shockwaves of Armageddon,* p. 113.

117. Lindsey, *Late Great Planet Earth,* p. 99; Bloomfield, *Before the Last Battle,* p. 69; idem, *How to Recognize the Antichrist* (Minneapolis, Bethany Fellowship, 1975), pp. 139–140; Rick Yohn, *What Every Christian Should Know about Bible Prophecy* (Eugene, Oreg., Harvest House, 1982), n.p., "The Great Holocaust." For more predictions of a coming Jewish holocaust, see in addition to the works already cited: LaHaye, *Beginning of the End,* p. 62; James, *Arabs, Oil, and Energy,* pp. 100–101; Salem Kirban, *Guide to Survival* (Huntingdon Valley, Pa., Salem Kirban, 1968), p. 198; Price, *Coming Antichrist,* p. 186; idem, *Last Word on the Middle East,* pp. 141; Ryrie, *Final Countdown,* pp. 63–64; Stedman, *What's the World Coming To?* pp. 35–36; Herbert Vander Lugt, *There's a New Day Coming!* (Eugene, Oreg., Harvest House, 1983), pp. 39, 66.

118. Lewis Sperry Chafer, *Systematic Theology* (Dallas, Dallas Theological Seminary, 1948), IV, 313, quoted in Rausch, *Zionism within Early American Fundamentalism,* p. 323; J. Palmer Muntz, "The Jew in History and Destiny," in Bradbury, *Israel's Restoration,* p. 94.

119. Author interview with J. Dwight Pentecost, July 13, 1989.

120. Kristol, "Political Dilemma of American Jews," p. 25.

121. Weber, *Living in the Shadow of the Second Coming,* p. 154; Rausch, *Zionism within Early American Fundamentalism,* passim (quoted phrases pp. 2, 3, 342). For a useful general study see David A. Gerber, ed., *Anti-Semitism in American History* (Urbana, University of Illinois Press, 1986).

122. Weber, *Living in the Shadow of the Second Coming,* p. 156 (*Protocols of the Elders of Zion*); Isaac M. Haldeman, *The Signs of the Times* (New York, Charles C. Cook, 5th ed., 1914; orig. publ. 1910), pp. 436, 437, 440, 441; Pink, *Antichrist,* pp. 278, 279; Pettingill, *God's Prophecies for Plain People,* p. 89; Gerald B. Winrod, *Mussolini's Place in Prophecy* (Wichita, Defender Publishers, [ca. 1933]), p. 25. See also Charles C. Cook, "The International Jew," *King's Business,* 12 (Nov. 1921), 1087, quoted in Wilson, *Armageddon Now!* p. 74.

A few pre-1945 prophecy writers strongly condemned anti-Semitism while acknowledging its presence in the genre. See, for example, Harry A. Ironside, *The Lamp of Prophecy; or, Signs of the Times* (Grand Rapids, Zondervan Publishing Co., 1940), pp. 109–115. J. Oliver Buswell, president of Wheaton College, an evangelical school near Chicago, in the *Sunday School Times* of the mid-1930s protested the anti-Semitism "manifesting itself among some of our Fundamentalist brethren"— Brooks, *The Jews and the Passion for Palestine,* p. 46. On the anti-Semitism of a leading fundamentalist, see William Vance Trollinger, Jr., *God's Empire: William Bell Riley and Midwestern Fundamentalism* (Madison, University of Wisconsin Press, 1990), pp. 62–82. On anti-Semitism among pentecostalists, see Robert Mapes Anderson, *Vision of* the Disinherited: The Making of American Pentecostalism (New York, Oxford University Press, 1979), pp. 218, 220. For useful general discussions see Leo P. Ribuffo, *The Old Christian Right: The Protestant Far Right from the Great Depression to the Cold War* (Philadelphia, Temple University Press, 1983), and George M. Marsden, *Fundamentalism and American Culture: The Shaping of Twentieth-Century Evangelicalism, 1870–1925* (New York, Oxford University Press, 1980), esp. p. 210.

123. Haines, *End from the Beginning,* chap. 2, pp. 17–27 (quoted passages pp. 16, 18, 24, 25, back cover).

124. Quoted in Lindberg, "A God-Filled Life," pp. 14–16; Blackstone's cite from Ezek. 20:32–38. For an essay that bears closely on the issues discussed here and in the following paragraphs see Jonathan Sarna, "'The Mythical Jew' and the 'Jew Next Door,' in Nineteenth-Century America," in Gerber, *Anti-Semitism in American History.*

125. Wilson, *Armageddon Now!* pp. 15, 217.

126. Weber, *Living in the Shadow of the Second Coming,* p. 154.

127. Charles O. Benham, *101 Roadsigns to Our Next Pearl Harbor and to Armageddon* (Washington, D.C., 1945), pp. 55–56, 132; Rimmer, *Shadow of Coming Events,* p. 41; Russell Bradley Jones, *The Things Which Shall Be Hereafter,* 1947, reissued as *The Latter Days* (Grand Rapids, Baker Book House, 1961), pp. 69, 77; William Ward Ayer, *What Goes On Here!* (Grand Rapids, Zondervan Publishing Co., 1947), p. 94.

128. John W. Bradbury, "To the Jew First," in Bradbury, *Israel's Restoration,* p. 12; Frank E. Gaebelein, "Arnold Toynbee and the Jews," in Culbertson and Centz, *Understanding the Times,* pp. 256–261; Van Impe with Campbell, *Israel's Final Holocaust,* p. 9; Lindsey, *There's a New World Coming,* p. 169; Hal Lindsey, *The Road to Holocaust* (New York, Bantam Books, 1989). See also Prince, *Last Word on the Middle East,* p. 110; Lindsey, *Late Great Planet Earth,* p. 35; David Allan Hubbard, *The Second Coming: What Will Happen When Jesus Returns?* (Downers Grove, Ill., InterVarsity Press, 1984), p. 81; Arthur W. Kac, "Prophetic Patterns in the World Today," *Moody Monthly,* May 1960, p. 29.

My argument here must be qualified by noting that blatant anti-Semitism of the crudest type still figures prominently in the apocalypticism of the extremist fringe groups known collectively as the Christian Identity movement. See Michael Barkun, "Racist Apocalypse: Millennialism on the Far Right," *American Studies,* 31 (1990), 127–128. These numerically minuscule groups, with their highly idiosyncratic—and frightening—notions of an Anglo-Saxon millennium, when the world will at last be free of Jews and people of color, vehemently reject the premillennialism espoused by John Darby, Cyrus Scofield, Hal Lindsey, and the other writers considered in this book.

129. Frederick J. Miles, *Prophecy: Past, Present, and Prospective* (Grand Rapids,

Zondervan Publishing Co., 1943), p. 20; Strauss, *God's Plan for the Future,* pp. 138, 142.

130. Stedman, *What's This World Coming To?* p. 59; Hyman J. Appleman, "A Suffering People," in Bradbury, *Israel's Restoration,* pp. 27, 28.

131. LaHaye, *Coming Peace in the Middle East,* p. 63.

132. Van Impe with Campbell, *Israel's Final Holocaust,* pp. 77–78, 81, 155. The specific passages quoted by Van Impe are Deut. 28:36, 47–48.

133. Chuck Smith, *What the World Is Coming To* (Costa Mesa, Calif., Word for Today, 1977), pp. 164–165; Coder, *Final Chapter,* p. 17; Unger, *Beyond the Crystal Ball,* p. 108; Paul Olson prophecy sermon, Madison Gospel Tabernacle, Madison, Wis., Nov. 1, 1989.

134. Gen. 12:3; Lindsey, *The 1980s,* p. 45; Bloomfield, *How to Recognize the Antichrist,* p. 124; Clark, *Shockwaves of Armageddon,* p. 93.

135. Quoted passage, Matt. 27:25; Stedman, *What's This World Coming To?* p. 101; Louis S. Bauman, "Many Antichrists," in Bradbury, *Israel's Restoration,* p. 69; Lindsey, *There's a New World Coming,* p. 170.

136. Van Impe with Campbell, *Israel's Final Holocaust,* pp. 77, 145; see also pp. 51–52, 55, 78–85; Jack Van Impe, *11:59 and Counting* (Royal Oak, Mich., Jack Van Impe Ministries, 1983), pp. 140, 141.

137. Rausch, *Zionism within Early American Fundamentalism,* p. 3.

138. Coder, *Final Chapter,* p. 16.

7. The United States in Prophecy

1. Herbert Lockyear, *Cameos of Prophecy: Are These the Last Days?* (Grand Rapids, Zondervan Publishing Co., 1942), p. 66.

2. Pauline Moffitt Watts, "Prophecy and Discovery: On the Spiritual Origins of Christopher Columbus's 'Enterprise of the Indies,'" *American Historical Review,* 90 (Feb. 1985), 102.

3. Edward Johnson, *Wonder-Working Providence* (1653) and Jonathan Edwards, "Thoughts on the Revival of Religion in New England" (1742), quoted in M. H. Abrams, "Apocalypse: Theme and Variations," in C. A. Patrides and Joseph Wittreich, eds., *The Apocalypse in English Renaissance Thought and Literature* (Manchester, Manchester University Press, 1984), p. 357; Jonathan Edwards, *History of the Work of Redemption* [1739], quoted in Ernest Lee Tuveson, *Redeemer Nation: The Idea of America's Millennial Role* (Chicago, University of Chicago Press, 1968), p. 100 (italics in original).

4. Nathan O. Hatch, *The Sacred Cause of Liberty: Republican Thought and the Millennium in Revolutionary New England* (New Haven, Yale University Press, 1977), pp. 3, 16, 139 (quoting the Reverend John Mellon, 1797).

5. Quoted in Tuveson, *Redeemer Nation,* p. 25.

6. Hatch, *Sacred Cause of Liberty,* p. 170, 174 (Tocqueville). James H. Moorhead offers an illuminating discussion of the tendency of nineteenth-century American Protestant theologians "to make the Republic itself an object of eschatological fulfillment" in his essay "Between Progress and Apocalypse: A Reassessment of Millennialism in American Religious Thought, 1800–1880," *Journal of American History,* 71 (Dec. 1984), 524–542, esp. pp. 531–533 (quoted phrase p. 531).

7. Nathan O. Hatch, *The Democratization of American Religion* (New Haven, Yale University Press, 1989), pp. 184, 185, 294n82.

8. Ibid., pp. 69, 184–185, 294n79; Tuveson, *Redeemer Nation,* pp. 125 (*U.S. Magazine and Democratic Review*), 156–157 (Melville). See also George Marsden, "Evangelicals, History, and Modernity," in Marsden, ed., *Evangelicalism and Modern America* (Grand Rapids, Wm. B. Eerdman's Publishing Co., 1984), pp. 94–102, esp. p. 96.

9. *Book of Mormon:* I Nephi 13:12; II Nephi 10:10–14; Ether 13:2–6; Tuveson, *Redeemer Nation,* pp. 176, 179–180. For a treatment of Mormon eschatology by an influential Mormon theologian, see Bruce R. McConkie, *The Millennial Messiah: The Second Coming of the Son of Man* (Salt Lake City, Deseret Books, 1982). For a historical treatment by a younger Mormon scholar, see Grant Underwood, "The Millenarian World of Early Mormonism" (Ph.D. diss., UCLA, 1988). See also Hatch, *Democratization of American Religion,* p. 187.

10. Benson J. Lossing to H. W. Bellows, Apr. 21, 1862, Bellows Papers, Massachusetts Historical Society; Tuveson, *Redeemer Nation,* chap. 6, pp. 187–208. My thanks to Harold Eugene Mahan for calling the Lossing letter to my attention.

11. Washington Gladden, "Migrations and Their Lessons," *Publications of the Ohio Archaeological and Historical Society,* 3 (1891), 195; Josiah Strong, *Our Country,* ed. Jurgen Herbst (Cambridge, Mass., Harvard University Press, 1963), p. 176, both quoted in Tuveson, *Redeemer Nation,* pp. 129, 166. See also Jean B. Quandt, "Religion and Social Thought: The Secularization of Postmillennialism," *American Quarterly,* 25 (Oct. 1973), 390–409, which argues for the persistence of a semisecularized postmillennialism into the early twentieth century. Quandt deals with both Josiah Strong (pp. 397–400) and the Social Gospel clergy (pp. 400–402).

12. Tuveson, *Redeemer Nation,* pp. 209–212 (Wilson quoted p. 211).

13. Arno C. Gaebelein, *As It Was—So It Shall Be. Sunrise and Sunset: A Study of the First Age and Our Present Age* (New York, Our Hope, 1937), p. 134.

14. Senator Dan Quayle, vice-presidential acceptance speech, Republican National Convention, Aug. 17, 1988.

15. Luke 17:26–30; Matt. 24:44.
16. Wilbur M. Smith, "The Cruelty of Modern Man," *Sunday School Times,* 91 (Feb. 5, 1949), 107–108; II Tim. 3:1–7.
17. David Webber and Noah Hutchings, *Is This the Last Century?* (Nashville, Thomas Nelson Publishers, 1979), pp. 115–118; Rev. 18 (quoted passage Rev. 18:2). See also Jack Van Impe, *11: 59 and Counting* (Royal Oak, Mich., Jack Van Impe Ministries, 1983), p. 161 (America as the "political Babylon"); David Wilkerson, *Set the Trumpet to Thy Mouth* (Lindale, Tex., World Challenge, 1985), p. 3.
18. Cyprian quoted in Jacques Lacarrière, *Men Possessed by God: The Story of the Desert Monks of Ancient Christendom,* tr. Roy Monkcom (Garden City, N.Y., Doubleday and Co., 1964); excerpt reprinted in William Griffin, ed., *Endtime: The Doomsday Catalog* (New York, Collier Books, 1979), p. 54.
19. Martin Luther quoted in Wilbur M. Smith, "Signs of the Second Advent of Christ," in Carl F. H. Henry, ed., *Prophecy in the Making* (Carol Stream, Ill., Creation House, 1971), pp. 190–191; Jonathan Mayhew, *Practical Discourses Delivered on Occasion of the Earthquakes in November 1755* (Boston, 1760), pp. 369–370, quoted in Ruth H. Bloch, *Visionary Republic: Millennial Themes in American Thought, 1756–1800* (Cambridge, Cambridge University Press, 1985), p. 35.
20. Gaebelein, *As It Was—So It Shall Be,* p. 152; Tim LaHaye, *The Beginning of the End* (Wheaton, Ill., Tyndale House Publishers, 1972), p. 128; Jack Van Impe, *Signs of the Times* (Royal Oak, Mich., Jack Van Impe Ministries, 1979), pp. 30, 31, 32.
21. David Hocking, *The Coming World Leader: Understanding the Book of Revelation* (Portland, Oreg., Multnomah Press, 1988), p. 167.
22. M. R. DeHaan, *The Days of Noah* (Grand Rapids, Zondervan Publishing Co., 1963), pp. 46–47; Van Impe, *11: 59 and Counting,* pp. 42–44 (backward masking); Jacob Aranza, *Backward Masking Unveiled,* advertised in David Webber and Noah Hutchings, *Computers and the Beast of Revelation* (Shreveport, La., Huntington House, 1986), back page.
23. DeHaan, *Days of Noah,* p. 43; William R. Goetz, *Apocalypse Next: Updated* (Cathedral City, Calif., Horizon House Publishers, 1981), p. 279; Roy Hicks, *Another Look at the Rapture* (Tulsa, Harrison House, 1982), pp. 18–19; Dave Hunt, *Peace, Prosperity, and the Coming Holocaust: The New Age Movement in Prophecy* (Eugene, Oreg., Harvest House Publishers, 1983), p. 69; James McKeever, "Father God and Mother Nature," *End-Times News Digest* (Omega Ministries, Medford, Oreg.), June 1990, p. 7.
24. Hunt, *Peace, Prosperity, and the Coming Holocaust,* pp. 35 (quoted passage), 52, 68, 80, 108, 122, 145, 180, 198, 232 (quoted passage); James

Montgomery Boice, *The Last and Future World* (Grand Rapids, Zondervan Publishing Co., 1974), p. 77; *Time,* June 19, 1972.

25. Harold John Ockenga, "Fulfilled and Unfulfilled Prophecies," in Henry, *Prophecy in the Making,* pp. 305, 306; Boice, *Last and Future World,* p. 54; Dan. 11:37. See also Smith, "Signs of the Second Advent of Christ," p. 200.

26. David Wilkerson, *The Vision* (New York, Pyramid Books, 1974), pp. 43, 44, 50, 79.

27. Idem, *Set the Trumpet to Thy Mouth* (Lindale, Tex., World Challenge, 1985), pp. 1–2, 20–21. Wilkerson gained fame in evangelical and pentecostal circles with *The Cross and the Switchblade* (1963) on his work with New York City street gangs. By the 1970s, says David Edwin Harrell, Jr., "no man's voice carried more authority in the charismatic revival"— Harrell, *All Things Are Possible: The Healing and Charismatic Revivals in Modern America* (Bloomington, Indiana University Press, 1975), pp. 186–187.

28. J. Vernon McGee, "The Crisis of This Present Hour," in *The Prophetic Word in Crisis Days* (Findlay, Ohio, Dunham Publishing Co., 1961), p. 39; Robert Glenn Gromacki, *Are These the Last Days?* (Schaumburg, Ill., Regular Baptist Press, 1970), pp. 64, 65; LaHaye, *Beginning of the End,* p. 89. See also Hal Lindsey, *The 1980s: Countdown to Armageddon* (New York, Bantam Books, 1981), p. 142.

29. Hunt, *Peace, Prosperity, and the Coming Holocaust,* p. 18; Roger Campbell and David Campbell, *Prosperity in the End Time* (Fort Washington, Pa., Christian Literature Crusade, 1983), p. 67 (quoted passage), 70, 73, 81, 94 (quoted passage).

30. Wilbur M. Smith, "The Exclusion of God and the Exaltation of Man in Education," *Sunday School Times,* 91 (Jan. 15, 1949), 43; Dan. 12:4. See also Campbell and Campbell, *Prosperity in the End Time,* p. 79; Goetz, *Apocalypse Next: Updated,* p. 263; M. R. DeHaan, *Coming Events in Prophecy* (Grand Rapids, Zondervan Publishing Co., 1962), p. 101.

31. Salem Kirban, *666* (Wheaton, Ill., Tyndale House Publishing Co., 1970), p. 248. See also Van Impe, *11:59 and Counting,* p. 150; Carl G. Johnson, *Prophecy Made Plain for Times like These* (Chicago, Moody Press, 1972), p. 47.

32. LaHaye, *Beginning of the End,* pp. 77, 107, 118, 136.

33. Ray C. Stedman, *What's This World Coming To?* (Ventura, Calif., Regal Books, 1986; orig. publ. 1970 as *What on Earth's Going to Happen?*), pp. 41, 42, 65.

34. Hicks, *Another Look at the Rapture,* pp. 16, 18. See also J. Barton Payne, *The Imminent Appearing of Christ* (Grand Rapids, Wm. B. Eerdman's Publishing Co., 1962), p. 160.

35. Wilkerson, *Set the Trumpet to Thy Mouth,* pp. 53, 55, 65.

36. Campbell and Campbell, *Prosperity in the End Time,* p. 79 ("many shall run to and fro"); Van Impe, *11:59 and Counting,* p. 165; Van Impe, *Signs of the Times,* p. 24; M. R. DeHaan, *Coming Events in Prophecy* (Grand Rapids, Zondervan Publishing Co., 1962), pp. 101, 108, 113 (quoted passages pp. 108, 113). The biblical passages quoted in this paragraph are from Dan. 12:4, Jer. 51:53, Luke 21:25, and Ps. 115:16.

37. Ray Stedman, *What on Earth's Going to Happen?* (Glendale, Calif., Regal Books, 1970), p. 44; William Ward Ayer, *What Goes On Here?* (Grand Rapids, Zondervan Publishing Co., 1947), p. 34; Paul Lee Tan, *Jesus Is Coming* (Rockville, Md., Assurance Publishers, 1982), p. 40. Cf. Mike Evans, *The Return* (Nashville, Thomas Nelson Publishing Co., 1986), p. 41: "Like enormous billboards beside the freeway, the dramatic prophecies of the Bible . . . cry out to us declaring that the days in which we live are the beginning of the end."

38. See, for example, Charles O. Benham, *101 Roadsigns to Our Next Pearl Harbor and to Armageddon* (Washington, D.C., National Forecast Magazine, 1945), p. 107; Ayer, *What Goes On Here?* pp. 68, 149.

39. John F. Walvoord, *The Nations in Prophecy* (Grand Rapids, Zondervan Publishing Co., 1967), reprinted in Walvoord, *The Nations, Israel, and the Church in Prophecy* (Grand Rapids, Zondervan Publishing Co., 1988), p. 174. See also Billy Graham, *World Aflame* (New York, Penguin Books, 1967; orig. publ. 1965), pp. 169, 192.

40. Charles R. Taylor, *The Destiny of America* (Van Nuys, Calif., Time-Light Books, 1972), p. 72; Merrill F. Unger, *Beyond the Crystal Ball* (Chicago, Moody Press, 1973), pp. 139–140; Carl Johnson, *Prophecy Made Plain for Times like These,* p. 39.

41. Lindsey, *The 1980s,* pp. 133, 141; Van Impe, *11:59 and Counting,* pp. 159–160. See also Hicks, *Another Look at the Rapture,* p. 18.

42. Wilkerson, *Set the Trumpet to Thy Mouth,* p. 18; author interview with John F. Walvoord, Aug. 8, 1989.

43. Pat Robertson, *The Secret Kingdom* (New York, Bantam Books, 1984; orig. publ. 1982), p. 14.

44. Idem, *America's Dates with Destiny* (Nashville, Thomas Nelson Publishers, 1986); idem, "A New Vision for America," Washington, D.C., address, Sept. 17, 1986; Stephen O'Leary and M. W. McFarland, "The Political Use of Mythic Discourse: Prophetic Interpretation in Pat Robertson's Presidential Campaign," *Quarterly Journal of Speech,* 75 (Nov. 1989), 433–452, esp. 438–449.

45. Robertson, *America's Dates with Destiny,* p. 444 (quoting "A New Vision for America").

46. Ibid., pp. 445–446.

47. Walvoord, *The Nations in Prophecy,* p. 174.
48. Taylor, *Destiny of America,* pp. 71, 72 (quoted passage; italics in original) Dwight Wilson, *Armageddon Now! The Premillenarian Response to Russia and Israel since 1917* (Grand Rapids, Baker Book House, 1977), p. 217.
49. Erling Jorstad, *The New Christian Right, 1981–1988: Prospects for the Post-Reagan Era* (Lewiston, N.Y., E. Mellen Press, 1987), p. 18 (Falwell); Arthur E. Bloomfield, *How to Recognize the Antichrist* (Minneapolis, Bethany Fellowship, 1975), p. 81. See also Ivor Powell, *What in the World Will Happen Next?* (Grand Rapids, Kregel Publications, 1985), p. 71.
50. Hilton Sutton, prophecy sermon, Shalom Christian Center, Madison, Wis., Aug. 20, 1988.
51. S. Maxwell Coder, "The Destiny of America," *Moody Monthly,* Jan. 1973, p. 58; idem, *The Final Chapter: Understanding What the Bible Says about the Last Pages of Human History* (Wheaton, Ill., Tyndale House Publishers, 1984), p. 89.
52. Walter K. Price, *The Coming Antichrist* (Chicago, Moody Press, 1974), pp. 48–49.
53. John Wesley White, *The Coming World Dictator* (Minneapolis, Bethany House Publishers, 1981), p. 76; Hunt, *Peace, Prosperity, and the Coming Holocaust,* p. 194. See also Hicks, *Another Look at the Rapture,* p. 104.
54. Edward Hoare, *Palestine and Russia* (London, Hatchard's, 1877), reprinted in E. L. Langston, *Great Britain, Palestine, Russia and the Jews: A Reprint of Canon Edward Hoare's Book "Palestine and Russia" Brought up to Date with Additional Chapters* (London, Charles J. Thynne, 1918), p. 103; Arthur I. Brown, *The Eleventh "Hour"* (Findlay, Ohio, Fundamental Truth Publishers, 1940), p. 78 ("young lions" as the United States); Doug Clark, *Shockwaves of Armageddon* (Eugene, Oreg., Harvest Books, 1982), pp. 10, 11. For "Tarshish" and the "young lions" as Great Britain, see A. Whitman, *Prophecy Opened: Illustrating the Character of God, as Shown in His Providential and Gracious Administration on Earth* (Carthage, Mo., Advance Book and Job Printing House, 1874), p. 477.
55. Goetz, *Apocalypse Next: Updated,* p. 145; Unger, *Beyond the Crystal Ball,* p. 90; Robertson, *Secret Kingdom,* p. 214.
56. Taylor, *Destiny of America,* pp. 57, 72, 110. See also pp. 222–225.
57. Clark, *Shockwaves of Armageddon,* pp. 93, 94.
58. Donald Grey Barnhouse, "Current Events in the Light of the Bible: P.S. No. 1 on the Splitting of the Atomic Nucleus," *Revelation,* Dec. 1945, p. 536.
59. Louis T. Talbot, "Unshakable Things," in John W. Bradbury, ed., *Israel's Restoration: A Series of Lectures by Bible Expositors Interested in the Evangelization of the Jews* (New York, Iversen-Ford Associates, [1952]), p. 184; Van Impe, *Signs of the Times,* pp. 15, 73.

60. Hal Lindsey, *The Late Great Planet Earth* (New York, Bantam Books, 1973), p. 150. The passage, Ezek. 39:6, is quoted from *The Amplified New Testament,* a modern translation much admired by evangelicals.

61. Isa. 18:1–2.

62. Hicks, *Another Look at the Rapture,* pp. 101–103; Van Impe, *11:59 and Counting,* pp. 163–166, 187 (quoted passage); Taylor, *Destiny of America,* pp. 65–68, 222–223. For an 1814 sermon by an Albany (N.Y.) Presbyterian clergyman linking Isa. 18 to the United States, see Peter Grose, *Israel in the Mind of America* (New York, Alfred A. Knopf, 1983), p. 9.

63. Isa. 18:5–6.

64. "Ted," *The Climax* (St. Petersburg, Fla., Gospel Truth, 1982; copy in Mosher Library, Dallas Theological Seminary), p. 38.

65. Wilkerson, *Set the Trumpet to Thy Mouth,* pp. 1, 6, 9.

66. A. G. Mojtabai, *Blessed Assurance: At Home with the Bomb in Amarillo, Texas* (Boston, Houghton Mifflin Co., 1986), pp. 167, 189.

67. Walvoord, *The Nations in Prophecy,* p. 172; Tim LaHaye, *The Coming Peace in the Middle East* (Grand Rapids, Zondervan Publishing Co., 1984), p. 162. For the same argument see Lindsey, *The 1980s,* p. 131; S. Maxwell Coder, "The Future of Nations," in Charles Lee Feinberg, ed., *Focus on Prophecy* (New York, Fleming H. Revell, 1964), p. 105.

68. See, for example, S. Maxwell Coder, "The Destiny of America," *Moody Monthly,* Jan. 1973, pp. 30, 56–58. For relevant biblical passages see Jer. 25:15–16, 26; Zech. 14:2 ("For I will gather all nations against Jerusalem to battle"); Rev. 16:13–16.

69. Margaret MacDonald's account of her vision quoted in James M. McKeever, *The Rapture Book: Victory in the End Times* (Medford, Oreg., Omega Publications, 1987), pp. 215–220 (quoted passage p. 215).

70. Robert Anderson, *The Coming Prince* (Grand Rapids, Kregel Publications, 1986; reprint of 1884 work), p. 191; Beverley O. Kinnear, *Impending Judgments on the Earth* (New York, James Huggins, 1892), p. 24; James M. Gray, *A Text-Book on Prophecy* (New York, Fleming H. Revell, 1918), p. 184 (quoting Haldeman).

71. Timothy P. Weber, *Living in the Shadow of the Second Coming: American Premillennialism, 1875–1925* (New York, Oxford University Press, 1979), p. 121.

72. Oswald J. Smith, *The Voice of Prophecy* (London, Marshall, Morgan and Scott, 1948), p. 13; William Culbertson, "Understanding the Times," in William Culbertson and Herman B. Centz, eds., *Understanding the Times: Prophetic Messages Delivered at the Second International Congress on Prophecy, New York City* (Grand Rapids, Zondervan Publishing Co., 1956), pp. 14–15; F. S. Donn, *The Israel Way to Peace* (New York, Exposition Press, 1957), pp. 69, 83, 134.

73. Stanley A. Ellison, *Biography of a Great Planet* (Wheaton, Ill., Tyndale House Publishers, 1975), p. 131; Chuck Smith, *Future Survival* (Costa Mesa, Calif., Word for Today, 1978), p. 46; idem, *The Final Curtain* (Costa Mesa, Calif., Word for Today, 1984), p. 58.

74. Donn, *Israel Way to Peace,* pp. 106–107, 108, 109; Wilkerson, *The Vision,* pp. 18, 99; Hal Lindsey, *There's a New World Coming* (Santa Ana, Calif., Vision House Publishers, 1973), p. 187; Salem Kirban, *Guide to Survival* (Huntingdon Valley, Pa., Salem Kirban, 1978; orig. publ. 1968), p. 118. See also Wilkerson, *Set the Trumpet to Thy Mouth,* p. 14.

75. Clark, *Shockwaves of Armageddon,* p. 20.

76. Dave Hunt, *Peace, Prosperity, and the Coming Holocaust,* p. 171; Coder, *Final Chapter,* pp. 63, 87; Joel 2:12.

77. Bill McKee, *Orbit of Ashes: Jesus Is Coming!* (Wheaton, Ill., Tyndale House Publishers, 1972), p. 60; author interview with John F. Walvoord, Aug. 8, 1989.

78. Lindsey, *Late Great Planet Earth,* pp. 155, 173; Rev. 16:19.

79. Lindsey, *There's a New World Coming,* p. 226. See also idem, "The Great Cosmic Countdown: Hal Lindsey on the Future," *Eternity,* Jan. 1977, p. 21.

80. Idem, *The 1980s,* pp. 132, 149; Michael L. Stine has contributed to my understanding of Lindsey's treatment of the United States, particularly in *The 1980s: Countdown to Armageddon.*

81. Lindsey, *The 1980s,* pp. 157–158.

82. E. Schuyler English, *The Shifting of the Scenes* (New York, Our Hope, 1945), p. 35; J. Dwight Pentecost, "The Prophetic Word and Europe," in Pentecost, *The Prophetic Word in Crisis Days,* p. 105.

83. Walvoord, *The Nations in Prophecy,* p. 173; Coder, "Destiny of America," pp. 56–57; idem, *Final Chapter,* p. 87; Rev. 13:7. See also Kirban, *666,* p. 136; idem, *Analysis of Worldwide News,* vol. I, no. 3 (1988), p. 3; McKee, *Orbit of Ashes,* p. 60.

84. See, for example, Charles C. Ryrie, *The Final Countdown* (Wheaton, Ill., Victor Books, 1982), p. 45: "The United States is not named, mentioned, or hinted at either directly or symbolically in any of the prophecies concerning the Western federation of nations of the Tribulation."

85. Clark, *Shockwaves of Armageddon,* pp. 21, 22.

8. Antichrist, 666, and the Mark of the Beast

1. Charles R. Taylor, *The Destiny of America* (Van Nuys, Calif., Time-Light Books, 1972), p. 236.

2. Leon Bates, *Projection for Survival* (Dallas, Bible Believers' Evangelistic Association; 3rd ed., rev., 1979), p. 129.

3. Timothy P. Weber, *Living in the Shadow of the Second Coming: American Premillennialism, 1875–1925* (New York, Oxford University Press, 1979), p. 55; David Wilkerson, *The Vision* (New York, Pyramid Books, 1974), pp. 63, 68, 70; Merrill F. Unger, *Beyond the Crystal Ball* (Chicago, Moody Press, 1973), p. 49; Bates, *Projection for Survival*, pp. 133, 139.

4. *End-Times News Digest,* Aug. 1989, p. 9; Roy Hicks, *Another Look at the Rapture* (Tulsa, Horizon House, 1982), pp. 111, 113 (quoted phrase).

5. Forrest Loman Oilar, *Be Thou Prepared, for Jesus Is Coming* (Boston, Meador Publishing Co., 1937), p. 121; Ernest Angley, *Raptured: A Novel on the Second Coming of the Lord* (Akron, Winston Press, 1950), pp. 2, 8, 25–26, 32, 44, 58; Salem Kirban, *Matthew: The Beginning of Sorrow* (Chicago, Moody Press, 1972), p. 69 (Rapture illustration); *Chaos* [comic book] (Chino, Calif., Chick Publications, 1975).

6. Douglas Ober, *The Great World Crisis* (Wheaton, Ill., Van Kampen Press, 1950), pp. 93, 97; Luke 21:25; John F. Walvoord, *The Nations in Prophecy* (Grand Rapids, Zondervan Publishing Co., 1967), reprinted in Walvoord, *The Nations, Israel, and the Church in Prophecy* (Grand Rapids, Zondervan Publishing Co., 1988), p. 13; Tim LaHaye, foreword, in Clifford Wilson and John Weldon, *1980s: Decade of Shock* (San Diego, Master Books, 1978), n.p. See also George Eldon Ladd, *The Last Things: An Eschatology for Laymen* (Grand Rapids, Wm. B. Eerdman's Publishing Co., 1978), p. 69; Wilbur M. Smith, "Storm Warnings on the Sea of Humanity," *Sunday School Times,* June 4, 1933, p. 341; and Frederic C. Jaher, *Doubters and Dissenters* (Glencoe, Ill., Free Press, 1964).

7. Donald Grey Barnhouse, "Prophetic Sidelights," *Revelation,* Sept. 1945, p. 363; Thomas S. McCall and Zola Levitt, *The Coming Russian Invasion of Israel: Updated* (Chicago, Moody Press, 1978), preface to 1st ed. [1974], p. 11; Daniel Berrigan, *The Nightmare of God* (Portland, Oreg., Sunburst Press, 1983), p. 109. See also Wilson and Weldon, *The 1980s,* pp. 87, 94.

8. Taylor, *Destiny of America,* p. 148; Charles R. Taylor, *Those Who Remain: 1980 Edition* (Orange, Calif., Today in Bible Prophecy, 1980), pp. 14, 62, 64; John Wesley White, *The Coming World Dictator* (Minneapolis, Bethany House Publishers, 1981), p. 96; David Wilkerson, *Set the Trumpet to Thy Mouth* (Lindale, Tex., World Challenge, 1985), p. 6, quoting Isa. 24:12,20; Mike Evans, *The Return* (Nashville, Thomas Nelson Publishing Co., 1986), p. 11. See also Herman A. Hoyt, *The End Times* (Chicago, Moody Press, 1969), p. 125; Pat Robertson, *The Secret Kingdom* (New York, Bantam Books, 1984), p. 215; Chuck Smith, *The Final Curtain* (Costa Mesa, Calif., Word for Today, 1984), p. 63.

9. *The Works of William Paley, D.D., Archdeacon of Carlisle: A New Edition with Illustrative Notes and a Life of the Author* (London, Wm. S. Orr and Co., 1849), p. 25; Paul Lee Tan, *Jesus Is Coming* (Rockville, Md., Assurance Publishers, 1982), p. 23.

10. Dan Betzer, *Beast: A Novel of the Future World Dictator* (Lafayette, La., Prescott Press, 1985), pp. 109, 151, 155, 156, 162.

11. M. R. DeHaan, *The Days of Noah* (Grand Rapids, Zondervan Publishing Co., 1963), pp. 41, 42; Lu Ann Bransby, *The Impending Hour* (Oklahoma City, Impending Hour, 1981), pp. 59, 64; Jack Van Impe, *11: 59 and Counting* (Royal Oak, Mich., Jack Van Impe Ministries, 1983), p. 116. See also Arthur E. Bloomfield, *How to Recognize the Antichrist* (Minneapolis, Bethany Fellowship, 1975), p. 121; David Edwin Harrell, Jr., *Pat Robertson: A Personal, Religious, and Political Portrait* (San Francisco, Harper and Row, 1987), p. 147, quoting a 1980 issue of Robertson's newsletter, *Perspectives,* which advised self-sufficiency and a shift of real-estate investments to smaller communities in preparation for the end.

12. Salem Kirban, *666* (Wheaton, Ill., Tyndale House Publishers, 1970), p. 55.

13. Ibid., pp. 57 (quoted passage), 95.

14. Betzer, *Beast,* p. 41. For the remembered joys of rural life see also Doug Clark, *How to Survive the Money Crash* (Irvine, Calif., Harvest House Publishers, 1979), p. 136.

15. Taylor, *Those Who Remain,* p. 9.

16. "Physical Preparation," *End-Times News Digest,* Nov. 1989, pp. 1–6 (quoted passage p. 6); ibid., Feb. 1989, p. 5; ibid., Jan. 1990, p. 7. See also James McKeever, *The Rapture Book: Victory in the End Times* (Medford, Oreg., Omega Publications, 1987), p. 36. McKeever was a leading spokesman for the so-called Post-Trib, Pre-Mill position, whose adherents hold that the Rapture will occur after the Great Tribulation, but before the Millennium.

17. Salem Kirban, *Guide to Survival* (Huntingdon Valley, Pa., Salem Kirban, 1978; orig. publ. 1968), pp. 26 (quoted passage), 87–89; Wilkerson, *Vision,* p. 100. See also A. Bekley Michelson, *Daniel and Revelation: Riddles or Realities* (Nashville, Thomas Nelson Publishing Co., 1984), p. 136: "The symbolic beasts of Daniel show [that] human government controls the people of the world by sheer force."

18. John M. Court, *Myth and History in the Book of Revelation* (London, SPCK, 1979), p. 130; Berrigan, *Nightmare of God,* p. 1.

19. Berrigan, *Nightmare of God,* pp. 12, 21, 58–59, 100.

20. Ibid., pp. 12, 23, 24.

21. Ibid., pp. 37, 38.

22. James M. Houston, "The Judgment of Nations," in Carl F. H. Henry, ed., *Prophecy in the Making* (Carol Stream, Ill., Creation House, 1971), pp. 366, 367; Michelson, *Daniel and Revelation,* chap. 5, pp. 129–141˙ (quoted phrases pp. 7, 134, 136); Wilbur M. Smith, "The Struggle for World Power," *Sunday School Times,* 90 (Dec. 4, 1948), 1083 (quoted passage); idem, "The Growth of the Worship of Power," ibid., 90 (Dec. 11, 1948), 1115–16.

23. Donald Grey Barnhouse, "The Church and Antichrist," *Revelation,* June 1945, pp. 249–250, 267–269; Alva J. McClain, "Significant Signs of the Times," in John W. Bradbury, ed., *Hastening the Day of God: Prophetic Messages from the International Congress on Prophecy in Calvary Baptist Church, New York City, November 9–16, 1952* (Wheaton, Ill., Van Kampen Press, 1953), p. 36; John F. Walvoord, *The Church in Prophecy* (Grand Rapids, Zondervan Publishing Co., 1964), reprinted in Walvoord, *Israel, the Nations, and the Church in Prophecy,* pp. 59, 65, 68, 166.

24. Hal Lindsey, *The Late Great Planet Earth* (New York, Bantam Books, 1973), pp. 118, 171; Unger, *Beyond the Crystal Ball,* p. 32; Chuck Smith, *What the World Is Coming To* (Costa Mesa, Calif., Word for Today, 1977), chap. 17, pp. 151–160 (quoted phrases p. 152). See also Ray C. Stedman, *What on Earth Is Going to Happen?* (Glendale, Calif., Regal Books, 1970), p. 90; Jack Van Impe, *Signs of the Times* (Royal Oak, Mich., Jack Van Impe Ministries, 1979), pp. 56–57; Herbert Vander Lugt, *There's a New Day Coming!* (Eugene, Oreg., Harvest House Publishing Co., 1983), chap. 7, esp. p. 74.

25. Oilar, *Be Thou Prepared,* p. 147, citing Isa. 5:8. See also F. W. Pitt, *Coming Events Cast Their Shadows in the Air* (London, Marshall, Morgan, and Scott, 1936), p. 128: "Few people would look for signs of the end-time in the London streets. Yet they can be seen in the mammoth stores that have sprung up in the last few years. A man of middle age can remember when there were no Harrod's, Selfridge's, Barker's, and Lyons', but there they are today, . . . the greatest municipal combine the world has ever seen. And what is true of London is true of every city everywhere, and what is true of commerce is true of politics and religion. Combines, federations, are the order of the day, and will be till commerce, politics, and religion are all vested in one head, which Scripture calls Mystery Babylon."

26. W. H. Rogers, *"The End from the Beginning": A Panorama of Prophecy; or, History, the Mold of Prediction* (New York, Arno C. Gaebelein, 1938), p. 215.

27. William Sanford La Sor, *The Truth about Armageddon: What the Bible Says about the End Times* (New York, Harper and Row, 1982), p. 3; Lehman Strauss, *God's Plan for the Future* (Grand Rapids, Zondervan Publishing

Co., 1965), p. 33. See also Wilbur M. Smith, *This Atomic Age and the Word of God* (Boston, W. A. Wilde Co., 1948), p. 198; Doug Clark, *Shockwaves of Armageddon* (Eugene, Oreg., Harvest Books, 1982), pp. 72–73; Frederick A. Tatford, *God's Program of the Ages* (Grand Rapids, Kregel Publications, 1967), p. 96.

28. Smith, *What the World Is Coming To,* p. 164.

29. Ibid., pp. 166, 167; Vance Packard, *The Hidden Persuaders* (New York, D. McKay Co., 1957). See also "Advertising—The Powerful Persuader," *Awake,* Feb. 8, 1988, p. 6.

30. Ray C. Stedman, *What's This World Coming To?* (Van Nuys, Calif., Time-Light Books, 1972), p. 66.

31. Walvoord, *The Church in Prophecy,* pp. 179–180; David Webber and Noah Hutchings, *Is This the Last Century?* (Nashville, Thomas Nelson Publishing Co., 1979), pp. 84–85; John 21:11. See also Hilton Sutton, *The Beast System: Europe in Prophecy* (Tulsa, Harrison House, 1981), p. 81; John F. Walvoord, "Is the End of the Age at Hand?" in Charles Lee Feinberg, ed., *Focus on Prophecy* (New York, Fleming H. Revell, 1964), p. 172.

32. Wilbur M. Smith, "Signs of the Second Advent of Christ," in Henry, *Prophecy in the Making,* p. 203; Van Impe, *11:59 and Counting,* pp. 218–221 (quoted phrase p. 221); McClain, "Significant Signs of the Times," p. 34 ("World State"). See also Wilbur M. Smith, "The Apocalypse: The Book of One World," *Sunday School Times,* 90 (Nov. 13, 1948), 1003; idem, "The Shaping of One World," ibid., 90 (Nov. 20, 1948), 1027–28; Chuck Smith, *Future Survival* (Costa Mesa, Calif., Word for Today, 1978), pp. 67–70; David Webber and Noah Hutchings, *Computers and the Beast of Revelation* (Shreveport, La., Huntington House, 1986), pp. 48–50; David Hocking, *The Coming World Leader: Understanding the Book of Revelation* (Portland, Oreg., Multnomah Press, 1988), p. 205; Willard Cantelon, *New Money or None?* (Plainfield, N.J., Logos International, 1979), p. 198.

33. Isaac Haldeman, *The Signs of the Times* (New York, Charles C. Cook, 1914, orig. pub. 1910), p. 345; Dave Clark, *How to Survive the Money Crash* (Irvine, Calif., Harvest House Publishers, 1979), pp. 41, 105; Dave Hunt, *Peace, Prosperity, and the Coming Holocaust: The New Age Movement in Prophecy* (Eugene, Oreg., Harvest House Publishers, 1983), pp. 47 (quoted passage), 52; Mary Stewart Relfe, *When Your Money Fails: The "666" System Is Here* (Montgomery, Ala., Ministries, Inc., 1981), p. 131 (Apollo mission); Tim LaHaye, *The Coming Peace in the Middle East* (Grand Rapids, Zondervan Publishing Co., 1984), p. 21 (energy crisis a fraud); Wilson and Weldon, *The 1980s,* p. 92; Gary North, *Conspiracy: A Biblical View* (Fort Worth, Dominion Press, 1986), p. 25,

back cover (Council on Foreign Relations); Salem Kirban, *Prophetic and Economic News Trends,* vol. I, no. 2 [1989], p. 2; idem, *Analysis of Worldwide News,* vol. I, no. 6 (1989), p. 38. See also *Salem Kirban's Prophetic Insights,* no. 1 (1989), p. 3; Clark, *Shockwaves of Armageddon,* pp. 18, 72–73. An early "exposé" of the Council on Foreign Relations was in Dan Smoot, *The Invisible Government* (Dallas, Dan Smoot Report, 1962).

34. Gaddis Smith, *Morality, Reason, and Power: American Diplomacy in the Carter Years* (New York, Hill and Wang, 1986), pp. 37–40. Illustrating his view that "the power of the Trilateral Commission has been much exaggerated" (p. 252n9), Smith cites Holly Sklar, ed., *Trilateralism: The Trilateral Commission and Elite Planning for World Management* (Boston, South End Press, 1980).

35. Hal Lindsey, *The 1980s: Countdown to Armageddon* (New York, Bantam Books, 1981), chap. 9, pp. 117–128 (quoted passages pp. 117, 128), 139; Salem Kirban, *Prophetic and Economic Trends,* vol. I, no. 1, 1989.

36. *Criminal Politics,* Apr. 1990, passim, esp. pp. 1 (Bush quote), 4, 8, 12, 13 ("pointed ears and sharp teeth"), 16, 19 (David Rockefeller). Books such as Cantelon, *New Money or None?* and North, *Conspiracy,* while they have a prophecy component, stand at the boundary between religious and secular apocalyptic writing, two genres explored and compared in Michael Barkun, "Divided Apocalypse: Thinking about the End in Contemporary America," *Soundings,* 66 (Fall 1983), 257–280. For the conspiracy theme in the millennialism of far-right racist groups, see Michael Barkun, "Racist Apocalypse: Millennialism on the Far Right," *American Studies,* 31 (1990), 127–128. For a general account of these movements see James Coates, *Armed and Dangerous: The Rise of the Survivalist Right* (New York, Hill and Wang, 1987).

37. DeHaan, *Days of Noah,* p. 134.

38. Samuel Wolgemuth, "Youth and the End of the Age," in Henry, *Prophecy in the Making,* p. 248.

39. Wilson and Weldon, *The 1980s,* p. 106.

40. Lindsey, *Late Great Planet Earth,* p. 101; Jack Van Impe with Roger F. Campbell, *Israel's Final Holocaust* (Nashville, Thomas Nelson Publishing Co., 1979), pp. 20–21; Webber and Hutchings, *Computers and the Beast of Revelation,* pp. 8, 34.

41. William R. Goetz, *Apocalypse Next: Updated* (Cathedral City, Calif., Horizon House Publishers, 1981), pp. 173, 181; *New York Times,* May 18, 1990: full-page AT&T advertisement featuring "One World/One Card" slogan.

42. Van Impe with Campbell, *Israel's Final Holocaust,* p. 21; Goetz, *Apocalypse Next,* p. 264; Webber and Hutchings, *Computers and the Beast of Revelation,* pp. 66, 125.

43. Bates, *Projection for Survival,* p. 45; Goetz, *Apocalypse Next,* p. 186.

44. Robertson, *Secret Kingdom,* p. 215; Webber and Hutchings, *Computers and the Beast of Revelation,* pp. 88, 123. See also, on computers and related technology, Cantelon, *New Money or None?* pp. 199, 204, 209, and Peter LaLonde, "What's New in Bible Prophecy?" Aug. 1990 flyer for his publication, *The Omega-Letter* (Dearborn, Mich.).

45. James McKeever, "Washington Watch," *End-Times News Digest,* Dec. 1988, p. 11 (quoted passage); ibid., Apr. 1989, p. 9; Evans, *The Return,* pp. 21, 22.

46. Wilson and Weldon, *Computers and the Beast of Revelation,* pp. 142, 149; Hunt, *Peace, Prosperity, and the Coming Holocaust,* p. 59.

47. Salem Kirban, *Countdown to Rapture* (Eugene, Oreg., Harvest House, 1977), p. 71; Wilson and Weldon, *The 1980s,* p. 144; Smith, *Future Survival,* pp. 4, 7; idem, *What the World Is Coming To,* p. 183; Kirban, *666,* p. 77 (convergence of U.S. and Soviet systems).

48. Smith, *This Atomic Age and the Word of God,* p. 217; Webber and Hutchings, *Computers and the Beast of Revelation,* p. 25; Wilson and Weldon, *The 1980s,* pp. 146, 149.

49. Lewis Sperry Chafer, "The Coming Destruction of Ecclesiastical and Political Babylon," in John W. Bradbury, ed., *Light for the World's Darkness* (New York, Loizeaux Brothers, 1944), p. 54; Dale Crowley, *The Soon Coming of Our Lord* (New York, Loizeaux Brothers, 1958), p. 69. See also, in the same vein, Billy Graham, *World Aflame* (New York, Penguin Books, 1967; hardcover ed. 1965), p. 195.

50. Walter Lippmann, *Drift and Mastery: An Attempt to Diagnose the Current Unrest* (Madison, University of Wisconsin Press, 1985; orig. publ. 1914), p. 24. See also David Brion Davis, ed., *The Fear of Conspiracy: Images of Unamerican Subversion from the Revolution to the Present* (Ithaca, N.Y., Cornell University Press, 1971); John Higham, *Strangers in the Land: Patterns of American Nativism, 1860–1925* (New York, Atheneum, 1963); Richard Hofstadter, *The Paranoid Style in American Politics and Other Essays* (New York, Alfred A. Knopf, 1965).

51. James Davison Hunter, *American Evangelicalism: Conservative Religion and the Quandary of Modernity* (New Brunswick, Rutgers University Press, 1983), pp. 60, 107–111. See also George M. Marsden, *Fundamentalism and American Culture: The Shaping of Twentieth-Century Evangelicalism, 1870–1925* (New York, Oxford University Press, 1980), pp. 206–211.

52. For Freud's account of a man gripped by delusional fears of "the imminence of a great catastrophe" in which (in Freud's view) "the end of the world" becomes "the projection of [an] internal catastrophe," see Sig-

mund Freud, "The Case of Schreber: Psychoanalytic Notes on an Auto-
biographical Account of a Case of Paranoia" (1911), in *Standard Edition
of the Complete Psychoanalytic Works of Sigmund Freud,* vol. 12 [1911–1913]
(London, Hogarth Press, 1958), quoted phrases pp. 68, 70. See also
"Delusional (Paranoid) Disorders" in *Diagnostic and Statistical Manual of
Mental Disorders* (New York, American Psychoanalytic Association
Press, 3rd ed., rev., 1987), pp. 199–203. Still useful is William James's
classic study of the psychology of religious belief, *The Varieties of Religious Experience* (Cambridge, Mass., Harvard University Press, 1985;
orig. publ. 1902). Norman Cohn in his study of millennial beliefs and
movements in medieval Europe, *The Pursuit of the Millennium,* notes
"the unmistakable syndrome of paranoia" and adds, "a paranoid delu-
sion does not cease to be so because it is shared by . . . many individuals." Quoted in John G. Gager, "The Attainment of Millennial Bliss
through Myth: The Book of Revelation," in Paul D. Hanson, ed., *Visionaries and Their Apocalypses* (Philadelphia, Fortress Press, 1983),
p. 149.

My understanding of the psychological aspects of prophecy belief has
been sharpened by conversations and correspondence with Daniel P.
Schwartz, Medical Director, Austen Riggs Center, Stockbridge, Mass.
Dr. Schwartz draws a helpful distinction between individual delusions
and belief systems shared by large groups, even when the two present
some structural similarities. The former are typically idiosyncratic, in-
congruent with the rest of the person's culture and experience, and im-
pervious to change or modification; they also thwart the individual from
functioning in society, and even isolate him or her from human contact
or association ("Everyone is out to kill me"). The latter, by contrast,
involve interchange and interconnectedness with others and, often, par-
ticipation in a group in which there is mutual caring; relate in at least
some way to a larger social definition of reality; and do not prevent the
person from living a fulfilling life in terms of meaningful work and the
capacity to give and receive love.

My sense is thereby confirmed that to understand prophecy belief one
must not only read the works in which these beliefs are set forth, but
also talk to their authors and, even more important, visit gatherings in
which such beliefs are promulgated in a social context. It was illuminating to me, for example, to attend prophecy services in Madison
churches and observe the parallelism between the theme of family and
social disruption in the end-time scenario and the manifestation of these
same concerns in the corporate lives of the congregations, with announcements of family retreats, potluck dinners, church-sponsored

nursery-care centers; tracts urging family togetherness; testimonies expressing love and concern for family members; acknowledgment of, and praise for, pastors' spouses and families, and so on.

53. F. S. Donn, *The Israel Way to Peace* (New York, Exposition Press, 1957), p. 135.

54. Key texts include Dan. 2:41; 7:7–8,24; 9:26–27; 11:31; Rev. 13:1,5; 17:12; Matt. 24:15–16,23–24; II Thess. 2:3; I John 2:18,22; I John 4:3 (quoted); II John 1:7. For discussions of Antichrist from a premillennial perspective see, for instance, Arthur W. Pink, *The Antichrist* (Swengel, Pa., Bible Truth Depot, 1923; reprinted Grand Rapids, Kregel Publications, 1988); Walter K. Price, *The Coming Antichrist* (Chicago, Moody Press, 1974); Paul Lee Tan, *The Interpretation of Prophecy* (Rockville, Md., Assurance Publishers, 1974), pp. 345–346; Warren Wiersbe, *Be Ready* (Wheaton, Ill., Victor Books, 1979), pp. 140–143. For a historical-critical approach see Wilhelm Bousset, *The Antichrist Legend: A Chapter in Christian and Jewish Folklore* (London, Hutchinson and Co., 1896; Eng. trans. of *Der Antichrist,* 1895); Shirley Jackson Case, *The Millennial Hope: A Phase of War-Time Thinking* (Chicago, University of Chicago Press, 1918), pp. 82–83, 148–150; T. F. Glasson, *The Revelation of John* (Cambridge, Cambridge University Press, 1965), pp. 7–10, 13, 79–83; F. L. Cross, ed., *The Oxford Dictionary of the Christian Church* (London, Oxford University Press, 1957), p. 61 ("Antichrist").

The "Antichrist" entry in Isidore Singer, ed., *The Jewish Encyclopedia,* I (New York, KTAV Publishing House, [1901]), 625–627, is useful on the Jewish roots of Antichrist belief. The amillennial, Reformed view of Antichrist is offered by Anthony A. Hoekema, *The Bible and the Future* (Grand Rapids, Wm. B. Eerdman's Publishing Co., 1979), pp. 154–163 ("The sign of antichrist, like the other signs of the times, is present throughout the history of the church . . . These are not, strictly speaking, signs of the end . . . Like the other signs, these, too, mark the entire period between Christ's first and second coming"—pp. 162–163).

55. Alan F. Johnson, *Revelation* (Grand Rapids, Zondervan Publishing Co., 1983), p. 136; Price, *Coming Antichrist,* pp. 19–31 (Irenaeus p. 22; Cyprian quoted p. 25); Case, *The Millennial Hope,* p. 182; Bernard McGinn, "Early Apocalypticism: The Ongoing Debate," in C. A. Patrides and Joseph Wittreich, eds., *The Apocalypse in English Renaissance Thought and Literature* (Manchester, Manchester University Press, 1984), pp. 20–21, 28–29 (on Augustine); Glasson, *Revelation of John,* p. 10; Norman Cohn, *The Pursuit of the Millennium: Revolutionary Millenarians and Mystical Anarchists of the Middle Ages* (Temple Smith, London, rev. ed., 1970), pp. 35–36, 75–84, 110–112, 136, 253–254; Marjorie Reeves, *The Influence of Prophecy in the Later Middle Ages: A Study in Joachimism*

(Oxford, Clarendon Press, 1969), p. 7 (Saladin as Antichrist), also many index entries under "Antichrist." For a general discussion see Richard K. Emmerson, *Antichrist in the Middle Ages: A Study of Medieval Apocalypticism, Art, and Literature* (Seattle, University of Washington Press, 1981).

56. Bousset, *The Antichrist Legend;* Case, *The Millennial Hope,* p. 148; John M. Court, *Myth and History in the Book of Revelation* (London, SPCK, 1979), pp. 128–137; Glasson, *Revelation of John,* pp. 8, 68, 79, 83.

57. Price, *Coming Antichrist,* pp. 29, 33–35; Ruth H. Bloch, *Visionary Republic: Millennial Themes in American Thought, 1756–1800* (New York, Cambridge University Press, 1985), p. 7 (Wycliffe); Cohn, *Pursuit of the Millennium,* pp. 80–81, 84, 206; Katharine R. Firth, *The Apocalyptic Tradition in Reformation Britain, 1530–1645* (Oxford, Oxford University Press, 1979), pp. 13, 27; Johann Rauw, *Weltbeschreibung: das ist, Ein schöne richtige und volkömliche Cosmographia des gantzen Umbkreiss der weiten Welt* (Frankfurt am Main, Johann Dreuttel, 1612), in my possession, end pages contain "RÖMISCHER PAPST" calculations totaling 666 (undated, possibly late eighteenth or early nineteenth century).

58. Robert Anderson, *The Coming Prince* (Grand Rapids, Kregel Publications, 1986; orig. publ. 1884), p. 134; James M. Gray, *A Text-Book on Prophecy* (New York, Fleming H. Revell, 1918), chap. 9, pp. 77–82; Pink, *Antichrist,* pp. 15, 18.

59. Raymond L. Cox, "Will the Real Antichrist Please Stand Up!" *Eternity,* May 1974, p. 16; J. Dwight Pentecost, *Prophecy for Today* (Grand Rapids, Zondervan Publishing Co., 1961), pp. 187–188. See also, for early postwar identifications of the Pope as Antichrist or the Harlot: Albert J. Lindsey, "God's Use of Types in Prophecy," in Bradbury, *Hastening the Day of God,* p. 159; Arthur I. Brown, *I Will Come Again* (Findlay, Ohio, Fundamental Truth Publishers, 1947), pp. 83–87; Tatford, *God's Program of the Ages,* pp. 93–95; Kenneth S. Wuest, *Prophetic Light in the Present Darkness* (Grand Rapids, Wm. B. Eerdman's Publishing Co., 1955), p. 78.

60. Lindsey, *Late Great Planet Earth,* pp. 173–174; Dave Hunt, *Whatever Happened to Heaven?* (Eugene, Oreg., Harvest House Publishers, 1988), p. 146; *Alberto, Four Horsemen, Double-Cross, The Godfathers, The Prophet* [anti-Catholic comic books] (Chino, Calif., Chick Publications, 1980s); *Battle Cry,* Chick Publications bimonthly periodical; "All Things Considered," National Public Radio, Oct. 11, 1988 (Paisley).

61. Carl E. Braaten, *Christ and Counter-Christ: Apocalyptic Themes in Theology and Culture* (Philadelphia, Fortress Press, 1972), p. 15; C. Allyn Russell, *Voices of American Fundamentalism: Seven Biographical Studies* (Philadelphia, Westminster Press, 1976), p. 44 (Norris).

62. Price, *Coming Antichrist,* pp. 37–38.

63. Cox, "Will the Real Antichrist Please Stand Up!" pp. 15–17, 60 (mentions Judas, Dayan, Kennedy, and Kissinger theories); Relfe, *When Your Money Fails,* p. 139 (Dayan); Zola Levitt, *The Cairo Connection: Egypt in Prophecy* (Irvine, Calif., Harvest House Publishers, 1978), pp. 93–104 (mentions—but does not endorse—Sadat, Kissinger, and Nelson Rockefeller theories); Taylor, *Those Who Remain,* pp. 22–26, 75–76 (Juan Carlos); *End-Times News Digest,* Aug. 1989, p. 3 (mentions Servan-Schreiber speculation); Anis A. Shorrosh, *Jesus, Prophecy, and the Middle East* (Nashville, Thomas Nelson Publishing Co., 1981), pp. 104–106 (Moon); Robert Glenn Gromacki, *Are These the Last Days?* (Schaumburg, Ill., Regular Baptist Press, 1970), p. 90 (Kennedy's 666 votes); David Ewert, *And Then Comes the End* (Scottdale, Pa., Herald Press, 1980), p. 77; Salem Kirban, *Kissinger: Man of Peace* (Huntingdon Valley, Pa., Salem Kirban, 1974).

64. "The Number of the Beast is 666" [Reagan as Antichrist], (n.p., n.d., 3 pp.), received in mail by Barbara Griffith, Amherst, Mass., 1988; CBS Evening News, May 9, 1988 (Reagan's address change); Robert W. Faid, *Gorbachev! Has the Real Antichrist Arrived?* (Tulsa, Victory House Publishers, 1988); Charles H. Dyer, *The Rise of Babylon: Sign of the End Times* (Wheaton, Ill., Tyndale House Publishers, 1991); Cox, "Will the Real Antichrist Please Stand Up!" p. 60 ("sick, sick, sick").

65. Price, *Coming Antichrist,* pp. 22, 24; Dan. 2:31–42 ("toes" v. 42), 7:24; Rev. 13:1, 17:12; G. H. Pember, *The Great Prophecies Concerning the Gentiles, the Jews, and the Church of God* (London, Hodder and Stoughton, 1881), p. ix (five Eastern and five Western kingdoms); Anderson, *Coming Prince,* p. 273. Complicating the picture, one interpreter pointed out that some ancient statues have *twelve* toes—Milton Terry, *Biblical Hermeneutics* (New York, Eaton and Mains, 1911), p. 323.

66. Herbert H. Ehrenstein, "The Common Market and Bible Prophecy," *Eternity,* Mar. 1962, pp. 18–20, 34 (Barnhouse's 1931 prediction recalled).

67. J. Vernon McGee, "The Prophetic Word and Europe," in *The Prophetic Word in Crisis Days* (Findlay, Ohio, Dunham Publishing Co., 1961), p. 78; Clarence E. Mason, Jr., "The United States of the Western World," in Charles Lee Feinberg, ed., *Prophetic Truth Unfolding Today* (Westwood, N.J., Fleming H. Revell, 1968), pp. 114–123 (quoted passage p. 122); Unger, *Beyond the Crystal Ball,* p. 69; John F. Walvoord, "Prophecy Serious, Not Sensational Stuff," *Christianity Today,* Dec. 11, 1981. The following are representative of a flood of similar commentary: S. Maxwell Coder, "The Future of the Nations," in Feinberg, *Focus on Prophecy,* pp. 103–104; Dale Crowley, *The Soon Coming of Our Lord* (New York, Loizeaux Brothers, 1958), pp. 67–68; Louis Goldberg, *Turbulence over*

the Middle East (Neptune, N.J., Loizeaux Brothers, 1982), pp. 119, 128; Pentecost, *Prophecy for Today,* pp. 186–187; Edgar C. James, "Prophecy and the Common Market," *Moody Monthly,* Mar. 1974, pp. 24–27; Lindsey, *Late Great Planet Earth,* p. 173.

68. Van Impe, *11:59 and Counting,* p. 106; Charles R. Taylor, *Bible Prophecy News,* Apr. 1988, p. 3; ibid., Apr.-May-June 1989, p. 9; Lindsey, *The 1980s,* p. 104. See also Chuck Smith, *Future Survival* (Costa Mesa, Calif., Word for Today, 1978), pp. 56, 63; Sutton, *Beast System,* pp. 90–92; Webber and Hutchings, *Is This the Last Century?* p. 25; Goetz, *Apocalypse Next,* pp. 117–118; Mary Stewart Relfe, *The New Money System 666* (Montgomery, Ala., Ministries, Inc., 1982), chap. 9, pp. 212ff.; White, *The Coming World Dictator,* pp. 26–28. The key texts in the debate were Dan. 7:8,24.

69. James Montgomery Boice, *The Last and Future World* (Grand Rapids, Zondervan Publishing Co., 1974), p. 104; Evans, *The Return,* p. 212; McGee, "Prophetic Word and Europe," p. 90.

70. Pentecost, *Prophecy for Today,* p. 112; Hunt, *Peace, Prosperity, and the Coming Holocaust,* p. 36. See also Roger Campbell and David Campbell, *Prosperity in the End Time* (Fort Washington, Pa., Christian Literature Crusade, 1983), p. 75; Hal Lindsey, *There's a New World Coming* (Santa Ana, Calif., Vision House Publishers, 1973), pp. 186–188; McGee, "Prophetic Word and Europe," p. 93; Mason, "The United States of the Western World," p. 120; Tom Westwood, *Palestine: The World's Last Battleground* (Redlands, Calif., Bible Treasury House, 1968), p. 26; Cantelon, *New Money or None?* p. 199.

71. Walvoord, *The Nations in Prophecy,* p. 96; Lindsey, *There's a New World Coming,* p. 192; Sutton, *Beast System,* pp. 53–54 (quoted passage), 82. See also, on the religious component of Antichrist's rule, J. Vernon McGee, "The Prophetic Word and Apostasy," in *The Prophetic Word in Crisis Days,* p. 177; David Hocking, *The Coming World Leader: Understanding the Book of Revelation* (Portland, Oreg., Multnomah Press, 1988), pp. 207–209; Herman A. Hoyt, "The Career and Calamity of the Superchurch," in Feinberg, *Focus on Prophecy,* pp. 203–217; Stedman, *What's This World Coming To?* p. 74; Coder, *Final Chapter,* p. 191; Goetz, *Apocalypse Next,* pp. 195, 207–209.

72. Kirban, *666,* p. 29; Betzer, *Beast,* pp. 87–92 (quoted passage p. 92); Unger, *Beyond the Crystal Ball,* pp. 48–49.

73. Walvoord, *The Nations in Prophecy,* p. 144; Lindsey, *The 1980s,* p. 109; Boice, *Last and Future World,* p. 72; Bill McKee, *Orbit of Ashes: Jesus Is Coming!* (Wheaton, Ill., Tyndale House Publishers, 1972), p. 107; Anderson, *Coming Prince,* p. 214; Haldeman, *Signs of the Times,* p. 355. See also, on Antichrist's political and diplomatic genius: Smith, *Future Sur-*

426 LG *Notes to Pages 279–284*

vival, p. 63; White, *Coming World Dictator*, p. 74; Sutton, *Beast System*, pp. 41, 95–96; Lindsey, *Late Great Planet Earth*, pp. 96, 141; Price, *Coming Antichrist*, p. 57.

74. Lindsey, *The 1980s*, p. 109; Smith, *Future Survival*, p. 63; White, *Coming World Dictator*, p. 68; Billy Graham, *World Aflame* (New York, Penguin Books, 1967), p. 194; Robert Glenn Gromacki, *Are These the Last Days?* (Old Tappan, N.J., Fleming H. Revell, 1970), p. 111; Hilton Sutton, *Revelation: God's Grand Finale* (Tulsa, Harrison House, 1984), p. 101. The key biblical passages are Dan. 7:8 and Rev. 13:5. See also Herman A. Hoyt, *The End Times* (Chicago, Moody Press, 1969), p. 120; Louis Goldberg, *Turbulence over the Middle East* (Neptune, N.J., Loizeaux Brothers, 1982), p. 128.

75. Gromacki, *Are These the Last Days?* p. 82; Stedman, *What's This World Coming To?* pp. 22, 27; White, *Coming World Dictator*, pp. 10, 35; Orlen L. Njus, *Time to Look Up* (Fulton, Mich., Orlen L. Njus, 1965), p. 64 (Beatles). See also McKee, *Orbit of Ashes*, p. 69; Kirban, *Countdown to Rapture*, p. 131.

76. Hunt, *Peace, Prosperity, and the Coming Holocaust*, pp. 47, 198, 204; White, *Coming World Dictator*, p. 54.

77. Kirban, *666*, pp. 31, 56–57, 61 (quoted phrase).

78. Betzer, *Beast*, pp. 18, 19, 23, 24, 30, 32, 41, 46 ("Italian-made boots"), 130 ("oozing charm"), 136, 168, 194 (extended quote).

79. Ibid., pp. 168, 215–216, 217.

80. Evans, *The Return*, p. 211.

81. Rev. 13:16–18.

82. Angley, *Raptured*, p. 126.

83. Tan, *Jesus Is Coming*, p. 28; Wilkerson, *The Vision*, p. 22. See also Smith, *Final Curtain*, p. 61; Clark, *Shockwaves of Armageddon*, pp. 43, 129, 142–143; Lindsey, *There's a New World Coming*, p. 194; David Allan Hubbard, *The Second Coming; What Will Happen When Jesus Returns* (Downers Grove, Ill., InterVarsity Press, 1984), p. 39.

84. Levitt, *Cairo Connection*, p. 106; Salem Kirban, *Rapture Alert News Report*, no. 9 [1987], p. 5; Van Impe, *11:59 and Counting*, pp. 116–117.

85. Lindsey, *The 1980s*, pp. 111, 112; Webber and Hutchings, *Computers and the Beast of Revelation*, passim, quoted phrases pp. 8, 25, see also esp. pp. 18–19, 53; Joel 2:7–8.

86. Bransby, *Impending Hour*, p. 84; Van Impe, *11:59 and Counting*, pp. 119, 121, 208; Jerry R. Church, quoted in ibid., p. 115 ("COMPUTER" = 666).

87. Jed Stevenson, "Among Canada's Notes Is a $1000 Bill that Shows a Diabolical Glitch in the History of Paper Money," *New York Times*, Mar. 25, 1990; Salem Kirban, *Rapture Alert News Report*, no. 9 [1987],

pp. 1, 2; idem, *News from Home,* n.d. [1989]; idem, *Analysis of Worldwide News,* vol. I, no. 3 [1988], p. 1. See also, in the same vein, Charles R. Taylor, *Bible Prophecy News,* Apr.-May-June 1989, p. 8. For background on the plan for a common European currency, see "Recent Crises May Help Cause of European Unity," *New York Times,* Oct. 21, 1990, p. 12.

88. John F. Walvoord with John E. Walvoord, *Armageddon, Oil, and the Middle East Crisis: What the Bible Says about the Future of the Middle East and the End of Western Civilization* (Grand Rapids, Zondervan Publishing Co., 1974), p. 144.

89. Webber and Hutchings, *Computers and the Beast of Revelation,* pp. 34, 62; Kirban, *666,* pp. 177, 195. See also Salem Kirban, *Questions Frequently Asked Me on Prophecy* (Huntingdon Valley, Pa., Salem Kirban, 1971), p. 12.

90. Campbell and Campbell, *Prosperity in the End Time,* pp. 48, 81; Kirban, *Analysis of Worldwide News,* vol. 1, no. 1, p. 3; White, *Coming World Dictator,* p. 95; S. Franklin Logsdon, *Profiles of Prophecy* (Grand Rapids, Zondervan Publishing Co., 1970), p. 50; Bransby, *Impending Hour,* p. 85 (baby with bar code on forehead). See also Webber and Hutchings, *Is This the Last Century?* p. 135; Goetz, *Apocalypse Next,* p. 173; Hocking, *Coming World Dictator,* p. 211; Lindsey, *The 1980s,* p. 111. In 1988 a group of parents filed suit in Federal District Court in Washington, D.C., challenging a government requirement that all children five years and older must have Social Security numbers in order to be claimed as exemptions for tax purposes. Explaining the suit, the group's lawyer mentioned his clients' belief that the law was a precursor to the Mark of the Beast—"U.S. is Challenged over Social Security Numbers for Children," *New York Times,* Aug. 21, 1988.

91. Van Impe, *11:59 and Counting,* p. 119 (*Omni*); Webber and Hutchings, *Is This the Last Century?* p. 137 (*Reader's Digest*). For a few of the many citations to the Sept. 30, 1973, cover of *Senior Scholastic,* see Relfe, *New Money System, 666,* p. 162; Goetz, *Apocalypse Next,* p. 184; and Van Impe, *Signs of the Times,* p. 46; David Jones, "Superficial Data," *Nature,* 346 (Aug. 2, 1990), 416.

92. Smith, *What the World Is Coming To,* pp. 126, 142. See also idem, *Future Survival,* pp. 4–7; idem, *Final Curtain,* pp. 13–16.

93. Webber and Hutchings, *Computers and the Beast of Revelation,* p. 129; Van Impe, *11:59 and Counting,* pp. 230–233 (quoted phrases pp. 230, 233); idem, *Signs of the Times,* pp. 47–52 (quoted phrases pp. 45, 52); *666 Jellybeans,* p. 48; Relfe, *The New Money System,* p. 58 (Apple Computer price). See also Campbell and Campbell, *Prosperity in the End Time,* p. 113: "Interestingly, the Number 666 is appearing frequently in connection with computer operations."

94. "Rev." Billy C. Wirtz, "Backsliders' Tractor Pull," Hightone compact disk HCB 8024 (1990).

95. Relfe, *New Money System,* front matter, pp. 205 (quoted passage), 253; idem, *When Your Money Fails,* pp. 62 (quoted phrase), 220.

96. Relfe, *When Your Money Fails,* p. 34 ("quietly, subtly, dangerously"), 35, 48, 51, 58 (IRS refund checks), 67, 68, 80 ("Oh, Nathan Hale"), 116, 124, 150.

97. Relfe, *New Money System,* pp. xxv, 32, 33, 34, 46, 49, 52, 58 (poem), 60, 153.

98. Ibid., pp. 69, 70; idem, *When Your Money Fails,* back matter.

99. Relfe, *New Money System,* pp. 73, 125, 157.

100. Relfe, *When Your Money Fails,* pp. 15, 68 (quoting another author), 150 (stray dogs and TV cable systems); *New Money System,* p. 52.

101. James Barr, *Fundamentalism* (Philadelphia, Westminster Press, 1977), p. 109 (Barr was Oriel Professor of the Interpretation of Holy Scriptures at Oxford University); Webber and Hutchings, *Is This the Last Century?* p. 139; cf. idem, *Computers and the Beast of Revelation,* p. 96. Revealing similar ambivalence, Mary Stewart Relfe in *When Your Money Fails* included a testimonial letter from the senior vice president of the First Alabama Bank of Montgomery, and in *New Money System* (p. 121) she denied that "the fine organization which markets the hand scan machine" was consciously part of Antichrist's conspiracy. Hal Lindsey, too, could be harshly critical of capitalism while at other times lavishly praising the "overwhelming benefits" of the free-enterprise system, denouncing socialism, and criticizing government social-welfare programs. See, for example, Lindsey, *There's a New World Coming,* p. 105; idem, *The 1980s,* pp. 141–145 (quoted phrase p. 145).

102. Rev. 18; Donald Grey Barnhouse, *Revelation; An Expository Commentary* (Grand Rapids, Zondervan Publishing Co., 1971; reprint of 1934–1942 *Eternity* essays), pp. 335, 340; Arthur I. Brown, *The Eleventh "Hour"* (Findlay, Ohio, Fundamental Truth Publishers, 1940), pp. 118, 119.

103. Lindsey, *There's a New World Coming,* p. 244; Clark, *Shockwaves of Armageddon,* p. 150. See also, for the same interpretation, Smith, *What the World Is Coming To,* p. 162; Houston, "Judgment of Nations," pp. 370–371; Price, *Coming Antichrist,* pp. 181–183; Coder, *Final Chapter,* p. 192; Vander Lugt, *There's a New Day Coming,* p. 92; Webber and Hutchings, *Computers and the Beast of Revelation,* p. 96. For the view that ancient Babylon will be literally restored, see Wuest, *Prophetic Light in the Present Darkness,* pp. 83–85, and Taylor, *Bible Prophecy News,* Apr.-May-June 1988, insert.

104. Wilbur M. Smith, "The Bible, the Book for This Hour of World Cri-

sis," *Sunday School Times,* 90 (Nov. 6, 1948), 969; E. M. Blaiklock, "The Archeology of the Apocalypse," *Eternity,* June 1955, p. 35.

105. Hal Lindsey with C. C. Carlson, *The Terminal Generation* (New York, Bantam Books, 1977), p. 90.

9. The Continuing Appeal of Prophecy Belief

1. Nathan O. Hatch, *The Democratization of American Christianity* (New Haven, Yale University Press, 1989), p. 184.

2. Quoted in I. B. Cohen, "Newton, Isaac," in Charles Coulston Gillespie, ed., *Dictionary of Scientific Biography,* x (New York, Charles Scribner's Sons, 1974), 81; Joseph A. Seiss, *The Last Times* (Philadelphia, Smith, English, 1863; "revised and enlarged" reprint of 1856 work), p. 13; George Marsden, "Evangelicals, History, and Modernity," in Marsden, *Evangelicalism and Modern America* (Grand Rapids, Wm. B. Eerdman's Publishing Co., 1984), p. 98.

3. Robert Anderson, *The Coming Prince* (Grand Rapids, Kregel Publications, 1986; reprint of 1884 work); Alva J. McClain, *Daniel's Prophecy of the Seventy Weeks* (Grand Rapids, Zondervan Publishing Co., 1969; reprint of 1940 work), p. 9; Timothy P. Weber, *Living in the Shadow of the Second Coming: American Premillennialism, 1875–1925* (New York, Oxford University Press, 1979), pp. 105–115 (quoted phrase p. 112); Ed Dobson and Ed Hindson, "Apocalypse Now? What Fundamentalists Believe about the End of the World," *Policy Review,* 38 (Fall 1986), 18 (citing Rimmer).

4. Arno C. Gaebelein, *The Prophet Daniel: A Key to the Visions and Prophecies of the Book of Daniel* (Grand Rapids, Kregel Publications, 1955; reprint of earlier work), p. 3; Milton B. Lindberg, *The Jew and Modern Israel* (Chicago, Moody Press, 1930; rev. Archie A. MacKinney, 1969), p. 7; Charles O. Benham, *Great Britain and the United States in Prophecy* (Joliet, Ill., National X-ray Publications, 1942), p. 11.

5. William H. Boyer mission report, *Evangelical Visitor,* Jan. 19, 1942, p. 8, quoted in Paul Boyer, *Mission on Taylor Street: The Founding and Early Years of the Dayton Brethren in Christ Mission* (Grantham, Pa., Brethren in Christ Historical Society, 1987), p. 139.

6. John F. Walvoord, "Prophecy as Evidence of Inspiration of Scripture," in John W. Bradbury, ed., *Hastening the Day of God: Prophetic Messages from the International Congress on Prophecy in Calvary Baptist Church, New York City, Nov. 9–16, 1952* (Wheaton, Ill., Van Kampen Press, 1953), p. 25. See also Charles R. Taylor, *Get All Excited—Jesus Is Coming Soon* (Redondo Beach, Calif., Today in Bible Prophecy, 1975), pp. 9–11; Lu

Ann Bransby, *The Impending Hour* (Oklahoma City, Impending Hour, [1981]), p. 28.

7. In one work, for example, Smith puts in quotes, as though from the Book of Daniel: "The final world-governing empire will be a federation of ten nations, as represented in the mixture of iron and clay of the ten toes"—Chuck Smith, *Future Survival* (Costa Mesa, Calif., Word for Today, 1978), p. 2.

8. Hal Lindsey, *The Late Great Planet Earth* (New York, Bantam Books, 1973), p. 141.

9. David Wilkerson, *The Vision* (New York, Pyramid Books, 1974), pp. 119–120. ˙

10. Author interview with John F. Walvoord, Aug. 18, 1989.

11. Anderson, *Coming Prince,* pp. 47–48; James McKeever, "When Is the Rapture?" *End-Times News Digest,* special introductory issue, ca. 1987, p. 9; author interview with John F. Walvoord, Aug. 8, 1989. On this point see also John J. Collins, *The Apocalyptic Imagination: An Introduction to the Jewish Matrix of Christianity* (New York, Crossroads Publishing Co., 1984), p. 87; and Klaus Koch, *The Rediscovery of Apocalyptic* (London, SCM Press, 1972; Eng. trans. of *Ratlos vor der Apokalyptik,* publ. 1970), p. 29.

12. Doug Clark, *Shockwaves of Armageddon* (Eugene, Oreg., Harvest Books, 1982), pp. 234–235. See also Lindsey, *Late Great Planet Earth,* pp. 174–175.

13. Cyrus I. Scofield, *Addresses on Prophecy* (New York, Arno C. Gaebelein, n.d.), p. 26.

14. Lindsey, *Late Great Planet Earth,* frontispiece; David Webber and Noah Hutchings, *Is This the Last Century?* (Nashville, Thomas Nelson Publishers, 1979), p. 51; Jack Van Impe, *Signs of the Times* (Royal Oak, Mich., Jack Van Impe Ministries, 1979), p. 4; John F. Walvoord, "Why Must Christ Return?" in Charles Lee Feinberg, ed., *Prophecy and the Seventies* (Chicago, Moody Press, 1971), p. 43.

15. "The Great Cosmic Countdown: Hal Lindsey on the Future," *Eternity,* Jan. 1977, p. 21.

16. John Wesley White, *The Coming World Dictator* (Minneapolis, Bethany House Publishers, 1981), p. 69; Hilton Sutton, *He's Coming!* (Tulsa, Harrison House, 1983), p. 96 (discussing Luke 21:36); Clark, *Shockwaves of Armageddon,* p. 139; John N. Darby, *The Hopes of the Church in Connexion with the Destiny of the Jews and the Nations as Revealed in Prophecy* (London, 2nd ed., 1842), p. 66.

17. Herbert Vander Lugt, *There's a New Day Coming! A Survey of Endtime Events* (Eugene, Oreg., Harvest House Publishing Co., 1983), p. 52; Ronald S. Toth, " 'Peace on Earth': Why Not?" *Plain Truth,* Jan. 1988,

p. 15. See also [James McKeever], "Personally from James," *End-Times News Digest,* Mar. 1990, p. 10.

18. William Robinson, *The Evanston Theme: Christ the Hope of the World; The Symbolic Nature of Biblical Eschatology* (n.p., Bethany Press, 1954), p. 12; James Barr, *Fundamentalism* (Philadelphia, Westminster Press, 1977), p. 205; Hans Schwarz, *On the Way to the Future* (Minneapolis, Augsburg Publishing House, 1972), pp. 154–155 (Schwarz was a professor at Lutheran Theological Seminary, Columbus, Ohio); R. Laurence Moore, *Religious Outsiders and the Making of Americans* (New York, Oxford University Press, 1986), chap. 5, pp. 128–149, quoted phrase p. 140.

19. Author interview with John F. Walvoord, Aug. 18, 1989; John Calvin, *A Commentary on Daniel* (Edinburgh, Banner of Truth Trust, 1966; reprint of 1852–53 ed. publ. Calvin Translation Society; 1st Latin ed. 1561), p. 135; Darby, *Hopes of the Church of God,* p. 55; James H. Brookes, *Maranatha: or, The Lord Cometh* (New York, Fleming H. Revell, 1889; orig. publ. 1870), p. 114.

20. Tim LaHaye, *The Beginning of the End* (Wheaton, Ill., Tyndale House Publishers, 1972), p. 172. See also Lindsey, *Late Great Planet Earth,* p. 176.

21. Thomas S. McCall and Zola Levitt, *The Coming Russian Invasion of Israel: Updated* (Chicago, Moody Press, 1989; 1st ed. 1974), pp. 74–75.

22. James Davison Hunter, *American Evangelicalism: Conservative Religion and the Quandary of Modernity* (New Brunswick, Rutgers University Press, 1983), pp. 79–81.

23. Carl F. H. Henry, *The Uneasy Conscience of Modern Fundamentalism* (Grand Rapids, Wm. B. Eerdman's Publishing Co., 1947).

24. Author interview with S. Maxwell Coder, Mar. 13, 1989.

25. Ray Gates, professor of biology and ecology at Grand Rapids Baptist College, quoted in Jim Morud, "Creation Groans: Are Christians Listening?" *Moody Monthly,* Oct. 1989, p. 16; Billy Graham, *Approaching Hoofbeats: The Four Horsemen of the Apocalypse* (Waco, Tex., Word Books, 1983), p. 74.

26. Author interview with Louis Goldberg, Feb. 23, 1989.

27. Dobson and Hindson, "Apocalypse Now?" p. 21.

28. James McKeever, *The Rapture Book: Victory in the End Times* (Medford, Oreg., Omega Publications, 1987), pp. 34, 49, 125, 238 (quoted phrase), and order form in back of book listing James McKeever, *Christians Will Go Through the Tribulation—And How to Prepare for It* (Medford, Oreg., Omega Publications); idem, "Personally from James," *End-Times News Digest,* Aug. 1989, p. 9; "May Conference for Bondslaves," ibid., Feb. 1989, p. 11.

29. Rousas J. Rushdoony, *Thy Kingdom Come: Studies in Daniel and Revela-

tion (Tyler, Tex., Thoburn Press, 1970); idem, *God's Plan for Victory: The Meaning of Post-Millennianism* (Tyler, Tex., Thoburn Press, 1977); David Chilton, *Paradise Restored: An Eschatology of Dominion* (Tyler, Tex., Reconstruction Press, 1985); *Journal of Christian Reconstruction,* passim; Pat Robertson with Bob Slosser, *The Secret Kingdom: A Promise of Hope and Freedom in a World of Turmoil* (New York, Bantam Books, 1984), chap. 14, pp. 198–210; David Edwin Harrell, Jr., *Pat Robertson: A Personal, Religious, and Political Portrait* (San Francisco, Harper and Row, 1987), pp. 148–149; Dave Hunt, *Whatever Happened to Heaven?* (Eugene, Oreg., Harvest House Publishers, 1988), chaps. 10 and 11, pp. 199–243, esp. pp. 204, 224, 276–277 (Jay Grimsted and Orange County), 205 (David Chilton quoted: "Our goal is world dominion"), 212 (Gary North quoted: "no-nonsense Christian values"). The key texts of the Dominionists are Gen. 1:26–28, in which God grants man dominion over the earth, and Matt. 28:18 ("And Jesus came and spake unto them, saying, All power is given unto me in heaven and in earth"). For a history of the interpretation of the Genesis passage, see Jeremy Cohen, *"Be Fertile and Increase, Fill the Earth and Master It": The Ancient and Medieval Career of a Biblical Text* (Ithaca, N.Y., Cornell University Press, 1989).

30. Hunt, *Whatever Happened to Heaven?* pp. 229–235; McKeever, *Rapture Book,* p. 197; Robertson, *Secret Kingdom,* pp. 203–204. For critiques of Reconstruction/Dominion eschatology see Hunt, *Whatever Happened to Heaven?* pp. 199–243; Thomas Ice and H. Wayne House, *Dominion Theology: Blessing or Curse?* (Portland, Oreg., Multnomah Press, 1988); Norman Geisler, "A Premillennial View of Law and Government," *Moody Monthly,* Oct. 1985, pp. 129–131; Dobson and Hindson, "Apocalypse Now?" p. 20; and [James McKeever], "Prophetic Heresy: Kingdom Now and Dominion Theology," *End-Times News Digest,* May 1989, p. 15. McKeever's precise command to the rainstorm was, "Rain, in the name of Jesus Christ, I command you to stop until after this wedding dedication is over"—*Rapture Book,* p. 197.

31. Trollope, quoted in Hatch, *Democratization of American Religion,* p. 210.

32. "The Liberation of Hal Lindsey," *Eternity,* Jan. 1975, pp. 31–34; Mike Evans, *The Return* (Nashville, Thomas Nelson Publishing Co., 1986), p. 163; "They Call Him the Walking Bible," *Perhaps Today* (Jack Van Impe Ministries magazine), May/June 1988, p. 3; "A Life Triumphant," ibid., Sept./Oct. 1988, p. 2; James McKeever, *Rapture Book,* p. 221; idem, "The Final Decade," *End-Times News Digest,* Feb. 1990, p. 1; Mary Stewart Relfe, *When Your Money Fails: The 666 System Is Here* (Montgomery, Ala., Ministries, Inc., 1981), inside front cover; McCall and Levitt, *Coming Russian Invasion of Israel: Updated,* back cover.

33. Edgar C. Whisenant, *88 Reasons Why the Rapture Will Be in 1988: New Expanded Edition* (Nashville, World Bible Society, 1988), front matter, "About the Author"; Leon Bates, *Projection for Survival* (Dallas, Bible Believers' Evangelistic Association, 1979), p. 187; Robert W. Faid, *Gorbachev: Has the Real Antichrist Come?* (Tulsa, Victory House Publishers, 1988), back cover; Gerald B. Stanton, *Kept from the Hour: A Systematic Study of the Rapture in Bible Prophecy* (Grand Rapids, Zondervan Publishing Co., 1956), front matter; John A. Sproule, *In Defense of Pretribulationism* (Winona Lake, Ind., BMH Books, 2nd ed., 1980), front matter; Texe Marrs, catalog of publications (Austin, Tex., Living Truth Ministries, n.d.).

34. Ray C. Stedman, *What's This World Coming To?* (Ventura, Calif., Regal Books, 2nd ed., 1986), p. 27; Van Impe, *Signs of the Times*, pp. 5, 57; Allen Beechick, *The Pre-Tribulation Rapture* (Denver, Accent Books, 1981), p. 18.

35. Quoted in Shirley Jackson Case, *The Millennial Hope: A Phase of War-Time Thinking* (Chicago, University of Chicago Press, 1918), p. 193.

36. Ruth H. Bloch, *Visionary Republic: Millennial Themes in American Thought, 1756–1800* (New York, Cambridge University Press, 1985), pp. 136, 137, 138 (quoting Simon Hough, *An Alarm to the World* [Stockbridge, Mass., 1792], p. 20).

37. Nathan O. Hatch, "Evangelicalism as a Democratic Movement," in Marsden, *Evangelicalism and Modern America,* p. 78 (Scofield); Albertus Pieters, "A Candid Examination of the Scofield Bible" (pamphlet, 1938, 27 pp.), p. 4, quoted in Loraine Boettner, *The Millennium* (Grand Rapids, Baker Book House, 1957), p. 358; J. Dwight Pentecost, *Prophecy for Today* (Grand Rapids, Zondervan Publishing Co., 1961), p. 14 (quoting an unidentified pastor). See also John W. Bowman, "The Bible and Modern Religion: II. Dispensationalism," *Interpretation,* 10 (Apr. 1956), 172. Bowman describes the dispensationalism presented in the Scofield Bible as "perhaps the most dangerous heresy currently to be found within Christian circles."

38. Hatch, "Evangelicalism as a Democratic Movement," p. 79; idem, *Democratization of American Religion,* p. 212; E. Ralph Hooper, foreword, in Oswald J. Smith, *The Dawn Is Breaking* (Grand Rapids, Zondervan Publishing Co., n.d.), front matter; Wilbur M. Smith, *World Crises and the Prophetic Scripture* (Chicago, Moody Press, 1952), p. 27; Lewis Sperry Chafer, "An Introduction to Eschatology," in John W. Bradbury, ed., *Israel's Restoration: A Series of Lectures by Bible Expositors Interested in the Evangelization of the Jews* (New York, Iverson-Ford Associates, 1952), pp. 155, 161.

39. E. W. Rogers, *Concerning the Future* (Chicago, Moody Press, 1962), p. 25; Salem Kirban, *Guide to Survival* (Huntingdon Valley, Pa., 1968; updated 1978), p. 248; Ronald Gladden, Seventh-day Adventist Church Prophecy Seminar, Madison, Wis., Mar. 10, 1990. For the jigsaw puzzle analogy, see also S. Maxwell Coder, *The Final Chapter: Understanding What the Bible Says about the Last Pages of Human History* (Wheaton, Ill., Tyndale House Publishers, 1984), p. 100; Derek Prince, *The Last Word on the Middle East* (Grand Rapids, Zondervan Publishing Co., 1982), p. 140; Hilton Sutton, *Revelation: God's Grand Finale* (Tulsa, Harrison House, 1984), p. 16.

40. Whisenant, *88 Reasons Why the Rapture Will Be in 1988*, p. 55 (Civelli); "Ted," *The Climax* (St. Petersburg, Gospel Truth, 1982); Mary Stewart Relfe, *The New Money System 666* (Montgomery, Ala., Ministries, Inc., 1982), p. 36; Anis A. Shorrosh, *Jesus, Prophecy, and the Middle East* (Nashville, Thomas Nelson Publishing Co., 1981), p. 4 (quoting a prophecy tract by a Montgomery author).

41. Relfe, *When Your Money Fails*, p. 220; Lu Ann Bransby, *The Impending Hour* (Oklahoma City, Impending Hour, [1981]), p. iii.

42. Evans, *The Return*, p. 61; Ivor Powell, *What in the World Will Happen Next?* (Grand Rapids, Kregel Publishers, 1985), p. 170.

43. Hilton Sutton, prophecy sermon, Shalom Christian Center, Madison, Wis., Aug. 20, 1988; idem, *Revelation*, p. 16.

44. Hatch, "Evangelicalism as a Democratic Movement," pp. 79, 82; Samuel Langdon, *Observations on the Revelation of Jesus Christ to St. John* (Worcester, Mass., 1791), cited in Bloch, *Visionary Republic*, p. 121.

45. Donald Grey Barnhouse, *Revelation: An Expository Commentary* (Grand Rapids, Zondervan Publishing Co., 1971; reprint of essays orig. publ. in Barnhouse's magazine *Revelation*, 1934–1942), pp. 206, 267; Wilbur M. Smith, *This Atomic Age and the Word of God* (Boston, W. A. Wilde Co., 1948), pp. 219, 271; idem, *World Crises and the Prophetic Scriptures*, p. 16.

46. Charles H. Stevens, "Israel in the Millennium," in Charles Lee Feinberg, ed., *Focus on Prophecy* (New York, Fleming H. Revell, 1964), p. 45. Many contemporary popularizers included snippets of quotations from a wide range of scientists, social commentators, and cultural observers, but showed little evidence of any real familiarity with the thought of the individuals in question. Although George Ladd was not a dispensationalist, he remained a premillennialist.

47. Barr, *Fundamentalism*, p. 120.

48. Smith, *Future Survival*, p. 28; Stedman, *What's This World Coming To?* p. 94 (Velikovsky); Webber and Hutchings, *Is This the Last Century?* pp. 121–129 (*Jupiter Effect*); Van Impe, *Signs of the Times*, [p. 2] (Paul

Harvey); Taylor, *Get All Excited,* pp. 4 (*Jupiter Effect*), 9 (*South Bay Daily Breeze*); Lindsey, *Late Great Planet Earth,* p. 180 (quoting Rimmer); Jack Van Impe with Roger F. Campbell, *Israel's Final Holocaust* (Nashville, Thomas Nelson Publishers, 1979), p. 106 (quoting John Walvoord); Kirban, *Guide to Survival,* p. 253 (quoting Pentecost); Evans, *Return,* pp. 29 ("mock 2.2"), 162 (Begin); Hal Lindsey, *There's a New Day Coming* (Santa Ana, Calif., Vision House Publishers, 1973), p. 131; idem, *Late Great Planet Earth,* p. 141; Clifford Wilson and John Weldon, *The 1980s: Decade of Shock* (San Diego, Master Books, 1978), p. 165 ("Albert Camu").

49. H. M. Baggarly, editor of the *Tulia* [*Tex.*] *Herald,* quoted in A. G. Mojtabai, *Blessed Assurance: At Home with the Bomb in Amarillo, Texas* (Boston, Houghton Mifflin Co., 1986), p. 147.

50. John L. McKenzie, *The Power and the Wisdom: An Interpretation of the New Testament* (Milwaukee, Bruce Publishing Co., 1965), extracted in William Griffin, ed., *Endtime: The Doomsday Catalog* (New York, Collier Books, 1979), p. 52; W. R. Wallace, "Shadows of Armageddon," in William Culbertson and Herman B. Centz, eds., *Understanding the Times: Prophetic Messages Delivered at the Second International Congress on Prophecy, New York City* (Grand Rapids, Zondervan Publishing Co., 1956), p. 182; George Eldon Ladd, *Jesus Christ and History* (Chicago, InterVarsity Press, 1963), p. 59. See, in the same vein, William Culbertson, foreword, *The Prophetic Word in Crisis Days* (Findlay, Ohio, Dunham Publishing Co., 1961), n.p.: "Sad, indeed, is the condition of the man who has no divine blueprint as to God's purpose in the world. Such an individual is shut up in the idea of a purposeless world or the empty hope of a man-made millennium."

51. Paul E. Billheimer, *Destined for the Throne* (Fort Washington, Pa., Christian Literature Crusade, 1975), p. 19; author interview with John F. Walvoord, Aug. 8, 1989; Alva J. McClain, "Premillennialism as a Philosophy of History," in Culbertson and Centz, *Understanding the Times,* pp. 23–24 (italics in original).

52. Dorothy Ross, "Historical Consciousness in Nineteenth-Century America," *American Historical Review,* 89 (Oct. 1984), 909–928; George Bancroft, *History of the Colonization of the United States,* 13th ed. (Boston, Charles C. Little and James Brown, 1846; orig. publ. 1834), I, v, 266; III, 468.

53. Stevens, "Israel in the Tribulation," p. 46 ("symmetry and continuity"); author interview with John F. Walvoord, Aug. 8, 1989. See also Charles C. Ryrie, *Dispensationalism Today* (Chicago, Moody Press, 1965), pp. 31, 43; McClain, "Premillennialism as a Philosophy of History," p. 23.

54. Roy E. Laurin, "Israel and the End of History," in Culbertson and Cenz,

Understanding the Times, p. 236; Elwood McQuaid, . . . *It Is No Dream! Bible Prophecy: Fact or Fanaticism?* (West Collingwood, N.J., Spearhead Press, 1978), p. 223. Useful on this point are Michael Barkun, "Divided Apocalypse: Thinking about the End in Contemporary America," *Soundings,* 66, no. 3 (Fall 1983), 275; and Anthony A. Hoekema, *The Bible and the Future* (Grand Rapids, Wm. B. Eerdman's Publishing Co., 1979), p. 28.

55. William Culbertson, "Why Prophecy?" *Moody Monthly,* Oct. 1958, p. 15. See also Barry Brummett, "Premillennial Apocalyptic as a Rhetorical Genre," *Central States Speech Journal,* 35 (Summer 1984), 88, 89; and Paul R. Alderman, Jr., *The Unfolding of the Ages: Prophecy Fulfilled, Prophecy Being Fulfilled, Prophecy to be Fulfilled* (Grand Rapids, Zondervan Publishing Co., 1954), p. 12.

56. Mojtabai, *Blessed Assurance,* p. 148; Chuck Smith, *The Final Curtain* (Costa Mesa, Calif., Word for Today, 1984), p. 56. For a few of many citations of Toynbee, see Hal Lindsey with C. C. Carlson, *The Terminal Generation* (New York, Bantam ed., 1977), p. 72 ("one of the greatest historians of our time"); Frank E. Gaebelein, "Arnold Toynbee and the Jews," in Culbertson and Cenz, *Understanding the Times,* p. 251 ("one of the key thinkers of our age"); William R. Goetz, *Apocalypse Next: Updated* (Cathedral City, Calif., Horizon House Publishers, 1981), p. 187; Van Impe, *11:59 and Counting,* p. 169. The definitive biography is William H. McNeill, *Arnold J. Toynbee: A Life* (New York, Oxford University Press, 1989).

57. Marsden, "Evangelicals, History, and Modernity," pp. 96, 99; John F. Walvoord, *Israel in Prophecy* (Grand Rapids, Zondervan Publishing Co., 1962), reprinted in Walvoord, *The Nations, Israel, and the Church in Prophecy* (Grand Rapids, Zondervan Publishing Co., 1988), p. 103; LaHaye, *Beginning of the End,* p. 25.

58. Peter Brown, *Augustine of Hippo: A Biography* (Berkeley, University of California Press, 1969), p. 317; James W. Davidson, *The Logic of Millennial Thought* (New Haven, Yale University Press, 1977), p. 168 (Edwards); Scofield, *Addresses on Prophecy,* p. 13; idem, *Reference Bible* (New York, Oxford University Press, 1917), quoted in Grace Halsell, *Prophecy and Politics: Militant Evangelists on the Road to Nuclear War* (Westport, Conn., Lawrence Hill and Co., 1986), p. 7.

59. David Allan Hubbard, *The Second Coming: What Will Happen When Jesus Returns?* (Downers Grove, Ill., InterVarsity Press, 1984), p. 19. See also Paul Stevens, *Revelation: The Triumph of God* (Downers Grove, Ill., InterVarsity Press, 1987), p. 58.

60. John F. Walvoord, "Where Is the Modern Church Going?" in Feinberg, *Prophecy and the Seventies,* p. 121; Billy Graham, "Turn to God in

Prayer," *Decision,* Jan. 1983, p. 1; Arthur S. Maxwell, *History's Crowded Climax: Prophecy Speaks to Our Time* (Mountain View, Calif., Pacific Press Publishing Association, 1940), p. 10; Goetz, *Apocalypse Next: Updated,* p. 75. For a more militant musical metaphor see Hubbard, *Second Coming,* p. 105: "It is as though God's creation were an ensemble . . . Just before the end, the master Conductor will purify the orchestra, wipe out the discordant instruments, and tune the whole ensemble to play his richest, finest strains for all eternity."

61. Cyrus I. Scofield, *What Do the Prophets Say?* (Philadelphia, Philadelphia School of the Bible, 1918), p. 160; F. W. Pitt, *Coming Events Cast Their Shadows in the Air* (London, Marshall, Morgan and Scott, 1936), p. v; Alderman, *Unfolding of the Ages,* chap. 20; Smith, *Final Curtain,* p. 1. See also Walvoord, *Israel in Prophecy,* p. 103.

62. Thomas S. McCall and Zola Levitt, *Satan in the Sanctuary* (Chicago, Moody Press, 1973), p. 90; Carl McIntire, *Christian Beacon,* June 24, 1965, p. 5, quoted in Erling Jorstad, *The Politics of Doomsday: Fundamentalists of the Far Right* (Nashville, Abingdon Press, 1970), p. 33; Hilton Sutton, *World War III: God's Conquest of Russia* (Tulsa, Harrison House, 1982), p. 29; Webber and Hutchings, *Is This the Last Century?* p. 59.

63. [John Wesley], "The Great Assize, or Day of Judgment" (broadside, London, 1774), reproduced in Griffin, *Endtime,* p. 195.

64. Rev. 21:4.

65. Scofield, *What Do the Prophets Say?* pp. 20, 159ff., esp. pp. 159–161; Zola Levitt, *The Cairo Connection: Egypt in Prophecy* (Irvine, Calif., Harvest House, 1978), pp. 125–126 (quoting Scofield). For useful studies see Millard J. Erickson, *Contemporary Options in Eschatology: A Study of the Millennium* (Grand Rapids, Baker Book House, 1977), esp. pp. 91–97, historical overview; Norman Cohn, *The Pursuit of the Millennium* (New York, Oxford University Press, 1970); John F. Walvoord, *The Millennial Kingdom* (Findlay, Ohio, Dunham Publishing Co., 1959); Loraine Boettner, *The Millennium* (Philadelphia, Presbyterian and Reformed Publishing Co., 1957); and Robert G. Clouse, ed., *The Meaning of the Millennium: Four Views* (Downers Grove, Ill., InterVarsity Press, 1977).

66. Billy Graham, *World Aflame* (New York, Penguin Books, 1967; orig. publ. 1965), p. xv; Clark, *Shockwaves of Armageddon,* p. 183. See also Kenneth S. Wuest, *Prophetic Light in the Present Darkness* (Grand Rapids, Wm. B. Eerdman's Publishing Co., 1955), pp. 117–118 (p. 117: "this will be earth's Golden Age"); Charles C. Ryrie, *The Final Countdown* (Wheaton, Ill., Victor Books, 1982), p. 116; James Montgomery Boice, *The Last and Future World* (Grand Rapids, Zondervan Publishing Co., 1974), p. 14 ("a golden age for mankind"); John F. Walvoord with John

E. Walvoord, *Armageddon, Oil, and the Middle East Crisis: What the Bible Says about the Future of the Middle East and the End of Western Civilization* (Grand Rapids, Zondervan Publishing Co., 1974), p. 180 ("the earth will enter a golden age"); Roger Campbell and David Campbell, *Prosperity in the End Times* (Fort Washington, Pa., Christian Book Crusade, 1983), p. 70 ("All economic and social problems will be solved in that golden age to come we call the Millennium"). In addition to Rev. 21:4 and 20:2,7 (the thousand-year binding of Satan), the key texts are Isa. 35:1–2; Jer. 31:12; Ezek. 34:25–27; Joel 2:21–27; and Amos 9:13–14.

67. White, *Coming World Dictator,* p. 116.

68. Cotton Mather, *Theopolis Americana: An Essay on the Golden Street of the Holy City* (Boston, 1710), quoted in Stephen J. Stein, "Transatlantic Extensions: Apocalyptic in Early New England," C. A. Patrides and Joseph Wittreich, eds., *The Apocalypse in English Renaissance Thought and Literature* (Manchester, Manchester University Press, 1984), p. 277; Van Impe, *Israel's Final Holocaust,* p. 155; Smith, *Final Curtain,* p. 61; Louis Goldberg, *Turbulence over the Middle East* (Neptune, N.J., Loizeaux Brothers, 1982), pp. 270, 271. See also Walvoord, *Millennial Kingdom,* p. 318, discussing Isa. 65:22.

69. Walvoord, *Millennial Kingdom,* pp. 302, 316; Goldberg, *Turbulence over the Middle East,* p. 271; Willard Cantelon, *New Money or None?* (Plainfield, N.J., Logos International, 1979), p. 234. See also Ryrie, *Final Countdown,* p. 116 ("No More Social Injustice"); Howard W. Ferrin, "Why Cannot Man Bring in Permanent Peace?" in John W. Bradbury, ed., *Light for the World's Darkness* (New York, Loizeaux Brothers, 1944), p. 116 (in the Millennium "no more will masses be arranged against the classes, labor against capital, man against man"); Merrill F. Unger, *Beyond the Crystal Ball* (Chicago, Moody Press, 1973), p. 149 ("in Christ's ideal kingdom . . . there is promised prosperity and blessing for all").

70. M. R. DeHaan, *Coming Events in Prophecy* (Grand Rapids, Zondervan Publishing Co., 1962), p. 149; "Is Someone Watching You? The 'Electronic Boss,'" *Awake,* Apr. 22, 1990, p. 20. See also Leon J. Wood, *The Bible and Future Events* (Grand Rapids, Zondervan Publishing Co., 1973), pp. 161–162.

71. Graham, *World Aflame,* p. 217; Hubbard, *The Second Coming,* p. 110. See also Herman A. Hoyt, *The End Times* (Chicago, Moody Press, 1969), p. 229, and Goldberg, *Tribulation over the Middle East,* p. 277 (the fulfillment of God's plan will enable us to "escape from ourselves, our loneliness, our frustrations, our lack of fulfillment, our meaningless lives").

72. Warren W. Wiersbe, *Be Ready* (Wheaton, Ill., Victor Books, 1979), p. 92; Vander Lugt, *There's a New Day Coming!* p. 129; Brown, *Eleventh*

"Hour," p. 125; Lindsey, *There's a New World Coming*, p. 294. See also Billheimer, *Destined for the Throne*, p. 35.

73. Hal Lindsey, *The 1980s: Countdown to Armageddon* (New York, Bantam Books, 1981), p. 175.

74. Walvoord, *Millennial Kingdom*, pp. 308, 316. For similar points see White, *Coming World Dictator*, p. 116; Smith, *Final Curtain*, p. 62; Robert Glenn Gromacki, *Are These the Last Days?* (Schaumberg, Ill., Regular Baptist Press, 1970), p. 104; Ryrie, *Final Countdown*, p. 117 ("peace on earth will also mean prosperity on earth"); Boice, *Last and Future World*, p. 18.

75. Rev. 21:2; Chuck Smith, *What the World Is Coming To* (Costa Mesa, Calif., Word for Today, 1977), p. 201; Clark, *Shockwaves of Armageddon*, p. 231.

76. Coder, *Final Chapter*, p. 53.

77. Wilson and Weldon, *The 1980s*, p. 181; Smith, *What the World Is Coming To*, p. 151; Arthur E. Bloomfield, *Before the Last Battle: Armageddon* (Minneapolis, Bethany House Publishers, 1971), p. 161. See also Walvoord, *Millennial Kingdom*, pp. 317, 319.

78. Hoyt, *End Times*, p. 224; Wilson and Weldon, *The 1980s*, p. 181; Hubbard, *Second Coming*, p. 59.

79. C. I. Scofield, "The Millennium," in Theodore H. Epp, ed., *A Brief Outline of Things to Come* (Chicago, Moody Press, 1952), pp. 93, 95; Walvoord, *Millennial Kingdom*, pp. 301, 317, 319; Isa. 11:4. See also Unger, *Beyond the Crystal Ball*, p. 151; White, *Coming World Dictator*, p. 117, which envisions "a flourishing world living under one King, with all the people living in harmony as in Eden."

80. Lindsey, *Terminal Generation*, p. 39; Smith, *Final Curtain*, p. 58; Vander Lugt, *There's a New Day Coming*, p. 119. See also Sutton, *Revelation*, p. 208; Ryrie, *Final Countdown*, p. 114 ("The Lord Jesus Christ will reign in the millennial theocracy . . . Here is the secret of peace on earth—a ruler who can enforce peace righteously").

81. Frederick A. Tatford, *God's Program of the Ages* (Grand Rapids, Kregel Publications, 1967), p. 139. Throughout the literature the structural similarities of accounts of Antichrist's demonic rule during the Tribulation and Jesus Christ's blessed rule during the Millennium are striking.

82. Paul Lee Tan, *Jesus Is Coming* (Rockville, Md., Assurance Publishers, 1982), p. 70; Wood, *Bible and Future Events*, pp. 176, 177; George Otis, *Millennium Man* (Van Nuys, Calif., Bible Voice, 1974), extracted in Griffin, *Endtime*, p. 149. See also Vander Lugt, *There's a New Day Coming*, p. 129; Sutton, *Revelation*, p. 208.

83. Coder, *Final Chapter*, p. 162.

84. Richard A. Elvee, "The Prophets Speak to the Twentieth Century," in Culbertson and Cenz, *Understanding the Times*, p. 107; Wood, *Bible and*

Future Events, p. 161; White, *Coming World Dictator,* p. 117. See also Smith, *Final Curtain,* p. 62.

10. Apocalyptic Portents in a Post–Cold War World

1. I Thess. 5:3; "Decade of Destiny . . . Peace and Safety or World War III?" Jack Van Impe Ministries mailing to supporters, [1990]; *Salem Kirban's Analysis of Worldwide News: Preview of Next Issue* (n.d., received by author Sept. 2, 1990). See also "Beware of the Soviets," *Bible Prophecy News,* Jan.-Feb.-Mar. 1991, p. 6.

2. Dave Hunt, *Global Peace and the Rise of Antichrist* (Eugene, Oreg., Harvest House Publishers, 1990); Christian Information Bureau, Bend, Oreg., promotional brochure for ibid., received by author summer 1991 (quoted phrase); "5 New Fulfillments of Bible Prophecy," promotional brochure for *Omega-Letter,* received by author summer 1991.

3. Lester Sumrall, *The Holy War Jihad: The Destiny of Iran and the Moslem World* (Tulsa, Harrison House, 1980); Wim Malgo, *Russia's Last Invasion* (Columbia, S.C., Midnight Call, 1980), p. 38 (Khomeini as Antichrist forerunner); William R. Goetz, *Apocalypse Next: Updated* (Cathedral City, California, Horizon House Publishers, 1981; 8th printing, Oct. 1987), pp. 103–110, 135–138 (p. 138: Iran "virtually in the Soviet camp"); [James McKeever], "The Muslims Have Declared War," *End-Times News Digest,* Apr. 1989, p. 10. See also Edgar C. James, *Arabs, Oil, and Energy* (Chicago, Moody Press, 1982), passim; John Wesley White, *The Coming World Dictator* (Minneapolis, Bethany House, 1981), pp. 82–83; Doug Clark, *Shockwaves of Armageddon* (Eugene, Oreg., Harvest Books, 1982), pp. 78–79; S. Maxwell Coder, *The Final Chapter: Understanding What the Bible Says about the Last Pages of Human History* (Wheaton, Ill., Tyndale House Publishers, 1984), chap. 2, pp. 25–29.

4. *Salem Kirban's Analysis of Worldwide News; End-Times News Digest,* Oct. 1990; Hilton Sutton Prophecy Hotline, recorded telephone message, Nov. 20, 1990; Scott Baradell, "Prophets of Doom: We're a Leg Up on Armageddon," *Dallas Times Herald,* Sept. 8, 1990, p. 1 (Lindsey).

5. *Bible Prophecy News,* Jan.-Feb.-Mar. 1990, p. 1; "Commentary," ibid., July-Aug.-Sept. 1990, p. 4; "When the Arabs Attack Jerusalem," ibid., July-Aug.-Sept. 1990, pp. 5–6; Charles R. Taylor, "Dear Friends of Today in Bible Prophecy," Sept. 28, 1990 (letter to supporters, with attached order form).

6. *Bible Prophecy News,* Oct.-Nov.-Dec. 1990, p. 2; Charles R. Taylor, "Dear Christian Friends," Jan. 22, 1991 (letter to supporters); idem, "Dear Friends of Today in Bible Prophecy."

7. "Persian Gulf Conflict Called Armageddon," *Wisconsin State Journal*

(Madison), Oct. 14, 1990, p. 5A; Russell Chandler, "Persian Gulf Threat Inspires New Warnings of Fiery Armageddon," *Minneapolis Star Tribune,* Sept. 21, 1990, p. 17A (reprinted from *Los Angeles Times*); Barbara Reynolds, "Is the End Nearer with Gulf Conflict?" *USA Today,* Sept. 21, 1990, p. 11A; Baradell, "Prophets of Doom: We're a Leg Up on Armageddon."

8. Michael Norman, "Seeking Signs in Headlines: Gulf Fighting Rekindles Interest in Armageddon," *Cleveland Plain Dealer,* Jan. 20, 1991, p. 1A; Molly Guthrey, "A Prelude to Armageddon?" *Minnesota Daily* (University of Minnesota), Jan. 16, 1991, pp. 1, 14–15 (p. 14 discusses Rev. 16:2—"noisome and grievous sore[s]"—and quotes graduate student James Quach); David Wilkerson, *Set the Trumpet to Thy Mouth* (Lindale, Tex., World Challenge, 1985), p. 14; National Public Radio, "Morning Edition," Feb. 25, 1991; Luis Munilla, unpublished nine-page letter to *Time* magazine, Aug. 24, 1990 (my thanks to Ronald Numbers for sharing a copy of this letter with me). See also Peter Steinfels, "Gulf War Proving Bountiful for Some Prophets of Doom," *New York Times,* Feb. 2, 1991, pp. 1, 10; Cal Thomas, "Armageddon? Mideast Events Are on Schedule," *Wisconsin State Journal,* Jan. 17, 1991, p. 15A; Jo Sandin, "Doomsday: A Source of Comfort for Many," *Milwaukee Journal,* Feb. 4, 1991, p. B1; Michael Hirsley, "Some Final Words on Armageddon," *Chicago Tribune,* Jan. 31, 1991; "A Revelation in the Middle East," *U.S. News and World Report,* Nov. 19, 1990, pp. 67–68.

9. Edwin McDowell, "World Is Shaken, and Some Booksellers Rejoice," *New York Times,* Oct. 22, 1990, p. C10; Baradell, "Prophets of Doom," p. 1A; Steinfels, "Gulf War Proving Bountiful for Some Prophets of Doom," p. 1A (Walvoord quote).

10. Steinfels, "Gulf War Proving Bountiful for Some Prophets of Doom"; author telephone interview with Robert Ibach (director of library, Dallas Theological Seminary), Feb. 12, 1991; Barbara Hanrahan (University of Wisconsin Press) to author, Feb. 12, 1991; *New York Times,* Mar. 18, 1991, p. A9, and *Boston Globe,* Mar. 28, 1991, p. 22 (Jews for Jesus ads).

11. Hal Lindsey, *There's a New World Coming* (Santa Ana, Calif., Vision House Publishers, 1973), p. 242; "Iraq—Rebuilding Babylon," *Christianity Today* (Nov. 18, 1988), 71; Charles R. Taylor, "The Crisis in the Middle East," Dec. 1, 1990 (letter to supporters); Charles H. Dyer with Angela Elwell Hunt, *The Rise of Babylon: Sign of the End Times* (Wheaton, Ill., Tyndale House Publishers, 1991); author telephone interview with Tyndale House marketing representative, Mar. 14, 1991. In a full-page advertisement in *Publisher's Weekly* (Mar. 1, 1991), Tyndale House noted that Dyer's book had a $50,000 advertising budget and was avail-

able in "a high-impact floor merchandiser." The role of publishers in feeding and stimulating popular interest in biblical prophecy must not be overlooked.

12. John F. Burns, "New Babylon Is Stalled by a Modern Upheaval," *New York Times,* Oct. 11, 1990, quoting Shafqa Mohammed Jaafar (chief archaeologist of the Babylon reconstruction project); "Works in Progress: Neo-Nebuchadnezzar," *New York Times Magazine,* Nov. 26, 1989, p. 94.

13. Rev. 6:12,14–16; 8:7–12; 16:2–3,8–10,13–14,18.

14. Isa. 34:1,2,9–10.

15. Salem Kirban, *666* (Wheaton, Ill., Tyndale House Publishers, 1970), p. 50; idem, *Guide to Survival* (Huntingdon Valley, Pa., Salem Kirban, 1968), p. 51; James M. Houston, "The Judgment of Nations," in Carl F. H. Henry, ed., *Prophecy in the Making* (Carol Stream, Ill., Creation House, 1971), p. 370; Charles R. Taylor, *The Destiny of America* (Van Nuys, Calif., Time-Light Publishers, 1972), p. 68; Isa. 18:2. For the same argument, see Jack Van Impe, *11:59 and Counting* (Royal Oak, Mich., Jack Van Impe Ministries, 1983), p. 163.

16. Lindsey, *There's a New World Coming,* pp. 130–131, 133. See also idem, *The 1980s: Countdown to Armageddon* (New York, Bantam Books, 1981), pp. 27–28.

17. Chuck Smith, *What the World Is Coming To* (Costa Mesa, Calif., Word for Today, 1977), pp. 143, 144; idem, *Future Survival* (Costa Mesa, Calif., Word for Today, 1978), pp. 21 (quoted passage), 28, 34, 36; Jack Van Impe with Roger F. Campbell, *Israel's Final Holocaust* (Nashville, Thomas Nelson Publishing Co., 1979), p. 125.

18. Billy Graham, *Approaching Hoofbeats: The Four Horsemen of the Apocalypse* (Waco, Tex., Word Books, 1983), bibliography, p. 195 (discussing the ridicule directed against the "rather controversial group of men and women known as ecologists," Graham comments, "With the sound of the fourth horseman's hoofbeats approaching, perhaps it is time we saw them in the light of Genesis and Revelation and took their warnings more seriously . . . I find myself becoming more and more an advocate of the true ecologists where their recommendations are realistic"); Roger F. Campbell and David A. Campbell, *Prosperity in the End Time* (Fort Washington, Pa., Christian Literature Crusade, 1983), p. 43; Matt. 24:7 ("pestilences"); Ernest Lee Stoffel, *The Dragon Bound: The Revelation Speaks to Our Time* (Atlanta, John Knox Press, 1981), pp. 42, 51, 56–57 (quoted passages). See also Mike Evans, *The Return* (Nashville, Thomas Nelson Publishing Co., 1986), pp. 47, 56; Clifford Wilson and John Weldon, *The 1980s: Decade of Shock* (San Diego, Master Books, 1978), chaps. 12 and 13, esp. pp. 110, 113.

19. David Wilkerson, *The Vision* (New York, Pyramid Books, 1974), pp.

105–108, esp. p. 105 (ozone layer); "5 New Fulfillments of Bible Prophecy," *Omega-Letter* promotional brochure, 1991. See also Chuck Smith, *The Final Curtain* (Costa Mesa, Calif., Word for Today, 1984), p. 51; Leon Bates, *Projection for Survival* (Dallas, Bible Believers' Evangelistic Association, 3rd ed., rev., 1979), p. 153. The Bible passages referred to by these authors include Rev. 8:8–9; 16:8–9.

20. Hal Lindsey with C. C. Carlson, *The Terminal Generation* (New York, Bantam Books, 1977), pp. 69–70; "5 New Fulfillments of Bible Prophecy"; James McKeever, "Father God and Mother Nature," *End-Times News Digest,* June 1990, pp. 1–9 (quoted passage p. 5); Exod. 7–10.

21. David Webber and Noah Hutchings, *Is This the Last Century?* (Nashville, Thomas Nelson Publishing Co., 1979), pp. 127–129 (quoted passage p. 129); Lindsey, *There's a New World Coming,* p. 130.

22. Isa. 65:17; Rev. 21:1; II Pet. 3:12–13; Adam Clarke, *The New Testament of Our Lord and Savior Jesus Christ—With a Commentary and Critical Notes* (New York, new ed., 1837), II, 892, 893; Edward Hitchcock, *Elementary Geology* (Boston, Crocker and Brewster, 1840), both quoted in Wilbur M. Smith, *This Atomic Age and the Word of God* (Boston, W. A. Wilde Co., 1948), pp. 147–148, 150; Joseph A. Seiss, *The Last Times* (Philadelphia, Smith, English and Co., rev. ed., 1863; orig. publ. 1856), p. 75.

23. James H. Brookes, *Maranatha: or, The Lord Cometh* (New York, Fleming H. Revell, 10th ed., 1889; orig. publ. 1870), p. 17; Walter Scott, *Future Events: With Numerous Prophetic Details* (London, Alfred Holness, 1881), p. 85; Cyrus I. Scofield, *What Do the Prophets Say?* (Philadelphia, Philadelphia School of the Bible, 1918), p. 171.

24. Herman A. Hoyt, *The End Times* (Chicago, Moody Press, 1969), p. 243; Lindsey, *There's a New World Coming,* pp. 270–271. See also Arthur E. Bloomfield, *Before the Last Battle—Armageddon* (Minneapolis, Bethany House Publishers, 1971), pp. 160, 161.

25. David Hocking, *The Coming World Leader: Understanding the Book of Revelation* (Portland, Oreg., Multnomah Press, 1988), p. 295. Italics in original.

26. Alvin Toffler, *Future Shock* (New York, Random House, 1970); idem, *The Eco-Spasm Report* (New York, Bantam Books, 1975); Barry Commoner, *The Closing Circle: Nature, Man, and Technology* (New York, Alfred A. Knopf, 1971); Lefton S. Stavrianos, *The Promise of the Coming Dark Age* (San Francisco, W. H. Freeman Co., 1976); Michael Barkun, "Divided Apocalypse: Thinking about the End in Contemporary America," *Soundings,* 66, no. 3 (Fall 1983), 258. See also Samuel McCracken, "Apocalyptic Thinking," *Commentary,* Oct. 1971, pp. 61–70.

27. Barkun, "Divided Apocalypse," p. 265; Smith, *What the World Is Coming To,* p. ix.

28. Toffler, *Future Shock,* p. 485, quoted in D. S. Russell, *Apocalyptic: An-*

cient and Modern (Philadelphia, Fortress Press, 1978), p. 61; Evans, *The Return,* pp. 9–10.

29. Pat Robertson, *The New Millennium: Ten Trends That Will Impact You and Your Family by the Year 2000* (Dallas, Word Publishers, 1990); McDowell, "World Is Shaken, and Some Booksellers Rejoice"; Ron Reese, "What in the World Is Happening?" tract (Brooklyn, Mich., [1990?]).

30. James McKeever, *The Rapture Book: Victory in the End Times* (Medford, Oreg., Omega Publications, 1987), p. 22.

31. Daniel Bell, *The End of Ideology: On the Exhaustion of Political Ideas in the Fifties* (Glencoe, Ill., Free Press, 1960), pp. 369–370.

32. Timothy P. Weber, *Living in the Shadow of the Second Coming: American Premillennialism, 1875–1925* (New York, Oxford University Press, 1979), p. 180.

ACKNOWLEDGMENTS

In the course of this project I have incurred many scholarly obligations, ranging from substantive critical readings of the manuscript to brief but often illuminating comments volunteered by members of my lecture audiences. Lynn Dumenil offered encouragement, acute suggestions, and my first forum (at Claremont McKenna College) at the beginning of the project, and, near its end, a critical reading of several chapters.

The other readers of all or significant portions of the manuscript, to whom I am especially indebted, are Dennis Martin of Loyola University of Chicago, Bernard McGinn of the University of Chicago Divinity School, Mark Noll of Wheaton College (Illinois), Ronald Numbers of the University of Wisconsin, and three anonymous readers for Harvard University Press.

Kai Erikson of Yale University, who commented on a paper about Salem witchcraft that Stephen Nissenbaum and I presented at the annual meeting of the Organization of American Historians in 1972, performed the same midwifery for the present project at the annual meeting of the American Studies Association in Toronto in November 1989. I hope it will not be seventeen years before we again share a platform!

Thanks, too, to others who provided an opportunity for me to sharpen my ideas in lectures and seminars: Robert Hostetter at Northwestern; Emily and Norman Rosenberg at Macalester College; Robert Frykenberg and David Knipe at the University of Wisconsin; Rabbi Moshe Re'em and Robert Skloot, who invited me to talk about Israel and the Jews in prophecy at Beth Israel Synagogue in Madison; and the history faculty at Southeast Missouri State University, who tendered an invitation to give the Harold Holmes Dugger Lecture in April 1991. An American Studies Conference at Haifa University in January 1990, organized by Leslie Fishbein and Ronald Robin, provided not only another forum but also an opportunity for visits to Megiddo and Jerusalem's Old City—geographic sites that loom large on the mental maps of prophecy believers. A conference on religion in American culture organized at UCLA by Daniel Walker Howe in May 1991 offered a splendid opportunity to meet others who share my interests.

At Northwestern University, Robert Jewett, Stephen O'Leary, and Michael L. Stine of Garrett Theological Seminary offered helpful advice and insightful comments. Carl Smith, director of Northwestern's Program in American Culture, encouraged the project with wry good humor.

A host of colleagues and friends offered suggestions; responded to queries; shared clippings, stories, or research; read specific sections; and otherwise generously contributed to this work. It seems insufficient only to list their names, but a full accounting would stretch this preface to chapter length. Thanks, then, to Babatunda Agiri, Michael Barkun, Benjamin Beit-Hallahmi, Alex Boyer, Kate Boyer, Mary Boyer, Jeremiah Brady, Jack Cahill, Eddie F. Carder, William Cronon, Yishai Eldar, Booth Fowler, Robert Griffith, Tom Hines, Nick Hook, Stephen Humphreys, Michael Kammen, Donald R. Kelley, Robert Kingdon, Clayton Koppes, Matthew Lee, Gerda Lerner, David Lindberg, Kimberly Little, Edward Linenthal, Harold Eugene Mahan, Roland Marchand, Carol Martin, Lucy Mathiak, Sheldon Meyer, Mark Pittenger, Calvin J. Roetzel, Emily Rosenberg, Bruce Schulman, Daniel P. Schwartz, E. Morris Sider, Stephen J. Stein, Susan Stevens, Charles Strozier, William Trollinger, Grant Underwood, and Margarita Zamora.

Ann Chapman Boyer (whose great-uncle Edward Mortimer Chapman figures in the text) provided bibliographic help and gave the manuscript a close critical reading.

Paul A. Ericksen, associate director of archives at the Billy Graham Center of Wheaton College (Illinois); Robert Ibach, director of the Dallas Theological Seminary Library; and Walter Osborn, reference librarian at Moody Bible Institute, were helpful in various ways. My thanks, too, to the librarians at Gordon Conwell Seminary, Fuller Theological Seminary, Oberlin College, the University of Wisconsin, and the public libraries of Cincinnati, Nashville, Philadelphia, Pittsburgh, and St. Louis.

I am especially grateful to Loretta Freiling, secretary of the Institute for Research in the Humanities, whose generosity of spirit and unfailing good humor facilitated this project in many ways.

I should like to express my appreciation to the authors, editors, and publishers listed in the credits section, who granted permission for the use of their photographs and other illustrative material.

At Harvard University Press, Aida D. Donald, Editor-in-Chief, has supported this work with gratifying enthusiasm. Carrie Curvin has been most helpful as well. And Vivian Wheeler's superb copyediting skills have improved the manuscript in countless ways. Lisa Clark brought imagination and a trained eye to the book's design.

A series of stimulating lunches with Merle Curti and Carl Kaestle over the span of this project enlarged my appreciation of the possibilities of both friendship and the life of the mind. My former editor Tom Engelhardt, unfortunately no longer at Pantheon Books, has maintained an active interest in my work.

Posthumous thanks are owed to my grandfather, William H. Boyer, whose sermons occasionally touching on prophetic themes at the Dayton (Ohio) Brethren in Christ Mission in the 1940s and early 1950s first introduced me to the subject. Well do I remember the awe aroused in my boyish consciousness by his sonorous allusions to the "antediluvian dispensation" and his frequent somber warning "Surely, these are the last days." I also want to acknowledge—again, sadly, posthumously—my father, Clarence W. Boyer, who shortly before his death in April 1988 shared his memories of prophecy articles published in the *Sunday School Times* in the 1930s and early 1940s.

CREDITS

The author thanks the following publishers and individuals who kindly granted permission for the reprinting of illustrations. (Credits are listed in the approximate order in which the illustrations appear.)

Thomas Nelson Publishers, Nashville, Tenn.: prophecy chart from John Phillips, *Exploring the Future* (1983); cover of *Israel's Final Holocaust*, by Jack Van Impe with Roger F. Campbell (1979).

Watchtower Bible and Tract Society of New York, Inc., Brooklyn, N.Y.: "The Mysterious Beasts of Revelation."

Bantam Books, New York: cover of Hal Lindsey, *The Late Great Planet Earth*.

Billy Graham Evangelistic Association, Minneapolis, Minn.: "Billy Graham TV Special" advertisement.

Salem Kirban, Huntingdon Valley, Pa.: Rapture wristwatch advertisement; Rapture in suburbia painting; "The Image of Daniel 2" painting; "Universal Numbering System" credit card; photograph of woman being tattooed.

Bible Believers' Evangelistic Association, Inc., Sherman, Tex.: Rapture painting with crashing cars; "Nuclear War/World Peace" chart; "Multitudes Missing" newspaper front page.

British Library, London: Psalter map.

J. Paul Getty Museum, Malibu, Calif.: illumination from St. Albans Abbey.

Otto Müller Verlag, Salzburg: Hildegard of Bingen illumination.

Moody Bible Institute Archives, Historical Collections: 1914 prophecy conference photograph; Cyrus Scofield photograph.

Oxford University Press, New York: Scofield Reference Bible advertisement. "Scofield" is a registered trademark of Oxford University Press.

Seminars Unlimited, Box 66, Keene, Tex. 76059: "Prophecy Seminar: The Cosmic Warfare in Daniel."

Moody Bible Institute of Chicago, Moody Press: cover of Thomas S. McCall and Zola Levitt, *The Coming Russian Invasion of*

INDEX